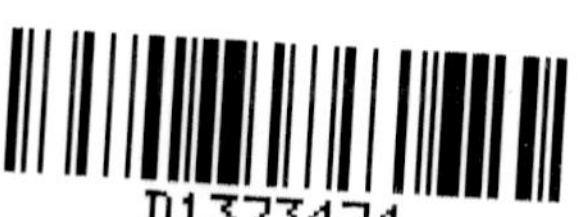

MONROE COUNTY COMMUNITY COLLEGE
301.431 B745s
Bossard, James Herbert Siward, 1888-1960
The sociology of child development
3 3131 00007 9495

THE SOCIOLOGY OF CHILD DEVELOPMENT

THE SOCIOLOGY OF CHILD DEVELOPMENT

FOURTH EDITION

JAMES H. S. BOSSARD
Late William T. Carter Professor of Child Development
University of Pennsylvania

and

ELEANOR STOKER BOLL
William T. Carter Professor of Child Development
University of Pennsylvania

HARPER & ROW, PUBLISHERS
NEW YORK AND LONDON

Title page: *Photograph by Dudley Blake*

THE SOCIOLOGY OF CHILD DEVELOPMENT, FOURTH EDITION.
Copyright 1948, 1954 by Harper & Row, Publishers, Incorporated. Copyright © 1960, 1966 by Eleanor Stoker Boll.
Printed in the United States of America. All rights reserved. No part of this book may be used or reproduced in any manner whatsoever without written permission except in the case of brief quotations embodied in critical articles and reviews. For information address Harper & Row, Publishers, Incorporated, 49 East 33rd Street, New York, N. Y. 10016.
C-1
Library of Congress Catalog Card Number: 66-11462

MONROE COUNTY COMMUNITY COLLEGE LIBRARY
Monroe, Michigan

To

Barbara

Constance

J. H. S. B.

CONTENTS

PART V CLASS AND STATUS DIFFERENTIALS

PART VI FAMILIES UNDER STRESS

PART VII EXTRAFAMILY GROUPS AND CHILD DEVELOPMENT

PART VIII THE LARGER SOCIAL SETTING FOR CHILD DEVELOPMENT

FOREWORD

Childhood is a universal human experience. A book about child development is therefore a book about all of us. The factors and problems involved in this process of growing up may be considered from different points of view. In this book the approach is primarily sociological; its chief emphasis is upon the social situations in which children live and grow from infancy to maturity. Since all of us grow up with other persons, these social situations, too, are a part of our common experience.

The steady production of valuable studies during the years since 1947, when the first edition was published, has presented a number of problems concerning the selection of material to be included. However, since the approach of this volume is distinctly sociological, only studies pertinent to that approach have been drawn upon. For summaries of other aspects of child development, such as the physical, psychological, or educational, the reader is referred to the excellent texts that devote themselves to those approaches. It is hoped that this brief comment will make clear both the continued emphasis of the sociological approach of this volume and the lack of specific mention of recent studies that fall outside this province.

With each revision of the original text there have been structural changes in the book as well as the inclusion of new facets of the child's life situation that have appeared as meaningful in his development. In this third revision the structure has changed considerably. The book has been condensed because of the growing practice, by teachers of child development courses, of using a variety of paperbacks along with a textbook. I have therefore omitted lengthy treatment of many of the topics included. I have not, however, omitted any subject that still appears to have a bearing upon child development at present. Also, new materials that have emerged as important recently have been added. Some of these concern the changing structure of the family, the high school marriage and drop-out situation, mass media, and children's heroes.

Since 1947, so many people have contributed help in the preparation of this book that it is impossible to include adequate acknowledgments. For earlier suggestions that have still been retained as parts of the third revision, I restate the acknowledgments made by Dr. Bossard in those editions.

"To Professors Ernest W. Burgess of the University of Chicago and Kingsley Davis of Princeton University, I am indebted for reading parts of the manuscript and for helpful suggestions. Professor F. Stuart Chapin, of the University of Minnesota, indicated additions to the original outline which have been included in its final form. Mrs. Frances C. Allen, of Philadelphia, contributed a revealing case study which is identified at the point of incorporation. Mr. Bradford Chambers has been most gracious in permitting me to examine his unpublished material on conflict gangs. The facilities of the Carter Foundation for Child Development at the University of Pennsylvania have been untilized at every turn, a debt which it is a pleasure to owe. *The American Sociological Review*, *The American Journal of Sociology*, *The Annals of the American Academy of Political and Social Science*, and the University of Pennsylvania Press have permitted the reproduction of material previously published by them. Finally, my two daughters have taught me so much about children that it seems only proper, for professional as well as for affectional reasons, to dedicate this volume to them."

For helpful suggestions incorporated in the revised editions, I am indebted to Professor Reuben Hill, Professor Jessie Bernard, and Dr. Evelyn Millis Duvall.

To the Administration of the Graduate School of Education, University of Pennsylvania, for the pleasant conditions under which this third revision was written, my thanks are expressed, as they are to Miss Polly Roberts and Mrs. Margaret Grosskurth for their assistance with the manuscript.

Great appreciation is felt for the continued interest and support of Mr. William T. Carter, Mr. William C. Dickerman, and Mrs. Joy St. John, without which the revision would have been impossible.

ELEANOR STOKER BOLL

November, 1965

INTRODUCTION

Photograph by H. Armstrong Roberts

PART I

THE SOCIOLOGY OF CHILD DEVELOPMENT

1

This is a book about children. Its central theme is the sociology of child development. In this respect it differs from either a psychological or pedagogical or psychiatric point of view. Since it is a book about children, the role of the child in contemporary thought needs to be considered; since it is written from the sociological point of view, the relation of child development to sociology and the meaning of the sociological approach should be explained. This chapter will discuss (1) a change, in the early decades of this century, in the focus of concern for and study of the child, (2) important past steps in the study of human behavior leading up to the development of the situational approach, and (3) some current emphases in the study of child development.

FROM WELFARE OBJECTIVE TO SCIENTIFIC CONCEPT

The child came to the serious attention of the modern world as an object of tender solicitude and of organized welfare endeavor. It was as such that the child was first regarded by sociologists. This was wholly natural, for the desire for social uplift was the background out of which sociology arose. With this original primary emphasis upon social amelioration, the welfare of the child became an obvious and logical objective. The emphasis in the scientific approach to human welfare was upon prevention; and the prevention of social problems, if it meant anything, meant the promotion of the well-being of children. Thus naturally, in the course of time, the child became the largest concern in the field of social work, both in the number of workers employed and in the amount of money expended. Thus, too, courses in sociology which dealt with the child were of the problem kind, and emphasized ameliorative measures. They have been referred to customarily as courses in child welfare.[1]

In recent years, a newer approach to child study and problems has come to be made by social scientists, and sociology has shared in this development. This newer approach can be summarized most tersely, perhaps, by saying that the child is regarded as a focal concept for scientific study rather than as a welfare objective. In other words, the child is seen as a human reality in whose development are combined the various specialized problems of particular groups of scientific students. The child, in short, serves as a project study, drawn from life rather than from the laboratory, in which may be observed the various processes of human growth and development. To say, then, that the child emerges as a focal concept for scientific analysis does not imply an approach that is theoretical or academic, as the phrase might indicate, but an intensely practical one, especially for the purposes of sociological analysis and research. It makes the child's social development a distinctive and legitimate scientific area for sociologists, just as it has been for psychologists and psychiatrists.

SOCIOLOGY AND THE AREA OF CHILDHOOD

To think in terms of the realities of a functioning society, there are a number of reasons for sociologists to center much of their work around the child. Whether one begins from the point of view

[1] Cf. Raymond Kennedy and Ruby Jo Reeves Kennedy, "Sociology in American Colleges," *American Sociological Review,* October, 1942, pp. 661–675, for the relative importance of such courses. In 1965, the American Sociological Association published a listing of types of courses offered by 127 graduate departments of sociology. An analysis of them suggests that few courses dealing directly with the child are courses on child welfare. The data included, however, are not of a nature to make accurate comparison with the 1942 study possible.

of group processes and analyzes them in terms of their simple beginnings, or whether he makes a lengthwise historical approach to the processes of personality formation and development, he is led in either event directly to the area of childhood. Some of the more obvious relationships between this area and the scope of contemporary sociological thought will be indicated in brief form.

The Sociological Conception of Personality

Contemporary sociologists conceive of the human personality as a product of social conditioning. In this process, two sets of conditioning factors are recognized as of outstanding importance. One of these is the interactive experience of life within the group. Sociologists discuss this currently under the heading of "social interaction" or "the role of the group." But the influence of relationships with other persons is modified or qualified constantly by what these other persons have learned, that is, their cultural heritages. Thus we identify the second set of conditioning factors as cultural ones, comprehending the more or less accepted group ways of doing and thinking. These, of course, are sociological commonplaces today. They are recalled here because of two important implications inherent in them. The first is the obvious fact that the social conditioning of the personality during the first years of life is of primary importance. Not only are the factors operating during this period the first to condition the individual, but there are few or no counterinfluences to overcome. All this is but another way of stating that the basic patterns of personality are laid during the period of childhood.

The second implication is that the sociological processes of personality formation can best be studied during the earlier stages. There are a number of reasons why this is so. The relative lack of counter and complicating factors has been referred to. There is a simplicity and directness about the process during the first years that is apt not to be duplicated later on. The process takes place on a smaller scale; the groups within which the child interacts and the culture-transmitting process operate on a smaller scale than is found in the later stages of life. Something akin to controlled conditions can be set up for children, an opportunity likely to be lacking when the subjects studied are older. In other words, the whole range of experimental studies in personality formation is confined in large measure to the area of child life.

In short, the social development of the personality is in large degree the story of the social development of the child. This is the inevitable implication of the sociological approach to personality—a conclusion similar to that of the psychiatrist and psychoanalyst. In this approach, the role of the family is predominant, and the family is the one institution whose scientific study falls most clearly within the province of the sociologist.

Cultural Continuities and Discontinuities

Viewed in retrospect, the culture of any society is a changing stream in which cultural continuities and discontinuities are occurring constantly. The more precise study of these, in their varying aspects and respective roles, falls ordinarily within the province of the culture historians and students of social processes. The point of emphasis here is that the child is the focal point of this recurring relationship between the cultures of successive generations.

Turning to cultural continuity, we see that the child is the carrier and connecting link between the cultures of succeeding generations. This is a fact of great importance; for, in terms of social process, it makes the relation of adult to child as important as, if not more so than, that of adult to adult. Kirkpatrick has already emphasized this in these words: "There has always been some awareness that important social continuities depend upon the parent-child relationship. . . . A considerable group of investigators representing the personality and cultural approach have turned the spotlight on childhood family experience . . . the dominant theme in this type of investigation is the relating of childhood family experience to the prevailing personality type engendered by such experience and to dominant cultural characteristics which reflect the prevailing personality type."[2]

Behavior Problems and the Socialization of the Child

The longer the sociologists' concern with crime, delinquency, and behavior of all sorts continues, the more one comes to be disturbed by the suspicion that our past approach has been from the wrong direction. We have, in times past, started with problem cases and worked back to general processes, and we have selected picturesque and intriguing factors and attempted to assess their role; whereas all the time we might have started more intelligently with the child and studied the normal processes of his development, ultimately coming to an understanding of deviant behavior in social relation-

2 Clifford Kirkpatrick, *The Family as Process and Institution,* The Ronald Press, New York, 1963, p. 62.

ships. In the medical field, the study of disease follows and is built upon an understanding of bodily structure and process; a similar procedure in sociology would make the study of juvenile delinquency a postscript to the study of the socialization of the child.

Group Relations and the Child

The sociology of child development is an important part of the science of group relations. Children are a definite population element. All societies recognize the distinctive existence of groups organized on an age basis. Anthropologists have shown the prevalence and importance of the age classificatory device in primitive cultures,[3] and more recently sociologists have come to emphasize its role in contemporary society.[4] The ascription of the child's status and the ways for the child and youth to achieve status—these are the heart of the class system of any society. The status of the child element in the population, the factors affecting its status, and its relationship to other population elements—these are a major part of the problem of group relations in sociology.

There are other and important phases of a sociology of childhood. The foregoing discussion is intended to be suggestive and illustrative rather than exhaustive. The essential fact to be emphasized is the child as a challenging pattern of operating actuality, thus making his social development a major area for scientific exploration and an intriguing project for pedagogical exploitation. For this is the stimulating challenge of the child as a scientific concept, that in it so many of the basic principles of sociology and of the unexplored problems of sociological research are combined into an operating pattern at a time in the life of the individual, and in a stage of simplified development, when they can be most readily understood.

FACTORS FAVORING THE STUDY OF CHILD DEVELOPMENT

One of the driving forces toward an emphasis upon the sociological study of child problems is what may be called the philosophy of the modern mind. The essence of this philosophy is the belief, so characteristic of the industrial-urban American culture, that

3 Melville Jacobs, *Pattern in Cultural Anthropology,* The Dorsey Press, Homewood, Illinois, 1964, chaps. 4 and 6.

4 Shmuel Noah Eisenstadt, *From Generation to Generation: Age Group and Social Structure,* The Free Press of Glencoe, New York, 1956.

man can in large measure control his own destiny. The contemporary American worships at the shrine of progress, meaning by that concept a controlled development of society in a direction believed to be desirable. Supremely sure of himself, he deems himself the master of his fate, contends that he need not submit, and that there really is no virtue in continuing to submit, to the limitations imposed upon him by the forces of nature or the follies of man.

This philosophy is deeply imbedded in our national way of thought because almost our entire history has been a living proof of its soundness. Three hundred years of continuous experience has made us the most confident and optimistic people in the world. We believe we can go to Heaven because, metaphorically speaking, for several centuries we have been doing so. We have occupied, exploited, and remade a very large and a very rich continent. As that process has gone on, civilization has repeatedly been reborn on its advancing frontier. The political philosophy which initiated our separate existence revolutionized the political tenets and structures of much of the world. Our own political ideas and forms have been repeatedly recast, always with the fond belief that the latest revision would just about usher in the millennium. Our industrial history is a dazzling record of miracles. We have already sent men orbiting around the earth and are preparing to send them to the moon. What, in view of all this, could the philosophy of the American mind be but what it is? How else could we proceed but in our confident roistering fashion?

The implications of such a philosophy for children are obvious. If society is to control and direct its development, then the place to begin is with the oncoming generation. The remaking of the world can never hold much point or hope of reasonable success if it is conceived in terms of the immediate present. It is essentially a process of trading in social futures, if the terminology of the market is permitted. Controlled and directed social movement implies a forward-looking philosophy with its eyes and its values focused on the future. And the future is the child. The child is the hostage which each generation gives to destiny, as a token of its behavior and its hopes.

THE PLASTICITY OF HUMAN NATURE

A second basic factor profoundly influencing contemporary thought in regard to the child has been the widespread acceptance of the idea of the plasticity of human nature. This idea, or principle, is the product of recent work in a number of sciences—principally psychology, anthropology, and sociology—and it is significant that the unorganized and originally unrelated efforts in these sciences have fitted together so aptly into the same pattern of conclusion.

One group of studies has emphasized the modifiability of human nature, how from the very beginning of life the original responses are modified by the particular requirements of the group in which the child lives. Moreover, this is a continuing process. Responses to stimuli in the environment are constantly in the process of formation and modification. Reinforcing these conclusions are the results of the accumulated material from anthropological sources revealing the diversity of group ways of living and thinking, i.e., the variety of cultural patterns into which children are born and by which they are conditioned. These studies have in turn been supplemented by the work of the sociologists, showing the relationship between culture and personality in a degree which led them to speak of personality as the subjective side of culture. In other words, modern scholarship has made it very apparent that everywhere throughout the world individuals are constantly being modified and conditioned for participation in their culture, that cultural unities vary from one group to another, as do the methods of cultural conditioning or the role of the respective agencies and persons who do the conditioning.

This principle, now an accepted foundation stone in the social sciences, is a revolutionary concept, once one turns to its implementation. It brings to the forefront, first and foremost, the whole process of childrearing and training, in both its individual and collective aspects. The meaning of education now comes to be reinterpreted to include the whole process whereby the child is inducted into his culture, that is, the whole transformation of the newborn infant into membership in a specific society with a specific culture. It comes to include, too, the transmission of the cultural heritage from one generation to another, and the process by which a society perpetuates and renews itself.[5]

Whether these contemporary convictions prove ultimately to be merely airy dreams in the realms of delusive grandeur, or the sterner stuff out of which better human beings and better worlds are destined to come, it must be clear that in all these efforts the child is the major objective; and an understanding of the child—his personality development, his socialization, his role as carrier of the culture, his cultural induction and his indoctrination—is the

[5] Harry M. Johnson, *Sociology: A Systematic Introduction*, Harcourt, Brace & World, New York, 1960, pp. 110–131.

enduring basis of any possible successful achievement. The modern mind, wrestling with the problems of human and social well-being, finds them where Plato dreamed his ideal state—in the directed development of the next generation. Science now dictates what our tender sympathies long have counseled. Society's "acre of diamonds" lies revealed in the cradle within the home, and social statesmanship finds its task in the rearing of the child.

THE STUDY OF HUMAN BEHAVIOR

Human behavior is a fascinating field for study. Understanding it has always intrigued human interest. Through the ages, man has observed the conduct of his fellows and utilized his generalizations as a guide for his experience. Thus must one interpret the fables, legends, myths, proverbs, sagas, sacred writings, literary tales, etc., which constitute the accumulated wisdom of the ages; they involved and reflected man's observations on what people did, and why. And this is the substance of human behavior.

With the passage of time, such observations grew in range and complexity; with the advent of writing and printing, they came to be recorded; with the growth of human learning, they became naturally more specialized. These developments coincided in point of time with the use of the modern sciences. The result was a natural one, no matter how slowly the logic of thought might move to its destined end; the study of human behavior came to be recognized as a legitimate field of scientific study. The point to be recognized (and it seems important by way of proper perspective) is that the modern sciences concentrating upon the problems of human behavior represent, then, so many current phases of man's abiding and age-old aspiration to understand his fellows and ultimately himself.

The scientific study of behavior did not begin as such. That is to say, there was no conscious recognition among the early scientists of the scope of the study of human behavior as a whole. The period of beginning was one of specialized sciences attacking some one particular field or group of problems involving human reactions, often working independently of other sciences in related fields, and at times having no appreciation of such relationships or of the larger implications of their work. Each of these specialized sciences staked off its own claim, as it were; developed its own tools and techniques; and, in course of time, arrived at its own conclusions. It is only in recent decades that an appreciation of the underlying field of human behavior has been recognized as the common core of these sciences.

TWO FUNDAMENTALLY DIFFERENT APPROACHES

When one surveys the various sciences studying human behavior, two fundamentally different approaches can be identified. One concerns itself with the individual who behaves, focusing attention upon his physical makeup, his biological heritage, his psychological traits, his personality trends, and the like. But all behavior is related to situations, in which the personality is developed and to which behavior is a response. The scientific study of the situations related to behavior is, then, the second fundamental approach to be noted.

The first of these is the one that has been followed generally by professional and scientific groups concerned with human behavior. Included here are the physical and biological sciences which have gathered a mass of information about the mechanism of the body—its structure, its physiological processes, the chemical role of the endocrine system, and the hereditary equipment of the organism. These foundation studies are highly important: first, because of the light they throw upon the physical equipment of the individual; and, second, in their emphasis upon behavior as the result of adjustment to the enveloping situation.

Second are the psychological sciences which occupy a central position in the studies of human behavior. The plural number is used because there are different approaches to the behavior of man which come properly within the scope of psychology, just as there are many systems of psychology. The scientific study of the child, from the psychological side, has been made in large measure via the psychometric approach, concerning itself with studies of capacity and thinking of behavior as a correlate or function.[6] Another group of psychologists have made what might be called the personality-testing approach. Their studies grew out of an interest in the correlation between intelligence and performance (i.e., behavior). The discovery that this correlation was not high led to an emphasis upon other traits and factors, such as temperament, character, and so on. Psychiatry may be included as one of the psychological approaches, even though it began as a branch of medicine. Concerned originally with the clinical treatment of the physiological causes of mental disorder, psychiatry represents today a framework of reference for behavior as a whole, with a variety of interpretations in sociopsychological terms and factors. The contemporary psychiatric point of view of mental disturbance as a

[6] As an example of this approach see, Irma R. Gerjuoy, "Discrimination Learning as a Function of the Similarity of the Stimulus Names," *Child Development*, September, 1964, pp. 677–684.

failure of the organism as a whole to adapt to the conditions of life can have no other meaning but that psychiatry becomes an applied science (or an art?) of human behavior. Similarly, one must include psychoanalysis in the psychological group. Like psychiatry, it began as a specialized therapeutic approach. As time has gone on, it too has become increasingly a study of the human personality, contributing concepts, emphases, and techniques, as well as conclusions distinctly its own.

Finally, there are the social sciences, which have turned increasingly in the past few decades to the study of human behavior. It is easy to understand the reasons for this development. In the first place, much of the work of the groups of sciences already mentioned has reached into, or has implications for, the social sciences; in the second place, the more one delves into the study of behavior, the more one sees that it is something which develops in relation to and with other people. Human personality is a product of social contact and communication, and its scientific study leads directly and inevitably to the study of the background situations to which behavior is a response.

THE SOCIOLOGICAL CONCEPTION OF PERSONALITY

Among the social sciences, sociology in particular has been interested in the general study of human behavior. This interest grows directly out of the sociological conception of personality. Such a conception naturally is conceived in terms of those social traits and relationships which distinguish the individual and differentiate him from other members of society. Virtually all sociological definitions of personality go back to that of Park and Burgess, who identify it as "the sum and organization of those traits which determine the role of the individual in the group."[7] Since such a role grows out of the ideas, attitudes, traits, and habits of the individual, these too must be included in the sociological meaning of personality.

The sociological insistence is that personality, thus defined, is not inborn but is acquired or achieved. On the basis of the individual's native or innate equipment, the human personality is a product of social conditioning. In the process of personality formation, two sets of conditioning factors operate. One of these is the interplay of person with person, which we term social interaction. Of outstanding importance in this connection, then, are the experiences of the person in his or her social contacts. But the influences

[7] Robert E. Park and Ernest W. Burgess, *Introduction to the Science of Sociology*, University of Chicago Press, Chicago, 1921, p. 70.

of relationships with other persons are constantly modified or qualified by what these other people have learned. Here is the second set of conditioning factors, namely, the cultural, embracing the more or less accepted ways of group doing and thinking. Hence personality is determined also by the conditioning power of the cultural heritage and by the social patterns of behavior which social groups develop, approve, preserve, and transmit from generation to generation. What this means, in substance, is that the sociologist sees personality as a reflection of the social situations in which the individual has been reared and to which he reacts. The self is a social looking glass.

THE SITUATIONAL APPROACH TO BEHAVIOR

For many years, references to the background factors in human behavior utilized the general term *environment,* and earlier applications of scientific methods to the problems of human behavior gave ample recognition to its importance. Thus Gabriel Tarde, one of the first students of crime to employ positive methods, championed the idea that the criminal was entirely a social product.[8] Among the earlier psychologists, John B. Watson had an almost complete disregard for inborn or constitutional traits.[9] William A. White, among the psychiatrists, early stated a clear and marked emphasis upon environmental factors in the causation of mental disorders.[10] Similarly, Alfred Adler, in the psychoanalytic group, wrote more than a generation ago of the relative importance of environmental conditioning.[11]

With continued progress in methodology, it became evident that some term other than environment was needed to identify specific combinations of environmental factors, and gradually the word *situation* came into use. This specificity of combination became evident in the work of such physiologists as Loeb, Jennings, and others, in their work with "tropisms," that is, reactions of organisms to light, electricity, heat, acids, and so on. Next it was applied by psychologists—Thorndike, Yerkes, Watson, Köhler—in their experiments with rats, dogs, monkeys, and babies. The procedure of both

[8] Gabriel Tarde, *Penal Philosophy,* translated by Rapelje Howell, Little Brown and Company, Boston, 1912.

[9] John B. Watson, *Psychology from the Standpoint of a Behaviorist,* J. B. Lippincott Company, Philadelphia, 1919.

[10] William A. White, *The Mental Hygiene of Childhood,* Little, Brown and Company, Boston, 1924.

[11] Alfred Adler, *Understanding Human Nature,* Garden City Publishing Company, Garden City, 1927. Consult his *The Neurotic Constitution,* Dodd, Mead & company, New York, 1917, for his explanation of how the individual compensates for his organic deficiencies.

of these experimental groups was the same: they prepared situations, introduced the subjects into a situation, observed the behavior reactions, changed the situation, observed the changes in the reactions, and so on.

It was a logical next step to apply this procedure to the study of human behavior, and much of the emphasis in recent years has been in this direction. Although the methodology was developed by comparative physiologists and psychologists, the foundation for its extension to human behavior was laid by Pavlov, Krasnogorski, Bekhterev, Watson, and others, in their work on the conditioned reflex. What this means is usually explained in terms of Pavlov's classical first demonstration with dogs. A dog is shown a piece of meat. His mouth waters in anticipation of eating it. The meat may be thought of as the original stimulus; the mouth-watering, as the dog's reaction. Pavlov's experiments showed that repeated association of other stimuli with this original stimulus in time brought out the original response. The reaction to the associated stimulus is called a conditioned reflex.[12] Such experiments when applied to children had similar results. Fears and prejudices were produced, especially by the behavior of other persons, and sometimes by a single association. The Thomases concluded that herein lies a most important approach to the formation of personality traits as dependent on situations.[13]

Sociologists saw in the situational approach very great opportunities for sociological emphasis. This particular approach to behavior rests upon the striking concepts developed by the late Professor Cooley. His ideas of "the self as a social product," "the looking-glass self," and "individual and society as two aspects of the same thing" had appeared as early as 1902, but it was destined to be another decade and more until the implications of these concepts began to be realized for purposes of sociological study.[14]

Following Cooley, the next major step in the development of the sociological approach to behavior problems came with the publication of Thomas and Znaniecki's monumental work on the Polish peasant.[15] In this, the peasant is studied in the process of moving from a European to an American situation, thus approximating the controlled change of situation with which, as has been pointed out,

12 I. P. Pavlov, *Conditioned Reflexes*, translated by G. V. Surep, Oxford University Press, London, 1927.

13 W. I. Thomas and Dorothy S. Thomas, *The Child in America*, Alfred A. Knopf, New York 1928, p. 507.

14 Charles H. Cooley, *Human Nature and the Social Order*, Charles Scribner's Sons, New York, 1902.

15 W. I. Thomas and Florian Znaniecki, *The Polish Peasant*, Richard G. Badger, Boston, 1919. (Current edition: Dover Publications, New York.)

the physiologists and psychologists had been working experimentally. Throughout their entire work runs the fundamental theme of the relationship between personality and the environing culture. "Personality is always a constitutive element of some social group; the values with which it has to deal are, were and will be common to many personalities, some of them common to all mankind. . . . Personal evolution can be understood only in connection with social life. . . . Personal life records, as complete as possible, constitute the perfect type of sociological material. . . . A social institution can be understood only if we . . . analyze the way in which it appears in the personal experience of various members of the group and follow the influence which it has upon their lives."[16]

Of particular significance in its effect upon subsequent sociological thinking was the emphasis upon the individual's definition of the situation. On the basis of his cultural and social conditioning, the individual meets the various social situations which confront him, and defines them with reference to his own behavior. Thomas further distinguishes between those definitions of the situation which are laid down for the individual by his culture—which Thomas calls the moral or public definition—and those which represent the individual's own conception—which he terms personal or hedonistic. The interplay between man and his culture is well stated in these words: "The human personality is both a constantly producing factor and a continually produced result of social evolution, and this double relation expresses itself in every elementary social fact; there can be for social science no change of social reality which is not the common effect of pre-existing social values and individual attitudes acting upon them. . . ."[17]

Following his work on the Polish peasant, which Burgess identifies as "the starting point for the sociological explanation of personality and culture."[18] Thomas carried forward his analysis of the cultural conditioning of personality in his paper presented to the American Sociological Society in 1926, with particular emphasis upon the role of "critical experiences." "Behavior traits and their totality," he wrote then, "are the outcome of a series of definitions of situations with the resulting reactions and their fixation in a body of attitudes or psychological sets. Obviously, the institutions of a society, beginning with the family, form the character of its members almost as the daily nutrition forms their bodies, but this is for everybody, and the unique attitudes of the individual and his

[16] *Ibid.*, vol. III, pp. 6, 10, 6, 7.

[17] *Ibid.*, p. 5.

[18] Ernest W. Burgess, "The Cultural Approach to the Study of Personality," *Mental Hygiene*, April, 1930, p. 310.

unique personality are closely associated with certain incidents or critical experiences particular to himself, defining the situation, giving a psychological set, and often determining the whole life direction."[19]

Two years later, in his presidential address to the American Sociological Society, he made a clear distinction between different approaches to the study of behavior:

In approaching problems of behavior, it is possible to emphasize—to have in the focus of attention for working purposes—either the attitude, the value, or the situation. The attitude is the tendency to act, representing the drive, the affective states, the wishes. The value represents the object or goal desired, and the situation represents the configuration of the factors conditioning the behavior reaction. . . . The situations which the individual encounters, into which he is forced, or which he creates, disclose the character of his adaptive strivings, positive or negative, progressive or regressive, his claims, attainments, renunciations, and compromises. For the human personality also the most important content of situations is the attitudes and values of other persons with which his own come into conflict and cooperation.[20]

Reinforcing Thomas' point of view were the conclusions of Faris, Bernard, and others. In 1921, Faris indicted the explanation of behavior in terms of instincts[21] and three years later Bernard's book on instinct appeared, followed by his analysis of environments in 1925.[22] In his paper for the American Sociological Society in 1925, Faris foreshadowed the later sociological dictum of personality as the subjective side of culture in these words:

Individuality may then, from one standpoint, be thought of as character, which is the subjective aspect of the world the individual lives in. The influences are social influences, but they differ in strength and importance. When completely ordered and organized with the conflicting claims of family, friends, clubs, business, patriotism, religion, art and science all ordered, adjudicated, and unified, we have not passed out of the realm of social influence, but we have remained where the social group, taken separately, can be invoked to explain the behavior. Individuality is a synthesis and ordering of these multitudinous forces.[23]

[19] W. I. Thomas, "The Problem of Personality in the Urban Environment," *Publications of the American Sociological Society*, 1926, vol. XX, p. 31.

[20] W. I. Thomas, "The Behavior Pattern and the Situation," *Publications of the American Sociological Society*, 1928, vol. XXII, pp. 1–2.

[21] Ellsworth Faris, "Are Instincts Data or Hypotheses?" *American Journal of Sociology*, September, 1921, pp. 184–196.

[22] L. L. Bernard, *Instinct: A Study in Social Psychology*, Henry Holt & Company, New York, 1924; "A Classification of Environments," *American Journal of Sociology*, November, 1925, pp. 318–332.

[23] Ellsworth Faris, "The Nature of Human Nature," *Publications of the American Sociological Society*, 1926, vol. XX, p. 29.

MEANING OF THE TERM "SITUATION"

One of the few organized efforts to define the term was made at the meetings of the Section on Sociology and Social Work of the American Sociological Society in December, 1930. In this symposium, Mrs. Ada E. Sheffield presented the idea of family case work as dealing, not with a client, but with "a dynamic field of experience, a field in which the individual or the family figures within an aggregate of interactive and interdependent factors of personality and circumstance . . . a segment of interactive experience involving clients in complex relationships with their physical and social setting." This new unit she spoke of as a *situation.*[24]

In defining the term for purposes of sociological analyses, Queen says: "A situation consists in relationships between persons viewed as a cross section of human experience, constantly changing in kaleidoscopic fashion, and affected both by material conditions and by relationships to other persons. Thus we made of the concept 'situation' an intellectual tool similar to the anthropologists' concept 'culture complex,' in that both are quite flexible as to content, both are capable of subdivision, both are something more than the sum of discrete elements, both convey the idea of relationships, both present nuclei about which configurations gather, and both are constantly changing."[25]

When one turns from formal definitions of the term, such as those just cited, to its actual use in the recent scientific literature, he finds that at least three general basic ideas seem to be included in the concept of the social situation.

The first is the idea that the stimuli included are all external to the organism. This implies at once that the term situation is not, properly speaking, synonymous with the word *environment.* As Mead points out, environment means all the factors to which the responding unit responds.[26] This obviously would include certain acquired internal aspects of the organism which would obviously operate as stimuli. These internal stimuli are not included in the concept of the situation; we are concerned only with those that are external to the organism.

24 Ada E. Sheffield, "The 'Situation' as the Unit of Family Case Study," *Social Forces,* June, 1931, pp. 465–474.

25 Stuart A. Queen, "Some Problems of the Situational Approach," *Social Forces,* June, 1931, p. 481.

26 George H. Mead, *Mind, Self, and Society,* University of Chicago Press, Chicago, 1934, pp. 245–247. Mead's concept was an important early step in clearly differentiating between the stimuli included in "environment," as defined by psychologists, and in "situation," as defined by sociologists.

The second basic idea involved in the term *situation* is that of the reciprocal relationship of these stimuli. In other words, they do not just operate; they operate with, upon, and in relation to, each other. In other words, a situation is an organization of stimuli in which each stimulus has a given relationship to every other one. It is the particular relationship of these stimuli to one another that gives them their meaning in any specific situation.

This basic principle, that any fact derives its attributes and meaning from its relation to other facts, is pertinent to all scientific study and indeed to the process of daily living. A union's right to call a strike, for instance, is a fact recognized by law. The extent to which a particular strike may endanger the public welfare, however, can so change the meaning of the right to call a strike, that the federal government may take steps to prevent it. So it is with the facts which serve as stimuli in a given situation. From the standpoint of the situation, the stimuli included exist in relation to one another, and from this obtain their meaning in the particular situation under consideration.

The third characteristic of the situation is that it is organized about, or in relation to, some focal point or person. It is this aspect of a special relatedness, with reference to some person or object, that has come to be the essence of the scientific use of the situation concept. On the basis of this specific unity of organization the situation becomes an emergent, by which we mean that this special relatedness becomes in itself an additional and effective factor.

The simplest illustration of the idea of an emergent is water—a combination of hydrogen and oxygen, in the very definite proportions of two parts of hydrogen and one part of oxygen. This special relatedness forms the liquid emergent known as water, which has quite different properties, that is, behavior, than either of its gaseous components. Concerning its reality, Mead speaks in these general terms: "Anything that as a whole is more than the mere form of its parts has a nature that belongs to it that is not to be found in the elements out of which it is made."[27]

The existence and importance of this factor of special relatedness were recognized by a number of thinkers in the nineteenth century. Such men as John Stuart Mill, Lester F. Ward, Spaulding, Wundt, and others were aware of it; and various terms, such as "creative synthesis," "evolutionary naturalism," "organicism," "holism," and "heteropathic causation" were used to identify it. C. L. Morgan's term *emergent* has, however, found most favor among contemporary philosophers, biologists, sociologists, and the like, who utilize the concept.

[27] *Ibid.*, p. 329.

By way of summary, then, a situation consists of a number of stimuli, external to the organism but acting upon it, organized as a unit and with a special relatedness to one another as stimuli of the specific organism involved. It thus becomes, as Lundberg suggests, a "field of force,"[28] or a segment of life to which the organism reacts as a whole. Thus conceived, it becomes a tool of precision for the scientist in studying the behavior of the organism, as definite and specific as the situation of the experimental physiologists and psychologists.[29]

THREE ASPECTS OF SOCIAL SITUATIONS

Social situations having been defined in terms of the basic ideas included, it is pertinent next to indicate the distinctive points of view from which they may be regarded. In speaking of these approaches for purposes of study, reference is intended not to the methodology to be employed, but rather to the nature and range of the phenomena considered. To clarify the distinction among these different ways in which social situations may be regarded they will be discussed separately.

Structure

A social situation is, from one point of view, a structure. Its analysis and description as such might be spoken of as a still-life picture. When we structurize a social situation, we see it in repose. Our interest is in the structural elements, their characteristics, and their position and relationships to one another. We are concerned chiefly with the relationships that are relatively continuous. What distinguishes a structure is the fact that it has form and that it is an organization, and the essense of both is continuity of relationship.

A classroom with a class in session, for instance, has a structure. It is composed of the size of the room, the size of the class, the sex makeup and age makeup of the class, and other such traits that are relatively static. Whatever the size and makeup happen to be

28 George Lundberg, *The Foundations of Sociology*, The Macmillan Company, New York, 1939 (pp. 217 ff.), 1964.

29 The reader should compare this characterization of the situation with that of Leonard S. Cottrell, Jr., in his article, "The Case Study Method in Prediction," *Sociometry*, November, 1941, pp. 358–370. See also Leonard S. Cottrell, Jr., and Ruth Gallagher, "Important Developments in American Social Psychology During the Past Decade," *ibid.*, May and August, 1941, for a statement of the main currents of change in contemporary social psychology. Another contribution by Cottrell is his "Analysis of Situational Fields—A Theoretical Orientation for Social Psychology," *American Sociological Review*, June, 1942, pp. 370–383.

they are related to one another in producing a specific result. A large room with few students creates one kind of atmosphere; a small room with too many students creates another kind. The whole nature of a course may have to be different if 95 rather than 15 students enroll in it. Teachers have strong feelings about the relative effectiveness of classes that are coeducational or that are segregated by sex, and their feelings often depend on the particular type of course given.

In the scientific study of a social situation structurally conceived, we take it apart, examine each part as to its nature, and inquire into the way these parts are organized into a unit. This is one separate but important step in understanding the situation. If I understand him correctly, it is this that Lundberg had in mind when he wrote: "After the field, i.e., situation has been selected, the problem is to structure it so that the relationship of the elements in the field can be accurately shown. The method of doing this with which we are most familiar is, of course, to name with words certain elements or factors in the situation and then by use of the adjectives or adverbs of ordinary language we attempt to give an accurate statement of the relationships within the field."[30] Similar would appear to be Mrs. Sheffield's thought in her paper of three decades ago: "The identifying of a pattern that is relatively constant helps us to bring order into our thinking about the variables which appear. It should clarify causative relations, should help us to follow social process, and to raise significant questions."[31]

Process

A second way in which a social situation may be viewed and studied is in terms of process. If the structural approach is a still-life picture, this second is a motion picture. We are concerned now with the interaction of the elements of the situation. The people in a class are not static. They behave toward each other and toward the structural elements of the classroom. In other words, action and interaction are taking place.

The term *social interaction* is used constantly by contemporary sociologists, currently as the generic name for a whole set of processes taking place between individuals; thus, social interaction denotes the set of processes by virtue of which society exists. Here, however, we are using the term *interaction* as a category of analysis, to identify the reciprocal or interdependent relationship among the

30 Lundberg, *op. cit.*, p. 108.
31 Sheffield, *op. cit.*, pp. 471–472.

elements in a situation. The basic idea involved is not one of a mere meeting or collision of these component elements, but something more pervasive and subtle, in the course of which each acts upon or somehow changes or modifies the other. Such interaction may take place between individual organisms, between persons, or between persons and their stimulating environment. Conceived thus in terms of process, the situation becomes an immediately related and functioning segment of human experience, as both Mrs. Sheffield and Queen have indicated in their definitions cited earlier in this chapter.

Content

Finally, from the third point of view, both structure and process are but vehicles or channels through which are transmitted a content of ideas, attitudes, words, and the like. To transmit these is the purpose of the class, and we speak of this content as "culture." The interactive process may be thought of, then, as a series of functioning operations conveying cultural items. Through this interactive process these cultural items are molded into a pattern which becomes the central core of the situation.

This cultural content is a very specific thing in the case of any given social situation. Although culture is comprehensive, like the air we breathe, nevertheless the human personality is constantly selecting items and elements from the current culture, and is channeling them through the interactive processes, so that any given social situation represents both a cross section and a cross selection of the contemporary culture organized about a given focal point.

The distinction between process and content, as well as the specificity of the cultural content, is well set forth by Kenkel.

> Of extreme importance in the development of personality is the manner in which the emotions of love and hate, of sympathy and hostility, are taught and displayed within the family . . . . Children can be taught to express their aggression or to conceal it, to co-operate or compete, and to fear or not to fear the external world in which they find themselves.
>
> Culture . . . is the key concept for understanding the broad configurations of behavior patterns as they vary from society to society. The simplest definition of culture is the "way of life" of a society, and an expansion of this definition shows that it includes an almost infinite number of specifics concerning what to do and how to do it, and even what and how to think . . . the common experience of society members during their formative years is thought to produce an essential same-

ness of personality. Since cultures vary one from the other, no society offers its members the totality of experience that is offered in another society.[32]

Although the three aspects of a social situation have been described separately, it must be remembered that they do not operate separately. Each affects the others, for they are all the stimuli which have a reciprocal relationship and are organized around some focal point, or person.

IMPLICATIONS OF THE SITUATIONAL APPROACH

Once the full meaning of the situational approach to behavior problems is recognized, it becomes important to consider the implications of such an approach, and it is to this discussion that we turn next.

1. It seems necessary to begin by emphasizing that the situational approach is distinct and separate, commensurate with the study of the personality that reacts to the situation. This fact would seem to require emphasis because such status has not always been given to it. Situations have often been considered as incidental to the organisms behaving within them even when the avowed purpose of a study was the analysis of a situation itself. The behavior of organisms is such a fascinating subject that it is apt to catch the eye and blind it to important situations which may have played a part in evoking that behavior.

2. The second implication of the situational approach to behavior problems, and complementary to the first one, is a recognition of the situation as a *separate* field for scientific investigation. In other words, situations need to be studied, inductively and by themselves, without any reference to the way in which organisms react to them. This is said with particular regard to social situations, with which we are primarily concerned.

Emphasis upon this second implication is also necessary because of the history of the situational approach to the study of behavior. Being first undertaken by physiologists and psychologists, the situations were created by the experimenters, were relatively simple, were "controlled," and were thoroughly understood. It was natural, therefore, that the investigators' chief concern was with the behavior that resulted. Pavlov, Krasnogorski, Bekhterev, for instance, give scant reference in their works to the situations employed in

[32] William F. Kenkel, *The Family in Perspective*, Appleton-Century-Crofts, New York, 1960, pp. 234–235.

experimenting with the conditioned reflex. All the emphasis is upon the reactions to these situations and the possible meaning of the observations.

Many of the sociological studies of child behavior have been carried out by psychologists, psychiatrists, and educators. It does not seem difficult to understand how such students would be prone (a) to minimize the role of the situation, or (b) to assume that social situations are understood adequately, and that the important fact is to see how the individual defines the situation and reacts to it. Most of them, naturally enough, have therefore been disposed to think primarily in terms of persons and their reactions; and when they have spoken of the situational approach, it has been with one eye turned toward it and the other toward the behavior reaction to it.

It is the emphatic insistence of this volume that a situational approach to human behavior is an entirely different matter. Social situations differ from mechanical or physical situations, and in a number of respects. In the first place, social situations are not created artificially as are those of physiologists and psychologists; they are accepted by the student as they are found. This changes the whole relationship of the student to the situation. He finds them ready-made and must learn to deal with them as they are. Second, social situations are more complex than the physical, nonhuman situations which have been dealt with prevailingly in behavior studies. The very nature of the human personalities involved excludes simplicity. The human personality is a very complex product; hence the simple combination of a man, a woman, and a child, in a family situation, would be far more complex than the combination of three chemical agents, for example. Again, the elements involved in a social situation cannot always be identified with clarity, nor can their role in the situation be expressed with the precision of a mathematical formula. For instance, the degree and nature of tension between the father and mother may be an integral part of a family situation and have profound significance for the child; yet these aspects may be difficult to identify or express with any kind of satisfactory accuracy. The emotional quality of a social relationship is as real a social fact as the temperature of water, but no statistical thermometer has yet been devised to measure and express it. Finally, social situations differ from nonsocial situations in the inexorability with which they change. Most of the situations utilized by students of prehuman behavior were fixed, or they changed slightly or slowly or both. This is not true of social situations; they are constantly changing, at times with considerable rapidity. From one point of view, social situations are functioning processes, which places them in a category quite different from standardized psychological tests, for example.

The scientific study of social situations is possible only if they are regarded as objective and separate realities. This is the first step in their scientific investigation. We must begin by disregarding the ways in which individuals define situations or react to them. Further progress involves their analysis with regard to the nature and range of the stimuli involved, the ways in which these stimuli operate, the cultural content of the interactive processes in situations, and the manner of organization, or special relatedness of all the stimuli involved, with special reference to the object or person considered. Each of these must be defined with precision and analyzed with an appreciation of all the complexities present. Only after social situations have been thus studied, with the slow laborious technique of the scientist, are we in a position to consider adequately their role in the behavior of the individual.

3. This is perhaps the place to emphasize the interdependence of sciences which the careful study of situations involves. This is an area where clear thinking has not always prevailed. The point of view presented here can best be explained through the use of examples. The physiologists, in their studies of the responses of organisms to varying situations, obviously drew upon the data of chemistry, bacteriology, physics, and the like, in order to create and describe accurately the situations to which the organisms were submitted; and quite as obviously, no question concerning such a procedure would be raised. Similarly psychologists, in creating situations or tests of a physical or mechanical sort to which their subjects are submitted, drew without the slightest hesitation upon the underlying physical sciences. That is to say, these earlier groups, who utilized the situational approach to the study of behavior, called upon all the scientific disciplines necessary in order to understand, as accurately as possible, the nature of the elements, which they combined to create the situations they utilized for their own specific purposes.

It seems pertinent, at this point, therefore, to call attention briefly to some current approaches and areas of investigation in child research which the reader may explore as supplementary to the situational approach, or as a part of it.

Since the most basic life situation for the child is that of the family, the work of Hill and Hansen describing the present conceptual frameworks used in family study by social scientists is of great value.[33] The following frameworks have been identified: (1)

[33] Reuben Hill and Donald A. Hansen, "The Identification of Conceptual Frameworks Utilized in Family Study," *Marriage and Family Living*, November, 1960, pp. 299–311.

The interactional approach, *sociology and social psychology,* which looks upon the person as an independent actor in a situation, as well as a reactor to it; (2) the structure-function approach, *sociology and social anthropology,* in which the person is considered as reacting to the social system, and independent action is rare and asocial; (3) the situational approach, *sociology,* in which behavior is purposive in relation to the situation that provokes it; (4) the institutional approach, *sociology and historical sociology,* in which institutions are considered as responses to human needs and values, and in which persons are active, as well as reactive within institutions; (5) the developmental approach, *sociology, borrowing from rural sociology, child psychology, and human development,* in which behavior is seen as a function of past and present social and individual developmental conditions.[34] It seems clear that, for a comprehensive understanding of the behavior and life situations of children, all of these approaches have contributions to offer. Each one emphasizes something currently considered to be an essential element in behavior. Familiarity with each of them can lead to both synthesis and perspective.

Equally important, to the student of child development, is an awareness of new types of research and new findings from any fields that have a bearing upon behavior. A popular type of research at the moment is the retesting of common conceptions by improved methodology and new insights. For example, an employed mother was once equated with maladjustment in the children. Yet this did not operate in all cases. By breaking down the factor of "employed mother" into a number of elements of which that is composed, it has been more nearly possible to predict which children of which working mothers might come to trouble. The same is true of juvenile delinquency. Computer research has made it possible to subject vast populations to the test of upholding or denying the allegations of former small and unrepresentative studies. While at the same time the small pioneer study of a new "guess" as to something that affects behavior is still significant in widening insight, and is a subject for retesting by the other methods. A knowledge of advances in biological and medical sciences is of growing value and should be taken into consideration. From the day of J. B. Watson to the present, there has been considerable modification in the idea that a child's social environment is totally responsible for what he is. There *are*

[34] *Ibid.* Hill and Hansen suggest the following, among others, as representing these approaches: the interactional, Leonard S. Cottrell, Jr., Reuben Hill, Mirra Komarovsky, Earl Koos, P. Wallin; the structure-function, William J. Goode, Carson McGuire, Talcott Parsons, W. Lloyd Warner; the situational, W. I. Thomas, Lowell J. Carr, James H. S. Bossard, Robert O. Blood, Jr.; the institutional, John Sirjamaki, Andrew Truxal; and the developmental, Evelyn M. Duvall, Robert G. Foster, Reuben Hill, and Lemo D. Rockwood.

biological forces known to be important, even in terms of sex-appropriate behavior, which has frequently been described as a purely cultural matter. The use of drugs in the treatment of severe mental disorders is another case in point.[35]

When one turns to the comprehensive, complex, and difficult task of dealing with social situations to which human behavior is a response, it ought to be clear that any sciences, any facts, should be called upon. Hence in utilizing the situational approach, sociologists should have no hesitance or compunction in drawing upon the work of physiologists, physiological chemists, endocrinologists, psychologists, psychiatrists, psychoanalysts, historians, economists, political scientists, cultural anthropologists, horticulturalists, statisticians, and the like, as the need may arise. The most extensive, and at times the most complete, utilization of the data of the complementary sciences by sociologists in developing the situational approach is entirely in keeping with the scientific folkways, and in this case peculiarly proper because of the difficulties of the material involved.

SUMMARY

1. The child came to the serious attention of the modern world as a welfare objective. In recent years, the emphasis in our thinking has changed the child into a scientific concept, as it were, making it a project study in which the processes of human growth and development may be observed and studied.

2. Two factors particularly have favored the scientific study of child development. One has been the modern belief that man can direct the development of the society in which he lives, as well as of its members; the second is the belief in the plasticity of human nature.

3. Two fundamentally different approaches to the study of human development can be identified. One concerns itself with the individual who behaves, the other with the situations to which behavior is a response.

4. The term *situation* is used in this volume to mean (a) a number of stimuli, external to the organism, but acting upon it, (b) organized and operating as a unit, and (c) bearing a special related-

[35] For the most comprehensive and current summary of many types and areas of research see, Martin L. Hoffman, and Lois W. Hoffman, *Child Development Research*, Russell Sage Foundation, New York, 1964. Of value, also, is the bulletin, *Research Relating to Children*, published periodically by the Children's Bureau, U.S. Department of Health, Education, and Welfare, U.S. Government Printing Office, Washington, D.C.

ness to one another as stimuli of the specific organism involved. It is, thus, a "segment of life to which the organism reacts as a whole."

5. Social situations can be studied from three distinct points of view. These are identified by the terms *structure*, *process*, and *content*.

6. The objective analysis of behavior along the lines just indicated constitutes an approach to behavior problems commensurate in importance to the study of the individual and his traits. It is a separate, distinct, and highly important approach, and needs to be recognized as such.

7. Social situations need to be studied objectively, and without reference to the way in which organisms react to them. This has not been done in the past because, for the physiologists and psychologists who first dealt with the role of situations, such situations were simple, ready-made, and thoroughly understood. Social situations, however, are not created as a rule by experimenters; they are accepted as they are found.

SUGGESTED READINGS

Abbott, Grace, *The Child and the State*, University of Chicago Press, Chicago, 1938, vols. I and II. These volumes are concerned with child problems, child welfare, and legislation for children and illustrate the emphasis of this earlier period.

Carr, Lowell J., *Situational Analysis*, Harper and Brothers, 1948. Intended as a textbook for introductory sociology, this book illustrates the use of the situational approach.

Flügel, John Carl, *Psychoanalytic Study of the Family*, Hogarth Press, London, 1939. (Current edition: Hillary House, New York.) An interpretative discussion of the psycho-analytics of family, marriage, and parent-child relations.

Gardner, D. Bruce, *Development in Early Childhood*, Harper & Row, Publishers, New York, 1964. Describes various approaches to the study of child development and emphasizes the growth task of the child in the preschool years.

Hurlock, Elizabeth, *Child Development*, McGraw-Hill Book Company, New York, 1964. A psychological approach to the study of child behavior with recognition of the influence of social factors.

Krogman, Wilton M., *A Handbook of the Measurement and Interpretation of Height and Weight in the Growing Child*, Child Development Publications, Evanston, Illinois, 1950. A study of children's development from the point of view of physical anthropology.

Mead, Margaret, and Martha Wolfenstein, *Childhood in Contemporary Cultures* University of Chicago Press, Chicago, 1955. This series of essays shows different ways in which to study the cultural aspects of child development.

Pollak, Otto, *Integrating Sociological and Psychoanalytic Concepts*, Russell Sage Foundation, New York, 1956. Dr. Pollak describes an interdisciplinary experiment in studying child behavior. Social scientists and clinicians cooperated. Family case records, diagnoses and therapy plans are included.

Thomas, W. I., and Florian Znaniecki, *The Polish Peasant*, Richard G. Badger, Boston, 1919, vols. I and II. (Current edition: Dover Publications, New York.) One of the earliest attempts to study behavior from the situational approach, this is a description of the situations and behavior of Poles who migrated to the United States.

Thomas, W. I., and Dorothy S. Thomas, *The Child in America*, Alfred A. Knopf, New York, 1928. Brought together in this book are the different ways of approaching behavior problems in children by physiologists, psychologists, psychiatrists, and sociologists.

Weill, Blanche, *The Behavior of Young Children of the Same Family*, Harvard University Press, Cambridge, 1928. This case-record study illustrates that siblings do not have identical life situations and therefore have different behavior responses.

FAMILY SITUATIONS AND THE CHILD

Photograph by Ronald Geraci

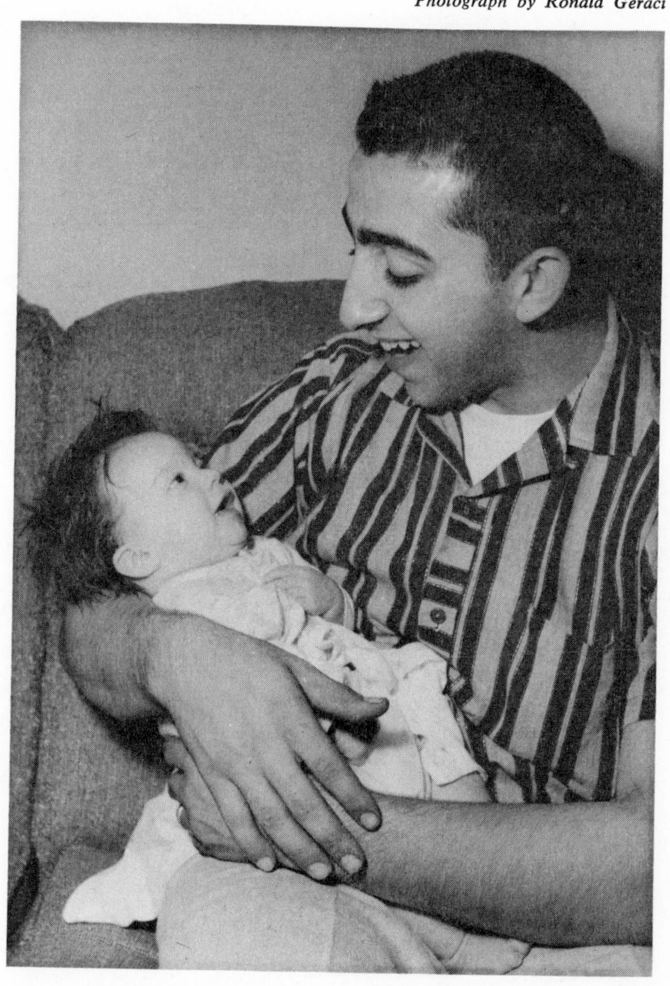

PART II

FAMILY STRUCTURE

A social situation was defined in Part I as an organization of stimuli, external to an organism and acting upon it, each having a special relatedness to one another, as stimuli of the particular organism involved. Furthermore, it was pointed out that social situations, thus conceived, could be studied from three points of view, identified by the terms *structure, process,* and *content.* Part II is devoted to (1) the meaning and importance of family situations in child development; (2) types of family structures and their varying significance; (3) family interactive processes as they affect the child; and (4) the cultural role of the family in child development.

FAMILY SITUATIONS: THEIR MEANING AND IMPORTANCE

The term *family situation,* as utilized in this book, involves the application of our definition of the phrase *social situation* to the specific family group. A family situation may be defined, accordingly, as a unit of stimuli operating within the confines of the family circle, and organized in relation to the person or object which serves as the focal point in the particular case being considered. Stated another way, the term *family situation* means a group of family stimuli operating as a unit with reference to some polar point. This polar point may be an outside object, a member of the family group, or a nonmember observer or student of the family. It is important to keep in mind the role of this focal point, for what is implied is that the family situation changes as the polar point is changed. To speak in general terms, the family situation of a child is the unity of existing stimuli within the family circle as they operate upon the child; that of the husband or wife in the same family will be quite different. The change in the polar point changes the entire situation, its involved stimuli, and the relationship of these stimuli.

There are two basic reasons for beginning the situational approach to child behavior with the study of family situations. One is their primary importance in the determination of behavior patterns; the second is their prior value for purposes of scientific analysis.

The importance of family situations in the formation of personality is emphasized today by all the sciences which are participating in the study of human behavior. The family is a society, the first in which the child lives, and the most powerful in conditioning original nature into the socialized personality.

This emphasis upon the family's primary importance in the socialization of the child must not be taken to mean, as frequently happens, that the personality is wholly and irrevocably formed during the first few years of life. Brown contends, for example, that far too much emphasis has been placed upon childhood experiences per se, that subsequent experiences determine the importance of these early activities, and that the individual, instead of being a product of his childhood, is the result of what adolescence, youth, and adulthood do to childhood experiences.[1] Similarly, Folsom points out that no one has yet proved that the total rate of personality development is faster in childhood than in later life.[2]

The prior value of family situations for purposes of scientific analysis derives from at least three characteristics. The first of these is the relative simplicity of family situations. To speak in quantitative terms, family situations involving only a few persons are a normal feature of our life. In the second place, family situations are of a continuing and recurrent nature. The interacting personnel remain normally the same, at least over considerable periods of time. Many of their characteristics, as well as many of their relationships, are relatively permanent and stable. Particularly is this true in the study of social situations with the child as polar point. Ordinarily, changes in personnel are limited in number, particularly when compared with such changes in other social situations; changes in the characteristics and relationships of this personnel tend to occur slowly and often imperceptibly. Finally, the relationships in family situations are peculiarly frank, intimate,

1 Lawrence G. Brown, *Social Pathology*, F. S. Crofts & Co., New York, 1942, p. 11.

2 Joseph K. Folsom, *The Family and Democratic Society*, John Wiley & Sons, New York, 1943, p. 323.

and private. Because of this, the family provides a unique opportunity for the free expression of personality; it is these characteristics which facilitate equally well the scientific study of family situations. In short, one is led to conclude that family situations are the most important of the social situations which determine behavior, and relatively the easiest to study.

THE FAMILY AS STRUCTURE

Since the time of Sumner, sociologists have recognized that a social institution consists of a concept and a structure, and that this structure is a framework which consists not of physical realities but of relatively permanent relationships.[3] The family is a social institution, and, therefore, it has a structure which depends on its personnel and their roles, its size, sex makeup and age makeup. To study the family as a structure is to view it in repose, that is, to consider it as a form of organization. Thus approached, there are many lines of inquiry which may be pursued. Attention is directed primarily to the different types of structural form, to recent changes in emphasis regarding these structural forms, and to their significance in the child's social development.

FAMILY PERSONNEL

People constantly use the word *family* as though there were no question concerning its meaning. When a small child, however, asks "Who is my family?" the answer depends largely on the culture within which he lives.

The student from a middle-class American home today, where the word *family* is synonymous with the reproductive unit of society, finds it difficult to realize that there have been many societies in which such units have not been so designated and in whose everyday life such a domestic structure has played a rather minor role. In translating the documents used in his study of the Polish peasant, Znaniecki found it wholly impossible to use the word *family* in the sense in which American students use it. The family, to the Polish peasant, was a social group which included all the blood and law relatives up to a certain variable limit, usually the fourth degree. To designate the smaller grouping which we call

[3] William Graham Sumner, *Folkways*, Ginn and Company, Boston, 1906, pp. 53 ff. (Current editions: Blaisdell Publishing Company, Dover Publications, and New American Library, New York.)

the family, Znaniecki used the term *marriage group.*[4] It is well to remember that in our own culture the transition in the concept of the family as a larger kinship group to that of the smaller household unit is rather recent, and is still found most typically in the middle class.

Thinking in terms of the contemporary American child and adapting our terminology to this point of view, we find that the following meanings of family stand out. First, there is the child with his father and mother. This is the biological and reproductive unit; in normal times and circumstances the parents are married and have established a home, where they live with their child or children. Thus the biological and reproductive unit becomes also a social unit in which develop the community and intimate features of social life. We shall call this the child's *family of procreation.*

In a great many households, however, the child grows up in a family which differs from the above. One or both of the parents may be missing; an aunt or uncle or grandparent or other kin, friend, boarder, etc., may be a continuing member of the child's family. This group is the household unit in which and through which the child receives his orientation in the social world. This it seems pertinent to call the child's *family of orientation.* In many cases, the child's family of procreation and the family of orientation are the same; but often this is not the case. In either event, both of these forms may be thought of as the child's *immediate family* in the sense of comprising the circle of his immediate, intimate, and continuing family contacts.[5]

Each child as he grows up discovers that he is also a member of a larger kinship group to which the term *family* is applied. William Brown, for example, is one of the Westchester County or one of the South Carolina Browns. This group contains all the relatives by blood or marriage up to a certain degree of relationship, a degree which varies from one family or culture to another. In our culture, when a marriage takes place, two blood lines are joined, and when a child arrives, both his mother's and his father's kin are the child's relatives. Whether or not they are all thought of equally as *family members,* however, depends upon the degree of social adhesion or isolation that follows the marriage. Frequently it happens that

[4] W. I. Thomas and Florian Znaniecki, *The Polish Peasant,* Richard G. Badger, Boston, 1919, vol. I, p. 87. (Current edition: Dover Publications, New York.)

[5] Some of the concepts here used are to be attributed to W. Lloyd Warner, of the University of Chicago. The reader should also consult a library edition of J. L. and J. P. Gillin's textbook, *An Introduction to Sociology,* The Macmillan Company, New York, 1942. Chapter 9 gives a summary of family-type groups, and a comparison will reveal our preference for the term *kinship group family,* rather than "extended family," as used there. Also, our use of the terms *family of procreation* and *family of orientation* is slightly different.

circumstances lead a child to consider one blood line as his family and the other as composed of comparative strangers. This distinction is important to the child and to the family's functioning in the development of his personality. For this larger circle of kinsfolk, the phrase *kinship group* is used.

In all of these answers to "Who is my family?" there is implicit the idea that a family is not merely a blood group but is also a social group. Though the biological function of the family has great importance in perpetuating the family, the society, and the race, the social function is of infinitely greater importance. Two lines of evidence might be cited. First, anthropologists claim that kinship groups exist in societies that know nothing of the biology of procreation. Second, there is an almost universal rule which permits the adoption as a family member of another person's biological offspring. This conception of the family as a social rather than a biological unit is particularly significant in the study of the child's social development.

Changes in Family Personnel and Their Significance

Two changes in the personnel of the American family stand out clearly in recent decades. One is the growing emphasis upon the immediate family rather than the kinship group family; the other is the increasing number of households which include no persons other than the family of procreation.

In the United States, urban and industrial life now dominates. This is a way of living in which it becomes almost impossible to maintain the kinship family pattern. One may illustrate the extremes by contrasting the historic Chinese family, with its several generations living under one roof as a matter of course, of pride, and of religious devotion, with the American woman who asks for and receives a divorce because her husband's parents moved into their house and he refused to ask them to leave. Urban life means relatively small and congested housing for most people. Industrial life has meant mobility, both horizontal and vertical. Family units move in space to obtain work, better opportunities, or are transferred by "the Company." A family in a situation that is not uncommon is the one in which the grandparents live in Pennsylvania, their married daughter lives in Connecticut, and her married sons live in Florida and Hawaii. Because of our continued economic prosperity and our fluid social class system many young married couples achieve socioeconomic status above that of their relatives and prefer to live and to rear the children away from the relatives.

Systems of social security and pensions make it less necessary for groups of relatives to act as mutual-aid societies, which was an important function of the older kinship group family. Even ethnic groups from Europe, who brought with them the tradition of the *Grossfamilie*, are succumbing more and more to the immediate family pattern, as they are caught up in the American way of life.

Along with the predominance of the immediate family has come a decrease in the number of persons, other than the biological unit, who live in the household. Servants are fewer because of the rising cost of their wages, negative attitudes toward the status of "domestic," smaller houses with laborsaving gadgets, and greater informality in family living. In our busy and congested world, privacy at home has become a prime value so that relatives, boarders, and other "outsiders" are seldom welcome except by necessity. Even the necessity is less. Grandmother, who once had no other place to go except to her children, now has the Golden Years Home or some other such institution. Maiden Auntie now becomes a career girl and has her own apartment. Orphaned cousins may find themselves in a foster home until such time as another family adopts them as members.

These two changes in family personnel have great meaning to children. The results may be both positive and negative. The family that houses and takes responsibility for only the procreative unit can give its children more of money, of time, and of attention. Decisions made for them are direct and are apt to be with the good of the child in mind rather than the welfare of the whole kin group. In concentrating on the children, however, parents may create tremendous pressures of expectation for them, or too much may be given with too little expected. By narrowing down the close affectional relationships to just a few, these relationships often become intense and overpowering. Fewer persons in the household mean fewer intricate human relationships to which a small child must orient himself, but he is also provided with less practice in living with and getting along with persons whose status or role is different from those of his own family of procreation. Perhaps most important of all is the fact that, though a family with fewer persons to support may mean better life chances for a child, it also means that the ledge of security for him is narrower. Should these persons die, desert or separate, his resources are far fewer than if he were a member of a close, protective kinship family. The high rate of marital breakup in America at present is creating a great deal of this kind of insecurity for children. Under happier circumstances, though, many of our children are developing and achieving to an extent that would be impossible were they simply small parts of the machinery of the *Grossfamilie.*

FAMILY SIZE

Ever since the beginning of the twentieth century there have been forces at work which have encouraged and enabled many parents to have few children. High standards of living, the need for more and more years of education in order to succeed in our society, the idea that parents owe something to themselves, among other things, have been the encouragement. The increasing efficiency of contraceptive devices has enabled families to realize their wishes and to institute what has become the common pattern—the small-family system.

Since 1950, however, it has become clear that there is an increase in the number of families who have more than two or three children. Table 1 reveals the extent of that increase. The fact is that,

Table 1 Percentage of Live Births by Order of Birth, 1950–1961

Year	1st Child	2nd Child	3rd Child	4th Child	5th Child	6th and 7th Child	8th Child and over
1950	33.3	32.1	18.4	9.2	4.8	4.7	3.6
1961	31.1	28.4	22.4	14.6	85.	7.8	4.5
% Change	−6.6	−11.5	+21.7	+58.7	+77.1	+66.0	+25.0

Live births per 1000 female population, aged 15–44 years in each specified group.
Data: Public Health Service, U.S. Department of Health, Education, and Welfare.
Source: *Statistical Abstract, 1963,* p. 55.

although we have more small families than large families, the number of children who grow up with many siblings is substantial. In 1961, an estimated 447,268 babies were born to mothers who had formerly given birth to 5 or more children. The Census Bureau reports 2,165,000 families, in 1964, having 5 or more children. It thus becomes apparent that there are many millions of youngsters in the United States who are growing up in large families.

Significance of Size of Group

All students of group dynamics attest to the fact that the number of people in a group influences the interaction and the behavior of the members. Bales and Borgatta,[6] for instance, suggest that in a group of two, agreement may be reached only by unanimity. If two people in a group of three are in agreement the third member has the unhappy choice of going along with the majority or trying to change someone's opinion. In the same-sized group, if two members disagree, the third is in a position to form a majority. Some of the conclusions of this study are that showing tension release, giving opinion, and giving orientation show fairly clear increasing trends by size of group.

Any college teacher or student is aware of the differences in procedures and organization of a classroom with 6 students and one with 60. As the size of the class increases, there is less opportunity for individual attention and individual expression. Greater discipline must be exerted, more lecture and less discussion becomes the rule. More formality and regimen become necessary, sometimes to the extent of assigning seats to reduce the time that would be consumed in taking attendance. The procedures, the organization, the interaction, the behavior, and the problems involved are all different because of the factor of size.

The same kinds of processes obtain in family life. A certain-size family is conducive to a certain way of life, a pattern of attitudes and a complex of values. We use the term "family system" to include all of these. The comparisons made between the small- and large-family systems[7] are in no way intended to suggest that one is "better" than the other. Each has its own special values that affect the development and personalities of the children growing up within them.

Contrasts in Family Systems by Size

In order to obtain broad comparisons between family systems the contrasts here are made in respect to 100 2-child families and 100 with 6 or more children, studies of which have been made at the William T. Carter Foundation.[8] Some of the most striking differences found are the following.

1. Childrearing practices differ in many respects. First, there is

[6] Robert F. Bales and Edgar F. Borgatta, "Size of Group as a Factor in the Interaction Profile," in A. Paul Hare (Ed.) *Small Groups—Studies in Social Interaction,* New York, Alfred A. Knopf, 1955, chap. 7.

[7] James H. S. Bossard and Eleanor Stoker Boll, *The Large Family System,* Philadelphia, University of Pennsylvania Press, 1956.

[8] James H. S. Bossard, "Large and Small Families—A Study in Contrasts," *Journal of the American Society of Chartered Life Underwriters,* Summer, 1959, pp. 222–240. Materials collected by the Carter Foundation, but not completely analyzed suggest that the four-child family system is a compromise between the extremes in childrearing practices of the large- and small-family systems.

the matter of who "rules the ranch." There are many current comments attacking the results of American matriarchal rule, and of the anarchy resulting from child rule. At the same time, some children complain about survivals of paternal autocracy.

In the families under study it was the large families which experienced the patriarchal survival, but the patriarch's authority was by no means direct. His wishes were known; they were impressed upon the children by the mother; but in the details of day-to-day living it was older children who saw to it that the younger children carried out the father's wishes. To a great extent it was the father who decreed, the mother who interpreted, and the children who exerted the authority.

The small families were the ones with matriarchal rule. Though in some cases Mother was following the father's wishes, in most instances she was the decision maker and in almost all cases the one who directly exerted the authority. Under only a very few special circumstances was one child ever put in authority over another; and if one tried to be authoritative, on his own, there was trouble.

Modes of discipline to enforce authority varied greatly. Physical punishment, or the threat of it, was mentioned more frequently by members of large families than small families. However, the threat seemed to be sufficient to make the actuality occur seldom. Johnny, for instance, would get the strap for a violation of the rules. Five or more other children witnessed the occasion. The message seemed clear to them: "If I misbehave, this is what will happen to me." In large families, a single punishment was usually a deterrent to misbehavior.

Almost as one voice, the respondents from small families reported little use of physical punishment. Instead there were two methods, one of which may be described as "Yak, yak, yak. Nag, nag, nag"—administered chiefly by the mother. The other was the withdrawing of privileges, such as allowances and movies or dating. This method was usually the father's.

The household organization and the children's roles within it were quite different. The larger the family, unless it was a completely disorganized and unhappy one, the greater the amount of regimentation and assigning jobs to the children. The success of a large family appeared to depend upon this systematizing, in order for the household and its relationships to run smoothly. The children themselves took a large part in demanding that their siblings stick to their jobs. If they did not, someone else would have to do the work. Thus, some of the traits applauded in siblings were conscientiousness, reliability, keeping in line. In small families, for the most part, regimentation was considered undemocratic and stifling to individual freedom. This was the kind of family that could afford to plan its work so as not to interfere too much with other pursuits of Mother, Father, and children. The children were often spared from all household chores in the interests of concentrating on their education, outside activities, and social life. Respondents in these cases stressed the talents and good social adjustment of their siblings. Credit was given to the parents for offering such advantages, although sometimes it was suggested that children were pushed into such activities unwillingly.

One can summarize the childrearing patterns in the following way. In the large family Father is the ruler, Mother is the administrator, and the children are public opinion. In the small family the father, like the Queen of England, reigns but does not rule. Mother is the responsible Prime Minister, and there is very little public opinion.

2. In some respects the large family is more vulnerable than the small family. Most large families experience economic hardship at some time. Even with an income that might appear ample to support a few children and their parents, the large family has to make it do for many. The difficulty is increased by the weight of numbers in other ways. There are *more* children to break arms, to have tonsils out, to receive shots. Measles spread to not a few but many. Someone always seems to have a cold. All of this puts pressure on parents and produces another kind of vulnerability.

Breakup of the large families before the children were independent was much higher than for the small families—with ratios of 1 to 3 and 1 to 10 respectively. Although the divorce rate was less for parents of large families, desertion and death of one or both parents was much higher, as was the rate of alcoholism among fathers.[9]

3. In spite of the vulnerability, certain kinds of anxiety over children appeared to be less in large families. For example:

Mrs. A. had two children. Her first baby walked alone at 13 months. Her second baby was not even trying to walk at 15 months. Yet Mrs. A. had read in a book on child development that two-thirds of all babies walk by the time they are 14 months old. First she tried supporting him, trying to make him walk. He screamed and refused to stand. Finally, in great anxiety, she rushed him to a physician to see if he might be

[9] Because of special problems related to large-family living, an organization, Parents of Large Families (POLF), has been formed so that such parents may pool their experiences. A news bulletin is issued from POLF Headquarters, P.O. Box 885, Norwalk, Conn., 06852.

retarded. The physician told her to go home and relax, that she was communicating her worries to the boy.

Mrs. B. had five children, their ages ranging from 7 years to 17 months, and was pregnant. The youngest child, fat and placid, simply sat on the floor and delightedly watched the excitement going on around her. When asked by a neighbor if she was not concerned that this baby wasn't walking, Mrs. B. replied, "Goodness, no! I wish she'd just sit for another year, it makes things so much easier."

A mother who has a number of children learns two things somewhere along the way. One is that each normal child develops at his own individual pace. The other is that all children go through certain maturational phases of life which are normal and temporary. She learns that the defiant negativist of 3 turns into a sweet, social little girl in a few years and that the dirty boor of a 13-year-old boy will pre-empt the bathroom as soon as he meets that first important girl. Such parents, instead of creating many needless anxieties for themselves and their children, learn to exercise a certain amount of "judicious neglect."

4. Children from the large and the small families had different ldeas of the sources of their security and of how it was related to family size. Although the literature on child development indicates that emotional security comes from the early relationship between mother and baby, large-family children seldom mentioned parents as the sources. They found security in the numbers of siblings who formed a cohesive group for defense, playing, confiding, teaching, even plotting *against* parents. This, they said, gave them emotional security and, incidentally, a sense of economic security. Though one's individual funds might be low, in childhood and even in adulthood, "the clan" could be counted on to help as a sort of mutual-aid society.

The comments of children from small families were almost the opposite. Security came directly from parents. It came from what they did for you and gave to you. Thus, the children expressed their feeling that emotional security came from economic security, or through the material advantages. A number of these respondents did remark that they thought they would have felt more emotionally secure had they had more siblings with whom to grow up.

5. Closely related to comments on feelings of security were comments on family integration and cohesiveness. Whereas large-family respondents thought of the family as a group to be maintained and served by each member for the good of all, those from small families thought of it more as a launching pad for the

projecting of adequate individuals into the outside world. Some of the former admitted that the closeness of family life had made it extremely difficult for them to relate to "outsiders" in later life. Some of the latter remarked upon their problems in becoming "cogs in mass society."

6. Problems of parent-child relationship were quite different in the two kinds of families. Large-family children sometimes spoke of emotional deprivation, of a parent not having enough time to satisfy all the youngsters. Though they felt this was compensated for, in part, by siblings, they still missed the close parent-child tie. Small-family children, when they complained, remarked about the intensity of the relationship, the concentration, the competition for affection, and the "apron strings" that bound throughout too many years. Most of them felt the pressure of too great expectations.

These contrasts in family systems indicate certain quite different influences on the children growing up within them. In the large family the emphasis is upon the group, not the individual. From this come both deprivation and security. The deprivation is in terms of thinned relationship with parents and lack of opportunity to develop individual potentials. The group cohesion, however, produces security, which is interpreted as coming from people and not from material things. Because of the repeated view of normally developing life processes, anxieties about oneself and others are reduced. Character traits valued are responsibility, loyalty, conscientiousness, doing one's share, taking one's place in the group. Siblings form the chief pressure in insisting upon these values.

In the small family the overriding emphasis is upon developing the full potential of the individuals therein. The family is thought of as existing for this purpose. Stimulation for creativity and success in a challenging world is a goal. Security is attained from parents who make this all possible by giving children all the advantages they need. Anxiety results when a child does not seem to be measuring up to "the average child," and this anxiety communicates itself to the young. Pressures on reluctant children are often necessary to achieve the desired ends. There is a reluctance to let go of children, both because much is expected from them and because they are few in number. With all the emotional eggs in two baskets the relationship is apt to be intense.

In conclusion, it should be emphasized that in these 200 families it is not the size by itself that has created varied systems of family living. Rather, it is life factors and personal values that arise in relation to a certain-sized group.[10]

FAMILY AGE STRUCTURE

Little research has been done concerning the family situations resulting from certain phases of the changing age structure of the family, although the changes themselves have received much attention. We know, for instance, that first marriages are contracted at an earlier age than they used to be. In 1890, the median age was 26.1 for males and 22.0 for females. In 1962, it was 22.7 and 20.3, respectively. The most popular age of first marriages for females in the United States is now 18 years. The percentage of people marrying has also increased slightly, from 91.9 to 92.8 percent. The population, too, has increased; so that if one thinks of numbers of children rather than of the percentage of youthful marriages, it would appear that there are more children being born to quite young parents. Statistics seem to bear this out. In 1940, there were 336,532 babies born to mothers who were 19 years old or under. In 1961, there were 609,182. Of these, 7462 were born to mothers under the age of 15, some of whom were also married "women." The birth rate for females 15 to 19 years of age in 1940 was 54.1 percent. In 1961, it was 88.7 percent.

In addition to these figures, it has been reported[11] that nine-tenths of American children are born before their mothers are 35 years old. This means that our pattern is to have children when we are young and to cease having them when we are still fairly young. Life expectency is becoming longer. In 1940, it was 62.8 years; and by 1960 it was 67.4. For men, it was 66.5 and for women, 73.0. Most parents, then, can expect to survive the independence of their last child for an extended period of years.

Since the beginning of this century both the rate of family breakup and the rate of remarriage has increased. A number of people, therefore, have been marrying at later ages, though it may not be the first marriage for some. During this same period medical science has decreased the danger of having first babies at later

[10] For a study of the effects of both size and sex structure of family on parent-child relations see, Glen H. Elder, Jr., and Charles E. Bowman, "Family Structure and Child-Rearing Patterns: The Effect of Family Size and Sex Composition," *American Sociological Review*, December, 1963, pp. 891–905.

[11] *School Service*, Lexington Kentucky, Bureau of School Service, College of Education, University of Kentucky, August, 1964.

ages. Whereas this was once considered perilous in the middle 30s, many women do have first babies safely now in the late 30s and early 40s. Thus, along with the situation in which babies are being born to younger parents, there is also the situation in which older parents start rearing families.

All of these changes would seem to have great meaning for children. Yet, as has been said, the consequences of these situations to them have not been widely investigated. The following discussion, for the most part, must then be framed as suggestions that might lead to further research.

The Young-Parent Family

The sight, so common today, of young parents with teenage children enjoying themselves at the movies, restaurants, or concerts and seeming to have so much in common, suggests a family situation full of healthy relationships. It is a great contrast to what often occurred in an earlier period when people married late; had children later; when there were more children, spread out over a greater number of years; and when the last child, particularly if a girl, was sacrificed to caring for an elderly, seemingly feeble, widowed mother who had long since disapproved of the "goings on" of that daughter's generation.

Most situations, however, have both their positives and their negatives, and some of the latter have emerged as problems in the lives of very young parents and their children. Not all young people who want to marry are interested in becoming parents, nor are they prepared for the realities and responsibilities of rearing children. The young husband and wife have been enjoying the freedom of their lives—freedom from the restrictions of parental authority. A baby arrives and is as restricting, in his way, as parents are in theirs. To such young people parenthood is a crisis, and for a time there may be considerable rejection of the child that changes life so drastically and attempts to force maturity on the youthful. It has been said by an experienced observer that "some people would be happy if they could put children into a barrel at the age of 2 and keep them there until they were eighteen."[12] Some of the ramifications of this attitude toward children are discussed at greater length in Chapter 3.

As the years pass, and the children grow into teen-agers, another problem sometimes arises—that of rivalry between parents and

[12] Edna Brown, "The Visiting Teacher Looks at the Rejected Child," *Mental Hygiene*, July, 1949, p. 432.

children who are close in age and interests. The youthful-looking 33-year-old mother of a 16-year-old girl remarked, "Babe and I can't get along together at all any more, and I know what causes the trouble. She is trying to act as if she were 21, and so am I."

Teenage girls have mentioned problems about bringing dates home to meet their parents. One commented, "I ask him in, and there is my attractive young mother. She is much more sophisticated than I am and knows better how to talk to young boys and put them at ease. So, *I* sit, and *they* talk."

Boys have described similar problems when they introduce their girls to young fathers. Some teen-agers have insisted that their parents refuse to let them grow up and act their age in order to evade such competition.

Others, girls especially, have voiced a quite different result of this age structure. Said one, "I wish Mother were older and farther away from her own dating years. She remembers them so well that she is trying to live them again through me. I'm not as keen on dating as she was, but she thinks there is something wrong with me if I don't run around and do all the things she did. She 'maneuvers' me and gets in my hair."

How widespread such difficulties are is not known. There is, however, little question that, as children grow even older, another problem is likely to occur. The young people are ready to leave home, for college, for employment, or for marriage. Mother has devoted her life to them, she is still feeling young and healthy and may have 20 or 30 years of life before her. Many women who have not cultivated broad interests and who have concentrated on children to the detriment of the marriage relationship discover, at that time, that their lives are empty—even of the husband who has remained with her only until the children are reared. This kind of situation creates concrete problems, as well as guilt feelings in the children. The problems may continue, even into the next generation where the parents—now grandparents—become the clinging and interfering kind. The popularity of new programs of continuing education is perhaps, in part, a result of the awareness of adults of the widening gap between active parenthood and death and an attempt to do something constructive with life in the interim.

The Older-Parent Family

The combination of prolonged education, frequent remarriage, and greater safety for first births at a later age is producing certain kinds of family situations which are deserving of more attention than has been given to them. Three types will be described here.

Although the rate of "campus marriage" has increased since the end of World War II,[13] it is still more usual for young people to postpone marriage until their education is completed—and this period of postponement is lengthening. In certain professions it is not rare for preparation to continue to the age of 28 or 30, and for a few more years to intervene before the responsibilities of marriage can be afforded. After that comes parenthood. What is the situation of the child born to such parents who have been "students" and "career people" for so long a time? How does it compare with that of the child born to young parents who practically grow up with him? That many facets of the two situations are different may be assumed. The longer one puts off parenthood for career life the more one becomes inevitably grooved into an adult-oriented and organized life. One may dislike it, and turn with joy to the very different organization of family life. Or, one may resent the unexpected demands that set the old routines topsy-turvy. Very young people may find parenthood upsetting because it takes away their youth too quickly. More mature persons, on the other hand, may have trouble renouncing long-established ways of living.

There is a great difference between the career woman who has a child rather late in life, and the woman who bears a child late in life, but who has been a mother since her youth. Their orientations to life have been dissimilar for years.

Another question relates to energy in dealing with young children and, indeed, with adolescents. Even young grandparents have uttered the almost classic remark, "It is so good to have the children come, and so good to see them go." The age at which the pressure of youthful energy begins to be exhausting is an individual matter, but the longer parenthood is delayed, the sooner this point is reached. One other fact may be pertinent to these situations. The world is changing faster every year. It is sometimes difficult for young parents to understand precisely the culture in which their children live. For more elderly parents the age-culture gap is even wider.[14]

The frequency of remarriage introduces two other kinds of older-parent situations for children. One is that in which a widowed or divorced man marries a younger unmarried woman who has never had children, who wants them, and who has them. The other

13 James H. S. Bossard and Eleanor Stoker Boll, "Campus Marriages—For Better or For Worse?" The *New York Times Magazine*, April 5, 1959, pp. 59, 83, 85, 86, 88.

14 James H. S. Bossard, *Parent and Child*, Philadelphia, University of Pennsylvania Press, 1953, chap. 10.

is the case in which both husband and wife have been married before. Some of the problems formerly mentioned apply to these families also, but still others enter the picture. There are the added possibilities of the "your children, my children, and our children" situation, with all of its complexities, and of the stepparent-stepchild relationships.[15] Also, in such families the age structure of the nuclear family and the related kinship group can become "abnormal," and is sometimes conceived as such by a child and by his friends. Mr. Brown, a widower at 52 years of age, married a single woman of 35. They had two children, two years apart. Mr. Brown, very happy after 20 years of his second marriage, was nevertheless eloquent about some of the family problems. His daughter by his first marriage had four children at the time of his remarriage. Feeling herself to be an expert in childrearing, she attempted to advise her new stepmother. The advice was not taken very kindly. Mr. Brown's father, a bit senile by the time the second round of children arrived, was constantly confused about which children belonged to whom and made many remarks to which others in the family were a bit sensitive. During school days, some of the children were teased because they had nieces and nephews older than they; others were teased for the opposite age arrangement. One exceedingly difficult time for father-children relationships, Mr. Brown reported, was during the children's adolescence. His wife insisted that they be permitted the ordinary noise and gang behavior customary to that period—and he agreed. He was, however, in the late 60s at that time and found it much more trying than during his first experience in fatherhood.

Age Relationships Among Siblings

Nature, unregulated by man, seems to plan that children be born at quite short intervals so that each one has siblings close in age. Infant mortality and other physical problems have always interfered with this plan and have made larger age differences between children in the same family. Parents themselves have usually found some means of attempting family planning according to their desires. The advent of more and more effective contraceptive devices, however, has made this planning a great deal more effective. It would seem to be of some significance, then, to explore sibling age relationships in the light of what actually is happening. Since such a study has not been made on a large scale,

15 *Ibid.*, Chap. 8. This chapter contains a detailed study of the effects of stepparent-stepchild relationships upon the child.

the following discussion, again, is based on data collected at the William T. Carter Foundation, and any conclusions are tentative.

In the 1920s some medical doctors became interested in birth intervals and suggested that babies should be born not less than three years apart. The decision was based wholly upon the health and welfare of the mother. Most children, though, have expressed to us that, in terms of happiness in their family relationships, the shorter the interval the better—regardless of the size of the family. There is some evidence that the present trend is in this direction. Dr. Reuben Hill has projected changes in the American family by studying three generations of 100 families.[16] He concludes that although birth intervals tended to widen for the generation married during the great depression, the pattern for both the grandparents and the present-parent generation is close to two years between births.

Much of what has been written about the contributions of sibling relationships to child development is more applicable if the children are close in age. They play together, work together, eat together, bathe together, share the same rooms, toys, clothes, and have many similar interests because of similar maturational phases. They may also fight more and engage in more rivalry and competition. Such experiences, in the protection of family life, are very good preparation for living in the outside world, and are apt to insure an abiding appreciation of one's relative place in life and of the rights of others. Children learn differently from slightly older siblings than they do from considerably older siblings or from adults. In the latter case, it is a more formal teacher-pupil situation. In the former, since the skills of the older child are only a little beyond that of the younger one, he stretches a bit—and learns. Siblings close in age can form a sort of union against parent management. They save each other from being with adults too much. The significance of this is that they are kept, to some extent, from the unnatural environment which the adult furnishes. Parents and other older people are less satisfactory companions for children than other children close in age—because children treat one another as equals. Older people are apt to be over solicitous, less understanding, more condescending, less interesting, more preoccupied, and in many ways less able to afford a healthy environment for a child's normal development.

Even some of the accepted data on birth order and child behavior are related to birth intervals in their effectiveness. It is true

16 Reuben Hill, "The American Family of the Future," *Journal of Marriage and the Family*, February, 1964, pp. 20–28.

that the first child is the only one ever to be an only child, but the extent to which this becomes important to him and the extent to which he experiences severe jealousy depends, among other things, upon how soon the next sibling arrives. The first child is also the experimental child, but if children come close upon each other, experience becomes intensive, and perhaps develops a clearer perspective than would be developed with more time. The oldest child is said to be the one in whom traits of responsibility for the others may be encouraged; and this may always operate to some extent. There is, however, much more opportunity for sharing responsibility when the whole brood differs little in years and capabilities. The in-between child, who is frequently described as having a neither-fish-nor-fowl position, is certainly not so isolated in in-betweenness if the birth intervals are short. The baby, or the spoiled brat as he is often called, has much less chance of becoming spoiled when parents are struggling to socialize two or three babies at the same time.

Though the general pattern may be to have babies a few years apart, there are, of course, other patterns which create quite different family situations for children. Several of them will be mentioned briefly. One is that in which parents decide to have one more experience in parenthood after their children are nearing the age of independence. A number of still-young mothers are choosing this way out of the dilemma of how to be occupied and useful for many years to come. Such children have both the advantages and disadvantages of being wanted for a particular reason, of the experience of their parents, and of their older age. A child born into this situation may be reared more like an only child than like a child with siblings. A 21-year-old girl, with three siblings older than she and a sister 7 years of age said, "We all come from a fairly large family. Yet my younger sister is much like an only child. We are more like aunts and uncles to her, and her nieces and nephews seem more like her brothers and sisters." Another girl spoke of her resentment when her much-older brothers came home to visit. "I never knew them very well because they left for college when I was a toddler. But when they come home, they take over. They have shared life with Mother and Daddy longer than I have, and they have more in common on an age basis."

Another set of age patterns among siblings results from the arbitrary motives of individual parents. There are many reasons, aside from physical ones, why children are spaced far apart—both financial reasons and deeply personal ones. In one family the third, and last, baby arrived when the first girl was 15 years old and the second was 7. Their births had been planned that way so that the very social parents would not have the problem of more than one preschool child at home at the same time. In this case, the oldest girl had never felt close to her younger sister until the new baby arrived. At that point, the 15-year-old was interested in real live babies, understood that the 7-year-old was going through the same feelings that she herself had formerly experienced, and took it upon herself to "mother" both of them. Data on age-spacing that have been gathered suggest that considerably older brothers or sisters sometimes play very important roles. They are halfway between parents and the younger child and have some understanding of the feelings and attitudes of both. They are also a bit closer to the changes in social norms and education that have come about since the parents' adulthood.

Finally, there is the matter of plural birth, a phenomenon which has been studied a great deal by biologists, physical anthropologists, and psychologists. The social significance of the rearing of multiple-birth children has been given comparatively little heed, although it is obvious that such children have always had a special status. So rare are triplets and children of higher multiple-birth cases that they reach headlines, are often made into "experiments," and have problems of attaining privacy and normal living. Twins are more frequent, enough so that they can be studied as a group, rather than as a special case, so that some generalizations about their situation can be made.

It has been pointed out by Dr. Ernest R. Mowrer[17] that even within the twin population there are important differences. Identical twins develop from one egg and are of the same sex and gene structure. Fraternal twins come from two eggs and may or may not be unisexed. Whereas the tendency is to treat identical twins as much alike as two people can be treated, greater differences are made between the other pairs, because of obvious dissimilarities in looks, abilities, and sex. This is, however, only a matter of degree. Twins are usually thought of as couples and are expected to have a unique relationship. Identical twins tend to develop this naturally. Frequently when very small, they form a sort of closed society. They often begin to talk later than single-birth children because they have a means of communication with each other. Sometimes they become socialized later and with more difficulty on the part of the parents. One aspect of this is seen in matters of discipline.

[17] Ernest R. Mowrer, "Some Factors in the Affectional Adjustment of Twins," *American Sociological Review*, August, 1954, pp. 468–471.

It is not easy to exert immediate punishment upon two youngsters who, almost by instinct, take off in opposite directions at the approach of it. The closed corporation learns to conspire in this kind of evasion. Another aspect is that playing with other children does not seem particularly intriguing. The twins are sufficient unto themselves. This twin-sufficiency comes to worry some of the very parents who have treated the children as one child. Then, there is an effort to separate them in play group and classroom, to stop dressing them alike. When this has been forced, it has been infinitely distressing to some identicals who have, indeed, experienced a rare relationship. One boy from such a pair, whose mother was very subtly (she thought) trying to spell out the advantages of their going to separate schools, said, "Mother, why don't you leave us alone? When we grow up we'll have different jobs and different wives, and we'll just have to grow more apart. Can't we go on being together till that happens?"

The mother retracted. The grown twins now have different wives, children and jobs—and an exceedingly close and satisfying relationship although separated by many miles.

Fraternal twins, and particularly those of different sexes, voice another problem. A number of them dislike being forced to be a couple in all respects. A lot more of competition and rivalry has been found between twins of this kind than between identical twins. Fraternal twins *are* more unlike; many of them rebel against the pressure to be alike; and they vie with each other in stressing their uniqueness or superiority.

The special status of being a twin has caused some problems in relationships with other siblings. Each set of children knows that the twins are "special." Even outsiders make that clear. "And how are the twins?" they beam. Single-birth siblings sometimes feel pushed too much into the background, and the twins too much to the fore. If twins are very close in their companionship this, too, can cause a sort of separation from other brothers and sisters.

In the family situation, it should be reaffirmed, no one factor acts alone in its effects upon the developing child. The size of a family has significant influences. These, however, may be modified and even cancelled out by the specific nature of the spacing of children. To six children, born within six years, family size cannot mean the same as it does to six children, born in sets of three children, several years apart.

FAMILY SEX STRUCTURE

One of the results of the small-family system is the number of homes in which the children are all of the same sex. With six or more in the family the probability is greater that there will be both boys and girls. According to the Census Bureau, parents in the United States are not giving the law of probability a chance as far as sex structure is concerned. It is reported that 28.8 percent of American families have just girls; that 30.2 percent have just boys; and that 41 percent, the minority, have both boys and girls. A consequence is that many children do not have the experience of growing up in the same house with siblings who are different physically, psychologically, and in their social training. In such cases there is not always a very realistic appreciation of what these differences are, or of what the results are in terms of behavior, attitudes, and values.

This lack of understanding of the opposite sex may be particularly true in a society like ours in which the romantic complex is so pervasive. At increasingly earlier ages the idea of "going with" or "dating" forms the basis of relationships between girls and boys, even though they are still too young to actually engage in these processes. Many of the tots on Art Linkletter's television program express love for, or expectations of marriage with, some other tot. It is a fact that such expressions are not rare in the first and second grades of school.[18] In a relationship of this sort, behavior is more in the nature of putting one's best foot forward and showing off than it is of being one's true self. The strength of this behavior increases with approach to actual dating age, and it creates an unrealistic image. It is not the way brothers and sisters and husbands and wives habitually act with each other.

Growing up with brothers, a girl is more apt to learn some of the important and fundamental differences between the sexes in our society. For instance, male muscles and bones equip boys for different kinds of activities, as do their senses. Boys are encouraged in such activities, too; for "sissiness" is a vice in our society, as it is not in all societies. Thus, boys are not too enthusiastic about entering into girls' interests and frequently make it clear that such interests are not very worthwhile. Though the male is muscularly stronger, he is biologically weaker. He is not built to "take it" in the same way that the female is and takes illness and certain kinds

[18] James H. S. Bossard and Eleanor S. Boll, "School Situations in Behavior Studies," *Sociology and Social Research*, 1947, pp. 423–429.

of crises with greater difficulty. He may have the same kinds of feelings of love and fear that girls have, but he is trained, early, to suppress the expressions of these. Little girls can express love freely, and fear much more easily. Girls have more training in the nurturing role and in the intricacies of human relationships—indeed it is possible that they are also better equipped by nature for these things. Many other examples of differences between the male and female could be cited which could cause problems if understanding is not acquired by the child. But these, perhaps, will suffice to illustrate the point that the girl who sees the boy growing up and being socialized—and the boy who has a parallel experience—has a more realistic preparation for association with the opposite sex throughout life.[19]

Another important aspect of the sex structure has to do with the fact that most fathers leave home during their work hours instead of working at home, with the whole family, as was characteristic in an agricultural economy. This leaves more of the responsibility of childrearing to the mother than was formerly the case. One result of this which has received much attention is the effect upon boys who are reared primarily by women. It is suggested that this tends to feminization of males, and it has been demonstrated that it has caused psychiatric difficulties.[20]

The possibilities of what such a situation means to girls, and other members of the family have been little explored. Two such effects might be suggested here. When girls have no brothers and a father who is rarely present, where do the girls get their image of the male and his role?

Also, one might think of the father as the focal point of this situation. One father explained that when he arrived home for dinner at night he felt like the fifth wheel on the wagon. His wife and two daughters were already occupied in feminine pursuits and feminine conversations. Said he, "I can't spend dinner hour discussing ways in which to get spots out of nylon blouses without ruining the blouse. I don't know anything about it, and I care less."

While considering the sex structure of a family and its meaning, the makeup of the family of orientation may be as important as that of the family of procreation alone. Consider, for instance, the case of a man who knew all the best methods and shortcuts in housekeeping, cooking, and sewing and who sought to win ap-

[19] For more detailed discussion of this subject see, James H. S. Bossard and Eleanor Stoker Boll, *The Girl That You Marry*, Macrae Smith, Philadelphia, 1960; and Eleanor Stoker Boll, *The Man That You Marry*, Macrae Smith, Philadelphia, 1963.

[20] Edward A. Strecker, *Their Mothers' Sons*, rev. ed., J. B. Lippincott Company, Philadelphia, 1946, 1951.

proval by constantly describing them. Though he appeared to be manly, men did not enjoy his company and women thought him rather strange. This man had been reared as an only child in a house with his widowed mother, his grandmother, and two maiden aunts.

SUMMARY

1. A family situation may be defined as a unit of stimuli operating within the confines of the family circle, and organized in relation to the person or object which serves as the focal point in the particular case.

2. Family situations should be studied with all possible scientific objectivity, first, because of their great importance in determining personality patterns; and, second, because they offer the best opportunities for the development of scientific techniques in the situational approach to behavior problems.

3. The structure of a family situation is composed of the personnel, size, age relationships, and sex makeup of the family.

4. Recent changes in family personnel are: (a) a growing emphasis upon the immediate family rather than the kinship-group family, and (b) the increasing number of households which include no persons other than the family of procreation.

5. Although the small family is most popular in the United States, there has been an increase in the number of large families. Size of family influences childrearing practices, the vulnerability of the family, emotional and economic security of the children, family integration and cohesiveness, and parent-child relationships.

6. The progressively younger age for first marriage has resulted in an increase of families with very young parents. At the same time, it has become less dangerous for women to have their first births at a later age, so that there has been an increase in the older-parent family. Improvements in contraceptive devices have enabled more parents to space their children according to their own individual motives, so that various patterns of age relationships between siblings and between children and parents result.

7. Twins have a unique age relationship which affects each twin, their relationship with each other, and with the rest of the family.

8. The small-family system creates a situation in which many parents have children who are all of the same sex. In such families the complementary nature of the two sexes does not operate among the children in the natural home setting and can cause a lack of

understanding of the opposite sex, physically, psychologically, and socially.

SUGGESTED READINGS

Blatz, William Emet, *The Five Sisters,* William Morrow and Company, New York, 1938. The birth of the Dionne quintuplets roused such interest that they were studied as unique specimens. This book is a psychological study of the quintuplets.

Cutts, Norma, and Nicholas Moseley, *The Only Child,* G. P. Putnam Sons, New York, 1954. Intended as a guide for parents, this book is based on data from 258 case histories of persons who were only children.

Drysdale, C. V., *The Small Family System,* B. W. Huebsch, New York, 1913. The first study of a then rather new phenomenon.

Gilbreth, Frank B. Jr., and Ernestine Carey Gilbreth, *Cheaper by the Dozen,* Thomas Y. Crowell Company, New York, 1949, 1963. An autobiographical novel about a couple who wanted a large family and had it. Then the father died.

Mead, Margaret, *Male and Female,* William Morrow and Company, New York, 1949. An anthropologist discusses patterns of living and attitudes that determine sex-appropriate behavior.

Neisser, Edith G., *The Eldest Child,* Harper & Brothers, New York, 1957. This book is written primarily for parents and people who work with children. It discusses the unique situation of the firstborn child in a family.

Newman, Horation H., Frank N. Freeman, and Karl J. Holzinger, *Twins,* University of Chicago Press, Chicago, 1937. An assessment of the relative weight of genetic inheritance and social environment on the intelligence and personality of twins.

Paton, Jean, *The Adopted Break Silence,* Life History Study Center, 222 North Hicks Street, Philadelphia, 1954. A life-history study of 40 adults who were adopted children tells the story of adoption from their point of view.

Reyher, Rebecca, *The Fon and His Hundred Wives,* Doubleday & Company, New York, 1952. A suffragette, columnist, and lecturer, visits a country where family structure is based on polygamy. She reports pros as well as cons.

Scheinfeld, Amram, *Women and Men,* Harcourt, Brace and Company, New York, 1944. Dr. Scheinfeld intended to show the social causes of sex-different behavior but found that biological factors were of equal importance.

Trasler, Gordon, *In Place of Parents,* The Humanities Press, New York,

1960. An intriguing study of foster children and their feelings toward their foster homes and their own parents.

Witmer, Helen Leland, et al. *Independent Adoptions*. Russell Sage Foundation, New York, 1963. Since many children are adopted through personal contacts rather than through social agencies, this follow-up study of such adoptions in the state of Florida is an important one.

FAMILY PROCESS AND THE CHILD 3

A family is more than a structure. It is a vibrant functioning reality, a group of persons living together in intimate continuing relationships. A second approach, then, to the study of family situations may be made through the objective analysis of the interactive processes which take place between the elements (chiefly persons) comprising the family structure. The purpose of the present chapter is to consider the family as a form of social interaction, with particular reference to the significance of these processes in the social development of the child. Accordingly, the emphasis here is upon the processes that are involved, the role of these processes, their more important constituent elements, and the nature of their operation. Specific problems created for the child and reports on research findings concerning these problems are reserved for a later chapter.

THE MEANING OF SOCIAL AND FAMILY INTERACTION

Sociologists speak a special language, as Waller reminds us,[1] because it facilitates precise communication in their specialized field.

[1] Willard Waller, *The Family*, The Dryden Press, Inc., New York, 1938, p. 15.

In this scientific jargon, the term *interaction* has the sanction of frequent usage and great emphasis; hence it seems necessary to say something more about its meaning. "The notion of interaction is not simple, but very complex," says Ormond.[2] It "involves, not simply the idea of collision and rebound, but something much more profound, namely, the internal modifiability of the colliding agents." For a complete analysis of interaction as a sociological process, the reader is referred to any standard work on systematic sociology.[3] For an interpretation of family life in terms of the interactive process, the reader will find most helpful Waller's book *The Family*, already cited.

For our purposes, it will be enough to identify the term as the generic name for the range of contacts between persons through which each influences the other, to the end that every new experience becomes part of a new totality. The term *family interaction* is used to include these reciprocal relationships between the members of a family in their continuing life with each other; and the results of this interactive family process, so far as the child is concerned, may be thought of as the child's familial sociopsychological heritage.

THE PECULIAR NATURE OF FAMILY INTERACTION

Family interaction is, as has just been pointed out, one form or area of social interaction and, as such, is part of the more comprehensive field of personal interrelationships. It is important, however, to point out that the family is also something more; it is a unique and distinctive kind of interaction. A family is a set of peculiarly intimate relationships, such as one finds perhaps nowhere else in the field of social interaction. Its intimacies are of many different kinds and degrees. They are mostly continuing in character. With few exceptions, they have the full sanction of society. They come to express themselves in a terminology which has meaning to the family members and to no one else. These intimacies and their peculiar tokens exist regardless of the degree of harmony within the family; in fact, family discord and tensions precipitate their own distinctive varieties of expression. Even when the family breaks up, some of these intimacies persist as do the

[2] A. T. Ormond, *Foundations of Knowledge*, Macmillan & Company, Ltd., London, 1900, p. 196.

[3] Excellent here is Leopold von Wiese and Howard Becker, *Systematic Sociology*, John Wiley & Sons, New York, 1932. See also Robert E. Park and Ernest W. Burgess, *Introduction to the Science of Sociology*, University of Chicago Press, Chicago, 1921, chaps. 5, 6.

tokens of their expression, so that this aspect of family interaction often continues long after the family's corporate existence.

Another reason for the distinctive peculiarity of family interaction is to be found in the composition of the family. The family community is made up of units dissimilar in age and sex, complementary in their nature, mutually responsible, and with the unifying bond of kinship for all but husband and wife; in the latter case there is the compensating bond of other relationships. Perhaps no one has described this phase of family life better than Bosanquet did almost 60 years ago:

> As with all organic wholes, its parts are admirably fitted by nature to subserve each other's needs, and to supplement each other's efforts. The need of the weak for protection finds its correlative in the pride of the strong in protecting; the clinging appeal of the child for affection elicits a response which might otherwise remain dormant for ever. The authority which all adults like to exercise finds a beneficent outlet in guiding the action of immature wills; and children who weary when left to the caprices of their undisciplined natures, find strength and contentment in a rule which is autocratic without having the impersonal rigidity of external law. And the man, again, who would prefer solitude to the constant clashing at close quarters of his own will with that of another man, finds it completed instead of thwarted when its functions are supplemented by those of the woman.[4]

Despite all this, the formal existence of a family does not, as everyone knows, guarantee a "condition of continuing harmony." There is about family interaction this additional distinctive feature: its naked incisiveness. One can dissemble only little in most phases of family interaction. Indeed, from more than one aspect, family interaction is a brutal process, the more so because of the very likenesses of the family members and the intimacies of the relationships between them. Here again it is worthwhile to quote Bosanquet at some length.

> A plain person finds no attraction in a mirror; and a person sensitive to his own defects of character may be inexpressibly jarred by seeing them reflected in another. I have known mothers whose irritation at the faults of their children was greatly enhanced by the fact that they recognized them as merely the faults of their own childhood recurring once again. And we fear no critic as we do the critic of our own Family, for has he not the key to all our weaknesses within himself? The stranger may be hostile and severe, but we can always console ourselves with the thought—which in nine cases out of ten will be perfectly true—that he does not really understand us. It is not being misunderstood which hurts most; it is being understood at our weakest, just as what helps the most

[4] Helen Bosanquet, *The Family*, The Macmillan Company, New York, 1902, p. 242.

is being understood at our best. And the member of our Family understands us literally "down to the ground," for it is the same ground upon which he himself stands.

Here, too, we may perhaps find an explanation of the strange bitterness which so often seems to attach to differences of opinion between members of the same Family. When an outsider differs from us we can accept it as something to be explained away by differences of experience, of surroundings, of education, above all of inherited temperament and disposition; in a sense it is possible to think of each being so far right that his opinion is the natural outcome of the sort of person he is. But when our brother differs from us there is no such escape from discord; this, we feel uneasily, is the same sort of person as ourselves, his opinion proceeds from the same nature as our own, and we cannot see any reason for the conflict. It is as if one's own judgment were divided against itself.[5]

LEVELS OF INTERACTION

It will help, perhaps, in clarifying further the nature of the interactive process in the family to point out that it takes place on several levels. Speaking generally, it may be said that interaction operates on as many levels as there are levels of communication; some idea of what this involves may be gathered from the fact that Sapir, in his analysis of speech as a personality trait, identifies at least five different levels of speech alone.[6] For our purposes, it will be sufficient to distinguish three main levels. The first is sensory interaction, a comparatively simple form confined to reciprocal reactions through the various senses—the sound of a voice, the sight of a gesture or facial expression, or a tactual contact between one person and another.

Nonverbal communication is of the highest importance in human interaction. Especially is this true in the more intimate forms of interaction such as one finds in the family. Much of the lovemaking between husband and wife is nonverbal, and certainly many of the signs of affection or the reverse between family members are of this kind. Many, perhaps most, signs of intimacy in long-continuing relationships are unspoken. It seems quite obvious that interaction on this level plays a particularly important role in the early life of the child, both because of the continuing emotional relationship between parent and child and also because of the child's lack of linguistic equipment for the first years. We wish

[5] *Ibid.*, pp. 249–251.

[6] Edward Sapir, "Speech as a Personality Trait," *American Journal of Sociology*, May, 1927, pp. 892–906.

to advance here the concept of *the facial personality of the parent* as a useful device to emphasize the child's first impression of the parents.

Second is emotional interaction, as in reciprocal joy, love, hate, etc. Everyone is familiar with the fact that the feeling reaction of one person, communicated to another, modified, and returned to the first person, tends to intensify the original emotional condition. This process is revealed most clearly in the development of mob psychology. In its saner and simpler forms, it is going on constantly between the members of the family group; it constitutes that intimate emotional responsiveness which is so uniquely the characteristic of family life.

Finally, there is interaction at the intellectual level, the process taking the form of a reciprocal exchange of sentiments, ideas, abstractions, judgments, evaluations, and the like. Here one person expresses an opinion or states an idea, to which another person reacts; this calls forth a reaction from the first, and so on. This process is clearly revealed in arguments, debates, and "bull sessions," but again the most common form of it is found in rational conversation such as recurs constantly in the normal relationships of family life.

The distinction between differing levels of interaction is particularly important when considered in relation to the child. It shows, first, that the interactive process begins long before the child has learned to speak. The foundations of parent-child relationships, therefore, precede verbal interaction. The implications of this are profound, both for child development and for mental hygiene problems. Second, the differing levels of interaction emphasize the variety and the subtle scope of the interactive process. Parent-child interaction is far more comprehensive than rational discussion based on the child's developing ability to participate. Third, the natural history of parent-child relationships, which remains to be written, must be based upon an understanding of the sequence in the differing levels of the interactive process.

GENERAL IMPORTANCE OF FAMILY INTERACTION

The constant interaction between the members of the family constitutes one of its fundamental features and gives it such great importance in the development of the personality of its members, especially its younger members. Moreover, it is this aspect of family life that is being emphasized by contemporary students, both because of an increasing appreciation of its importance in the study of personality and also because, in a rapidly changing society constantly becoming more complex, personal relationships within the family become increasingly important. Recent literature on the family emphasizes this, particularly in the case of its adult members, chiefly husband and wife. The growing prevalence in our society of specialized groups into which one puts but part of his personality, the increasing formality and impersonality in our social relations, make the family virtually the one place where one may be at ease. This is particularly true in regard to the emotional aspects of our lives. Man is not a perfunctory, rational animal. It has been said that what distinguishes man from other animals is drinking without being thirsty and making love at all seasons. The essence of both, obviously, is emotional.

It is the general importance of family interaction for the child that chiefly concerns us here. It is in this unit of interacting personalities that the child learns to live, in which his personality first takes form, and in which this personality continues for a number of years to be confirmed and enriched. There are at least three reasons why this family experience is of such overwhelming importance in molding the child's personality. In the first place, the family gives the child his earliest or first experience in living, and first things always have a special significance. A girl's first beau, a boy's first kiss, an author's first book—these always have a peculiar meaning. Second, family experiences are repeated over and over again. By the fifteenth birthday, for example, a boy or girl may have spent as many as 5475 days or parts of days with his or her family. This repetitive aspect alone is enough to give the family an overwhelming importance. Third, family interaction is tinged from the beginning by an emotional coloring that places its interrelationships in a distinctly specialized class. This is particularly true in the case of parent-child or intersibling relationships.

COMMON CONTRIBUTIONS OF FAMILY INTERACTION TO THE CHILD

Extended consideration has been given to the interactive aspect of family life, not only in the recent literature on the family and on parent-child interaction, but also in the more generalized studies of interpersonal relations. One group of such studies is concerned primarily with determining what it is the child gets from this interactive experience, particularly as it affects his sociopsychological needs and development.

1. One of the basic things which the family gives its members is the satisfaction of what W. I. Thomas has called "the desire for intimate response." Every normal human being—and this includes every normal child—wants to be wanted, to be understood, to be appreciated, to be loved. This desire can best be satisfied in the family. Normally children get this satisfaction from their parents, and it is because of this that so much of their experience with their parents is so meaningful. It is this that is so instrumental in creating the bond which binds the child to his family emotionally. This affectional bond between members of the family, particularly between parent and child, is of vital importance under any circumstances of family life; it is increasingly and correspondingly important as other bonds—economic, protective, educational, and religious—become less effective.

There is some reason to think that this aspect of the family interactive process has increasing meaning for the child in contemporary culture. This observation is based on the growing complexity and impersonality of social life, particularly in urban centers. We recognize that these changes have great meaning for the adult members of the family. The recent literature on the family, with its emphasis upon the role of the family as a cushioned retreat for its members, leaves no doubt of this. Little thought, however, has been given to the significance of these changes for the child. The urban child's life is complex and impersonal, too. A 7-year-old, for example, may be in a second-grade class of 50 members in a school with hundreds of pupils. To get to that school means coping with many persons and running the gauntlet of incessant traffic. He may spend a considerable part of his day with people who are comparative strangers to him and who are not wholly dedicated to his welfare and comfort. Such a child needs a home as a "cushioned retreat" from his activities outside the family even more than an adult does.

2. The family provides a sense of both social and biological identity that is not offered by any other kind of group life. Two examples of the importance of this to the child may be cited. Adopted children may have the most satisfactory relationship with their adoptive parents, yet so many of them wonder about, ask about, and seek for their own blood parents. Though these children have social identity, they lack biological identity with the family. Again, persons who take children away from families where they are badly and cruelly treated and place them in better homes where they are loved and cared for are frequently chagrined to find the children longing to return to the parents who abuse them. They want to be with "their own."

3. The family sets the stage to develop and utilize the child's abilities. Through its selection of toys, games, and playmates, the family establishes the first situations in which the child performs. At first these situations are apt to be centered around him, to encourage and stimulate him alone; later, the element of competition is allowed to enter. Usually the earlier forms of competition are artificial or protected in character, devised for the purpose of showing what the child can do. Later this may be changed, and the children may be introduced gradually to, or left to wander into, a natural or unprotected competition. It is the art of parenthood to manage these changes deftly and aptly, and for the best development of the child. Obviously the difficulties of many children are due to the fact that they have grown up without being "emancipated" from a protected competition.

4. A desire for the approval of one's kind is a basic human need. Here again the family is important because it is our first audience. The giving or withholding of the approval of this audience operates as a powerful selective force in determining the goals upon which the child concentrates and around which he develops skills. There is much stress in child-development literature at the present time on the importance of parental "stimulation" in determining a child's progress and even in preventing mental dullness. A part of this stimulation is the presenting of possibilities for learning and action for the child; another very important part of it is the approving of the results. The role of the family audience may be shown easily in regard to manual skills; there seems to be no reason why the same is not true of other forms of behavior.

5. The child receives from the family his first lessons in living with other persons and in making adjustments to them. The family is a miniature society in which the child comes slowly to discover that there are other persons whose presence, needs, and rights have to be considered. Gradually he finds that he must limit his demands in the presence of others, and must adjust to them. The transition from the egocentric to the socialized stage takes place gradually and at varying times and rates in different children. Sometime, between the eighteenth and thirty-sixth month, true social behavior develops, and chains of response of both the linear and the circular type described by Allport put in their appearance.

Certainly the child receives plenty of practice in this process of adjustment. He has to adjust, first of all, to the adults in his family group—parents, relatives, servants, etc.—and each of these adults is apt to be a good deal of a law unto himself. Then, if there are other children in the family, adjustment must be made to them on the basis of their personalities, age, and status in the family group. In other words, the young child has to learn early to shift gears continually, as it were, in dealing with the other persons in the family group.

Part of this experience is the child's introduction to the study of human behavior. He learns how people act, how they react, how they differ. He learns that one adult talks much and does little, another is exactly the reverse; one threatens but does not punish, another does neither, a third does both. It is amazing to discover at how early an age children classify their elders on the basis of their behavior types. "My daddy don't spank, he just be cross," a 2½-year-old told her governess when the latter threatened to report the child's conduct to her father and made the added threat that he would punish her. Then, too, children sense early how members of the family group differ in the ways in which they meet situations and deal with other persons, which techniques succeed and which do not. Mother has her own ways of dealing with Daddy when he is angry; this is what Grandma did to her neighbor; Sister manages to win usually, because of her technique; brother Charles seems to lose out so often because he acts thus and so. The family, in other words, is a psychological laboratory and a school which is always operative, and in which human nature and relationships are most often seen in the raw, that is, on the basis of that intimate and uninhibited responsiveness which is the essence of family life.

6. It is perhaps here that the role of the family in the determination of personal attitudes should be discussed. The reality and importance of attitudes, as well as the prior and basic importance of the family in their determination, have been much emphasized in recent years by the social sciences. Among the attitudes formed through family experience are those which its members develop toward each other on the basis of their intimate and emotional relationships. Each member of the family group comes to develop an attitude toward every other member—child toward child, parent toward parent, parent toward child, and child toward parent. It is in this way that the child obtains his patterns for a varied number of later personal relationships.

The attitude of the child toward the parent has been particularly emphasized by students of behavior problems, chiefly because it has in it more than a person-to-person relationship; it involves also the relationship of one person to another who has greater powers. The parent, in other words, is not only a person but also the symbol of authority, and the child's attitude toward the parent becomes his attitude toward authority.

The importance of adjustment to authority as a pattern of behavior can best be appreciated when we remember that every individual lives his life constantly in the presence of forces greater than he. These forces may be cosmic, such as the forces of nature; or political, such as the state; or occupational, such as the employer; or domestic, such as one's mate; they may be all of these, and others, existing at the same time. All of us must adjust all through our lives to persons and forces greater than we.

Modern psychiatrists who contend that much adult behavior is the result of childhood patterns formed through family experience have emphasized greatly the role of the family in the creation, through parent-child relationships, of patterns of reaction to authority.

7. The child gets from the family interactive process many of the tools with which he acquires his beyond-the-home education. Particularly important here is the acquisition of language. The role of language is recognized in the sociological literature primarily as a vehicle (a) in the accumulation and transmission of culture, and (b) in the development of personality. Basically, language is a symbolic technique that permits communication among individuals. The ability to use this technique is the key to contacts, interactions, and relationships which are involved in social organization. To express it in another way, words are the symbolization of experience; and the number, variety, and adequacy of the words the young child learns through his family experience, and the meanings which are fixed upon these words, become the tools of his subsequent instruction. A more extended discussion of the child's linguistic acquisitions in the family, and their importance, will be found in a later chapter.

8. Finally, the child obtains through his family experience his first living habits; and because so many of these first habits remain through later life, this acquisition is of great importance in the development of the person. Living habits are specific things, both as to the area of life they comprehend, and as to the particular procedures involved. That is to say, eating habits revolve around the food needs, and they include the foods relished and eaten, how and when eaten, with what regularity, in what combinations and amounts. We are dealing here not with vague general notions but for the most part with very definite, concrete aspects of living. John develops the habit of gulping down his food; it is Mary's habit to eat a scanty breakfast, or none at all; Bill never eats liver.

It must not be assumed that these living habits have to do only with eating, sleeping, bathing, bowel movements, and the like. They include many other things, such as manner of walking, manner of speaking, gestures, grimaces, carriage, way of sitting, use of eyes and hands, care of personal appearance, etc. Detailed studies of human interaction reveal the surprising importance of many such matters, which unfortunately are often considered trivial by parents.

Out of the vast amount of scientific data of recent years, two facts stand out in clear relief. One is that the foundations of human personality are laid in early childhood; the second, that the chief molder of personality thus becomes the family. It is in family experience that we find the origin and fixation of the reactions of one individual to another. As Anderson has put it, "The behavior of the adult toward persons has its genesis in the behavior of the child toward persons. Social behavior is of a piece with all other forms of behavior and is governed by the same laws."[7]

FAMILY INTERACTION AND THE FAMILY CYCLE

Family life is never static. It is always changing, and, presumably, in certain predictable stages. This idea utilizes the natural history method, so successfully applied in the biological sciences, and involves the concept of the family life cycle, now utilized in some form by most contemporary students of the family. The concept is fundamental to a consideration of family interaction.[8]

In the early years of this century, Rowntree described a regular economic cycle in the life of the British working family. Its financial status went down with the arrival of several children and remained low until the children were of working age, at which time the family income increased and remained higher until the children left home. After this, at a later age, the family was again left in reduced circumstances. Later studies substantiated the concept of a family economic cycle, and showed that it is not restricted to British working families. For sociologists, these researches became significant for the deeper fact that lay behind them: that the family goes

[7] John Anderson, in W. F. Dummer, *The Unconscious*, Alfred A. Knopf, New York, 1927, p. 90.

[8] For more complete discussion, see B. S. Rowntree, *Poverty*, The Macmillan Company, London, 1901; Edkar Sydenstricker and W. I. King, "The Income Cycle in the Life of the Wage Earner," *Public Health Reports*, Washington, 1924, pp. 2133–2140; Evelyn Duvall and Reuben Hill, *Report of Committee on the Dynamics of Family Interaction*, National Conference on Family Life; Paul C. Glick, "The Family Cycle," *American Sociological Review*, April, 1947, pp. 164–174; James H. S. Bossard and Eleanor S. Boll, *Ritual in Family Living*, University of Pennsylvania Press, Philadelphia, 1950, chap. 7; Paul C. Glick, *American Families*, John Wiley & Sons, New York, 1957, chaps. 3, 4, and 5.

through successive stages of development as it progresses from youth to old age, and that this means successive changes in family relationships, needs, and interaction.

Out of this dynamic point of view has come the division of the family cycle into certain stages. A recent classification of them is (1) Beginning Families: Establishment Phase, (2) Beginning Families: Expectant Phase, (3) Childbearing Families, (4) Families with Preschool Children, (5) Families with School Children, (6) Families with Teen-agers, (7) Families as Launching Centers, (8) Families in the Middle Years, and (9) Aging Families.[9] Obviously, the history of the life of a family is a continuum, even if changing ceaselessly. But the stages thus far identified do serve as a convenient framework for the analysis of family life, and particularly of family interaction. Each stage has its own preoccupations and tasks, its own peculiar satisfactions and frustrations.

The Law of Family Interaction

The concept of the family cycle is, like all other conceptual tools, a useful and meaningful device which nevertheless has its limitations. Families do not always develop through these nine stages, nor at times fit into any of them. Another concept, the Law of Family Interaction, may be used as an additional aid in understanding the relative complexity of interaction in any one family at any stage in its development. Quintilian, the famous Roman rhetorician of the "Silver Age," once remarked that "for exploring human nature, one household is large enough." In keeping with this observation, the thesis is here presented that the relation of the size of the group to the complexity of its interrelationships may be stated with the precision of a mathematical law.

By way of preliminary explanation, what happens within the family with the coming of each child may be stated simply and graphically as follows:

The relations of husband and wife are like this:

Those of a husband, wife, and child can be diagramed like this:

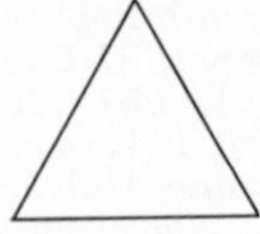

[9] Evelyn Millis Duvall, *Family Development,* J. B. Lippincott Company, New York, 1957.

Those of a husband, wife, and two children look like this:

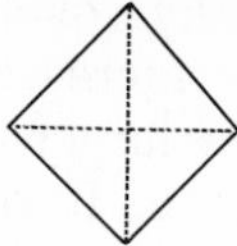

Those of a husband, wife, and three children look like this:

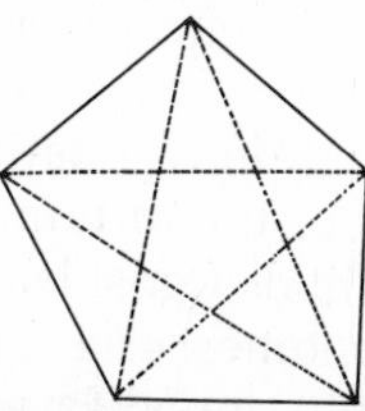

Within every family, there are two variables which submit to precise mathematical determination. One of these is the number of members in the family, i.e., the size of the group; the other is the number of personal relationships between its members. If these two variables are considered mathematically, what happens with the addition of each new member of the family group may be set forth in the following two sets of numbers:

Number of persons	2, 3, 4, 5, 6, 7, 8
Number of personal relationships	1, 3, 6, 10, 15, 21, 28

Family life begins customarily with two members, husband and wife, and one set of personal relationships. The advent of a new member, such as a child, increases the number of persons by one, to a total of three, but the number of personal relationships by two, i.e., from one to three. The coming of another member increases the size of the group from three to four, but the number of personal relationships from three to six, i.e., by three.

Considering these two series of numbers, the first is a series of ordinary numbers, changing in the simplest arithmetic progression in whole numbers; the second is a series of triangular numbers. The law may be stated, then, as follows: *With the addition of each person to a family or primary group, the number of persons increases in the simplest arithmetical progression in whole numbers, and the number of personal interrelationships within the group increases in the order of triangular numbers.*

The mathematical formula involved may be set forth as follows:

$x =$ the number of personal interrelationships
$y =$ the number of persons

$$x = \frac{y^2 - y}{2}$$

The basic implication of this law is that every increase in the number of members of a family (or other primary group) results in more than a corresponding increase in the number of personal interrelationships, and that the larger the group becomes, the more disproportionate is the increase. It seems obvious that this fact should have great meaning in a study of the interactive process, with applications not only for the family but for various types of group functioning. We shall concern ourselves, however, with its meaning for family life.

1. Applying this law to family relationships, one is impressed with the actual complexity of life in families of even moderate size, especially for the young child. Consider, for example, a family of five, consisting of father, mother, and three children. A total of ten sets of personal relationships prevails within this family; and because of the close proximity and intimate nature of family life, there is a continuing awareness of each of them on the part of all the members of the family group.

One is apt to overlook the significance of the mere size of the household for the young child. The writer has recently studied the case of Helen K., who at 5 years of age is nervous, high-strung, and overstimulated, with spells of nervous vomiting. Helen is an only child; but in her two-and-a-half-story home of moderate size there live, in addition to her father and mother, two grandparents, one paternal, the other maternal. Two servants are also in the home daily. With 7 persons in the home, there are 21 sets of personal relationships. In at least 10 of the 21, there is some emotional strain and tension. Helen is the person most constantly present in the household. It seems apparent that the size of this household unit, when translated into the number of personal relationships, tells much about Helen's problem.

2. On the other hand, the proposed law clarifies what the loss of one member may mean to the interactive process of a family. Just as the addition of one member increases the number of relationships in exact keeping with the number of members already in the group, so does the withdrawal of one member similarly decrease the range and complexity of the interactive process. This becomes particularly significant in a small family. In a family of three, the loss of one member reduces the number of relationships by two-thirds of the former number; in the case of a family of four, the reduction amounts to one-half. The law has peculiar significance, then, in analyzing the effects of the loss of a parent, for example, in military service, or through death, divorce, desertion, and the like. The family's loss of one of its members has its quantitative dimensions, dependent upon the size of the group.

3. The Law of Family Interaction throws peculiar light upon the nature and role of the larger families of former days. Consider, for instance, some families of colonial America. Benjamin Franklin came from a Boston family of 17 children. In a family of 19 members, there would be 176 sets of interrelationships. One wonders whether Franklin was led as a young man to leave his family to seek a career or to escape the complex life of his primary group setting. Patrick Henry was one of 19 children. If all these and both parents were living, there were 210 sets of interactive relationships in the Henry household; and again one is led to wonder if this complex setting may not have conditioned his vehement insistence upon liberty. There is Chief Justice John Marshall, who was the first of 15 children. May not his judicial temperament have developed through his experiences as the oldest son in carrying adjudicating responsibility for the 105 relationships which existed among the Marshall children?

4. The larger family of former generations is often compared with the small, immediate family of today. Usually, such comparisons are vague and expressed in rather general terms. The proposed Law of Family Interaction enables a precise mathematical comparison between the two in terms of the exact number of interactive relationships. In a family of 4 members, which is a typically sized contemporary family, there are 6 sets of personal relationships; in a family of 12, such as was characteristic of a century ago, there are 66 sets. Such a comparison reveals the precise nature of the revolutionary change in the intimate response pattern of the average family member which has come about as the result of the small-family system.

The enormity of such a change in the intimate life of the individual precipitates questions of great importance. What is its significance for the social development and needs of individuals? What is the significance of the small-family system of today, thus mathematically appraised, in the socialization of the child? What is its meaning in terms of the socioemotional security of the individual family member? Does this revolution in the intimate interactive life of the individual explain the devotion of contemporary youth to the larger economic and political associations? Does it explain the eagerness of the emotionally isolated person of today to participate in mass emotional movements?

5. Finally, the Law of Family Interaction emphasizes the fact that with each child there is an increasing extension and complexity of social experience within the family, with more possibility, on the one hand, for satisfactory stimulus and response. What this means for the individual member of the family depends on his ability to

enlarge the capacity for such intimate relationships as the family makes possible. Some persons have this ability to a great degree, others almost wholly lack it. This is why the coming of children enriches the life of one family and results usually in the disorganization or disintegration of another.

FAMILY HABITS OF INTERACTION

One of the basic facts affecting the pattern of family interaction is that the family life in which one grows up consists to a considerable extent of a series of habit patterns. Families do many things invariably in the same way. There are family patterns of eating, talking, greeting people, and behaving toward each other. In fact, most aspects of family living come to be routinized, and this applies to social interaction as well as to other forms of behavior.

Families differ decidedly in the nature of these living patterns. In one family, for instance, there may be much light-hearted banter; in another, quarreling is the rule. One family fosters free and easy conversation; the members of another family tend to be preoccupied; in the third, there is a consistent pattern of tight-lipped silence. The Jones family is noted for good-humored teasing; the Browns are known as a sensitive group that explodes at the drop of a hat. There are families that do things together; in other families, activity consists of a series of individual appearances in public with a petulant domestic recovery from such appearances.

It is these patterns of interaction that the child absorbs in the course of his or her family experience. Many of these habits are taken over, through a process much like osmosis in the world of plant life, with little or no awareness of what is going on; others are modified as the growing child evaluates them on the basis of experience; some, perhaps a relatively few, come to be rejected, with substitutions of a quite different kind. It is this process which ingrains the family patterns of interaction into the growing child, which explains in large measure the emphasis that predictive studies of marriage success and failure place upon the total configuration of reactive tendencies. Stated simply, young people who grow up in happy families form happy families in turn. Equally simple is the explanation. Persons who grow up habituated to patterns of interaction making for happy relations carry over such habits to the families they form in turn.

ATTITUDES TOWARD PARENTHOOD

A second basic factor affecting family interaction, particularly so far as the child is concerned, consists of the attitudes of the parents, first, toward parenthood, and second, toward children.

It is one of the pleasing fictions of our culture that every baby is a "bundle of joy," brought to eager, loving parents; fortunately the fiction becomes fact often enough to justify the retention of this pretense. Proceeding into the realm of reality, one finds that parenthood often is not voluntary, as the recurring role of infanticide and the age-old search for effective contraceptives so clearly prove. Recently, there have been a good many references to parents' acceptance or rejection of the child after its birth, and undoubtedly such reaction is a basic factor affecting the interactive process in the family as well as the child's personality development. However, the matter is by no means so simple as is implied in most of these references, and it is suggested here that the larger question is actually that of the parents' whole attitude toward parenthood.

Some researchers have questioned college students in the classroom as to whether they wish to have children, how many, what sex, and so on. On the basis of the answers it has been concluded that the students will become accepting or rejecting parents. It seems to us that this is naive, to say the least. The time when attitudes toward parenthood come to focus is when parenthood is anticipated or becomes a reality—and in relation to circumstances as they exist at those times.

The specific attitudes derive from many sources. The coming of a first child to a young married couple makes such a change in their lives as many of them cannot completely visualize. E. E. LeMasters[10] found that the coming of a child to a middle-class American couple constitutes a crisis event, mainly because they romanticize the idea of parenthood but have little actual preparation for the more mundane realities of it, such as sleepless nights, a great deal of hard work, loss of social life, and the like. A recent study of similar nature[11] corroborated LeMaster's conclusions. In time, most of the couples recover from the shock of parenthood and those who experience least shock recover most quickly. For all women, pregnancy is a physical and psychic shock. They come face to face with the biological destiny from which it is exceedingly difficult to run.

[10] E. E. LeMasters, "Parenthood as Crisis," *Marriage and Family Living*, November, 1957, pp. 352–355.

[11] Everett D. Dyer, "Parenthood as Crisis: A Re-Study," *Marriage and Family Living*, May, 1963, pp. 196–201.

Whether the reaction is pleasurable or unpleasurable depends upon many circumstances.

Still another source of attitudes toward parenthood, if a child is wanted, is the reasons why it is wanted. The ability to plan families has brought with it a greater importance in the motives for having them. What *is* wanted? A child, or an object to make up for something that the parents have missed in life? The answers to these questions have a fundamental bearing upon the acceptance or rejection of the child, not as they affect the assumption of overt parental responsibilities, but as they bear upon the emotional reaction to the particular child. There is a cold, calculating acceptance of a child, based on economic or personal advantage, a wanting of children because it is the thing to do; and there is a warm, personal, innermost acceptance of them, the essence of which is love.

A further source of the attitude toward parenthood is to be found in the parent's reaction to the changes in family life which result from the coming of children. The completeness of this change is indicated by the frequency with which one hears parents say: "What did we ever do before the children came?" The coming of a child is like the advent of a new sun or planet into the solar system. The center of family life shifts. A reorientation of relationships follows. The relationship between husband and wife changes. Part of the affectional output is transferred from mate to child. This is particularly likely to happen with the mother, as the common complaint of husbands indicates. If the erotic relationship suffers, there may be a compensating increase of feelings of respect. Many couples vow never to do so, yet they invariably address each other as Father and Mother after they have children. Each comes to see the father or mother stereotype in the other. Everything in the home comes to be viewed in relation to the children. Conversation is changed as to objectives, inclusions, and avoidances. In the home there is increasing pressure upon the parent to live up to the stereotype of the parent. To all these changes and demands each parent reacts, and this reaction runs deep into the ultimate attitude toward the child. Such reactions may vary from an almost self-persecuting acceptance to a complete unwillingness to accept; they may result in a parent who is intensely jealous of his child or a genial-appearing one who sits by and in reverie recounts the trips he could take "if it weren't for the children."

There is also the parents' willingness or unwillingness to accept the social aureole of parenthood. This term is used to identify society's projection of the idealization of parenthood upon the individual father or mother. The mother and her child in the park, the father and his sons at the football game, the matron and her daughters at the opera—these arouse a distinctive reaction from onlookers. These parents are regarded quite differently from what they would be if they were alone. There is something in the appearance of parent with child that calls forth the warming glow of our approval. We accord them the pathos of the mores.[12]

To this social aureole of parenthood there is a reaction of the individual parent. Some parents simply revel in it and take advantage of the "privileges and immunities thereunto appertaining." "Many women," says Waller, "base their whole claim to consideration in this world and the next on the process of parturition."[13] On the other hand there is the young mother who resents being a *jeune fille* no longer, and there is at least one taproom keeper who said to his 8-year-old daughter: "Don't call me Daddy when there are ladies about." The pattern of attitude toward parenthood is not a simple thing; indeed, it is quite complex, and for any child it is the *combination* of those of both of his parents with whom he has to live.

THE ATTITUDE TOWARD CHILDREN

There is an attitude toward children, distinct from that toward parenthood, which operates to affect the family interactive process. This attitude again is a complex product, but in all, perhaps, a part of the larger pattern of one's philosophy of life. Philosophy follows experience and seeks to justify it. One's philosophy of life may be defined, therefore, as one's personal rationalizations upon the facts of life. In other words, it is a more or less well-defined and -developed system of beliefs, values, principles, etc., which we hold, through which we unify life and give it meaning. It is this philosophy that orients us toward the polar star by which we steer the course of our lives.

Part of this philosophy consists of our conception of people—what they are like, what motivates them, how to deal with them, and so on. Children, of course, are people; hence the philosophy of life, and particularly of human nature and of childhood, which the parents hold is a powerful factor in the creation of their attitude toward children. Does the parent think that children are little animals or that they should be treated like young adults? Does the parent harp constantly on the virtue of obedience, or does self-

[12] Waller, *op. cit.*, p. 462.
[13] *Ibid.*, p. 463.

control seem the higher good? Can the child be molded according to plan, or is what "is in the blood" his irrevocable destiny?

Important, too, is the parent's adjustment to his own philosophy of life. The simplest way to express this is in terms of the parent's conscience. Glueck wrote about one aspect of this a number of years ago:

> Individuals who bring into the marital and parental relation a too rigid and inflexible conscience, whose neurotically exaggerated sense of guilt and need for expiatory punishment exposes them to a life of mean and purposeless denial and asceticism, create a domestic atmosphere that distorts and scars those who are obliged to live and grow within it. A parent of this type is apt to instill in his children a form of perverse morality and ethics that is destructive of happiness. His notions of the duties and privileges of parenthood are of a kind to exclude from the child-parent relationship any possibility of naturalness, of a free interchange of trust and confidence, and to breed secretiveness, distrust, and deception.[14]

THE SPIRIT OF FAMILY INTERACTION

"It is within the family emotional climate," writes Sheldon Glueck in a summary of the work of the Gluecks on juvenile delinquency, "that the most deeprooted and persistent character and personality traits and distortions of the growing child are developed."[15] This observation calls attention to the fact that, underlying all the other factors in family interaction is the spirit or atmosphere of family life. This is one of the intangibles of life which students, preoccupied with scientific analysis and measurement, tend to avoid. And yet it is far too important a reality to pass by. It is something so real that it strikes the observer almost as soon as he appears upon the family scene. The sacred writings of various people, as well as the masterpieces of literature, have not overlooked these realities of the spirit, and neither should sociologists studying the intimacy of family life. In recent years, students of problem children have said much about the effects of troubled and strained and disturbed "psychic atmosphere" in the family backgrounds of their cases. If psychic atmosphere is important in the study of nervous or delinquent children, it seems equally important to emphasize the role of family spirit in normal child development.

14 Bernard Glueck, "The Significance of Parental Attitudes for the Destiny of the Individual," *Mental Hygiene*, October, 1928, p. 734.

15 Sheldon Glueck, "The Home, the School and Delinquency," *Harvard Educational Review*, Winter, 1953, p. 25.

Santayana, the philosopher, writing at the close of his life, gives us an excellent illustration of this.

After my mother and sisters left, my uncle Santiago, with his wife Maria Josefa and his daughter Antonita, came to live with us, and a new and distinct chapter begins in my experience. The scene, the persons, the events are still present with me most vividly. I didn't feel deeply or understand what was going on, but somehow the force of it impressed my young mind and established there a sort of criterion or standard of reality. That crowded, strained, disunited, and tragic family life remains for me the type of what life really is: something confused, hideous and useless. I do not hate it or rebel against it, as people do who think they have been wronged. It caused me no suffering; I was a child carried along as in a baby-carriage through the crowd of strangers: I was neither much bothered nor seriously neglected: and my eyes and ears became accustomed to the unvarnished truth of the world, neither selected for my instruction nor hidden from me for my benefit.[16]

The spirit of family life is compounded of many ingredients, some obvious and clear in the consciousness of the members of the family, but others buried in the unawareness of a deep mental hinterland. The turned-up nose of daughter Sue, the son's mischievous brown eyes, the mother's forgotten experience with a brown-eyed lover, the deepness of father's voice, sister Kay's lilting laughter, the wiggling stump of the tail of the family's cocker spaniel, the peaceful glow of candlelight at the evening dinner table, a roaring fire in the grate, father's deep satisfaction with his work, and Mother's patent satisfaction with Daddy—to some these may appear as incidental minutiae of family life. Clearer insight may recognize them as of the greatest importance. Moreover, it is not only the persons and elements which are present in the interactive process, but each is the focal point of past experience. As Dollard has reminded us, to the concept of the family as a unity of interacting personalities should be added the phrase, "each with a history."[17] It is, then, out of this miscellany—of persons and things, present and past, obvious and subtle, remembered and forgotten—that there emanates from and pervades the family interactive process a certain essence which is the spirit of the family process. It is one of the basic realities of family life.

[16] George Santayana, *Persons and Places*, Charles Scribner's Sons, New York, 1944, p. 119.

[17] John Dollard, "Needed Viewpoints in Family Research," *Social Forces*, October, 1935, p. 110.

THE SPECIFICITY OF FAMILY INTERACTION

It is often assumed that a single or unified family pattern of interaction exists which is the same for all its child members. Manifestly this is not the case. The interactive process within the family group is an individual one, varying from one individual to another. Each member has a specific relationship to every other member. Particularly is this true of each parent to each child, and some of the reasons for this are quite obvious.[18] Father has one attitude toward his son, another toward his daughter. Mother, who detests her mother-in-law, and her daughter, who is the image of her paternal grandmother, develop patterns of interaction quite different from those existing between Mother and her son, who is the image of Mother's father, whom she reveres. Little Jane, who has red hair and a temper like her father, clashes with him, while sister Sue, with the conciliatory passiveness of her mother, never squabbles with her daddy. Obviously sex, physical appearance, temperament, and other differences between the members of the family play their respective roles in the determination of these specific patterns. Moreover, the life of any family is a changing stream, so that its patterns of interaction would change from one stage to another in the family cycle.

WHAT THE CHILD GIVES THE PARENTS

A family pattern of interaction is not a one-way street with the arrow pointing from parents to children. Parents do things to and for children, it is true; but children reciprocate. This fact is amazingly slighted in material on the family, written during the past several generations; and probably this is because we feel our culture is so child-centered that we think only in terms of what children get, or should get. Nevertheless, a part of parental attitudes about parenthood and children is a result of what children give to them. Passing mention, at least, should be given to the contributions of children to married couples.

The Expansion of Family Interests

Just as the coming of children broadens and complicates the interactive processes within the family, so there occurs a similar de-

[18] For an interesting study of mother-child interaction, see Barbara Merrill Bishop, "Mother-Child Interaction and the Social Behavior of Children," Psychological monographs, vol. LXV, no. 11, 1951.

velopment in regard to its interests. With the birth of the first child, parents become attentive to a number of matters they had not considered before; or, if they have considered them previously, they do so now with new meaning and intentness. One is reminded here of Popenoe's statement that a man who does not marry is only one-third alive, that married people may be two-thirds alive, but that only those who experience parenthood may be alive fully.[19]

First to arise are often problems of family finance, with particular emphasis upon future prospects. Occupational ambitions of the father may be sharpened, and long-range plans for careers may be made for the first time. Interest in life insurance often becomes vital at this stage of a family's history, or enlarged insurance programs may be undertaken. What kinds of insurance should be purchased—for immediate protection, for the future education of children, to meet the ordinary hazards to life and limb? Next to receive attention are questions concerning the home. Is home ownership desirable? Is it feasible under existing conditions? What kind of home is it best to purchase? What financing plans are most desirable?

Interests like these quickly shade into questions concerning the community. What kind of community is this? Is this the place to rear children? To buy a home? What, if any, are the zoning restrictions? What kind of people live in this community? Who are the people that dominate it? How politician-ridden is this place? What is the tax rate? What is the status-conferring rating of this area? One particular aspect of the organized life of any community, which many parents consider of great importance, is its educational facilities. Are there nursery schools in the neighborhood? Is there a publicly maintained kindergarten? What is the quality of the instruction in the school system? How do the schools of the particular district rate educationally? Roman Catholic families will consider the availability of parochial-school instruction. Upper-class families may be interested in private-school facilities. In addition to the school system, many parents will want to know about Sunday School and church facilities, provisions for playgrounds, public libraries, community sports programs, and a great variety of other community resources and facilities.

Moreover, it is not simply the local community and the larger society of the present which become of interest and importance to parents with the birth of their children; it is also their future development and welfare. The child is the future of the family; and no parent with the slightest interest in his child can ever be wholly

[19] Paul Popenoe, *Modern Marriage*, The Macmillan Company, New York, 1927, p. 26.

unconcerned with the world of tomorrow, for it is in that world that his child will become, like the parent, an adult member. "After me the deluge" may be the philosophy of a cynical bachelor; it can never be the sentiment of a normal parent.

Emotional Satisfactions of Long Duration

The child not only broadens the interests of parents in community and social matters of all kinds, but gives to most parents emotionally satisfying interests of lifelong duration. Nothing is perhaps more essential to a happy life than such interests. Many people are fortunate in acquiring an interest or interests of this kind. They may be of many different kinds. One person may find such an interest in the quest for political power, climbing from one post of political preferment to another; the next person may find it in the winning of wealth and its use for the acquisition of a few selected objectives; a third may find it through his creations on an artist's canvas, the pages of a book, the test tube of the laboratory. For vast numbers of people, life interests of a satisfactory sort are difficult or impossible to obtain. Such persons may find, as can all others and as many do, abiding life interests in the careers of those whom they conceive to be like themselves—their children and their children's children. Of a truth are such interests lifelong in duration and emotionally satisfying in kind.

Emotional exploitation of children is news; behind the news are innumerable parents who find in their interests in children deep and abiding satisfactions without exacting any crippling bondage. This is the essence of normal and happy parenthood. Particularly do these emotional satisfactions tend to grow in importance as parents and children grow older. Earlier in life, parents are more active, more concerned with their own achievements and hopes. Life's compensations tend to come more adequately from the range of one's own activities. It is only with the passing of time, the hardening of circumstances, the reconstruction of values, and the greater need for emotional satisfactions from without that one turns normally to the developing careers of one's own children.

The Opportunity to Relive Life

This acquisition of lifelong interests suggests another of the child's possible contributions to his parents. It is the opportunity, in a sense, to live their lives over again. This is something which most persons, including those who will not admit it, would like to do; it is something which, in the literal sense of the phrase, is obviously impossible. What every modern student of parent-child relationships emphasizes, however, is that the parent sees in the child his nearest approach to such an opportunity. This tendency of parents to seek to relive their lives in those of their children often leads to a foisting upon the children of activities and pursuits not of their own choice. This practice is spoken of in mental hygiene circles as projection. It is a practice extensively indulged in by parents, and it has much meaning for educators and for students of behavior problems. Lost almost to view are the many parents with accepting, live-and-let-live attitudes who guide their children gently into the lives which *their children* want and for which they are best fitted. These parents, no less than the others, have an opportunity to live life over again and to enjoy it to the utmost.

The Control of Human Development

The parents' effort to relive their lives through their children is in turn but part of a larger story. This is that the child gives to the parent control over another person, and of a most intimate and comprehensive kind. It is a control that is all-pervasive. Arising as a form of physical control because of the infant's complete helplessness, it comes, as time goes on, to cover every aspect of the child's life and to be supported by the entire range of society's sanctions.

The acquisition through parenthood of control over another person is one of life's major experiences, and its significance may be considered from various points of view. There can be no doubt, for example, of its emotionally satisfying nature. Control of a child satisfies the parent's will to power. This is a deeply rooted desire. All persons have it, and they seek to satisfy it in many ways. We begin to seek it as children in playing with dolls and animal pets. Much of our adult life involves its quest. It is this age-old, universal desire which is satisfied in the parent with the coming of children, and the entire range of parenthood is from one angle a constant exercise of the power of control over another person.

A good deal has been said in recent years about the fact that some parents utilize this power over their children to secure relief from personal thwartings and maladjustments in their lives outside of the home. In other words, the disgruntled parent can come home and take it out on his child. The father who is forced into insignificance and obscurity in his job returns home to restore his ego in an exaggerated obedience from his son. The employee who is "barked at by the boss" all day can compensate at night by "laying down the law" to his little William. The mother who was "cut" at her bridge club in the afternoon takes it out on her daughter that night. In these and in many other similar cases, the child becomes for the parent a vehicle for the transposition of satisfactions.

To those who see in their control over a child an opportunity to direct the development of a human being, this responsibility may lead to a deep and continuing search for life's values. What do I want my child to be? So far as I can influence and direct his development, what are the important and worthwhile goals to be sought? These questions arise with the birth of the first child; they persist throughout its infancy, adolescence, and into early manhood and womanhood. Parenthood is a daily round of decisions on the question of what things are important, and in what order. These involve choices—in expenditures of time and effort, in schools, in social contacts, in occupations, in forms of behavior, in spheres of activity. These decisions represent value judgments. From one standpoint, all life is a constant series of choices of life values. These choices come to be made more definitely as they are the more consciously imposed upon those for whom we have assumed responsibility.

Insight into Life's Processes

This survey of the child's contributions to his parents would be incomplete without reference to the fact that children give parents an intimate insight into the processes of life—its appearance, growth, and development. Because of our inability to consider ourselves with sufficient objectivity, we need to see this process at work in other persons and in other forms of life. Through the long centuries of "man's rough road," he has seen it constantly in the seeds he sowed, the harvests he reaped, the animals he domesticated, as well as in the abundant progeny he brought into the world. Today, an increasing percentage of people live in cities where they neither sow nor reap—crops; where a cow can be seen only in the zoological garden, and where even a pup is a luxury, and a nuisance, to be spayed or boarded out periodically in order to keep domestic and neighborly peace.

This change in the range of many people's contacts with living things makes experience with the birth and rearing of children all the more important if the processes of life are to remain part of the content of conscious thinking. Let it be emphasized here that there is a difference between an abstract understanding of a process, and constant contacts with its concrete manifestations. The insight into the processes of life development, which the nurture of one's own children gives, covers much of what in academic circles constitutes the substance of biology, psychology, and the related life sciences. Constant contact with growing children gives meaning to the findings of scientists in these fields; also, such experience acts as a corrective for much of what passes as scientific achievement.

Insight into the Meaning of Life

What parenthood brings to one, in the ultimate analysis, is some comprehension of the meaning of life and of the individual's role in the cosmic scheme of things. Stated in its simplest form, it is this: Each person is but a temporary trustee of the life stream.

One comes to sense this first, perhaps, with one's possessions. Yesterday, you owned them absolutely. Today, your child uses them carelessly, and destructively perhaps. You squirm a bit at first, but, after all, it is *your* child violating *your* possessions; and you resolve the conflict finally so that the violation of what was yours dissolves into the development of your child that is. Somewhat later, you experience the same changing evaluation of your energy. Originally, your energy was yours, to expend for your pleasure and your development. With continuing parenthood this, too, changes. Your energy becomes the small change you pay to satisfy the passing needs of your children. It is at such moments that there comes to a parent the true meaning of one's relation to life: that each generation is but a trustee of life, for all its values and possessions. This is what society requires of mankind, that it carry the torch from one generation but ultimately turn it over to the next generation. This it is that the child brings, in some varying form of expression, to each parent who has the capacity to perceive it.

SUMMARY

The salient points in this chapter may be summarized briefly as follows:

1. Family life may be viewed as an interactive process between its members. As such, it is a peculiar form of social interaction, distinguished by the intimacy, deep community, and brutal incisiveness of its relationships.

2. Family interaction proceeds not only at the intellectual but also at the sensory and the emotional level. This tripartite nature is responsible for its fundamental importance.

3. In the constant interplay between family members, the child's

personality takes form. Common contributions of the interactive process to the child are (a) satisfaction of the desire for intimate response, (b) a sense of both social and biological identity, (c) a stage for the development of the child's ability, (d) the approval of one's kind, (e) the first lessons in living with other persons, (f) determination of personal attitudes, (g) tools for the acquisition of an education, and (h) living habits.

4. Family interaction varies from one stage to another in the family cycle.

5. Family interaction increases in range and complexity with each additional member.

6. Parent-child interaction is greatly influenced by the parents' habit patterns of interaction and by their attitudes toward parenthood and children.

7. Underlying all other factors in family interaction is the spirit or atmosphere of family life—subtle, difficult to measure, but all-pervasive in scope and fundamental in importance.

8. Patterns of family interaction are individual and specific, varying from one child to another, and changing often in the course of the life cycle.

9. Common contributions of children to parents include (a) an expansion of family interests, (b) emotional satisfactions of life-long duration, (c) the opportunity to relive life, (d) the control of human development, (e) insight into life's processes, and (f) insight into the true meaning of life.

SUGGESTED READINGS

Burgess, Ernest W., and Harvey J. Locke, *The Family,* American Book Company, New York, 1953. In this textbook the family is described as having changed from an institution to a mere companionship group.

Duvall, Evelyn Millis, *In-Laws, Pro and Con.* Association Press, New York, 1954. An interesting analysis of three-generation family interaction.

Duvall, Evelyn Millis, *Family Development,* J. B. Lippincott Company, New York, 1957. The family interactions to fulfill the developmental tasks of members at each stage of the family cycle is described in detail.

Hess, Robert D., and Gerald Handel, *Family Worlds,* University of Chicago Press, Chicago, 1959. A psychosocial study of the complexities of family emotional organization.

Levy, Marion Joseph, *The Family Revolution in Modern China,* Harvard University Press, Cambridge, 1949. (Current edition: Octagon Books, New York.) Although the book deals primarily in changing kinship structure, changing family interaction is implicit in the material.

Lin, Yoa-hua, *The Golden Wing,* Oxford University Press, New York, 1947. A sociological study of Chinese familism.

Marmey, Carlyle, *Dangerous Fathers, Problem Mothers, and Terrible Teens,* Abingdon Press, New York, 1958. A book written by the pastor of a Protestant church.

Parsons, Talcott, and Robert F. Bales, *Family, Socialization and Interaction Process,* The Macmillan Company, New York, 1955. This collection of papers treats family interaction and child socialization in its psychological and psychoanalytic aspects. Its approach is interesting as a contrast, though the language is somewhat technical and abstract.

Shaw, George Bernard, "A Treatise on Parents and Children," in *Misalliance,* Brentano's, New York, 1914. A cynical but perceptive essay on children's attitudes toward parents.

Thomas, Father John, *The American Catholic Family,* Prentice-Hall, Englewood Cliffs, New Jersey, 1956. A specialized study of family life in one American religious group.

Van de Water, Frederic F., *Fathers Are Funny,* The John Day Company, New York, 1939. An autobiography of a father's relationship with his son, written by a popular journalist.

FAMILY CULTURE AND THE CHILD 4

A third approach to the study of family situations concerns itself with their cultural content. Although family structure and family process are distinct social entities, each with its own significance, from the larger point of view both are but means to an end, and that end is the content which they serve to convey. This content is culture, and it is in many ways the most significant aspect of a family situation. Accordingly, the present chapter is devoted to a consideration of the meaning of family culture, its relation to the larger culture system, the differing versions of this larger system, the cultural role of the family, and the nature of the contemporary problems precipitated for children by these cultural factors and processes.

THE SOCIOLOGICAL EMPHASIS UPON CULTURE AND THE FAMILY

Culture is another of the words which sociologists have come to accept as part of their scientific terminology, investing it with rather precise meaning. In contrast to popular parlance, which uses it as synonymous with good manners, proper etiquette, or refinement of artistic taste, it is defined by sociologists and other social scientists as "that complex whole which includes knowledge, belief, art, morals, law, custom and other capabilities acquired by man as a member of society."[1] Expressed more simply and tersely, culture is the sum total of the ways of doing and thinking, past and present, of a social group.[2] From the standpoint of the child, culture is the social heritage to which he is born and in which he is reared. This social heritage includes the answers which his group has made and is making to the problems of life.

It is an accepted sociological principle that culture, thus conceived, is one of the chief determinants in the formation of personality. In fact, so great is the relative importance which sociologists attach to the conditioning power of the cultural heritage that personality is continually spoken of as the subjective side of culture. Equivalent in meaning is the other frequently cited dictum of the self as a social looking glass. The foregoing principle was emphasized in Chapter 1 and is recalled here because of its background importance to the discussion in the present chapter. Stated usually without reference to or qualification for age, the application of this principle to the child would seem to be particularly obvious. In other words, if culture determines personality, certainly it does so with particular force and effectiveness in that period of life when it is accepted and absorbed with little or no hesitation or questioning. Thus, hand in hand with the sociologist's emphasis upon cultural data and the principle that personality is culturally determined goes his concern with the family group.

THE FAMILY CULTURE PATTERN

In making a cultural approach to the study of family situations, it is important to distinguish between family life as part of the culture system and the family as a medium through which the larger cultural heritage is transmitted to the child. These are two distinct social realities; it is important to identify and remember the difference between them.

The pattern of family culture is our first concern. Speaking generally, this consists of the ways of living and thinking which constitute the family and sex aspects of group life. This is one of the patterns which is part of the culture system of all societies. It includes marriage and courtship procedures, sex mores, husband-

[1] E. B. Tylor, *Primitive Culture,* 7th ed., Brentano's, New York, 1924, p. 1.

[2] Emory S. Bogardus, *Contemporary Sociology,* University of Southern California Press, Los Angeles, 1931, p. 68.

Table 2

	USSR	Thailand	Scandinavia	Brazil
Marriage	Based on mutual attraction and consent. Illegal to force marriage against will. No formal barriers to intermarriage. Recent increasing interest in ceremony.	Parental selection of mate with some latitude. Ceremony arranged by elders—ritualistic. No prohibition of polygamy. Intermarriage permitted.	Mutual attraction and consent. Ceremony usually religious. Intermarriage accepted but population is highly homogeneous.	Traditionally by parental arrangement. Father's choice given legal preference. Law requires civil ceremony. Church requires religious ceremony. Intermarriage extensive, but usually within same class and lighter individuals of different blood groups.
Divorce	Greatly simplified in 1966 from former costly and legally intricate procedure.	Legally permissable. Wife may divorce on grounds including cruelty or nonsupport.	Increasing permissiveness. Very high rate among the younger marriages. Legal separation possible through mutual desire.	Not sanctioned.
Premarital Sex Activity	Traditional double standard.	Double standard.	Single standard. Very permissive. "Going steady" usually marks beginning of sex relations. Rate of illegitimacy high.	Double standard. Girls chaperoned when away from home. Premarital intercourse, if discovered, results in forced marriage or banishment of girl.

Husband–Wife Relations	Symmetrical with some remaining spheres of sex-typed specialization.	Women serve men, may not interfere with men's activities outside home. Pattern changing for some educated women. Husband and wife legally responsible for supporting each other.	Equality of sexes. Husband the assumed breadwinner.	Traditional duality of roles very strong. Patriarchal dominance, becoming modified among upper-class urban families.
Childrearing	Delegated to other parents, if possible, because of maternal employment.	Father, moral trainer. Mother delegates duties to older children if possible. Docility and obedience stressed.	By mothers. Physical and intellectual resourcefulness stressed. Girls reared for marriage; boys, for job.	By many adults in extended type family. Godparents play significant role. Great affection shown but with rigorous discipline, stressing etiquette.
Household	Three-generation family acceptable under one roof.	Customary for newly married couple to live with parents. Household may include other relatives and nonrelatives.	Typically huband, wife, and two children. No in-laws.	Traditionally of the extended type. Nuclear families appearing in urban areas.
Religion	?	Buddhism.	Primarily Protestant.	Catholic.

wife relationships, status of men and women, guardianship, parent-child relationships, divorce, disposition of the children's earnings, family solidarity, responsibility toward aging parents, attitudes toward unmarried mothers and children born out of wedlock, and various other matters. In short, there exists in each society a series of socially accepted attitudes and forms of behavior centering around the sex, procreative, homemaking, childrearing, and family relationship activities of the group which social scientists today speak of as the family and sex culture pattern.

Selected Family Culture Patterns

How family patterns vary can be shown, as in Table 2, by comparing a few important aspects of these patterns in different societies.[3]

No part of the entire culture system seems quite so important for the child as the family culture pattern. It is peculiarly the child-centered aspect of the culture; in fact, the child is what gives meaning to the pattern as a whole. The family culture consists of all the stages involved in the child's birth and rearing; it includes virtually every feature of the child's life for a number of years. Other aspects of it can be viewed from the child's standpoint with a certain objectivity: the child is introduced to those parts of the culture. But he lives the family culture, and thus one must regard it as the most subjective, the most deeply embedded part of the cultural heritage: the one which carries over longest in the life span. The family life in each of the societies described above is distinctive and different from the others. These differences are the essence of what the children absorb with such intimate completeness as to seem the nature of human nature.

THE FAMILY AND THE LARGER CULTURE SYSTEM

The family culture is, of course, only a part of the larger culture of society. A second, and fundamental, cultural role of the family is to transmit this to the child. It is through his family that he gets his first introduction to it, and for a number of years remains the chief agency through which he has contacts with the larger cultural milieu.

[3] For original source of these comparisons see *Marriage and Family Living*, November, 1954.

This larger culture is made up of a number of patterns involving the fundamental aspects of the communal life. Recent students of culture have identified 13 patterns as generally present in the cultural system or configuration of a society. They are as follows:

1. Patterns of communication: gestures and language.
2. Methods and objects for providing for man's physical welfare.
   a. Food getting.
   b. Personal care.
   c. Shelter.
   d. Tools, instruments, and machines.
3. Means or techniques of travel and transportation of goods and services.
4. Exchange of goods and services: barter, trade, commerce, occupation.
5. Forms of property: real and personal.
6. The sex and family patterns.
   a. Marriage and divorce.
   b. Forms of kinship relation.
   c. Guardianship.
   d. Inheritance.
7. Societal controls and institutions of government.
   a. Mores.
   b. Public opinion.
   c. Organized state: laws and political officers.
   d. War: institutional form of conflict of tribes, societies, or states.
8. Artistic expression: architecture, painting, sculpture, music, literature, dancing.
9. Recreational and leisure-time interests and activities.
10. Religious and magical ideas and practices.
11. Science (in civilization chiefly).
12. Mythology and philosophy.
13. Cultural structuring of basic interactional processes, such as competition, conflict, cooperation, differentiation, stratification, accommodation, and assimilation.[4]

VARYING VERSIONS OF THE CULTURE CONFIGURATION

The Ethos, or National Culture

Children are born customarily into a particular system or configuration of culture patterns, usually national in scope, and of a

[4] Kimball Young, *Sociology—A Study of Society and Culture,* American Book Company, New York, 1942, p. 39.

definite historical epoch. The distinguishing culture system of a particular society was called the *ethos* by the ancient Greeks; and William Graham Sumner, pioneer American sociologist, utilized the term to apply to the totality of characteristic traits by which a society is individualized and differentiated from other societies.[5] It is in the ethos, then, that the United States differs fundamentally from Nazi Germany, modern Persia, ancient Judea, or the interior of China in 2000 B.C.

A comparison between the United States and India in the early part of this century will reveal how comprehensive these differences are. That the material culture of the two countries was completely dissimilar is well known. Less emphasized are the differences in nonmaterial culture, which really were the characteristic features of the two countries. As suggested by Young, they are as follows:[6] Our American culture is dominated by (1) belief in individual material success and national progress; (2) belief in universal literacy and education as the means of solving social and personal problems; (3) acceptance of the idea that there is advantage and virtue in rapid movement through space; (4) faith in the virtue of constant change in all, or most, aspects of life; (5) confidence in man's ability to control and direct his destiny, in both a personal and a social sense. In India, by way of contrast, there is less belief in progress, or none, in our sense of the word; mere bigness has no special merit; there is no virtue in rapid movement; calm deliberation is the height of desirability; and the desire for forgetfulness of the self and of the wish to be somebody is the ultimate good, rather than material success.[7]

To this ethos, or national cultural pattern, the child is introduced by his family. This introduction is in part formal, but much more it is incidental and imperceptible. The ethos surrounds the child at every turn; he learns it because he knows no other. It is like the air he breathes or the landscape he sees. To him it is but a natural part of the scheme of things. And all the time, as he learns the culture he absorbs the family attitude toward it. He shares this attitude with his parents, and because of his emotional relationship to them his attitude toward the culture becomes emotionally tinged. Thus originate those feelings toward one's country, and about other countries whose cultural pattern is different, with which we have been so much concerned in recent years. One recalls here Sumner's

5 William G. Sumner, *Folkways*, Ginn and Company, Boston, 1911, pp. 37–38. (Current editions: Blaisdell Publishing Company, Dover Publications, and New American Library, New York.)

6 Young, *op. cit.*, pp. 42–43.

7 K. Shridharani, *My India, My America*, Duell, Sloan & Pearce, New York, 1941.

remark that the ethos furnishes the point of view from which one group criticizes the ways of another group.

The identification of the family version of this natural culture pattern is highly important in any country; it is peculiarly so in the United States because of the heterogeneity of our population. In studying family situations from the point of view of cultural content, it becomes important to ask questions such as those which follow. Is the family verson of the ethos of this American-reared child an American version, an American-Sicilian one, or an American-Bulgarian one? Do the father and mother represent the same national culture? Are the versions held by the immediate family and that of the larger kinship group family the same? Here, concretely speaking, is a young man, born and reared on the lower East Side of New York, son of an Italian father and an Irish mother. What is his national culture pattern as transmitted by his family?

The Regional Culture

Recently, social scientists have broken down the nation into regions. The region is a unit part of the larger society, identified first in geographical terms, subsequently on the basis of trade and other economic considerations, and now increasingly on cultural bases —each region being identified for its own peculiar social system, significant for family life and child development.

These cultural areas are not mere academic distinctions. Under one name or another, they have long been recognized in popular parlance as well as in more intellectual discussions. The Southerner differs from the Maine Yankee, and the Iowan in Hollywood is unlike both; the Prussian and the Bavarian have never "spoken the same language"; the northern Italian is different from the Sicilian in many respects, in his ways, his speech, and his ideas. The region, in other words, is a distinctive social system that supplies a plan for personality patterning. It is this regional or sectional variant of the national cultural pattern that is imposed on the child through the family. This regional variant is in many respects more intimately meaningful to him than the national culture. When the family moves from one region to another, the transition for the child may be very difficult. Consider, for example, the child of North Carolina Piedmont parentage who is thrust overnight, as it were, into the school and social life of a second-generation Irish or Portuguese section in New England. Such a child appreciates, if parents and child behavior students do not, the reality of differences in the regional culture.

The Class Culture

The population of any national and regional society is divided in turn into class and other interest groups, and the more these groupings become distinct and fixed, the more prescribed and predictable are the patterns of attitudes and behaviors associated with them. These class culture patterns have become so important in the social development of the contemporary American child that a separate chapter is devoted later in this volume to their analysis. The one point to be emphasized here is that the family transmits to the child the culture pattern of its own class, together with the class attitudes toward other classes. The family influence upon the child is particularly significant in its rating of social classes, placing its own class in the scale and determining its attitudes toward other classes. Here one finds marked emotions, for these matters of class distinctions go far below the surface. Prejudice and appreciation, antagonism and cooperation, pride and a rankling sense of injustice —these develop as by-products of the transmission of the class culture. Class bias has its roots in the family setting of the child, and it has taken form before the family turns him over to other culture-transmitting agencies.

In other words, the child gets from the family pattern a way of living, based on the fact that he is born in a certain class in a given region in a particular nation. He learns the life of Boston rather than of Burma; of the flat or the farm; of the slum or the suburb; of the Sicilian concrete mixer or the Fifth Avenue surgeon. In short, the child gets from the family his class cultural orientation. Thus as a functioning element in the cultural content of any given family situation, there must be considered the family version of the class culture which has been transmitted to the child.

The Religious Culture

A religion constitutes a way of living and thinking and therefore is a culture. It is fairly obvious in a comparison of the family patterns of Sweden and Brazil that the values of the predominant religion influence many other aspects of life. Children, by necessity, are inducted into the religious culture of their parents and it colors much of their behavior and thinking about all sorts of things.

The extent to which this is true has been spelled out very clearly by Gerhard Lenski[8] who inspected the religious factor and its influ-

[8] Gerhard Lenski, *The Religious Factor: A Sociological Study of Religion's Impact on Politics, Economics, and Family Life*, Doubleday & Company, Garden City, N.Y., 1961.

ence on four different groups within the United States. Studying Jewish, Catholic, White Protestant, and Negro Protestant groups, he found significant differences of attitude and behavior in the following areas and in others.

1. Work—whether you like work for work's sake or whether you work because you must, in order to eat.
2. Installment buying—whether it is proper or unwise.
3. Savings from income – whether you should save even if you have to deny yourself something you want, and the *reasons* for saving.
4. Political behavior—whether it is important to vote and for which party you will vote.
5. Political attitudes—as to the sanctity of the Constitution, the effects of communism, the importance of world problems, spending abroad, spending for the national defense, school desegregation, residential desegregation, the welfare state, government control of big industry, health insurance, price controls, the unions, union membership.
6. Family—whether one chooses to live where many of one's relatives are; how often one visits one's relatives; willingness to move away from one's own home town.
7. Childrearing—whether you are more interested in his future or his present: attitudes toward physical punishment or symbolic punishment; attitudes toward monetary rewards or symbolic rewards; values of strict obedience as contrasted with independent thinking; how *many* children should be reared.
8. Sin—how wrong is gambling, birth control, moderate drinking, Sunday business, divorce, and so on.

In considering a family situation and its influence on the child, then, it is wise to remember that children in the United States are born into various religious cultures, each with its own special significance to his rearing and behavior, and each with its own interpretation of the rest of the child's culture. When religion is considered in this light, some pertinent questions come to mind. What are the effects on children of moving from one religion to another? What are the effects of having two religions represented in his family through interfaith marriage?

The Family Version

The culture to which the child is born is too vast, too comprehensive, too diverse, to be transmitted in its entirety, either by the family or by other agencies subsequently assisting it. This is particularly true of ideas, beliefs, and values in the culture. From the beginning of the child's induction into the culture, the family does more than merely transmit the culture. To speak more precisely, the family customarily performs three additional or supplementary functions: (1) it selects from the existing surroundings what is transmitted; (2) it interprets to the child what is transmitted; and (3) it evaluates what it transmits. In other words, the child sees the cultural heritage through the eyes of his family; he learns of it through the symbols which the family uses; and he shares the family's feelings toward it.

There are a number of factors which in turn determine this selective and evaluating process. Obviously, the family is limited in these respects to the culture which it has come to know; in part, it depends on what in the culture it has access to; third is the effect of its experience with different aspects of the culture; and, finally, there is the influence of the family's hopes. Each family is prone to see its children as its future, so that domestic hopes and ideals are imposed upon the children, often with more emotional accompaniment than are the realities of the culture. In other words, every family transmits the cultural heritage in its own way. More than that, it transmits its own version, compounded out of what it can see of the culture, how it sees it, and how it wants to see it.

The result of this selective and evaluating process on the part of the family is the formation of the child's sense of values, in regard to both personal pursuits and social behavior. The culture to which the child is born has its folkways, its mores, and its scale of rewards for differing schematizations of living. But it is within the bosom of the family that judgments are formed, conflicts of culture are resolved, choices are made or at least influenced. Life is varied and complex, infinitely full of possibilities. Personality development is a constant series of choices. These choices represent the person's values, and modern scholarship concludes that these values are in large part the result of family conditioning.

So fundamental is the role of the cultural values transmitted by the family and operating in any given family situation that the fullest consideration must be given to their identification and operation. Though the study of values is so difficult that it is avoided frequently, it is an implication of the outline of study proposed in this chapter that cultural values can be studied objectively.

THE FAMILY AND THE CHILD'S PLACE IN THE CULTURE

As the child is being introduced to his cultural heritage, there arise other questions of a more personal nature. Who am I? What am I? What is my own particular relation to this cultural situation in which I find myself? What is my peculiar place in it? What is my status?

These questions arise early, and are insistent. Parents may sense them before children develop to the point of formulating them. Social workers recognize the craving of adopted and foster children to learn about their own parents—who they were, what sort of people they were—regardless of how they were treated by them. The press is replete with stories of grown persons seeking knowledge of parents they never knew. The study of genealogy is a very human and understandable quest.

One of the most important things which the family does for the child is to give him status. Rather, one should speak of the statuses which he gets from the family. There is, first of all, his status in the family of procreation. With the coming of another child, this status is modified, often quite materially so. Again, the child has his status in the family of orientation, if that differs from the family of procreation. In these statuses in the immediate family, sex, age, and age relationship are the determining factors.

It is with reference to the child's status in the large society that the family serves a most important function. In this connection both the immediate and the kinship group types may be of great importance in giving the child his status in the world of his fellows. The family does this by means of two things: it gives him a name and a social position. Without a name, the child is only an undifferentiated human organic unit. When he is named he becomes "somebody." Then, by virtue of his family, he obtains a place in the social group. He is now what sociologists call a "person," that is, an individual with status.[9]

The family name is particularly important in the United States, with its many large population groups of recent foreign extraction. These family names quickly identify the child as a member of a particular group, and since these groups are apt to have a distinctive status, the child is assigned that status. What may result from this is described by Schettler. "Persons of minority nationality

[9] Robert E. Park and Ernest W. Burgess, *An Introduction to the Science of Society*, University of Chicago Press, Chicago, 1925, p. 35.

groups learn through experience that certain names always awaken certain prejudices. These persons realize that it is their names that constitute the common enemy for them as well as for members of the majority group. Evaluation of themselves stops with the judgment placed upon their names. Without consideration, much of their personality has been thereby discarded. These persons act upon the lesson learned, and they decide that a new or false name is an effective mask for disguising themselves. They change their names, Taraskevicia is translated as Rasko, Strakovsky is recast as Stark, Berkovitz evolves as Burke, Trofinov turns up as Travis, and Keidansky is shortened to Kay."[10]

This factor of status is related closely to two other concepts much emphasized in the recent literature of social psychology and psychiatry. One of these is the matter of security. We all seek security throughout life. Very early in life the child senses security or insecurity as a member of the family group. He feels that he was wanted or not wanted; that he was a boy when his mother wanted a boy, or the reverse; that he came too soon, or when he was wanted. Later on, he seeks security through membership in secondary groups, through achievement of one sort or another. Many a personality pattern of extreme aggressiveness or incessant restlessness or an insatiable drive for power results from deep-seated insecurity formed during this period. Still later, people seek security in marriage. The pattern of many marriages is not one of romance, but of a drive for the security which the chosen mate may give. Part of the quest for security is for physical and economic safeguards against the threats of an external, foreboding world; but much of it is psychosocial—a wanting to belong.

Status has a great deal to do with conduct through its effect upon one's conception of oneself. The role of the conception of oneself has been grasped by many students of human nature. William James used to remark that a man had as many selves as there were persons who recognized him and carried an image of him in their minds. The poet Masefield writes:

And there were three men went down the road,
  As down the road went he.
The man they saw, the man he was,
  And the man he wanted to be.

Status is a factor in the determination of a person's conception of the self, and this conception in turn is a determinant in his be-

[10] Clarence Schettler, "Does Your Name Identify You?" *Social Forces*, December, 1942, p. 172.

havior. This, then, is another element in the cultural content of a family situation which should be considered.

SOCIAL CHANGE AND THE FAMILY'S TRANSMISSION OF CULTURE

The culture-transmitting role of the family has been growing in importance in recent times and in a number of ways. First, the culture to be transmitted has been accumulating rapidly. Cultural expansion in the past century and a half has been phenomenal, and the rate of growth shows no signs of abatement. Rather, all the evidence points to its acceleration, particularly the part which is the result of modern science. During the past century or more, there has developed a pattern of science, invention, and discovery which has become thoroughly embedded in our cultural configuration and which has resulted both in very rapid cultural change and in its cumulation in precise and available form. All of this means not only that there is much more for the family to transmit to the child, but also that the task of selecting and interpreting and evaluating the culture has grown correspondingly.

This expanding task of the family in turn necessitates a longer period of time, so that with the accumulation of culture there needs to be a corresponding lengthening of what has been spoken of traditionally as the period of infancy. Actually, what is meant is the period of preparation for life during which the child remains under the supervision of the family. It is obvious, too, that the lengthening of this period is primarily a social fact, rather than a biological one as has been assumed so often. The lengthening of this period of the child's dependence upon the family is a change of outstanding significance, both in the history of the family and in the social development of the child.

This longer period and the more extensive culture markedly change the culture-transmitting role of the family. Time was when the culture was simple and the time available for its transmission was short. What the family did was largely to impose this culture upon the child. Today, the family increasingly becomes the manager or administrator of the child's induction into the culture. A part, and a highly important part, of its function remains what it has always been, but in addition there are increasingly the tasks of selecting parts of the culture to be emphasized, establishing necessary and advantageous contacts with specialized cultural agencies, detouring around some aspects of the culture, depreciating others

—in short, manipulating and assessing the expanding process of inducting the child into an accumulating culture.

Our rapidly changing and accumulating culture places other responsibilities upon the family. Several of these will be identified.

1. The family must play its role in preparing the child for change. In times past, the time span of change, especially for important changes, was longer as a rule than a generation or even a single human life. As a result, man was trained to adapt himself to fixed conditions. This meant emphasis upon the acceptance of the family culture. Today, this time span is very short. Important changes, even epoch-making changes, are frequent; a number occur within the period when the individual is being reared. What this means is that part of the culture-transmitting role of the family is to prepare the child for change, i.e., for novelty of circumstance. If the family is too backward and resistant to change and transmits this attitude to the child, he may grow up to live in a world of unreality. There are such families, and their children often pay the price of continuing maladjustment.

2. On the other hand, not all changes are important or desirable. The death rate of changes is high. Their life span is short. A certain resistance to them is both essential and wholesome. The family, in other words, needs to play a stabilizing role in a rapidly changing culture.

3. In a rapidly changing world, the family must give the child a sense of stability and security. There are other institutions and agencies which tend to play a stabilizing role, but they do not afford the comprehensiveness and the intimacy of the family relationship. Change, confusion, and uncertainty have their psychic aspects and implications, and the insurance and insulation against them need to be in kind. The family, it will be recalled, has always served as a refuge and an insurance. In times past, it has been the physical and economic side of this that has been emphasized, first because those were the chief hazards confronting its members, and second because no other agency afforded adequate protection against them. Today, both of these circumstances have changed; it is against the hazards of the spirit that the family offers its chief protection. A child's home still is his castle, even if the light within it has become more important than the moat and wall without.

4. Finally, mention must be made of the fact that the relationship between culture and family is reciprocal. During periods of marked cultural changes, or cultural maladjustment, the family, as a primary agency in cultural transmission and continuity, tends to be weakened and to be rejected by its individual members. "Pe-

riods of violent change," writes Zimmerman, "are those in which the family is lifted from its former influence, so that the individual and the older culture can operate on principles independent of each other . . . the illusion arises that the culture of the age has no family necessity."[11]

SUMMARY

1. A third approach to the study of family situations concerns itself with their cultural content. This, in many ways, is the most significant aspect of family situations; it is the aspect which contemporary sociologists emphasize.

2. The pattern of family life is part of the larger culture system of society. These family patterns differ markedly from one group to another, as studies of selected patterns clearly reveal. From birth, the child is inducted into his particular family culture.

3. Another cultural role of the family is to serve as agent in the transmission of the larger culture systems to the child. For a number of years, the family remains the chief agency through which the child has his contacts with the cultural milieu.

4. There are varying aspects of the larger cultural configuration: (a) the national culture, (b) the regional culture, (c) the class culture, (d) the religious culture, and (e) the individual family's version.

5. The family fixes the child's place in the larger cultural configuration through the ascription of status, the assignment of a name and traditional place, the bestowal of a sense of security and a conception of one's role.

6. The culture-transmitting role of the family increases in importance in a changing society. With the rapid accumulation of culture in the contemporary age, the family tasks of selecting, interpreting, and evaluating the culture grow correspondingly.

SUGGESTED READINGS

Benedict, Ruth, *Patterns of Culture*, New American Library, New York. A comparison of the cultures and personalities in three North American Indian groups.

[11] Carle C. Zimmerman, *The Family of Tomorrow*, Harper & Brothers, New York, 1949, p. 69. For a more complete elaboration of this point of view, see the same author's *Family and Civilization*, Harper & Brothers, New York, 1947.

Brown, Ina Corinne, *Understanding Other Cultures,* Prentice-Hall, Englewood Cliffs, 1963. A popularly-written and readable book that compares many important aspects of life among different peoples.

Lenski, Gerhard, *The Religious Factor,* Doubleday & Company, Garden City, N.Y., 1961. A sociological study of the influence of religion upon attitudes in politics, economics, and family life.

Lewis, Oscar, *The Children of Sanchez,* Vintage Books, Random House, New York, 1961. The autobiography of a Mexican family.

Mangione, Jerre, *Mount Allegro,* Houghton Mifflin Company, Boston, 1942. A story of Sicilian-American family life.

Orme, Alexandra, *Comes the Comrade,* William Morrow and Company, New York, 1950. A novel that describes the billeting of Russian soldiers in a European manor during World War II. Their lack of understanding of any but Russian culture makes them misinterpret the behavior of others.

Spiro, Melford E., *Children of the Kibbutz,* Harvard University Press, Cambridge, 1958. A report of the effects of an experiment in Israel in which parents and children do not live together all of the time.

Smith, Elmer Lewis, *The Amish Today,* Schlecters Publishers, Allentown, Pa., 1961. An analysis of the beliefs, behavior, and contemporary problems of an old and stable religious sect.

Whiting, Beatrice B., *Six Cultures,* John Wiley & Sons, New York, 1963. A detailed study of childrearing in widely different cultures.

Whiting, John W. M., *Becoming a Kwoma,* Yale University Press, New Haven, 1941. A very readable and detailed description of the teaching and learning processes that produce a type of personality in a primitive culture.

Whiting, John W. M., and Irvin L. Child, *Child Training and Personality,* Yale University Press, New Haven, 1953. An excellent cross-cultural study of methods of childrearing and their consequences in various cultures.

Zimmerman, Carle C., and Richard E. Du Wors, *Graphic Regional Sociology,* The Phillips Book Store, Cambridge, Mass., 1952. The authors describe personality characteristics, or types, related to different regions within the United States.

FACETS OF
FAMILY LIFE

Photograph by Ed Norgord

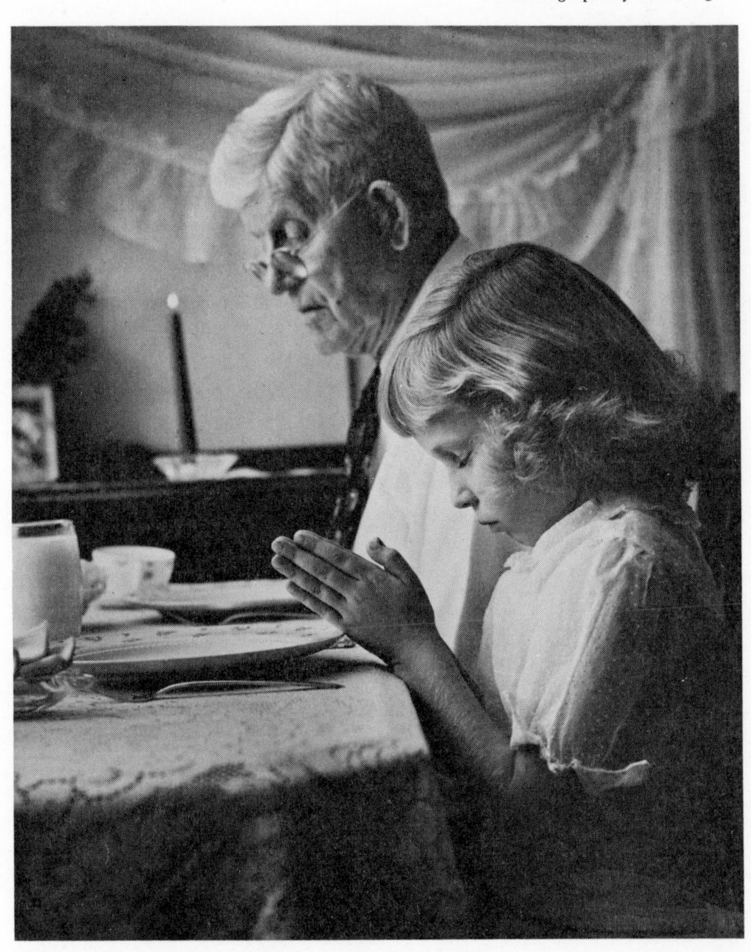

PART III

THE EMPATHIC COMPLEX AND CHILD BEHAVIOR 5

Various studies of child behavior, and conferences of workers dealing with particular cases, focus attention chiefly upon the mother, as though she were synonymous with the child's family background. In still other instances, the child's family is interpreted to mean father and mother. Obviously the mother and/or the father customarily are the key persons in the child's family situation. According to the federal census, of all legitimate children under 18 years of age and living with one or both parents, approximately 91 percent were living with both parents, 8 percent with the mother only, and 1 percent were living with the father only.[1] However, when one is concerned with the role of the family in an understanding of the child's behavior pattern, the parent or parents are by no means the whole, or even at times the major, part of the family situation. It is the purpose of the present chapter to examine the larger meaning and scope of the term *family situation,* and its relation to child behavior.

[1] U.S. Bureau of the Census, *Statistical Abstract of the United States: 1963,* Washington, D.C., 1963, p. 73.

THE FAMILY OF ORIENTATION: ITS COMPOSITION

The child's family of orientation was defined in Chapter 2 as the circle of his immediate, intimate, and continuing contacts. Utilizing this concept, of whom and what may this family of orientation consist?

First there are other children in the family. In more than 68 percent of the completed families in this country, two or more children grow up together.[2] It is but emphasizing the obvious to point out that children influence each other, particularly when growing up in the same family.

Second, there are other adults in the family background, by which we mean adults other than the parent or parents.

Stepparents might be singled out as a special group of these. In many ways they differ in their role from that of blood parent. The role of stepparents is a phase of child development increasing in extent but relatively unexplored.[3] A brief factual summary will indicate the proportions of this problem. About 23 percent of marriages in the United States in recent years have been remarriages for one or both of the spouses;[4] in approximately 1 out of every 14, both have been married before. Moreover, remarriage has been increasing in extent in all age groups, but particularly in the ages from 25 to 34 inclusive. These, it will be noted, are the likely years of parenthood. Then, too, the previous conjugal condition of those remarrying has changed considerably in the past few generations. Formerly most persons remarrying had been widowed; today about 73 percent have been divorced.[5] How many children are involved in these marriages is not known. Scattered state reports show that more than one-half of the divorced persons who remarry have children, and there is little reason to assume that the proportion among the widowed remarrying is much different.[6]

Kinsfolk are the largest group of other adults that the child contacts during the early and more formative years. Despite changes in the relationship between the immediate and the extended families in recent years, kinsfolk still come to each other's aid, particularly in the sharing of living quarters. Census data reveal to some

[2] *Ibid.*, p. 43.

[3] For a valuable study in this area, see William C. Smith, *The Stepchild*, University of Chicago Press, Chicago, 1953.

[4] U.S. Bureau of the Census, *op. cit.*, p. 71.

[5] *Ibid.*

[6] For a summary of the data on remarriage and its significance in child development, see James H. S. Bossard, *Parent and Child*, University of Pennsylvania Press, Philadelphia, 1953, chap. 8.

extent the presence of relatives in the household at any one time, but these show the situation only as of the day of the given survey, and hence do not answer our question: How many children grow up with relatives living in the home as the child is growing up?

To throw some light on the question as stated, a study of 410 university students may be of interest. Only one item of information was called for: List all the persons who lived as members of your household prior to your tenth birthday. The results follow:

1. An even 100 were families which had consisted of parents and children only. This is roughly 1 out of every 4.
2. In 30 cases, or 7 percent, there had been but one parent or a stepparent, for at least a part of the time.
3. In 50 cases, or 12 percent, servants, but no other persons, had lived in during that period.
4. In 230 cases, or 56 percent, relatives and/or other persons had lived in the household as members of it. Families, with servants living in, and other persons, have been listed in this category.

It may be pointed out at once that university students represent a selected group, and this is true. There can be little doubt, however, that the number of families with only parents and children living in the household would be larger than in the general population. Unfortunately, too, this sample, while suggestive, is too small to be definitive.

Kinsfolk need not live in the same household to have importance in the child's development. Despite certain individualizing influences affecting the modern family and the rising predominance of the immediate family, a study of 68 students at a large eastern university suggests that there is a marked degree of identification with kinsfolk as such, regardless of what they are like or how well one has known them previously. Two aspects of this are particularly noticeable. First are the differences in allusions to relatives and to friends. Although there are many references to friends, there are no suggestions of identification with friends or neighbors at all comparable to those with any or all relatives. This seems significant in that our friends are of our choosing, but we are born to our kin. Close identification, then, was with the people "inflicted" upon the informants. In cases where the relatives were acceptable people, this was a source of satisfaction and ego-inflation. Many wrote of talented relatives who visited and glamorized their very homes with their presence. On the other hand, those who were immoral, peculiar, faddish, infantile, the shabby, the uncouth, and the uneducated—these are sources of deep shame, personally.

Children normally contact still other persons within their homes with a frequency and/or under circumstances which make them a definite part of the family scene. These include guests, family friends whom the child and his family visit, servants, other caretakers of the child, and, as we shall attempt to show later, also domestic pets within the household. Because these receive separate consideration in the next chapter, mere mention of them will suffice at this point.

TWO CONCEPTS: THE FAMILY COMPLEX AND THE EMPATHIC COMPLEX

To assume, as is often done, that the child's family which molds his behavior consists wholly or mainly of his parents, seems rather remote from reality. Actually the child ordinarily contacts, from infancy on, a wide array of persons within his home or through family contacts. Besides the parents, there are the other siblings, kinsfolk, guests, servants, and others, all of whom are a part of the family environment and may, and ordinarily do, play a role in influencing the child's behavior. To designate this larger group, we shall employ the term *family complex*. The word *complex* is used here to mean a whole made up of integrated parts, a system of particulars like, for example, the B complex in vitamins. When, therefore, we shall refer henceforth to the child's family background we shall do so as meaning this broader concept of the family complex.

A second complex we shall use is that of the *empathic complex*. This has particular reference to the child's relation to the family complex. The word *empathy* is defined in current dictionaries as "the imaginative projection of one's own consciousness into another being," or "the ascription of our emotional feelings to the external object which serves as their visual and auditory stimulus." It was the late Harry Stack Sullivan, a psychiatrist, who sparked the term into use in connection with the study of human behavior. "Empathy," he wrote, "is the term that we use to refer to the peculiar emotional linkage that subtends the relationship of the infant with other significant people."[7] Sullivan primarily utilized the term *empathy* in connection with the subtle process whereby certain emotional states, like anxiety, are transferred from mother to infant, but he did recognize that as the child grew older he came to per-

[7] Harry Stack Sullivan, *Conceptions of Modern Psychiatry*, The William A. White Psychiatric Foundation, Washington, D.C., 1947, p. 8. (Current edition: W. W. Norton & Company, New York, 1953.)

ceive through this same emotional linkage more overt manifestations in regard to behavior. In fact, he sensed the role of this emotional linkage throughout the life of the individual. "We do not know much about the fate of empathy," he wrote, "in the developmental history of people in general. There are indications that it endures throughout life, at least in some people."[8]

We shall define the term *empathic complex* to mean the particular or specific emotional linkage between a child and the significant persons in his background. For a number of years, this means primarily persons who live in the same household, and the range of his family's contacts.

THE THEORY OF THE EMPATHIC COMPLEX

The theory of the empathic complex is presented in three parts.

1. As the child grows out of infancy and his more or less exclusive contact with the mother, he develops close relations with a selected few other persons. Some of these are members of his immediate family; some, of his kinship group; still others are selected from family contacts, such as guests, servants, and the like. Data presented later in this chapter suggest the possible number and range of such persons.

2. These persons are selected by the child, within the limitations that this situation imposes. In doing so, he considers primarily the total personality of these "other persons," and only secondarily the details of his relations with them, that is, their methods of child-rearing. Behrens, in a highly significant study, has shown this in the case of the mother. "The study indicates that evaluations of child-rearing practices are of little value unless understood as aspects of a dynamic process of socialization dependent on the social interaction of those individuals concerned." The results of this study show that "the child's adjustment to socialization was significantly related to the 'total mother person' and specifically to her character structure, but insignificantly related to the mother's specific rearing techniques."[9]

In selecting "total persons," the child does so on the basis of his needs of them, and not as they are viewed by other persons. For example, a quiet, serious, hard-working father, whom adults characterized as a good father, a good husband, and a good provider, appeared to the child as a cold and forbidding total person. In

[8] *Ibid.*

[9] Marjorie L. Behrens, "Child Rearing and the Character Structure of the Mother," *Child Development*, September, 1954, pp. 225–238.

another case, an impressive-looking, vigorous lawyer, coming to the home to visit, impresses a lonely, daydreaming boy with the way other persons kowtow to him.

To illustrate still more concretely the nature of this process of selection, we cite a case from a considerable collection of similar cases, as yet unpublished.

Marcia is the youngest of four children. She is 4 years old. Helen, next to her, is 6 and has started school. Tom, her brother, is 10, looks with disdain upon all females, and spends as much time as possible away from home. Jane, the oldest of the four, is 13, old enough now to be companionable with her young and attractive mother. Marcia is lonely. Time drags for her. Meanwhile Mrs. Adams, a charming widow, has moved next door. She and Marcia's mother quickly become friends, visiting back and forth. Mrs. Adams lives alone, has no children of her own, but is very fond of them. Marcia begins with short visits to Mrs. Adams. Then they become longer and more frequent. Soon Marcia stays for dinner with Mrs. Adams, and a little later stays overnight. Mrs. Adams has a way with children. Soon Marcia spends as much time as possible "next door." She has "taken over" Mrs. Adams completely.

Above all, and pervading all, influencing the child's selection is the emotional rapport which develops between him and these "other persons." And this, be it emphasized, is a two-way relationship. Children, because of their dependence, want to be loved, to be recognized for themselves, but they also want to love in return. Years ago, Charles Dickens expressed this latter factor, so often overlooked, we believe, in contemporary studies. In *Great Expectations*, Pip, who had been reared by Mr. and Mrs. Joe, has just been freed of the guilt for having stolen Mrs. Joe's pie. "I do not recall," he says, "that I felt any tenderness of conscience in reference to Mrs. Joe. But I loved Joe—perhaps for no better reason in those early days than because the dear fellow let me love him."[10]

3. These "other persons," or empathic complex, become the primary factors in the child's behavioral development, and for three main reasons.

a. They serve as the polar points around which the details of child rearing are organized. The theory of the empathic complex is not meant to ignore or to depreciate the constant repetitive processes that go on in the child's life, the multitude of continuing details of family life and habits of childrearing, but to add to their consideration the idea that there are polar points, highly magnetized as it were, around which they tend to swirl and become organized.

[10] Charles Dickens, *Great Expectations*, Holt, Rinehart and Winston, New York, 1955, p. 6.

b. They become the motivating forces which strengthen or weaken the methods of childrearing. The child decides that he wants to be like one or more of these other persons, and, to become so, will respond cooperatively to certain aspects of his rearing. Or he will think, as a young person said to us recently, "the key to my behavior is the strong desire not to be like my older sister."

c. They serve as the mediating agents between the child and his environment. Zimmerman and Broderick have shown how family friends serve this purpose with families as a whole.[11] Our theory contends that a similar function is served by his empathic complex for the child.

It should be made very clear that the thesis advanced in this chapter is supplementary and not opposed to the cultural study of patterns of childrearing and development. Each culture and subculture has its distinctive modes of childrearing and personality formation. Our thesis suggests that, within the cultural configuration of the area of the family, it is the empathic complex which accounts for the selective aspects of the individual child's behavioral development, thus explaining the wide variations that obtain within a seemingly common background. Simply stated, what we are proposing for the study of behavior is that it is people, and not methods of childrearing, that are significant in explaining the differentials within a culture or subculture. It is on this basis, too, that the negative findings of Sewell and his associates may be explained.[12]

SOME SUGGESTIVE LINES OF EVIDENCE

In support of the thesis which we have advanced, we submit four lines of evidence, selected from our studies in the sociology of child behavior.

1. Examination of published autobiographies reveals that almost without exception the authors explain their own development in terms of a relatively few persons toward whom they developed marked feelings of like or dislike when quite young. The number of such persons usually is limited, ranging from two to as many as seven. They frequently include persons other than members of

[11] Carle C. Zimmerman and Carlfred B. Broderick, "Nature and Role of Informal Family Groups," *Marriage and Family Living*, May, 1954, pp. 107–111.

[12] William H. Sewell, "Infant Training and the Personality of the Child," *American Journal of Sociology*, September, 1952, pp. 150–159; William H. Sewell and Paul H. Mussen, "The Effects of Feeding, Weaning, and Scheduling Procedures on Childhood Adjustment and the Formation of Oral Symptoms," *Child Development*, September, 1952, pp. 185–191; and William H. Sewell, Paul H. Mussen, and Chester W. Harris, "Relationships Among Child Training Practices," *American Sociological Review*, April, 1955, pp. 137–148.

the immediate family, sometimes animals, and sometimes objects such as books.

2. Six hundred life-history documents written for the William T. Carter Foundation show clearly that the writers believe their behavior to have been influenced by a selected few persons, whose personalities stand out vividly and to whom the writers feel strong emotional attitudes of either appreciation or aversion.

3. A group of 150 undergraduates and adult students were asked to identify all persons in their maternal and paternal kinfolk group, and to rate their feelings for each person as "close," "disliked," or "neutral." The "neutrals" composed over 48 percent of the group of relatives; the "disliked" another 11 percent. Clearly the emotional responses to the members of the family group were limited and highly selective.

4. Finally, another experimental study was made with 38 graduate students in the field of human behavior. When asked to identify, by the same categories of emotional feelings, the chief influences in their own development, they mentioned from three to eight persons. A thumbnail personality sketch of the students and the persons was obtained. The results were striking in that the students obviously tended to share traits of the liked persons and to resist traits of the unliked ones.

Each of these studies, however limited in number of cases and superficial in character, suggests that adults who analyze the outstanding influences in their earlier behavioral development emphasize a selected few persons whom they contacted in those early years: toward whom they developed strong emotional attitudes; who came to personify certain traits, values, habits, occupations, and behavior patterns; and whom they more or less consciously sought to emulate or, in the case of feelings of aversion, to develop opposing traits, etc. On the basis of these contacts, the boy or girl reacts toward the methods of childrearing that constitute his or her experience, and evaluates other conditioning factors encountered.

SUMMARY

1. In studying the role of the family in the development of the child's behavior, the family must be conceived to include more than the parents.

2. The family of the child's orientation to life includes, in addition to the parents and possible stepparents, siblings, kinsfolk, guests, servants, and household pets.

3. To comprehend this broader range of family personnel and influences, the term *family complex* is suggested.

4. For the peculiar emotional linkage between the child and significant persons in his background, the concept of the empathic complex is suggested.

5. The theory of the empathic complex holds that (a) as the child grows out of infancy he develops close relations with a few other persons, mostly adults; (b) these persons are selected on the basis of the child's felt needs of them; and (c) these other persons become the primary factors in the child's behavioral development.

6. Suggestive lines of evidence include autobiographical material, life-history documents, data on personal contacts within the family complex, and an experimental study in cooperation with 38 graduate students in a large university.

SUGGESTED READINGS

Dickens, Charles, *Great Expectations*, Holt, Rinehart and Winston, New York, 1955. This classic is one of the best novels through which to examine the few significant people in the life of a boy deprived of his parents.

Sullivan, Harry Stack, *Conceptions of Modern Psychiatry*, The William A. White Psychiatric Foundation, Washington, D.C., 1947. (Current edition: W. W. Norton & Company, New York, 1953.) The source of the original development of the concept of the empathic complex as it applies to human behavior. There is no literature that applies it extensively to child development.

SOME NONFAMILY MEMBERS: THEIR ROLE IN CHILD DEVELOPMENT 6

It has been pointed out in the preceding chapter that the child's family background actually consists of the whole segment of life that is organized around the immediate family. Guests, people who are visited by the family, domestic servants, and even domestic pets are included in this complex. The present chapter is devoted to a consideration of them and of their role in child development. Various other persons in the child's background might be considered here, but these few, it is hoped, will be sufficient to illustrate the concept of the empathic complex.[1]

[1] See Oscar W. Ritchie and Marion R. Koller, *Sociology of Childhood,* Appleton-Century-Crofts, New York, 1964, chap. 7 for references to other adult nonfamily participants.

FAMILY GUESTS

Families vary greatly in the amount and type of entertaining which they do in their own homes while the children are growing up. Extremes run from the house that is always a bit like Grand Central Station to the one in which guests are so few as to be frightening or exciting; from the family in which all sorts of people are welcomed to the one in which guests are very carefully screened; and from the family in which children are rigidly excluded from participation in adult entertainment to the one in which they are considered on an equal footing or made the center of attention. As these situations vary, so do the influences of guests upon child development.[2]

There are, however, certain general features of the guest situation that set it apart from chance meetings with other persons outside of the home. Guests are "selected" people, selected usually by the parents. Guests are usually "approved" persons—approved in the sense that no matter how much certain things about them may be disliked they are invited and welcomed into the family milieu, with all the rights and rules that pertain to guests. They are with the family for a definite period of time, become the spotlighted person to whom attention is due and toward whom it is largely directed, and at the same time, are seen against the backdrop of family and house that has become so familiar it is seldom consciously seen. A guest creates a difference in this familiar locale which is often marked and noted by children. Analysis of several hundred published autobiographies and other life history documents has revealed at least three purposes which guests serve for children.

A Broader Perspective on Parents as People

In the eyes of children, at home with their own family, parents are just parents. Or, as Rosamond Lehmann has put it: "When we are children, we do not see people close to us as themselves—only as our need for them, our habit of them. When something happens to make us realize that they have an enormous life going on apart from us, we feel rather resentful."[3]

[2] For a more detailed discussion of family guests see James H. S. Bossard and Eleanor Stoker Boll, "The Role of the Guest: A Study in Child Development," *American Sociological Review,* vol. XII, no. 2, April, 1947, pp. 192–201.

[3] Rosamond Lehmann, *The Ballad and the Source,* Reynal and Hitchcock, New York, 1945, p. 100. (Current edition: Harcourt, Brace & World, New York.)

George Bernard Shaw has said much the same thing: "A contemporary stranger is a novelty and an enigma, also a possibility; but a mother is like a broomstick or like the sun in the heavens, it does not matter which as far as one's knowledge of her is concerned: the broomstick is there and the sun is there; and whether the child is beaten by it or warmed and enlightened by it, it accepts it as a fact in nature and does not conceive it as having had youth, passions, and weaknesses, or as still growing, yearning."[4] Being present while adult guests are being entertained is one of the earliest means by which children begin to see that Mother and Father are human beings who play roles other than that of parent. The newness of a guest's behavior, as contrasted with the familiarity of the parent's personality, sometimes makes children very sensitive to traits which they had either taken for granted or had not been aware of before. Here are some examples:

Vivian Hughes used to listen to her mother entertaining. She was pleased and amused by her mother's intelligence and sense of humor as compared with the stupidity of the "usual female visitors" who enjoyed only worries and grievances.[5] Edgar Lee Masters was much gratified by the frequent visits of his teacher to his mother, who had had no great amount of formal education but had read widely and was a match for the schoolmistress.[6] But another writer went through agonies watching his father "show off" and "tell tall tales" to the very respectable men he brought home.[7]

"I always found it very profitable," wrote a college student, "to ask for a dime and was sure of receiving a quarter, especially if my mother's relatives were there. (My father's relatives were more money-wise than my mother's.) It was a twofold purpose. My father took the opportunity to show off, and this was indicative of his financial status."

Children often have the opportunity to observe in the privacy of the family circle that parents do not always practice what they preach. But the social gathering together of adults can increase the opportunity for such observations when those adults are being companionable or convivial, and forgetful of the penetrating scrutiny of the younger generation. In both morals and manners, guests revealed adult inconsistencies to the authors of the autobiographies.

4 George Bernard Shaw, "A Treatise on Parents and Children," in *Misalliance*, Brentano's, New York, 1914, p. xcv.

5 Vivian Hughes, *A London Child of the Seventies*, Oxford University Press, London, 1934, p. 89.

6 Edgar Lee Masters, *Across Spoon River*, Farrar & Rinehart, New York, 1936, p. 66.

7 *Sherwood Anderson's Memoirs*, Harcourt, Brace and Company, New York, 1942, p. 45.

An actor's daughter writes about the night that she was wakened by the noise of a party, got out of bed, and slipped in among the guests unnoticed. Beer and rye were abundant. Members of her family were dressed in their wrappers. A man was holding Mamma's hand. Another was trying to kiss Nana, a favorite aunt; he was "nosing" into the lace cascade on the front of her wrapper.[8] One autobiography tells of a boy watching a series of scenes between the Jewish stepfather-in-law and his mother. The man, who had come to visit, had to have his food prepared in the orthodox manner, which made a lot of trouble for the lady of the house. After a time, he suspected that she was only *pretending* to prepare his food properly. The youngster knew that these suspicions were correct—his mother was only pretending.[9]

Often members of the family disagree in their estimates of a guest or of his behavior. In some cases, in these narratives, such differences became acute and caused family conflict. Harriet Munroe used to enjoy watching the games of the men who came to play cards with her father. But her mother did not approve of these people, who filled the house with smoke and required spittoons. The poet writes that she noticed the men came less and less often and that finally her father went out in the evenings to the home of a widower instead of bringing his friends home.[10]

Yet another inconsistency in parents that is shown up when guests are present concerns matters of social behavior. How people behave and talk "in family" is not always considered proper with outsiders. This often comes to a child's attention with somewhat of a shock. A number of writers remembered being sent from the room for behavior which they had not known would get them into trouble. One, when a little boy, was absorbed in listening to some breezy gossip of his mother's when the vicar came to call. He waited patiently for the vicar to be welcomed and seated and then asked his mother to go on with the story about ——. He was promptly sent upstairs.[11] Another tells of hearing the cook say that if the vicar came to tea much oftener he would eat Auntie out of house and home. The girl thought the vicar ought to know, so she told him. But she was sent to bed without any supper.[12]

Guests act as a focus not only upon family members but also

[8] Aline Bernstein, *An Actor's Daughter*, Alfred A. Knopf, New York, 1941, pp. 142–149, 108–110.

[9] John Cournos, *Autobiography*, G. P. Putnam's Sons, New York, 1935, pp. 26–30.

[10] Harriet Munroe, *A Poet's Life*, The Macmillan Company, New York, 1938, p. 24.

[11] Charles Finger, *Seven Horizons*, Doubleday, Doran & Company, New York, 1930, pp. 10–11.

[12] Jeanette Gilder, *The Autobiography of a Tomboy*, Doubleday, Doran & Company, New York, 1901, p. 91.

upon the family background. A family has status only in comparison with the status of others. Small children are often well insulated from a recognition of their family's standing by a lack of that comparison. The daughter of a well-to-do Russian patriarch reveals that she did not know she was living in luxury, so accustomed to it was she. But on Christmas, when all the peasants from her father's estate came to be entertained and to receive gifts from him, the girl gained a conception of her family's position in that country.[13] A farm boy, though, tells of his resentment over the yearly visits of his town aunts, because they let it be seen that their sister had married beneath her. He disliked to see his mother put on airs for them, and then become subdued in spirit before their superiority.[14]

Acquaintance with Varying Personalities and Situations

For the same reason that the novelty of the guest introduces children to new facets of family life and parent behavior, so does it introduce them to different kinds of people with strange behavior, ideas, religions, occupations, and so forth. In fact, to the extent that guests come frequently and the child participates, this can be a rich and early learning experience.

Young men and women who wrote about their early childhood frequently mentioned their first conceptions of personality types from seeing, as guests, wives who tyrannized their husbands; couples who made a real marriage, with little in the way of worldly goods; well-groomed career women without an ounce of maternal warmth in them; little, wrinkled old ladies of youthful spirit and animated conversation; rollicking bachelors who took on sobriety with married life; relatives who fought each other and fawned on the uncle who had a large fortune; good sports in adversity; persons who had little or nothing to complain about but did so unceasingly; fair-weather visitors; those who used others for their own selfish ends; self-absorbed bores; conversational extroverts; "snobs and democrats"; those who never imposed upon hospitality and those who always did; the pretenders; and the genuine. Boys, particularly, noted the occupations of guests, and how certain occupations were regarded by their parents and the other guests.

Most young children seem to be strongly convinced that there is only one true religious faith, one honest political party, one right

[13] Princess Catherine Radziwill, *It Really Happened*, Dial Press, New York, 1932, pp. 28–29.

[14] Cyrenus Cole, *I Remember, I Remember*, State Historical Society of Iowa, Iowa City, 1936, pp. 67–69.

code of ethics, one "proper" way of doing a certain thing, and they believe that people who believe and do differently are not themselves "proper." Often, this is not so much the result of personal smugness or of deliberate parental indoctrination as it is of a lack of intimacy with people whose beliefs and customs are unlike their own. The guest who was accepted by the parents as a "proper" person often disclosed to the children during visits a point of view different from, or directly opposite to, that which the family entertained. Sometimes the children were much shocked by these revelations, but nevertheless they came to see that people they knew and liked acted differently and held views different from theirs.

Just as children are not equally impressed and influenced by all family and kinsfolk, so are they "selective" about guests. To some they are neutral, with little or no impact upon the child. Other guests are loved, and still others despised. These did have an influence. They were identified as what the children consciously wanted to be like, or as the living image of what they wanted to avoid being. In both cases, it is clear that the guests had become a part of the child's empathic complex. To illustrate, there was "the catty spinster who hated women and pawed over my father"; the lawyer, with "the brusque manner and large head who always dominated our household"; "the perfectly groomed and poised woman, whose every little movement I watched and tried to emulate"; the handsome "singer-actor whose gleaming teeth were responsible for the faithfulness with which I brushed my teeth for years"; the actor with "the flowing tie and the story of the lion-taming act"; the mayor of the town who "got down on the floor and played with me."

Fulfillment of Children's Needs

Quite apart from being a possible rich source of learning for children, guests often do contribute things that have been lacking in children's lives. Only children living in isolated areas mentioned the companionship of visitors as being high spots in their lives. The warmth of a guest to a child of rather formal parents was remembered into middle age by some. Small attentions, praise and gifts helped to build up the self-esteem of others. Especially noticeable was the number of people who reported on the good advice they received from guests during adolescence. During teenage rebellion, when parents seem more ignorant and less understanding than ever before or after, a guest who is identified with positively, but who has no actual authority over the child, appeared to be an acceptable person and one who was helpful with problems, with questions about schooling, and about future occupation.

CHILDHOOD VISITING

Consideration of the role of guests in the home, in child development, tends to emphasize the complementary experience of childhood—visiting in other homes. Life-history documents, autobiographies, and interviews contain frequent reference to its importance. Here, obviously, is another area of behavior analysis calling for extended research.

A pioneer study of childhood visiting made under the auspices of the William T. Carter Foundation and based on 100 written case records or personal interviews offers the following suggestions as to the role visiting plays in child development.[15]

1. The amount of childhood visiting in other persons' homes varies as much for individual children as does the entertaining of guests in their own homes. There are cases in which there is much visiting and much entertaining and in which there is little. There are also the cases in which parents prefer to confine their children's contacts with others to their own homes, so that they may supervise and be aware of what is taking place. Then, there are parents who are only too happy to accept any invitation for their children that will get them out of the way for a while; but who do not entertain in return. For the children, there are represented quite different opportunities in early introduction to the outside world. Some youngsters who have no such introduction, frequently find abrupt entrance into the school world quite difficult. Others are thrust into the new experience without thought or supervision on the part of parents. Characteristic comments on such experiences are references to: "the house in which the Jewish dietary laws were made light of, and I broke them with subsequent horrible conscience pangs," "my hostess who, I found, was mistress of a prominent lawyer," "Mrs. X.'s children who taught me to steal little things from stores," "the boy, a year younger than me, who ran around naked all the time." Other children, for whom parents planned more thoughtfully, found visiting to be a broadening and pleasant experience, for the most part.

2. Among this last group of children, visiting appeared to act

[15] The entire study is presented in James H. S. Bossard, *Parent and Child: Studies in Family Behavior*, University of Pennsylvania Press, Philadelphia, 1953, chap. 13.

not only as a process of socialization but also as a social weaning process—a gentle beginning of separation from home and of self-confidence with other people in strange places.[16] For most of these cases there were definite and progressive steps in the process. As babies and very small children, they visited parents' friends with parents. Later they went to relatives' and playmates' homes for short times alone, then for overnight or weekend stays. At the same time, distances for visits were lengthened from a walk, to a bus ride, to an overnight train or plane trip. These youngsters were gradually conquering both dependence and distance. One of them wrote, "When I was finally allowed to go by train half way across the continent to stay with my grandmother for a month, I *really* felt grown up." This might be compared to the comments of a girl who had never been permitted to stay away from home overnight until she went to college in a distant city. She became actually ill from panic and homesickness and left college after one miserable month.

3. Childhood visiting offered the same broadening knowledge of types of people as did entertaining guests. The difference was that this learning took place in new settings under unfamiliar circumstances and, therefore, stimulated much comparing between one's own family and household and those of others. Children are apt to believe that "everyone does just like us," unless they have some basis for comparison. Sometimes the grass seems greener on the other side of the fence: "The house is bigger and prettier"; "the mother and daddy never fight"; "the kids are allowed to do as they please." Just as often, came comments such as: "The filthy house where I got nits in my head"; "the father who swore all the time and hit his son"; "those funny Quakers who go to a church with no preacher"; "food that I had a hard time to eat"; "they just live and think completely different from us." In these last cases, children returned home wiser, but more consciously appreciative of their own homes than they had been before.

DOMESTIC SERVANTS

In the early years of the twentieth century, servants formed a significant part of the lives of young children. Domestics were of many kinds, from the hired hands and hired girls in the farm family with whom the children romped and worked, through the cooks and maids who lived with the middle-class family, to the

16 *Ibid.*

staff of carefully chosen servants and tutors and governesses of well-to-do people. Since that time, servants of all kinds have become scarcer and more expensive. Many people of the working class who can secure only unskilled jobs prefer such jobs to the status of "domestic." An enjoyment of less formality in family living has decreased the need and desire for servants. Yet, in many instances, they still do exist in a child's family of orientation. It seems pertinent, then, to take a brief look at what they have meant to children of the present generation.

For this purpose, 500 life-history documents have been collected and analyzed by the authors since 1950, all of them from persons not over 25 years of age at the time of their writing.[17] From this largely middle- and upper-lower class sample, over one-half (56 percent) had never had domestic help in the homes of their childhood. Of the other 44 percent, 40 cases mentioned day workers who, once or twice a week, came and went and had not the slightest effect upon the writers. The rest were quite emphatic about the contributions, both positive and negative, made by servants in the household.

1. Most frequently mentioned was the motherly woman, or the sympathetic young girl or young man, who was warmer toward the child than the parents. Obviously, these servants did not have the vested interests in careful childrearing that the parents did and took it less seriously. However, when children felt wronged or disciplined too harshly, they complained to the servants, were comforted by them; and the servants often interceded for them with good results in the child's eyes. These servants became to the children the "confidantes," the "companions," "a person I'd rather be with than my own mother." Strong and mutual emotional bonds were made in many cases; the child felt "lost" when the servant left, or was still "keeping in touch" at the time the life-history document was written. Time was when more adults were present in the household and a child who felt persecuted or unloved by his parents could seek consolation and security in other adults. It seems clear that present-day servants sometimes serve children in this way.

2. Second in importance was the servant's role in forming children's opinions about races other than their own. Over 80 percent of the servants mentioned were Negroes, most of them "had a knack with children" and were well liked or devotedly loved. Typical

[17] For an earlier study see James H. S. Bossard and Eleanor S. Boll, "The Role of the Guest: A Study in Child Development," *American Sociological Review*, April, 1947, pp. 192–201.

comments made were: ". . . so I never had any racial prejudice"; or "She had only second-grade education but much wisdom, and I respected her"; or "There were awfully tense moments when I would leave the maid and go to my mother, but I never developed race prejudice."

As important, but less frequently mentioned, was the early lesson that all people of the same race are not alike. A boy, for instance, tells of a Negro couple who let the house and his little sister get greasy and smelly. He resented this and despised the servants. In contrast to them, a subsequent Negro couple "came from a family of teachers, were ambitious, had a fine attitude toward life, and discussed movies, philosophy, and God with us kids." If it is true, as the studies say, that basic prejudices are set early, in the home, then these servants have played an important role in the formation of attitudes toward another race.

3. Some children saw servants as means to more companionship with their own parents since the latter were freed from chores that consume much time. A 20-year-old girl, about to be married, was so impressed with this role of the servants in her own upbringing that she discussed it with her fiancé. They decided that if they had to live with secondhand furniture and no rugs they would have domestic help, so that they would have plenty of time and energy for their children. This seems to be an interesting instance of value selection—a difficult subject to study and, therefore, too often ignored.

4. A relatively new role of the servant, at least in scope, appeared as that of the person who cared for children of gainfully employed mothers. The comments made were definite and of two kinds. When the servants were well-chosen, warm, and efficient, the children not only identified them as parental substitutes but felt positively about their mothers' employment. "I think that Mother was happier working than she would have been housekeeping, and that made all of us happier"; and "Us kids were able to have a lot more of the things money can buy than we could have if Mom hadn't worked," were some comments. If, however, the servants were not fitted for their job or the children did not like them as people, the feelings expressed were quite different. Deep antagonism toward both servants and parent was obvious in such cases. For example: "Mothers have *no business* going off to work and leaving their kids at the mercy of somebody who doesn't really care. I sure suffered from this. I just never had a proper upbringing in all the little things that matter so much when kids are in school"; or "My brother and I hated Hettie intensely. We

used to talk to each other about things, and we were sure that our parents didn't really care anything about us—to go off all day and leave us with her like that."

The literature on the results of maternal employment, though conflicting in its conclusions, frequently suggests that it is not so much the employment in itself that causes family adjustment or maladjustment. Rather, it is the feelings of the parents, the attitudes of the children, and the specific arrangements made for child care. It would seem that these three things are much related. If successful arrangements are made, children are apt to be happy about the situation, and the parent is more carefree and less conscience-ridden. Thus, such servants may, indeed, play a very important role in family interaction as well as in child-rearing.

5. Servants were almost exclusively of a race, religion, ethnic group or social class different from that of the family employing them. Often children had their first lessons in status rankings and the ways of living in other cultures right in their own families of orientation. They learned about loyalty to people other than one's own, dedication to service, humility, poverty, and unmercenary values. They also learned about new words, superstition, illegitimacy, reproductive processes, alcoholism, illiteracy, "how frightening it is to be devoutly religious," "ephemeral marital relations," murder, the segregation problem—among a host of other things that helped to prepare them early for some of the realities of the outside world which they would someday enter.

In summary, two points might be stressed in order to relate the role of domestic servants to sociological concepts stated in earlier chapters. First, it is clear that the child's empathic complex may extend beyond the family of orientation. Some of the above cases have identified with servants—positively and negatively—and have been greatly influenced in their development by them. Second, in the family situation of a child no one stimulus is a determinant of his behavior or attitudes. All stimuli interlock and act upon the child who then assesses them. The domestic servant, whatever he may be like, is one stimulus, acting in relation to the specific family and child. One illustration of this is the child first learning about illegitimacy. In one family where a girl servant from a reform school "was raped" and became pregnant, the parents were silent on the whole subject, and their little son was intrigued and "preoccupied" with the situation. In another, the parents were loudly and harshly analytical about what had happened, frightening the child badly about the matter of sex in which he was little informed.

In still another, "Dad gave her money so that she could have the baby in a hospital. I sensed that it was a very sad thing to get oneself into such a mess and was pleased that Dad was so nice about it."

DOMESTIC ANIMALS

One wonders, at this point, whether domestic animals should be included under the heading of nonfamily members—so much a part of family life have they become. About 11.3 million families have cats and almost 18 million own dogs. The dog, apparently the more popular pet and therefore selected as "case material" here, is expensive to some people. Well over half a billion cans of dog food are sold every year in the United States—more than any one other canned-food product. Canines are big business to others—dog breeders, veterinarians, pet-supply dealers, even dog psychologists. *Changing Times* reported in 1959 that television stations take in about $15,000,000 annually from commercials about pet products and that other media sell about $350,000,000 worth of pet items per year. It is not, however, the quantity of dogs in our country nor their commercial value that is of interest here. It is, rather, the peculiar quality of their relationship with human beings, and their influences upon child development and family relationships.[18]

Mythology and folklore, fables and fiction, interrelate man's life with dogs and other animals. Novelists, journalists, playwrights and television-script writers are well aware of, and take advantage of, the dramatic popular appeal of the feeling between dogs and humans. Social scientists have been relatively slow to study or to appreciate the possible significance of its place to the individual in group life. As far back as 1935, modern scientists were criticized for deliberately blinding themselves to the tender relationships in life, feeling that they might appear to be sentimental, and for avoiding the subject of love, lest they be thought emotional.[19] Gordon Allport has written that "a persistent defect of modern psychology is its failure to make a serious study of the affiliative

[18] James H. S. Bossard, "I Wrote About Dogs," *Mental Hygiene*, July, 1950, pp. 385–390; James H. S. Bossard, "The Mental Hygiene of Owning a Dog," *Mental Hygiene*, July, 1944, pp. 408–413; Nelson Foote, "A Neglected Member of the Family," *Marriage and Family Living*, August, 1956, pp. 213–218; Marcel Heinman, "The Relationship Between Man and Dog," *Psychoanalytic Quarterly*, vol. XXV, no. 2, 1956, pp. 568–585.

[19] Ian Sutti, *The Origins of Love and Hate*, Kegan Paul, Trench, Trubner and Company, London, 1935.

desires and capacities of human beings."[20] General Omar N. Bradley, addressing an audience, commented that we are a race of nuclear giants and ethical infants, knowing more about war than peace, and more about killing than living. Many people have complained that social scientists, prefer to study the spectacular and critical (such as hostility, rejection, frustration, racial antagonism) rather than a host of small, healthy, constructive processes that make up a large part of the daily life of the average citizen and help form him into what he is. Because of these challenges a systematic and continuing collection of materials on the role of the dog has been undertaken by the William T. Carter Foundation, and some of the conclusions follow.

1. A dog can fulfill the need to be loved. All literature on child development stresses the fact that, without love, children cannot survive as normal people. Parents are the ones who are supposed to give this love, but some do and some do not. For parents who are incapable of this gift there is little suggestion as to how to obtain substitutes. Therapists who work with unloved children, able to relate only to things and not to persons, are well aware of what sometimes happens when a puppy is taken into the family. He jumps up in excitement when the child appears; tail wagging, he licks the child's face; romps with him; goes to bed with him; and snuggles beside him. The puppy does this no matter how much the child's behavior has displeased the parents, no matter how unpopular the child is with his own peer group. A feeling of warmth and consolation, a sense of personal worth can be born in this experience. The same thing is true for normal children, who often *think* that they are unloved, or wronged, or not very worthwhile to other people. This holds not just for youngsters. Adults require being loved also, and in our tremendous, individualistic society there are so many who are not. One reason for the growing popularity of dogs may well be a result of our changed sex ratio. A large surplus of single, widowed and divorced women over the number of eligible men of corresponding ages has created much loneliness and sense of worthlessness for the so-called "nurturing sex." Though adults who are devoted to their pet animals are often suspect, Dr. Lawrence S. Kubie, former president of the New York Psychoanalytic Society says, "Compulsive behavior in humans is no more triggered by dogs than it is by food. We see compulsive eaters and compulsive dog owners, but these are symptoms; neither the food nor the dog's presence is causative."[21]

[20] Gordon Allport in Pitirim A. Sorokin (Ed.), *Explorations in Altruistic Love and Behavior*, Beacon Press, Boston, 1950, pp. 145–146.

[21] Mary Jean Kempner, "Money, Votes and Psychiatry Are Going to the Dogs," *Sports Illustrated*, May 11, 1964, pp. 72–79.

2. Human beings need not only to be loved but also to be able to give affection without reservation. This is often made difficult. People can be so unsatisfactory in their response, this is hurtful, and reservation becomes an established pattern in order to prevent more pain. A young married woman who frequently mentioned her feelings for her husband was told, "I know you love me or you wouldn't have married me. You needn't tell me about it all the time." She ceased telling him. A teenage girl who had been longing for a first date was finally asked by a boy for an engagement. In spite of her excitement, she calmly answered, "Wait until I look at my calendar to see if I already have a date that evening." Few of us are wholly free of inhibitions in our relations with humans. Dogs do not put up such defenses. They eagerly absorb all the devotion given to them and, as a 4-year-old on Art Linkletter's TV program said, "A dog is man's best friend because they don't back-sass you." The giving of unreserved affection to an animal may be a temporary solace; it may also be a learning experience which can be transferred to relations with people.

3. The dog contributes to the development of many a human being the challenge of a continuing responsibility. This matter of a continuing responsibility is one of life's major experiences—sobering, exacting, maturing, character-forming. Not all of us have it. Many persons go through life without it; others find it first when parenthood comes to them. This experience may come early in life, to a growing child, when a pet is consigned to his care. A doll or an electric train can be cast aside when the child is tired of it. A dog has to be walked, fed, watered, given shots, supplied with a license, guarded from dangers *constantly*, or it will die or be lost to the family.

4. The dog is an excellent vehicle for parents to use in training children in toilet habits. The pup must be housebroken. The family walks him, scolds him for making a puddle, and constantly talks about the pup's toilet habits. The parallel between puppy behavior and human behavior gets through to the child.

5. In the same way, a dog may serve to educate children about sex and physiological processes. In families that tend to be too inhibited about the latter, to live with the needs of animals is to gain a net impression of their naturalness. Animals have long been used to educate children concerning sex relations and the birth processes. Less appreciated has been the possibility of instilling attitudes about promiscuity and dysgenic marriage. A purebred female dog comes into heat, and must then be walked on a leash. Mother explains that this is to prevent her from having puppies. The children *want* some puppies. "But you want puppies that are

as nice as our dog, don't you?" Mother replies. "In that case, we have to choose a good father for them. We can't let her run around with any old dog." Even in the matter of the natural process of death, the dog has often served as a child's first introduction to the meaning of it.

6. The dog is a satisfactory victim of personal needs for power and ego satisfaction. The child who is commanded all day long may be commander over his dog. The child who is full of resentment over what he believes is his bad treatment by adults may kick at his dog. Though this use of a dog, if carried to extremes, is not exactly commendable, there is some therapeutic effect for children when indulged in within reason.

7. Walking an attractive dog has been a means through which some overly shy children have been enabled to make friends. Such is the attraction of dogs to children and adults that they will stop, talk, ask questions, play. For a youngster in a new neighborhood, a dog is often a wedge into the already formed play group.

8. Finally, a dog is a satisfying companion. He follows you around, indoors and out, and does not leave you as people do. He is silent, responsive, uncritical, patient, more affectionate than you deserve, and appreciative beyond what anyone could expect from a human being. Perhaps this is why there is always "a boy and his dog."

SUMMARY

1. In the early life situation of the child, there are others than family members and kinsfolk who have influence in his development.

2. Family guests may present a broader perspective on parents as people, acquaint children with varying personalities and situations, and fulfill needs of children that are not met by parents and siblings.

3. Visits to the homes of other people serve as a process in social weaning and broaden the horizons of knowledge in many ways.

4. Domestic servants may serve as parent substitutes or confidantes, are responsible for forming racial attitudes, free parents for more companionship with children, affect their attitudes toward maternal employment, and provide lessons in status and cultural differences.

5. Dogs may fulfill the need to be loved and to love in an uninhibited way, give the challenge of continuing responsibility, pro-

vide instruction concerning many natural processes of life, become an instrument for power and ego satisfaction, provide "contacts" for shy children, and afford constant companionship.

SUGGESTED READINGS

Ackerley, Joe Randolph, *My Dog Tulip,* Secker and Warburg, London, 1956. A popularly written book about one canine friend.

Davis, Allison, B. B. Gardner, and Mary R. Gardner, *Deep South,* University of Chicago Press, Chicago, 1941. This book contains much interesting information on domestic servants in the South, with references to their relationships with children.

Judy, Will, *Don't Call a Man a Dog,* Judy Publishing Company, 1949. An interesting book with a provocative title.

Steinbeck, John, *Travels with Charley,* Viking Press, New York, 1962. An appealing tale of the relationship between a man and his dog while exploring America.

Sullenger, Thomas Earl, *Neglected Areas in Family Living,* The Christopher Publishing House, Boston, 1960. The author has collected and reprinted materials from both scientific and popular sources on areas of family life that he feels are important but that have seldom been subjects of serious study.

Weygandt, Cornelius, *On the Edge of Evening,* G. P. Putnam's Sons, New York, 1946. This autobiography is of interest here because of the relative weight given to a relationship with a dog, and with other persons.

(Since little has been written on the subjects of guests, visits, servants, and animals in child development literature, it is suggested that the student explore published autobiographies. Those that deal extensively with childhood are often full of references to these subjects.)

MODES OF FAMILY OPERATION

Photograph by A. Devaney Inc., N.Y.

Photograph by Ed Norgord

PART IV

FAMILY TABLE TALK

7

Preceding chapters have emphasized two basic steps in the social development of the child. One is his introduction into the process of living with other persons; the other, his contact with the accumulated modes of living and thinking which constitute the cultural system in which he lives. Both of these are acquired by the child first through his family. These two processes are the essence of childrearing and, on the cultural side, comprise the family's role as the connecting link between successive generations. Much has been written about the importance of what the family does in these respects, but far less attention has been given to the mechanism by which the family achieves these ends. It is to a consideration of this mechanism and some of its more important aspects that this and the succeeding five chapters are devoted.

FORMAL INSTRUCTION THROUGH THE FAMILY

The helplessness of the human infant requires a long period of nurture and protection, and it is part of the economy of nature that parents conserve and transmit their experience, knowledge, and understanding to their children during this time. Thus the family is destined by its very nature to be the primary educational agency in the life of the child, and in simpler forms of society a large part of the child's education is obtained from the family. The ancient Jewish household, for example, was the only educational institution for most Jewish folk until the time of Christ, when, for the first time, through the leadership of Rabbi Joshua ben Gamla, schools apart from the home were instituted in the towns and villages of Palestine. Similarly, in colonial American times, both industrial and intellectual training were largely given in the home. It is only as cultural resources and economic means accumulate, and the social organization becomes more differentiated and complex, that specialized educational institutions develop to which the family turns over many of its functions.

Part of this educational process in the family life of more primitive societies, while lacking the formality of present-day schools, was relatively concrete and direct: a projection of the family routine upon the child. To understand the nature and scope of this educational process in earlier times, two facts must be kept in mind. One is the concrete and vocational nature of what the child was taught. The primitive family was engrossed in the all-absorbing task of making a living, and the child was taught as early and as effectively as possible to do his share. The other is the fact that earlier the child was reared in the extended or kinship group form of family in which there were likely to be many more pupils and teachers than in the immediate family of our contemporary urban culture.

FAMILY EDUCATION THROUGH INDIRECTION

The greater part of the family's role in childrearing, however, is achieved through indirection, in ways that are subtle and devious, for the most part unconscious, and as a by-product of family routine. The family might be spoken of as a conditioning agency, and what happens to the child is by way of absorption from the life of the family as a whole. In other words, the family lives its collective life—it eats, talks, laughs, argues, wrangles, its members go about their allotted tasks—and in this life the young child grows and learns to live.

There are, then, two ways in which a child learns from his family about processes of interaction and about the culture of his society: (1) through formal indoctrination and (2) through absorbing them from daily living.

Because of the continuousness and pervasiveness of the latter, it can be assumed that it has an enormous influence upon the child. Unfortunately, it is precisely this subtle and comprehensive process of learning from family living that is most difficult to study. To attempt this by interviews or through check marks on a questionnaire is obviously impossible. While most formal instruction is consciously planned, the daily life of a family is very largely an unconscious process. A family *is, does, talks* in the same way that a family breathes—without thinking much about the process or the results.

THE VALUE OF FAMILY TABLE TALK

Experimental studies made by the William T. Carter Foundation at the University of Pennsylvania suggest the value of transcripts of family table talk for purposes of studying family operation. When this is recorded without the knowledge of the family, one is able to study the family routine much as the scientist observes amoebae swimming about in beef broth.

The significance of the family meal has long been recognized by nonscientific groups. Religion has long recognized its intimate importance. Divine family worship at mealtime has been a common observance and is still continued in the offering of "grace." Christianity immortalizes it in the ceremony of the Last Supper, and renews this recognition endlessly in the continuance of the communion rite. Dramatists stage it with frequent effectiveness. To the novelist it is a constant device for character delineation or plot facilitation. Even the essayists, like Dr. Holmes, build their sage observations around the framework of the breakfast table.

Students of family and child problems may regard family table talk from two main points of view. One is as a form of family interaction. Here the concern is with the relationships between the personalities in the family group, with particular reference to the functioning and formation of personal traits. Also, as far as the children are concerned, there is a good deal of emphasis upon habit formation, such as habits of eating, sitting, speaking, and the like. A second approach sees the family meal as a vehicle for the transmission of the family culture to its younger members. Here the chief point of interest is the role and techniques of family table talk in this continuing process. Before proceeding to the two main points of view just identified, certain general considerations concerning the social nature of the family meal should be noted. Accordingly, the main body of this chapter is presented in three parts: first, the social nature of the family meal; second, its analysis as a form of family interaction; and third, its role in the transmission of the family culture to the younger members.

THE SOCIAL NATURE OF THE FAMILY MEAL

1. The family meal is a distinct aspect of the family's life, especially the main meal of the day. It holds the members of the family together over an extended period of time. The length of time, and the details of the occasion, naturally vary from one family to another; but, in general, a meal is an extended session of the family personnel, with a relatively high rate of attendance. Mealtime is the family council time, particularly today when under the stress of the differing interests of its various members the family is not likely to get together at any other time. In many families the dining table is the focal point for most of the family interaction.

2. It is at the dining table that the family is most apt to be its true self. This may mean that it is at ease, relaxed, friendly, enjoying itself. It may also be the family in haste, operating with direct bluntness, tense, or at war. The family meal, in short, represents the family in action, focused upon a common interest and a task so absorbing as to let it operate off-guard in other important aspects.

3. It is significant, in any attempt to appraise the social significance of the family meal, to recall that its role is one of continuing repetition. Many families meet around the table three times a day; most families do so at least once a day. Over a period of years, the simple arithmetic of the situation is enough to emphasize its quantitative effectiveness.

4. Finally, it is obvious that the social significance of the family meal and the role of table talk, vary from one social class to another. In a study made in the Philadelphia Metropolitan Area,[1] many of the lower-social-class families had only one meal together during the week. Others had no meals together, their housing accomodations being too small to permit it. Eating was an individualized affair of a hit-or-miss nature. In a number of the upper-class families the complexities of the rather formal dinner period were considered too great for young children, who were fed elsewhere by "Nannies." When children were permitted at the table the interaction was somewhat formalized because of the ritualistic nature of the meal and the presence of servants. It was the middle-class meal that featured the constant, repetitive interaction of the whole family, each member taking his particular role in every aspect of family dinnertime.

[1] James H. S. Bossard and Eleanor S. Boll, *Ritual in Family Living*, University of Pennsylvania Press, Philadelphia, 1950, pp. 116–117.

TYPES OF FAMILY MEALS AND TABLE TALK

Families differ a great deal in their behavior at mealtime. Analyses of recordings of table talk in 200 families reveal at least 5 main types.

First there are the hurried meals, where the members of the family act as though they were engaged in an unavoidable process of refueling. Food tends to be served as though eating were a mere physiological necessity, and gulped down as though the time required was time wasted. Conversation is scant, blunt, and direct. There is a liberal sprinkling of "yes," "no," "uh-huh," "bread," "more," "salt," and the like. Over and over, as one studies these transcripts, there arises the picture of a number of half-snarling dogs cleaning out a trough. In both cases, the gatherings break up with the last morsel of food.

A second type consists of those family meals which are devoted largely to recurrent domestic warfare. Squabbling is a habit, not an episode. Often as high as 80 to 90 percent of all conversation is of this kind in these families. The children are taken to task for past and present misdeeds, parents quarrel with each other, the food is criticized, or its preparation is disparaged. Or there may be constant nagging about table manners. Frequently some member of the family leaves the table in tears, anger, or disgrace. Obviously, we have here a family trait, and mealtime offers such families full scope for its expression.

Then there is a third group or type of families whose critical conversation is turned outward. They are "talking about" someone all the time. The Smiths down the block drive a car they can't afford. The neighbor's child is a brat. Mrs. Green's coat looks shoddy. The Brown girl runs around with a fast crowd. Policeman Brady is not honest. The teacher plays favorites. Here we have a family habit of disparagement—"always belittling." We found families in our study whose grist for the conversational mill was almost wholly of this kind. Yet the parents wonder why son Jack has no friends and wants to stop school.

Fourth are the family meals which abound in human-interest talk. Members of the family tell their experiences of the day. Choice bits of news are saved for mealtime. Ellen speaks of a forthcoming basketball trip; Mother talks about the price of meat; and Daddy brings home a funny story he heard at luncheon today. The personal triumphs, disappointments, and pleasantries of the day are related. Public issues may be discussed. One of the most interesting of our case records comes from the home of a well-known public figure who propounded at the beginning of dinner each evening some topic of public interest. The members of the family discussed this topic as the meal progressed until Father summarized, after the coffee was served, the various points that had been brought out. While few families are likely to formalize their mealtime conversation this way, many families in this fourth group do devote some time to public questions of current interest.

Finally, there are the family meals which become occasions for family rituals. These tend to be characterized by order and impressive decorum. Prayers may be said by way of prelude. Candles gleam on the table and the surrounding surfaces. Perhaps everyone stands until Mother is seated. Various other conventions are observed. Coffee in the living room may follow the meal. In these families, mealtime becomes a sort of private tradition for its members. People listen to one another. Such a procedure involves self-discipline, and this bodes well for discipline in other areas of behavior. Self-discipline is a habit which must be acquired, and mealtime ritual may be a helpful beginning.

It is important to add that most families in this study talked habitually in the same way, many invariably, about the same things. Members of these families usually seemed unaware of the habitlike character of their family table talk, nor of its possible importance in the life of the family and the development of the child members. These type differences are particularly significant in the general discussions that follow, and the reader should keep this constantly in mind.

TABLE TALK AS A FORM OF FAMILY INTERACTION

The role of the group in the determination of personality is a recognized sociological dictum. The primary character of the family as a group, and its fundamental importance in the development of personal traits, particularly of children, are equally well established. From what has been said concerning the social nature of family table talk, it is obvious that much of the family's interactive process takes place during the family meal. Certain aspects of this process call for special comment.

1. The individual's role in the family group comes to be clearly defined around the table. Since the entire family is together, relationships between individual members are brought out into the open. Feuding members are seated at opposite sides of the table,

for example. Covenants secretly arrived at become manifest. Group choices are made—in seating arrangements, in the serving of food, in the assignment of leftovers, in priorities in conversation.

Transcripts of family table talk may reveal with unmistakable clarity the dominating role of one member. The following record, taken from the files of the William T. Carter Foundation, will serve for purposes of illustration.

The family consists of Mother, Father, and their only son Robert. The table is set in the kitchen, where Mother is cooking. Father is already sitting in his place at the table, and Robert is in the living room.

MOTHER. Robert! Everything is ready. Come in and eat. (*to Father*) Go call Robert.

FATHER. Robert! Everything is ready. Come in and eat. (*Robert goes to the bathroom to wash his hands.*)

MOTHER, *a few minutes later.* Robert! Come and eat now. Everything is getting cold.

ROBERT. O.K.

MOTHER, *filling Robert's plate.* I cooked asparagus that you like and pork chops that you like. Do you want coffee or milk?

ROBERT. Both.

MOTHER, *to Father.* Get him the milk and a glass.

ROBERT. I can do it, I'm not helpless or paralyzed. (*Mother is still filling Robert's plate.*)

ROBERT. That's enough. (*Mother puts more asparagus on plate.*)

ROBERT. I said that's enough! (*The family begins to eat. After a few minutes of silence, Robert goes to the refrigerator to get the milk.*)

MOTHER. Don't keep the refrigerator door open too long.

ROBERT. Do you have to keep telling me the same thing over and over? You know I don't keep the door open.

MOTHER. Gee, I can't even speak any more! The sons boss the mothers and fathers these days. (*to Father*) Besides, I told you to get the milk. (*silence for some minutes.*)

MOTHER. Do you like the asparagus, Robert?

ROBERT. Yes.

MOTHER. How are the pork chops.

ROBERT. Good.

MOTHER. Do you want some bread?

ROBERT. No.

MOTHER. Are you sure?

ROBERT. I said no.

MOTHER. Bread is good for you. You should eat more bread. Don't you want some?

ROBERT. I said, "no!" Besides, the bread is right in front of me, if I'd wanted some, I would have taken it.

MOTHER. Have some more asparagus.

ROBERT. I don't want any more.

MOTHER. Have another pork chop.

ROBERT. I don't want another pork chop.

MOTHER. Is that all you are going to eat?

ROBERT. If I had wanted more, I would have taken more.

FATHER, *to Mother.* Will you leave him alone and let him eat as he pleases?

MOTHER. I think the coffee is ready. (*to Father*) Will you pour it out? (*Robert rises to get the coffeepot. Mother sees this and rushes to the range to get it herself.*)

MOTHER, *to Father.* God, but you're lazy.

ROBERT. *I'm* the one who's ready to drink the coffee! (*Robert fixes his coffee.*)

MOTHER. Is that all the milk you're going to put in?

ROBERT. I like it that way.

MOTHER. I don't see how you can drink it like that.

ROBERT. I'm the one who's going to drink my coffee, not you. I'll fix it the way I like it.

MOTHER. My God! Mothers can't even talk to their children any more. (*Robert picks up his cup of coffee and takes it upstairs to his bedroom.*)

MOTHER, *calling to Robert on his way upstairs.* Don't you want some fruit and cake?

ROBERT. No! (*Goes into bedroom and closes door.*)

2. The family is an audience for individual performance, chiefly conversational. Through these performances family members reveal their abilities to, and try them out on, each other. One is reminded here again of Dr. Holmes's observation, "There are little-minded people whose thoughts move in such small circles that five minutes of conversation gives you an arc long enough to determine their whole curve." Even silences in table talk are an important part of its art. Again Holmes reminds us that "talking is like playing on the harp; there is as much in laying the hand on the strings to stop their vibrations, as in the twanging them to bring out the music."[2]

3. This table audience, both in the responses which it gives to, and in those which it withholds from, its individual members, carries the greatest weight in the molding of personal traits. Its intimate nature and repetitive force make it often the family's best corrective disciplinarian. Children especially are frank—frequently quite brutally so—in their reactions to one another, and perhaps

[2] Oliver Wendell Holmes, *The Autocrat of the Breakfast Table,* James Osgood and Company, Boston, 1878, p. 71.

nowhere are they so with as much self-assurance as under the protective custody of the family meal.

4. One of the distinctive services of family interaction at mealtime is the development of the symbols of expression—again, particularly those of the children. All the members of the family participate in family table talk—from the youngest to the oldest and most erudite. Through this process, the family members enlarge one another's vocabulary. Children in particular acquire symbols to use in learning and in speaking. Much of one's knowledge about the precise meaning of words comes as a by-product to participating in family conversation. In other words, the family meal is a class in oral expression. In a family of any size, meals become gabfests. Two or three persons may be talking at the same time. Facility and quickness in expression constitute the price of admittance to the conversation.

5. The family meal represents the family's interaction in its most democratic mood. Now, more than at other times, the younger members get a chance to blossom verbally. Well-fed elders accept with good humor remarks from juveniles which otherwise would not be tolerated. Side conferences prevail also while the main program continues.

6. The family meal is a kind of personality clinic, with both students and clients in attendance. Especially is this true if the family is of any considerable size. Each member comes to be analyzed, dissected, catalogued, and processed by the other members. This is all the more devastating because it takes place before the entire group. Undesirable traits and personal weakness may be particularly identified and castigated.

7. Table talk serves a definite purpose in aiding children to learn the relative roles of the parents and adults in the family. Aunt Minnie jabbers away, does three-fourths of the talking, says little, and tends to be disregarded in family decisions. Mother defers to Daddy as a rule, but takes an emphatic stand at times. Daddy talks very little at the table. Even when they correct the children, Mother and Aunt Minnie turn to him for support. Repeatedly they suggest to him that he take disciplinary measures. Deference to him is constant and repeated. But Father is silent, his face is immobile. His few words to the children at the table, or even a look, suffice. The stereotype of the strong, silent father has been created. Under no other circumstances could the full-length process of this creation be so effectively imprinted upon the child's mind as at mealtime. A family meal, in other words, is like the scene from a drama in which the personalities identify themselves to each other.

FAMILY TABLE TALK AND THE TRANSMISSION OF CULTURE

Sociologists agree that the family is the chief culture-transmitting agency in our society. The family introduces the child not only to his own particular culture, but also to that of the larger society. In this latter capacity, it not only interprets this larger culture, it creates attitudes toward it. Much of this happens as a by-product of family table talk. In this process the following aspects may be identified.

1. The family meal, particularly dinner, is the clearing house for most of the family's information, news, and experiences. Jack tells about the substitute teacher; Jane about the neighboring girl's new coat; Daddy refers to the fact that Mr. Davis is complaining about the number of government questionnaires, and threatens to go out of business; Mother thinks that Bill is coming down with the grippe. The dining table is like a crossroads through which flows the news of the world as the respective members of the family see it and experience it. Much of this traffic of information and ideas flows swiftly and unobtrusively past, noticed more in its absence than in its presence; but it is there for all to see, hear, and assimilate.

2. The family meal constantly serves as a forum for the discussion of matters of interest and concern to the various members. Questions are asked, answered, or evaded in turn. The range of topics covered may be wide and varied, or monotonous in the recurrence of a few items of interest. Significant for all are the topics meticulously avoided as well as those assiduously discussed. The selection of topics for the family forum is in itself highly indicative.

Considered as a forum, the family meal may take several different forms. First, it may be quite formal. Questions are obviously posed, and discussion is patently stimulated. Second, the mealtime forum may be informal and spontaneous. This is much more frequently the case. Questions arise in the course of the family conversation, and the discussion proceeds out of the fullness of the heart rather than from the prodding of the parent. Topics tend to succeed each other in kaleidoscopic fashion, and the argumentation most often is both brief and direct. Finally, the family forum is often entirely incidental, scarcely recognized as a forum, in which views are expressed by a word, a silence, or a facial expression. Each family tends to have its own words, phrases, idioms, grimaces, signs, gestures, and the like, that are eloquent with meaning for all the members even if somewhat unintelligible to outsiders.

3. The family meal serves constantly as an evaluating confer-

ence, especially on the experiences, needs, and interests of the members. There is group discussion. Individual views are expressed, modified, and reconciled often as a family judgment, choice, decision, or attitude emerges. Whether arrived at experimentally in democratic conference or imposed by an autocratic parent, these evaluations are absorbed on the basis of their emotional relations to the family, so that the line between the two is often indistinct.

As far as the induction of the child into the culture of the family is concerned, this evaluating process in family table talk serves two purposes which Dr. Holmes long ago suggested in his *Autocrat of the Breakfast Table* as requirements for satisfactory conversation. One is agreement upon the ultimate beliefs; the other is agreement upon the secondary questions that depend upon these ultimate beliefs. In other words, table talk not only inducts the child into the fundamental idea patterns and values of the family culture, but also, because of its concrete nature, clarifies the concrete applications which follow thereform.

4. The family meal often functions as a substitute for classroom instruction. This happens in several ways. First, there are the well-known staged conversations—as a rule, for the benefit of the younger children. Says Mother: "I heard today about a little boy who ran across the railroad tracks"; to which Father replies quite seriously: "I am glad that my children don't do things like that." Or Mother refers to a visit from Mrs. Terry and her daughter, who was very polite. "Oh, yes," says Father, "you can tell that she is going to be quite an attractive young lady."

Again, "lessons" for class instruction may be introduced by one of the children. Helen, aged 12, tells of a neighbor's daughter, a proverbial and perennial scapegoat. Father, who is envious of the neighboring father's business success, expresses himself freely concerning the conduct of his neighbor's daughter. Mother, who dislikes the mother, is equally heated. Without understanding the motives involved, Helen is quite impressed. The neighboring girl's conduct *was* reprehensible.

Finally, many of the lessons learned at family meals are unplanned and spontaneous. "Katie kissed John," pipes up the well-known little brother, and in the wake of this disclosure there may follow either an eloquent silence, or a colorful discussion concerning kissing, John's intentions, John's job, Katie's prospects, and Mother's attitude toward early marriages. Such is perhaps the most common grist in the family round-the-table mill as it grinds, now slowly, now rapidly, but always exceeding fine.

5. Akin to these pedagogical functions are the stimulation and

direction of the child's interests. If he has literary or artistic or mechanical interests, family table talk does much to stimulate or dampen their development. One is reminded again of Dr. Holmes: "Writing or printing is like shooting with a rifle; you may hit your reader's mind, or miss it—but talking is like playing at a mark with the pipe of an engine; if it is within reach, and you have time enough, you can't help hitting it."[3]

In many respects, family table talk may be likened to a university seminar on family culture that continues for a number of semesters. Both are similar in that there are designated reports (at times unscheduled), criticisms which vary with the prestige of the person making them, an exchange of points of view, and boredom for the more sophisticated members of the group. There is teaching, too, and inculcation of point of view; but these follow more from the give-and-take of informal discussion than from formal admonition. As is the case in most seminars, the discussion often rambles; assigned topics are disregarded; the procedure departs from the program which the seminar master (instructor or parent as the case may be) has devised; and seminar members leave the table before the discussion is concluded. Finally, the ultimate effects are, for the most part, subtly devious and intangible.[4]

COMMON ILLUSTRATIONS OF CULTURE TRANSMISSION THROUGH FAMILY TABLE TALK

1. Much of the family's sense of economic values, and the child's training in them, is indicated in the following sentences that appear repeatedly in the case material in the files of the Carter Foundation.

"Go easy on the butter, it's fifty cents a pound."

"Eggs are sixty cents a dozen now."

"Bill's shoes have to be soled."

"What, again? Why I just paid two dollars for soles three weeks ago."

"I think you ought to be ashamed to waste bread when thousands of Chinese children are starving."

"Mother, Mary soiled her new dress."

"Well, she had better take care of it. We can't buy another until after Christmas."

It is lack of the absorption of values of this kind, so constant in normal family life, which constitutes such a big gap in the training of the child reared in an institution.

3 Holmes, *op. cit.*, p. 30.

4 For a discussion of how this process may operate in inculcating prejudices, see Eleanor S. Boll, "The Influence of Family Conversation on Children's Attitudes." *Growing*, April–June, 1962, pp. 2–5.

2. Political attitudes crystallize early in children's minds as a by-product of table conversations such as the following.

BILL. Mother, Jack made $1.05 playing the machine down at Louey's store.

MOTHER. Jack had better get a job after school instead of playing the machines.

FATHER. Well, Jack comes by that honestly. His old man is a gambler if there ever was one.

OLDER SISTER. There must be money in it. I saw Mrs. Haggerty [Jackie's mother] and she had one of those new fur coats on.

MOTHER. Why don't they raid Louey's place? I saw in the paper about some judge saying they [the machines] were illegal.

FATHER. Guess the police are fixed. (*Bill looks at his father, apparently not wholly clear on what was implied.*)

MOTHER. Bill, that shirt has got to go into the wash.

FATHER. Hank O'Brien was telling me yesterday that the police "take" on these machines ran into thousands of dollars a week. He said the lieutenant drove a Cadillac coupe to work, but parked it two blocks away from the station house.

Light seemed to dawn on Bill as he finished his dessert. The boy next door entered the house and Bill rushed from the table.

3. The multiple implications, for a child, of what may seem to the parents merely a routine conversation appears from the following.

FATHER. Well, I'm sorry, but I forgot to bring home some whiskey for the cocktails tomorrow night.

MOTHER. It's all right, I don't think we better serve cocktails.

FATHER. How come?

MOTHER. Well, the Pearsons are coming, and you know him.

SON. Is Dr. Pearson coming, Mother, is he? Is he, Mother?

MOTHER. Yes he is, and Mrs. Pearson is coming too.

DAUGHTER. Why don't we serve cocktails when Dr. Pearson comes?

MOTHER. Well, Dr. Pearson is a doctor, and he thinks cocktails aren't good for people. He says too many people have the cocktail habit.

SON. I like Dr. Pearson.

FATHER. Well, I like him, too. But this means a stupid party. (*This to wife.*)

MOTHER. I think I'll serve tomato juice. Do you think that will be all right? The red glasses will look nice on that black tray.

FATHER. If Pearson doesn't want to drink that's O.K. with me, but I don't see why that should spoil the party for the rest of us.

MOTHER. Well, I do think out of deference to his views we should have a dry dinner.

SON. I like Dr. Pearson. Is he a good doctor, Mother?

This conversation carries these implications for the children: (a) A doctor whom I like does not approve of the social use of alcohol; (b) Father thinks a dry party is dull; (c) Mother sees her obligation as a hostess; (d) a difference of opinion is resolved with deference to a guest, regardless of the wishes of the host and hostess. There is no preaching, no moralizing. All the ideas are transmitted in a matter-of-fact way, incidental to a table conversation, chiefly between the parents, concerning a small dinner party.

SUMMARY

1. It is important to understand the mechanism by which the child is inducted into the life of his family and by the family into the life of the larger society.
2. Part of the family's function in this respect is discharged through formal instruction. This was done more extensively earlier than it is today.
3. The greater part of the family's function is performed through indirection, that is, through a subtle conditioning process. This can best be studied by means of records of family life recorded in the first person.
4. Transcripts of family table talk are particularly valuable for purposes of scientific study.
5. Family table talk is a form of family interaction, important in the identification of personality roles and the development of personality traits.
6. The culture-transmitting function of the family operates with effectiveness during the family meal.

SUGGESTED READINGS

Day, Clarence, *Life with Father,* The Modern Library, New York, 1944. The writer uses the dining room as a center of family interaction for obvious dramatic purposes.

Hart, Moss, and George S. Kaufman, *You Can't Take It with You,* Farrar & Rinehart, New York, 1937. Another example of the way a literary artist, like Clarence Day, uses the dining table as a focal point.

Holmes, Oliver Wendell, *The Autocrat of the Breakfast Table,* James Osgood and Company, Boston, 1878. A classic essayist has things to say about the importance of this locale.

(Family table talk is a subject one should explore through autobiography.)

FAMILY MODES OF EXPRESSION 8

Civilization is a verbal complex. The ability to use language and other symbols of communication is what differentiates man from the lower animals because it permits not only the communication of ideas and experience, but also their accumulation, first through memory and then through the recorded word. These symbols of communication are an element in the cultural systems of all societies, and the study of the child's induction into his culture must begin with, and to a large extent center about, their acquisition by him. Accordingly, this chapter is devoted, first, to a brief summary of the role of language in the development of society and the child; second, to the various forms of symbolic communication; and, third, to the role and functioning of family situations in the child's linguistic growth.

THE SOCIAL ROLE OF LANGUAGE

Language is a prerequisite for the development of society and its culture. Its role is essentially twofold. First, it is the basis of the interactive relationships which are involved in social organization.

As such, it serves many purposes—to give vent to feelings, to gratify the craving for sociability, and to bring about action on the part of others, as well as to convey thought to others. Similarity in modes of expression quickly becomes a bond which holds people together, and perhaps nothing else in the range of human experience is more important in the formation and cohesive strength of social groups. It is operative, not only at the level of national organization, but also in such groups as the family, a college fraternity, a labor union, a social club, and an underworld gang. "They speak the same language" is a common descriptive expression, and it means that within these units of organization there have developed peculiarities of speech which serve to distinguish them from other groups.

The second function of language is to serve as a vehicle for the transmission and preservation of culture. This statement, so fraught with sociological significance, yet fails to tell the whole story. Language is not just a series of objective symbols for the transmission of ideas; it becomes so indelibly associated with these ideas as to be virtually part of them. To express the content of a culture, words must be developed to identify it, and thus the two from the beginning are inextricably associated with each other. In short, words do not just develop parallel to experience; the two interpenetrate—so much so, that among many peoples there develops a virtual identity of the word and the thing which it represents. This is the basis of the magic of spells. Even in our contemporary culture, the line between the two is not sharply drawn. "It is this constant interplay between language and experience," writes Sapir, "which removes language from the cold status of such purely and simply symbolic systems as mathematical symbols of flag signalling."[1] Language is therefore both part and symbol of a culture, reflecting its essence in such a way that another language cannot serve as a substitute. Just as many aspects of a culture cannot be expressed in another language because no words exist to do so, similarly many words can be understood only by explaining them in their cultural setting. In other words, language and all communication are culturally colored.

One other fact concerning the social role of language should be noted, and that is the priority of its development. Because of the nature of its role, it is obvious that language must be the first aspect of the culture to take form, and that its perfection is a prerequisite to the development of the culture as a whole.

[1] Edward Sapir, "Language," *Encyclopaedia of the Social Sciences,* The Macmillan Company, New York, vol. IX, p. 157. See also in this connection George C. Barker, "The Social Function of Language," *A Review of General Semantics,* Autumn, 1945, pp. 228–234; includes bibliography.

The role of language in the development of the child is similar to that in society, for society and the child are but two aspects of the same thing. Language is the key to the child's participation in group life and his introduction to the prevailing culture. In other words, the acquisition of language is necessary to set into motion the two conditioning factors of social interaction and cultural background which mold the personality of the child. With the child, then, as is the case in societal development, the linguistic acquisition comes first and consequently has a pervasive primary significance.

SELECTED FORMS OF COMMUNICATION

The word *language* has been used thus far in a very general sense as though it comprehended the whole range of interhuman communication. Literally speaking, this is not true, as the following brief description of the forms of communication that are significant in the early life of the child well reveals.

First, communication is not a human monopoly. Dogs bark, horses neigh, snakes hiss, and birds warble. Many of the sounds made by animals express needs, desires, or emotions. Similarly, infants utilize a variety of vocal signals, such as calls for food, gurgles of delight, or cries of discomfort. Chapin speaks of these as laryngeal cries which constitute a "halfway" or "pre-linguistic" stage of communication.[2]

Second are what might be called the nonsymbolic forms of communication, such as gestures, facial expressions, and the like. In part, these are an aspect of preverbal communication, utilized particularly by parents in their relations with children who have not yet acquired speech habits, and they must be regarded largely as physical expressions of emotions and their accompanying demands. There is, of course, a second aspect to these forms of communication, and that is their recognition as physical accompaniments of speech that serve the double purpose of releasing tension for the speaker and adding an expressive overtone for the listener.[3]

Most communication between humans, however, takes the form of articulate speech in which there is what Ogden calls "objective reference."[4] This is a distinctly human achievement, and involves

[2] F. Stuart Chapin, *Cultural Change*, D. Appleton-Century Company, Inc., New York, 1928, pp. 35–36. See also Charles Morris, *Signs, Language and Behavior*, Prentice-Hall, New York, 1946.

[3] Herbert Blumer, "Social Attitudes and Nonsymbolic Interaction," *Journal of Educational Sociology*, May, 1936, pp. 515–523.

[4] C. K. Ogden, *The Meaning of Psychology*, Harper & Brothers, New York, 1926, p. 150.

the reduction of experience to familiar terms which come to have general acceptance. This common core of communication symbols constitutes the language of a people, and "phonetic language takes precedence over all other kinds of communicative symbolism, which are by comparison either substitutive, like writing, or merely supplementary, like the gesture accompanying speech."[5]

FAMILY MODES OF EXPRESSION

Turning now to the more specific aspect of child development, we can note three additional facts in the child's acquisition of his linguistic culture. First is the existence of a family version of the modes of expression. Early in the history of most societies, the total number of symbols and other forms of communication exceeds the needs and capacities of the average person, so that he comes to select from the common storehouse of social forms in developing his own version. Most students of language point out that there is a common or composite, and an individual or family, version of these socially accepted forms of communication. The former consists of the more or less impersonal mass of symbols which reflect the accumulated experiences of society; the latter, of the selections and modifications of this common storehouse made by the individual or family unit which reflect the accumulated experience of the particular individual or family.

Second is the fact that this family version includes all the various forms of communication. In other words, a family not only selects its own words and gives them their distinctive meanings, but supplements them with its own system of gestures, facial expressions, and even laryngeal cries, as Chapin calls them. Moreover, none of these elements in the family version is simple. For example, Sapir, analyzing speech as a personality trait, identified at least five levels at which this form of expressive behavior develops. In addition to vocabulary, there are voice quality; voice dynamics, such as intonation, rhythm, and speed; pronunciation, where again there is an individual and a social pattern; and style, which is a facet of everyday speech just as it is of literature.[6] Similar complexities characterize other aspects of the family version.

Third—and this needs particular emphasis—is the fact that the child first learns the family version of the linguistic culture. This means that he comes to know his world first, and for a number of

[5] Sapir, *op. cit.*, p. 155.

[6] Edward Sapir, "Speech as a Personality Trait," *American Journal of Sociology*, May, 1927, pp. 892–905.

years, through the symbolic tools which the family gives it. In other words, he identifies things and ideas by means of the words which his family supplies, so that the two are interwoven from the start. This, it should be noted, is both a facilitating and a limiting process, for words not only enable us to grasp ideas but also limit our conception of them. Thus it happens that while the child is learning from his family the mediums of communication through which he comes to know his world, he is learning, too, the limitations and handicaps inherent in this family version. Plant emphasizes in particular the dangers inherent in these limitations. "Our people," he writes, "have learned to manipulate word and number symbols, rather than to understand the relation of these symbols to reality. Anyone who works much with adolescents knows their inability to use meaningfully the symbols which they have so carefully learned by rote."[7]

The child's acquisition of language has been studied in the past chiefly by psychologists and educators, who were interested primarily in the development of the child's verbal competencies, with particular emphasis upon the stages or age levels with regard to the numbers of words and the length of sentences used. Our approach here is the situational one, in which the chief concern is with the variations in the situations in which the child acquires his expressive behavior. Studies of such family situations, made under the auspices of the William T. Carter Foundation at the University of Pennsylvania, include 51 case records of family modes of expression, and this material is drawn upon heavily in the remainder of this chapter.

INFANT CONDITIONING SITUATIONS

The child's contacts with family modes of expression begin at birth. Particularly important is the mother's response to the child. Observations of the mother's communication behavior with her infant were made in 16 cases, all of them during the first 10 months of the child's life. The observed behavior of the mothers revealed three distinct communication patterns. The first was one chiefly of sounds. This type of mother for the most part coos, gurgles, laughs, talks, and makes other sounds to her baby. Her behavior, as she bathes or "changes" or feeds the infant, is of an outgoing, verbal kind. In the second pattern, the mother's communication behavior

[7] James Plant, "Adolescents in Wartime," *Annals of the American Academy of Political and Social Science*, November, 1944, p. 5.

is much more one of facial expressions. She catches the child's eye, smiles, frowns, or makes grimaces of one kind or another. There are verbal accompaniments, to be sure; the difference in this respect between the first and second type of mother is wholly one of degree. In the third type, the mother is predominantly active and intent. The face is relatively immobile, action is swift and efficient, and there are fewer sound accompaniments as a rule.

Such are the differences in the earliest situations of expression in which infants find themselves. It is interesting to speculate on the significance of these first conditioning influences. This, however, falls more properly within the province of the psychiatrist; we merely report in the briefest form these first family modes of expression as evidenced in the mothers' linguistic or communication behavior. Our findings here, based on a small number of cases, are presented as highly tentative, and for suggestive purposes only.

Dr. Leo Kanner, child psychiatrist, reported on an unusual type of mental illness affecting children of intelligent parents which may have some relation to the observations just presented. These young patients, nearly half of whom come from families represented in *Who's Who* or *American Men of Science*, or both, seem to live in a strange world of their own, completely without people. Hands that dress and care for them are just hands—objects not belonging to any person. Dr. Kanner raises the question as to whether the gifts of the parents might not have actually contributed to the illness of their children. For the most part, the members of these families are strongly preoccupied with abstractions of a scientific, literary, or artistic nature and are limited with regard to genuine interest in people.[8] This, it is obvious, would particularly characterize the treatment of the young infant.

PREVERBAL EXPRESSION IN THE FAMILY

Another point to be emphasized is the importance, in the young child's development, of preverbal forms of expression within the family. A good deal of the earliest communication from adult to child consists of facial expressions—smiles, grimaces, frowns, and so on—with some sound accompaniment at times. Until the child has acquired some words, communication with adults must be achieved in this way. Not only moods but ideas and commands are thus transmitted. The parent frowns and utters sharp, staccato sounds; or the mother smiles or gurgles, and food follows. These

[8] Leo Kanner, "Unaware of Others," *Science News Letter*, August 11, 1945, p. 92.

differing sights and sounds come to define behavior for the child before words are understood. Moreover, this mode of expression is retained after words are used. The child observes the facial expressions of his parents for some years and associates pleasure, anger, happiness, irritation, or annoyance with them. He learns, too, that these are often advance notices of more aggressive behavior on the part of the parent.

It is doubtful whether the role of facial modes of family expression for the child has been recognized adequately in the study of human behavior. Two of its implications seem particularly important. One is the fact that the child's earliest impressions of the parents are those of visual memory. This suggests that the parent has a "facial personality," and that this is the first personality which the child comes to know. A second implication is that these facial expressions and the accompanying sounds are chiefly expressive forms of emotions. Here, in other words, are to be found early conditioning factors in the child's emotional development, as well as the basis of the emotional accompaniment with conversation. Studies in the beginnings of gesture patterns might be made appropriately at this point.

THE RANGE OF FAMILY SEMANTIC SITUATIONS

From the time the child learns his first word until he learns to read, the acquisition of words is by ear, that is, by hearing the spoken word. This period covers about six years, and for children who show only slight interest in reading it remains the predominant one. During this period the family is the chief group in which the child acquires words, its relative importance depending upon the extent to which his contacts during the preschool period are confined to the family group. Transcripts of table talk for 35 families in which there were children, gathered through the facilities of the William T. Carter Foundation, permit certain tentative generalizations concerning family linguistic situations. They are presented here in summary form.

1. The amount of conversation per family per unit of time varies tremendously. At one extreme are several families who had almost no talk during a 40-minute dinner. There are long spells of silence. The air is one of marked restraint and formality. Conversation is confined almost wholly to requests for food. The parents are described as "tight-lipped" adults. At the other extreme are records of continuous table talk, often with several members of the family

talking at the same time. In other words, the amount of talk to which a child is exposed within the family group varies tremendously.

2. There is a marked difference in the extent of the vocabulary used in the table talk of families. Some families use a very limited number of different words; others reveal what is commonly referred to as an excellent command of language, that is, they utilize a wide variety of words. To a considerable extent, these differences coincide with variations in the subject matter. Many family conversations are confined largely to trite, routine matters, or to personal and kinship affairs. The language here tends to be as drab and limited as the topics discussed. In varying degrees of contrast are the family conversations which cover many subjects. In table talk records that are equal in the total number of words recorded, there are differences of more that 800 percent in the number of different words used.

3. The process of acquiring a vocabulary is twofold. One involves the learning of new words; the other, the association of meaning with them. Since words do not have a single correct meaning but have what Hayakawa calls "areas of meaning,"[9] the family's role in identifying the meaning of words for children during this early period is particularly important. A careful reading of the case material reveals considerable differences in the meaning given to the same words in different families. Some of these differences have to do with shades of meaning; others are so obviously incorrect that they reveal only the family's ignorance.

There are, however, other factors than knowledge and ignorance. Our material reveals highly significant family attitudes toward words and their meaning. In one of these families, with two children aged 7 and 9 years, there is a continuing attempt on the part of the parents to enlarge the children's semantic grasp. In the course of the family conversation, the children are asked if they understand the words used, or they interrupt to ask, for example, "Daddy what does *emphasize* mean?" Both the father and the mother in this family leave the dinner table to consult the dictionary, with a statement like: "Well, we might as well find out now." In contrast, there is the family where John, aged 13, used the word *preference*, only to have his father curse him and say, "Preference, Preference, I'll Preference you. You with your fancy words. You can't highhat me as long as I pay the bills." Then there is the family in which the child said, "I don't know what that means," to which the parent replied, "If I get the razor strap, you'll understand what I'm saying."

[9] S. I. Hayakawa, *Language in Action*, Harcourt, Brace and Company, New York, 1939, p. 71. (2d ed., Harcourt, Brace & World, New York, 1964.)

One particular aspect of this family interpretation of words calls for special comment. The child gets from the family not only the meaning of words, but also often a meaning charged with emotion. One semanticist refers to these as *loaded*[10] words. They are words that carry emotions as well as ideas, such as *dago, kike, hunkie, louse, crackpot,* and so on. And there are the words which families use to epitomize a set of conceptions or evaluations and which, transmitted to the child, become barriers to shield them from reality. *Capitalism* is synonymous with *exploitation; Communist* means a wild-eyed, unreasonable person; a *fascist* is a person who disagrees with you; *politics* explains any public or semipublic miscarriages of your ideas of fair play.

4. Family semantic situations vary on the basis of the role permitted to the child. Roughly speaking, families fall into two main types in this respect, differing from each other in degree. There are the child-centered and the adult-centered table conversations. In the former, the child or children dominate the conversation, or it centers around them. Adults direct the talk toward the children, toward subjects that interest them, and seek to stimulate their participation in the conversation. In contrast are the family conversations that tend characteristically to be adult-centered. Here subjects of adult interest only are discussed, child participation is ridiculed or dismissed as incidental prattle, or the children are admonished to "be quiet and let your elders speak." Differences of this kind presumably have a great deal to do with a child's acquisition of the linguistic culture.

5. One cannot but notice variations in the child's participation in the family table talk on the basis of interruptions by other members of the family group. Family life records show that some children are seldom allowed to finish a sentence. In some families this happens because another person, most often the mother, interrupts to say what the child is trying to say. In other cases, the child's attempts are lost in the general welter of the family's words. In one of these families, a 6-year-old girl was not once allowed to finish a sentence without interruption or verbal help. It is pertinent to raise the question of the relationship of such situations to stammering and other speech defects in the child. Certain kinds of stammer, for example, might well be regarded as a mechanism for holding the floor, conversationally speaking, and having time to think and formulate words. Even savants do this at times, when momentarily at a loss for words.

6. A careful study of family conversations reveals that the mother is the most important factor in the transmission of the

[10] *Ibid.*, p. 46.

child's linguistic culture. This is most apparent when family conversation records other than table talk are considered. In many families, particularly in the lower-income groups where she prepares and serves the meal, the mother often comes to the table after the others are seated, and she may leave it several times during a meal. Records of family table talk in such cases fail to do justice to her importance, especially with the younger children. Considering the situation as a whole in normal homes where the mother devotes herself largely or wholly to the job of homemaker, she converses more with the young child than anyone else. This relative importance of the mother in the child's major scholastic attainment, that is, learning a language, has never been fully assessed. The significance, at home, of the role of the mother who is gainfully employed many hours a day also needs to be examined.

The semantic situations which prevail in different families are presented here as of basic importance in the child's linguistic development. The number of words that a child can use, and use in their accepted meaning, determines in large measure his school progress, especially in the earlier years, and this initial success or failure speedily becomes cumulative in its effects. Again, there are those psychologists who emphasize the role of word equipment in intelligence measurement scores. This again would be particularly true in the earlier years. Finally, words are the mediums through which the child learns about his world. They are avenues by which the world we do not see comes to us. We interpret these reports on the basis of what the words in them mean to us. To the extent that our grasp of words is inadequate, our interpretation of this world is incorrect or incomplete. Moreover, this matter of interpretation is of much greater importance today than it used to be. The colonial child, and adult, could function satisfactorily with much more limited semantic equipment. Today, by contrast, we live in a global setting, mostly in areas of dense population, and with means of communication which deluge us with words. Our lives are filled with words, and to live satisfactorily we must know many words and be able to use them within the framework of social acceptance. Words are therefore a mechanism of social adjustment.

LEVELS OF LANGUAGE

Students of language often speak of language levels, using the term to indicate that language takes different forms at varying levels or strata in the larger society. Four such sets of language levels may be identified in the records of family conversations.

One of these results from an age-graded use of words in families in which there are children. At least three age levels can easily be distinguished. The first one tends to prevail when the children are quite young; much of the family conversation is at the "baby-talk" level. Later there develops a layer which extends up to the eleventh or twelfth year. During this period, the words customarily used in family conversation, especially by the children, are relatively simple, and are of the kind that seem most easily learned by ear. Still later, as the children progress in school and acquire many words through outside contacts, a third or youth level is obtained. In families where there are no children, another or wholly adult level can be identified.

Two problems suggest themselves in a further analysis of these age levels. One of these concerns the younger children. Such children tend to be ignored in these changes. The family seems to adjust its age level to the older children and to ignore the younger ones, especially if the age differential is not large. Questions about word meanings asked by the younger children are given less consideration, even in our most intelligent families. Apparently this is another example of how family situations differ for individual children in the same family.

A second problem implicit in this material grows out of the differences in children in their capacity to learn by ear. The child's acquisition of words by means of these recurring family conversations is wholly by ear. Some children's apprehension of words is visual: they must see what they hear; in others it is auricular: like Santayana, they must hear what they read.[11] What this means is that children who acquire new words by sight are generally handicapped during this period. One cannot but reflect, too, on the significance of this difference in the many lands and during the long years in which almost all learning took place by ear.

A second set of language levels is based on sex differences. There is a sex-appropriate language for boys and one for girls. The recorded conversations of all the families in which there are children bear witness to these differences and to the family's consciousness of them. "Little girls do not talk that way." A lady never raises her voice." "He sounds like a boy all right." "Her voice will be a great asset to her." This sex distinction is evident at every turn—in the words used, habits of exclamation, intensity of expression, and stock phrases, as well as the subjects discussed. The child learns early and is reminded constantly that there is prestige in learning the sex-appropriate forms of expression.

The third set of language levels is based on the quality of expres-

[11] George Santayana, *Persons and Places*, Charles Scribner's Sons, New York, 1944, p. 156.

sion as determined by social usage. It is in this sense that professional students of language usually speak of levels of language, and three such levels are customarily identified. The first is *informal English,* which is most generally encountered in the ordinary life of people of good social standing. "It is the typical language of an educated person going about his everyday business." The second is *formal English,* which is informal English "refined, tidied up," and "shorn of its looseness"; it partakes more of the written language of educated writers. Here one says "presently" instead of "soon," "prematurely" for "too soon," and "it is to be regretted" instead of "it's too bad." Finally, there is *vulgate English,* the everyday speech of less educated people, bristling with "vulgar" words and "bad grammar": "I ain't got none." "I seen it." "You'll see it wrote on the door."[12]

While the main distinctions between these types are quite clear, there exist marked variations from one family to another. There are children in families whose recorded conversation contains few grammatically correct sentences; at the other extreme are the families in which the parents are meticulous regarding the children's good English. These differences are a matter not only of the intelligence and verbal equipment of the parents, but also of their consciousness of and attitude toward the problem. Because of a certain informality that characterizes much of our life today, and the contact between children of all classes in the public-school system, many children in language-conscious families bring into their homes the vulgate language of their associates. Some of the comic strips do likewise, and with the prestige of the printed word. The case is similar in regard to slang, which may be regarded as a variety of the vulgate language that grows out of a desire for novelty or vivid emphasis. In our so-called better homes, there are constant efforts in family talk to correct or restrain these lapses. Although the number of our cases does not warrant a generalization, it appears that the higher the family's social level the more standardized its conversation will be at the level of informal or formal language.

Again one cannot but speculate on the significance of these language levels for the child's school progress. The schools use a relatively formalized type of English. The complex ideas and dignified subjects taught necessitate the use of this type; hence the schools naturally lay great emphasis upon proper linguistic behavior. Our

[12] Leonard Bloomfield, *Language,* rev. ed., Henry Holt & Company, New York, 1940; Porter G. Perrin, *Writer's Guide and Index to English,* Scott, Foresman & Company, Chicago, 1942; H. L. Mencken, *The American Language,* 4th ed., Alfred A. Knopf, New York, 1936; Leonard Bloomfield, "Literature and Illiterate Speech," *American Speech,* 1927, pp. 432–439.

records clearly identify the children who are reared in homes in which the language of the school is used, so that no linguistic difference or effort is involved in passing from one to the other. Similarly, one sees the handicap of the child, especially the younger child, who is reared in a family that uses vulgate English and who must constantly pass back and forth from one level to the other in school and at home. Many of these children live a kind of linguistic double life during their school years which cannot but be a handicap to their school progress. Subsequently many of them take jobs where vulgate English will suffice and where any other kind would be conspicuous. How stable the family form of speech may be is indicated by the question of one high-school senior to another: "Is ya done y're Greek yet?"

LANGUAGE AS A SOCIAL INDEX

The more one reads records of family talk, the more he sees language as an index of family social characteristics. Four aspects illustrative of the use of family language as a social index will be presented briefly.

Occupation

Many occupational groups develop distinctive forms of expression. Some of these consist of "shop talk," which includes the lingo of the job, from psychiatry to panhandling; some are figures of speech suggested by the occupational experience. To the extent that an occupational group is isolated from other folks, its members come to use clearly marked varieties of speech. Thus, seafaring men speak their own type of nonstandard English; the hobo has his own speech forms; so do circus people, soldiers in foxholes, and professors who live in ivory towers.

Our records of family conversations are replete with illustrations of the role of the occupational background. This influence may be direct, i.e., through shop talk at home; it may determine the general or nonoccupational topics talked about; or it may dictate the imagery used. People naturally draw on their daily experience for the grist for their conversational mill. Moreover, our limited number of cases suggests that the role of such experience is greater at the lower occupational levels. The professional and executive types of families, many of whom live in suburban communities, make an apparently conscious effort to draw a line, as it were, between the job (office, plant, shop, etc.) and the home. Some parents pride themselves on not "bringing the office" into their family life. In such cases there is less infusion of occupational terminology than there would otherwise be.

Religion

It is rather surprising to find the number and variety of religion-identifying references in family conversation records. These are clearest in Roman Catholic and Jewish families. References are either direct, or in the imagery employed, or by implication. Religious holidays, religious observations in everyday life, and relations to other cultural groups are alluded to frequently. In two of our cases words are used that obviously have some religious implication but are meaningless to us. Requests for explanation are evaded. We are reminded here of Bloomfield's observation: "If the special (religious) group is at odds with the rest of the community, it may use its peculiarities of speech as a secret dialect, as do the English-speaking gypsies."[13]

Geographical Area

Linguistic diversities based on geographical sections have long been emphasized by students of language. Although most clearly revealed in audible speech, they appear also in written form in the use of identifying words and expressions. Even a person with an excellent mastery of the common language will keep some feature of the "dialect" of his place of origin and "with a certain coquetry flaunt" it before us. However, Jespersen contends that, generally speaking, the more commonplace a person is, the more will his language bear the stamp of the community in which he lives. Obviously, this will also hold true of the family unit.[14] These geographical speech marks appear repeatedly in our records. The family that uses a "lift" and listens to the "wireless" is obviously British. The 13-year-old miss who "is fixing to go" with "you-all" is manifestly not from Vermont. "The potatoes are all" identifies the upstate Pennsylvania German. The family who drives to "the end of the cement" came a year ago from the mountainous West. Words and phrases bearing the mark of geographical origin are on almost every page of this material.

[13] Bloomfield, *Language*, p. 49.

[14] Otto Jespersen, *Language: Its Nature, Origin, and Development*, G. Allen and Unwin, London, 1922, pp. 75, 204. (Current edition: W. W. Norton & Company, New York, 1964.)

Social Class

The phrase *social class* is used to denote general social status as indicated by plane of living, educational attainment, occupational status, and certain additional cultural attainments. Thus conceived, social class is the most striking line of cleavage in our language records. First are the distinctions in the words commonly used. At one level you go to "tea." You "eat supper" in some homes; in others you "are at dinner." At one level, you say. "Oh, I say"; at another you hear "Cheez" every fourth word. A girl may be a "goil," a "moll," a "cutie," a "lassie," or "Miss Helen." In different circles you are invited to "have one," to "have a skittle of suds," or to have a "shot on the run," or a "Scotch and soda."

Again, social classes differ markedly in the use of imagery in conversation, that is, in the degree to which figurative expressions are used. Families at the lower social levels seem much more figurative in their language, less rational, and less logical than other people. Our conclusions here are highly tentative, and reflect chiefly an impression.

We are on somewhat firmer ground with this case material in pointing out a certain class difference in the use of words. Families in the lower social classes show a tendency to slur words, to run them together, so that the combination of words and sounds comes to be the important thing. These families also tend toward the removal of irregularities in language, a process often referred to by language students as leveling. In families in the higher social strata, particularly among intellectual persons, every word tends to be used more in an individual sense. Sentences consist of individual units. They can be taken apart, put together again, and combined in different ways. The distinctions and subtleties in language are emphasized. In other words, as students of language put it, humble folk create language, but the upper classes develop, refine, and systematize it.[15]

Language obviously is a peculiarly revealing form of behavior. It identifies a person more effectively than almost any other form, because it is the result of slow accretion over long periods of time. In its existing version it is the combination of habits that are so deeply ingrained and so unconscious a form of expression as to permit of little consistent dissembling. Language habits not only are singularly persistent; they also reveal life's past content. Language is the

[15] Further references to class differences in language will be made in Chapter 11, "The Child and the Class Structure."

verbal aspect of personality, announcing its source and history with every word. Language is behavior; speech, its vocal declaration.

FAMILY LINGUISTIC SYSTEMS

Reference to the social determinants of language must not blind us to the fact, so clearly brought out in these studies, that each family has its own linguistic system. The conclusions that follow are based not only on records of conversations but on a large number of supplementary interviews.

1. Each family has its own word peculiarities. These may be words or expressions in common use but with a distinctive family meaning or form, peculiar turns of expression, or words which are not used elsewhere and have meaning only for the family. Karen G., who has an M. A. degree and teaches English in the high school, still says "acrosst" for *across*, as does her entire family. Ruth always says "replentish" for *replenish*, as did her mother and her grandmother. The Powers family uses the word *copistatic*, which means, to them only: "Well, everything went well today." The Turners use: "We must have gotten that with cigarette coupons," to mean: "I can't understand how that damned thing got into this house (or room, or box)." In other words, each family has a kind of shorthand or dialect which often serves far more effectively than ordinary words to convey meaning, to give praise, or to apply the verbal lash. These word peculiarities are a product of the family history and derive their distinctive meaning from this fact.

2. Each family has its own terms for certain aspects of its life. The most obvious illustrations are the words or phrases that have to do with certain parts of the body, toilet habits, and toilet accessories. As a rule, a family develops these when the children are quite young, and they are retained as a matter of habit. But the list of instances which we have found are far more extensive. They have to do with going out at night, sleeping late on Sunday morning, family chores, social obligations, and many other aspects of life. Several of our families insist that much of this family terminology, especially that dealing with more intimate matters, needs to be studied on the basis of age levels; i.e., children have their own words which they communicate to each other at certain age levels just as adults have their words when they discuss these matters, and this age division coincides with parent-child groupings.[16]

3. Each family has its word taboos or word avoidances. In part, these are reflections of the social patterns, and include words per-

[16] For an interesting case of age (i.e., parent-child) distinction, see Jerre Mangione, *Mount Allegro*, Houghton Mifflin Company, Boston, 1942, pp. 54–55.

taining to certain parts of the body and to certain of its functions; there are also religious taboos upon taking in vain the names of those worshiped or revered; even the names of certain animals may be taboo, usually because of their application to individuals. Among the latter, our families identified such words as *bitch, snake, wolf,* etc.

Within the social pattern is the family pattern of word taboos. Our material emphasizes that these vary a great deal from one family to another, often with no consistency or underlying principle. One family speaks frankly about sex but strictly avoids religious words and names. A family that is openly and habitually profane punishes a younger member for the inadvertent use of the word *whore*. Any reference to bowel movements is labeled as distinctly in bad taste by several of our families who are not otherwise conspicuous for the "cleanliness" of their conversation. The word *bitch* is used normally by Philadelphia suburban families engaged in dog breeding. Another family permits no reference to alcoholic drinks or habits in any form. An adolescent in one family knew only the word *rum*. Beer was rum; whiskey was rum; wine was rum. And one drop of rum defiled. Finally, we cannot avoid mentioning the family in which the word *grandmother* was taboo. In this case, the husband's mother was a tall, statuesque blonde who was not at all willing to be thus reminded that her "salad" days had passed.

It is our observation that a large part of a family's distinctive pattern of word taboos is based on the aversions of the adults or on the marked prejudices of some one member of the family, so that the taboo is maintained as a matter of deference. A family does not use words as a rule which remind its members of things they do not want to think about. These omissions are significant, then, in that they identify the family avoidances, based chiefly on the past experiences, or lack of experiences, of its adult members. They are usually deeply embedded and show strong emotional association.

Lengthy interviews with a number of families whose modes of expression were studied seem to warrant the following conclusions regarding these taboos. First, the word taboos which prevail in families are an important factor in determining the reaction of the members of the family to other people. We think that persons who violate these taboos are crude, uncouth, ill mannered. Or, at least, their violation arrests our attention in a less than favorable way. Second, children learn these taboos quite early, and by the time adolescence is reached they have become firmly fixed. Our families report various school difficulties growing out of the fact that children from different families observe varying word taboos, and teachers with still other taboo patterns become involved. Third, there arise problems of adjustment between persons who establish intimate and continuing relationships with each other, as in marriage, on the basis of their respective word taboos. "Rapport," one matron pointed out in the course of this study, "is verbal in part. These word taboos are much more important than behavior taboos, because so large a part of our social relationships is verbal." Finally, one is impressed by the fact that word taboos mean subject avoidances. This in turn results in areas of ignorance, at least as far as family instruction or insight is concerned. Betty Smith, the novelist, has reminded us that when children ask questions about sex the parents do not know how to answer them because they do not have the words, mutually known and understood, to do so.[17] The program of sex education might well begin with some concern with family modes of expression.

The study of family word taboos leaves one with a profound conviction of the importance of language as a social discipline and culture-transmitting device. Through the processes of word selection and word reaction, the family does much to introduce the child to the social, and, of course, the family, code. This substantiates the conclusions of Groves when he says: "Conventions are in large measure built into the child as attitudes toward words. Some are unseemly, and as a result emotional reactions similar to primitive taboos get tied to certain acts and ideas. Other words are encouraged, and the approval helps establish a favorable disposition toward a different set of behavior and thoughts. Much of this language fellowship of child and parent is carried on without self-consciousness."[18]

FAMILY PATTERNS OF CONVERSATION

In reviewing the material on family conversations, one is impressed by the fact that most families show a specific totality or pattern which is characteristic of that particular family. These are spoken of here as family patterns of conversation, and although a phase of family linguistic systems they are reserved for separate comment. Summary types or classifications, based on a total of 82 cases, are presented briefly.

[17] Betty Smith, *A Tree Grows in Brooklyn*, Harper & Brothers, New York, 1943, p. 223. See also, Cyril Bibby, *Sex Education: A Guide for Parents, Teachers, and Youth Leaders*, Emerson Books, New York, 1946.

[18] Ernest R. Groves, *The Family and Its Social Functions*, J. B. Lippincott Company, Philadelphia, 1940, p. 152.

1. Family conversations may be subjective or objective. By the former are meant those cases in which the conversations are family-centered. That is, the family talks chiefly about itself, its experiences, its achievements, its misfortunes, and its problems. In contrast are those families in which the talk centers largely upon matters outside the family. This group may be divided into two subgroups: (a) those who talk chiefly about other people—friends, enemies, relatives, business or work associates, or public personages; and (b) those who talk about objects—airplanes, tanks, automobiles, books, trucks, and the like.

2. Family conversations may be summarized as analytical or evaluating. The first type consists of conversations in which the general approach is the analysis of a person, object, or event. There are description, analysis, and interpretation. The emphasis is chiefly upon telling about the subject at hand. The contrasting type is concerned with judgment; motives are imputed, purposes and results are evaluated. The conclusions are chiefly (in this study) critical, depreciatory, and denunciatory. These are the families that are "always talking about somebody." In some of the families studied, whose social ambitions were strong, the overwhelming part of the conversation is devoted to the depreciation of the social clique or group they hope to enter.

3. A rather distinctive type of family conversation is the sharp, rapierlike kind. Here the emphasis is upon sharpness and brilliance of execution. It may take the form of making wisecracks, being smart-alecky, or being keenly clever. In any event, the main consideration is fast, sparkling, adroit expression. Further varieties within this type may be identified. In some cases, statements are made as if to attract attention primarily to the speaker. Talk is a kind of exhibitionism or showmanship. It is as though the speaker sought to give a clever performance rather than attempted to convey a thought. He is interested in juggling deftly, no matter whether the balls he juggles are of tinsel or of gold. In some cases there is a sadistic performance. Sometimes a habitual phrase is clearly indicative of a sadistic intent. For example, one adult in the study habitually used the phrase, "So I stuck my knife in there and turned it around to see how they would squirm," to indicate his participation in a discussion. The main purpose is apparently to hurt. Here one finds the cutting speech, the stinging remark. You say something to put someone in his place. In the case of three persons included in this study, more than nine out of every ten remarks recorded for them were of this kind.

4. Family patterns of conversation vary greatly in regard to their

general tonal quality. At one extreme are conversations which abound with "snarl words," and much of the talk consists of spasmodically throwing verbal bites at each other as one throws sticks at a dog. There are loud noises, yelling, wrangling, constant interruptions, so that the whole performance partakes of the nature of static on the radio. At the other extreme are the family conversations which suggest, by way of contrast, the Sunday afternoon symphony. A quiet and polite exchange of ideas goes on, "purr words" dominate, there is politeness and consideration when disagreement arises. People are allowed to finish a sentence. Even the children are accorded these courtesies.

The topics of conversation in these 82 families show a rich variety, but the topics discussed by any one family seem as a rule rather limited. In other words, most families talk habitually about a few things. One cannot escape the conviction that the range is determined not so much by the intellectual capacities of the persons involved as by their predilections. For example, some of the highly intelligent families devote their conversational prowess to a very limited number of topics which are discussed both *ad infinitum* and *ad nauseam*. Some families, for example, talk constantly about the neighbors' children; others, about the boss; others, about the movies. It is interesting to note to what extent certain topics of conversation become a matter of habit, a fact which has great meaning for the child and his induction into the culture.

When one notes these and other characteristics of family conversations, he cannot but be impressed with the distinctness of the pattern in any individual family. Family conversation is, from one point of view, a series of habits—in the things that are talked about, how they are discussed, the attitudes which prevail, the kinds of words that are used, and the degree of conversational etiquette reciprocally accorded.

SOME CHARACTERISTICS OF SPEECH

Language is above all a matter of sound. Through the long ages of man's past, most people were illiterate, and to them language was exclusively a vocal form of expression. Today, the recorded form of language is used increasingly; nevertheless, the most frequently used form remains the spoken word. Although this study was concerned chiefly with written records of family conversations, some notes were made regarding certain characteristics of speech which seemed of importance to the child and his induction into the culture.[19]

Pronunciation

Through commonly accepted usage and standard works of reference, society establishes certain forms of word pronunciation. Departures from these accepted forms, more than those due to individual variations in voice timbre, serve to attract attention. These have been noted in this study. They occur constantly, and with marked frequency in certain families. Some of the errors recorded are slight, so that the meaning is still clear; in other cases, families use words which leave one wholly at a loss to understand what is meant. Further observations suggest two conclusions. First, families in which the adults aspire to better speech (and to a higher social position) offend frequently in this respect. Apparently, they see words in print and make an effort to use them; and since they have not been learned by ear, they are mispronounced. The self-educated are particularly apt to mispronounce words. Second, one notes repeatedly a sensitiveness to having one's pronunciation corrected. These records reveal several cases of considerable tension between members of families that resulted from attempted corrections.

Considering the mispronunciations noted as a whole, we are impressed with two further facts. First is their significance for children in their educational progress, particularly in its early stages before the school can reorient the use of vocabulary; the second is the significance of these word mistakes in social relationships. Consistent or conspicuous mispronunciation of words identifies the speaker as ignorant or uncouth, or results in his being misunderstood or misunderstanding others. The old saying, "She looked like a lady until she opened her mouth," is at least partially applicable here. The relationship between security in word pronunciation and a sense of personality security is for the psychiatrist to determine.

Accent

There is a stress or increased force given to certain syllables in speaking which, together with certain habits of pronunciation, is spoken of here as accent. This is an easily noticeable characteristic

[19] See Edward Sapir, "Speech as a Personality Trait," pp. 892–905, for reference to such characteristics.

of speech in those whose accents differ from that of the observer. Methods for its scientific recording and analysis are rather undeveloped. Although a number of observations were made, the conclusions presented here are highly tentative. It appears that accent is largely a matter of geographical or national origin and of social and educational status, and to a lesser extent a family and individual product. One is particularly impressed by the fact that, in the heterogeneous life of America, with its diverse nationality and linguistic groups, accent is peculiarly indicative of social type. This latter phrase is used to mean the constructs which the group arrives at by selecting and abstracting accentuated forms of conduct displayed by some of its members and having specific connotations in terms of interests, concerns, and dispositions of the group.[20]

Gestures

This term is used here to mean bodily accompaniments of speech used for purposes of emphasis or explanation. Gestures accompany all speech; in kind and amount they differ with the individual speaker, but to a large extent they are governed by social convention. Students have regarded gesture generally as a culturally patterned development, that is, certain gestures characterize entire groups. Thus Child reports, "Gestures are an important part of the Italian's equipment for communication. They are used a great deal as an accessory to ordinary conversation, especially when speech is excited or emphatic. There are also a number of special gestures which convey a specific meaning by themselves."[21] In our civilization, people of the privileged class gesticulate least.

Observations made in the course of this study suggest that there is also a family pattern of gestures. Our notes indicate repeated instances of some habitual distinctive use of the hands or body by several members of the same family. These similarities occur generally between parent and child and at times are so identical as to be almost uncanny. The use of gestures strikes one in particular as a kind of barometer of nervous output in conversation. Gestures are accompanied usually by a heightened or intensified expression of energy. This multiple form of expression, with its increased demands upon nervous energy, would seem to be of great significance in relation to the other forms of expenditure of energy by the individual.

[20] Samuel Strong, "Social Types in a Minority Group," *American Journal of Sociology*, March, 1943, pp. 563–573.

[21] Irvin L. Child, *Italian or American?* Yale University Press, New Haven, 1943, pp. 22–23.

SUMMARY

1. Language is a distinct form of culture and needs to be considered separately as such.

2. Language is a mechanism or medium for social interaction and for the transmission of all forms of culture. It is a symbolic technique enabling communication between individuals.

3. Modes of expression constitute a distinctive aspect of family situations. Each family has its own words, signs, gestures, pet phrases, humorous references, special words of condemnation, favorite topics, and characteristic forms of expression.

4. Language is behavior, much like manners or dress, whose standards and requirements vary on the basis of class, origin, occupation, activities, and the like.

5. Language, learned early and constantly associated with every other aspect of culture, comes in a peculiar way to serve as a symbol of home, family, class, state, status, and country. This explains why, as Lowie puts it, "Nowhere is the difference between tweedledum and tweedledee a more powerful barrier than in language." Students of behavior, and of international relations, will do well to remember this.

SUGGESTED READINGS

Brown, Ivor, *Mind Your Language,* Dufour Editions, Philadelphia, 1964. A commentary on changing language patterns and language fads of today.

Lewis, Morris M., *How Children Learn to Speak,* Basic Books, New York, 1959. A description of what happens in speech development from crying to talking. Takes account of the influence of adults and emotional factors.

Mitford, Nancy (Ed.), *Noblesse Oblige,* Harper & Brothers, New York, 1956. A series of humorous essays on the speech and manners of the British upper class.

Peal, Elizabeth and Wallace E. Lambert, *The Relation of Bilingualism to Intelligence,* American Psychological Association, Washington, D.C., 1962. A study which would be of value to the student interested in the psychological development of children.

Piaget, Jean, *The Language and Thought of the Child,* Routledge and Kegan Paul Ltd., 1952. A psychologist interrelates the child's inner needs and his social world as they affect his language and thought.

Putnam, George N., *The Status Significance of an Isolated Urban Dialect,* Linguistic Society of America, Waverly Press, Baltimore, 1956. A study of the relationship between language and status in one specific situation.

Sapir, Edward, "Speech as a Personality Trait," *American Journal of Sociology,* May, 1927, pp. 892–908. This article was one of the first writings in a sociological journal to identify speech as an important aspect of personality.

Warfel, Harry Redcay, *Language, a Science of Human Behavior,* H. Allen, Cleveland, 1962. The strong relationship between behavior and language is developed here in detail.

FAMILY RITUALS AND CHILD DEVELOPMENT 9

The more one comes to observe and study families firsthand, the more apparent are the existence and operation of certain prescribed forms of group behavior which constitute an important part of family life and the personality formation process of its younger members. These are spoken of as family rituals, and they are one of the means by which the family operates to socialize the child. The meaning of family rituals, their changing nature and extent, the general role of ritualistic behavior, and the significance of ritual in family life and child development constitute the content of this chapter.[1]

THE MEANING OF FAMILY RITUAL

The Term Ritual Defined

Ritual is a very old word, but it has been utilized throughout its history mainly by two groups of persons. One of these has consisted

[1] For a more extended discussion of this subject, the reader is referred to James H. S. Bossard and Eleanor S. Boll, *Ritual in Family Living*, University of Pennsylvania Press, Philadelphia, 1950. For a summary of selected aspects, see "Ritual in Family Living," by the same authors, in the *American Sociological* Review, August, 1949, pp. 463–469.

of students of religion, who have seen it as the origin of religion, or as a technique of magic or worship, or as a part of the ethical or control system of religion. The other group has comprised anthropologists, who have stressed ritual as one of the obvious and inescapable characteristics of primitive culture, with forms that are highly visible and that pervade every field of human activity. But they, too, have emphasized chiefly its role in the development of religion, so that references to ritual are everywhere interwoven with discussions of magic, taboo, totemism, and the like.

The result of all this has been that ritual is identified, especially at the more popular level, in terms of worship and public ceremonials, with forms that are imposed by some authority other than that of the lay participants. When the popular notion of ritual carries over into the secular, it usually concerns the rites of fraternal organizations and clubs that are found in a sort of religious twilight zone. Most of these rituals are crises or initiation ceremonies and as such are solemn, spectacular, rigid, and imposed by outside authority. An example of this everyday conception of ritual is found in the 1959 edition of Webster's *New Collegiate Dictionary:* "**1** The form of conducting worship; religious ceremonial. **2** A code of ceremonies observed."

When one ignores the traditional uses of the term and looks at its basic meaning, there is nothing awesome or mysterious or religious about it. What ritual really is, is a system of procedure, a form or pattern of social interaction, which has three unvarying characteristics. First, it is definitely prescribed. This is the way a thing is to be done. Ritual means exactness and precision in procedure. Second, there is the element of rigidity. The longer the prescribed procedure continues, the more binding its precision becomes. And finally, there is a sense of rightness which emerges from the past history of the process, i.e., the oftener the repetition of the prescribed procedure occurs, the more it comes to be approved. This distinguishes it from mere habit. To deviate from the procedure is wrong, not wholly on utilitarian grounds but also because it breaks the rhythm and the rapport. Ritual is conceived, then, primarily in terms of social process, with definite forms of interaction and a specific cultural content. Thus interpreted, it is not confined to any one field, such as religion, but may develop in any aspect of social life, and especially in one where relatively continuing relationships are maintained.

THE NATURE OF FAMILY RITUAL

Obviously, the family is an aspect of social life in which ritual inevitably develops. It is a social process. It has a definite cultural content. Its relationships are intimate, repetitious, and continue over long periods of time. Many patterns of its behavior come to be prescribed, both for its individual members and for a family as a functioning unit. Routine, habit, rigidity, sense of rightness and wrongness are inevitable accompaniments of these patterns. They also are the essence of much of the life of the family. Just as ritual has been identified as the core of the culture of a people, so it would seem also to be the hard core of family living.

A family ritual may be defined, then, as a prescribed formal procedure, arising out of family interaction, involving a pattern of defined behavior which is directed toward some specific end or purpose and which acquires rigidity and a sense of rightness as a result of its continuing history. Thus defined, ritual develops in connection with many aspects of family life, but clusters particularly about such things as holidays, anniversary days, meals, vacations, religious worship, and collective ways of working out household routine and using leisure time.

Possibly the most effective way to clarify the concept of family ritual is to cite selected illustrations in briefly summarized form. Three cases, drawn from a large collection of source material gathered under the auspices of the William T. Carter Foundation, are presented here.

1. *The Saturday Afternoon Gift Ritual.* Saturday afternoons held a very special ritual: the bringing home of the Reading Terminal (a well-known Philadelphia market) package. My father would leave his office at noon, go to the Terminal for his lunch, and then shop. Mother and sister and I waited for him in the den, and he would come straight up and put a huge parcel on Mother's lap. The scissors were ready on the table beside her. There was always a pound of Wilbur Buds for Mother: her favorite candy. There were always two ½ pound boxes of hard candies for sister and me. The other contents varied from week to week, but usually included all sorts of exotic fruits, fresh, candied, and preserved; nuts; dates; and cookies. We all sat still until each package had been opened and exclaimed about, sampling a bit of this and that, and then the party was over until next Saturday. At the end of the party, Daddy handed my sister and me our allowances, and we rushed out as fast as we could to spend them.

2. *The Hair-Washing Ritual.* Thursday night was always hair-washing night at our house. Religiously, when that night of the week

rolled around, mother would march me upstairs and make sure I got into the tub before I had a chance to jump into bed. I usually knew when it was time for this ordeal by listening to the radio. It never failed that when Rudy Vallee would come on the air, Mother would call: "Come on, sister, it's time for your hair washing." To me this was worse than a dose of castor oil. "But all little boys and girls have to have their heads washed," Mother would say. "Look at Daddy and me, we are grown people and we have to wash our hair." "All right," I would say, "but my little girl won't ever have to wash her hair." This would make Mother laugh, but all the same, she would dump me into the tub and start scrubbing away. When the Rudy Vallee program went off the air, I was delighted, for I knew the job was over and I would not have to go through such torture for another week. But now it is many years later, and other radio programs are on the air, but Thursday night is still hair-washing night in my life.

3. *The Morning Ritual.* As long as I can remember, at least since we children started school, we have had a very set ritual in the morning. It really begins the night before when Dad sets the alarm for 6:45. When it goes off Mom gets up and wakens us children, and then goes into the bathroom. I lie in bed until I hear Mom come out and go downstairs. Then it is my turn for the bathroom. My sister lies in bed until I come out, and then she goes in. By the time she is finished I'm dressed, but before I go downstairs, I check to see if Dad is really awake. He gets the bathroom last because he has to shave and takes longest. We don't have any time limit on occupying the bathroom but none of us varies much. Every morning Dad appears at 7:20, and breakfast is ready.

This ritual may sound like just a routine, but it is much more than that. We are all people who aren't very "sociable" for a while after we get up. All, except Mom, have to leave the house at an exact minute. This ritual works like a breeze. It is efficient, we "avoid" each other until breakfast, and by that time we are all in a good mood and ready to be "one happy family."

The *nature* of family ritual is obviously related to the nature of the family and its collective life. A study of 400 families and their ritual, over a period of 80 years, has suggested some conclusions about this relationship.[2]

1. Along with the secularization of modern society and family has come the increase of rituals of a secular type.

2. These secular rituals are described as intently and viewed as seriously as the more spectacular and religion-based rituals of an earlier era. An appreciation of this is important to an understanding of the significance of such family forms. Once ritual is thought of as generic process of interaction rather than in terms of some pietistic end, then sherry before dinner may become as much a

[2] For the original study see James H. S. Bossard and Eleanor Stoker Boll, *Ritual in Family Living*, University of Pennsylvania Press, Philadelphia, 1950.

ritual as family prayer before going to bed; and watching Sunday night TV programs may become the center of a ritual complex, as much as the reading of the Bible.

3. The case records give evidence of an actual increase in the number and range of rituals in many families. The reasons for this seem fairly clear. The modern family, and particularly the city family, has more leisure to devote to the refinements of family living, and ritual quite obviously involves the ceremonial use of leisure. Again, the enriched variety of contemporary life offers a greater number of things for families to do together, if they are so minded. Also, there is the pressure of mass advertising, which seeks to build up and exploit the commercial aspects of many rituals, such as gift giving, observance of holidays, and the like.

4. As well as being more numerous and more varied, family rituals are also more flexible. In many cases they do not continue as long and may be altered more quickly and frequently. These facts are closely related to our society's attitudes toward democracy, individualism, and flexibility in childrearing. In days when children and even wives were more rigidly controlled, family rituals tended to more rigidity and less cooperative creativity. At present, even the youngest member may feel free to suggest or to rebel. This seems to have had the effect of increasing the pleasure in both long-term and short-term family rituals, for they have been shaped and tempered according to the needs of all those participating.

CLASS DIFFERENTIALS IN FAMILY RITUALS

The concept of social class, as representing differences in ways of living, has come to be recognized by contemporary sociologists and will constitute the basis of the next two chapters. Suffice it to say here that the question of class differentials in family rituals rose early in the research study here reported and was set up as a separate phase of the project. A total of 156 families were included, selected from people who lived in neighborhoods, used services, had occupations and belonged to associations that are unequivocally lower, middle, or upper class. Examples of the sources from which these families were recruited included patrons of a social settlement, residents in a community in which most of the women were employed in a domestic service, a public school in a middle-class suburban district, the Junior League and the Social Register.

The overall conclusion was that family rituals increase in number, variety, richness, and willing cooperation by individual family members as one moves upward in the social scale. Also, rituals differ in character from one class to the other. After all, rituals take their shape from the culture in which they arise, and different classes develop different cultural levels. Very briefly generalized, the conclusions for each class level are as follows:

1. The lower class is one in which there is little connection with the past. The present is composed of individuals crowded into a space too small for comfort. The economic situation is not one of affluence. Children see little, if anything, in their families to stimulate a desire to perpetuate what they see. Opportunities for emotional satisfactions in the home are few, even for the adults. The rituals arising from these situations are, for the most part, rituals of expediency to keep the home going and to facilitate escape from home into a more exciting or promising outside world.

2. The middle class is more comfortably situated. There is enough physical space to permit of frequent family interaction, but not enough to allow much isolation of family members. Family finances are such that each member can hope to benefit by close cooperation. The past of the family is in their minds, but usually the present is better and gives challenge for the future. The family tone is one of hopefulness and optimism. There is a scorning, therefore, of habits that might lead in a downward direction, and a pressing forward toward a higher one which tends to both moral and social carefulness. The rituals here show a cooperativeness of a desire to reach these goals, as well as a genuine family "togetherness" in a home where there is need and opportunity for it.

3. The upper class is guarding a way of life which is considered by them, and many others, to be the desirable way of life. They have the time, for the most part the wealth, and the physical surroundings in which they can perpetuate it. The history of their families is something to conserve and in which to take pride. Their way of life can be preserved by taking seriously the social symbols which are generally acknowledged as standing for it. Their rituals converge around these. They are more formalized than in the other classes, and they are more easily perpetuated from generation to generation because of the fortunate circumstances in their lives.

FAMILY RITUAL AND THE FAMILY CYCLE

Reference has been made in Chapter 3 to the concept of the family cycle and its significance in the study of family interaction.

It is equally important for an understanding of family rituals. Not only do rituals change from one stage in the cycle to another, but the periods of change appear to be times of crisis and heightened emotions over the ritualistic procedures themselves. Sometimes the emotion is excitement and joy: at other times it is irritation or worse. But the change has to occur if the family is to mature normally. Some of these stages and changes will be identified briefly.

1. Marriage is a time for a new deal in family ritual. It involves at least three different processes: (a) a conscious deliberation by each person to be married concerning certain rituals which must be abandoned and others which must be kept; (b) an adjustment of two separate ritual systems between the new husband and wife; and (c) the emergence of new family rituals. Couples devise their own rites consciously, in the excitement of their new freedom, surroundings, and belongings, and find others forming inevitably in the daily process of living together.

2. With the childbearing stage comes normally a deep sense of a changing role and status of the family. Ritual, among other things, takes on a new meaning. It is no longer a repressive procedure to be freed from, or a practice to promote pleasure and to cement relationships between married lovers; but it is a means through which the heritage from the past is to be handed down to the future. It is at this time that many religious rituals, holiday customs, and kinship celebrations come into interest for redefining and, where mates do not agree, create new difficulties. Moreover, a wholly different orientation leads new parents to consider rituals appropriate not just to themselves but to the coming generation. The new parents become noticeably more orthodox in their views with the advent of children and tend more toward the traditional, which pleases their kinsfolk; to show off the new baby, the parents reenter kinsfolk celebrations. All this combines to reassert an emphasis upon the continuity of family patterns.

3. The preschool family period is particularly rich in the formation of many trial-and-error procedures which crystallize into set forms. These are the years when the new two-generation family is learning to live together. Parents and children, siblings and new siblings, are working out a pattern of family life. Disciplinary rituals, in particular, arise, as do many mother-child rites. Many, perhaps most, of these arise as trial-and-error attempts at expediency. Proving their worth, they become rigid and are consciously approved and cultivated.

4. The family with teen-agers comes gradually to revise its

rituals. It is now that rites stressing maturity and responsibility appear. The upper-class girl makes her debut. The Jewish boy is feted through the Bar Mitzvah. Boys and girls receive a front door key and a driver's license—all at a definite age. Rites now tend to become sex-divided. Father and mother assume new roles with their grown children. Many rituals come to be on an equality or near-equality basis, often devised to create moments of family intimacy in which to foster child frankness and confidence.

5. Serving as a launching center for the children, either for marriage or a career, brings the family to a stage in its cycle which is prone to be tension-creating and disruptive of family rituals. Parents overeagerly try to perpetuate rituals, and children overzealously try to be free of them. The results are that ritualistic situations are strained and that children often reject what they later redefine and readopt. There is one outstanding exception to this, which appears in cases where children are earning their own money and have a high degree of independence-feeling. In these cases, there is the development of rituals which have the purpose of repaying the parent, usually Mother, of presenting gifts at specific times, of entertaining her on certain days, or of taking over the household to free her once a week.

6. There is a stage which may be called that of the Aging Family, where the children have departed for establishments of their own and the parent couple are left alone. Family rituals now become important because: (a) older people are physically and psychologically disposed to such regimen; (b) there is an opportunity to return to rituals that enriched married life before the children arrived; and (c) grandparent-grandchild rituals arise to gratify both generations. This is a type of ritual which has been largely overlooked in child development.

THE FUNCTION OF RITUAL

It has been pointed out that the study of ritual has been confined in past years to its role in the field of religion. Certainly the old and abiding religions such as Mohammedanism, Judaism, and Roman Catholicism have been highly ritualistic in character. Perhaps the most penetrating analysis of the role of religious ritual in its generic sense is that given by Emile Durkheim, the French sociologist.[3] It will be briefly reviewed here because of its striking applicability to the role of family ritual.

[3] Emile Durkheim, *Les formes élémentaires de la vie religieuse*, Librairie Félix Alcan, Paris, 1912, book III.

Rituals, Durkheim points out, have four very significant functions. First is its disciplinary and preparatory function. Ritual prepares an individual for social living by imposing upon him the necessary self-discipline without which society is impossible. Social life is possible only as individuals are able to accept controls, and ritual aids in the development of such controls and does so in a relatively painless kind of way.

Second, and of particular importance, is its adhesive function. Ritual, being a group procedure, serves to bring beings together, to reaffirm their common bonds, and to enhance the social solidarity. Rituals are occasions of social communion and afford the means by which the group reaffirms itself periodically. They are particularly necessary in the modern world because the workaday, private, and personal interests of the individual occupy so large a part of life, and it is only in their joint observance of rituals that their common pool of values is re-established.

Third, according to Durkheim, is the vitalizing function of religions. If society is to be kept alive, its members must be made keenly aware of their social heritage: traditions must be renewed, faith must be renewed, values must be transmitted and deeply imbedded. A large number of rituals involve a recalling of the past, in happy and dramatic form, thus serving to recall the social heritage from lapsing into the limbo of the forgotten. Finally, there is the euphoric function of rituals, meaning that they serve to establish a condition or feeling of social well-being. This function takes on a special significance when a group is faced with an actual or threatened crisis. Ritual is very valuable in such a situation because it makes it necessary for people to have and express certain sentiments and to declare them together.

In the case records of family rituals which have already been cited these functions of discipline and preparation, of adhesiveness, of vitalizing, and of well-being can be seen in operation.

FAMILY RITUAL AND FAMILY INTEGRATION

The foregoing summary serves as an excellent background for the remaining discussion of this chapter, which is devoted specifically to the role of ritual in family living and in child development.

Returning to the study made by the Carter Foundation, there is one thread running through all the material that was gathered, and that is the fact that ritual is a form of regularized personal relationship between members of the family group. This regularization may involve all the members of the family, such as a national holiday or a family anniversary observance. Most family rituals are of this kind, anticipating and ordinarily obtaining the cooperation of all of the members of the family. But rituals also develop between individual members. There are, for example, husband-wife rituals. These begin to develop usually in the newly established family, and especially with the coming of the children, but they may appear at any stage or in any area of the husband-wife relationship. The sex life of married couples appears to be ritualized in many families.

Just as between husband and wife, so the relations between parent and child may be ritualized. Many of our cases are father-daughter or mother-son rituals. These might be a fruitful source of study for the psychoanalytically minded. Here we must content ourselves with the citation of two simple illustrations:

Frank S. lives in a suburb but maintains his office in the nearby city. Every Saturday since his daughter's twelfth birthday, she takes the suburban train and comes to his office by noon. The two then go to a well-known eating place for lunch. After lunch there is a matinee, football game, or other event. This continued for six years until the daughter left to enter a New England college. On these "dates," father and daughter almost never included another person. Most of the problems involving the daughter's school, social, and family life, were talked over by father and daughter on these occasions.

When Richard was married he and his wife began the custom of going to his parents' home every Sunday for dinner. When the dinner was over, Richard and his mother did the dishes. The help of other persons was always rejected. Richard always washed and his mother dried. Each Sunday, he would tease his mother about the same things, pretending to complain about the abundance of dishes and playfully accusing his mother of not having done any dishes since the preceding Sunday. Halfway through the process, his mother heated the coffee and she and Richard sat to sip it, and talk about happenings of the preceding week. When all matters had been discussed, the kitchen chores were finished. Often this task and talk would cover a period of two hours and more. At the end of the period, they would rejoin the others with Richard always telling some fantastic tale of how his mother had exploited him during the interval with work saved up during the preceding week.

Considering the personal relationships described in our case material, what happens in this regularizing of behavior? Four aspects can be identified. First, there is a strong sense of continuity about these relationships. The assumption of the participants is that they will go on and on, being repeated at regular intervals.

Second, the relationship becomes standardized, and, like a worn rock, becomes smoother as time goes on. There is the prescribed form and sequence, each step leading to the next with the precision, as it were, of a timetable. Behavior becomes predictable, which makes for ease and comfort in the relationship. Third, the relationship is glamorized. There is the effort to make it attractive, and often to make it impressive. The persons involved seem to say: We like what we are doing, we want to do it well and happily. Finally, the emergence of the ritual and its continuance seem to deepen the relationship. As Dunlap has written recently about the role of ritual: "Faith develops from ritual, rather than ritual from faith. The development of faith from ritual, as an interpretation of ritual, and with further progressive reinterpretations, is obviously consonant with the fact that ritual is a group product."[4]

Rituals, however, are more than patterns of personal relationships. They are procedures which have a purpose: they represent choices and values. They are approved ways of doing and thinking, and this means culture. The more one succeeds in getting on the inside of families, the more one sees them not as mere units of interacting personalities but as having each its own distinctive ways of living. These constitute the family culture, and it would seem that ritual is the one best starting point for the study of family culture patterns, just as it has long been recognized as the best point from which to begin the study of religion. Ritual obviously comprises much of the behavior of which the family is conscious and of which its members definitely approve.

Perhaps the overall conclusion that emerges from the assemblage of the material is that ritual is a relatively reliable index of family integration. What do we mean by family integration? Does it mean absence of discord? Obviously this is an aspect or index of it, even if negative in character. Is it ability to withstand shock or strain? Possibly, but this would seem to be somewhat a matter of accepted values and character traits of the constituent members rather than an interactive product or structural strength. The word *integrate* means to bring together and to make into a whole, and we use the term *family integration* to mean the welding or unification of its diverse elements into a complex whole or harmonious relationship. An integrated family means to us a well-knit family, one bound together with strong and continuing ties and functioning smoothly as a unit.

If one conceives of family integration in generic terms, there

[4] Knight Dunlap, *Religion: Its Functions in Human Life*, McGraw-Hill Book Company, New York, 1946, pp. vi, vii.

are many indexes which may be utilized to identify it. These include the effective meeting of common problems, the ability to resist major crises, smoothness of operation, lack of tension or conflict, evidences of family pride, criteria of family cooperation and continuity, and continuity of family planning. Thinking in terms of process, family integration is unrelated to moral purposes or cultural values. A well-integrated family may evidence its integration in recurrent feuding with another family, in packing boxes for shipment to displaced persons, in periodic outbursts of drunkenness, or long-range planning for the successive education of the children in a large family.

Ritual indicates many things and serves many purposes in the life of a family. The existence of well-established ritual implies, for example, a considerable amount of like-mindedness among the members of a family. Take such a simple yet basic fact as a common interest in family life. The development of a ritual by a family is an index of the common interest of its members in the family as a group. Parents who are conscious of the family as a group, who wish to make a success of family living, who think of their family as a continuing and permanent arrangement, are the ones most likely to initiate and continue the cooperative procedure which yields a ritual. One can detect, therefore, at the very beginning, a selective process between those family members who develop and utilize ritual, and those who do not. One must be interested in his family, want to make a go of it, and think of it as a permanent relationship, to look forward to the establishment of family rituals and traditions.

Again, rituals are developed cooperatively. This gives and stimulates a sense of group participation, a further sharing of intimacies, and a sense of lively satisfaction. As Adams pointed out years ago, the feelings of satisfaction that accompany the performance of ritual, and the "pause of satisfaction" that follows the achievement of ends in mind, constitute the essence of the aesthetic experience. In other words, the aesthetic experience is a concomitant of successful participation in the ritualistic act.[5] "The rite is performed; control is achieved; the participants rest satisfied."[6]

Third, common participation is a ceremony that carries with it a sense of rightness that makes for family pride. One senses this feeling of pride in almost all of our case records. Even if there was a sort of playful apology or grumbling pose of feminine coy-

[5] Elizabeth Kemper Adams, *The Aesthetic Experience*, University of Chicago Press, Chicago, 1907.

[6] Frederick G. Henke, *A Study in the Psychology of Ritualism*, University of Chicago Press, Chicago, 1910, p. 84.

ness in the lines of the case record, it was easy to detect the shades of smug satisfaction between the lines which described the family rituals. Apparently family pride makes for ritual; ritual makes for family pride.

Next, many of our rituals involve refinements of living, and adherence to them implies, and stimulates, a common interest in such refinements. Ritual necessitates a certain formality in social relations, and complementary to this are consideration for the rights of others and the discipline of self, all of which makes for good group relations. It is obvious from our material that ritualism and formalism in family relations make for predictability of behavior response, and this tends to reduce strain and disorder.

FAMILY RITUALS AND CHILD DEVELOPMENT

It has been pointed out that many, perhaps most, family rituals develop with the coming of children. Often the rituals partake of the nature of a family drama, designed to impress the children. Many rituals center about them; usually they participate in them. Naturally, the impression of many family rituals upon the children is very vivid. Proof of this appears constantly in the clarity with which rituals are recalled, the pride shown in pointing out their details and features, by young people with whom the subject is discussed. Similar is the tendency of autobiographers to view their early family life in terms of recurring family rituals.[7]

Again, a large proportion of family rituals have pleasant associations. Often they center about holidays, birthdays, anniversaries, and other happy occasions. Because of the nature of family rituals—their recurrence, the sense of rightness that accompanies them, the pleasurable associations—they groove themselves deeply and pleasantly into the accumulating layers of the youthful mind, which constitute the essence of the unconscious. Considered in more specific terms, this process may be viewed in operation along six selected lines.

1. Rituals as group habits. From the point of view of child and youth development, a significant characteristic of ritual is its habitual character. Rituals are habits, group habits. Moreover, they are the habits of the first, most exclusive and enduring group to which the child belongs, and the one in which emotional ties are deepest. Pressure from such close association is heavy: infraction

[7] Bossard and Boll, *Ritual in Family Living*, chaps. 3 and 4.

by members most upsetting. Family ritual, then, assumes power both from its own nature and from its special setting.

The meaning of habit has been well stated by Bogardus. He writes: "Habit means to have. Habit gives possession; it gives permanency to one's experiences. . . . It is strangely true that nothing is well done until it is done by habit. Reliability and thoroughness depend on habit."[8] Obviously, much of the disciplinary role of ritual, of which Durkheim speaks, flows from the repetitive character of its operation, and nowhere is this more manifest than in childrearing.

One ritual which illustrates this habit-forming and disciplining role in child development is the following:

> My family makes a ritual of sending its thank-you notes for Christmas presents received. As the gifts are opened, the cards from them are collected and stacked. The evening after Christmas, the whole family gathers around a table with the cards and writing equipment. The atmosphere is light, with much chatter. "What was that thing that Aunt Sophie sent me, and what can I possibly say about it that is nice?"
>
> This sort of thing goes on through the evening, but when it is over, one kind of social obligation has been fulfilled, promptly, without nagging, in a pleasant sort of way. The youngest see that this is not a chore that Mother metes out to them—that she and Daddy share this social obligation too—and that they, too, have their problems of expression about certain gifts and certain obligations but have learned the controlled behavior necessary to meet this situation.

2. THE STANDARDIZATION OF AFFECTIONAL RESPONSE. Rituals make for standardized affectional responses between members of the family. This is important because individuals demonstrate affection unequally and differently. Though depth or sincerity of affection may be quite unrelated to any visible display of it, the former, unannounced, is often overlooked completely by a person accustomed to recognizing it by certain overt symbols. This fact is provocative enough of trouble in families to make significant the question: how do we come to be demonstrative or undemonstrative in certain set ways? The study of family rituals contributes an answer to this question. In many families, the expression of affection is a definite, imperative part of their rituals, was performed without question, and came to be, for the children as well as the parents, the accepted mode of behavior.

Three different kinds of demonstration appeared. First, there

[8] Emory S. Bogardus, *Essentials of Social Psychology*, 4th ed., Jesse Ray Miller, Los Angeles, 1923, pp. 45 and 46.

were the families who ritualized, to them, the high value of physical contact in affection, through kissing or caressing. Such patterns, once established, come to be the *normal* way to behave, and it is the *omission* of the symbol at the proper time which is the conscious act, is noticed, and has a hurtful connotation.

A different kind of affectional demonstration ritualized by certain families is the prescribed thoughtful act to anticipate the comfort of a family member. One such rite, selected from the case material upon which this summary is based, follows:

> Each night before Dad would retire, there would be placed on the stand beside his bed a tall glass of orange juice. No one in particular was designated to perform this task, but as each of us came home or went upstairs to bed we would check on this "must." Forgetfulness on our part shamed each of us. The only mention on Dad's part would be a reluctant, "Missed my orange juice last night, everyone must have been tired." That hurt us because we hurt him.

Other such examples were: The preparing of a breakfast in bed for Mother on Sunday mornings; the cocktail made and served to Father by his eldest daughter immediately upon his arrival home from work each evening; the regular brotherly romp with the baby just before bedtime. In some families, this sort of "fore-thoughtful" rite extended even to the family dog, and required special feeding, a definite play hour, or an automobile ride.

The most frequently mentioned ritual for the expression of affection concerned the giving of presents. In some instances, every holiday or anniversary is a mutual family present-giving event, and sometimes other special occasions were devised regularly for this kind of affectional display:

> Rarely did any of us return home from in town, a trip, a holiday, or even from the corner groceries without bringing Mother a remembrance, such as a handkerchief, pastry, and so on. So when at dinnertime, three of us presented her with three different boxes of sweets and cakes, she would smile and thank us. Other than that, such courtesies were taken for granted in our home.

There is no evidence that families which had these rituals were more or less warmly affectionate that other families having no such definite procedures. The significance of them lies in the fact that the symbols used habitually in the home and unconsciously taken for granted come to stand for the thing they express. They may establish habits of expression which mark a certain kind of personality; they may also establish attitudes that make an individual incapable of understanding or finding comfort in a different symbol.

3. Family Etiquette. Relations between persons, at any above the starkest levels, involve the observance of certain prescribed forms of behavior. These forms or codes vary a great deal and tend to become both more rigid and more important as life becomes more complex and social standards rise. A part of the social development of every person is training in these codes of conventional behavior, and in this the role of the family is fundamental, particularly so through the patterns of family etiquette that are maintained.

An excellent illustration of family etiquette is found in the mealtime rituals that take form. A study of these shows widely differing habits of social graces, table manners, and customs of dress that are distinguishing marks and that have a bearing upon an individual's qualifications for acceptability in particular social spheres. Significant differences are indicated in the two excerpts of case material that follow:

a. Our dinner gong sounds 10 minutes before dinner is ready so that we can finish washing and dressing promptly. . . . If a member of the family is not on time for dinner he is told that breakfast is the next meal. . . . We join hands around the table and say grace, and then sit down all together. Dad sits at the head of the table, Mother is at the foot, and the children are ranged between them according to age. . . . Our dinner table is always set with a white tablecloth and the best china and glassware. The maid passes the plates to each person as Dad carves, and then serves the vegetables from silver dishes. She helps the children who are too young to serve themselves so that they will not stain the cloth. . . . We eat what is put in front of us and no questions asked. We are not allowed to interrupt each other, especially Mother and Dad. We are never allowed to fight or argue during the meal, and the violator is sent to the kitchen to finish the meal. . . . No one can ever get up and leave the table for any reason and come back again. . . . At dinner, we always have four courses, served in order. The first time my brother saw salad served with the main course, he made an embarrassing comment. We could no more think of serving salad with the main course than we could make the mistake of using a salad fork for our meat. Spode service plates are used at dinner, so that the place in front of us is never bare when one course is removed, and the flower on the plate shows up prettily while we wait for the next course. . . . There is no smoking permitted at our table. After we have finished dessert, Mother and Dad look at each other, nod, and we all go into the living room. The maid then brings in the silver service which belonged to Mother's mother, and those of us who are old enough have coffee and cigarettes.

b. Hands are washed after the meal is placed on the table, delaying same. After my mother places dessert on the table, she always stops to make tea, thus forcing the rest of us to plumb the depths of impoliteness and begin without her. . . . Father gets the paper first and reads it during breakfast. We are not allowed to touch it until he is finished. I sit there watching him, between sips of coffee, waiting till he is through and wondering when I can get at the funnies. . . . Father does the carving out in the kitchen, because he has had some sad experiences in letting the gravy splash on the table. . . . When we are going to the movies we have our food from the kitchen all on one plate to save dish-washing. . . . We never know when the whole family will arrive, so if they're not all there they eat whenever they come in. . . . When company comes we use our good china and silver. . . . The first one finished is the first one out, but she has to take her own plates into the kitchen and scrape and rinse them. . . . Mother and I always wear a dress for dinner (this is to be distinguished from "dressing for dinner" in that it means one does not appear at dinner in housecoats, jeans, or slacks). . . . The first thing Father does when he comes home for dinner is to take off his shoes and put on his house slippers.

4. THE ORGANIZATION OF LEISURE. Leisure-time activities constitute a recognized problem in present-day family life. In their experimentation with the problem, many families find patterns of activity so satisfying that they become ritualized. The by-products of these rites are significant in respect to child development.

There are, for example, the reading rituals—of the "funnies," the daily paper, the weekly issue of *Life*, the Bible, the classics, and selected holiday stories like Dickens' *Christmas Carol*. Another frequently found ritual of family leisure centers around the radio, television, and the hi-fi. Procedures are strict in many instances, involving the program listened to, the place of seating, who tunes in, and under what circumstances someone else may take over. Other families have definite times and places for the entire family to go to the movies, with set procedures perhaps before and after the show. Still other families approach the rite of the family council in the late evening with an "evening snack": a gathering of the family in the kitchen, around the refrigerator, for pickup eating, with a recapitulation of the day's events. Finally, there are the families in which summer vacations have become a part of the family's ritualistic life.

5. PRACTICE IN GROUP ADJUSTMENT. All family living is education for group living, but homes vary in the stability of practice situations presented. A highly ritualized home is one in which there is much repetition in the same kinds of situations and group relationships. For family ritual means that the members must be together: at specific times; for certain purposes; to fulfill definite roles and

obligations; to perform them in relation to others' roles and obligations. The continuance of the ritual usually means that these conditions are met and performed unfailingly. It would seem from the very nature of ritual that the more family life is formalized by them, the less haphazard would be the socializing process, regardless of whether a family's rites were healthfully socializing or not. The analysis of rituals suggests the molding of many personality traits through repeated practice of obligatory actions which, taken in combinations, tend to habits of social stability and adaptability. It may show one means by which some individuals come to be the ones who are constantly called upon because they are ready and willing to work, are dependable, punctual, and understand their role and status in relation to a group; or why others come to be the ones who are shunned because their performance in all these respects is so perfunctory. Social habits of cooperation, regularity, punctuality, and recognition of the rights of others are offered here as being related to ritualistic procedures. Rights of others come to be ritualized in many families as do, unfortunately, deviations from these.

6. FAMILY CONTINUITY. The study of family rituals in 400 families emphasizes not only their role in the promotion of family solidarity and in the training of children to patterns of valued behavior, but they serve also to show to the child that his own family circle is but the living link in a chain of generations that composes "the family." This concept of the family is important to the individual not only in respect to his own sense of worth and security, but also in respect to his attitudes toward responsibility for the future of the family.

Three well-defined types of family rituals which are important in this connection will be noted. One is the family reunion, customarily an annual gathering to which every living member of the kinship group is invited, and with formal programs of business and social items. Another is the formalized family gathering, held upon stated holidays, for the purpose of "catching up with each other." Such meetings are less formalized, more restricted in personnel, and more frequent than family reunions. Finally, there are the festive Sunday breakfasts each week, when the married siblings return home with their spouses and children to discuss family affairs and to tell what happened during the week. These Sunday breakfast rites are the most frequent and the least formalized of all. If there is a tribal elder, it is apt to be just "Grandma."

A FINAL NOTE ON THE ROLE OF FAMILY RITUALS

As one analyzes the rituals of families, one comes to be impressed with how large a part of the behavior and personality of its individual members is revealed. A thumbnail sketch of a man could be drawn on the basis of his behavior and attitudes toward work, play, leisure, sex, illness, religion, affectional response, etiquette and social graces, responsibility for future generations, and so on. Carrying this consideration one step farther, it can be seen what may be the results to subsequent home life from the combining of two ritual systems. A bride, for instance, who had long looked forward with pride to the time when she could call in her own husband on baking day to "lick the bowl," as the men of her family had always done, was reduced to tears and prolonged resentment when her groom responded "What? That raw stuff!" Superficial as it may appear, this sort of thing, as well as whether to vacation separately or together, to send the children to camp or not, how to celebrate Christmas and Sunday, who does the dishes and the shopping, how one behaves at meals, are not things that are frequently reasoned out before marriage. They are patterns unconsciously *expected* and raise emotional temperatures when observed differently. They become even more important when there are children to be considered, and each parent wants them to perform the "right" way. For these reasons, a careful analysis of family rituals, so individualized and so obscure in the modern family, seems a significant part of the study of that group.

It should be repeated that in this discussion of the influence of family ritual upon children and their development there has been no attempt to suggest sole causation of specific effects. It is all too obvious that a single critical event may completely turn the course of conditioning set by rituals, and further, that rituals themselves are, for the most part, just the channeling of certain deep-seated desires and attitudes into habitual behavior patterns. The conclusion of this study has been merely that: (1) the ritual is a means of communicating overtly the ways of doing things and the attendant attitudes that a family has found to be most satisfactory for its own use; (2) this ritual behavior is practiced repeatedly, unchanged, and is often unconsciously performed; (3) it covers many areas which are native to family life, and will continue in the next generation of the family; (4) rituals symbolizing the same phases of life are observed very differently from family to family and are a part of what makes individuals noticeably different from each other; and (5) these individual differences, as crystallized in, and influenced by, rituals are just as significant as comparisons of ritualistic differences from primitive to civilized cultures, or from one national culture to another.

SUMMARY

1. A family ritual is defined as a prescribed formal procedure, arising out of family interaction, involving a pattern of defined behavior which is directed toward some specific end or purpose and which acquires rigidity and a sense of rightness as a result of its continuing history.
2. Ritual develops in connection with many aspects of family life, but clusters particularly about such things as holidays, anniversary days, meals, vacations, family work, religious worship, and collective ways of using leisure time.
3. Modern rituals have become secularized in large measure, but contemporary family rituals are viewed as seriously as those which obtained a century ago.
4. Family rituals vary on a class basis. Those in the lower classes are chiefly rituals of expediency, arising to solve lower-class family problems. Those in the middle classes stress discipline, "togetherness," and achievement. Those of the upper classes tend more toward the refinements of living and the maintenance of past forms of life.
5. Both the nature and variety of family rituals vary from one stage of the family cycle to another, as do also the attitudes of the family members toward rituals. The coming of children and the years of their early maturing are particularly rich in ritual development.
6. Ritual serves many purposes in social life—disciplinary, adhesive, vitalizing, and euphoric.
7. Ritual is a relatively reliable index of family integration. Its acceptance by family members makes for predictability of behavior response, thus reducing strain and disorder in the family group.
8. Family rituals are particularly important for child development. They serve as group habits, they standardize affectional responses, they become the core of family etiquette, they help to organize leisure time, they give practice in group adjustment, and they make for family continuity.

SUGGESTED READINGS

Bossard, James H. S., and Eleanor S. Boll, *Ritual in Family Living,* University of Pennsylvania Press, Philadelphia, 1950. An analysis of life history reports on the rituals in the lives of authors and students.

Durant, Will C., *The Age of Faith,* Simon and Schuster, New York, 1950. The meaning and importance of ritual to the endurance of religious institutions is a thesis in this book.

Durkheim, Emile, *Les Formes Elementaires de la Vie Religieuse,* Librarie Felix Alean, Paris, 1912, book III. (Current edition: Crowell-Collier Publishing Company, New York.) Durkheim analyzes the relationship between religious ritual and behavior.

Fromm, Erich, *Psychoanalysis and Religion,* Yale University Press, New Haven, 1950. Although psychiatrists have been conscious chiefly of compulsive rituals of a pathological nature, Dr. Fromm appreciates the purposes of ritual in any normal group life.

Henke, Frederick G., *A Study in the Psychology of Ritualism,* University of Chicago Press, Chicago, 1910. Although this is a study of primitive ritual, much of the content, like that of Durkheim's book, is quite applicable to family life.

Sinclair, Jo, *Wasteland,* Harper & Brothers, New York, 1947. A novel in which the effects of the ritual of the Passover on the members of the family are described.

Sumner, William Graham, *Folkways,* Ginn and Company, Boston, 1906. (Current editions: Blaisdell Publishing Company, Dover Publications, and New American Library, New York.) A sociologist describes many primitive rituals and comments on the decline of ritual in our society.

10

CHANGING ROLES AND FUNCTIONS OF PARENTS

Until quite recently in human history, people were forced to function in rather compact groups in which the relation of the individual to his group was all or nothing. Such was the nature of tribal society in which kinship, real or fictitious, was the bond which held its members together. Later, the feudal system combined land tenure with closely knit personal relationships. Still later, and in the United States, an agricultural economy maintained this compactness in the family group. An industrial economy, however, gave rise to a form of social structure the ultimate unit of which is the individual. The late Professor Ross used the term *individuation* to designate this process which "pulverized social lumps and released the action of its members."[1] Today, the immediate family has responded to this liberating process so that Mother, Father, and child tend to function separately in many areas of their lives in addition to those differences which result from the respective status ascribed to each on the basis of their age and sex.

The present chapter seeks to consider: (1) some of the factors responsible for the changing roles of parents; (2) mothers' roles; (3)

[1] E. A. Ross, *Principles of Sociology*, The Century Company, New York, 1920, p. 439.

fathers' roles; (4) intrafamily-role relationships; and (5) society's expectations.

BACKGROUND FACTORS IN CHANGING ROLES AND FUNCTIONS

There are at least four conspicuous movements in American life that deserve special attention as they concern changes in role and function of family members.

The Change from the Producing to the Consuming Family Pattern

Fewer than 100 years ago, more than 7 out of every 10 American families lived in agricultural areas. Today, nearly 7 out of every 10 live under urban or suburban conditions. This has had a revolutionary effect on the general pattern of family roles and functions. Agricultural life tends to breed patriarchy. The muscularly stronger male becomes the head of the family business, which is the direct production of necessities for family consumption. Women and children are valued workers in such an enterprise, but they are subordinate in position to, and economically dependent upon, the male director of the business. This producing type of family life is self-contained, having relatively little need of contact with, or reliance upon, outsiders. It has the appearance of a "social lump," in which the group and its maintenance is the important value. The individual achieves status in proportion to his or her contribution to the group and not in projecting his talents upon the outside world. A number of sociologists have used the term *familism* to describe the fundamental attitude about the relationship between individual and group in such a family. A strong we-feeling is developed, and the members are conceived as a team working together in all their life activities. Interdependence is stressed, and the welfare of all supersedes the welfare of any individual. As in any well-run business organization, roles and functions are clearly defined. Women are childbearers, childrearers, housekeepers, and part-time laborers. They have no function apart from family life. The lives of children are contained almost wholly within the family group.

Urban living has created, for most families, the necessity of the members leaving the family group to earn a salary. Outside contacts become very important, sometimes to two or more wage-earning members of the same family. They are not working together physically as a team at the most basic function of life—sustenance. The we-feeling weakens; a member has needs and rights and responsibilities in relation to people outside the family; and the family lump begins to pulverize with the emergence of the individuated lives of family members. In such a situation, attitudes change, too. The importance of the family becomes relative to the particular situation of the individual within it. Who is head of the family no longer depends upon who has the strongest muscles but upon who is able to take command. Thus women need not be subordinate, nor need they have their roles and functions dictated to them. Indeed, at present, it is impossible to state what *is* the proper role and function of a specific woman or mother in the United States. The possibilities are so varied that there is no longer a set pattern and the question of what it *should* be is highly argumentative.

Mass Compulsory Education and the Gainful Employment of Women

A very significant factor affecting the various roles is the American emphasis upon educating girls in the same way and according to the same standards that we educate boys. In parts of the world, past and present, where girls are educated only for traditional woman's work, they have little opportunity for job competition with men. In the United States, women can, and have competed successfully in almost every type of employment except in the heaviest type of labor and the Presidency. Added, then, to the present emphasis upon the individual, there has come about the possibility of partial or complete economic independence of the female. Employment statistics indicate the extent to which she has availed herself of this opportunity. Between 1940 and 1962 the percentage of the female population in the labor force rose from 27.4 to 35.7. During the 1950's the female labor force grew in number more than did the male labor force—4.8 million and 3.5 million respectively. Only one-fifth of the employed women in 1960 were widowed or divorced, and the number of single women employed actually decreased. In the same year, of 23.5 million husband-wife families with children under 18 years of age, 6.2 million had both the husband and wife in the labor force. About 3 million women with children under 6 years of age were employed.[2] Another important aspect within the picture of female employment is this. It is generally conceded that before World War I, the large majority of women who worked outside their homes did so because they were obliged to, to maintain their families. This is no longer

[2] *Population Bulletin*, Population Reference Bureau, Washington, D.C., May 1964, pp. 64–65.

true. Women, in growing numbers, now seek work as personal careers, to raise the level of family living, or for the sake of financial independence. Marriage counselors are well aware of the manner in which this has altered the married woman's role with her husband. Once she was totally dependent upon him and, for the most part, fulfilled such functions as he saw fit. Now, if he does not approve of her activities, she can say, "What does it matter what he thinks. I earn my own keep."

Laborsaving Devices and Size of Home

At just about the same time that homes began to shrink in size from the four-story mansion to the ranch house, industry started producing an increasing multitude of devices to make housekeeping less physically draining and time-consuming. The results of the captains of industry's altruistic attempts to make life easier for "the little woman" have become big business. Small homes with "standard equipment" now include kitchens with wall ovens so that mother will not have to stoop; mechanical refrigerators which have no ice pans and do not even have to be defrosted; automatic dishwashers to eliminate the perpetual historical chore of women; deep-freeze units to decrease trips to market; disposal units which save many steps outdoors and some very disagreeable cleaning; power washing machines that reduce what was once a full day's work to a few hours—including ironing with the electric mangle and steam iron. The coal range and coal furnace are almost defunct. Vacuum cleaners, electric mixers, not to mention the whole modern production of frozen, half-cooked and ready-to-eat foods, have changed the nature of housekeeping for the average mother. It has been referred to by many people as "push-button housekeeping." As one man put it: "I, who remember my grandmother spending two hours washing the dishes after a family meal, now hear my own daughters arguing about whose turn it is to put them into the dishwasher."

Family Size

Partly because of the increased status of woman, the small-family system has been instituted during this century. Not only does the average family have fewer children now, but there are fewer relatives welcomed into the household as permanent members. Unmarried daughters and maiden aunties can find employment and support themselves. When social security does not suffice, "convalescent homes" take care of many aged relatives. Indeed, the

American family ideal has become a small, nuclear family living alone without "interference from relatives." This, then, has decreased the number of dependents upon Mother's services. Census figures show that the average-sized family has decreased from 5.79 persons in 1790 to 3.4 persons in 1964. This is a decrease of more than two persons per household on the average.

It seems clear that along with such changes in family living come changes in role and role-relationship within the group.

Functions of the Modern American Family

The subject of family functions has received much attention from sociologists during the past 25 years and has become an almost standard inclusion in textbooks on the family. Current thinking on this subject is the larger background for attitudes as to how parents are functioning at the present time.

In 1929,[3] and again in 1933,[4] Ogburn spoke of the *declining* functions of the family. He and his followers have maintained that most of the historic functions of the family are no longer performed by that group, but by other institutions and agencies. Production, recreation, protection in illness and dependency and danger are taken over by industry, big business, commercialized amusement, the doctors, hospitals, police, and so on. Education is now the province of the schools, colleges, and universities. According to Truxall and Merrill, even the important family function of conferring status upon the child is no longer a significant part of family life. In a time of such great family mobility, they feel, no one knows enough about family backgrounds to confer status on that basis, and each individual earns his status for himself. A textbook by Burgess and Locke, entitled *The Family: From Institution to Companionship*, indicates the extent to which the institutional aspects of family life are considered to have slipped away from it, changing it to a companionship group whose definition is "A unity of interacting personalities." The three basic functions remaining to the family are those of procreation, affection, and socialization. It is pointed out that even the biological function of giving birth is not fulfilled quantitatively as it once was, since families are smaller. The affectional function, however, is assumed to be more important than ever in a time of mobile and rather anonymous living. The few stable affectional relationships a child has, become

[3] William F. Ogburn, "The Changing Family," *Publications of the American Sociological Society*, vol. XXIII, 1929, pp. 114–133.

[4] William F. Ogburn, *Recent Social Trends in the United States*, McGraw-Hill Book Company, New York, 1933, vol. I, p. 661.

extremely significant. Since no other institution has ever been found to socialize the child as the family does, that important function, too, remains with the family.[5]

These conclusions concerning family functions are based largely on statistical indices of actual and possible activities outside the home (such as employment of married women with children, enrollment of children in schools and other agencies for education, child care, and recreation) and on estimates of the decreased time necessary for homemaking because of the growing use of laborsaving devices in the home. Goods produced for sale and services to the family rather than by the family is another source of evidence. The results paint a picture of little interdependence and extreme individuation in the current American family. The *decline* of functions is clearly emphasized.

In 1934, Bossard suggested that family functions were in a state of *change,* that the historic ones were not so much lost to the family and taken over wholly by other groups as that the family's part in them has had to change with changing times.[6]

The voices of professional women who are themselves mothers have recently been raised, emphasizing this interpretation of what is happening to parents' functions.[7] A summary of the comments runs something like this. Though the family does not produce most of the goods for its own consumption, someone has to produce the wherewithal to buy the goods—or go on relief. Fortunately, it is still the minority of American families which resort to that. Furthermore, consuming patterns have become so increasingly complicated with the addition of new brands and new products that wise selection becomes an important family function. For example, when the first women's college was instituted in the United States, there were no closets, but only three hooks on the walls of the students' rooms. One was for the Sunday dress; one for the nightdress, and one for the school dress. Most of these were painstakingly made at home. Now, in late August and early September, women's clothing stores are bombarded by entering college girls and their mothers,

[5] Representative of the views of many authors on the subject of family functions are the following books: Ernest W. Burgess and Harvey J. Locke, *The Family: From Institution to Companionship,* American Book Company, New York, 1953, pp. 462–479; Andrew G. Truxall and Francis E. Merrill, *Marriage and the Family in American Culture,* Prentice-Hall, New York, 1953, pp. 312–354; Robert F. Winch, *The Modern Family,* Henry Holt and Company, New York, 1952, pp. 50–176 (revised edition: Holt, Rinehart and Winston, New York, 1963); William F. Ogburn and Meyer F. Nimkoff, *Technology and the Changing Family,* Houghton Mifflin Company, Boston, 1955.

[6] James H. S. Bossard, *Social Change and Social Problems,* Harper & Brothers, New York, 1938, pp. 606 ff.

[7] Among others representing this point of view are Margaret Mead, Sidonie Matsner Gruenberg, Evelyn Millis Duvall, Dorothy Barclay, and Dorothy Thompson.

spending hours in careful selection of this year's college wardrobe. In much the same way, the earlier family menu was the result of choice from what had been grown on the farm and whatever meat, fish, and poultry were available. Now, it would seem that in order to make the best nutritional choice for one's family, one should have at least a course in elementary physics, chemistry, and home economics.

Dr. Margaret Mead writes of the modern mother:

> She shops, she markets, she chooses, she transports, she integrates, she coordinates, she fits little bits of time together so as "to get through the week," and her proudest boast often has to be "it was a good week. Nothing went wrong."
>
> The average young American woman is very cheerful over these tasks. They are a drain on her nervous energy rather than on her physical strength, time-consuming rather than back breaking. . . .[8]

Dr. Nimkoff, summarizing a survey made at Bryn Mawr College, shows that "push-button housekeeping" may give rise to misleading ideas. Women with more laborsaving devices were found to spend more time, not less, on housework. The typical farm mother spends 60.55 hours a week in housework; the typical mother in cities under 100,000 spends 78.35 hours a week in such work; and the mother in cities over 100,000 spends 80.57 hours. Dr. Nimkoff adds:

> The reason seems to be that the farm woman has more varied household and out-of-the-home duties and therefore devotes less time to any particular duty. . . . Perhaps the fact is that the household labor-saving devices make it possible for the modern housewife to be a better housekeeper than her predecessor, with fewer economic functions to perform, and with efficient machines at her disposal for cleaning, cooking and washing, the modern housewife can perform her domestic duties in less time and with less energy and is therefore in a position to perform them more often. The availability of the labor-saving devices invites their use as does the ease of operation. The result is that the modern wife who has a vacuum cleaner probably cleans her house more often, and the one who has a washing machine does the wash more often. The effect of the household appliances is, then, to make it possible for the housewife to do a more thorough job of housekeeping *as well as* to provide her with more leisure for out-of-the-home pursuits.[9]

Dorothy Thompson, after making a survey of products bought by the American family, came to the conclusion that modern technol-

[8] Margaret Mead, *Male and Female*, William Morrow and Company, New York, 1949, p. 330.

[9] Meyer F. Nimkoff, "What Do Modern Inventions Do to Family Life?" *Annals of the American Academy of Political and Social Science*, November, 1950, p. 56.

ogy is leading to greater self-sufficiency within the family unit. The question, she insisted, is what people *do* with the time technology has handed back to them. Her answer was:

> In the conventional picture they sit at television sets, go to the movies, play canasta, and that is about all. In reality they also paint pictures, set out gardens, decorate and even build their own houses. . . .
>
> The Singer Sewing Machine Co. recently reported that today 30 million American women make at least some of their own and their children's clothes. Last year home dressmakers bought a half billion dollars' worth of yard goods. In 1950, the last year for which figures are available, they bought over 100 million dress patterns. Women not only sew to get more for their money. They sew to get clothes that are "different."
>
> Of the billion and a half dollars' worth of paint sold last year, 65 per cent was put on walls by housewives or their husbands—at a fifth of the cost of hiring someone to do it. . . .
>
> The net effect of the division of labor and the enormous efficiency resulting from the gadgets we have developed is to return man to himself and to his home, to increase his self-sufficiency and range of activities.[10]

As for the educational function, much of this is done at home, for better or for worse, throughout the life of the child. Not only is socialization a part of the educational process, but a great deal of formal education takes place at home both before and after the child goes to school. Every time (as has already been suggested in former chapters) a child's question is answered, every time a child is told what to do, every time a child "observes" something that happens in his own family circle, he is being educated. In recreation and in protection a great deal of guidance is the family's function. Does Mary attend burlesque or opera? At what age may she begin to date? What does she do about speaking to strangers on the street? Who decides whether she should go to school with that cold? Does she have the operation that the school doctor recommends or does she not? What church, what school does Mary attend, and how often? All of these matters and literally thousands of others are, in the last analysis, in the hands of the family. Either the family gives the guidance and makes the decisions or no one does, until Mary is old enough to make them for herself.

Also, at least two students of the family have pointed out that the small-family system does not necessarily add to the leisure time of the mother. One writes:

> In small families the parents are called upon to do for their children, especially when they are young, what in the old-fashioned family the

[10] Dorothy Thompson, "Our Gadgets Set Us Free," *Ladies' Home Journal*, May, 1953.

other children of various ages and other adults did casually and incidentally. Parents have to double as friends and playmates while remaining fathers and mothers. They have to find sibling and cousin substitutes as well as aunt or grandmother substitutes. Where children in the past somehow picked up their companions and formed their own play groups casually and informally, parents today have to proceed deliberately. They have to find a day nursery or nursery school, or even find neighbors who will join to start one where there never has been any before. The anomaly reaches a climax in that new social phenomenon known as the sitter. In a large family there was always somebody who could "mind" the baby while going on with other business about the house or yard. The sitter, however, is a special functionary engaged to be around chiefly as an emergency resource, and has only minimal concern with the infant in question.

The need for parents to make special plans to be able to go out of an evening or to have a safe place in which the child can play of a morning or to find the child suitable companions or to do any of the things that took care of themselves automatically in a large family, seems to reflect upon their competence. Outsiders, with old-fashioned notions of the family and its workings, openly reproach these parents for "shifting their responsibilities" to others. Yet it is the most conscientious parents who do such planning, who make the special effort to provide for their children what they need beyond the constant companionship of the mother.[11]

To which Dr. Mead adds:

Each home has been reduced to the bare essentials—to barer essentials than most primitive people would consider possible. Only one woman's hands to feed the baby, answer the telephone, turn off the gas under the pot that is boiling over, soothe the older child who has broken a toy, and open both doors at once.[12]

So, according to this line of thought, though there are at present other agencies which aid the family in its more extensive job, the successful parent still has these functions to perform and in many ways they are more difficult and complex than ever before.

There is more to these differing points of view than mere pedantic quibbling. As far as the future functioning of the family institution is concerned two different types of service are implied. If the family now serves only to give birth, to love, and to socialize its children, then services of the government, the church, the school, welfare agencies, and so on, must continue to be increased, strengthened, and supported in order to take over the rest of childrearing. If, on

[11] Sidonie Matsner Gruenberg, "Changing Conceptions of the Family," *Annals of the American Academy of Political and Social Science*, May, 1947, p. 130.

[12] Mead, *op. cit.*, p. 334.

the other hand, there are families which function well with the type of assistance already available (and it is obvious that there are such families) then a program of education is implied—the education of families in the manner of performance that is successful in the twentieth century.

THE ROLES OF THE MOTHER

In spite of controversies over what functions are being fulfilled in modern American families, there has been little interest in surveying them to discover precisely what are the roles played therein. For this reason a small study was made at the William T. Carter Foundation which gives a picture of the actual activities of a limited number of mothers.

A Study of Mothers' Schedules

Twenty-one mothers were given notebooks in which, for a period of two weeks, they wrote diary-like accounts of what they did during each 15-minute period of the waking day.[13] No effort was made to find a representative sample of the entire population. Rather, mothers were selected who were not marked as conspicuous failures, but who were of varying economic status, with different-sized families and ages of children.

Certain characteristics of the population are important in understanding the roles that the mothers played. *First* is the employment status. Sixteen husbands and five wives in these families were regular salary earners. In three cases, both had regular earned salaries. One of the mothers had just given up full-time employment because of the problems it created for her young son. Three more of the wives, whose husbands were employed, had incomes of their own from investments. Two mothers were the sole family support. In one case the mother was on public relief with some help from a relative, and in another a college-student husband, who earned very little, received ample support from his parents. Table 3 shows the occupations of the major breadwinners in the nuclear families. *Second,* salaries and incomes combined for the families are shown in Table 4. The data on income and occupation indicate that these families are above the national average (as they are, also, in education). This is a difficulty usually found in the type of study

[13] A part of the study was financed by a grant to Dr. Boll from the Committee on the Advancement of Research, University of Pennsylvania.

in which lengthy written records are required and means that the results of it cannot be projected upon the total population of modern American mothers. However, this does not deny the fact that valuable depth records are received, individually, from persons ranking

Table 3

Occupation	Number of Cases
Professional	4
Proprietor, manager or official	4
Clerk and kindred worker	3
Skilled workman and foreman	3
Semiskilled workman	1
Unskilled	3
Unclassifiable	1
None	2
Total	21

Table 4

Salary and Income	Number of Cases
Over $10,000	7
$6,000– 7,999	3
$5,000– 6,999	4
$3,000– 4,999	2
$1,000– 1,999	3
Under 1,000	2
Total	21

very high and very low in the income-occupation scale. These give basic leads for further investigation of larger and more representative samples.[14]

Finally, the ages of the mothers in the study ranged from 54 to 21; and the ages of the fathers, from 60 to 23. In terms of marital status, 18 mothers were married, 1 separated, 1 widowed, and 1 divorced. This is a slightly lower rate of broken families than is found in the general population as viewed cross-sectionally by the United States Census. Numbers of children, their ages, and their current activity are shown in the following tables.

[14] For more detailed observations upon this method of research see: James H. S. Bossard and Eleanor S. Boll, *Ritual in Family Living*, University of Pennsylvania Press, Philadelphia, 1950, pp. 208 ff.

Table 5

Number of Children	Number of Families
1	6
2	9
3	4
4	2
Total	21

Table 6

Age Range of Children	Number of Children
Under 6	9
6–12	11
12–18	13
18–21	6
Over 21	5
Total	44

Table 7

Activity of Children	Number of Children
Preschool	9
School	25
College	5
Employed	4
Adult dependent	1
Total	44

A large majority of these mothers, then, are involved with school and preschool children though other cases included serve to reveal the continuing functions of motherhood at later stages of the family cycle.

The Mothers' Schedules

The average waking day of the mothers ranged from 17 hours and 24 minutes to 13 hours and 54 minutes. These hours were divided into the following categories:

1. Work directly concerned with service to family and home.
2. Socializing with family (this included mealtimes spent together).
3. Personal service, rest and recreation for the mother herself (this

included activities of an exceedingly wide range, from a manicure, to reading the daily paper, to napping, to bathing and dressing).
4. Social recreation with other than family but sometimes including family members.
5. Community work.
6. Services to friends and kinsfolk.
7. Mother's hobby.
8. Religious activities.
9. Mother's education (student mothers).
10. Employment.

Average numbers of hours per day spent in the above activities gave no picture of the actual role of any one mother—as is often true of averages. Their patterns of activity varied greatly and it was the organization and values inherent in the individual patterns that were significant.

Some highlights of the findings, of which there were too many to include all in this chapter, are summarized as follows:

1. Time spent on homemaking functions was closely related to family needs, organization, and values. Only one mother spent as little as 2 hours and 54 minutes per day on work directly concerned with service to family and home.

Mrs. A. had one child, a teen-aged boy. Her husband had just bought a store and had started in business for himself. Since he had no other employees, she spent four and a half hours every day working in the store while the boy was at school. This was her "employment," for which she was paid only in terms of family income from the business. In return for this sorely needed help, her husband had hired domestic help twice a week to do all housework except marketing and cooking. This family placed high value upon being together and upon socializing with friends. This they accomplished during the evenings and weekends, so that the daily average spent on these activities was over 3½ hours each. This left the mother less than 2 hours per day for any activity by herself and for all personal service for herself. Community and religious organizations and service for friends and relatives were cut from Mrs. A.'s schedule during this particular time of family life.

The patterns of the two mothers with the highest daily average of home and family service hours show an interesting contrast.

Mrs. B., 24 years of age, had twin sons 15 months old and a 3-month-old daughter. Her husband's salary was $1700. She spent nearly 9¾ hours per day in direct service to her family, "played" with them for 4¼ hours more, found 1¾ hours for her own personal needs, a half hour apiece during the two weeks for social and religious activities, and managed to get rest by spending nearly 10-hour nights with intermittent rises to feed and change babies. Her life was almost entirely contained within her own home.

Mrs. C. was a registered nurse who had recently given up employment to be with her 8-year-old son. Her interfaith marriage was not an entirely happy one, and her desire was to have her son identified with her own side of the family. This, and her hospital training, resulted in a program of a 10-hour-and-54-minute daily "home service" routine. The house was kept in an almost sterilized condition as were the occupants, their clothing, and their dog. Her 1¾-hour daily period of socializing with her family involved only eating well-balanced meals and watching TV. The 24-minute average of socializing with others meant taking the boy to visit his maternal grandmother; the only other activity was the 1¾ hours per day kept for herself, primarily taking short rests after a series of household chores.

Twelve of the 21 mothers had no help at all, either from domestic servants or relatives. Of these, 8 spent more than an 8-hour day on home services, and none spent fewer than 4¾ hours.

2. The amount of time spent in relaxed socializing with family bore no relation to age of family, number of children, income, or even hours of housework. The mothers who enjoyed such periods found time for them. One might say, more correctly, that they planned so as to make the time for them. These mothers apparently created an atmosphere that made other family members also enjoy such periods. There was a marked contrast, here, with other families, in that weekday dinners and most weekend meals were prolonged and social. Two other observations were made. The families that socialized together most did so least by means of watching TV programs. Also, those among them who had higher incomes, help, and older children found more time than other families for socializing with friends and relatives. It seemed that the family trait of "liking people" included both family members and others.

3. The amount of time that the mothers spent for their own personal needs and for those quiet solo moments of "restoring one's soul" was appallingly little. Especially so since this category included such a wide range of "personal services." Only three mothers had as much as three hours a day to bathe, dress, repair their clothes, have a midday snack, nap, relax, read, watch TV, and so on. Two of these mothers had only adult children, and the other had domestic help and two teen-agers who were active in school organizations. For mothers of young children, with or without help, such moments were rare and not often consecutive. One mother of three boys in the strenuous years of age, who also had a strong

sense of social, religious, and community responsibility, managed to account for an average of 36 minutes per day to take care of her own needs.

4. Daily averages of time spent socializing with friends and relatives ranged from 12 minutes to 4 hours and 6 minutes. Several distinct patterns were seen. The young mothers with preschool children, with low incomes and no help did not find much time for such activity. They talked with the neighbor over the fence, or a friend dropped in for a cup of coffee, and that comprised their "social life." Mothers in the same circumstances but in medium-income brackets lived in neighborhoods composed of other families like them. Here, after the household chores were done, several young mothers would meet together in one home with all of their children, thus pooling child care and taking advantage of adult companionship, for averages of from an hour to 2½ hours per day. Mothers of preadolescent school children found time for socializing while their youngsters were in school. For those whose children did not come home to eat in the middle of the day, "lunch with friends" was a popular activity. Evening socializing, however, was rare. In fact, there were almost no social engagements for husband and wife together in the evenings in families with preadolescent children. One exception was in the case of a woman with three of them, but with a high income, a reliable babysitter, and a strong sense of social obligation. There was rarely a dinner in the home without guests and she was also able to accept evening engagements, so that she averaged over 4 hours a day of "social life" (this added to nearly 6 hours of service to home and family, and more than two socializing with family members alone). With the adolescence of children, the rate of socializing with others increased for all income brackets. In some families most of it included the children, but in all cases the husband and wife found occasions to "escape" alone with their own friends.

5. Nine of the cases performed no community service during the two-week period. Three of these women were employed outside the home, two had very recently moved into new neighborhoods and were not yet "at home," one was living on public assistance with an "emotionally disturbed" daughter, two more had very small babies, and one of these mothers was also a college student. The last was the former registered nurse, whose situation has already been described. All of the others performed some community service, ranging from 3 minutes to 1 hour and 18 minutes per day. A general pattern emerged here, too. The mothers of younger children served by making telephone calls, baking cakes for charity

sales, and other chores which could be done at home in the course of their regular routine. The other mothers were much more active outside the home as chauffeurs, PTA and Scout workers, Red Cross aides, and so on. The mother with the most hours of community service had two grown sons. After over 5 hours of housework a day, she still had more time than any others for service to others, her own personal services, and her hobby.

6. Fifteen of the cases found some time during the two weeks to perform some service (other than social) for friends or relatives. The nature of the help was quite varied, but most of it went to relatives. Elderly parents and grandchildren were the most time-consuming recipients. One mother spent an average of 1 hour and 10 minutes a day doing "good deeds" for other than immediate family members. She was a woman who had grown up in the same community in which she now lived, knew many people in it, and had many elderly relatives living nearby. At the moment, immediate family demands upon her were decreasing in time. She thus increased her hours of aid to others and to her community.

7. Only five mothers stated that they had no hobbies. Of the other 16, only 6 of them mentioned any hobbies which would take them outside their own home. The hobbies of the other ten were of two sorts: those that added to the attractiveness of their homes, such as sewing, crocheting, painting, interior decorating, gardening, and flower arranging; and those that could be enjoyed during short intervals of quiet and relaxation, such as piano playing, reading, taking pictures of the children, listening to hi-fi recordings, making family scrapbooks, and raising African violets. In spite of their reports of having such hobbies, however, only three mothers had any time to spend on them during the recorded weeks. A woman with two small children spent an average of 18 minutes every evening crocheting after the youngsters were in bed. Another, with school-age children, found half an hour a day to hook a rug. The third, with older children, was readying her garden for the winter and spent half an hour a day on it. Thirteen mothers found no time for such indulgence.

8. Religious activities were reported by ten of the mothers. All of these attended Sunday morning church services with the father and/or the children. Three more mothers drove the children to Sunday School and back. Two others commented that the family usually went to church together on Sundays but did not during these two weeks for specified reasons. One was a family emergency and the other, the weekend visit of friends. The other six made no mention of church attendance and none of the mothers reported

any during weekdays. Seven of the mothers, however, supervised the saying of bedtime prayers by the children daily.

9. Only two of the mothers were pursuing formalized education. Their life patterns were quite different.

Mrs. D., 22 years old, was married to a medical student. They had an 11½-month-old son. She was finishing her senior year at college under circumstances unusually fortunate in such a situation. Though her husband earned only $682 a year, the D.'s lived with his parents, where they gave "partial help" including a nursemaid for the child, and a cleaning woman who also did the ironing. Mrs. D. had the shortest waking day of all the cases, was second lowest in hours spent on service to home and family, spent over 4 hours a day socializing with friends and family, and 4 hours and 24 minutes a day in the classroom and in studying. Religious, community and other service activities were not on her schedule.

In contrast was the second case.

Mrs. E. was a registered nurse with one son, 15. Gainful employment accounted for 4 hours and 24 minutes a day and "homework" the same amount of time. Another 2 hours and 48 minutes were spent in the classroom and in studying for a master's degree in nursing. Mrs. E. also spent nearly 4 hours daily socializing with family and friends, and managed a few minutes of community and other service daily. Only three other mothers had a longer waking day than did Mrs. E.

10. Of the five mothers who were gainfully employed, only one spent appreciably less time on "homework" than on the job, and she had more domestic help than any of the others. Four of these five mothers had waking days of slightly over or under 17 hours. In these cases there seemed to be an emphasis upon "making up to the family" for the hours spent in employment, for all of them recorded more hours socializing with family than was average for the whole group of mothers. The reasons for employment of the women were these. One was filling in, in a family emergency; two, a widow and a divorcee, were the supporting heads of their families; another had resumed her "career" upon the adolescence of her only child; and the last took a chauffeuring job to supplement her husband's $5000 income, which seemed to them insufficient for a family of four.

The mothers in this study represent the kinds of parents who are *not* contributing to juvenile delinquency in their children. What roles such mothers fill, how they distribute their time, and what their values are concerning the relative merits of their various activities may indicate some successful patterns of functioning in

America at the present time. Certain few generalizations may be made about the group as a whole.

Except in one case, where the mother was very young, new to motherhood, and still a student, these people were primarily family-oriented and adjusted their time with that prime value in mind. In the exceptional case, it was obvious that the in-laws were still maintaining the role of parents during temporary emergency. This, too, is a parental function.

Wherever the needs of the family were greatest (young children, low finances, current family problems, lack of other help, etc.), the mothers spent least time for and by themselves. Except where the pressures were extreme, they did not necessarily curtail social life with family and others. Employed mothers, and ones with very demanding preschool children, went out of their way to find time for such activities, though the latter could not spend as much with friends as the former. It was also apparent that the social life of husband and wife together suffered with the presence of young children and became more active as the children grew in independence. It would seem that a second value of the mothers was relaxed socializing with "people," including family members. This implies an attempt at family "togetherness," a sharing of family recreation, and a community of friendship with others which, among other things, is a means of social control. It may also imply that mothers feel they can be better mothers if they can manage such periods of recreation. Their days were long; their functions varied; their lives complex, often hectic. Perhaps the conscientious modern American mother needs to seek relaxation from nervous strain more than an earlier type of mother did from heavier physical work in a more placid world.

These parents were community-conscious. Those who performed no such services during the two weeks had very clear family reasons for not doing so. For the others there was a very clear pattern. Service to the community increased as family demands decreased. The fact is, however, that only one mother gave over an hour a day to the community, and most of them measured such service in minutes. This points to a current question asked by many parents whose communities make many demands upon them and who feel somewhat shamed by not being more civic-minded. They wonder what they should do. The mothers in this study have answered the question for themselves. They give for the community what they can after family needs and recreation are taken care of. To the community this might indicate that the soliciting of such services might be, successfully, adjusted to specific families, in terms of types of service and amount of time requested. Ordinarily, it is the mothers of school-age children upon whom the greatest demands are made by the community. There may be other kinds of women and mothers who could serve more and as well.

The mothers in this study did not seek employment or higher education "in spite of" their families. In every case in which the mother worked or went to school there were very adequate provisions made for the children, and in most cases the employment was either necessary or thought of as benefiting the family. In no case were young children left alone, and with the exception of time spent normally in school, none of them had to be accommodated by any other agency while their parent was at work. This might, perhaps, serve as a guide to the many women college students who want a categorical answer to the question "Should we continue school or work after our children arrive?"

After examining the 21 schedules in the light of discussions on the waning functions of the family, one thing would seem clear. If the only remaining functions are biological, affectional, and socializing, the term *socializing* covers a multitude of activities not usually considered under that heading. The most time-consuming function of the mothers, "Service to home and family," includes not merely the routine housekeeping chores of shopping, cooking, washing, cleaning, mending, and so on, but also many hours of chauffeuring, conferring with teachers, overseeing homework, taking children to doctors and dentists, attending sick children, patching up wounds, disciplining and so on *ad infinitum*.

The average time for all mothers spent on counseling children was three hours a week, in spite of the fact that our sample included babies and adult children. Some of this counseling concerned discipline. It is quicker to spank, but these mothers "talked it over" instead. One mother described such an hour spent with her son in this way: "He is apt to be rather grumpy around home, especially if things don't go the way *he* wants them to go. It means a more tactful approach on so many things, and if things are presented right there isn't a better little worker. But his personality definitely requires more patience on our part." Most of the maternal counseling, however, illustrated the kind of guidance needed by children living in a complex and individuated society. Many hours were spent trying to weigh the values of a desired activity, type of recreation or education, the best way for a child to spend money he earned, difficulties with playmates, dating behavior. This sort of guidance was not confined to the younger children. Married ones brought their problems to parents for discussion, and one mother wrote, "My husband and I spent the whole evening talking over the complications of the latest love affair with the 20-year-old son." It seemed clear that both modern theories of childrearing and the nature of our society have increased the importance of the parental function of guidance.

SOME PROBLEMS OF THE MODERN AMERICAN MOTHER

Although the role of the good homemaker has become more complex and demanding of nervous energy, her status in that role has not been rated high by the society. The term "only a housewife" is a familiar one. A penalty that women have had to pay for their "emancipation" is that if they do not use it they are often considered to be shirking an important responsibility. One mother, for instance, had been working for two years on the problem of getting her twin sons into college. Along with the usual routine of caring for a family of six, she had seen to it that the twins got a remedial-reading course, she sent for and examined dozens of catalogues, filled in as many application blanks, drove the boys hundreds of miles to visit various colleges and the deans of admission. Finally, the boys were accepted into a college of their choice. While checking upon a questionnaire which was sent to them, their mother noted that both boys had written "Mother's Occupation—Nothing."

At the same time the society's expectations of her role have become greater in at least two ways. The first has been very aptly described by Dr. Margaret Mead who feels that through the pressure of advertising the housekeeper is expected to keep up to standards never thought of before.

> She doesn't give the sort of party where she is admired because of the heaps of food that she has ostentatiously prepared, but instead she is admired just in proportion to the way she "looks as if it had taken her no time at all." As our factories move towards the ideal of eliminating human labour, our home ideals have paralleled them; the successful home-maker to-day should always look as if she had neither done any work nor would have to do any; she should produce a finished effect effortlessly, even if she has to spend all day Saturday rehearsing the way in which she will serve an effortless Sunday-morning breakfast. The creativity that is expected of her is a creativity of management of an assembly-line, not of materials lovingly fashioned into food and clothes for children.[15]

[15] Mead, *op. cit.*, p. 333.

To the extent that she is successful in this respect, the effort that she puts into it is apt to be underestimated by others. The second heightened expectation is one that she shares with school teachers, who have been complaining recently that their role is now supposed to include that of psychologist, psychiatrist, policeman, health officer, crime-prevention officer, referee, educational theorist, sociologist, and so on. The same is true of the mother, and perhaps to a greater extent.

Added to this, there is evidence that education for women in the recent past has not been designed so as to ameliorate these problems. College-graduated women have themselves expressed the opinion that college gave them "culture" but did not prepare them, in skills or in attitudes, for the parent role which has become their life's work.[16] They graduate expecting to be "outstanding women" and find themselves "bogged down" in motherhood.

The combination of these facts causes resentment, uncertainty, or a sense of unworthiness and failure in many mothers, none of which feelings are aids to healthful child rearing. In some mothers, it produces a confusion of values that results in neglect of children. One such case is Mrs. Adams, a civic worker *par excellence* who always knows the latest in current events, literature, science, and the opera, but has two petty-thieving, unhappy, and undernourished children. Other mothers, who know Mrs. Adams' family only casually, admire her greatly and wonder why they cannot organize their lives as she does.

THE ROLES OF FATHER

Roles of mother and father have always been regarded as serving complementary functions in the family. The roles, however, have not been the same at all times nor in all societies, as has been indicated in previous pages in respect to the mother's role. Although the mother, as the key person in the family, has been the subject of much interest for students of the family, the father has received less attention. It is true, nevertheless, that his role, too, changes as a society changes; that he has been affected also

[16] John Willig, "Class of '34 (Female) Fifteen Years Later," *The New York Times Magazine*, June 12, 1949, pp. 10 ff.; Mirra Komarovsky, *Women in the Modern World: Their Education and Their Dilemmas*, Little, Brown and Company, Boston, 1953; Simone de Beauvoir, *The Second Sex*, Alfred A. Knopf, New York, 1953; Lawrence K. Frank and Mary Frank, *How to Be a Woman*, Bobbs-Merrill Company, New York, 1954; Lucius F. Cervantes, *And God Made Man and Woman*, Henry Regnery Company, Chicago, 1959; and Betty Friedan, *The Feminine Mystique*, W. W. Norton and Company, New York, 1963.

by the individuating process; and that as the mother's behavior in family life alters, so must the father's if the conplementary relationship is to be maintained. Consideration will subsequently be given to: (1) the status of the father; (2) his primary function as seen by the society; (3) changes in the role and functions of the father; (4) certain aspects of father-child relationships; (5) increasing expectations of the father role; and (6) parental roles and social change.

FATHER, THE FORGOTTEN MAN

One of the most striking changes for the American father as the traditional family has changed in form is the way in which society as a whole regards his place in family life. Once he was the most significant figure in the family, the head of the household in all important matters. Roman law gave him control over his wife and children. In the event of crises or problems, he was the decision maker. If conflict arose between a family member and the society, the father was the person called upon as responsible for the behavior. Though the legal power of the "paterfamilias" over his family members weakened in time, the tradition of the father as authority was passed down from the Romans to the British, and hence became part of early American life.

Today, his situation is much altered. Every aspect of social change discussed earlier in this chapter has tended to produce a less obvious and less potent position in the family for the male parent. As women have assumed a stronger and more active role, the man's has seemed to decline correspondingly as concerns family life.

This has had considerable effect on the way in which the society regards the father. Advertisers, appreciating that it is women who do most of the buying for their homes, carefully attempt to catch the female eye and interest in the area of household purchases. "Women's magazines" crowd the newsstands. Their content covers all aspects of homemaking, childrearing, and family relationships. For men, magazines deal chiefly in sports, science, and do-it-yourself projects. If a child gets into trouble at school, it is rarely that the father is called upon by the school authorities. The mother has become the important contact to the extent that if she does not care to inform her husband of the problem he may remain entirely ignorant of it. Parent-teacher associations and other family-community organizations have been largely populated by mothers and until recently have made little attempt to draw the attendance of fathers. Child-guidance clinics, particularly those operating through the concepts of psychiatric therapy, have dealt almost exclusively with the mother and child and have done the father and the family great injustice by considering him and his relation to his family only as it has been reported by his wife and child. Though there is a plethora of scientific and pseudoscientific books intended to educate women for their roles as wives and mothers, there is a lack of such materials for husbands and fathers. Except in the books on sex techniques and methods of infant care which are written for both sexes, the male has been largely ignored. Such a glaring omission was noted by the psychiatrist Dr. O. Spurgeon English and Constance J. Foster in 1951, when they published a book entitled *Fathers Are Parents, Too.*[17] Even before then World War II served to remind students of the family that fathers were an important part of the group relationship. Suddenly, so many men were taken away from their families. Hundreds of boys became fathers, precipitately. Not a few had children born whom they never saw for a year or more while the men were overseas. Father's presence had been rather taken for granted, but his absence and subsequent return to his family were noted with interest.[18] From that time on there has been a slowly growing attention given to fathers in both scientific and popular literature. As is the case with mother, the current opinions vary widely as to what is happening to the role and functions of the father, and as to the results of the changes to him, to his wife, to their children, and to the society. The picture is confused, but Father at least has a place in it.

FATHER'S FUNCTION—BREADWINNER

Available evidence points to the fact that the prime duty of a father is regarded to be the support of his family financially. Various studies have indicated that the male parent, the family members, and the society in general concur in this feeling. Dr. Evelyn Millis Duvall writes: "Now as always, a man is expected to be the primary breadwinner and set up his little family in the style to

17 O. Spurgeon English, M.D., and Constance J. Foster, *Fathers Are Parents, Too,* G. P. Putnam's Sons, New York, 1951.

18 See: Virginia Van Meter Underwood, "Student Fathers with Their Children," *Marriage and Family Living,* Summer, 1949, p. 101; Rex A. Skidmore, Therese L. Smith, and Delbert L. Nye, "Characteristics of Married Veterans," *Marriage and Family Living,* Summer, 1949, pp. 102–104; Lois Meek Stolz, *Father Relations of War-Born Children,* Stanford University Press, Stanford, California, 1954.

which he wants them to become accustomed."[19] In a study of 416 adolescent boys who were questioned as to whether they expected their future wives to work, over three-fourths of the answers were an unqualified "No." Only one in eight responded in the affirmative.[20] Another investigation of 85 fathers by depth interview concluded that "the concept of the father as one who makes material provision for his family appears to be basic to thinking about what the father's role is. . . . It ranked first in discussion of 'concept' and second in discussion of father's own performance and in his advice to future fathers." In relating the findings of the study to other literature on this subject, the author wrote:

At first glance, the reiteration of this function by so many fathers of this study might seem to identify it as one common only to modern urbanized man, reinforced as it is by the writings of modern authors. Among others, Parsons . . . writes that the kinship system of modern industrial society is characterized by the "relatively isolated conjugal family" in which wife and children depend upon the occupational status of husband and father for their own status and income. Social status itself hinges on "earning a living" in "an approved occupational role." . . . Failure to have an adequate job, "earn a living," and thus to provide for the family, may have consequences that go beyond loss of status. In view of the "alteration in basic masculine role in the direction of occupation," . . . the husband and father does not measure up to our accepted notion of what a man should be when he fails in this "fundamental" function. . . . Thus, Parsons observes that to be an economic provider is "virtually the only way to be a real man in our society." . . . Such a man is thought of as "real," "normal," . . . and more matured and experienced than his wife. . . . Hollingworth expresses a similar view when he writes that "in the course of time a man tends to become his occupation." . . .

Yet, students of social organization among human and animal communities assure us that "nurturing behavior" was unique to the human male as long ago as the dawn of human history. They take special pains to point out that such behavior is distinctively "human." . . .

Thus, when the fathers of this study placed emphasis on the function of economic provider, they were not merely giving expression to the approved stereotype of the "basic masculine role" in modern urban industrial society, but to a historical function that is peculiar to the human male.[21]

[19] Evelyn Millis Duvall, *Family Development,* J. B. Lippincott Company, Philadelphia, 1957, p. 197.

[20] Raymond Payne, "Adolescents' Attitudes Toward the Working Wife," *Marriage and Family Living,* November, 1956, pp. 345–348.

[21] Ruth Jacobson Tasch, "The Role of the Father in the Family," *Journal of Experimental Education,* June, 1952, p. 348. The author's quotations are from: Talcott Parsons, "Age and Sex in the Social Structure of the U.S.," *American Sociological*

Deeply rooted social tradition as well as the exigencies of present-day life, then, seem to make the idea of the "adequate husband and father" also that of "the main family provider."

The majority of American fathers are fulfilling this function. There are the others, however, who do not; and their number cannot be easily estimated for they are of many types. The department of public assistance in just one state reported a 1-month payment of 2½ million dollars for families whose fathers had deserted them. The courts often find it difficult to do more than "order" support from divorced fathers. Some men cannot find gainful employment; others will not and much prefer to depend upon the salary or income of wife and children. Then, too, there is a growing number of young marriages in which one of two things happens. The couple is supported by their own families, or the husband is "treated" to an education by his young wife. If it is true that social tradition about fathers' function is still strong, then these fathers are to some extent seen by themselves and others as failures.

FATHER'S DOMESTIC ROLE

There are two different conceptions at the present time as to what the father's role actually should be in respect to domestic duties while he is not at his place of gainful employment. The traditional conception is that of a definite division of labor between male and female. The man must not be expected to do what is considered as "woman's work." The companionate conception is quite different. The man and wife are to be helpmates to each other in all areas of life. Responsibilities should be shared not on a sex-delineated basis but according to the most efficient, healthy, and pleasurable organization of the family's life.

The first concept, the traditional, is a heritage from the past. It was strong when father was head of the family business, when families were large, and domestic servants available. Under such circumstances there were a number of females available (older daughters, female relatives, hired help) so that the mother need

---

Review, October, 1942, pp. 604–616; "The Social Structure of the Family," in R. N. Anshen (ed.), *The Family: Its Function and Destiny*, Harper & Brothers, New York, 1949, pp. 173–201 (revised edition: Harper & Row, New York, 1959); H. L. Hollingworth, in C. M. Morgan, *The Attitudes and Adjustment of Recipients of Old Age Assistance in Upstate and Metropolitan New York*, Archives of Psychology, no. 214, Columbia University Press, New York, 1937; and S. Zuckerman, *Functional Affinities of Man, Monkeys and Apes*, Harcourt, Brace and Company, New York, 1933.

not ask the men and older boys to help very much with household chores and routine child care. Their job was the work that supported the family.

Now, the traditional concept is being questioned by many who see the emergence of the companionate role in the family. Not only does this make for closer relationships and better understanding in the home, they say, but the more complex role of the mother outside of the home requires assistance from her husband at a time when other sources of help have decreased. The depression of the 30s and World War II both made their effects felt in the changing attitudes of some men about household chores. With incomes depressed, many fathers considered it quite manly to help their wives at home. War veterans who had learned to peel potatoes, darn socks, and do their own wash under circumstances in which they were considered heroes, often felt no hesitation about continuing these duties at home—and some were interested enough to learn and teach their wives new short cuts in housekeeping. A noted family-life consultant writes:

> Now that men have a reasonably short working week (as compared with 60 or more hours in the nineteenth-century work week), they have more time at home. Household tasks in the modern home, with its electrified equipment and packaged goods, are less arduous, more fun, and require less technical knowledge. Any man who wants to can whip up a tasty meal in today's kitchen. And many of them do. Now with wives out of the home carrying the variety of roles characteristic of modern women, husbands are finding a new place for themselves in the family.[22]

There is not 100 percent agreement as to whether this change in father's role is desirable or healthy. One example of remonstrance against it in popular literature is an article entitled "Husbands: The New Servant Class," in which the author states the results of three polls as follows:

> Crosley says that more than a third of the husbands in several of our northeastern states do the dishes, clean house and look after the children, and more than half of them do a lot of the shopping. The Gallup poll insists that 62 per cent of American husbands are intimate with dishwater and about 40 per cent help with the cooking. Kenneth Fink, director of the Princeton Research Service, has discovered that in New York 87 per cent of the young men from 21 to 29 help with the housework, but there seems to be some slight advantage in growing older—only 70 per cent of men over 45 are part-time women.[23]

[22] Duvall, *op. cit.*, p. 164.
[23] Russell Lynes, *Look*, December 14, 1954.

The attitude of the writer is one of frank disapproval of "the man in the apron." He believes this a weakness, of man's own making, but taken advantage of by women who demand "a husband and also a part-time wife." Attitudes of students of family life have been summarized by Dorothy Barclay, New York *Times* columnist.[24] One group decries the demasculinizing of the father, believes that the pattern will be passed on to their sons, and feels it creates a confusion of sex roles in children. The other group see these changing roles (of both husband and wife) as complementary adjustments to modern civilization which should not be judged on the basis of what was "right" in a different sort of world. Children, they say, are bound to reflect these changes as they grow up, not only because of the model but because of the kind of life they will be living. The attitudes of several hundred college students (male and female) about this role of their father have been found in their written family case records.[25] They complain mildly about the father who is a good provider but will not lift his hand to any housework, and about the "lazy" mother who expects her husband to do her work when he comes home, tired, from his own. The real tirades against father, however, are reserved for the men who do not give enough economic support to afford any help for their wives, and still insist upon playing the part of the patriarch who sits and is served by his womenfolk. In the minds of these particular young men and women, this behavior is not only passé, but arbitrary and unjust. In general they look with approval upon the parents who work as a team, each helping the other as much as possible. They see this as a sign that their parents are devoted to, and happy with, each other. In the minds of these college students, such behavior also makes for good family organization and they express their intention of establishing such a pattern in their own homes when they marry.

To don the apron or not, however, is only one aspect of the father's domestic role. Another is his part in infant and child care. Here, again, the traditional conception has been that this is women's responsibility—though there have always been individual fathers who enjoyed this role and were well fitted to it. In general, though, feeding, bathing, and diapering babies had not been considered a manly art. It was also assumed that the mother should rear the young children in such a way that the disciplining, which was father's realm, would not often be necessary. Apparently, many of

24 Dorothy Barclay, "Trousered Mothers and Dishwashing Dads," *The New York Times Magazine*, April 28, 1957, p. 48.

25 Materials being gathered for a research project by the authors under the sponsorship of the William T. Carter Foundation for Child Development.

the forces which have changed some men's attitudes toward housework have led them to think differently about the childrearing function. In the Tasch study,[26] 77 of the 85 fathers reported active participation in childrearing duties; and in their advice to future fathers they indicated their attitude that this was part of the requirement of the father role. Added to this, their image of the father as guide and teacher of his children was mentioned more frequently than any other aspect of his role.[27] Representative of the findings in the studies of World War II veteran fathers are those in the Underwood sample.[28] The 20 fathers, with one child each between the ages of 2 and 5, spent a mean time of 1 hour and 11 minutes per day with their children, and 17 of them stated that they thought of their relationship with the child as guide and teacher. It was also noted that problems over child care caused these fathers their greatest "headaches." They did not read the books—which are written largely for women—and resorted to their own "experience" or that of their fathers. Better education for a generation of fathers involved in child care was clearly implied.

In the materials collected for a study of family ritual,[29] veteran student fathers of young children expressed delight in the period they set aside from their work each day at a special time in order to take over the care of their offspring. Some of them indicated that war experience had done something to their value system—that "society" came to be thought of not in terms of "things" but in good and intimate relationships with one's family. Here are some actual comments from World War II veterans concerning the effects of their service on attitudes toward the family:

> "I realize more what the family means and what the children mean in my life." "I was father to so many young kids in service that I feel I was educated to help adolescents." "I used to think I didn't want the responsibility of my family any more, but after seeing German kids wanting to eat scraps from my mess kit, I decided that I should accept the reponsibility for my own family." "I saw things that I didn't want to have happen to my family; it stabilized what I want and made me more sensible."[30]

Perhaps the coming of the atomic age has had the effect of continuing this attitude in the postwar generation. Educated young

[26] Tasch, *op. cit.*, p. 352.
[27] *Ibid.*, p. 349.
[28] Underwood, *op. cit.*
[29] James H. S. Bossard and Eleanor S. Boll, *Ritual in Family Living*, University of Pennsylvania Press, Philadelphia, 1950.
[30] Rachel Ann Elder, "Traditional and Developmental Conceptions of Fatherhood," *Marriage and Family Living*, Summer, 1949, p. 106.

people not only *say* they want more children than has been the average national pattern, but they *do* have more. J. M. Mogey of Oxford University has this comment to make:

> All the evidence available points to an increase in the participation of fathers in the activities of the household over the past two decades. . . . This newer father behavior is best described as participation, the re-integration of fathers into the conspicuous consumption as well as the child rearing sides of family life. And in a family unit where, over and above marital and mother-child relations, there also exists harmonious father-child relations, stability should ensue.[31]

He adds that the continuing baby boom is largely concentrated among the educated, urban, white-collar workers in the United States, and that such births must be desired by both partners since these people are most sophisticated about contraceptives. He feels that "A change in the position of the husband from a rigorous insistence on responsibility with its concomitant of social distance to a more active participation in domestic routines helps to explain these new developments."[32] He also foresees a continued drop in the divorce rate with this new definition of the father role.

What happens about Father's participation in childrearing as the child grows to school age and older? This question deserves much more empirical study than has been devoted to it for the answer is important. There is some slight indication that Father's involvement decreases. Philip Wylie, the famous social critic, looks with a stern eye at the American father and writes: "There are 168 hours in a week. The average man spends about 40 of them at work. Allow another 15 hours for commuting time, lunch, overtime, etc. Then set aside 56 hours, eight each night, for sleep. That adds up to 111 hours—leaving Dad 57 hours for eating, relaxing, or whatever he wants to do. Surely in those 57 hours he could find time to be a father to his children."[33] To indicate that Dad does not, he cites an experiment by Gordon Schroeder. Three hundred seventh- and eighth-grade boys kept an accurate record for two weeks of the time spent together by father and son. The average time was found to be seven and a half minutes per week.

If this picture of the decline of the childrearing function as children grow is a true one, there may be two reasons for it. First, it has been said that it is not the initial cost of a baby but the upkeep that is expensive. Young fathers, with enthusiasm about having

[31] J. M. Mogey, "A Century of Declining Parental Authority," *Marriage and Family Living*, August, 1957, p. 238.
[32] *Ibid.*, p. 239.
[33] Philip Wylie, "American Men Are Lousy Fathers," *The American Weekly*, November 27, 1955.

babies rather than things, come to discover in later years that children do require many things. One does not have to look far to see the obviously overworked father, struggling to keep up with the financial demands of his maturing family. He has little time and less physical and nervous energy for "fathering" them. Secondly, wholesale participation by Dad in childrearing is rather new. Methods of childrearing are more intricate than they used to be because of "scientific insistence." Children themselves become increasingly complicated mechanisms as they age. A father then, who enjoys, and feels competent in, the care of a cuddly and relatively uncomplicated young child, may be completely unable to cope with the guide and teacher function later. Since many mothers express a growing sense of inadequacy in this respect, it is understandable if the same is true of their husbands whose training has not been so heavily directed toward parenthood as has their wives'.

INTRAFAMILY ROLE RELATIONSHIPS

Although the roles of mothers and fathers have been treated separately here, they do not operate separately. Family interaction is a *network* of relationships, and what changes one person affects the whole group. Several aspects of this interlocking nature of role changes will therefore be suggested.

Parents and Children

There is little question that, as production has been removed from the home, Mother has assumed a more dominant role in it. She is the one who is on hand during most of the childrearing process, and being there, she must make all the hundreds of quick decisions that are required during this process. Eddie Cantor illustrated how this operates when he said, "I make all the major decisions for my family, and my wife makes all the minor ones; but there hasn't been a major decision in the past 20 years." This means that in many families the mother becomes the authoritarian parent, and not the buffer between the children and the patriarch, as pictured in Clarence Day's *Life with Father.* That this is a general trend in our society is suggested by Dr. Campisi's study of the Italian family, in which patriarchy is a strong tradition.[34] His con-

[34] Paul J. Campisi, "Ethnic Family Patterns: The Italian Family in the United States," *American Sociological Review,* May, 1948, pp. 444–445.

clusions are that after two generations in the United States there is only a slight survival of the once supreme dominance of the Italian father.

This decline in authority is especially true in the home with young children since so much of decision making for them requires prompt action. One cannot wait till father comes home to decide whether the toddler may go out in the snowstorm, to play with the neighbor's children, or what to do about the ink bottle that is poised over the living-room rug. One acts, immediately. The rearing of small children is composed of thousands of such details that require authority and discipline. Such being the case, the mother who is there attends to such details in the way that she sees fit, and through much experience may become, or fancy herself, as an expert in this respect. Some very good mothers and loving wives have fitted so well into this role of decision maker and discipline dispenser that they come to regard their husbands as "interfering" when they take a hand in such matters. As one mother put it:

> I guess I got used to being boss when the kids were little. Now that they are older I just keep on helping them decide, or telling them, what they can or cannot do. After all, I'm with them much more than Dave is and they naturally come to me. The children and I talk things over during the day, then Dave comes home for dinner and disagrees with some plan they've made. It annoys the children, because he doesn't know all the pros and cons that we talked over, and we have to go all through it again. I must admit it annoys me sometimes, too. I wish he would just trust my judgment. But then, a father really ought to have *some* say in what his children can do.

Apparently, fathers feel they should, too. In the Tasch study "the traditional concept of the father as 'head of the house,' the person in whom authority resides, the law-giver, arbiter, and disciplinarian, was given a good deal of support . . .[35] Certain doctors, clergymen, and social scientists agree that paternal authority should be maintained to a considerable extent for the health of the family relationships and the development of the children. Dr. Strecker's book on "Momism" is a case in point.[36] Too much mother domination is creating a group of weaklings among the lads in America. Little recognition has been given to the fact that there may be serious effects for daughters, too; but the authors feel that the influence of male authority is exceedingly important for girls in respect,

35 Tasch, *op. cit.*, p. 350.

36 Edward A. Strecker, M.D., *Their Mothers' Sons*, J. B. Lippincott Company, Philadelphia, 1946.

among other things, to dating, marriage choice, and marital and occupational adjustment. Male authority may be discounted at present in some homes, but it certainly cannot be in the outer society. Rabbi Robert L. Katz expresses with strength his opinion on the subject of fathers' authority.

The power of the father has been broken. But we ourselves must still learn how to be fathers and to fulfill many of the functions traditionally assigned to the father. We have so long protested the abuses of fatherly authority and we are so imbued with the traumas of the father-son relationship that we have been all too prone to neglect its creative and necessary side. In psychiatric literature, too . . . the fatherly role has been greatly overshadowed by the motherly role and the stress on the emotional security of good mother-child relationships. . . . A religious view holds out the possibility of the father's combining authority and love. It emphasizes his role in helping the child to achieve a sense of integrity and individuality at the same time that he learns to participate in the community. There is no irreconcilable conflict between these two goals. The good father is the symbol, the embodiment of this type of personality. He gives to his son an example to follow, he is the father and the teacher. . . ."[37]

The results of changes in authority roles to parent-child relationships is not entirely clear, but there are some indications that authority provokes hostility and conflict. Psychiatric literature has supported this notion for some time, but more recent sociological studies have indicated that same thing. One showed that "a much higher percentage of parents who are more dominant than their spouse is reported to have conflict relationships with their children." This does not hold merely on the Freudian principle of mother-daughter and father-son hostility, but in any combination (father-daughter and mother-son, also). The author of this study comments that this would result in a society like ours because of our attitudes about authority itself, whereas it might not in such a situation as the traditional Chinese family where a great respect for, and subservience to authority, is a strong tradition.[38] The problem of authority without conflict and rebellion, then, may be a particularly difficult one for the American family with its traditions of individualism, permissiveness, and "democracy" in human relations. Another, a study of college girls' conflicts with their parents, revealed that father-child difficulties centered around choice of date and mate; but mother-child conflict covered so many life areas that

[37] Rabbi Robert L. Katz, "The Role of the Father," *Mental Hygiene Quarterly*, October, 1957, pp. 519–520.

[38] Yi-Chuang Lu, "Parental Role and Parent-Child Relationship," *Marriage and Family Living*, November, 1952, pp. 294–297.

it seemed like a general unrest in relationship.[39] This may be another price the American woman must pay for her increased status, particularly in a society whose traditional philosophy is to rebel against authority.

One analysis of hundreds of family case records has revealed certain authority patterns as they actually exist in families at the present time. In one, the mother attempts to maintain the father's authority by saving the disciplining of children for him whenever he is at home. According to the children's reactions, the plan is not too healthy. Their comments range from "I was always scared for Dad to come home," to "I didn't have much respect for him. Mother told him what to do and he did. But he didn't know what it was all about." In patterns where one parent or the other clearly dominated, children seemed, for the most part, resentful of the one parent and sorry for, or scornful of, the other. There was an exception to this attitude if one parent took over the authority because the other was actually incapable of it. There, children seemed to sense that some authority was needed, and they had some appreciation for it, especially if the father was taking over because of an ineffectual mother. Very much resented was the arbitrary, autocratic father who insisted upon being the head of the household whether he was fitted for it or not. Finally, children reacted most agreeably in cases where they felt that both parents shared equally in the command of the home.

In family situations in which the father is freed from the tyrannical role of the patriarch, he has more opportunity to develop that of "pal" to his children. In the very recent past, and to some extent today, this is a role which has been applauded and encouraged by "experts" and mass media.

Some voices have been raised in protest over this role. Dr. Otto Pollak questions whether the child needs a pal as much as a father figure, and if the pal role may not interfere with normal Oedipal development.[40] Rabbi Katz writes: "At best, dad or pop is the captain of the team. Sometimes he is cast in the role of a gray-haired sibling. Less jealous for the authority and responsibility of his office than for the freedom and self-expression of his children, the modern father chafes under the burden of his increasing years, envies the youth of his children, and struggles to remain their peer."[41]

The attitudes of children toward the pal role seem to be that

39 Margaret S. Wilson, *Conformity and Nonconformity of College Girls to the Standards of Their Parents,* University of Pennsylvania dissertation, 1952.

40 Otto Pollak, *Social Science and Psychotherapy for Children,* Russell Sage Foundation, New York, 1952.

41 Katz, *op. cit.,* p. 518.

though they enjoy "romping with Dad" when they are small, the thing can be overdone. Adolescent children prefer to look upon their father as a man rather than as a perennial Boy Scout and often feel shamed by the antics of the latter. Continuing companionship they do enjoy, but not as a pal; nor are they always agreeable to much "participation" with teenage activities. Yet, a pattern has been set which may be difficult for Dad to change. A common complaint of such fathers is that their children seem to be growing away from them—when their children are wishing that Dad would grow up.

Dorothy Barclay, in writing of the high-pressured city father whose "pal" activities with children almost must be artificially produced, says: "A father needn't be expected to play baseball with 'the gang' every Saturday to prove his belief in the value of vigorous action. The way he meets a request for a new ball or glove, for a tennis racket or a book of tickets to a nearby pool, will reflect his real valuation of children's sports activities."[42] And a college student comments: "I think this business of parents being pals came up because kids need someone to play with and there are so few playmates around. I think it would be better if parents had more babies and saw to it that the kids had nice children next door. Then the parents could relax and just be parents."

All of these writers agree that although the amount of time given to a relationship is meaningful, the quality of it is much more important. The quality, they believe, of the father's role should be that of a good father and not just that of a good pal.

With fathers working away from home and mothers increasingly taking jobs outside of it, a question has arisen about the effects on children when both parents are absent during much of the day. Many studies have predicted dire consequences. In recent years, however, because of refinements in the methods of examining this situation, conclusions are more specific. Maternal employment is not a single unit in family life but is made up of a cluster of significant factors. One of these is the arrangements that are made for substitute supervision. Another is the meaning and value of her work to the mother. There are mothers who insist that they are happier, more creative and better family members when they can broaden their interests and knowledge through outside employment—and there are children who agree with them. Still another matter to be considered is the reason for the mother's working. Some mothers must work because the father is not fulfilling his

[42] Dorothy Barclay, *Understanding the City Child*, Franklin Watts, New York, 1959, p. 131.

role as provider; some find outside employment because they dislike the mothering job; some wish to earn wages for some definite family goal. When Mrs. Gregg, after years of being a housewife, took a position so that her 16-year-old daughter could be put through college, the results were a closer unity in the family. Her efforts were appreciated, her problems understood, all members of the family came to her aid as they never had before, and the children suddenly became more mature and independent. The age of the children is also an important factor in maternal employment. Ordinarily, children who are of school age experience less psychological shock when mothers leave home, although there are also cases in which a very small child is better off with a warm mother substitute than with an unwilling mother.

Unfortunately, the opportunities to consider the weight of all these aspects of maternal employment are unequal between the mother who *has* to work and the one who does so for other reasons. The first seldom has the resources to time her work to the demands of her children and to find an adequate substitute for their care. Added to the problem of her absence, there is often a broken home and very low socioeconomic status. Until the depression of the 1930's, preschool group care of children was largely in the form of nurseries for the offspring of families of some means who wished to have their youngsters "socialized" early. Since that time the need for all kinds of day-care centers for children who would otherwise be inadequately cared for has increased greatly, and the need has increased much faster than have the facilities. It is in such situations that children suffer most from the absence of their parents.[43]

Husband-Wife Relations

Whatever affects the relationship between their parents has a direct influence on children. There are at least three results of changing roles which should be mentioned here.

First, the wife of today, especially if she is a housewife, often stands in position to determine the relative importance of her husband in the eyes of the whole family. What she does for them is obvious. What he does, is not. She takes them to school, to the doctor, feeds them; and it is she who is called when they get into trouble. He leaves home to do something that most small children cannot even visualize; and somehow, miraculously, the things that Mother buys for them get paid for. In the middle of this situation

[43] Eleanor Stoker Boll, "The Family and Society," WAY *Forum*, April, 1963, pp. 26–29.

is Mother. If she is the kind who wants her children for herself and wants to be the most-admired person in the family, she does have some opportunity to build herself up in the children's eyes and to let their father be a relatively shadowy figure on the periphery. An example was the wife of a renowned juvenile court judge. From the moment of their birth, the mother spent most of her time playing with and loving her youngsters. When their father was at home and would talk about his work or some honor that had come his way, she immediately changed the subject to something involving herself and the children. Before long, he became the silent member of the family. His children grew up thinking of him only as the person who paid the bills and who complained when they were too high. Never did his son and daughter have any conception of how hard he worked, the great service he performed, or how much he was revered by many people, until they grew old enough to understand this for themselves.[44] There is hardly a need to describe the opposite kind of situation, in which a wife deliberately builds up an important image of her husband to the children who see relatively little of him and who would be unable to grasp, by themselves, his specific role in family life.

Second, the separation in space of the roles of housewife and employed father has sometimes had the effect of glorifying the other one's job and creating dissatisfaction with one's own. This attitude can be deepened if the connotation of "housewife" is a person who has little to do except to push buttons and turn switches.

Mr. Z., for example, arrives home at 6 P.M. on a torrid August day and finds Mrs. Z. and the children waiting for him on the terrace where an evening breeze has just sprung up. He looks at his wife and thinks, "What a life! Home all day in the cool suburbs and no endless routine of deskwork."

His wife looks at him and thinks, "What wouldn't I give for a few days freedom from constant chores and chaos, and to sit in an air-conditioned office with nice clean paperwork."

Finally, to the extent that the husband of a working wife joins with her in satisfying the demands of the family while they are at home, they may both have a greater appreciation of each other's roles. She understands his life because she herself is subject to some of its rigors and pressures. He sees that running a family can be dull, chaotic, challenging, and tremendously rewarding. The children see them as a unity of parents with roles which are tightly interlocked.

[44] Eleanor Stoker Boll, *The Man That You Marry,* Macrae Smith Company, Philadelphia, 1963, pp. 161–164.

SOCIETY'S EXPECTATIONS

The expectation of our society as to parental roles, especially the roles of those who are not financially depressed, can create great pressures and feelings of inadequacy for both father and mother.

The ideal of the good father includes the good businessman, the good family man, and the good community man. An article on "The New Burdens of Masculinity"[45] points out a change in expectations of father as a breadwinner. He still carries burdens surviving from the past but also has new ones created by a modern age, through emphases on occupational mobility, the importance of education, vocational adjustment, and new traits such as "politicking" which are required for high-level positions. At the same time, "men are now expected to demonstrate the manipulative skill in interpersonal relations formerly reserved for women under the headings of intuition, charm, tact, coquetry, womanly wiles, etc. They are asked to bring patience, understanding, gentleness to their human dealings. Yet, with regard to women they must still be sturdy oaks."[46] They are also supposed to honor the new position of their wives without "castrating" themselves, and be heads of their families by democratic means.

At the same time, the community is reaching out increasingly for fathers. One hears comments that men are endangering their society when they leave the community largely in the hands of women. It becomes a community scandal when no father is found willing to be leader of the local Boy Scout troop or organizer for the Little League.

As has been mentioned formerly, there is a great deal of negative comment about the woman who is just a housewife and who does not fulfill herself and make her contribution in the larger society. The role of ideal mother itself, though, is considered as covering a wide range of knowledge and talents. She should be a nutritionist, pediatrician, psychologist, sociologist, expert buyer, budget wizard, philosopher, educator—among other things. Added to which, she, too, should take her place in the community. The League of Women Voters, the Bloodmobile, the PTA, and many other such organizations want her services. To the extent that she cannot spare much time from family obligations, she often feels that she is not really doing her job.

[45] Helen Mayer Hacker, "The New Burdens of Masculinity," *Marriage and Family Living*, August, 1957, pp. 227–233.

[46] *Ibid.*, p. 229.

A serious problem of parents as to their roles and functions at present is that there are no 100 percent positive answers as to what these should be in order to be most effective. Once roles were simpler and much more clearly delineated. Right or wrong, most parents felt they knew how the "good mother" and the "good father" performed. Now they are, in a sense, pioneers. There are few guideposts, and those that exist are often conflicting. Essentially each family is experimenting in a pattern of group living in an unknown land. During this process, many of them fail completely and add to the disequilibrium of the complex and changing society. At the other extreme are the notable successes, developing behavior patterns in family life which are satisfactory adjustments to the present and to social change itself. The ways these families have found are, probably, the best answers to "what are the roles and functions of modern American parents."

SUMMARY

1. Whereas the basic unit of function used to be the compact group, through a process of individuation mothers and fathers have come to function more separately in their roles as parents.

2. The changed status of women during the past century has affected the role she plays and the functions she fulfills. Some of the factors influencing her new status have been: (a) a change from the producing family to the consuming family pattern; (b) mass compulsory education and gainful employment of women; (c) the increase in laborsaving devices and decrease in size of homes; and (d) the small-family system.

3. As the society has changed, so has the nature of the historical functions of the family become altered. Some of them, such as the recreational, educational, and protective, have been partly assumed by other agencies. Others, like the affectional and socializing, have achieved greater importance. The functions of counseling and guidance have assumed great significance and are increasingly complex and difficult.

4. A study of the total activity of 21 "successful" mothers for a period of two weeks illustrates the manner in which these women are adjusting their roles and functions to present-day family life.

5. Problems are created for the mother as a parent because, though the title of "homemaker" carries low status, more is expected of her in that role than formerly. Not only are standards of housekeeping higher, but the mother is expected to be a director

of human relations and an expert in child development. Her education, up to the present, has not been oriented toward helping her fulfill these roles.

6. As a society changes, so must the role of the father, in order to adjust to new family needs, and also to retain the complementariness of function with the mother.

7. For some time the importance of the father role has been overshadowed by that of the mother. This is true in respect to the community as well as to those concerned with the study of, and therapy in, the family and behavior. Quite recently, there has been a growing interest in total group interaction, which has aided increasing interest in fathers' role and functions.

8. Attitudes toward the domestic role of the father have been changing, not only in respect to sharing of household chores but also as concerns early and late childrearing. Opinions vary as to the effects on children of the so-called "demasculinizing" of the male parent. The changes that have come about, however, seem to have arisen as new family situations have developed.

9. The roles of mother and father do not operate independently. Family interaction is a network of relationships, and what changes one person affects the whole group.

10. The passing of patriarchal authority and the emergence of mother control may lead to the following: (a) more conflict with the mother, (b) an accentuation of the pal role for the father.

11. The effects of maternal employment on children depend upon many factors other than the employment itself. The specific combination of them may produce results which are healthy or unhealthy.

12. Husband-wife relations are significant in the development of the children. Recent changes in parental roles may (a) give the mother a key position in building up a strong, positive image of the father or in excluding him as a family contributor, (b) cause dissatisfaction for husband and wife in their own roles and a glorifying of the other's role, (c) create more understanding of both domestic and employment roles, in the case of working wives and "domestic" husbands who are also employed.

13. Society's expectations for parental roles are broad and complex. Such expectations, if they cannot be fulfilled, can cause feelings of unworthiness in the most conscientious of parents.

SUGGESTED READINGS

Bossard, James H. S., *Social Change and Social Problems,* Harper & Brothers, 1938, chap. 25. One of the first reactions against Ogburn's theory that the American family was no longer fulfilling the historic functions. The thesis here, is that the functions are changed but not defunct.

Campisi, Paul J., "Ethnic Family Patterns," *American Sociological Review,* May, 1948, pp. 443–449. Changing roles of parents are described in the Italian family through three generations, in Italy and in the United States.

English, Spurgeon, and Constance J. Foster, *Fathers Are Parents, Too,* G. P. Putnam's Sons, New York, 1951. One of a very few books on child care and development written for fathers.

Landis, Judson, "A Re-examination of the Role of the Father as an Index of Family Integration," *Marriage and Family Living,* May, 1962, pp. 122–128. An investigation of the relationship of closeness with the father to the type of family life.

Lindbergh, Anne Morrow, *Gift from the Sea,* Pantheon Books, New York, 1957. A sensitive expression of the conflicts in the life of a loyal wife and good mother of six children.

Malinowski, Bronislaw, *The Father in Primitive Psychology,* W. W. Norton & Company, 1927. An interesting comparison with discussions of fathers' roles in modern America.

Ogburn, William F., and Meyer F. Nimkoff, *Technology and the Changing Family,* Houghton Mifflin, Boston, 1955. A thorough discussion of a phase of social change that has affected both roles and functions of the family.

Perry, Joseph, "The Mother Substitute of Employed Mothers," *Marriage and Family Living,* November, 1961, pp. 362–367. Three Guttman scales for measuring certain phases of children's adjustment showed no difference between that of preschool children whose mothers were employed and nonemployed.

Stolz, Lois Meek, *Father Relations of War-Born Children,* Stanford University Press, Stanford, 1954. A study of the relationship between fathers and small children who were born during the father's overseas service.

Zimmerman, Carle C., *Family and Civilization,* Harper & Brothers, New York, 1947. An historical survey of forms of family life since the rise of civilization shows a recurring cycle from cohesive to individuated family life, and relates these forms to the strength or weakness of the civilization.

CLASS AND STATUS DIFFERENTIALS

Daily Herald Copyright Photograph

PART V

THE CHILD AND THE CLASS STRUCTURE 11

Thus far, the family background of child development has been analyzed in general terms with only slight reference to those major differentiations, known as social classes, which exist in all but perhaps the most primitive societies. It is the purpose of this chapter, first, to survey briefly the nature of these differentiations in our contemporary society, and then to consider, somewhat more at length, their meaning for child development.

THE CONCEPT OF SOCIAL CLASS

Origins of Stratification

The concept of class came into the literature of sociology from economic sources and until recently has been considered chiefly in its economic implications. The differences between classes were expressed largely in terms of wealth and income, and what these have been able to command by way of goods and services. In line with this emphasis, the processes of social stratification were identified in terms of economic competition and conflict, until a considerable number of students of society, following the lead of Marx and Engels, interpreted the whole social process in terms of the class struggle. "The history of all hitherto existing society," they wrote in the *Communist Manifesto,* "is the history of the class struggle."

Because of the common assumption that social classes are primarily economic in origin and character, the findings of Landtman are significant. After examining a vast amount of anthropological material, he emphasizes rather the fundamental importance of such original factors as age, sex, and differences in personal endowments. Through the maze of ceremony and customs of various societies, he traces the rise of certain elements in the population to positions of superiority, showing how differences in personal traits break down the utopian equalities of primitive culture. Differences in wealth are of subsequent importance (1) in enabling certain classes to acquire various prestige symbols which become identifying characteristics, (2) in the acquisition of advantages which can be turned into sources of new distinction, and (3) in the transmission of class advantages from one generation to another. Wealth, in other words, tends to reinforce and to perpetuate inequalities which result from the operation of other factors.[1] More recently Davis and Moore have explained the same phenomenon in these terms: (1) to any society some functions are more important than others; (2) not all members are capable of performing these functions; (3) training for these functions requires time and self-sacrifice; (4) privileges and special rewards are required to induce the able to undergo the training and the sacrifice; (5) with access to privileges and rewards comes prestige and social inequality in the society.[2] Important in order to understand the stratification system in different countries is the fact that not all countries find the same function to be the most important. At least one report on the Soviet Union describes that "classless society" as being composed of the upper classless, the middle classless and the submerged masses. The prestige group is composed of the party and state elite and the approved group of writers, scientists, artists, and such.[3] Communism, statesmanship, science, and developing "culture" are obviously prime values in the Soviet Union. A man from the immigration service in Israel states that in his

[1] Gunnar Landtman, *The Origin of the Inequality of the Social Classes,* University of Chicago Press, Chicago, 1938.

[2] Kingsley Davis and Wilbert Moore, "Some Principles of Stratification," *American Sociological Review,* April, 1945, pp. 242–249.

[3] Flora Lewis, "Love among the Upper Classless," *The New York Times Magazine,* July 20, 1958, p. 111.

country greatest prestige and rewards go to those who are adept in the planning and managing of a relatively new experimental state. In Japan, in the seventeenth century, bankers, merchants, and traders were at the lowest status level. As Japan industrialized, the status of people in those occupations rose to near the top. Whatever the function that is stressed, the material gains acquired thereby tend to maintain the prestige and power of the group even after their role in the society has diminished in importance. In a sense then, social stratification is based upon function, reward, prestige, power, and status, relative to that of others.

Class as a Culture Concept

There is another possible way to approach the study of social classes and that is to conceive of them as selective cultural groupings, each with its identifying mode of living and habits of thought. Such a conception takes the direction of Max Weber's unfinished definition of class in which he includes the possession of economic means, an external standard of living, cultural, and recreational facilities, and the possibilities of communal action.[4] It tends to coincide with Werner Sombart's emphases upon common interests, ideology, consciousness of cohesion, and particularly ways of thinking which are representative of particular systems of economic organization.[5] It embodies Ginsberg's definition of a social class as a group of individuals who, through common consent and similarity of occupation, wealth, and education, have come to have a similar mode of life and a similar stock of ideas, feelings, attitudes, and forms of behavior and who, on any or all of these grounds, meet one another on equal terms and regard themselves, although with varying degrees of explicitness, as belonging to one group.[6] Or, put more pithily, it makes a social class "the largest group of persons whose members have intimate access to each other."[7] Hodges has noted that social scientists have explored many different areas in our country. Some of these scientists hoped to prove the nonexistence of social classes. Yet, they usually discovered a community to be divided into a number of life-style and prestige layers. People in each layer are more like each other (and more unlike others) in values, beliefs, aspirations, childrearing practices, speech and

[4] C. W. Mills and H. H. Gerth, in *Politics,* October, 1944, pp. 271–278.

[5] Werner Sombart, *Der moderne Kapitalismus,* Munich, 1924–1927.

[6] Morris Ginsberg, "Class Consciousness," in the *Encyclopaedia of the Social Sciences,* vol. III, p. 536.

[7] Allison Davis, B. B. Gardner, and Mary R. Gardner, *Deep South,* University of Chicago Press, Chicago, 1941, p. 59.

dress customs, consuming patterns, ways of spending leisure time, and many other aspects of life.[8]

A social class, thus conceived, is a cultural reality. Its identification is not an academic exercise in snobbery or a subjective evaluation, but a recognition of the fact that people live and work and play and think at different levels. The differences between classes are not merely financial or ostentatious. They encompass a wide range of social behavior. Once social classes are thought of as cultural entities the subject of the content of those cultures can be opened for objective study.

How distinct and fixed class patterns are varies a good deal from place to place and time to time. Some of the more important factors affecting this process, as identified by Cooley years ago,[9] are: (1) marked differences in the constituent parts of the population; (2) little communication and enlightenment; and (3) a slow rate of social change. Others include differences in wealth, increasing division of labor, and size of community. Generally speaking, the more a social class is segregated and isolated, the more definitely do its members tend to develop their own distinctive activities and interests. In other words, the more social classes become distinct and fixed, the more do their respective members reveal a fixity and predictability of class behavior.

THE CONTEMPORARY CLASS PATTERN IN THE UNITED STATES

Common usage has long recognized three social classes—upper, middle, and lower. This tripartite system roughly classifies the rich, the poor, and those who are in between. In 1941, Warner and his associates found this classification inadequate and divided each of the classes into two divisions: upper and lower.[10] Hollingshead found it necessary to divide at least the upper class into old families and new families when describing differences in family stability.[11] Some researchers have used a fivefold classification, or as many as they thought they discerned when studying a specific area. Still

[8] Harold M. Hodges, Jr., *Social Stratification: Class in America,* Schenkman Publishing Company, Cambridge, Massachusetts, 1964, p. 12.

[9] Charles H. Cooley, *Social Organization,* Charles Scribner's Sons, New York, 1922, pp. 217 ff.

[10] W. Lloyd Warner and Paul S. Lunt, *The Social Life of a Modern Community,* Yale University Press, New Haven, 1941.

[11] August B. Hollingshead, "Class Differences in Family Stability," *Annals of the American Academy of Political and Social Science,* November, 1950, pp. 39–46.

others insist that such groupings cannot be identified at all in our society currently.

Much of this confusion and difference of opinion results from certain distinguishing features of the American class system which can be best explained by referring back to the factors stated by Cooley.

1. There are marked differences in the constituent parts of our population, but these have been shifting. Earlier in our history large immigrations of unskilled peoples constituted lower social class groupings on an economic and ethnic basis. The separateness was stressed by religious differences. Although this situation remains to a certain extent today, successive generations of these immigrants have achieved the life style and prestige of groups higher in the stratification system. Thus, ethnic origins and religious conviction are not status determinants as decisively as they once were.

2. Because of mass education and the mass media, communication between the elements of the population is much greater than formerly. Ideas and ways of living and thinking are passed more easily from one group to another. With good communication, comes more cultural diffusion.

3. Our rate of social change is fast, and the change is continuous. This includes increasing wealth for many kinds of people, increasing division of labor (with a shift of emphasis on the importance of certain jobs and the elimination of others), and a large growth in the size of our community. This last factor has the effect of creating less uniformity in the life patterns of a social-status group. For example, if the entire elite group of a society lives in face-to-face relations with each other they tend to remain similar, or to change in similar ways. When the group is too large to interact in this manner, there come to be subdivisions and differences in behavior even though the same prestige ratings are attached to them.

Finally, the American class system includes a caste, which may be thought of in general terms as a class which has become hereditary and occupies a relatively fixed place in the social structure. Specific features of a caste system include: (a) an entrenched arrangement whereby the privileges, duties, and obligations are distributed unequally between an upper and lower group; (b) the lack of opportunity to change from one caste to another; and (c) the complete absence of any social sanction of marriage between persons from different castes. This identification of a caste as a part of the class system of the United States has been made by sociologists with particular reference to race and certain supplementary physical traits as the criteria of caste identification. It is quite clear, however, that social class statuses exist within a caste. Some students have inferred that class differences cut across and outweigh the caste system.

SOCIAL CLASS VALUES

In a fivefold classification, McKinley draws thumbnail sketches of what he sees as the dominant values of modern American social classes. The upper classes stress "gracious living," skills in consumption, and skills in public service. The upper middle class is career oriented. "Respectability," morality, and productivity typify the lower middle class. In the working class, goals develop in response to realistic situations; they are concerned with getting by and keeping out of difficulty. In the lower class there comes apathy and resentment toward the values of the other classes with an emphasis upon living for the present and getting all the pleasure possible out of it. This last, McKinley adds, is often exaggerated in the minds of people of other social classes, to the extent of ignoring the fact that there is much of organized and responsible behavior among the members of the lower class.[12]

It has been noted by many students of social class that life in the working class (wage earners) and in the middle class (salaried persons) is coming to be more alike since wage rates have been increasing. Yet, Handel and Rainwater, after a study in five different cities, came to a more specific conclusion. Certain parts of the lives of these two groups have a "surface similarity," but different meanings. For instance, it is much more common than formerly for working-class parents to want their children to go to college. The emphasis is on the *sons'* going. College education is conceived as vocational training to prepare boys for a good job. In the middle class, higher education for both boys and girls is thought of as a broad humanistic experience that is valuable, even if not put to direct use. Also, increasing homeownership in the working class signifies their desire to escape from the subordination of landlords and from restrictions. The middle class *have been* homeowners. To them this signifies their class position and their desire to live among similar responsible persons. Again, in terms of income in these two classes which it is presumed are growing closer together, differences in expenditures are marked. Working-class parents buy more dur-

[12] Donald Gilbert McKinley, *Social Class and Family Life,* The Free Press of Glencoe, New York, 1964, pp. 20–22.

able goods than formerly, such as houses and automobiles. They also service them by themselves more frequently than do the middle class. In fact, wage earners appear to be the "do-it-yourself" group. They spend less on many kinds of services—repairs, dry cleaning, restaurants. They vacation at home or with relatives more often than the middle class, and go to hotels and motels less often. Although an increasing number of their children do go to college, they are more apt to go to publicly supported junior colleges or state universities than are the children of the middle class.[13] When considering social classes as cultural entities, the material aspects of these cultures are perhaps of least importance in comparisons. It is the values and meanings behind them that are of greatest significance in their "ways of living."

CLASS DIFFERENCES IN CHILD DEVELOPMENT

Our chief interest in class differentials lies in their significance for child development. It must be obvious that this significance is great, and for at least three reasons. First, the conception of classes in terms of cultural levels means that class differences are both fundamental and comprehensive. Thinking of a social class as a mode of life and of thought, means that it pervades every aspect of life. Second, such cultural levels express themselves, then, nowhere more clearly than in the intimate, everyday details of family life, from which it follows that the family becomes the chief vehicle in the transmission of the class culture. This means, third, that class differences enter the childrearing process from the beginning of the child's life, and continue as operating factors as long as the child has any relationship with his family. In other words, just as the child is inducted by his family into the ethos or national culture and into a regional culture, so he is also inducted into a class culture.

Survival and Health

It seems proper to begin this analysis of class differentials in family life by considering their relationship to the child's chances of survival. Being a child is a dangerous occupation. Despite recent reductions in infant mortality rates, the death rate of children in the earlier age groups is relatively high. These early life hazards, how-

[13] Gerald Handel and Lee Rainwater, "The Working Classes—Old and New," *Trans-action, Social Science and the Community*, November, 1963, pp. 25–27.

ever, are not evenly divided. They vary in part on the basis of class differences. The probability of neonatal death, for instance, is heightened in communities where at least half of the people are in the lowest socioeconomic brackets.[14]

Sickness rates and other health aspects of child life vary on a class basis. Persons in the lower classes are sick more frequently; their sicknesses are of longer duration and tend to be more disabling; the adequacy of medical attention may be less, so that the sequelae of the major sicknesses at least are also more frequent and more serious. With these differences go other class differentials. The nature of the family insight into the child's health problems and their implications for his daily life; the availability of resources, other than medical, for dealing with these problems; the possibilities of working out satisfactory life adjustments—all of these tend to vary on a class basis, so that some children tend to enter adolescence and adult life much better equipped physically than others.

As regards mental health, Hollingshead and Redlich found a correlation between its incidence and social class status. The lower the class standing, the greater was the proportion of psychiatric patients.[15] Severity of mental illness showed the same trend, the rate of psychotic patients being highest in the lowest classes.[16] Their treatment is different and takes place in different types of institutions,[17] and the mean cost per day is significantly greater for the higher classes.[18] In the lower classes there are more feelings of shame about having this kind of sickness in the family and therefore a greater reluctance to use psychiatric services.[19]

Behavior Rewarded

The rewards given by significant people in the child's life for approved behavior are a potent influence on development. This process begins to operate during earliest infancy and continues, to a considerable extent, throughout life. It has been noted by many writers that the particular types of behavior rewarded vary on a social-class basis.

14 Charles V. Willie and William B. Rothney, "Racial, Ethnic, and Income Factors in the Epidemiology of Neonatal Mortality," *American Sociological Review*, August, 1962, pp. 522–526.

15 August B. Hollingshead and Fredrick C. Redlich, *Social Class and Mental Illness*, John Wiley and Sons, New York, 1958, p. 216.

16 *Ibid.*, pp. 248–249.

17 *Ibid.*, pp. 300–302.

18 *Ibid.*, pp. 330–331.

19 *Ibid.*, chap. 11.

Albert Cohen describes the middle-class parent as rewarding children (primarily sons) for ambition, a high level of aspiration, and for having difficult long-run goals which mean deferred gratification. Individual responsibility is important, even though it minimizes generosity, as is the achievement of skills and outstanding performance. Examples are athletic and academic achievement and skills of potential economic and occupational value. Even recreation should be "constructive," and not just a waste of time. The middle class emphasizes rationality, forethought in budgeting time and resources in an efficient way, and respect for property (meaning a proper regard for "mine" and "thine"). Manners, etiquette, being "personable" are important. Physical aggression is frowned upon. The result is the producing of persons who are controlled (sometimes to the point of lack of spontaneity), regulated, diligent, and able to forego the pleasures of today for the rewards of tomorrow.[20] Aberle and Naegele found that middle-class fathers were concerned about "lack of responsibility and initiative, inadequate performance at school, insufficiently aggressive or excessively passive behavior, athletic inadequacies, overconformity, excitability, excessive tearfulness, and the like . . ." in their sons.[21]

In contrast, Hodges' summary of studies of social class describes what occurs in the lower-status group. Levels of achievement are regulated to what it is felt can be attained. A quest for some security is the important thing. Toughness in boys is admired as a form of ability to get ahead of other people. Intellectualism appears to be unmasculine. Living for the moment is not frowned upon in a group in which opportunities for "living it up" are relatively rare.[22] Social workers have complained that their lower-social-class clients do not know how to budget their money properly when they have it. This may be easier to do at an income level in which wise budgeting can also include periodic hedonistic satisfactions.

Although there are many other differences in attitudes toward behavior as between the social classes, this may suffice to illustrate that from the beginning of life the children are molded into the ways that seem most appropriate to their own social culture.

[20] Albert K. Cohen, *Delinquent Boys,* The Free Press of Glencoe, New York, 1955, pp. 88–93.

[21] David F. Aberle and Kasper D. Naegele, "Middle-Class Fathers' Occupational Roles and Attitudes Toward Children," in Norman W. Bell and Ezra F. Vogel (Eds.), *A Modern Introduction to the Family,* The Free Press of Glencoe, New York, 1960, p. 132.

[22] Harold M. Hodges, *op. cit.,* chap. 10.

CLASS VARIATIONS IN FAMILY STRUCTURE

One of the most clearly established facts in contemporary population data is the variation in the size of the family of procreation from one social group to another. To some considerable extent, these variations occur on a class basis. There has long been a differential birth rate in the United States, based on both economic status and education. The parents with lowest income and education had the most children, the largest families. There has recently occurred a change in the size of the differential, with the growth in size of family in the upper income and educational groups. A difference still remains, however. The size of the lower-class family is larger than that of the middle class. This means, basically, that there is a class differential in the size of the child's most intimate socializing group. The Law of Family Interaction, presented in Chapter 3, permits a more concise consideration of this fact.

A second aspect of the family structure that seems to vary on a class basis is the composition of the family household unit. Are children in the upper classes reared prevailingly in homes occupied only by the family of procreation? Is the family of orientation more prevalent among the lower classes? Does the larger kinship group appear in the same household more frequently in the lower classes? Here again it is impossible to write with satisfactory precision; but on the basis of economic differences as well as of ethnic factors, all these questions can be answered in the affirmative. Speaking generally, the immediate family and the procreative form of it tend to prevail in the middle classes, in large measure, because ambition dictates; in the lower classes, however, larger families, lower incomes, and shorter working-life spans necessitate, in greater measure, the inclusion of kinsfolk in the household unit. These differences, combined with differentials in space per person within the home, have great meaning in the childrearing process.

THE SETTING OF FAMILY LIFE

Elsewhere in this book are discussions of the effects of the physical basis of home life upon child development and attitude toward his family. It is pertinent, therefore, to comment upon certain differences in the setting of family life that occur on a social-class basis.

There is, to begin with, the physical appearance of the home;

that is, how it looks and compares with other homes, both inside and out. This really involves a dual comparison: first, with homes of other families within the person's class, and second, with homes in general. Such comparisons are related to the conception which members of a family have of themselves and of their relations to others.

Second, there are the number and size of rooms in the home, particularly in relation to the number of members in the family. Does each person have his own room? If not, how many share a bedroom? its drawer space? the living room?

It is significant to note the extent to which the members of the family, particularly the children, have an opportunity within the home to be by themselves—to have their own bedroom, bed, drawer space, room to study, room to listen to their own choice of radio program—and to what extent these must be shared constantly with others.

Does the family own its home? Are the words *my* or *our* applied constantly, even if unconsciously, to the place in which the child grows up? Or are his relationship to his home, and the behavior of the adults which he observes, those of the renter? It is commonly understood, among persons competent to make the comparison, that the behavior patterns of homeowning families differ in many respects from those of renters, particularly in their treatment of the home in which they live, and that in many instances the differences are marked. "Acting like a renter" is a common expression in certain parts of the country.

Homeownership is related closely to duration of occupancy, and both must be thought of as having particular importance, not only for the feeling (or lack) of permanence of family life, but also for the degree of the child's sense of security, in school and community.

Again, there are what are here called the *facilitating aids* in home life. This term is used to indicate the range of material equipment and services whose presence or absence affects the atmosphere and tempo of home life, particularly the processes of child development. These include servants in the home; mechanical appliances of a laborsaving nature; specialized rooms, such as game rooms, study nooks, space for a laboratory set or a hobby; the number of radios and victrolas; and home recreational facilities. Factors of this kind determine not only the child's activities within the home but also, often, the whole nature of parent-child relationships.

Just as there are facilitating aids, so there are special handicaps which hamper normal family life. Many families live in a physical setting which presents particular difficulties for children—cramped apartments, lack of play space, a home dominated by adult activities, fastidious concern with household furnishings, and the like.

Another special phase of the setting of family life is the degree to which purely family relations and parent-child relations are isolated from other activities of the members. There are families, as in some suburbs of large cities, in which the family life of their members is cut off almost entirely from other activities. Business or "the office" is not brought home, even on the telephone. In other cases, by contrast, storerooms, professional offices, candy shops, display rooms, etc., are operated in the home and their activities constantly intrude, on both a time and a space basis, upon the family's life.

Finally, there is the spatial relation of the home in relation to other homes. How near in terms of distance do other families live? How near in terms of sound? How much separateness and distinctness of family life are possible, measured in terms of the physical setting of the home? These and other aspects of the physical setting of home life vary a great deal from one social class to another, with the result that family and child life flourish under significantly different conditions.

The middle and upper classes have a high rate of homeownership, and the upper class the highest rate of permanency of domicile. In general, it may be said that amount of space per person, as well as possibility for privacy, is directly related to class status. Facilitating aids depend, to a large extent, on amount of income. Insulation, or isolation, from neighbors increases with class status. Effects of these things upon children in their family life are not always as obvious as they appear. Much has been written concerning the large family in a small yardless house where the street is outside the window, the neighbors are on the other side of thin walls, neighborhood feuds are common, there is little quiet and relaxation. Little attention has been given to the other extreme, the situation in which a child is reared on a huge estate, in a 40-room house, with few or no siblings, and his own private suite with Nannie's rooms close by.

THE BOND OF KINSHIP

The term bond of kinship is used here to cover the nature and role of intrakinship relations and attitudes, with particular reference to the child. Four aspects will be emphasized: (1) the family's attitude toward the child; (2) the relations between the immediate family and the larger kinship group; (3) the sense of family solidarity, and (4) family stability. In each of these, significant class differentials are apparent.

The Family's Attitude Toward the Child

1. The attitude of upper-class families toward the child is characteristically one of possessive pride and hope. This is a product, in large measure, of two factors. The first is family pride, pride of present achievements or past histories or both; the second is the economic means enabling one to luxuriate in the satisfactions of parenthood. Children, therefore, tend to be wanted in specific numbers to guarantee and fortify the family position, but to be limited to the number in keeping with the family's capacity for childrearing on its class plane. The child is regarded, commonly and consciously, as the carrier of the family name, its traditions, heritage, and status. Fathers who have established businesses, for example, expect or hope that their sons will carry on; mothers with an assured social position are concerned as a rule that both sons and daughters will maintain it, if not better it.

This fundamental attitude toward the child, coupled with the relative ability to carry the costs of childrearing and the facilitating aids in the home, all combine to work for a pleasant home life and for high standards of child care. The child receives the best that the family knows of, his development is closely watched, and he is received early on a basis of equality. Coupled with this care and interest is a strong sense of group pressure in the child's development. Upper-class children are expected to measure up to the class culture and to the traditional performance at the level of their particular family. In fact, as the child grows into maturity, he is given to understand that he must not merely retain the family place but, if a male, he must retain or regain the material resources required, and, if a female, "marry them." Four further facts may be noted about these family pressures. First, the selective factor which operates most strongly is social prestige; there is much less concern about the moral aspects of behavior. Second, the higher up one moves on the social scale, the stronger these family pressures become. Similarly, as the child grows older, the stronger the pressure becomes. Finally, there is the important fact that at the upper-class level these pressures derive not only from the immediate family but from the whole range of kinsfolk. In many cases, this includes kinsfolk who are dead. "What would your Grandmother Elson say?"

Many of the problems peculiar to upper-class children are the result, directly and indirectly, of these pressures. Children may not have the ability to measure up to the level of their family's performance. After all, the next generation has a biological heritage of abilities and disabilities partially different from that of the parent. Or the children may not possess the health or energy needed to function at the family level. There may not be the interest or inclination to do so. Again, parents and other kinsfolk may fail to realize that situations have changed and that what they expect is both difficult and futile. Persons familiar with the problems of students in universities and professional schools know the number, variety, and often the tragic role of these family pressures.

2. Family attitudes toward the child in the lower classes are in sharp contrast in many respects. To begin with, lower-class parents, while not lacking in love and affection for their children, become concerned about the number of them. With incomes and housing facilities sharply limited, each additional child, after a given point is reached (and it is reached early in the family's life), takes on elements of a crisis. Out of this grows in large measure not only the multitude of tragic family problems which plague lower-class families but also the prevailing attitudes toward and treatment of their children.

The chief emphasis in lower-class childrearing is upon not being an annoyance or a nuisance. Children must keep quiet and not disturb the adults in the home or the neighbors nearby. The reasons for this emphasis are obvious. Houses or apartments are small, families are large, walls are thin, neighbors are close. Many people must live within a small area, the adults are occupied with the pressure of making a living, and the children must be trained to adjust to the requirements of these conditions. What this really means for the child has been well stated by Davis and the Gardners: "In a sense, there is no 'child's world' in the lower classes; children are expected to behave as adults at an early age. Fewer concessions are made to immaturity, and the child's pattern of behavior differs from the adult pattern less than in other class groups."[23]

Such emphases and purposes in childrearing naturally lead to a considerable premium upon obedience and on the further virtue of promptness. The well-brought-up child is the one who "stops what he is doing," and at once. In securing this promptness and obedience, the chief reliance is upon physical punishment. Since often this is administered by the male head of the family, and since

[23] Allison Davis, B. B. Gardner and Mary R. Gardner, *op. cit.*, p. 129.

the number of stepchildren in these classes is relatively high, the effect upon "father"-child relations is again obvious.

A second emphasis in lower-class childrearing is upon being helpful. Children are taught early to run errands, to do chores, and to assume responsibility for the care of the home and the other children. Lower-class daughters become "little mothers" early in life; where circumstances permit, boys are expected to go with the father and help him. Here, again, necessity is crowned as a virtue. Children are reared, not with an eye to the development of their capacities, but to meet the dictates of the family's need. It is at this point that lower-class family standards and the requirements of child labor and compulsory school attendance laws conflict.

3. The attitudes of middle-class families toward the child range between the two already noted. The child is wanted, perhaps, chiefly as a form of marriage fulfillment. There is, however—especially in the upper middle class—marked interest in planned parenthood through the use of contraceptives. Family limitation is desired, not generally as a matter of sheer economic necessity as in the lower classes, but as an aspect of family planning. The number of persons to plan for is the basic criterion of the planning process.

But there is a second aspect of the middle-class family's attitude: the fact that the child is seen as the possibility of the fulfillment of hopes. Reference has been made to this in an earlier chapter; it is pointed out here that such cases are probably most prevalent in the middle-class groups. This fact has a particular bearing upon family conceptions of childrearing.

The chief emphasis in childrearing in the middle classes grows out of their place in the class configuration. Above them is the appraising challenge of the upper classes; below, the enticing envy of the lower classes. The former stand ready to reject them; the latter threaten to engulf them. The natural result is a marked emphasis upon "appearances," upon "what people will say" and "how things will look." The middle-class code thus becomes one of rigidly controlled behavior, with a strong insistence that children conform to the formalized patterns of behavior.

Obviously, this cannot be brought about by physical punishment alone. Children at this class level are more likely to be reasoned with, the values of such conduct are pointed out, self-interest is appealed to, nonphysical forms of discipline are invoked. Although childrearing in the middle classes is of necessity carried on largely by the mother, there is considerable cooperation from the father. There are family consultations, definite programs are initiated, outside help may be solicited. Here are the parents who take children to clinics, who go to hear lectures, who want to read books on "child psychology." Many of these parents become confused and others become skeptical in their effort to substitute these newer methods for the old-time disciplines; unfortunately some, in their despair, reduce their efforts to a minimum.

The Relationship Between the Immediate Family and the Larger Kinship Group

The immediate family's relationship with the kinship group is a fundamental factor in the family background of the child, and it varies considerably on a class basis.

1. The upper-class pattern, particularly of the upper division, is quite definite. The kinship group rather than the immediate family tends to be the focal point and the ultimate consideration in the life of its members. Pride in the family name stems from the history of the larger group; individuals and immediate family units bask and share in its reflected glory; to it rather than the immediate family is given prior loyalty. It is within the kinship group that a general pattern of behavior develops which sets the norms for its constituent members; to it the immediate family unit is subordinate.

This type of relationship is perhaps most strongly developed in the area of the old South, and its nature and social significance can best be studied there. Its clarity and frequency in other parts of the country vary a good deal, depending upon the age of the region and the horizontal mobility of the upper-class population, as well as its vertical mobility. Its relative importance also is probably less in the lower upper class, since the families at this level are more recent arrivals in the social sense, and have less of an idealized past in terms of family history to utilize and exploit.

Some of the significant implications of this dominance of the kinship group will be stated briefly. First, it involves pressure upon the immediate family to conform to the general kinship behavior patterns, with particular reference to the field of childrearing. Second, it follows that relatives share to some extent in the process of childrearing. The role of grandparents is considerable, especially of those who are the particular personification of the family glory or the holder of the family fortunes. Third, there is much emphasis upon respect for older relatives, which comes to be generalized into respect for one's elders. Fourth, the "family's" influence in the choice of matrimonial mates is great, as it is also in the choice of professional or business careers. Fifth, close relations with the circle of kinsfolk are common after marriage. Sixth, as the younger members of the family grow up, there is emphasis upon the examples set by earlier members in regard to community, political, military, and other forms of public service. This emphasis, so marked in older cultures where vestiges of feudal life and the responsibilities of the liege lord prevail, is perhaps less operative in American life. It may develop as a phase of the democratic way of life in this country as time goes on.

2. The middle classes put more emphasis upon the immediate family, although there is a considerable variation between the extreme ends of this social span. In general it may be said that as we go from the top of the upper middle class toward the lower classes, the immediate family grows in importance as the focal unit in the life of its members.

Two basic factors possibly account for its relative position in the middle classes. The first is the individualizing aspect of middle-class life, with its emphasis upon individual effort, achievement, and acceptance of responsibility in the democracy of the home. The particularizing of relationships with kinsfolk is thus only another phase of the same tendency. Second is the fact that middle-class families are socially mobile; many of them have "arrived" recently, and many hope to move higher. This means that collateral branches of the same kinship group have acquired a differing status. Families living in the city have "country" relatives; prosperous families have poor relatives; "newly elegant" families have crude cousins. This tends to be particularly true of members of ethnic groups who have recently acquired middle-class status. The combined effect of these two factors is to make for a rather highly selective process in the relations between the middle-class immediate family and its wider circle of kinsfolk.

The implications for child development follow correspondingly. The middle-class child is reared by his parents; relatives are not expected to interfere. His attitude toward relatives is individual, not general and inevitable. Choices involving the child's training and career and his matrimonial mate are made within the immediate family. Relations between generations after his marriage are dictated more by mutual respect than by "family" duty.

3. In the lower classes, too, the focal point is the immediate family; its relative lack of permanence has been referred to previously in this chapter. What importance attaches to the larger circle of kinsfolk is called forth by the needs of its members, and not as a rule by their sharing in an idealized past. The form taken by this relationship beyond the immediate family is most frequently a close association between brothers and sisters, who after marriage

may live near each other and share their common problems and experiences.

There are, however, notable exceptions to what has just been said. These are found chiefly in the ethnic groups in our larger cities, where the lower-class status coincides with Old World vestiges of kinship family structures. But even in these families, the secondary group life prevalent in contemporary urban centers has tended to dissolve the cohesive bonds of these extended family structures, so that the younger generation tends to ignore them, even as their elders seek tragically to maintain them.

The Sense of Family Solidarity

Family solidarity is an intangible thing, however tangible its manifestations may be from time to time. On the positive side it may be defined as a consolidation or union of interest of the members of a family; on the negative side it involves chiefly the rendering of aid in time of crisis. Thus conceived, some sense of solidarity prevails in every family; the chief concern here is with significant variations in its nature or extent from one class to another.

1. In the upper classes, family solidarity is a product primarily of the self-interest of its members. Three factors in its production readily suggest themselves. First, there often exists in upper-class families common participation in business or other projects; second, there are often family fortunes to conserve; and, third, there is the family honor or good name which must be preserved. In time of crisis, the family prestige must be preserved; in good times, it must be enhanced. The family name is a stock in trade whose value must be protected; this is the common interest of the upper-class family. What the family does for its children, and what is expected of the younger generation, is dominated by considerations of this kind.

2. Family solidarity in the middle classes is more voluntary, social, and selective. It seems more like the friendly participation of independent persons, rather than the common effort of the crew of a smart yacht. Possibly economic considerations are effective here. Middle-class families are concentrated largely in the stabilized occupations. They are members of the professional and salaried groups. There is a relative security, even if not an imposing amount, of family income. Middle-class families tend to participate with relative adequacy in the insurance features of modern life; there is as a rule some surplus to draw on. The result of all this is that crisis situations are less prone to arise in the middle classes, and no class pattern develops in this respect.

3. Family solidarity in the lower classes is characterized chiefly by three facts. First, it concerns itself for the most part with crisis situations. These are common in lower-class families. Needs are urgent and have to do often with the essentials of life—food, shelter, and refuge in case of illness. Furthermore, these families are large in size. Responsibility for aid in time of crisis is expected and generally accepted. Second, family solidarity tends to be matrilinear. This is the result of what has already been said concerning the relative role of the mother. Not only is she a more constant factor in the family's life, but she is also more often the basic person involved in the need situation. Reciprocal demands between mother and child, and the demands of the sister upon her brother, are more common. Third, there is again the pattern of family solidarity in lower-class ethnic groups where there is the relative subordination of the individual, particularly the individual child, to the family group, and the ideal of economic security for family members through family solidarity.

Family Stability

The term "family stability" is used here to mean the endurance of the procreative family personnel throughout the term of dependence of the child. It is of considerable importance in the development of children whether or not they remain, during this period, within the upbringing of both of their own blood parents. The chances of having the family remain intact varies on a social class basis. Descriptions of these variations and their causes have been given most ably by Dr. Hollingshead, and the following discussion is in most parts a summary of his report.[24]

1. Families that have been established in the upper class for two or more generations are stable to a high degree. Some of them pride themselves on the fact that no divorces have ever occurred in their families. It has already been stated that the upper class is an extended kinsfolk group where all members are quite powerful when it comes to making critical decisions for its minors. The prestige of all elders, plus the prospect of exclusion from inheritance and social relations enhances this power. Thus, an intended marriage which seems inappropriate is severely condemned and brings pressure from the entire group. In order to forestall such a crisis, the old upper class has ways in which to assure a fairly narrow field for mate selection from the beginning of their children's

[24] August B. Hollingshead, "Class Differences in Family Stability," *The Annals of the American Academy of Political and Social Science*, November, 1950, pp. 39–46.

lives. Examples are private schools and colleges, private summer homes where children vacation with others of their own status, and the debutante season for the girls when, at late teenage, social relations are intensified within the group. The fact that the debutante list has become extended to others than the old upper class has not completely defeated its purpose for them. As in any large group, there tend to be rather strict subdivisions in social relations. Along with the pressure to marry "properly," there is the pressure to keep the marriage going in order not to disgrace the family name. Thus, stability in the established upper-class family springs not necessarily from greater happiness in marriage but from control and a sense of responsibility.

2. The new upper-class family is one that has achieved economic success in a relatively short time and has a high rate of instability. The power of the kinsfolk group does not apply here, since sudden upward mobility usually requires a sloughing off of relatives who have not climbed the ladder at the same pace. Also the new families are not often welcomed into the established family cliques or clubs. Frustration takes the form of conspicuous consumption and fast living, which is frowned upon by the more prestigeful group. In a desire to flaunt their economic status, new-family parents frequently overindulge children to the point of catering to their every wish. Thus, even parental control over their actions is weakened. Divorces and remarriages are common in these families, as are other signs of instability such as alcoholism.

3. Middle-class families are more stable than those of the new upper class. This is in part a result of "middle-class mores"—self-discipline, respectability. There is also the fact that they *may* move upward in the status system, and they *fear* falling downward. There is much to gain by working together, behaving properly, and being productive. If children are to maintain the family position, or raise their own through hard work or marriage, they require a strong, stable family to help them attain this.

4. Lower-class families have the highest rate of family breakup and incomplete family structure because of divorce, separation, desertion, death, and illegal unions which produce children. These families live with economic hardship, crowded conditions, sporadic unemployment, a high rate of maternal employment, and other conditions which cause frequent crises. Divorce is not the most usual means of breaking the family. This requires money and lawyers. It is easier to simply walk out. A later union is therefore not a legal marriage although it may become a family. Children of such a family may belong to the man, to the woman, to both. Fre-

quently such families break up, and another one is formed, with a redistribution of children and "parents." Sometimes blood relationships in such families are extremely confusing. Although this picture of family instability prevails in the lower class, it is not characteristic of all families at that level. Dr. Hollingshead describes the situation as a continuum, with very stable relations at one end and very loosely-knit relations at the other. Kinsey, in fact, reported that the lower-class male, who has the highest incidence of premarital and extramarital intercourse in his early years, becomes an increasingly stable husband in this respect as he grows older, more so than husbands at higher social levels.[25]

Among the young women, there was little difference between educational levels in this kind of behavior. As they grew older, it decreased in the lower level and increased at higher ones.[26] It might be concluded from this that the age at which many children are subjected to breaks and tensions in their parents' relationship varies on a class basis. One can only conjecture at what age this is most traumatic and influential in the development of their own behavior patterns.

THE EDUCATIONAL PATTERN

In discussing the educational process as an aspect of child development, something broader than classroom instruction is implied. The term *educational pattern* is used to identify this broader concept, and includes such elements as the linguistic equipment which the child obtains in the home, the family attitude toward education, the nature of the school curriculum, the length of the school experience, the child's social status in the school world, and the values emphasized in the course of school life. Variations in these and other elements on a class basis are obvious in the educational pattern, and serve both as an expression of the social stratification in the adult world and also as the mechanism for its perpetuation.

1. Reference has been made in a preceding chapter to class differentials in the linguistic culture. Upper-class children come to school with a language equipment which both adequately serves their school progress and promptly identifies their social background. The words used, the habits of expression, the shades of

[25] Alfred C. Kinsey, Wardell B. Pomeroy and Clyde E. Martin, *Sexual Behavior in the Human Male*, W. B. Saunders Company, Philadelphia, 1948, p. 355.

[26] Alfred C. Kinsey, Wardell B. Pomeroy, Clyde E. Martin and Paul H. Gebhard, *Sexual Behavior in the Human Female*, W. B. Saunders Company, Philadelphia, 1953, pp. 421–422.

meaning, the subtleties of expression, the range of topics discussed, all reveal the upper-class home training. The importance of education is taken for granted. It is the thing to do. Going to college is looked forward to, not only in preparing for a vocation but also in equipping one with the interests and standards of his class. Curriculums are selected and shaped toward this end. Upper-class children for the most part go to private schools—boys to private preparatory schools and girls to finishing schools that have preparatory and collegiate features. Throughout this school process, the child is indoctrinated with the attitudes, manners, rituals, and routines of his class. Upper-class children usually do not work while going to school. Financial allowances tend to be adequate, although as a rule they are more conspicuously generous in the lower upper class.

2. In most communities the American public-school system is a middle-class product. Its teachers are drawn chiefly from this group, the language it utilizes in its instruction and the values it emphasizes are representative of the middle class. Its directive control is middle class. When the middle-class child goes to public school he goes into a typical middle-class institution. The linguistic equipment he brings from home fits into the school life, and without attracting attention to itself. Middle-class pupils and middle-class teachers speak the same language. Especially is this true when the children come from professional, semiprofessional, and junior executive homes. There is more than a friendly attitude toward education; it shades into a marked emphasis upon its value, not as a social grace but as a tool with which to rise in the world, particularly in an economic or professional way. Middle-class children go to high school. They tend to elect classical and scientific courses; many plan to go to college. Where state universities, scholarships, and stipends of various sorts are available, the percentage who go to college is high. The incidental values emphasized during their school experience, simply stated, are these: Behave yourself, do well in your studies, be a go-getter, search out all the facilitating aids that society offers for higher training, and you will get along in the world, i.e., raise your status.

3. Lower-class children have handicaps in their educational process from the very beginning. Their linguistic equipment is not that of the school. Words, grammar, forms of expression must be relearned. They identify themselves as lower class to teachers and pupils. Their home background tends to make them critical of or unsympathetic to the idea of education. Their milieu furnishes few incentives to the learning process which are not direct and obvious.

The courses selected therefore are those designed for immediate and practical use. A large number of these children work during the school term, often to the point of interfering with their school work. Attendance is less regular than that of children in the other classes. The incidence of disturbances in the family background is high. Changes in schools attended are frequent. Retardation is more common. Economic pressure and lack of sympathy lead to an early withdrawal from school. The school's emphasis on "getting on in the world" is twisted into bitter cynicism. Lacking the middle-class graces, these children rationalize the situation by depreciating their importance. Delinquent behavior and contacts with "the law" on the part of either their parents or themselves are common.

SOCIAL ACTIVITIES AND PARTICIPATION

Class differences, so evident in the family and school life of the child, are fully maintained throughout the range of out-of-the-home activities.

1. The social activities of upper-class children tend to be full and varied. A wide range of choices is open to them, as a result of the economic position of their families, the relative leisure of the members of this class, and their ability to contact the necessary sources of information about interesting things to do. Sports are much emphasized, for sports' sake. There is concern with playing the game and, whatever else may betide, playing it well.

One of the distinctive features about the social activities of upper-class children is their relative exclusiveness. For them, social participation, no matter how full and varied, tends to be segregated. In their recreational pursuits, they go or are taken to areas, resorts, hotels, summer camps, etc., patronized by their own class. Although they mingle freely, it is with their own kind. Part of this aloofness, no doubt, is consciously created and maintained, but in large part it is the result of a sorting process carried out by like-minded and like-financed people. Common interests, common traditions, and common capacities make for a way of socializing which is exclusive.

2. If the social participations of upper-class children are exclusive, those of the middle class tend to be selective. Middle-class families on the whole do not have the resources to maintain the foregoing features of aloofness in the lives of their children, but they tend rigorously to impose standards of selection. In upper-class families, relative isolation accomplishes rather unconsciously what middle-class parents must achieve consciously, that is, sorting out

and selecting the proper associates and activities for their children; hence the superficial student may conclude that social snobbery is primarily a middle-class weapon.

Middle-class children utilize public (as opposed to private) facilities, although there is care to select suitable ones. The distinction between the upper and lower middle classes becomes noticeable here, as in the whole range of social activities. Upper middle-class families tend to be much more discriminatory, calculating, and ambitious in the pressures which they exert upon their children, with the result that the children's activities are more purposive and have more of an air of strain and effort rather than sheer enjoyment.

Special mention should be made of the scientific interests and pursuits of many middle-class children, especially those in the upper middle class. This is clearly manifested in the high school courses chosen by middle-class children, and is echoed in the hobbies and avocations of the adolescent stage. The reasons for this are fairly obvious. A rapidly changing and developing science is replete with the opportunities which are the basis of the middle-class hope of a rise in status.

3. The social participations of lower-class children may be characterized as residual. These children do chiefly what is available for them, which often is meager enough. Parents have neither the time, the leisure, nor the knowledge to be of much help; they are too preoccupied with their own problems and insecurities. True, there are selective factors at work here, but they operate within the confines of their class configuration. Ethnic considerations weigh heavily. Welfare projects, whose opportunities were once regarded with scant skepticism, are now considered a public service. Athletic and other recreational activities are particularly emphasized, both as a means of achieving individual status and also as an escape from the drab routine of lower-class existence. For lower-class children there is no insulation against the rawness and rough edges of life, only the immunity which comes from constant exposure.

PARENTS' OCCUPATIONS AND THE CHILD[27]

Occupation has often been used as an index to the social status of the individual. Although it is not always an accurate index, "Each occupational group . . ." Ogburn and Nimkoff pointed out,

[27] A part of this section is based upon a study by James H. S. Bossard in *Parent and Child*, University of Pennsylvania Press, Philadelphia, 1953, chap. 11.

"has its own special cultural context. There is a distinct set of activities and even vocabulary for each vocation, which results in unique 'vocational attitudes'."[28] Pitirim Sorokin wrote:

> Occupation determines considerably the place and district of our dwelling, its character and type, its furniture and equipment. Occupation determines our budget of income and budget of time: the hours of our working, recreation, getting up, and going to bed. It influences the character of our meals, and recreations, that of our reading and amusements. It fashions our habits, our ethics, our manners, our etiquette. It determines considerably with whom we are associated, whom we meet, with whom we talk and are in contact. All this being taken into consideration makes apparent the enormous influence of occupation on the whole physical, mental, moral, and social nature of man.[29]

It is pertinent, therefore, in discussing social-class differences to give some consideration to parental occupations and their meaning to children at various levels.

1. Children are always making comparisons between their own families and others. "What does *your* daddy do?" is a common question. In the upper social class, occupations are both prestigeful and at a high-income level. From the comments of children of this group one senses a feeling of family pride, emotional security, social assurance—or smugness and snobbery. For example:

> I was conscious always of my father's position. I was proud to tell people who he was. I learned early in life, too, that the men in my father's family had all been prominent in the business or professional world.
>
> From childhood on, I was impressed by the fact that my father had his own business and his own office. The nature of his business, and the contacts he made, were such as to emphasize the high social status of the family. Our family also has a history filled with persons in the professions.

Children are aware also of the fruits of their parents' high-income occupations. One wrote:

> Father's position made family life possible at a satisfactory level. We always went to summer camps, our home was one to be proud of, and my brother and I have gone through college in comfort.

Others have appreciated the fact that their fathers' occupations did not entail weekend work, nor many evenings away from home. Since their mothers were not gainfully employed, this meant that the whole family had considerable leisure time together.

[28] William F. Ogburn and Meyer F. Nimkoff, *Sociology*, Houghton Mifflin Company, Boston, 1940 (pp. 205–206), 1964.

[29] Pitirim Sorokin, *Social Mobility*, Harper & Brothers, New York, 1927, p. 322.

The children of very prominent parents have expressed some negative attitudes, as well as pride, in the effects upon themselves and their family life. Most of them speak of a "goldfish bowl" existence, in which their every action and activity is scrutinized and commented upon by people outside the family. Outsiders also attempt to exploit their relationships with children from famous families, fawning on them, giving parties for them, and fussing over them. Mrs. Eleanor Roosevelt wrote that this was one of the problems in the lives of her children. They were never permitted to start at the bottom, but were given jobs with high returns when they were too young and too inexperienced to know that the jobs were offered only because of Franklin Roosevelt's name and position. If the children had not taken the jobs, they would have been considered ungracious by their father's followers. When they accepted the jobs, they were accused by their father's opponents of feathering their own nests. Because of being given too much, too soon, said Mrs. Roosevelt, only John developed a proper perspective.[30]

Intrafamily relations are also affected. The matter of "too little time" with parents applied in these cases. A part of this was because of the preoccupation of parents with work, to the extent that some children had to make appointments with their fathers in order to discuss a personal problem. Another part was being reared largely by servants, with a specific period only, each day, to visit with parents. The Duke of Windsor wrote of this—of being never really alone with his parents—and commented also on the tremendous expectations that prominent parents have of their children. They were considered as little images of the adults. It was also impressed upon the children that they must never think of themselves as better than anyone else; yet it was made clear that they should behave better and achieve more because of their status.[31]

2. Middle-class children express pride in their parents' employment, not always so much because of the prestige of the occupation itself as because of how hard they work for the good of the family. Gainful employment of mothers is more frequent in the middle than in the upper class, but it is not necessary for mere economic survival. Children are given advantages that they could not otherwise have because of an income-earning mother; and this, to some extent, is understood and appreciated.

It is in the middle class that most complaints are made about

[30] Eleanor Roosevelt, *This I Remember,* Harper & Row, New York, 1949, pp. 15–16.

[31] The Duke of Windsor, *A King's Story,* G. P. Putnam's Sons, New York, 1951, p. 29.

too-long hours of work, no free weekends, father or mother always being too tired or preoccupied.

Typical statements follow.

We rarely had meals with my father, and had little opportunity to share experiences with him. He was always so busy, working even on Sundays. When he came home from work he was usually too tired to pay much attention to us.

My father's work took him away from the house early in the morning. He would be gone all day. When he came home he was extremely tired, and mother would be tired, too. He rarely played with us or amused us with stories. The most he did for us was occasionally on Sundays he would read the funnies to us.

My father was too busy developing his business to pay any attention to us. He tried to substitute for this by buying our affection.

My father was so busy when I was younger that I never developed any affection for him. It was not until in my teens, and later when I saw how much he had accomplished, that I began to respect him. Now it is too late because my father died from the strain of too much work. One of the things I have learned from my father's occupation is that a man should never allow an occupation to take him away from getting to know his family.

Father's business took him away over long periods of time. When I did see him, it was over weekends. He was never around when I needed him. What home life we had was without him for the most part.

What children seem to like is an occupation that allows a parent the time and nervous energy to be a parent.

It is in this group also that most complaints are made about the invasion of the occupation into the privacy of the home. Three cases are presented briefly.

My father is a clergyman. We live in a relatively new home, bought by my father's congregation. We have little or no privacy in our home life. Everyone seems to think they can come to see the "pastor's home" any time they want. Some of the church officials walk in without knocking or ringing the doorbell. Our telephone is ringing from morning to night. We can seldom finish a meal without interruption. People come to our house for all kinds of reasons: to get married, to tell their troubles, to ask for advice, or to complain about another member of the church. Sometimes it takes us several days to finish a conversation. One thing I am sure of, and that is that I'll never marry a minister.

My mother keeps a store that is a part of our house. Business interrupts everything, especially our meals. Often my mother must leave the table to wait on the trade. The fact that I disliked most was that we never closed the door from the store to the home: the customers thus were able to invade our privacy at all times. It was not unusual to see customers' children playing in our living room.

My father is a doctor, with his office at home. In addition to his office, there is a large waiting room. But his patients early took over the living room across the hall. From there, they come upstairs to the bathroom. When they are on the second floor, they walk around, opening doors and looking into the rooms. There is not a square inch of privacy on the first two floors of our home. Often, patients have come filing into the living room and the dining room while we are still at dinner. I have even met patients on the third floor when I come out of my room.

3. Lower-class children seem to be least aware of their parents' long hours away from home and of their fatigue. These, perhaps, are things which are simply taken for granted. Maternal employment is assumed to be a matter of necessity. As long as the work is "decent" and enough money comes into the family, there is satisfaction but not much pride expressed. On the other hand, dangerous jobs do prey on the minds of some of these children; and shame is often admitted, as illustrated by the following records.

I came to feel a sense of shame and embarrassment about my father's job, not because of the lack of money, but because of the lack of status. I recall being very impressed with the status of occupations of other parents and secretly wishing that my father could achieve that status so that I could impress other boys and girls.

Both my mom and dad worked at dirty jobs and came home every day filthy and smelly. It was something to see them after being in school all day with grownups who were clean and nice looking. I didn't want my friends to see them. I hope I can take courses at a school of beauty culture, and sometime have a beauty shop of my own. Above all, I want a job where I can stay clean.

FAMILY RANK ORDER

For purposes of a generalized summary, it has been somewhat assumed thus far that all the families in the same social class enjoy the same status. Actually, this is far from true. Each family tends to have a rank order in its class, and this order determines not only the extent to which the family is representative of its class culture but also its attitude toward other social classes and other families in its own class. Everyone with social experience can identify the family that fawns upon the families that obviously outrank them in their own class and treat with derisive scorn those in the class immediately below them. Lower-ranking families in the upper classes are under considerable pressure as a rule, feelings of insecurity manifest themselves in many ways, and the whole atmosphere of the home becomes one of extreme tension. In contrast are the middle-class families who are firmly established in the higher rank orders and who maintain their position with comfort and confidence, secure in the prestige of their relative rank order. The home atmosphere here may be one of ease and contentment. Finally, we may identify the upper lower-class immigrant family, hard-working, living carefully, realizing its class status for the time being but hopefully anticipating the future. Here is a family obviously on the up.

The family's rank order in its class is of the highest importance in the creation of the psychic atmosphere of the home which psychiatrists are wont to emphasize in their study of juvenile behavior disorders.

THE CHILD AND HIS CLASS NURTURE

Two basic premises are inherent in the relationship between the child and his class setting. The first is that child rearing is the social mechanism in the maintenance of the class structure; the second, that childrearing is utilized as the chief social device for attaining a rise in class status. Each of these has great social significance.

Childrearing as the Social Mechanisms in the Maintenance of the Class Structure

Social classes live in different worlds, and families reflect the world of their class. This world, or class culture, they transmit to their children from the beginning of the child's life. From infancy on, children are conditioned to certain modes of behavior, so that by the time they reach adulthood they have the techniques for living at their class level. Two further facts need emphasis. One is that this behavior includes relations not only with one's own class, but also with persons in other classes—or out-groups, as the sociologists term them. Second, this class culture includes ways of thinking as well as ways of doing. The child is reared in the mental world of his class; thus he absorbs, as from the air he breathes, the beliefs, prejudices, attitudes, and values which characterize his class.

An appreciation of this process explains the pervasive persistence of the class culture. So deeply ingrained and so strongly emotionalized is it that its hold upon the individual often exceeds the force of other cultural pressures. History is replete with examples where the class hold has been stronger than that of the ethos. One such illustration comes from the history of France. There is much reason to believe that that country's debacle, and the development of Pétainism, resulted from the convictions of the dominant classes in France that coming to terms with the historic foe from across the Rhine was preferable to a rapport with Frenchmen of other classes.

Childrearing as the Social Device for Attaining a Rise in Class Status

To most parents, children personify another chance at life achievement. From this it follows that the key to much parental effort in a country with a high rate of vertical mobility is a desire to secure for the child opportunities denied to the parents; and the driving force in parental pressure upon the child, to achieve a status the parent never attained. It is a definite feature of the American social class system that the child becomes the spearhead of parental ambition.

This creates many problems for American children, problems permeated by a series of cruel dilemmas. For the child who succeeds in attaining a status higher than his parent's, there is the problem of parent-child relationships. What inevitably follows is that successive generations find their lateral associates at different social levels. The continuity of family life is broken. The price of vertical mobility is the disorganization of parent-child relationships. For the child who fails, there are frustration and the aftermath of isolation or bitterness, or both. Some of the failures reject their parents' class and the class to which they aspire rejects them, with the resultant loneliness of a social no-man's-land. Others, dropping back to their original status, develop strong feelings of class bitterness. This ambition to utilize children to achieve a higher social status leads to much unhappiness, and for many children.

Even when upward mobility is desired and attained there may be problems of an individual nature. To live with the pattern of social living in which one was born and reared is, in a sense, living kinesthetically—without much thought about it. In change there must come a consciousness of behavior in its most minute details—of etiquette, apparel, equipment, food, mannerisms, and a host of others. In *Noblesse Oblige,* a series of essays, there are hundreds of examples of uses of words, or pronunciations of words, which alone would betray the nonupper-class person to the British upper classes.[32] Lack of awareness of such details may cause rebuff.

[32] Nancy Mitford, *Noblesse Oblige,* Harper & Brothers, New York, 1956.

Constant awareness of them, until they become natural habits, can cause stress. Jackson has found several respects in which status inconsistencies are psychologically disturbing to the individual.[33] Hodges reports on several studies that indicate a relationship between social mobility, neuroses and psychosomatic symptoms.[34] Finally, a personnel officer in an expensive private girls' school made the following diagnosis. "The attempt to rise socially creates behavior problems." In her school there were three groups of children: the "self-assured" upper class; the "comfortable" middle class, who were sent there only because their parents felt the education to be superior; and the "uncomfortable" middle class, who were there as spearheads for parental ambitions and who knew it. Over 90 percent of her behavior problems, she reported, came from the last group.

SUMMARY

1. The concept of class came into sociology from economic fields. Contemporary sociologists define class primarily in terms of status. It can also be thought of in terms of cultural levels.

2. Three social classes—upper, middle, and lower—are usually recognized. Recent studies have divided each into an upper and a lower division and show a distribution that does not wholly conform to the figure of a truncated pyramid.

3. The American class system is characterized by (a) shifts in the population elements that become socially mobile, (b) greater cultural diffusion because of the impact of the mass media, (c) shifts in the status ranking of certain occupations, (d) its relative mobility, and (e) the inclusion of a caste system.

4. In spite of some increasing similarities in the outward modes of behavior of certain social class groups, differences are still found in the values attached to material goods and expected behavior.

5. Class differentials are both obvious and important in child development. They are manifest in (a) the child's chances of survival, and physical and mental health; (b) types of behavior that are rewarded; (c) the family structure; (d) the setting of family life; (e) the bond of kinship, including the family's attitude toward the child, the relations between the immediate and the kinship group families, the sense of family solidarity and family stability; (f) the educational pattern; (g) social activities and participation, and (h) the effects of parents' occupations on the children.

[33] Elton F. Jackson, "Status Consistency and Symptoms of Stress," *American Sociological Review*, August, 1962, pp. 469–480.

[34] Hodges, *op. cit.*, pp. 227–229.

6. The child's family not only is a member of a given class, but also has a rank order in that class, which has an effect upon the family life, particularly its psychic life.

7. Two basic processes inhere in the relationship between the child and his class setting. One is that childrearing serves as the social mechanism for the maintenance of the class structure; the other, that childrearing is utilized as the chief social device for attaining a rise in class status.

SUGGESTED READINGS

Amory, Cleveland, *The Last Resorts,* Harper & Brothers, New York, 1952. Mr. Amory describes the invasion of resort places by the new upper class and the retreat of the old upper class. He shows also the servant hierarchies within the resorts and the houses.

Baltzell, Edward Digby, *Philadelphia Gentlemen,* The Free Press of Glencoe, New York, 1958. The subtitle is "The making of a national upper class."

Burt, Nathaniel, *The Perennial Philadelphians,* Little, Brown and Company, Boston, 1963. The history, development and changes in the upper class of an old and growing community.

Davis, Allison, *Social Class Influences upon Learning,* Harvard University Press, Cambridge, 1948. An early Ingles lecture discusses a problem of growing concern today.

Dobriner, William M., *Class in Suburbia,* Prentice-Hall, Englewood Cliffs, N.J., 1963. Many books have been written recently about the suburbs. This book is one of a few that recognizes that there is no such thing, that each suburb has its own history and present character.

Havighurst, Robert J., *et al, Growing Up in River City,* John Wiley and Sons, New York, 1962. An analysis of various phases of the lives of youth, as influenced by the social class of their parents.

Hodges, Harold M., *Social Stratification,* Schankman Publishing Company, Cambridge, 1964. A very readable book, more descriptive than statistical, on social class differences in life style, past and present.

Lipset, Seymour M., and Reinhard Bendix, *Social Mobility in Industrial Society,* University of California Press, Berkeley, 1959. Summaries and interpretations of international studies of social mobility include conclusions at variance with generally accepted ones.

McKinley, Donald G., *Social Class and Family Life,* The Free Press of Glencoe, New York, 1964. A careful, analytic review of past studies on social class influences on childrearing. It explodes some enduring myths about differences in childrearing practices.

Marquand, John P., *B. F.'s Daughter,* Little, Brown and Company, Boston,

1946. A novel, written by a prize-winning novelist, that shows some of the problems of intersocial-class marriage.

Marquand, John P., *Point of No Return,* Little, Brown and Company, 1949. An interesting novel that gives Mr. Marquand's picture of American upper-middle-class life.

Mills, C. Wright, *White Collar,* Oxford University Press, New York, 1951. A detailed examination of changes within the middle class in the U.S.A. up to the middle of this century.

Walker, Charles R. and R. H. Guest, *The Man on the Assembly Line,* Harvard University Press, Cambridge, 1952. A study of life in the working class.

THE INDIVIDUAL CHILD AND HIS STATUS

12

The concept of status, implicit throughout the entire preceding chapter, has its individual as well as its group and class aspects, and it is to a consideration of the status system of society in relation to the individual child that the present chapter is devoted. Three main topics will be considered: first, the meaning and types of status; second, factors and problems in the ascription of status; and third, status achievement in contemporary American society.[1]

THE MEANING AND TYPES OF STATUS

The simplest way to define individual status is to say that it means a person's relative social position, assumed by him and

[1] For an excellent summary, in readable form, of features included in this discussion, the reader is referred to Ralph Linton, *The Study of Man*, D. Appleton-Century-Crofts, New York, 1936, chap. 8; Kingsley Davis, "The Child and the Social Structure," *Journal of Educational Sociology*, December, 1940, pp. 217–230; Allison Davis, "American Status Systems and the Socialization of the Child," *American Sociological Review*, June, 1941, pp. 345 ff.; Ralph Linton, "Age and Sex Categories," *ibid.*, October, 1942, pp. 589–603; Talcott Parsons, "Age and Sex in the Social Structure of the United States," *ibid.*, pp. 604–616; Leonard S. Cottrell, Jr., "The Adjustment of the Individual to His Age and Sex Roles," *ibid.*, pp. 617–620.

acknowledged by his fellows in their reciprocal relationships. Another way of expressing it, from the standpoint of formalized behavior, is to say that it means one's polar position in the patterns of reciprocal behavior in a functioning society; from the individual's standpoint, it is a collection of rights and duties; and from a neutral point of view, it may be described as a specific social position which carries with it definite privileges and obligations.

Considered specifically, a person has many statuses, as many as there are groups with whom he has relations. For example, John Smith as a practicing attorney has a status as a lawyer among the fellow members of his guild; as a deacon in the Methodist Church, he has a status among churchgoers, especially among Methodists; as a Knight Templar, he has a status in the fraternal world; and as the burgess of his borough, he has a status in his suburban neighborhood. In addition to these particularized statuses, he has also a composite or general status, which is the emergent total of all the particular statuses and which represents his polar position in the generalized life of society.

It is generally assumed that the latter is the significant status, and under certain conditions this is so. However, in the specialized secondary group life of our larger urban centers, the particularized status is often the only one that is known within the group; hence to its members, it, rather than the general status, is the important one. It might be added here that one of the problems of the individual in contemporary secondary group society grows out of the rather complete distinctness between the various groups of which he is a member and within each of which he has a separate status. Many people have to make sharp adjustments as they pass from one group to another in which they hold widely differing statuses.

Another and basically important distinction is that between the ascribed and the achieved statuses. The ascribed statuses are those which are assigned to individuals on the basis of certain facts about them other than indicated ability. Some of these facts exist from birth; others follow in a more or less prescribed sequence during individual development. The importance of this, for child development, is that they can be predicted and trained for from birth. The achieved statuses, as the term implies, are those which must be earned. They are not assigned as a matter of course, but are left open to be attained through competitive individual effort.

FACTORS AND PROBLEMS IN THE ASCRIPTION OF STATUS

In organizing the outstanding factors in the ascription of status, we see that they seem to fall into two main groups. In the first are those which ascribe status to the individual child because of his membership in certain population groups. These factors may be thought of, for purposes of contrast, as operating along vertical lines, as ascribing a relative status to an entire population group. The factors of color, ethnic origin, and class readily suggest themselves. The second series may be thought of as operating horizontally, that is, within each of the vertical categories. These include sex, age, age relationship, order of birth, plural birth, and the like. Membership in a given kinship group runs through and serves as a connecting link between all of them.

The Color Complex

For one who takes a realistic view of life, color is one of the two factors which fix permanently, from the beginning of life, and in more ways than one, the status of the child. Associated with color are certain other physical traits which combine to constitute the essence of social visibility. These may be spoken of as the color complex. Here is a factor which determines the child's status as a world citizen, i.e., not only in relation to other color groups distributed throughout the world, but also in relation to well-defined color complex groups within the United States. Since the predominant color group here is white, this factor has particular meaning for children who are born into nonwhite groups.

The basis for the ascription of status to these nonwhite groups is a product in large measure of their history in this country. All the numerically important groups were brought here either as slaves or as less-skilled laborers. As a result, a definite status was assigned to them, with resultant attitudes on the part of the dominant group. In the course of time these attitudes hardened, became emotionalized and persistent. Since deeply rooted attitudes in the dominant culture change slowly, they are operative today to a marked degree.

Ethnic Origin

The ethnic factor operates along the lines of the color complex, except that it is neither so definite nor so pronounced. In the United

States, the status significance of ethnic groups differs considerably from one group to another, and for the same group from place to place. Students of minority groups tend at times to overlook these variables in an apparent oversimplification of their problems. The status of the Irish as a group differs from that of the Poles, and that of the French Canadian may be quite different in Quebec from what it is in Connecticut. Here again one sees the role of historical development, as well as the divergence of the culture of the particular ethnic group from that of the dominant element. There is an extensive literature on minority group relations, and there is no thought here of summarizing it; the one point of emphasis is that the individual child has ascribed to him the status of his ethnic group at any particular time and place.

Class

The factor of class has been discussed in the preceding chapter; it is mentioned here only to complete the threefold linkage of the factors which operate on a vertical basis, each involving large segments of the population.

Sex

Sex is in many ways the simplest and most universally used of the reference points in the ascription of status. Sex is apparent from birth, it remains fixed for life, and all societies prescribe the various attitudes and roles on a sex basis. The age at which this differentiation begins, however, and the extent to which it develops vary from one culture to another. Parsons concludes that in this country the distinction develops relatively late and to a lesser degree than in many cultures, and that this is particularly true of sex privileges and responsibilities.[2] Whatever the time and degree, there is from the beginning of life an association, in the minds of the responsible members of society, of the two sexes with different functions, training, and responsibilities. The entire, even if intangible, weight of family and other group expectancies differs on a sex basis.

This sex typing of behavior and privileges is not only rigid and lasting but covers an extensive range. In most societies, the male is typed and trained for the superordinate role; the female, for the subordinate role, but with social allowances for certain forms of devious aggression against, or sabotage of, the male role. Modes of expressing fear and affection, as well as aggression, are socially typed for each sex. There are sex-appropriate language, clothes,

[2] Parsons, *op. cit.*, pp. 604–605.

gait, intonation of voice, play, recreation, and occupation. There is a noticeable difference in the control of the sex life, or events leading up to sex experience, girls being much more rigidly supervised in this respect. In this country, and probably in most societies, the crucial definition of the sex-appropriate role is formulated at adolescence, and it occurs earlier for girls than for boys.

It is, then, one of the essentials in the social development of the child that the social personality of each one shall match his sex in the biological sense; that is, boys must be boys and have masculine habits, and girls must have girls' habits. This typed behavior is largely a social creation. Earlier there was a good deal of rationalization to the effect that these different social roles were assigned on the basis of physiological differences, but their changing character from place to place and time to time can only mean that they are culturally determined. Similarly, they are socially enforced. The system of rewards for sex-appropriate and punishments for sex-inappropriate behavior constitutes a large part of the social code of any society. It operates with relative severity, begins early in the family's treatment of the child, and is reinforced later by the controls of the school, the gang, the social clique, and the adult world. For the child, particularly the female child, the road to prestige is paved with the rewards of observing the sex-appropriate code, especially as one moves from the lower to the higher social classes.

Age

Another obvious, highly visible fact about the child is his age; and its use as a reference point in the ascription of status is as old and universal as that of sex. Unlike sex, it is a constantly changing condition and as a result cannot give rise to permanent lifetime statuses. Age works on a developmental basis, with each person passing through a series of positions and pressures on an age basis.

Age grading is much emphasized in primitive societies. The age grades constitute distinct groups whose members are especially identified. Definite ceremonial rites mark the entrance into and exit from each group. Behavior appropriate to the members of each group is defined and often ritualized, and each group is organized into a hierarchy. In this country, age grading is obviously present, but it is characterized by a certain informality and lack of ceremonial observance which, however, in no way detract from its reality and effectiveness. Much of the learning process of the contemporary American child comes through his experience in conforming to the requirements of his age group,[3] for each group has its own pattern of expected behavior, privileges, and opportunities. In brief, each age group has its own status.

To achieve conformity of behavior in the specific age category, a system of rewards and punishments is used. Ridicule or ostracism, particularly by the members of one's age group, is usually employed for not "acting your age." Similarly, there are rewards by way of increased authority, privileges, and opportunities for a prompt advance to the next age category.

Society utilizes all sorts of prestige symbols which operate on an age basis. A child's hair is cut differently from that of the adolescent and adult. A very young child sits at the table on a high chair; later he has an adult chair but sits on the side of the table. Upper-class homes may have a special dining room for children up to a certain age. Certain words and phrases are forbidden to children before they reach a certain age. The time for retiring at night, crossing the street alone, going out after dark, having your own door key—these are but a few of the many privileges which vary on an age basis.

Both home and school emphasize age as a reference point for behavior. Much of the competition among children for the parents' favor, and the parents' emphasis on child behavior, operates through a system of age privileges. To beat customary age privileges is to gain from the parents more recognition or responsibility than one's age accords. But the present-day school is our most thoroughly age-graded institution. With compulsory promotion now operating widely, there results a form of automatic age grading which has few parallels, even in primitive societies. In the social life of many elementary- and secondary-school children, there is wide variation in rank and clique behavior among children separated by only one-year age grades.

Certain problems of child behavior which grow out of the operation of the age factor in the ascription of status may be noted briefly. First, children differ markedly in their adaptation to the age hierarchy prevalent in the family's life, as well as in that of the larger society. Some children accept the customary age roles and move along with changes in them. Others strive desperately for the privileges of a higher age group. Still others retreat to the demands of a lower level. There is considerable reason to believe that the second group is the most likely to develop behavior problems, particularly during the adolescent period.

A second problem is the relative abruptness of change from one

[3] John Dollard and Neal E. Miller, *Social Learning and Imitation*, Yale University Press, New Haven, 1941, pp. 184–188.

age category to another. This varies greatly from one society to another. In some it is very gradual, with no clear lines of demarcation from one to another. In others, "it is more nearly comparable to a string of beads, each period being set off sharply from those that precede and follow it."[4] In this country there are certain of the latter type of change. One is the sudden change for many children at the age of 6 from living entirely at home to going to school full time. The gradual transition through nursery school and kindergarten would seem to be much easier and more satisfactory. Even more abrupt is the change from a full-time school status, at ages 16 to 18, to full-time employment in the world of industry. This happens with particular frequency among lower middle-class urban children. Rural children usually have no such difficulties.

A third problem grows out of the difference between the physical passage from childhood to maturity and the social transfer of the child to the status of adult. This problem does not arise in primitive societies which observe rites to signalize the outstanding landmarks in the life of the individual. In our society, the lack of such rites, combined with the high standards of compulsory school attendance and social protection, results in a situation in which grown young people retain the legal status of children long after they have become adults in other respects.

Age Relationship

If age operates on a developmental basis with but temporary status, the age relationship between given persons remains fixed and carries with it the implications of a permanent status. "Will I always be two years younger than Betty?" wails a 4-year-old. "Yes. always," replies the mother to her disconsolate daughter.

This age relationship is a status-fixing factor of tremendous significance in the relationship between closely associated persons. It has, for example, a very definite role in the kinship group structure. From birth on, each child has a fixed relationship, based on the age differential, with every other person in the prescribed kinship circle. This relationship covers a constant and comprehensive series of the detailed aspects of the life of the individual child, and of the adult as well. In the child's school life, this age relationship, reinforced by class affiliations and numerals, becomes the basis of much of the social life of students. Among the most frequent comments by one student about another are such as these: "Oh, she is in ninth grade," "He was a sophomore when I was a freshman,"

[4] Linton, "Age and Sex Categories," p. 602.

"She graduated the year before I did," "I was a grade ahead of her." How significant these comments are can be seen from the fact that they may be made in old age in reference to early school associates.

Order of Birth

Order of birth is in large measure only another name for age relationship, except that at times it has significance because of the particular order of birth in the family or social configuration as a whole. The middle child, and also the oldest and the youngest, may be said to have a status resulting from that fact, not covered wholly by the fact of age relationship.

Primogeniture

Particular mention should be made of the special status, both legal and social, of the eldest child over the centuries. The source of this goes back far in human history, probably to religious conceptions of the special value or virtue of first fruits. Its social importance has been considerable, and in a variety of ways. First, it has been utilized as the general method of monarchial succession. Second, it has served the great landowning families in maintaining their position, through the inheritance both of titles and of landed estates. For many centuries, especially during the feudal stage of history, this maintenance of unity in family estates served as a prop for the stability of the social and economic order. Third, its operation has made for family unity during long periods of time when lack of the principle and its resultant family unity could only have resulted in social disintegration. Fourth, it has tended within the family group to fix the occupation of the oldest male, as well as his range of responsibilities toward other members. Its importance has declined greatly in recent decades, in large measure because of the greater degree of security afforded by the larger society.

Plural Birth

The general significance attached to multiple birth today is wholly social—the assignment of a special social status. On the one side, this status involves an almost complete lack of individual identity. A twin is never just John Smith or Mary Jones, but always one of the Smith or Jones twins. Similar, but more so, is the case with triplets, quadruplets, and quintuplets. On the more positive side, plural birth confers an attention-getting or publicity status which in certain cases is exploited by the parents or some other interested agency. The ramifications of this type of ascribed status have been discussed at greater length in Chapter 2.

Adoption

Adoption is a legal fiction by which an individual, usually a young child, who belongs by birth to one kinship group acquires an equivalent status in another one. It was very common in the earlier stages of cultural development, often occurring on almost a mass scale. This was due undoubtedly to such factors as a high death rate among younger parents, large families, and generally unsettled conditions of life which created large numbers of orphaned children. To meet this problem, large-scale rationalization developed the institution of adoption as a family duty and a social virtue. In other instances, as among the Romans, the prevailing emphasis upon family continuity emphasized the desirability of adoption for those cases where the barrenness of the wife meant the lack of a natural heir.

Adoption in this country seems to have been on the increase ever since World War I. The details have been brought more and more under the regulation of the law and the surveillance of public authorities, to the end of safeguarding the dual process of conferring the privileges of parenthood upon the childless and securing a satisfactory home for the parentless. Thus protected, the status of the adopted child is one that has certain intangible social implications. These are indicated by such statements as the following: "Fred is one of the Smith boys. He is the adopted one." "The Browns have two children. You know, they are both adopted." "Mother, who really am I? What were my people like?" Such statements; and their significance, possibly vary considerably on a class basis.

Illegitimacy

Illegitimacy of birth affects the status of the child in many ways. Suffice it here to refer to the general conclusions of anthropological research that one of the universal social rules is that no child, if he is to have full legal and social status, shall be brought into the world save within the limits of socially approved arrangements. The history of childhood furnishes the complement to this, for it indicates how throughout human history the child born outside of these socially approved limitations has had a special status as a social pariah. One of the most unpleasant aspects of man's inhumanity to man is the way in which the established order has vented its disapproval of the offending parents upon their helpless child.

Kinship Unit

Membership in the kinship unit is the initial factor through which the entire system of ascribed statuses operates. Not only is it the oldest, it is also the most universally accepted determinant of status. Originally, man obtains his status through his personal traits and exploits. Frequently, and in time, these come to be extended to his family, and then to his descendants. In a manner like the inheritance of biological traits and accumulated possessions, status is transmitted from one generation to another.

The ascription of status through membership in a kinship unit operates in several ways. First, the child has ascribed to him at birth a status within his kinship group. This involves the socialized pattern of his relations to his parents, brothers, sisters, and relatives to a certain degree of kinship. This is particularly significant because it involves his relationship with a whole series of persons with whom he will have, for a number of years, his most constant and intimate relations. These prescribed patterns are both positive, indicating how he is to act toward certain people, and negative and prohibitive, including what he may not do. In all societies the initial status of every normal individual, according to Parsons, is the child's status in a given kinship unit.[5]

Second, membership in the kinship unit determines the status ascribed to the child in relation to other kinship groups. In this way, the family serves as the vehicle through which ascriptions of the bases of the color complex, ethnic origin, and class are made, as well as the rank order in each of these categories.

General Importance of the Ascribed Statuses

An amazingly large part of the ordinary business of living is included in the operation of these ascribed statuses, particularly those of age, sex, and membership in the kinship unit. The relative importance of the ascribed statuses is not the same, however, in all societies. It seems evident that in small and comparatively stable groups they are emphasized a great deal. In such societies, social

[5] Parsons, *op. cit.*, p. 604.

habits are fixed, and the reciprocal patterns of behavior are so clearly defined that they are readily imposed upon the young child. His induction into his culture takes the form of his acceptance of the age, sex, and other subordinations which are involved. But in a large and rapidly changing society, reliance upon the ascribed statuses is more difficult. Old statuses become specialized and new ones appear; hence the family's initial role in introducing the child to the status system is more complicated and comes to be shared with other agencies whose conceptions and emphases may be different.

In addition to the customary differences in social complexity and rates of social change, a society sometimes passes through an age of iconoclasm when the status systems, among various other aspects of the social structure, are destroyed or recast. There may be a deliberate mass urge to let girls behave as boys do; young men are placed in authority over old ones, members of subject races are raised to pinnacles of power, and the common man is glorified to the exclusion of all others. These developments seem to take the form of outbursts so impulsive and irrational as to suggest that they are a therapeutic mass drainage of resentment against conditions far removed from their manifestations.

The problems involved in the socialization of the child, which is only another term to identify the adjustment processes of the individual, vary directly with the rate of change and the clarity with which the requirements of the ascribed statuses are defined. This clarity is increased by similarity between what a child is told and what he sees in practice, by lack of contact with other culture groups which maintain different ascribed status requirements, and by uniform conformity with the status pattern on the part of the adult members of the child's social world. In other words, if a child grows up in a society in which the patterns of reciprocal behavior are clearly defined and universally practiced, his socialization is relatively simple. The reverse of these conditions naturally increases the difficulties.[6]

ACHIEVED STATUSES AND THEIR ATTAINMENT

Every society has a number of statuses which are open to individual achievement. Their number and the difficulty of attainment vary a great deal, as does their importance in the functioning of any particular society. Linton insists that most of the statuses

[6] Cottrell, *op. cit.*, pp. 617–620.

open to achievement do not touch the business of living very deeply and that, although satisfying to the persons who achieve them, they are designed, from the standpoint of society, chiefly "to serve as bait for socially acceptable behavior or as escapes for the individual."[7] Such a judgment seems to run counter to the great emphasis on status achievement in this country, where the more recently arrived ethnic groups have been particularly concerned that the road to this end be kept open and that the status-achieving devices be made available to them. This makes all the more striking the relative absence, in the literature on status systems, of a consideration of the achieved statuses and the devices utilized to attain them. The subject has amazing ramifications and requires a vast amount of study and research. By way of a move in this direction, some status-achieving devices significant for the younger age groups are presented briefly.

Athletic Skill

Activities of an athletic nature play a large part in American life. This is true particularly in the segment of the population which is under 25 years of age. Much of the life of American youth is organized around scholastic and collegiate athletic programs, from which it follows that a considerable part of the comparative rating which takes place in the child's and youth's world is based on athletic achievement. Naturally this is more marked among boys than girls, and it is rather more significant in the lower than in the upper classes. This does not mean that there is less participation in sports among upper-class boys, for often the reverse is true. Reference is intended rather to the variations in the interpretation and exploitation of success in athletic competitions among the different classes. Thus upper-class children tend to engage in sports for sport's sake, lower-class boys, to achieve status, i.e., honors, social recognition, and prestige.

Artistic Achievement

Achievement in the arts operates somewhat along the lines of athletic ability, but is more significant for girls than for boys, and seems in many ways to be more effective as a status-achieving device. Warner has written about one aspect of this.

> One of the usual methods by which the children of members of the lower groups raise themselves is to exercise various semi-artistic talents.

[7] Linton, *The Study of Man*, p. 128.

So-called schools of dancing, music, and elocution are attended by such children where they learn how to tap dance, play a saxophone, or recite pieces. Such trained talents are utilized by the various associations, clubs, and lodges for their entertainment, and the growing youth comes to their notice and frequently to membership. He thus climbs out of his lower status to a higher group and stabilizes his rise by becoming a member of an association in a higher group. This method of rising is, of course, not confined to the lower groups. The middle and lower upper classes also use their occasional talents as equipment for raising their class participation. The wealthy son or daughter of a "recently arrived" textile manufacturer, after completing his or her training at one of the older colleges with its higher social prestige, goes to an art school in Paris, or trains his or her voice "on the continent," or goes to New York to learn to write. If such attempts succeed in launching a generally recognized artistic career, his status is raised and his sphere of behavior enlarged in the field of upper-class activity. If he fails, he frequently becomes emotionally unstable and in some cases develops psychoneurotic behavior.[8]

Success on the stage has been, for a long time, a short cut for many young girls to the achievement of a higher social status. In recent decades, television and radio and the movies have offered similar opportunities, and on an extensive scale. How effective artistic achievement of a high order may be as a status-achieving device is indicated by the fact that in "café society," so-called, the Social Registerite accepts only the equality of the artist.

Educational Attainment

"Go to school, study your lessons, and you won't have to work as I do"—so speaks the ambitious lower-class parent to his child. "Be an outstanding student, and you'll find your way to the top"—this is the advice of the middle-class parent. "Why, of course, Bill's going to the university," for both child and parent in the upper classes assume that this is the thing to do. These statements, at differing levels, express the American attitude toward education. Education everywhere is an outstanding agency chiefly to raise status and, incidentally, to prevent loss of it. It is part of the American creed that intellect and talent can be educated and therefore improved, that people doing so should be rewarded, that the rewards should include prestige and money, which can be transformed into social status.[9]

In the United States, all of this becomes particularly significant

[8] W. Lloyd Warner, "Formal Education and the Social Structure," *Journal of Educational Sociology*, May, 1936, p. 520.

[9] W. Lloyd Warner, *Environment and Education*, Supplementary Educational Monograph No. 59, University of Chicago Press, Chicago, 1942, pp. 16–28.

because of the mass migrations into this country. Education has been utilized, on the one hand, by us to assimilate the masses of European children, and on the other by these children and their parents to raise their own status. In other words, for them our system of public instruction ceases to be a vehicle for transmitting the accumulated traditions and skills of the group, and serves instead to develop new cultural values, new loyalties, and in many cases a status higher than that of the parents. This is most marked in the field of higher education, which is being profoundly influenced and possibly even transformed in certain areas under the impact of larger numbers of second-generation American students. The application of these students is unusual, in selected aspects of the higher education pattern; their hopes are particularly forward-looking; their expectation is specific. There is particular concern with the prestige symbols in education, such as grades, honors, and degrees. The doctor's degree is especially esteemed; and colleges of pharmacy and the like, in which its attainment has been relatively easy, have proved particularly attractive, as enrollment data clearly indicate.

It should be emphasized, however, that this interest in education as a status-achieving or -maintaining device is not confined to any nativity group in the population. A large proportion of the students in the American educational system, as well as their parents, regard a school or college as a place to go to make advantageous contacts, to gain the proper entree, to get in with the right people, and ultimately to secure the right of identifying themselves with a particular institution, as one of its accredited representatives. Many educators do not like to face these implications.

Group Membership

The joiner is a product of an open class system, and this device is utilized early in the child's life, when membership in certain groups is sought in order to raise his status. This may begin early with enrollment in a given Sunday School, or later with confirmation in a given church. Later, there are selected dancing classes, private schools or particular public schools, social clubs, high school and college fraternities, and cliques. This aspect of the child's socialization will be discussed in a subsequent chapter; the reference here is solely to their utilization as status-achieving devices.

Place of Residence

Early in life, status comes to be assigned on the basis of place of residence. The right and wrong sides of the railroad track are identified for children almost from the time they enter school; the comparative status of selected areas in large cities and suburbs becomes known to most children as a by-product of competitive school athletics, as well as of their mixture in centrally located high schools. All of this is, of course, an extension into the early age period of what obtains among adults. An example of its operation in the nation's capital follows:

Like any other socially ambitious newcomer, Mrs. Toy would like to move immediately into the embassy circle and pass from there into the more powerful Cabinet group. To accomplish these aims she must know the right people, and the right people are found, of course, only in the right places. Washington's most correct residential districts are Massachusetts Avenue, where most of the embassies are; Arlington across the bridge; or Georgetown, the one-time Negro colony whose old brick houses are now occupied by such celebrities as the Harry Hopkinses, the James B. Forrestals, the Francis Biddles, and Mrs. Edward B. McLean. The newcomer whose husband can afford it (and if he can't, she'd better stay home) can rent a small furnished house in Georgetown for about four hundred dollars a month.[10]

Status-crossing Romances

The role of marriage as a status-achieving device has been emphasized recently in sociological literature.[11] Obviously, in this respect marriage is only one step in a process which begins before marriage and does not culminate with it. The whole range of romantic relations may be considered from the standpoint of their role in the status systems of society. This process begins with courtship. To become the favored one of a member of the opposite sex who belongs to a higher prestige group is an effective and frequently successful way of moving across a class line. The method of operation is somewhat as follows: The boy or girl of higher status intercedes with his or her crowd in behalf of the chosen one. Tolerance of the chosen one may follow. Subsequently, there are invitations from the higher-status crowd. Such invitations create a special opportunity. If the neophyte measures up to requirements, group acceptance may follow, and the newly arrived one becomes a member of the clique, especially in the eyes of outside observers.

10 Margaret Case Harriman, "How to Woo Washington," *Harper's Magazine*, August, 1944, pp. 227–228. See also Walter Firey, "Sentiment and Symbolism as Ecological Variables," *American Sociological Review*, April, 1945, pp. 140–149.

11 James H. S. Bossard, "Marriage as a Status Achieving Device," *Sociology and Social Research*, September–October, 1944, pp. 3–10. For a more complete analysis of marriage as a status-achieving device and its significance for marriage and child development, see James H. S. Bossard and Eleanor S. Boll, *Why Marriages Go Wrong*, The Ronald Press Company, New York, 1958, chap. 8.

There are various specific aspects of such class-crossing romances. One consists of the cases where relationships are with or between minority groups. As in marriage, so in premarital romantic attachments there is often the opportunity for escape from an ascribed status. Another aspect involves premarital sex relationships. Studies of sex delinquency among girls reveal how frequently the girl of lower status seeks to "put herself across" with a higher-status boy on the basis of sex relationships. The relative status of the mothers and fathers of children born out of wedlock is an illustration in point. Similar in implication are Whyte's studies of Italian attitudes. He writes: "In the social and ethnic group category, the most desirable woman for nonmarital sex relations is the girl of old American stock background, preferably blonde, who has a higher status than the corner-boy."[12]

RELATIVE EMPHASES IN STATUS SYSTEMS

One of the continuing problems in every society, of special significance for those in the lower age groups, is the proper relative emphasis upon the ascribed and the achieved statuses. The foregoing analysis should have made it clear that a great deal of the business of living is taken care of by the ascribed statuses, that the behavior involved in these roles is socially typed, and that the child can be trained for it. Clarity and definiteness in group expectancies, and habit in behavior patterns, seem necessary for survival and desirable for the development of stable personalities. The individual child does need a cultural ledge sufficiently broad and stable to permit satisfactory performance and adequate security.

On the other hand, too much limitation in the achieved status is a curb on the ambitions and development of the child. A curb on the former makes for feelings of frustration; limitation of the latter entails a loss of social efficiency and leadership. In younger societies, and where conditions are changing constantly, this may prove particularly serious. As a society matures, and the adjustive relationships between groups and between the society and its physical environment come into being, such limitations may be considered of less importance.

[12] William F. Whyte, "A Slum Sex Code," *American Journal of Sociology*, July, 1943, p. 28.

SUMMARY

1. Status may be defined as relative social position. Thus conceived, it has its individual as well as its group and class aspects.

2. There are two main groups of statuses: the ascribed and the achieved.

3. The factors underlying the ascription of status include the color complex, ethnic origin, social class, sex, age, age relationship, order of birth, primogeniture, plural birth, adoption, illegitimacy, and membership in a kinship unit.

4. A large part of the ordinary business of living is included in the operation of the ascribed statuses. Their relative importance is greatest in small and relatively stable societies.

5. Every society includes a number of achieved statuses which are open to competitive achievement. Some of the status-achieving devices which are particularly significant in child and youth development are athletic skill, artistic achievement, educational attainment, group membership, place of residence, and class-crossing romances.

6. The proper relative emphasis upon the ascribed and achieved statuses is a continuing problem in every society. The essential requirement is balance, and this point seems to change wth the development of the particular society.

SUGGESTED READINGS

Eisenstadt, Shmuel N., *From Generation to Generation,* The Free Press of Glencoe, New York, 1956. This anthropological study shows the relationship between age groups and social structure.

Fletcher, Alice M., *The Child and the Tribe,* Proceedings of the National Academy of Sciences, vol. I, no. 12, December, 1915, pp. 569–574. The place of the child in a society of North American Indians.

Joshi, Sastris, *The Child Marriage Restraint Act,* Law Book Company, Allahabad, 1962. Reports the current status of child marriages in India as compared with the status described in Rathbone's book, cited below.

Linton, Ralph, *The Study of Man,* D. Appleton-Century-Crofts, New York, 1936, chaps. 8, 15, and 26. A discussion of status and role as related to social systems, culture and personality.

Miller, Nathan, *The Child in Primitive Society,* K. Paul, Trench, Trubner and Company, Ltd., 1928. Although this book shows the place of the child in primitive conditions, the student might use almost any anthropological study of children in its place.

Moore, Fred, *Child Health,* University of Iowa Press, Iowa City, 1933. A survey that illustrates the growing concern over children's life situations at a time when their status in the United States was changing.

Powell, Marvin, *Age and Sex Differences in Degree of Conflict Within Certain Areas of Psychological Adjustment,* American Psychological Association, Washington, D.C., 1955. Age and sex are here related to certain psychological processes. Certain aspects of status may be inferred.

Rathbone, Eleanor F., *Child Marriage,* G. Allen and Unwin, London, 1934. The book describes the earlier situation in India. It should be read in conjunction with Joshi's book, cited above.

FAMILIES UNDER STRESS

Photograph from Pasadena City Schools

PART VI

SOME PROBLEM FAMILIES 13

Thus far, the approach to the sociology of child development has been through the analysis of family situations, with reference to their significance for children. The effort has been to show how the family operates to mold the personality of the child, how the family inducts him into the prevailing culture, what differentials in this process occur from one class to another, and how behavior requirements and stimuli are typed at different status levels. Speaking generally, these discussions reflect the changes in child study from the earlier emphasis on problems of social misconduct and economic need to the contemporary stress on the processes of child-rearing, and from a primary concern with socially disadvantaged children to concern with those at all cultural levels.

Some emphasis should be given, however, to the problem approach; and this chapter and the next will be devoted to family situations which have been identified as the problem-creating kind. Following the basic approach of this book, it seems proper to think of these as problem homes with children rather than as homes with problem children.

THE RANGE OF FAMILY SITUATIONS

Before proceeding to a discussion of selected groups of family problems, it should be stated that the range of specific family situations is endless. The study of family situations began with an analysis of the more conspicuous problem-creating cases. At first, these were considered chiefly from the standpoint of the good of the child, with emphasis upon broad moral factors. Gradually, however, other factors which could be easily detected as well as tested and measured, such as health, education, and economic status, were included. The procedure for studying the family developed into an examination of the situations of individuals with specific behavior irregularities, in order to find which of these measurable factors were most constant in the homes of these individuals.

Although many types of family situations in terms of these factors were identified, two discoveries led to the formation of a new approach. The first was the realization that selected unhealthy factors do not inevitably produce unhealthy home situations; the second was the development of newer insights into the processes and significance of personality formation, especially through family interaction. The result has been the emergence of an approach to the study of family situations as groups of interacting persons influenced by special sets of circumstances, to which the family reacts in specific ways.

The very number of these studies has led to attempts to systematize and classify family situations. Particularly helpful and suggestive are the classificatory schemes proposed by Weill and Symonds.[1] Our own classification[2] is reproduced in Table 8 as an inductive summary of the literature from 1926 to 1940.

PARENTS WITH PROBLEM ATTITUDES

Reference was made in Chapter 3 to the role of parental attitudes toward parenthood and children, and to the chief sources of these attitudes. A few problem-creating attitudes will be discussed here.

Parents Who Reject Their Children

This is the first of the problems of family personnel to be considered in this chapter.

This type of problem home first came to the attention of students

[1] Blanche Weill, *Behavior of Young Children in the Same Family*, Harvard University Press, Cambridge, 1928; Percival M. Symonds, *The Psychology of Parent-Child Relationships*, D. Appleton-Century Company, New York, 1939.

[2] James H. S. Bossard and Eleanor S. Boll, *Family Situations*, University of Pennsylvania Press, Philadelphia, 1943, pp. 111–112.

Table 8 A Classification of Family Situations

	Intrafamily Relationships
Excess of affection	The possessive home
	The oversolicitous home
	The overindulgent home
Normal affection	The companionable home
Discrimination in affection	The divided home
	The favored-child home
	The "impartial" home
Inconsistency of affection	The bickering home
	The unreliable home
Displacement of affection	The home with a new member
Lack of affection	The nagging home
	The frigid home
	The neglectful home
Frank rejection	The home of the unwanted child
Repression	The mother-controlled home
	The father-dominated home
	The overly demanding home
Anarchy	The child-dictated home
Confusion	The home with too many bosses
Approaching balance	The democratic home
	Family Patterns
Size	The large family
	The one-child family
Organization	The cooperative family
	The independent family
	The incomplete family
Activity	The nomadic family
	The "joiner" family
	The family of the intelligentsia
	The "cliff-dweller" family
	The community-benefactor family
Values and goals	The social-climber family
	The materialistic family
	The overly religious family
	The scientific family
	The superstitious family
	The conventional family
	External Factors
Socioeconomic status	The inadequately financed home
	The suddenly wealthy home
	The large-inheritance home
	The mother-supported family
	The family marked by peculiar occupational characteristics
	The home of culture conflict
	The disgraced home
	The family in the public eye
Neighborhood	The farm family
	The small-town family
	The city family
	The summer resort family
	The misfit-in-the-neighborhood family
	The family in a substandard neighborhood
Health	The home of the invalid
	The home of the defective

of social relations because of the resultant behavior of the children involved. After reviewing the literature on the subject, Symonds concluded that when either or both parents reject a child, he is likely to be characterized as aggressive, annoying in school, attention-getting, hostile, hyperactive, jealous, or rebellious; and that he may commit such delinquencies as truancy, thieving, or lying.[3] There is every evidence that such children are driven abnormally by two quests: one, to attract attention, i.e., to gain group acceptance; the other, to see their teachers and parents upset about them. Obviously, both of these are compensatory.[4]

More recently, the subject of child rejection has been emphasized in the literature on planned parenthood. Because of the lack of knowledge, or the unavailability, of reliable contraceptives, it is pointed out that many unplanned pregnancies ensue, with the subsequent birth of children who are not wanted by their parents. The facts on abortion bear eloquent testimony to the urgent desperation of such parents.

The chief concern here is with the nature of the family situation in child rejection. This, we contend, needs considerably more careful analysis than has been given to it. Parental rejection of the child has been referred to generally as though it were relatively simple, effective from birth throughout the child's life, and involved similar attitudes for both parents. Obviously, this represents an oversimplification of the facts. While such situations do exist, they are only a minor part of a much larger situation. It may help, therefore, to conceive of rejection situations as having at least three dimensions. First, there is the matter of who it is that rejects the child. He may be in the situation of having loving parents and being rejected by a sibling or grandparent. He may be rejected by both parents or just one. Each of these cases has its own specific meaning to the child.

The Black family illustrates rejection by the father and acceptance by the mother.

Mr. and Mrs. Black were married when they were 26 and 22 years of age, respectively. They lived in a three-room apartment in a large city. Mr. Black earned a relatively high salary. Mrs. Black stayed at home and kept house. Their relations, including their sex life, were mutually satisfactory. But Mrs. Black became lonely after a time, and "tricked" her husband, as she put it, into parenthood. From the beginning of her pregnancy, he was not interested in the coming of the child, apparently

[3] Symonds, *op. cit.*, p. 45.

[4] For an excellent study of parental acceptance and rejection, see *ibid.*, chap. 2, and Hilde Bruch, *Don't Be Afraid of Your Child*, Farrar, Straus and Young, New York, 1952, chap. 5.

indicating a resentment against it for breaking into a happy, carefree relationship with his wife. After the child was born, he lost interest in her, and finally, when the child was 7 months old, deserted. Some time afterwards, he began living with another woman. For a time, he made occasional payments in support of his wife and child. Mrs. Black seems devoted to her child, and does an excellent job of mothering it. Recently, after her divorce, she has remarried. There have been no children with the second husband, who seems somewhat lukewarm toward his stepchild.

Some obvious cases of families' division in regard to acceptance of a child appear in remarriages when one or both mates have children. Smith[5] has summarized the literature on the stepchild, and much of the material available can be viewed from the standpoint of child acceptance and rejection. In addition to remarriage there is the informal shifting of mates, so prevalent in the lower classes. Here, too, the problem of rejection looms large, with added implications for the child because of his knowledge of the extramarital relationship. The reconstruction of a home, whether through remarriage of the parent or not, often means that the child is "bounced here and there like a ball and does not know to whom he can go or where he belongs."[6]

In summary, the basic fact in regard to this first so-called dimension is that family attitudes toward a child involve the attitude of all the members of the family of orientation. While the mother's acceptance-rejection response is in many ways of primary importance, the response of the other members is also significant, both in its meaning for the child and also in the effect which rejection by one member has upon the other members.

A second dimension of rejection situations involves their time aspect. The rejection of a child may be permanent or temporary. Here, as elsewhere, there is the possibility of an honest change of attitude. This seems to be illustrated in the following case:

Mrs. King did not want to have a child. This attitude may have been created largely by her mother, who repeatedly had expressed the hope that her daughter would not "have to have a child." When Mrs. King became pregnant, she was both frightened and resentful, and her mother continued to express her hope that "something" might happen. However, the child was born after a rather difficult delivery. After the birth, Mrs. King gave clear evidence of her rejection of her child, and turned rather frigid toward her husband. About two years later, while taking her child to a public park one day, she met two other young mothers, both of

[5] William C. Smith, "The Stepchild," *American Sociological Review*, April, 1945, pp. 237–242.

[6] *Ibid.*, p. 241.

whom were quite proud of their motherhood. The three speedily became quite friendly, and gradually Mrs. King began to absorb the attitude of her two friends. Gradually, she seems to have relaxed and her attitude toward her husband changed. Meanwhile, her child was developing into a very attractive young person. At this time, Mrs. King had a prolonged illness, and during her convalescence she did some serious thinking. Something in the nature of a complete change toward life seems to have occurred. She freed herself from her mother's influence. A year and a half later, she had a second, and planned, child. She says that the coming of these two children, and especially the first, were the turning point in her life.

As was pointed out in Chapter 3, the birth of the first child to an American middle-class couple often is a crisis situation. Parenthood has been romanticized, but the realities have not been foreseen, causing some disenchantment with the parental role. Usually, this feeling changes to one of subsequent wholehearted acceptance.

There are cases in which the age of the child makes a difference in a parent's feelings toward him. In a clinic for emotionally maladjusted children, a mother and her four small youngsters were being treated. They were very clearly the victims of maternal rejection. During therapy, however, the mother decided that she wanted to have another baby. She loved small, dependent, cuddly babies. By the time they became negativistic and self-willed 3-year-olds she was through with them. On the other hand, there is the college-educated young wife who handed her infant over to a nursemaid. Before the little girl was born her mother collected a library for her which she will not be able to read until she is a teen-ager. The mother can hardly wait until the child grows up and can have "intellectual communion" with her.

A third dimension of rejection situations concerns the form or nature which the rejection takes. This is in part a matter of degree, but is much more a form of expression. For example, rejection may be physical, involving the child himself, as in the case of abandoned children. Ordinarily, physical rejection occurs with illegitimate children and may take the form of abandoning the child on a doorstep or a dump pile or along a country road; or it may involve surrendering him to an agency or relative or adopting family. In some instances, however, married couples turn their child over at birth or soon afterward to a relative or some other person "to raise." Rejection later in the child's life may involve placement in an institution, reform school, boarding school, convent, or military school. Again, it may express itself chiefly in economic ways, in a failure to provide adequately—lack of toys, inadequate clothing, no personal allowance, and the like. The mink-coated mother and the daughter in the frayed dress tell their own story. In other cases, the rejection is of an educational nature, chiefly omission. There is a lack of guidance, supervision, or educational facilities. The parents have other interests, and delegate the training of their children to servants, nurses, or relatives. Finally, rejection may be emotional in character; this is by far the most emphasized form in recent years. Contemporary students seem to think that emotional rejection of the child has more serious consequences than any other parental fault. What it means above all else is that the child's basic craving for intimate response, his desire to be loved, is not satisfied. It is this that hurts most, and gives meaning to other forms of rejection. In other words, there is a spiritual inadequacy in such homes, and the child's payment for it is a basic lack of security.

Although there has always been some physical abuse of children by parents, there appears to have been an increase of parental violence toward very small children recently. Battered children, when brought to hospitals and X-rayed, reveal series of broken bones which, because they were soft, have knitted together by themselves. Physicians call it "the battered child syndrome."[7] In January, 1962, the Children's Bureau called together a group in order to consult on what might be done about the seeming increase in such incidents.[8] By 1963, at least 18 states had introduced some kind of legislation on this matter and 13 states enacted laws requiring the mandatory reporting of such cases, under certain circumstances.[9] It is a rather appalling thought that such measures are necessary in a so-called "child-centered" and "affluent" society such as ours. Perhaps these very two attributes add to the problem. Affluence creates a hedonistic spirit in some adults, and a hatred in those who do not share the affluence. Both of these feelings are easily turned against a small child who requires time, patience, and financial outlay. In a child-centered society that values all children, it is not easy to dispose of the unwanted child. In earlier eras, there were socially approved ways which, though cruel, did not prolong the cruelty. These are discussed in a later chapter. Today, however, the lives of all children are protected by law, and "what the neighbors will think" is a strong pressure against making

[7] Charles Flato, "Parents Who Beat Children," *Saturday Evening Post*, October 6, 1962, p. 30.

[8] *The Abused Child,* U.S. Department of Health, Education, and Welfare, Children's Bureau, Washington, D.C., 1963.

[9] Vincent De Francis, *Review of Legislation to Protect the Battered Child*, Children's Division, The American Humane Association, Denver, 1964.

some other arrangements for them outside the family. Thus, it appears that at all socioeconomic levels, there are parents who have, who keep, and who violently reject their children.

A final word should be said about parents who reject their children. Not all are heartless and selfish, as is often assumed. Many young people who become parents and reject their children are themselves the victims of maladjustment; hence they are only the transmitters of what was done to them. Some of these parents may appreciate their own ineptitudes, so their fundamental unwillingness to be parents represents a reasoned judgment rather than a selfish whim. Again, some young people are highpressured into being parents, and their resentment against this pressure may find expression in their attitudes toward their children. Such pressure may be exerted within the circle of kinsfolk, as in the case of upper-class families which put marked emphasis upon family continuity. Or it may be community pressure, such as one finds in small towns, where persons are paired off, married, and become parents, under the innuendos and suggestions of their friends. Again, a parent's rejection of a particular child may grow out of that child's relation to the sex balance within the family. A couple with four girls may be none too pleased when the fifth child is a girl. Five boys and a husband may give a wife strong feelings of resentment against a sixth son. Finally, rejection of a child may symbolize the parents' deep-seated rejection of the world. To many thoughtful people, the world today is not a happy or pleasing prospect to give the bearer of a new life. To reject a child may only express resentment at one's cosmic destiny. Perhaps all that has been said suggests that parental rejection of a child is not a simple factor, operating alone, but is a phase of a larger pattern of attitudes and values. Parents who reject their children need understanding, too. Moreover, parental rejection is often partial, and is modified by misgivings of various kinds. This is a highly significant fact, for it means that the rejection of a child leads to feelings of guilt which express themselves in a marked solicitousness concerning the child. Such a combination results in a family situation which combines the evils of rejection and of oversolicitousness. It is to the latter type of situation that we turn next.

PARENTS WHO MAGNIFY THEIR RESPONSIBILITIES

A second group of problem parents stands in direct contrast to those who reject their children. In part, these parents reveal a tendency to overaccept their children, but the group envisaged here involves a somewhat broader and perhaps more significant concept. In going through the literature on child-behavior problems, one finds a number of family situations in which the common element is the tendency on the part of parents to magnify their parental responsibilities in one or more ways. As a group, these parents take themselves too seriously. Obviously, this is again a matter of degree, with a cultural determination of the point at which it is considered a problem. The concrete expressions of such situations, as well as their particular emphases, come to attention in a variety of ways, the more important and common of which will be identified briefly.

1. First are the parents who overprotect their children.[10] The mother is the most common offender. Overprotection, in its milder forms, is quite prevalent. Frequently, too, it is temporary, ceasing with the birth of another child or with the advancing maturity of the parents. Probably the most serious type, and certainly the most frequent clinical type, is maternal overprotection which masks or is compensatory for a strong rejection of a child.

Maternal overprotection, which is synonymous with the mother's excessive care of her children, manifests itself usually in three ways. First, there is excessive contact—"the mother is always there." This involves continuous companionship between mother and child, prolonged nursing care, excessive fondling, and sleeping with the mother long past infancy. Second is infantilization, which means prolonging infancy by rendering services to the child far beyond the customary age. Illustrative of such services are breast feeding, bathing, feeding, punishing, and the like. In short, what these cases involve is an undue prolongation of the "waiting-on" period. Third is the prevention of social maturity—"she won't let him grow up." Here one finds an active prevention of the child's growth in the direction of self-reliance. Within the home, there is no emphasis upon family chores, self-care, or the care of rooms or personal possessions; outside the home, there is prevention of experiences which make for growth in social adaptation, which lead to meeting one's own problems and fighting one's own way.

Two specific problems, frequently encountered, may be noted here. One relates to the child's school experience. The overprotecting mother coaches the child, may prepare his lessons, makes frequent visits to the school, conflicts with the teacher, and at times becomes an interfering nuisance. In the more extreme forms, she tries to set the child against the teacher. It is as though she resented

[10] In the voluminous literature on this type of parent, Levy's analysis is a model of insight and clarity of presentation, and his findings are heavily drawn upon in the next few paragraphs. Cf. David M. Levy, *Maternal Overprotection*, Columbia University Press, New York, 1943.

the school and the teacher, seeing in them a threat to her monopolistic control of her child. The second problem results from the child's formation of friendships. Here again, the overprotecting mother tends to reach out as if to combat the process, or at least to direct and control it to her child's advantage. Many parents apparently seek to narrow the social contacts of their children.

2. A distinct form of overprotection is often found among the parents of children who present health or physical disability problems. That such children should evoke more parental care and concern than healthy ones warrants no explanation in terms of neuroses. Levy does not think that illnesses per se are productive of maternal overprotection, but he concludes that they may intensify a tendency to overprotect that is already present; i.e., illness gives an added push to an attitude present before the appearance of the illness. Also, one should recognize the difference between serious illnesses and others, between illnesses which require prolonged nursing and those which do not. Moreover, certain mothers may have been "sensitized" by experience with other very serious illnesses.

In the case of deformed or defective children parental attitudes and behavior seem much more pronounced. "In the mental and emotional attitudes of parents toward the physically defective child in the family," writes Laura Hood, "there were characteristics so constant that they might fairly be considered as representing a 'psychology of parents of a crippled child.' To have a little child paralyzed or otherwise physically defective is an experience probably more devastating to mind and spirit than to suffer grave physical impairment one's self, and the phychological adjustments required may be more complex."[11]

In many of these cases, parents are filled with a sense of hopelessness that finds expression in an emotional pattern based on pity. When these disabilities occur in families which have no conception of the possibilities of modern orthopedic work, these patterns take a permanent form. Often, too, the parental reactions are complicated by feelings of guilt over an imagined responsibility or proof of a family taint. From this complex of circumstances there result family situations which not only impair the possibilities for any constructive program dealing with the child's condition or defect, but also create serious difficulties for his personal and social development.

3. Some parents magnify their responsibilities because of their

[11] Laura Hood, "On Interviewing Parents of Crippled Children," *Social Service Review*, March, 1928, pp. 62–63.

own life experiences. These are persons who may have gained some degree of success in life, but at considerable cost. They have come through, but in the hard way. Their experiences have been such as to leave psychic scars which, even though they have healed, are always visible by way of reminder. Such parents develop at times an almost neurotic susceptibility to human competition. Some of them tend to withdraw from it to lead an isolated life; others seek to project such a pattern upon their children. They seek to insulate their children against the raw edges of life, as it were. "I never want my child to go through what I did."

4. Akin to overprotecting parents are those who interfere too much with the lives of their growing children. They want always to know what the children are doing, where they are going, with whom, who said what and to whom. Here is a form of parental aggressiveness which may take many forms and stem from various roots. There may be elements of jealousy and resentfulness, a desire to put the children on the defensive for stepping outside the range of family activities. It may derive from an overly active imagination or glandular system. At times it may be the expression of a personality trait, a tendency to take oneself too seriously. Such parents extend the range of their concern over too wide an area of their children's lives. This frequently leads to parent-child conflicts during adolescence, for it is then that the child's own area of operation broadens, and the tendency to exclude adults from this area begins to manifest itself. Most students of behavior problems in children have regarded this as the effort of parents to extend the period of infantile dependence; the emphasis here is on a somewhat different situation, in which parents face the growing-up process of their children but insist on sharing their experience, actually or vicariously, while doing so.

5. Finally, there are the parents who work too hard at the craft of parenthood. Looming large among these are those who are always reading books or attending lectures on "child psychology," are always rejoicing in the "latest theory" of "psychoanalysis," and applying it to their own children. The particular "theory" seldom remains the same over any considerable period of time; but while it is in favor, its acceptance is exclusive and complete. It is to be understood, of course, that there is intended here no reference to the efforts of serious-minded parents who seek to equip themselves for obligations whose importance they recognize. Rather the problem involves a sort of dilettantism, or pseudoscientific faddism, which reminds one at best of the truth of the statement, "A little learning is a dangerous thing."

Some Sources of Tendencies to Magnify Parental Responsibilities

Parents who have been through a long period of sterility, or a series of miscarriages or still births may naturally tend to give a heightened evaluation of the child, coupled with unduly apprehensive and protective reactions. Unhappy marriages, also, can create this situation. Just as a wife devoted to her husband cannot be exclusively a mother, so the child bears the brunt of his mother's unsatisfied or unsatisfactory love life.

In addition to the foregoing, there are three other factors in contemporary society which suggest that the parents who magnify their responsibility are on the increase. One is the increasing prevalence of the small-family system which, coupled with early marriage, means that the period of childbearing is over relatively early in the life of the mother. Another factor is the increased longevity of the mother, together with the general rise in standards of positive health and vitality in the middle and older age brackets. At the same time, the separation of home and occupation means that the husband is away from home the greater part of the day. In combination, this means that for many present-day mothers the period of childbearing, and even of childrearing, is over while life is still at the flood tide for them. Confronted with this situation, an increasing number of mothers are finding an outlet in employment or in public-service careers. There are those, however, who can find no form of satisfactory adjustment save in an intensification of their parental duties. It is here that danger lurks for the child.

Basic Aspects of Families who Magnify Their Responsibilities

A final word should be said concerning the basic aspects of the group of families under discussion. Three such aspects stand out clearly, both from a descriptive analysis of family situations in general and from the literature on behavior problems as it deals with the products of such situations. The first of these is a life situation or configuration which is weighted unduly in the child's favor. To put it another way, there is a lack of balance in the pattern of personal relationships. The child receives more than a properly proportionate share of attention, affection, and service. The cards of personal relationships are stacked in his favor. When early developed and long continued, this results in the creation of the egocentric psychopath who wants to be the beloved tyrant in every situation. When this feeling is of lesser degree or shorter duration, there appears the demanding type of person who expects and anticipates all kinds of special attentions and services, or the aggressive, bullying, resentful type who seeks to compel special consideration. A second basic aspect is the interference with the growing-up process. The child is not allowed to develop responsibility, to stand on his own feet, and above all, to experiment with life. Growing up to be an adult is a hard, long, slow process, which is best done the hard way. Hence when parents magnify their responsibilities, they either do the experimenting themselves or interfere with the child's learning-from-experience process by interposing themselves into it. The incidental but serious effect for the child is the maintenance of infantile or subage responses. A third and quite obvious aspect is the impediments placed in the child's relations with his friends. The children in the group of families under consideration reveal a general difficulty in making friends, for the obvious reasons that their parents keep them away from the necessary experimental contacts, or interfere in the process, or have built up in them a dependence on their parents and other adults which precludes friendships with their own age group.

PARENTS WHO DISREGARD THE PERSONALITIES OF THEIR CHILDREN

A third main group of problem parents are those who tend to disregard the personalities of their children. These are the parents who cannot see their children as separate and distinct personalities but at best see them as vest-pocket editions of themselves.

First are the families dominated by acquisitive-minded parents who have a strong sense of the "mine and thine" aspects of life. For them, objects and people fall into two groups: those that belong to them and those that do not. The latter are rather strictly abjured; they do not register except incidentally in the orbit of their attention. But the things which belong to them are completely and wholly theirs. It is *my* car, *my* house, *my* wife, *my* child. Life is a series of possessive relationships, of which they are the center, from which it follows that the relationships are to be shaped in accordance with this fact. Some of these parents are driven by a desire to possess and manage someone in order to gain assurance of their own importance. There is another type, the successful parent who has a rather conscious assurance of his own abilities and who discharges his parental duties with the same aggressive vigor that distinguishes him in his occupational relationships. Consider, for example, a certain type of successful executive. His breakfast is served at his order. Then he confers with his gardener and gives instructions for the tasks of the day. A chauffeur drives him to his office, where a touch of a button summons people all day long. Today he "handles" a dozen difficult situations involving many persons, and does so exceedingly well. Returning home, a problem concerning his child is presented to him. He acts promptly, feeling very confident of his judgment, his insight into life, and his knowledge of life's values. There is not only his confidence, but also his assumption of the dominant role in every situation. There are those persons who carry as their sole responsibility the complete range of life, and who think of everything—perpetual masters of ceremonies. Obviously, here one is confronted with a character complex rather than a neurotic pattern. Such individuals manage their children because they are the type of people who always manage.

Second are the family situations dominated by parents who have strong ideas, convictions, or philosophies. They may be successful executives who generalize their experience, they may be academic introverts who have arrived at a theory, they may be "crackpots" who have absorbed some singular notion; their common condition is their exclusive devotion to an idea. Such ideas may be of any type. Two types are of particular significance here: those which relate to childrearing, and those which relate to careers.

The field of childrearing is the peculiarly happy hunting ground for faddists with their momentary theories of human development. "What children need is—" is their positive cry, although their agreement ends with this unfinished sentence. One such theory and what it means in a child's life may be ascertained from the following case:

Frank Pierce is vice-president of a bank. He has risen to his present position from the ranks. He is devoted to his job, his church, and his family. For some time now, he has been friendly with a colonel in the infantry during World War II. What children need, he and the colonel keep on telling each other, is discipline—strict, severe, rigorous. Children should be taught to obey, promptly and completely. The way the father applies this theory is illustrated by the following incident. His 3-year-old child is engrossed in play on the floor. The father watches for the moment when he is completely absorbed in his play, to say: "Junior, get Daddy a drink of water." For failure to obey at once, Junior is punished.

Another type of fixed ideas which prevail among parents concerns the careers of children. These are the parents who, from the day the children are born or from early infancy, have "plans" for them. They are to go to this school, college, and professional school; they are to engage in this particular sport or acquire that selected skill; they are to go into a certain occupation or make a certain kind of marriage. Such positive ideas or plans spring from various sources. At the upper-class levels, where the incidence of such situations is high, they often derive from family pride and a wish for the continuance of traditional performance at the family level. The longer such traditions have prevailed, the greater the pressure upon the child may be. At times it is not only the pressure of the living members of the family; the influence of the deceased members still remains. At slightly lower social levels, the parents may be social climbers who bear down upon their children to complete an unfinished program of class ascent. At the lowest-class levels it is perhaps more often in regard to the selection of an occupation that an ambitious parent, perhaps the mother, seeks to exert undue influence. Throughout this entire range of situations, the unfulfilled wishes of the parents come to be projected in many cases upon the children; i.e., the parents seek to relive their lives in those of their children.

A third variety of family situation in which the children's personalities tend to be disregarded are those in which the children are utilized to satisfy the emotional needs of the parents or other adults in the family. This includes the well-known "silver cord" cases, where a parent, most often the mother, binds the children to her to satisfy a thwarted emotion. Strecker has discussed these situations in relation to the problems of military service. Silver cords, he writes, come in varying lengths. Sometimes they are very short, but much more often they are very long, often extremely long. Seldom is a silver cord an obviously binding tie. It appears in many guises. There is the oversolicitous mother whose gentle, sacrificing manner hides a dominance that is hard and arbitrary; and the frail, weak little mother who, after giving her health and strength to "the children," wants at least one to find happiness in never leaving her side; and the artificially "happy" home where everyone loves each other too much to quarrel.[12] In addition, there is the mother who is so unhappy that only the devotion of her children "keeps her going"; the unmarried aunt who "devotes herself" to a niece or nephew; and the father who, denied recognition in his adult world, emphasizes over and again the respect and obedience that are a father's due. Parental disregard of the personalities of children may take the form of stark dominance, harsh and cold and

[12] Edward A. Strecker, "Psychiatry Speaks to Democracy," *Mental Hygiene*, October, 1945, pp. 591–605.

exacting against the canvas of family life; but much more often it is a soft and loving tyranny, the satisfaction of parental demands as a debit due for services rendered. The variety of family situations under discussion here are chiefly of this kind.

Finally, there are the parents of today who are still steeped in the authoritarian lore of the past. Here we find not a pose, or an occupational habit, or of necessity a disguised emotional need, but a traditional conviction. Children must obey; it is the responsibility of the parents to compel it. "You do this because I say so. I am your father." This, it is well to remember, was the prevailing principle of childrearing in the family of past centuries. The dominating authoritarian father was only part of a larger pattern of family life which included the exercise of paternal authority over all the members, rigorous discipline, and the subordination of the individual to the family group, all to the end of family solidarity. Such powers on the part of the father were recognized in the law and hallowed by the church.[13]

FAMILY PROBLEMS CREATED BY EXTERNAL FORCES

There are two distinct approaches to the study of the family and its problems. One is to consider it, relatively speaking, as a unity in itself with emphasis upon the family situations of its members—their interaction with each other and their cultural relatedness. The other approach sees the family as part and parcel of the larger society, stressing the continuing interrelations between the two, and giving particular emphasis to the ways in which the family reflects and reacts to changes and forces in the social organization as a whole. It is clear that family situations cannot be considered without reference to the impact of external forces; and obviously, the section on problem families would not be complete without recognition of the large number of families in which problems of internal relations arise from the stress of outside influences. Some of these will be considered in the remainder of this chapter.

THE PHYSICAL BASIS OF HOME LIFE

Family life has a physical setting, a material structure within which the family functions; and the character of this structure

[13] For studies of authoritarianism, consult T. W. Adorno, and others, *The Authoritarian Personality*, Harper & Row, New York, 1950.

affects in many ways the nature of the functioning process. Perhaps no aspect of family life is exempt from its conditioning influence. This is the real essence of the housing problem. There is a sociology as well as an architecture of home planning. A house or an apartment has too long and too largely been considered as a physical shelter to which the family must adjust its life. There is much more to be said with propriety about the adaptation of a physical structure to the life of its occupants. Just as we have come to emphasize the family as the matrix out of which develop the personalities of its members, so must housing be conceived as the means of providing facilities adequate for the family to function in these respects.

Thus considered, and viewed more particularly from the standpoint of the child, many aspects of the family's physical setting fall into their proper perspective—the possibility of a room of his own, with space for clothes, toys, and books; the nature of the sleeping arrangements; quietness for rest; sleep unbroken by household, adult, and neighborhood noises; separation of adults and child; a place to prepare his schoolwork; a place, amid proper surroundings, to bring his friends; a place for all the members of the family to live their own lives, both as members of a family group and as individuals. Each of these items, and many others, could be separated for more complete analysis; they are both the minutiae and the substance of family life and of child development.

It is one of the tragic realities of life that many families live under the stress of housing inadequacies, and that these bear with particular heaviness upon the life of the children in these families. Included here is the home where privacy is unknown; where crowding imperils health and prevents comfort; where activity must be subdued because of the immediate presence of others; where the sick, aged, or irritable cannot be segregated; where the child must prepare his schoolwork in the only room available for the entire family group; and where the entertainment of friends, and even courtship, must be carried on in a room shared by the parents or next to their sleeping quarters. Both the size and the arrangement of living space are important.

Similarly important, particularly for the child, is the outside appearance of the home. This advertises the family's status to all who pass by or come to call. Children comment at an early age on the appearance of their friends' homes, and the attitudes of adults are revealed by studies of family budgets which show that in the lower-income groups preference is given to housing over food. To young and old alike, but especially to adolescents preoccupied with desires for social recognition and prestige, the appearance of the home flaunts their identification to all who have eyes to see. The key to the behavior problems of many adolescents is a home-avoidance technique; they select their friends, conduct their courtships, and organize their lives in general so as not to bring their friends home.

There is evidence that the amount of space provided for a given number of human interactive relationships has a bearing on the quality of those relationships.[14] Emile Durkheim's *De la division du travail social* (1893) points out that increase in the number of contacts multiplies the occasions when people find themselves interrelated, when problems arise necessitating adjustment, and when life has to be lived in conformity with rules and regulations.[15] This implies rather clearly the basic importance of the spatial setting of social interaction.

More specifically, the thesis advanced here is that the spatial dimensions of living quarters are related to the stresses, strains, and frustrations of family living.

THE IMPACT OF RESIDENTIAL MOBILITY

The term *residential mobility* is used here to mean changes in family location or residence. It is estimated that over 34 million people in the United States moved from one place to another in 1962. Since 1950, annual reports indicate that approximately one-fifth of the population changes residence each year, about 1 out of 15 moves outside of the county each year, and in excess of 3 percent cross a state line in their moves. These yearly migrations now include approximately 6 million children between the ages of 5 and 13.[16]

Residential mobility obviously has great meaning for family life. A change in residence for a family is like transplanting a tree or plant; for both plant and family it involves a separation from the matrix, a disturbance of the root system and consequently of the functioning of the organism, followed by the problems of adjusting to a new setting. In both cases, too, the specific consequences depend on various factors—the extent to which the plant or family has developed and spread out its root system, the skill with which

14 James H. S. Bossard, *Parent and Child*, University of Pennsylvania Press, 1953, chap. 7.

15 Cf. George Simpson, *Emile Durkheim on the Division of Labor in Society*, The Macmillan Company, New York, 1933, book II.

16 Bess B. Lane, *When Children Move from School to School*, Membership Service Bulletin no. 105, Association for Childhood Education International, Washington, D.C., 1960, p. 3.

the transfer is made, the similarity or dissimilarity of the new soil (in the case of the plant) or culture (for the family), and the frequency with which such transfers occur. The culture differential involved in residential mobility is of the highest importance; it is the key to the relative significance of such movements as those from one farm or one city street to another nearby, from one region to another, from farm or village to metropolitan center, and from one country to another.

For mobile families, the common problems may be summarized as follows: (1) maintenance of social participation in the new community, (2) continuance of subjection to community controls of behavior, (3) retention of social status, (4) readjustment of traditional attitudes toward the demands of new cultural situations, and (5) maintenance of family solidarity in the readjustment process. When these problems are not worked out satisfactorily they cause maladjustments in contemporary American families.

An additional effect of mobility deserves special mention. Duvall has pointed out that with the increasingly early age of marriage more help is required from the in-law, grandparent generation.[17] Much as one hears of the interference of in-laws, there is a reverse side to this. For many younger families in particular, the presence of kinsfolk nearby confers many beneficial advantages. In case of need, there is someone to advise, to aid, to comfort, to encourage, to admonish, or to restrain. A study by Litwak has shown that geographical distance between white, younger, middle-class, native-born individuals and their kinfolk does not necessarily destroy family identification.[18] Yet, if the distance is great the identification must be maintained by mail, telephone, or occasional visits. This is not quite the same as living in a close, cohesive, extended family group.

Residential Mobility and Child Development

Turning to the role of residential mobility in the development of the child, one finds at least six aspects that seem to be of primary significance.

1. Change of residence breaks the continuity of life as expressed in the tangible tokens of family possession. This has its meaning for all the members of the family, but one who understands the concreteness of child thinking and feeling will quickly sense that

[17] Evelyn Millis Duvall, *In-Laws: Pro and Con,* Association Press, New York, 1954, pp. 13–16.

[18] Eugene Litwak, "Geographic Mobility and Extended Family Cohesion," *American Sociological Review,* June, 1960, pp. 385–394.

the physical symbols of family unity and continuity mean more to him than to any but the very old members of the family. Adults are far too prone to overlook this fact, with glib references to the "adaptability of the child." The house and street where one lives are symbols, too, of stability. Their unchanging continuance simplifies life, and the child, especially when younger, is not fitted to grapple with complexity. Unless a child is distinctly unhappy in his present home, it is usually with some reluctance that he moves from it to face a new and unknown situation. He may, or may not, adjust quickly, once the move is made.

2. Residential mobility often means a change of school for the child. This is apt to precipitate many problems, considering for the moment only the scholastic aspects of the situation. Involved are adjustment problems to new courses, tasks, methods, and teachers. Some work may have to be repeated; in other cases subjects, either in whole or in part, will never be covered. In such subjects as mathematics and languages, this lack of sequence may be serious for the child's progress. A grade may be lost or gained, with varying consequences for his attitude toward his studies. His rank order in his class may be changed, upward or downward. Furthermore, many changes in school enrollment are made during, instead of at the beginning of, the year, and in such cases the danger is particularly great that the child's school work may be disturbed and tend to become fragmentary and disconnected. This is particularly true when the moves are frequent. As one person put it, "Because we moved about so much when I was a child my education was snippity, and I think I suffered from its polka-dot pattern during all my high-school years, and perhaps now."[19]

3. The child neither lives nor studies in a vacuum. Change of residence means also change in friendships, social contacts, and social acceptances. First, there is the break with old friends. To try to hold on to them may impede the child's adjustment to new situations; to terminate the contact may constitute a real loss. "All my life," writes Sheila, who moved eight times with her family before she was 17, "I have felt emptiness because certain people I liked passed out of my life." These losses, comments a teacher of wide experience, seem less important for the younger child, but become increasingly serious after the eleventh or twelfth year.

Second, there is the immediate problem of social contacts and acceptance in the community and school system the child enters. For the boy, this may mean a series of fights to try out the newcomer, with the resultant assignment of status. For the girl, the

[19] Lane, *op. cit.*, p. 5.

struggle may be less physical but by no means less stark and cruel. The assignment of the newcomer to the proper pecking order is not confined to barnyard society.

4. In this process of finding his social place in a new community, the problems of the mobile child must be considered against the background of his family. His family, too, is mobile. One result of this may be that the family is of little or no help. Parents have their problems, too, in settling into a new community. They have to learn it, the people, the new job, etc.; and they may be preoccupied with these things. Also, the family may be mobile because the father is dead, or the parents quarrel or are shiftless or have separated or been divorced. The mobile child may have been shifted from the home of one relative to another, or from kinsfolk to institution and back again, or from one foster home to another. Human problems have a way of becoming interwoven in the fabric of family life.

5. Residential mobility often involves a change from one cultural setting to another for the child and his family. The significance of this has been emphasized thus far chiefly in regard to migrations from Europe to America. However, with the increasing identification by sociologists and anthropologists of, and emphasis upon, subcultural areas, it becomes evident that changes of residence within the United States, at times within the same state, may be a more radical procedure than has commonly been supposed. Certainly one would not depreciate the problems of a North Carolina Methodist farm boy who comes to live in an Irish Catholic urban area. Changes in cultural milieu may be defined more narrowly than this, however. Whitney in a study of the families of 501 undergraduate liberal arts students described 90 percent of the local moves as "status moves"—to "a better street," "a more desirable" neighborhood, etc.[20] This type of move also requires some adjustment to community, school, and other children.

6. "Don't forget the cumulative aspect of this problem of moving from place to place," writes a young wife who herself moved more than a dozen times before graduation from high school. The point is well taken. It is to be remembered that we have been considering not the effects of a change of residence, but of their recurrence. Whatever the meaning to the child of any particular change of residence, whatever the similarity or difference may be, the significant fact is that both these experiences and his definition of

[20] Vincent H. Whitney and Charles M. Grigg, "Patterns of Mobility Among a Group of Families of College Students," *American Sociological Review*, December, 1958, pp. 643–652.

them accumulate. "There comes to be," writes the above young woman, "a vagueness about places where you have lived, of apartments and neighborhoods you didn't know well, or had come to dislike. Perhaps there were some you had liked. But after a time there comes to be an unreality about them, so that sometimes you are not quite sure whether this is something you have known in life or only in dreams." Obviously, the results of residential mobility are not all undesirable. Landis has pointed out general aspects of the reverse side.[21] The mobile child learns to be alert, adaptable, resourceful, democratic. A graduate student in a large university commented, "My life has consisted of perpetual moving around. It has made me able to understand and get along with all kinds of people and to adapt easily to all kinds of situations." Nevertheless, Everett Lee, who has for 25 years studied the relation between migration and mental disease, concludes that there are many more migrants than nonmigrants who are admitted to mental hospitals. He adds that moving appears to be more disturbing to the child than to his parents.[22]

ECONOMIC PRESSURES

Most families are under economic pressure of one sort or another; we are concerned here with a degree of pressure which has a considerable meaning for child-family relationships. Such pressures are conceived here as being of two kinds: first, those which arise from economic inadequacy, and second, those deriving from sudden economic changes and dislocations.

Economic Inadequacy

The concept of economic inadequacy includes many different kinds of concrete situations—the inadequately financed home,[23] the mother-supported home,[24] the home with heavy drains upon its financial resources, the family with many young children, the family with unemployment,[25] the family on relief,[26] the white-collar

21 Paul Landis, "The Case for Mobility," *The Survey*, March, 1943, pp. 74–76.

22 Joan Cook, "When Move You Must," *The New York Times Magazine*, January 5, 1964, p. 52.

23 Bossard and Boll, *op. cit.*, pp. 185–188.

24 *Ibid.*, pp. 194–197.

25 Ernest W. Burgess, "Unemployment and the Family," *Marriage and Family Living*, Autumn, 1945, p. 87; also James H. S. Bossard, *Social Change and Social Problems*, rev. ed., Harper & Brothers, New York, 1938, chap. 12.

26 Ruth S. Cavan and Katherine Ranck, *The Family and the Depression*, University of Chicago Press, Chicago, 1938; Bessie H. McClenahan, "The Child of the

poor, the improvident family, and the family whose spending routine is a complete pattern of unwise expenditures. It is well to warn the reader here against one of the common faults in so much of the recent socioeconomical writing, which assumes that economic inadequacy is wholly or primarily a matter of insufficient wages. Inadequate income does exist, but unwise outgo and general financial ineffectiveness are both prevalent and productive of similar results. Moreover, ineffective management of finances is not simply a factor, but also a symbol of various character traits of the parents. Similarly, it should be recalled that economic inadequacy is a relative term, and as far as family planes of living are concerned it can be measured by the yardstick of ordinary working-class patterns (i.e., how one's friends and associates do live) and by the foot rule of need as established by scientific investigation (i.e., how scientists think they ought to live).

Economic Changes

One specific aspect of the problem of economic inadequacy results from the rapidity of changes in the price and wage levels. A few statistical facts will serve to illustrate the general situation. The wholesale price index for all commodities shows a rise from 43.8 in 1940 to 100.7 in 1960 (1957–1959 = 100). The purchasing power for consumer goods, with the same base, fell from 204.8 in 1940 to 94.9 in 1962.[27] True, wages and personal and family incomes have risen during these years, but such changes have been far from evenly distributed.

It has long been the contention of economists that there is no particular merit or demerit in either high or low prices, but that the change from one price level to another always involves serious consequences. Much the same can be said about the economic status of the family; sudden changes are highly significant, and in proportion to the extent and speed of their occurrence. Here the suddenly wealthy family is one with the suddenly poor. Both types of change have been the fate of a relatively large number of American families. One of the results of the churning waves of social change that have surged back and forth over this country during its history

---

Relief Agency," *Social Forces*, May, 1935, pp. 560–567; James H. S. Bossard (Ed.), "Children in a Depression Decade," *Annals of the American Academy of Political and Social Science*, November, 1940; Horst Mendershausen, *Changes in Income Distribution During the Great Depression*, National Bureau of Economic Research, New York, 1946.

[27] U.S. Bureau of the Census, *Statistical Abstract of The United States: 1963.* (Eighty-fourth edition.) Washington, D.C., 1963, p. 351.

is the sudden rise and fall in economic status of individual families. The fortune-making periods of American history in particular furnish their full quota of this kind of family. The history of the immigrant stream is replete with illustrations, particularly of families by whom the path from Old World peasant status to urban mansion has been traversed in a relatively few years. In more recent years, the sequence of two world wars and a world-wide depression has continued these rapid turns of the economical wheel.

The effects of economic income, as concerns inadequacies in housing, have been mentioned. As important are effects of economic pressures of this kind upon the attitudes and conceptions of the child. The economic status of the family does much to influence the ideological development of its younger members. The child in a low-income home sees himself as such in comparison with other children and homes. Economic inadequacy expresses itself in concrete deficiencies whose values are largely social, i.e., comparative. Out of these comparisons grow the child's conceptions of himself and his attitude toward others, including his family. We are reminded here of Samuel Johnson's dictum, "Poor people's children never respect them."[28] Meltzer has thrown light in the same direction with his study of children's attitudes toward their parents, and his conclusion that children living at the lowest economic level had the least pleasantly toned attitudes toward their parents.[29]

"SO LITTLE TIME"

There is a dimension of family life which has to do with the time and energy, nervous and physical, that the maintenance of satisfactory family relations requires. Students of the family tend quite generally to ignore this dimension, although its basic importance is obvious. It is a particularly necessary requisite today for wise and effective parenthood because of the nature of childrearing in our contemporary culture. Not only is our culture, especially our urban culture, a highly complicated one, presenting many opportunities and problems to the child, but the role of parenthood has changed with the development of numerous specialized child-serving agencies and institutions. Confronted with the realities of the present child culture, the parent is cast more and more into an administrative role in which he becomes adviser, assessor, interpreter, and selector of the child's experiences and opportunities.

28 Joseph Wood Krutch, *Samuel Johnson*, Henry Holt & Company, New York, 1944, p. 4 (Current edition: Harcourt, Brace & World, New York, 1963.)

29 H. Meltzer, "Economic Security and Children's Attitudes to Parents," *American Journal of Orthopsychiatry*, October, 1936, pp. 590–608.

Elsewhere, in analyzing the changing protective functions of the modern family, it has been pointed out that "instead of the overt dangers of two centuries ago, those of our contemporary society are more subtle and insidious, and thus inevitably call for new protective methods. Now, instead of physical force, there is needed keen judgment; instead of brute strength, there must be wise counsel; instead of regulation, the demand is for instruction; and suggestion must replace compulsion."[30]

In other words, the contention here is that parenthood in the modern family, calling for the tactful management of the children in relation to the diverse opportunities and range of contacts of all kinds now open to them, needs considerable time and energy if it is to function effectively; for these are tasks which require investigation, analysis, judgment, planning, decision—and none of them can be hurried or performed effectively with tired nerves.

It would be an avoidance of reality to overlook the many aspects of contemporary life which tend to reduce the time-energy dimensions of parenthood below the normal requirement. Moreover, it is in the upper social, economic, and often educational brackets that one must begin the identification of these aspects. William Healy, philosophizing after a lifetime of studying child-behavior problems, points out how the pressure of business and of social affairs greatly outweighs concern about structuring the personalities of children. "As I interview parents," he writes, "I find that comparatively few of those who are on the quick upgrade financially are in any measure alive to what they may be doing to their children."[31] Nor are the fathers who are putting themselves under pressure to amass a fortune or to attain professional or political leadership the sole offenders in this respect. In many such families, the mothers, seeking to complement the ambitious design for the family, devote their time and energy to projects of public service or social prestige or even child welfare, all the time neglecting their own maternal responsibilities and permitting their children to run wild or handing them over to the care of domestic servants, at times not of a high order.

DISGRACED FAMILIES: THE STRESS OF SHAME

The role of shame in human relationships is far more important than contemporary students have recognized. Both the psychology

[30] James H. S. Bossard, *Social Change and Social Problems,* Harper & Brothers, New York, 1938, p. 609.

[31] William Healy, *Personality in Formation and Action,* W. W. Norton & Company, New York, 1938, p. 145.

and the sociology of shame have yet to be written. Its significance in the development of the child, especially in the adolescent stage, is particularly great.

A disgraced family is one which experiences a decline of status because of an adverse attitude on the part of the community toward the behavior of some one or more of its members. Since these attitudes involve the mores of the specific group which reacts to this behavior, it follows that the type of behavior condemned, and the degree of social disapproval expressed, vary a good deal from one social class to another, as well as from region to region. However, for purposes of general discussion, the following types of behavior commonly tend to affect unfavorably the social status of families: crime, especially major penal offenses; imprisonment; illegitimacy; drug addiction; chronic drunkenness; mental illness; and suicide. The number of families thus affected is large, as any inclusive index of these forms of behavior would show. Moreover, one must think in terms of the proportion of families which go through such experiences, not merely the number to be found at any one moment. Human problems are cumulative, not merely cross-sectional.

Many factors determine the meaning of family disgrace for child development. First, there is the family's definition of its own behavior. Data on the family backgrounds of delinquent children show that a large proportion come from homes in which criminal behavior is a more or less accepted pattern. Often, too, families of this kind tend to live near each other, so the neighborhood pattern may coincide with that of the family. This means that neither in the family nor in the neighborhood is there any critical sensitivity to a criminal record. "Marie is such a good girl," her mother tells the probation officer; "she always brings home everything she steals." Second, there is the degree of unity and emotional interdependence which exists between family members, particularly the degree of attachment between parents and children. Third, loss of status resulting from family disgrace becomes more serious as one moves upward in the social scale—"the higher they come, the harder they fall." Fourth, the size and anonymity of the community are significant. Family disgrace in a stable, rural, primary-group community tends to be much more serious than in a mobile, urban, secondary-group area. Fifth, the age of the child is important. Family status means more in adolescence than in any other age span.

Obviously, disgraced families and their significance for the child are a highly individual matter, but again certain common aspects may be identified. First, one would expect a loss of self-assurance, both for the child and for the other members of the family. Status is inextricably associated with self-confidence and self-respect, so the loss of the former cannot but involve modifications of the latter. As time goes on, accompanying feelings ranging from vague frustration to bitter resentment may develop. At an early age, the child of normal insight cannot help sensing that he is paying the price for the misdeeds of others. Second is an inevitable preoccupation with one's problems. For the child this may range from mere abstraction to worry to obsessive reveries. One result of this in turn may be a lack of social or scholastic effectiveness, which brings further problems and complications in its wake. Parents and other older members of the family, too, are likely to be preoccupied, so they fail the child at a time when he most needs reliance on their comfort and help. Third is the effect upon relationships within the family. These may take several different forms. There is, for example, the situation in which the members form a conspiracy to conceal the family skeleton, trying to hide the act, the offender, or the knowledge of what has occurred. Or the situation may resolve itself into a conflict between the erring one and the rest of the family, with the possibility of all kinds of complications. Also present frequently may be feelings of sorrow. These prevail most often in families with strong affectional ties. Foremost in its meaning for the child in such cases might be the disappointment in the parent, the feeling of disillusionment that comes with the shattering of the childhood ideal of the parent or other offending kin.

Perhaps the most generally observed consequence of family disgrace is the social isolation of the family. Such isolation often is self-imposed. The child or the entire family may withdraw from normal contacts. There is a conscious effort to avoid former associates and friends. A great variety of avoidance techniques are developed to meet such situations. Or the isolation may be imposed by the group. Particularly does this happen in the case of children. The child from the disgraced family may be avoided, or snubbed by friends, or dropped by the clique, or disbarred from the playground. Such isolation may take a positive form or the negativism of the silent treatment. Anyone who observes juvenile behavior cannot but see that children often are very cruel to each other, especially at a time in life when the wish for social recognition is very strong. Frequently, the isolation is imposed upon the child before he is of an age to have developed the spiritual resources which could enable him to cope with such situations.

Complementary to this isolation from the group, there often develops the tendency to form new social contacts at a lower status level. Actually this is a ready adjustment to an existing situation. Since the community has changed the person's status, the thing to do is to form compensatory contacts at a lower level.

Unfortunately, the element of disgrace does not operate alone as a rule. Most often disgrace is an expression, in "the public relations" of the family, of a whole complex of disorganizing circumstances. An illustrative study is that by Treudley, showing how mental illness interferes with family routines.[32] In addition to withdrawal from social participation because of feelings of shame, the following additional complications may arise: (1) The family income and plane of living may be lowered. (2) Different members of the family adjust or react differently to the arrangements necessitated by the illness. (3) The mentally ill member projects his discomfort, illness, or complaint on the rest of the household. (4) The public peace of the neighborhood may be disturbed by the ill person. (5) If the mother is ill, the management of the appearance and functions of the home may deteriorate. (6) Eating and other dining-room routines are broken or upset, with subsequent effects upon the digestion of the children. (7) There is unpredictability of household routines. Meals are served at irregular times, for example. (8) Tensions develop between family members over these irregularities. (9) The mentally ill person becomes notional about food, clothing, bed, etc. (10) The mentally ill individual may become sadistic, deliberately seeking to destroy the family pleasure. (11) The sleep of the members of the family is broken. (12) The children are not disciplined or supervised. (13) There is no cooperation between home and school. The children may miss school, be late, or be unable to study. (14) The children's play life and other forms of spontaneity may be interfered with seriously. (15) The pet notions, aversions, prejudices, etc., of the mentally ill member may interfere with the normal lives, friendships, and activities of the children. (16) Feelings of nervous strain are inevitable. (17) The behavior of the mentally ill member either is not predictable or is unpleasantly predictable.

MINORITY-GROUP FAMILIES

A minority group is defined as "a subgroup within a larger group (ordinarily a society), bound together by some special ties of its own, usually race or nationality, but sometimes religion or other

[32] Mary B. Treudley, "Mental Illness and Family Routines," *Mental Hygiene*, April, 1946, pp. 235–249.

cultural affiliations."[33] It is evident, then, that in our society there are many minority-group families of varying kinds. Since child development in relation to national, religious, and social class cultures is discussed elsewhere in this book, it seems pertinent at this point to relate it to certain specific groups which are identifiable because of racial characteristics and/or linguistic culture.

A racial group is in a distinctive category because of its visibility. Due to a fluid class system in the United States and a history of economic opportunity, there are today in the Social Register the names of people from various ethnic groups whose ancestors were unknown peasants in Europe not many generations ago. The family may have entered America with minority-group status, but that is in the past. Who knows, for instance, whether the forebears of that attractive blonde came from Sweden, Poland, or Germany, unless her name identifies them? This process of upward mobility and of becoming merged with "native American" culture does not operate in the same way upon racial minorities. The fact of skin color and other characteristics means that they remain identifiable. In addition, those people, for the most part, entered the country as either slaves or unskilled laborers. This is true of the Negro, Japanese, and Chinese. The American Indian, who was here when the white man arrived, was considered a savage from whom the land should be taken. When a group is clearly visible, ideas concerning its status do not fade quickly in the eyes of the majority group.

Variables in Minority-Group Status

The census of 1960 reported a total of 20,491,443 nonwhite persons in the population. They cannot, however, be considered as one group with the same problems, although they do have the formerly mentioned problems in common. Some important variables are the size of the group, the area of concentration, their order of arrival into the United States, and their economic achievements. The ways in which these variables operate may be illustrated by a few examples.

1. THE NEGRO. To the majority group, the larger a minority is the more threatening, and more vocal, it may seem to be. Negroes are by far the largest minority racial group in the United States, numbering 18,871,831 in 1960. Whereas they once were largely concentrated in the rural Deep South, 73.2 percent of them now

[33] Henry Pratt Fairchild, Ed., *Dictionary of Sociology*, Philosophical Library, New York, 1944, p. 134.

live in urban areas—preponderantly in the eastern part of the country. Although they were the first of the racial minorities to be brought into the United States, slavery and subsequent conditions have prevented most of them from high economic achievement even as of today.

2. THE CHINESE AND JAPANESE. The Chinese and Japanese, partly because of restrictive immigration laws, have never formed a large part of the population. The 1960 census reports 607,691. They concentrated chiefly on the southwest coast, and it is significant that at least until after World War II, the words "race problems" meant different things to a Westerner and an Easterner—Orientals and Negroes, respectively. Many of the Chinese and Japanese, without the bonds of slavery, and with strong family institutions, became independent shopkeepers and owners of small farms. They entered the country early, and many of them prospered with its growth. Much hardship was undergone by the Japanese when they became "the enemy" and were put into camps during World War II.[34] If there was any positive result of this experience, it was that some of these people were subsequently dispersed into parts of the country that had a more favorable attitude toward them than was the case on the west coast.

3. THE AMERICAN INDIAN. Today, the American Indians number approximately 530,000. This is the only racial minority group that is preponderantly rural. Being the initial foe to the white invaders, once they were conquered they congregated where the majority group permitted them to—on reservations in the West, on land that was considered to be of not much value. Thus segregated and made wards of the government, they had relatively little opportunity to escape from their tribal culture and to achieve economic success. Segregated government schools which attempted to teach white culture yet could not find general acceptance for Indians in "white man's jobs" for some time, created further problems. Though progress has been made, the Bureau of Indian Affairs estimates that in 1960 there were still 158,580 Indians living on the largest reservations. There were also 219,418 additional Indians living in rural areas, many of them, presumably, on smaller reservations.

34 For the story of the Japanese minority during wartime, see Dorothy S. Thomas and Richard S. Nishimoto, *The Spoilage*, University of California Press, Berkeley, 1946.

4. THE PUERTO RICANS. The most recent entrants in large numbers into the United States are the Puerto Ricans. In the history of immigration, new arrivals have always been looked upon with suspicious eyes, especially when their principal language is not English. The Puerto Ricans are largely concentrated in cities. The 1961 estimate is that there are, in New York City alone, 720,000 persons of Puerto Rican birth or parentage. Their birth rate, too, is high—40 per 1000. For nonwhites as a whole it is 30.[35] In addition, the Puerto Ricans have come largely from rural areas, with little education, little or no knowledge of the English language, and few skills that promise immediate economic achievement.[36]

From an examination of these variables, it becomes obvious that each group has its own uniqueness in history and in current conditions.

THE WEIGHT OF THE PROBLEMS

The external and problem-creating forces, which have been discussed formerly in this chapter, press with unequal weight among families. Some families bear a few such forces, for a time, and find the resources to overcome them. In the case of the Negroes and the Puerto Ricans, in general, all of these forces are acting upon them together and with little chance of spectacular relief in the near future. This is probably one reason why much of the literature on minority-group problems concentrates at present on these two groups.

Their housing is inadequate, unhygienic, crowded, and lacking facilities to provide quiet and privacy—or in some instances, good nutrition. Not only can there be little pride in such homes, rather they are places to stay away from as much as possible. Unfortunately, for both adult and child, the only nearby places of escape are the streets of the city slums and such commercial pleasures as they afford. It is surprising that under such conditions many families are able to create attractive homes.

The residential mobility of these groups has four significant aspects. One is that so many of the families have but recently

[35] Nathan Glazer and Daniel Patrick Moynihan, *Beyond the Melting Pot*, The M.I.T. Press, Cambridge, 1963, pp. 91–94.

[36] As this is being written a radio news report announces that California, which was the greatest source of the tomato crops, can no longer find enough cheap labor for it. New Jersey is about to take the lead because of a good supply of Puerto Rican labor. New Jersey awaits a ruling on the wages of migrant labor.

moved from rural areas to crowded cities. From 1910 to 1960, the Negro population of New York City alone increased from 97,721 to 1,088,000. It is clear that country and city people live in quite different environments. The urban environment is highly mechanized, rational, mobile, impersonal, commercialized, cynical, and heterogeneous; the rural environment involves more physical but less nervous effort, there is a closer adjustment to nature, relationships are personalized, there is more stability and informality. These differing environments call forth different ways of living, different sets of values, different personality traits and types. The urban type is identified as intellectual, mercenary, calculating, reserved, sophisticated, and precocious, in contrast to the rural personification of the opposite of these qualities. The children whose families have moved from country to city live in a world which their parents do not fully understand with the result that many such children are caught between an emotional allegiance to their families and an intellectual conclusion that their parents cannot help and do not understand. This seems like an invitation to run riot. Nobody knows, and nobody seems to care. A second aspect is enforced mobility within the slum environment because of the condemnation of houses, a change in location of employment, or lack of funds to pay the rent. The rate of both unemployment and turnover in employment is high. Moving, under such circumstances, can break any neighborhood ties that have been made, and can offer little opportunity for bettering the physical basis of the home. Neighborhood friendships may mean a great deal to people who are restricted socially otherwise. One of the complaints about the large apartment-housing projects is that the community spirit is lost. A third problem in mobility is created when occupancy in a housing project is dependent upon a certain maximum income, above which the tenants are not permitted to remain. This means that those families that are progressing economically must find other homes, even though adequate housing is unavailable. The fourth problem is closely related. It concerns all those families in the groups that are the more stable and less financially depressed. It is difficult for them, because of residential segregation, to find places to live in which a healthier and more optimistic family life can be attained. On a recent television program there was interviewed a Negro family that could afford such a place, but had been trying to find a home outside of the slums for four years, without success. As an example, a report on the city of Philadelphia, for 1960, gives the following figures. Of all the residential blocks, 4.6 percent were inhabited by only nonwhite households; 17 percent, by a majority of nonwhite; 15.3 percent by a majority of white; and 63.1 percent by white households only.[37] Well known is the story of the Negroes' attempts to find housing in family suburbs where there is space for children to play and schools that are less congested. Many have found such homes, but not without problems in the doing and after the move.

Economic pressure falls with very heavy weight upon the majority of the families in these groups. At the basis of it are a lack of education, the resulting lack of skills in an increasingly automated society, and a continuing discrimination against them in jobs for which they are capable. In Philadelphia, in 1960, average family income was $6269 for whites, $4248 for nonwhites, and $3435 for Puerto Ricans.[38] A long history of hopelessness and of the acceptance of relief breeds apathy into many of the young people. Teachers in slum areas are familiar with the kind of pupil who comes to school in physical being only and cannot be stimulated to take advantage of whatever education he might acquire. This has been the life of his parents and grandparents and many of his neighbors. How can one fight it?

In many of these families the time-dimension of family life is almost nil. Housing conditions do not inspire children to come home and play after school where mothers can supervise them. Furthermore, Mother may not be there. The women, able to find types of employment unsuitable for men, have a higher rate of gainful occupation. Also, since the Negro family has tended to be matriarchal in its structure since slavery days, there frequently is no male head of the household. Under such conditions family life is sporadic and offers little opportunity for parental interaction with children.

It seems an obvious conclusion that, under the pressure of all these external forces, many people try to find relief through crime, delinquency, drug addiction, alcoholism, and the like. This is a depressed-area pattern that becomes a familiar part of the group life. Because it is so familiar, it comes to be accepted as inevitable by some, and the sting of disgrace is lessened. The shame, however, and the anger are great when this kind of behavior is identified by an out-group as "typical" of minority families, as if it were a part of the inherited genetic structure. It has been cogently demonstrated that, in many cases where some or all of these pressures are removed, the families cease being problem families.

Basic to the elimination of these minority-group situations in

[37] *Philadelphia Public Schools: Educational Survey*, The Board of Public Education, Philadelphia, February 1, 1965, p. 24.

[38] *Ibid.*, p. 26.

the future is adequate education of the young children. This subject has been neglected here because of its inclusion in a later chapter.

TWO FUNCTIONS OF THE HOME

The more one studies the problems of children in families under stress, the more one comes to consider and evaluate the child's home from two different but complementary points of view. First, the home is the place from which the child goes to participate in the larger social life; and, second, it is the place to which he returns after his social experience. This suggests the basic importance of two functions of the family in the child's development: the family's role, first, as a status-defining agency; and second, as an experience-defining agency. It seems appropriate to conclude the part of this volume devoted to the analysis of family situations in child development with a brief consideration of these two functions.

The Home as a Status-Defining Agency

When the child begins making social contacts outside his family, he is identified at first largely in terms of the home from which he comes and to which he brings his friends. The home serves, therefore, as a very important factor in the process of his social identification and the ascription of his status. This factor operates in the social development of all children, and at all social levels; but it is particularly important for girls, for they must operate, socially speaking, more in terms of the home basis than must boys. This is especially true during the adolescent stage, when the drive for social recognition is strongest.

Once the universality of the foregoing process is recognized, one is in a position to understand a number of things about child behavior. It explains, for example, that oft-noted critical attitude which adolescents, particularly adolescent girls, manifest toward their parents—their efforts to "bring up father," to make over the family and the home. Similarly, too, it enables one to assess the stresses and strains of family life which have been described in the preceding pages. The essential tragedy of so many of the young people in these homes is that their families are a social handicap, or are believed to be so, during those years when the children's chief interest is their social acceptance outside the home. It is our considered judgment that the behavior problems of many adolescents should be reinterpreted and restudied as attempts to work out an adjustment to the social isolation or discrimination which they experience because of their family origins. This would be particularly true, and keen, in a country with traditions of social democracy and with a large population of recent immigrant origin. More will be said about this in a later chapter.

The Home as an Experience-Defining Agency

Complementary to the role of the family as a status-defining agency is its function in defining the experiences of its members. Much has been written recently of the importance of the home as a cushioned retreat for husband and wife; obviously the larger aspects of such use have great meaning in child development. Home is the place the child comes back to, with his experiences. It is the lair to which he retreats to lick his wounds; the stage to which he returns to parade the glory of his achievements; the refuge he finds in which to brood over his ill treatment, real and fancied. Home, in other words, is the place to which one brings the everyday run of social experiences, to sift, to evaluate, to appraise, to understand, or to be twisted, to fester, to be magnified, or ignored, as the case may be. Here again one sees a universal process in child development, with families under stress often scoring their most signal failures in this respect. Such families are families in which the parents are preoccupied with problems other than those arising in the social development of their children. From this it follows that parental failures in these families most often take the form of "sins of omission." Childrearing, let it be emphasized again, is for the parents a teaching process, and teachers under stress do not make good teachers.

SUMMARY

1. The range in family situations is extensive, and has led to attempts to classify them. One of the more comprehensive classificatory schemes has been presented by way of example.

2. The first problem-family situation discussed is that of the parents who reject their children. Rejection situations are very complex. The rejecting person may be any member of the family group, and the attitude is subject to change at any time, often extremely so. Rejection may be physical, economic, or emotional in character. The latter type is particularly emphasized today.

3. A second type includes parents who magnify their responsibilities. This may take the form of overprotecting the child, usually on the part of the mother. Overprotection takes a distinct form in the case of children with health or disability problems. Parents take their parental duties too seriously, sometimes because of their own bitter experiences and sometimes because they have too aggressive an interest in their children's affairs.

4. A third main type includes parents who disregard the personalities of their children. These may be acquisitive-minded parents, with an overly developed sense of possession; they may be parents with very strong ideas, convictions, or philosophies which involve child development; parents with strong emotional needs, whose children are exploited; or authoritarian-minded parents, who insist upon being master in the family.

5. Family situations cannot be considered without reference to the impact of external forces. In many families, problems of internal relations result from the stress of outside influences.

6. The physical setting of family life affects its functioning processes. Many families live under the stress of housing inadequacies, which often bear with particular heaviness upon the life of the child.

7. Residential mobility affects the child in many ways. It breaks the continuity of life; and involves a change of school, adjustment to new social contacts, lessened family help and guidance, and, at times, marked changes in cultural contacts.

8. Economic pressures on family life include both economic inadequacy and the impact of sudden changes and dislocations.

9. Satisfactory parent-child relationships require adequate time and energy. Many families, especially at the upper economic and social levels, are under stresses which result in inadequacies in this respect.

10. The role of shame is very important in child development. Disgraced families are a serious handicap to their child members, particularly in their social contacts. Outstanding illustrations of such families are those in which imprisonment, illegitimacy, drug addiction, chronic drunkenness, and so on, occur.

11. Minority group families in the United States have specific problems relating to (a) the size of the group, (b) the area of concentration, (c) their order of arrival into the country, and (d) their economic achievement.

12. The Negro and Puerto Rican groups, at present, are the ones selected primarily in the literature as having the pressure of all the

external factors operating in their family life with serious consequences to it.

13. The problems of children in families under stress must be considered in the light of two basic functions of the home for the child: (a) the home as a status-defining agency, and (b) the home as an experience-defining agency.

SUGGESTED READINGS

De Francis, Vincent, *Review of Legislation to Protect the Battered Child,* Children's Division, The American Humane Association, Denver, 1964. The title speaks for itself.

Deutsch, Martin, *Minority Group and Class Status as Related to Social and Personality Factors in Scholastic Achievement,* Society for Applied Anthropology, Monograph No. 2, 1960. The title is self-explanatory.

Drake, St. Clair, and Horace R. Cayton, *Black Metropolis,* 2 vols., Harper & Row, New York. A study of the Negro in Chicago after the great emigration from the South to northern cities had begun.

Gordon, Milton M., *Assimilation in American Life,* Oxford University Press, New York, 1964. The author sees the United States not as an assimilation of cultures, but as a primarily white, Anglo-Saxon, Protestant culture with subgroups still remaining within it.

Frazier, E. Franklin, *The Negro Family in the United States,* University of Chicago Press, Chicago, rev. ed., 1957. A history of the American Negro, written by a Negro college professor.

Hill, Reuben, *Families Under Stress,* Harper & Brothers, 1949. The effect of the crisis of war separation on families is the subject of this study.

Jacobs, Jane, *The Death and Life of Great American Cities,* Random House, New York, 1961. A complaint against city improvement that betters housing but destroys community cohesion.

Koos, Earl L., *Families in Trouble,* King's Crown Press, New York, 1946. A study of 62 low-income families living in one block in New York.

Morrison, J. Cayce, *The Puerto Rican Study,* New York City Board of Education, New York, 1958. The author reports on the education and adjustment of Puerto Rican public school pupils in New York from 1953–1957.

Radzinski, John M., *The American Melting Pot,* International Association for the Advancement of Ethnology and Eugenics, New York, 1959. The eugenic theory of race was popular early in this century. This is the modern version of that theory.

Thomas, Dorothy S., and Richard S. Nishimoto, *The Spoilage,* University of California Press, Berkeley, 1946. A description of the experiences of the Japanese and Japanese-Americans during World War II.

Thomas, Dorothy S., Charles Kikuchi, and James Sakoda, *The Salvage,* University of California Press, Berkeley, 1952. A continuation of the story of the Japanese after the end of World War II.

Williams, Robin M., Jr., *Strangers Next Door,* Prentice-Hall, Englewood Cliffs, 1964. Investigators lived in chosen areas to study the neighborhood patterns of prejudice and interaction between racial and ethnic groups.

Wynn, Margaret, *Fatherless Families,* Michael Joseph, London, 1964. An analysis of current arrangements to aid fatherless families, with recommendations for further help.

HOMES WITH CONFLICT SITUATIONS

14

The family is a miniature society, it has been pointed out, that is unique for the continuing intimacy and the naked incisiveness of the interrelations between its members. From this, it follows that one of the most important groups of family problems has to do with the harmonious adjustment of these interrelations. These problems, in turn, may be considered from the point of view of husband-wife relationships, or of their bearing upon the processes of child development. This chapter is devoted to homes with conflict situations, with particular reference to child development. Four separate groups of such situations are selected because of their importance for children: (1) excessive quarreling between members of the family, (2) culture conflicts between the parents, (3) intergenerational conflicts, and (4) broken homes.

PARENTS WHO QUARREL

The literature on family problems gives due emphasis to the problems of personality adjustment within the family and to the fact that, as marriage becomes more and more a romantic, personal affair rather than a socially controlled institution, these problems grow increasingly important. Most of this emphasis, however, is devoted to the relationship between the marital partners. Family discord and conflicts are thus considered as a form of interaction between the adults in the family, with reference chiefly to the durability of the marriage and the personality development of the conflicting parties, and only incidental mention of any significance for child development.

Summary reports of cases brought to behavior clinics show remarkably little mention of children from homes with quarreling parents. This is, perhaps, another evidence of the selective nature of clinic cases, resulting chiefly from the fact that it is parents and not children who decide upon clinic contacts. Obviously, quarreling parents do not bring their children to clinics nearly so often as overprotective parents or those who show feelings of guilt over rejecting their child.

Similarly sparse are the references to quarreling homes in juvenile-delinquency studies. A notable exception is to be found in Healy and Bronner's summary of 4000 cases, presented 40 years ago. "Excessive quarreling in the home," they wrote, "is one of the conditions that has been cited both by delinquents and relatives as making directly for bad conduct. We have come to know that in 12 percent of our total 4000 cases there was excessive quarreling at home. Without any means of gauging in what percentage of families among our general population good temper gives way to quarreling in excess, we nevertheless feel that the proportion in our group must be unduly large."[1] Ten years later, Healy emphasized that in many cases of delinquency only the more superficial factors are stressed, that among the deeper causes are the emotional experiences of the delinquents, and that one of the most common of these is intense feelings of discomfort about family disharmony.[2]

Quarreling an Interactive Process

Conflict is a process, and quarreling is a form of conflict. Quarreling must be studied, therefore, as an interaction concept, which means that we are concerned not with the behavior of the individuals who quarrel but with their interrelations. Their behavior may take any given form, and may differ from one person to another. The essential fact is that each person directly and inten-

1 William Healy and Augusta F. Bronner, *Delinquents and Criminals: Their Making and Unmaking,* The Macmillan Company, New York, 1926, p. 126.

2 William Healy and Augusta F. Bronner, *New Light on Delinquency and Its Treatment,* Yale University Press, New Haven, 1936, chaps. 6, 14.

tionally opposes the other. Thus conceived, quarreling must be recognized as a normal process in family life. Students of the family no longer think of the happy family as one in which there is no discord. Conflict within limitations is a process whereby problems are faced and frequently resolved. As with so many other things, it is the degree or extent of the process that is pathological.

This conception of quarreling is inherent in the interesting distinction between destructive and productive quarreling made by Duvall and Hill.[3] Destructive quarrels are those which concentrate on the ego of the other, tending to destroy the illusions and fictions by which people live. Productive quarrels, on the other hand, are concerned with issues and problems; they involve redefinitions of situations; they relax the strain of emotional intimacies of the honeymoon period of marriage; and they often reveal the underlying strength of relationships between quarreling family members.

In the study of marital discord two terms, conflict and tension, have customarily been identified. Each has its own particular meaning. Conflicts are fights which arise in families over all possible kinds of differences, but which tend to be solved or to terminate; tensions may be defined as unsolved conflicts which may find open expression or be repressed, with accumulating emotional force.[4] Both of these terms represent social realities; the latter seems particularly pertinent in the analysis of marital relations, and the former conforms to the pattern of thought presented in this chapter.

As a process of interaction, family conflicts may be *acute* or *chronic*. Acute conflict is characterized by a sudden outbreak, often taking a violent form and, when it results in a settlement, leaving no emotional scar. In chronic conflict, the conflict becomes constant, often at a certain level. Families in chronic conflict are in what the poet calls a "constant state of warfaring condition." Folsom speaks of *habituated* conflict as a form of conflict which reaches a certain level and continues there indefinitely. He also uses the term *progressive conflict* for conflict that "grows worse and worse."[5]

Quarreling as a process may be considered also in terms of the precipitating agents or circumstances. It may result from the presence in the family of a disorganized personality who cannot meet the trivial annoyances of the day, or the faultfinding of a shrew

[3] Evelyn M. Duvall and Rueben Hill, *When You Marry*, D. C. Heath & Company, Boston, 1945, pp. 188–190. (Current edition: Association Press, New York, 1962.)

[4] Ernest W. Burgess and Harvey J. Locke, *The Family*, American Book Company, New York, 1945, p. 560.

[5] Joseph K. Folsom, *The Family and Democratic Society*, John Wiley & Sons, New York, 1948, pp. 445–446.

who distills her chief joy in life from continually reminding her husband and children of some neglect of duty. It may be the work of a crass nagger, or of an ego that makes extremely stringent demands upon other members of the household. At times it is a daughter who reacts with automatic negativism to every effort to help her, or an adolescent who is trying to make her family over. Similar in kind is the wife who pinpricks her husband incessantly about minor points of etiquette so that she need not feel ashamed of him in their "crowd." Not infrequently older brothers and sisters, who ought to be leaving home to establish their own families, stay and raise the family pot to the boiling point. Much of the significance of family quarrels for children stems from the nature of those who precipitate and stage the quarrels.

Family Quarreling and the Child

From the standpoint of the child, there are at least five aspects of family quarreling which merit special consideration. First is the scope of the quarrel. How many members of the family are involved? Is it one parent indulging in his daily habit? Do both parents actively participate? Are the children drawn into the quarrels, and to what extent? Are other adult members of the family involved? How large is the family, and how many of its members are engaged, and to what extent? Second is the stage setting of the quarrel. Do the parents quarrel in "the secrecy of their boudoir," or is the scene staged at the dinner table? Many families do their quarreling at mealtime, with the result, in addition to other consequences, that nutrition and the digestive process are interfered with. Studies of the effects of fear, anger, and other emotional states upon the chemistry of the body are highly pertinent here. Another important fact about the staging of family quarrels is the extent to which the neighbors can hear them. This is particularly pertinent in the thin-walled houses and apartments in congested areas, for it means that the child's sense of shame is involved, and shame is a social factor as significant as it has been ignored in the literature of behavior. Third, there is the nature of the quarreling. The various forms of quarreling remain to be explored. They include half-irritated wrangling; a series of venomous, sharp-tongued exchanges; an icy repartee; a succession of sly thrusts; the fury of high anger; a crescendo of threats; and, finally, the climax of physical violence. Perhaps the basic dimension of parental quarreling, as far as its meaning for children is concerned, is its emotion-provoking character. A fourth significant aspect of family quarrels is the extent to which they consume the attention, time, and energy of the parents. The childrearing process is highly exacting, and the essential problem of many children grows out of the fact that the best efforts and energy of their parents go into fighting with each other, leaving only the husks of a spent passion for the children. Akin to this are the cases in which the emotion aroused in the quarreling parent is projected upon the child. Taking one's spite out on the children is very common, as is the habit of many parents of showing their disdain for each other by neglecting or being cruel to their children. It is quite clear that many cases of cruel treatment of children by their parents are only distorted expressions of hatred between the parents. The mother who has been beaten by her husband *can* in turn beat her child who is the image of the offending father. On the milder side, quarreling parents lose the sense of calmness, judgment, and insight necessary for normal and helpful relations with children. They are too occupied with their own emotions and problems to be of help to the children with theirs. Finally, there is the child's evaluation of parental quarrels. There may be a vague, uncritical acceptance of it all as the way of life. Santayana speaks of this in his own case in these words:

> After they [my mother and sisters] left, my uncle Santiago, with his wife Maria Josefa and his daughter Antonita, came to live with us, and a new and distinct chapter begins in my experience. The scene, the persons, the events are still present with me most vividly. I didn't feel deeply or understand what was going on, but somehow the force of it impressed my young mind and established there a sort of criterion or standard of reality. That crowded, strained, disunited, and tragic family life remains for me the type of what life really is: something confused, hideous and useless. I do not hate it or rebel against it, as people do who think they have been wronged. It caused me no suffering: I was a child carried along as in a baby-carriage through the crowd of strangers: I was neither much bothered nor seriously neglected: and my eyes and ears become accustomed to the unvarnished truth of the world, neither selected for my instruction nor hidden from me for my benefit.[6]

Similar to this is the child's acceptance of quarreling as a habitual form of interaction. Quarreling parents make quarreling children who grow up to be quarreling mates—this is but a restatement of some of the findings on adjustment in marriage.[7] Other children

[6] George Santayana, *Persons and Places*, Charles Scribner's Sons, New York, 1944, p. 119.

[7] Ernest W. Burgess and Leonard S. Cottrell, Jr., *Predicting Success or Failure in Marriage*, Prentice-Hall, New York, 1939, chap. 7.

lose respect for their quarreling parents, or confidence in their ability. Often the parental bickering comes at the very time that the child has a problem and needs help, or has had an experience which needs to be evaluated in the light of calm adult insight. Particularly difficult is the situation for an older child, perhaps most often a son, who sees a mother beaten or threatened. He may be physically too small to interfere but mature enough to feel highly frustrated. He may be perplexed as to his duty, torn by internal conflict. He may interfere, only to aggravate the whole sorry situation. These are the children who become hard, bitter, calculating, revengeful, full of hate for a parent or an entire family group. There are children who have killed a parent thought to be physically dangerous to the other parent.

Finally, it should be emphasized that both the process of quarreling as a form of family interaction and the assessment of its meaning for child development must be approached in terms of class differentials. At lower class levels, quarreling is much more likely to involve physical violence. The physical mistreatment of mates and children is more common. In fact, a frequent justification for living with a man without benefit of clergy is that he is less given to physical violence when a lover than when he has the status of husband. In the upper classes, the more verbal forms of quarreling predominate, perhaps in large measure because an adequate linguistic equipment is available for quarreling purposes. The sharp slur or the stinging sentence takes the place of a poke in the eye. There is some evidence that very small children are less frightened by the latter. This is a pattern of hostile behavior which they at least understand, for it is their own. It is later, if ever, that they acquire the verbal dexterity to understand and engage in linguistic fisticuffs.

There are also class differentials in the extent to which children and neighbors are drawn into or become aware of the quarreling. These depend, in part, on the size of the home and its physical isolation or nearness in relation to other homes and families. Although parents are usually advised not to quarrel in front of their children, the children are not always sure that this is the best procedure. One girl commented that if her parents had gone to their own room to quarrel and she had overheard their tones of voice without seeing them and hearing their words, she would have been scared to death. Another reported that she never saw her parents quarrel and took it for granted that husbands and wives did not "spat." During the "adjustments" of her own first year of marriage she became so upset that she went back to her parents, who informed her that such things happen in "the best of families."

CULTURE CONFLICTS BETWEEN PARENTS

No two persons ever have exactly the same cultural background; hence every marriage represents, in the strictest sense of the word, the union of two personality types between whom there are instances of culture conflict. Many of these, however, are minor in character and can be adjusted with a modicum of difficulty; some are more serious and rend the family life in twain. Our present concern is with the more serious of such culture conflicts between parents, with reference to the processes of child development. Three kinds of these conflicts will be considered briefly.

Religious Differences in Marriage

In the United States freedom of religion and freedom of individual choice in mate selection produce a situation in which there are many religious sects among which there are many intermarriages.

Though it is known that there are over 265 different religious bodies, accurate statistics on interfaith marriage are not available. Estimates suggest that about 50 percent of Catholics marry non-Catholics and that more than 50 percent of Protestants marry outside their faith or into a different Protestant denomination. According to Dr. Erich Rosenthal, the rate of Jewish out-marriage is greater than has been assumed and is rising. He polled 23,313 Jewish families in Washington, D.C., and found that 13.1 percent consisted of couples with only one Jewish partner. In Iowa, he reports, the rate is nearly 1 in every 2.[8] It is quite clear, then, that a great many children in the United States have parents who were reared in different religious cultures.

1. CHURCH ATTITUDES AND MIXED MARRIAGES. Injunctions against intermarriage between religious groups are age-old and well-nigh universal. All of the principal religious groups in the United States have declared their opposition to mixed marriages. Only the degree of opposition varies. Most positive and clear-cut is that of the Roman Catholic Church. Because of its conception of marriage as a sacrament and of the church as the divinely appointed custodian of all sacraments, the Roman Catholic Church cannot accept the principal of state control and regulation of marriage, and has imposed its own requirements upon its mem-

[8] Report in *Newsweek*, October 7, 1963, p. 97.

bers. The existing policy is based on the revised code of the canon law of 1918 which, while it reiterates opposition to mixed marriages, permits them under the following conditions: first, that the Catholic partner be allowed free exercise of his religion; second, that all the offspring be baptized and reared as Catholics; third, that the Catholic partner promise to do all he can to convert the non-Catholic; fourth, that the non-Catholic make his promises in writing; and fifth, that the marriage take place in the presence of an accredited priest and two witnesses.[9]

The union of gentile and Jew has been frowned upon from the beginning, as witness Deuteronomy vii, 1–3: "When the Lord thy God shall bring thee into the land whither thou goest to possess it, and hath cast out many nations before thee, . . . thou shalt make no covenant with them, . . . Neither shalt thou make marriages with them; thy daughter thou shalt not give unto his son, nor his daughter shalt thou take unto thy son." These prohibtions were repeated with equal directness by the later prophets, such as Ezra and Nehemiah, and established the policies laid down by rabbinical authorities since. While the degree of opposition has varied from the rabbis who followed the more lenient German Reformed movement to the more strict attitude of Orthodox and Conservative rabbis, there is no doubt concerning the fundamental opposition of Judaism to marriages outside of the faith.

American Protestantism had no definite policy toward mixed marriages for many years, chiefly because of the Protestant emphasis upon the role of the individual conscience and the American tradition of civil control of marriage. In recent years, however, the opposition of many Protestant clergymen has been succeeded by formal declarations of attitudes. Chief among these are those of the Presbyterian, Methodist, Lutheran, Protestant Episcopal, Northern Baptist, Southern Baptist, Disciples of Christ, and the Evangelical and Reformed churches.[10]

2. THE SOCIAL SIGNIFANCE OF RELIGIOUS DIFFERENCES. To appreciate the significance of such marriages, it is necessary to recall the social significance of religious differences that was discussed in Chapter 4. In all religions, there is an interpenetration of religion into the other aspects of social life and organization.

[9] Clement S. Mihanovich, Gerald J. Schnepp, and John L. Thomas, *Marriage and the Family*, Bruce Publishing Co., Milwaukee, 1952; John J. Kane, *Marriage and the Family*, The Dryden Press, New York, 1952; and the Ave Maria Report, "What You Should Know About Mixed Marriage," *The Ave Maria* (Catholic Home Weekly, Notre Dame, Indiana), November 24, 1956, pp. 8–13.

[10] For a full statement of these see James H. S. Bossard and Eleanor S. Boll, *One Marriage Two Faiths*, The Ronald Press, New York, 1957, chap. 5.

This is particularly true in regard to family life and the mores of behavior, both of which are areas which organized religion considers as fields for its special authority. This interrelationship is most marked in a country like India, where religion is identified with the caste system and involves the whole range of social life. In the United States, the interrelationship, while less marked, is still of great importance. In some cases, religion is identified with group history and class status; in others, it is intertwined with ethnic origin, and in still others, with the general paucity of compensations of life, the church involving a large part of the organized life of the group. How important even the smaller sect may be in this connection has been pointed out recently by Clark in his analysis of Canadian experience. Sects, he says, arise usually as revolutionary forces in social as well as in religious life, they are often dominated by a personnel recruited from one class, and not infrequently they are forced into politics, so that, in the course of its history, the sect becomes a culture complex of religious, social, and political ideas.[11]

What all this comes to is that the religious labels which men use are symbolic of fundamental cultural differences. Roman Catholicism, sociologically considered, is not merely a theological system or a traditional ritual; it is a culture complex. Methodism is not just a form of worship; it is a way of living and thinking. The name Quaker or Friend serves to identify more than simplicity in church architecture; it is a demeanor, a way of dealing with life situations, a set of values. These larger aspects of religion, intertwined with the minutiae of living, are centered particularly in the intimate, familial aspects of life, an area which organized religious groups invariably reserve as their own special field of dominance. In other words, a marriage between members of different religious groups is not merely a union between two persons who happen to "go to different churches," to be resolved with no more effort than a casual broad-mindedness about a place and form of worship; it represents a supposedly permanent relationship between people who have been reared with fundamental differences in ways of living and thinking.[12]

3. Significance for the Child. It has been pointed out that religious differences are cultural in character, that they are perva-

[11] S. D. Clark, "The Religious Sect in Canadian Politics," *American Journal of Sociology*, November, 1945, pp. 207–217.

[12] See Jerold S. Heiss, "Interfaith Marriage and Marital Outcome," *Marriage and Family Living*, August, 1961, pp. 228–233 for a discussion of varied outcomes of Jewish, Catholic, and Protestant mixed marriages.

sive in scope, that they find expression in the minutiae of daily living, and that they center chiefly in family life. To the extent that the personalities of the parents have been molded by their religious culture, and to the degree with which they identify themselves with their religious groups, religious differences between the parents become significant, both for marital relations and for child development. From the standpoint of the child, it means that the family's cultural background is divided, with inevitable conflicts in family life.

These conflicts come to a focus more sharply in the rearing of children than in any other aspect of the family's life, for childrearing, as pointed out in an earlier chapter, is essentially a series of decisions by the parents. Two periods of the child's life in particular are involved: one is early childhood; the other, adolescence. In both periods, crucial decisions have to be made; both periods are emphasized as of outstanding importance in the process of personality formation. The problems at issue may begin with the practice of birth control and the child's coming; they include the religious rites of infancy, such as baptism; the selection of a name, a Sunday School, a school, a church, social contacts; and patterns of behavior and moral teachings of all kinds.

The conflict between the parents may take many forms. Most frequently, perhaps, it is a struggle to control the child's development; often, too, the undertones indicate that the parents are trying to dominate each other through their child. Since these conflict situations are often accompanied by the separation of the parents, the conflict frequently takes the form of a struggle for the possession of the child, in which the larger kinship group may join. Sometimes this struggle takes the form of seeking to select, on the basis of religious affiliation, the child-caring agency to which the child is to be committed. In many cases the conflict expresses itself in less overt form. One parent may submit, ostensibly, to the demands of the other but seek to undermine the latter's hold over the child. In still other cases, one parent acquiesces, but with an obvious air of defeatism which may not be lost or without effects on the child. There are the families of toleration, so-called, in which both sets of demands are accepted. The child goes to mass at the Roman Catholic Church in the morning, and to the Methodist Sunday School in the afternoon. One Sunday the family plays cards and drinks beer with one set of relatives; the next Sunday the Sabbath is observed with meticulous correctness in the company of another group. To younger children especially, all this may be highly confusing. There are also tolerant families in which nothing is settled, nothing accepted. There is the tolerance of a neutral indifference. Finally, we must include those apparently unsatisfactory arrangements in families whereby all the children of one sex follow the religion of one parent, and those of the other sex, that of the other parent.

Marriages Between Ethnic Groups

A second group of family conflict situations grows out of the intermarriage of ethnic groups in the United States. The extent of it is difficult to determine accurately at present for two reasons. First, the census classifies as foreign-white stock all those who were born in another country, or those who were born in the United States but who were of foreign or mixed parentage. The succeeding generation becomes native-born white of native-born parentage, and their ethnic roots are unidentifiable. Secondly, there is not as much interest in studying interethnic marriage as there was formerly. This is because the rate of immigration has declined and because it is felt that the third generation has assimilated to American ways so that little culture conflict is involved. There are some reasons, however, to think that the problem is still of a size to warrant attention.

1. THE STATISTICS. Native-born whites of foreign or mixed parentage, according to the 1960 census, totaled 23,784,347, or 15 percent of the total population. This compares with 23,589,485, or 15.6 percent of the total 1950 population. It might be pointed out that though the percentage is less in 1960 the number is greater.

It is customary in discussions of this kind to add the foreign-born white population to the above nativity class. The term *foreign-white stock* is used to indicate these two nativity classes. The 1960 census reports 33,078,380 persons in this category, comprising 20.8 percent of the total population. This compares with 1950 census reports of 33,750,653 persons, or 22.4 percent of the total population.

The concentration of these population elements in a relatively small part of the nation is also significant. In 1960, 63.3 percent of native-born whites of foreign or mixed white parentage were located in seven states (California, Illinois, Massachusetts, Michigan, New Jersey, New York, and Pennsylvania). Almost 7 out of every 10 (67.8 percent) of the foreign-born whites resided in these states. In fact, half of the foreign-born whites were in four states (California, Illinois, New York, and Pennsylvania), and 43.5 percent of the native born of foreign or mixed parentage resided in these four states. Moreover, it is chiefly in the large cities in these states (Los

Angeles, Chicago, New York, and Philadelphia) that these population elements are found.

The composition of the foreign-white stock in terms of national origin is particularly important in the present discussion, in that it reveals its cultural diversity. It should be recalled, before assessing the meaning of the following figures, that until the middle of the last century the large majority of the people who came to this country and who settled it were from western Europe. The culture that they established here was one of western European nature modified by life in the United States. It was relatively recently in our history that large numbers of people of quite different cultures (in family system, religion, and political beliefs) immigrated to our country. Of the 9,294,033 foreign-born whites in 1960, roughly one out of three (31.7 percent) was of western European origin; 46.0 percent came from eastern Europe; 18.8 percent from America (Canada, Mexico, etc.); 2.2 percent from Asia; and 1.4 percent from other areas. Of the 23,784,347 native-born whites of foreign or mixed parentage, 39.4 percent had their ancestral roots in western Europe; 43.3 percent in eastern Europe; 14.8 percent in America, chiefly Canada and Mexico; 1.2 percent in Asia; and 1.2 percent in other areas. Comparing the percentages of 1960 with those of 1920 the proportion in both of the nativity classes whose cultures were western European has been declining, while the proportion of people with eastern European culture has increased.

Some idea of the cultural diversity of the foreign-white stock may be obtained by a look at the totals by principle countries of origin. There are 24 countries that have contributed more than 200,000 of this population element; 10 countries, more than a million each; 6 countries, more than 2 million; and 2 countries (Italy and Germany), more than 4 million each. Nor does this summary include such groups as the Puerto Ricans. In 1961, it was estimated that there were 720,000 persons of Puerto Rican birth or Puerto Rican parentage in New York City alone.

Many Americans are prone to think of immigration as something that terminated a number of years ago as a result of restrictive legislation. It is pertinent, therefore, to point out that from 1921 to 1962 a total of 8,741,265 immigrants have been admitted to the United States.

2. The Assimilation. One need only to walk through a large city to see that the persistence of foreign culture is greater than the American Melting Pot theory prophesied. Quite apart from neighborhoods of a ghetto nature, there are those with definite ethnic flavor. The foods and other wares in the store, the newspapers on the

stands, the furnishing of the houses, the customs of the people all identify the origins of their forebears. Furthermore, assimilation takes place first in outward forms and last within the confines of private family life. There are people who wear American clothes, smoke American cigarettes, and drive American cars who wish to preserve for their children the values of a family system they consider superior to the American.

At one time the United States Census attempted to study the role of assimilation by reporting on *Mother Tongue*. In 1940, it was discovered that almost one out of every five white persons in the United States grew up in a home in which some language other than English was the principal one spoken during childhood. Most of these persons were foreign born or of foreign-born or mixed parentage. There were, however, 2,929,060 who were native-born white of native-born parentage; and they constituted 3.5 percent of this nativity class in the population.

To appreciate the full significance of this the sociological role of language should be recalled. First, language is part of the culture of a people comparable to its family system, its economic life, or its religious institutions. Second, it is also a mechanism which transmits the remainder of the cultural system. Because of this function, it comes to be peculiarly interrelated with the details and spirit of the entire culture. Language is therefore both part and symbol of a culture, reflecting its essence in such a way that another language cannot serve as a substitute. Just as many aspects of a culture cannot be expressed in another language because there are no words to do so, similarly many words can be understood only by explaining them in their cultural setting. Words represent not things but our behavior with regard to things. It is through words that we organize our thoughts about things. Speech, which may be thought of as the active, individual expression of language, is the vocal aspect of personality. It is particularly revealing, first because it is vocal, and second because, being learned early in life and thoroughly ingrained from constant use, it betrays, as almost nothing else does, the origin and background of the person. The linguistic culture is, then, a peculiarly pervasive aspect of the entire cultural background of the personality. Since the question on *Mother Tongue* was dropped as of the 1950 census, we do not have a comparable measure of assimilation today.

Marriages Between Social Classes

Recognition of the reality of social classes, as well as of their cultural significance, came rather late to the United States, but has been receiving increasing attention. Little is known about the extent of such marriages and their meaning for marital relations and for child development. Enough is known, however, to indicate the fruitfulness of this area for research studies. Some of the problems which need to be considered will be mentioned here. To what extent are class lines crossed in marriage? What is the social distance between the classes united? For example, in any particular case does upper upper mate with upper lower, or is it lower upper with lower middle, or merely upper upper with lower upper? What are the cultural elements which differ? For example, the religious element may be the same but the linguistic and artistic elements may differ widely. Obviously, too, differing elements in the culture have differing significance for family life. The sex pattern, for instance, will be highly significant. Studies now being made reveal the most striking differences in the forms of sex behavior at various class levels. The sex mores differ, as do the concept of the sex role in marriage, the requirements of sex adjustment in marriage, the aspects of sex relationships which are considered important, sex experience in marriage, the use of contraceptives, and many other points. Culture differentials in the rearing of children have been indicated in Chapter 4 and will serve to suggest how numerous may be the points of issue in interclass marriages in the field of child development.[13]

GENERAL OBSERVATIONS ON BICULTURAL FAMILIES

Highly important as the crossing of the cultural line in marriage is, whether religion or class or nationality, the resultant family situations are not easy to study, especially in their deeper meaning for the personality development of the members. Three complicating factors seem to be of primary importance. First, such marriages usually are at first based on a good deal of love and affection, strong enough to overcome the resistance of cultural differences. Common observation suggests that often a strong physical attraction is involved in such unions. As a result, many intercultural marriages begin with certain added elements of attraction, especially significant in the earlier years when physical and romantic bonds in marriage are relatively more important. Second, another unusual bond in these unions is the pride of the partners, equivalent in

[13] For further discussion see James H. S. Bossard, *Parent and Child: Studies in Family Behavior*, University of Pennsylvania Press, Philadelphia, 1953, chap. 9.

many cases to stubbornness. This arises from the fact that these marriages have usually been consummated in the face of contrary advice from friends and relatives. If this pressure is strong enough, the partners may proceed to marry in a spirit akin to defiance. Subsequently, unwillingness to admit that a mistake has been made may keep these marriages from disruption or may hold them together longer than might otherwise be the case.

The third complicating factor has to do with the personalities of those who consummate mixed marriages. Is there a selective process? Slotkin's study of Jewish-Gentile intermarriage concluded that there were eight types of persons involved: demoralized, promiscuous, adventurous, detached, rebellious, marginal, acculturated and emancipated. Only one-third of the mates were in the first three classifications, which suggests that two-thirds of them were persons who wished to be free from, or were not well integrated into, their own group.[14] Anselm Strauss studied American-Japanese war-bride marriages and discovered the following. The mates had no romantic commitments to any persons of their own race. They were independent of family, neither supporting them nor being supported by them. They had "jobs," but were not career-minded people. They were not "joiners," in that they did not belong to clubs, churches, and other groups.[15] These people appear to have a sort of rootlessness from a group that is characteristic of those in the Slotkin study.

Finally, there is a phenomenon of adolescence which appears to add to the numbers of mixed marriages. For many youths, adolescence is a period of rebellion from parents, from their culture, from all the values they hold. Then, a mate who personifies all that the family does not stand for seems desirable and exciting. With the passing of time and a re-evaluation of one's own attitudes, it sometimes becomes clear that the mate was chosen more because of a mistaken idea than for devotion to him as a person.

Bicultural families are perhaps more likely to have in-law troubles than other families, for it is among the two kinship groups that the cultural differences appear without the softening or restraining influence of romance. In many cases the kinsfolk of one or both mates may have tried to prevent the marriage, or at least counseled against it, a fact which is not forgotten after the marriage has taken place. In those cases where the relationship between one mate and his own kinsfolk is close, the latter's opposition to the mar-

[14] J. S. Slotkin, "Jewish-Gentile Intermarriage in Chicago," *American Sociological Review*, February, 1942, pp. 34–39.

[15] Anselm L. Strauss, "Strain and Harmony in American-Japanese War-Bride Marriages," *Marriage and Family Living*, May, 1954, pp. 99–106.

riage is correspondingly meaningful. Even when he rejects his kinship group along with their mores, strong in-group feelings may drive the kinsfolk to seek to regain the errant one.

Again, bicultural marriages as a rule involve the union of groups with differing statuses. What is the status of the new family? Does it have a marginal position, occupying a sort of social "no man's-land?" Is it rejected by the superior and accepted by the inferior cultural group? How uncertain is the situation in the eyes of friends and relatives? Is their attitude aloofness, hesitance, or condescension? Is one member accepted and the other rejected? What status is ascribed to the children? How does each mate react to the attitude toward himself and the other? To what extent are cultural differences seized upon, by friends, relatives, and the couple themselves, as pretexts to disguise other differences? Cultural differences are seldom unrelated to other aspects of family life. What seems to happen in many bicultural families is a continuing disagreement, coupled with a determined effort to stay together. There is attraction between the parents, and they could be happy if it were not for these irreconcilable differences. They cannot agree to agree, nor can they agree to disagree.

All these differences, cultural and personal, within both the immediate family and the kinship group, come to a focus on the children. They become particularly pronounced in relation to specific decisions which tend to fix the relatively permanent status of the children. Such decisions become involved with the self-respect of the parents and the pride of the respective kinship groups, as well as their deepest cultural values. Behind the crisis periods thus precipitated, the "feel" of the conflict situation is ever present. This has been expressed poignantly by one who was reared in a bicultural family. "There never was a time in my life," he writes, "when I first became conscious of religion. Like the concept of 'mother,' it seemed always to have been present as a great and awful question upon which adults did not agree, and upon which they would brook no discussion."

The conflicts may focus upon one cultural element, as in the case of religion, or they may comprehend the entire ethos. They may express themselves in a continuing tug of war, with overt recognition of the points at issue; or they may reach a compromise in ways and degrees which vary with the intricate complexities of human situations. The significant fact here is that the children come to personify the problems at issue, and their personalities reflect the conflicts, compromises, and adjustments that are made. To restate somewhat the fundamental principle of this volume, the personality of the child is the reflection of the family culture, of its conflicts and tensions and differences, as well as of its agreements and harmonies.

INTERGENERATION CULTURAL CONFLICTS

Second Generation Children

The rearing of American-born children in foreign-culture homes has been the perennial result of the stream of immigration flowing into this country. The dimensions of this stream have been mentioned earlier in this chapter, as has the fact that foreign-born persons tend to assimilate most slowly in matters of family life.

Some Problems That Arise

For the children in these families the situation is considerably different. Being young, their integration into the parents' culture is not so complete and fixed, to begin with. Moreover, their contacts are chiefly with the school and other peer agencies in the new culture which are concerned with the world of ideas, attitudes, values, philosophies, and patterns of parent-child relationships. In short, the cultural pressures in America upon the children of immigrants differ materially from those exerted upon their parents, being strongest for the children in the elements of the culture in which they are weakest for the parents.

What happens as a result of these pressures is that the younger generation grow away from their more conservative and culturally persistent elders, so that, as time goes on, they come more and more to live in different cultural worlds. But for the younger generation there is the added complication that they are forced, to the extent that they are subject to the control of their elders, to live in both worlds.

This situation has been considered by a number of sociological students. Some of them, following Thomas[16] and Park and Miller,[17] have viewed it primarily as a transitional process in which the immigrant slowly learns to adjust to his new social heritage. These earlier treatises are particularly valuable in showing how extensive and pervasive are the necessary changes—from one set of values to another, from a primary-group form of living to one consisting

[16] W. I. Thomas and Florian Znaniecki, *The Polish Peasant,* Richard G. Badger, Boston, 1919. (Current edition: Dover Publications, New York.)

[17] Robert E. Park and Herbert A. Miller, *Old World Traits Transplanted,* Harper & Brothers, New York, 1921.

largely or wholly of secondary-group contacts, from the extended kinship group to the immediate form of family, from tradition to education as a regulating principle of behavior, and from communal to individual habits of life, all of these expressing themselves not in the form of broad principles but rather in the minutiae of everyday living.

Other students have viewed the process in terms of conflict between successive generations. Writing of his own experience, Mangione says: "The more aware I became of the great differences between their [the parents'] Latin world and the Anglo-Saxon world, the more disturbed I was; nor was I the only child of Sicilian parents who was disturbed. We sensed the conflict between the two worlds in almost everything our parents did or said. Yet we had to adjust ourselves to their world if we wanted any peace."[18] One of Pauline Young's cases speaks similarly: "You see, we young people live in two worlds, and learn the ways of both worlds—the ways of our parents and the ways of the big world. Sometimes we get mixed up and we fight. . . . Many times I get mad, and then I leave the house. You see, I don't want to hurt my parents and still I want to live like I see is right—that is, right according to American ways. They can't see it my way, and I can't see it theirs."[19] To epitomize the process just described, a number of sociologists have utilized the concept of culture conflict, which may be said to be compounded out of the sociological emphasis upon culture and its role in the determination of personality, the idea of conflict as a social process, and the psychiatric emphasis upon mental conflict as developed by Healy[20] and others. This concept has been used particularly as a tool in the analysis of behavior problems of children of the second generation.[21] Its essential idea is a conflict between successive generations so comprehensive and pervasive in character as to warrant the use of the term cultural.

Another problem that arises, apart from that of cultural conflict, is parental inadequacy. What of the capacity of these elders in their role as parents? The rearing and guidance of children in modern America, particularly in the larger cities in which so many families of foreign stock have congregated, include a great many

18 Jerre Mangione, *Mount Allegro*, Houghton Mifflin Company, Boston, 1942, p. 228.

19 Pauline V. Young, *The Pilgrims of Russian Town*, University of Chicago Press, Chicago, 1932, pp. 114–115.

20 William Healy, *Mental Conflict and Misconduct*, Little, Brown & Company, Boston, 1917.

21 Louis Wirth, "Culture Conflict and Misconduct," *Social Forces*, June, 1931, pp. 484–492. Consult also Maurice Price, "The Concept 'Culture Conflict,'" *ibid.*, December, 1930, pp. 164–167.

things—the satisfaction of their physical needs, the selection of clothing and other essentials in a socially acceptable form, the choice of a school, supervision of school progress, guidance in selecting school and other peer companions, appreciation of recreational needs and their proper selection in an urban setting, and judgment of surrounding influences and of both overt and insidious dangers to be avoided. Adequate parenthood has become a complex and difficult challenge in all families, requiring knowledge not only of the intricacies of the world in which the child lives, but also of its social resources and how to use them effectively. This knowledge the foreign-born parent, or even the second-generation parent, often does not have. This is especially true of the mothers in these families, upon whom so large a part of the responsibility in the child's earlier years must of necessity rest. Such mothers are apt to labor under two particular difficulties. One is the fact that, often, they make so little progress in mastering the English language; the other results from the traditions of their culture, which frown upon their development of out-of-home contacts. As a result, in many of these families there is a relative, and often a complete, lack of parental capacity. What happens all too often is a reversal of the process: it is the child who comes to the aid of the parents, the child who acts as interpreter, the child who becomes the intermediary between parent and landlord, the child who learns where the parent can find a job. Thus, whereas all children pass through the stage where they think they know more than their parents, these children *know* that they know more. This may be one of the basic factors in the subsequent development of their personalities.

One of the most perplexing problems for parents of more recent foreign extraction has to do with the techniques of parenthood. The idea is widespread in this country that a child should not be trained and disciplined to be subservient to the parent, but should be helped to develop his own personality. This involves a democratic-experimental approach to child rearing, a greater respect for the child's intelligence and his capacity for self-discipline. These ideas are, to be sure, of comparatively new formulation, many of them dating from recent developments in the sciences of human behavior. They are still understood by a relatively small proportion of the community, but they are acted upon in general by a much larger part of the population. The problems which this changing philosophy of child rearing creates are not easy for intelligent American parents who are capable emotionally of accepting the ideas involved; they are particularly difficult for many parents who are still dominated by ideas of another and older sort. The majority of the immigrants who have come into this country since 1900 hail from countries whose culture was not imbued with democratic family ideals, where standards of behavior were more fixed and exacting, and where rigorous training during youth was supplemented by the practices and traditions of compulsory military training. Their American-born and -reared children, going to American schools in which these newer ideals and techniques were applied, and mingling with other children reared in such an atmosphere, have looked to their parents for similar treatment. Their parents, on the other hand, informed poorly if at all about the new, naturally cling to the traditions of a lengthy past in which they have been reared, and which to them seem as natural and inevitable as the rising and setting of the sun. Not that the issues on this score were ever fought out on the grounds of abstract principles and philosophies. In the families under consideration they give rise to concrete wrangles over the age at which the child will go to work, the control of his earnings, expenditures for clothing and recreation, and other vital realities in everyday family life. Bewildered parents attempt to enforce Old World ideas with Old World methods; restive children respond with anger and ridicule.

Not all families of recent immigrant origin stick resolutely to the old. Many of them hasten with undue speed and aggressiveness to reach for the new. They reject the old before they understand or attain the new. At times, the path from the steerage on the immigrant ship to the gilded mansion and to aspiration to membership in the exclusive social club has been traversed within a single generation; more often, it has been done within only two. The problems of children in such families arise primarily from a too rapid adjustment to American culture and a too intense climbing of the social ladder. As emphasized in an earlier chapter, it is the child who in this driving process becomes the spearhead of the family's ambitions; it is upon him that the resistance, and perhaps resentment, of the older and established groups focus. Thus the child in these families is caught in a cross fire of pressures, one from his kinsfolk, urging him to "make it"; the other from the groups to which he aspires, rejecting his aspirations.

Considering the situation of families of foreign stock as a whole, the basic process seems to be one of cultural mobility; and the basic resulting problems, those of family and individual disorganization. In the transfer from the Old World culture to that of the New, different members of the family progress at unequal rates. To speak in general terms, the children tend to move more rapidly than the parents; examined more specifically, what occurs most often is that the father moves more rapidly than the mother, and the younger children more easily and rapidly than the older ones. Under the individualizing influences of American life, every member of the family moves at his particular rate. A result is the disorganization of the family and the development of conflict situations based on the difference not merely in personality traits but also in cultural allegiances.

Some Patterns of Response

It is impossible within the confines of a few pages to assess the response patterns of millions of children to crises of cultural mobility such as have been described in families of foreign white stock. Life is too complex and richly varied to do this. We can at best attempt only to identify some of the more apparent of their responses under the following five headings:

1. THE CHILD'S REJECTION OF HIS PARENTS. One basic reaction in the field of parent-child relationships that runs like a recurrent theme through the responses of so many of these children is rejection of their parents. In some cases, there is refusal to tolerate the parent's presence or to remain under the parental roof. This is the child who runs away from home, who engages in delinquencies which promise or express his independence, or who merely drops out of sight. More often, however, the rejection is partial and symbolic. For example, the child changes his name from a foreign-sounding one to one more accustomed to native American ears. Or, the child may reject the parental religion. Most frequent of all is rejection of the parents' authority. Sometimes this rejection becomes chronic and rebellion against authority becomes a habit of response. Once formed and exercised against the first embodiment of authority that the child knows, the transfer of these habits to subsequent forms of authority—in the schoolroom, the workshop, and one's own home—frequently follows. Thus, the second-generation child often develops into the type of social rebel that is clearly identifiable in contemporary society by an unfailing willingness to rebel against anything, once it is recognized as part of the established order of things.

2. THE MARGINAL MAN. The child's rejection of his family is but part of the larger transition process from immigrant to American status and culture. In the course of this process, which is generally slow and often painful, there is characteristically an

intermediate stage in which the immigrant, or his child or even his grandchild, lets go of the old culture, but not wholeheartedly, and takes on the new, but not completely. The result is the emergence of a person who lives and shares the cultural life of two peoples without being entirely identified with either one. To designate this type, Robert E. Park coined the phrase *marginal man*, and it has found widespread acceptance. As defined by Park, a marginal person is "a cultural hybrid, a man living and sharing in the cultural life and traditions of two distinct peoples; never quite willing to break, even if he were permitted to do so, with his past and his tradition, and not quite accepted . . . in the new society in which he now seeks a place."[22] In other words, he is in a marginal position between two cultures that have not fused and that may be in conflict with each other.

A marginal status leads to frustration, and the behavior responses to frustration are varied. They include hypersensitivity, a tendency to want more than is one's due, conspicuous behavior in order to attract attention, openly aggressive behavior and philosophies, and other compensatory measures.

3. Leaving the Marginal Status. The marginal position is not ordinarily a stationary one. Most such persons, especially those in the younger age groups, tend to move in one direction or another. The direction and speed of this movement have considerable bearing as a rule upon the behavior pattern of the individual, so a brief summary of the prevailing situations is next in order.

Most marginal persons, both children and parents, tend to move toward the dominant group and its culture until relative or complete acceptance is obtained. This happens, of course, most frequently where there is no biological barrier.

Movement from the marginal position may be in the opposite direction, involving a withdrawal from earlier aspirations and a return to one's own group. There are some second generation children who, as adults, have become more loyal to the foreign culture than their own parents. The first child of the foreign-born parents, especially if it is a girl, may find it impossible to win in the conflict with them. Then, disappointment and defeat may lead to a strong compensatory allegiance to their original culture and group, and its expression may take several different forms. Some become leaders of their national culture groups, serving as teachers, editors, lawyers, clergymen, or labor leaders. They act as spokesmen for

22 Robert E. Park, "Human Migration and the Marginal Man," *American Journal of Sociology*, May, 1928, p. 892.

their people and fight for an improvement in their condition and status. Commonly there is a commercialization of the compensatory drive which they have developed. Others turn hard and bitter, utilizing their influence to rebel against the dominant group and its culture. Such people often develop into aggressive nationalists or revolutionists in the class struggle. Since the dominant group has generally a higher class status, the marginal rebel focuses the resentment he has built up upon the existing class structure.

A third possible movement is away from both groups and culture. Here one finds the lonely, isolated person who organizes his life in the solitude of a social no-man's-land. Sometimes such individuals harness all their energy to some occupational goal, devoting themselves with a zeal akin to genius to the achievement of some task, finding in its completion the satisfactions that life otherwise denies. But the isolated person does not always turn to constructive achievement. Here again is the other fork of the road, with its inevitable accompaniments of delinquency, suicide, alcoholism, occupational drifting, and the like.

4. CULTURAL AND MENTAL CONFLICT. Some years ago, William Healy introduced the term *mental conflict* into general usage among students of behavior. He defined it as "a conflict between elements of mental life, and [it] occurs when two elements or systems of elements are out of harmony with each other."[23] The concept *cultural conflict* which social scientists have developed in recent years is similar in nature; and their principle that personality is the subjective aspect of culture makes mental and cultural conflict two aspects of the same fundamental situation. Obviously, then, the cultural conflicts which have been shown to characterize so many children of foreign white stock are a fruitful source of mental conflicts.

Healy found mental conflict an important factor in the production of juvenile delinquency, and he became increasingly impressed with its relative significance as his work with delinquents continued. Sutherland and others, making their approach from the social side, conclude that culture conflicts are the "stuff" out of which much misconduct develops, and that "the conflict of cultures is . . . the fundamental principle in the explanation of crime."[24]

[23] Healy, *op. cit.*

[24] Edwin H. Sutherland, *Principles of Criminology*, J. B. Lippincott Company, Philadelphia, 1939, p. 52. See also Thorsten Sellin, "Culture Conflict and Crime," Bulletin, Social Science Research Council, New York, 1938; Louis Wirth, "Culture Conflict and Delinquency," *Social Forces, June*, 1931, pp. 484–492; Eleanor Glueck, "Culture Conflict and Delinquency," *Mental Hygiene*, January, 1937, pp. 46–66.

Thus we return again, on the basis of both approaches, to the relatively high rate of delinquency in the second-generation group.

But mental conflicts produce other patterns of response. Here one enters the field of the neuroses and psychoses which are the special province of the psychiatrist. However, the mental symptoms which they identify have significance for sociologists, too. The individual who is neurotically exhausted by the inner conflict of his divided cultural loyalties is a socially uneffective person; mental conflicts are often resolved by rash and impulsive forms of escape which deviate from the commonly accepted social norms.

Not all culture conflicts lead to misconduct, nor are the majority of children of foreign white stock to be thought of as problem children. The effort in the foregoing pages has been to analyze a life process involving a large number of Americans, basically important in its implications yet usually given only limited and superficial attention. One cannot but recall here the words of Santayana: "Fixity of tradition, of custom, of language, is perhaps a prerequisite to a complete harmony in life and mind. Variety in these matters is a lesson to the philosopher and drives him into the cold arms of reason: but it confuses the poet and the saint, and embitters society."[25]

Age-Culture Conflict

Another factor in the creation of cultural differences between successive generations is to be found in the rapidity of cultural change which has characterized our society. The consequences of this have been touched upon briefly in Chapter 2. The fact is, however, that this factor operates to some extent in all but a few relatively isolated cultural pockets in this country. Its nature, therefore, is general, though differing in degree from one family to another; and it should be re-emphasized at this point.

Cultural change increases the cultural distance between successive generations. Since the time interval between generations is relatively fixed at about 30 years, the difference between the cultural milieus in which their personalities are formed depends wholly upon the rapidity with which cultural change occurs. Other things being equal, the more rapid the processes of cultural change, the greater the cultural distance between generations.

The significance of this for parent-child relations has been well stated by Davis.

[25] Santayana, *op. cit.*, p. 103.

Extremely rapid change in modern civilization, in contrast to most societies, tends to increase parent-youth conflict, for within a fast changing social order the time-interval between generations, ordinarily but a mere moment in the life of a social system, becomes historically significant, thereby creating a hiatus between one generation and the next. Inevitably, under such a condition, youth is reared in a milieu different from that of the parents; hence the parents become old-fashioned, youth rebellious, and clashes occur which, in the closely confined circle of the immediate family, generate sharp emotion. . . . Our rapid social change has crowded historical meaning into the family time span, has thereby given the offspring a different social context from that which the child acquired, and consequently has added to the already existent intrinsic differences between parent and youth, a set of extrinsic ones which double the chance of alienation, Moreover, our great social complexity, our evident cultural conflict, and our emphasis upon open competition for socioeconomic status have all added to this initial effect. . . . They have disorganized the improper relation of parental authority by confusing the goals of child control, setting up competing authorities, creating a small family system, making necessary certain significant choices at the time of adolescence, and leading to an absence of definite institutional mechanisms to symbolize and enforce the progressively changing stages of parental power.[26]

Another approach to the significance of cultural change in parent-youth relations is to consider its effect upon the respective roles in society of the old and the young. It tends to depreciate the value of experience. It discredits precedents, traditional ideas, and techniques. The older person is at a disadvantage by reason both of what he must unlearn and of what he may not yet have mastered. The emphasis is upon experimentation, and a premium is put upon youth as being more versatile and adaptable. Old-fogeyism becomes a popular cry.

The experience of China through centuries of her history offers striking evidence of the foregoing in reverse. Lang has pointed out how the dependence upon agriculture, the importance of the public official, and the static nature of Chinese civilization all combined to strengthen the position of the elders. "The old man represented an accumulation of wisdom. The young man wanted to imitate him, not to fight him. For hundreds and thousands of years there was no conflict of generations in China."[27]

The current dislocation and reversal of the roles of old and young

[26] Kingsley Davis, "The Sociology of Parent-Youth Conflict," *American Sociological Review*, August, 1940, pp. 523–535.

[27] Olga Lang, *Chinese Family and Society*, Yale University Press, New Haven, 1946, p. 10.

naturally come to a focus in family life. Children as always question their parents' understanding, only more so; what is particularly significant is the extent to which modern parents question their own capacities and judgments. In most societies, parents bring up their children in their own way of life, and the task is reasonably clear. But the contemporary parent succumbs not only to the confusion of rapid change but also to what might be called the great American fear of being naïve. This is a current dread of upholding an old virtue or point of view or method of doing a thing, lest it imply that one does not know the new one; and large numbers of parents permit this to become an inferiority complex of the first magnitude. Living in a small immediate family, free from the domination of the elder kinsfolk, lacking authoritative sources of information other than the radio or the attractive young doctor down the street, looking askance and sidewise at the neighbors who are similarly confused, many a present-day parent feels nothing as much as uncertainty, a feeling which his children may sense before he is aware of it.

There are, of course, other families in which the situation takes a different turn. Here the parents adhere resolutely to old ways and values and seek to impose them upon their resistant offspring. At times, the very insecurity of the parents in a changing world leads to their compensatory devotion to the old, and then the conflicts are even more bitter. In many of these families, the cultural conflicts become involved with questions of family loyalty, the parents demanding loyalty not only to themselves on the basis of family affection, but also to the attitudes, ideas, and values which they set up as part of the family pattern. Such situations often become painful and disturbing, especially to the children, and they result in internal conflicts between emotional loyalty and intellectual judgment.

A final word should be said about the stabilizing role of the family in a period of rapid cultural change. It is easy, and it has been customary in certain quarters, to criticize parents for being old-fashioned and too resistant to new ideas in the school and youth culture of their children. Such an indictment, whatever its merit in any individual case, must be weighed against the family's responsibility as a conservator of old values and as a stabilizing force in a world in which so little remains true to itself through the space of a decade. After all, the mortality rate of new attitudes, ideas, and values is relatively high, perhaps as high as that of inventions in other fields; and a certain sheer resistance to change, quite apart from critical evaluation, seems both wholesome and essential. Moreover, there are things that are permanent. Courtship customs may be revolutionized by the automobile, and in turn by the airplane, but the way of a man with a maid has about it certain unchanging aspects. "There are values," Groves reminded us, "aside from those that come from human adjustment to mechanical processes or even to social organization. We sometimes call these spiritual values. The important thing is to recognize that they are basic in any program for human satisfaction. . . . In times of social flux the family becomes more than ever the final refuge for those who can find little sense of security elsewhere."[28]

BROKEN FAMILIES

The fourth group of family situations with which this chapter deals comprises those in which personal or culture conflicts between the parents have led to a termination, for the time being, of the family relationship. The termination may be permanent, as in annulment or divorce; it may be uncertain and unsettled, as in desertion or separation.

Extent of the Problem

The United States Census Bureau, in 1960, reported that there were 3,435,501 children living with a mother or a father who was separated or divorced. Another 863,849 children were living with a mother and stepfather. Thus, there were more than 4 million children who had been involved in the breakup of their families. It might be noted that these figures cover only one year and do not include other forms of marital separation, such as desertion or "absence from home," which has not yet reached the point of formal separation or divorce.

Broken Homes and Child Development

To understand what the breakup of a home means to a child, one must go back to the fundamental functioning and values of the monogamous family. These grow out of a relatively permanent union between a father and a mother, each of whom plays a basic role in the culture-transmitting and personality-forming processes of family life. Not only does each parent bring his heritage, but

[28] Ernest R. Groves, *The Family and Its Social Functions*, J. B. Lippincott Company, Philadelphia, 1940, pp. 450–453.

each also colors on a sex basis what is transmitted. That is to say, the father brings a male, the mother a female, culture. Thus each parent is not only an addition but also a complement to the other in the childrearing process. When a family breaks up, this normal process is interfered with, to an extent and with a significance which vary on the basis of the particular circumstances involved.

Sequences to Family Disruption

Three general sets of such circumstances are of basic importance. First are the new family relations which the parents establish. Parents may live apart and not remarry, but this situation is relatively rare in our society. It is more usual that one parent, or both of them, takes a new mate. It is also usual that children are born of the remarriage.

A second set of circumstances of basic importance involves the disposal that is made of the children in the broken family. There are a number of possibilities. The child or children may live with one parent, by agreement of all concerned. Such an agreement may be observed with varying degrees of good faith. Second, there may be an agreement for the children to be shared, with a shifting from one parent to the other, such agreements again varying in fidelity of observance by either parent. Third, there may be a struggle, acute, chronic, or intermittent, for the custody and control of the child's development. The struggle may take place between the parents, or it may be between the opposing groups of kinsfolk. Fourth, the child may be placed in an institution or a foster home, such cases constituting a large proportion of dependent children thus cared for. Finally, the court may award custody of the child. In many cases, decrees for maintenance and custody are necessary; they are often followed by appeals, modifications, and extensive litigation. The courts supposedly award custody on the basis of the welfare of the child, but the decision as to what this means depends on the judgment of the court. No uniform standards exist to guide such decisions, so in actual practice they depend on the judge's special knowledge and experience, his knowledge of the family, the number of cases handled, the time available for each case, and the general attitude of the community. One principle usually observed is that custody goes to the so-called innocent party. This status of "innocence" grows out of the American legal principle that a divorce must be granted not on the basis of mutual consent, but as an award to an innocent or aggrieved party. Obviously such "innocence" has nothing to do with the security and best interests of the child.

The third and possibly the most important set of circumstances involves the attitudes and behavior of separated or divorced parents toward their children. A number of well-defined patterns can be discerned. There are the parents who compete for the affection (and perhaps custody) of the child. This competition is prone to take unwise forms—an undue playing up to the child, overindulgence, displays of extravagance, and the like. Again, in many cases, the parents continue to fight each other through their children. Either or both parents, in part as an expression of personal animus and in part as a compensation for marital unhappiness, seek consolation, revenge, release, prestige, or security through their children. The result is that the child becomes the special victim of parental interference. As the only remaining link between former mates, he becomes the agency through which they can express their resentment toward life and each other. Such exploitation of a child takes many specific forms—he may be utilized to spy on a parent, the mother may incite the child to make all sorts of expensive demands on the father, or the child may be utilized to bear tidings of one parent's new-found happiness with another mate. Third, the parent may utilize the breakup of the family as the occasion to reject physically a child who was never wanted. It is particularly true that the child who is rejected is identified with the marital partner who is rejected. Finally, it must be emphasized that the experience of passing through marital crises is enough to lessen the parental effectiveness of many persons. In places where a stigma attaches to divorce, the parent must face and adjust to this. In any event, there is for the parents a continuing awareness or consciousness of their crises. Under the stress of all this, the child and his problem may be forgotten or neglected. Parental absorption in their own crises poses many a child problem. At times, the child not only sees his problems neglected, but is further utilized to bolster a faltering ego; that is, his loyalty is sought to atone for the self-condemnation of the marital failure.

Family Disruption from the Standpoint of the Child

Finally it is essential to consider all these marital and family situations from the standpoint of the child. The aspects which appear most generally in these cases will be summarized briefly.

1. Perhaps the basic situation which a broken home creates for a child is internal conflict. A child ordinarily has some emotional attachment to both parents. This feeling is independent of what other persons think of the parents, and of the parents' relations with each other. In many cases, people, including parents, do not

understand this. When the family is broken and the parents separate, the child is called upon to make a decision which he finds difficult to make, which he is unwilling and often unprepared to make. Yet the very fact of his parents' separation necessitates it. Often the parents further complicate the situation by demanding that the decision be made. The problems thus created may be particularly difficult for older children who have an insight into the merits of the case and are also aware of their own economic necessities or personal advantages.

2. In many cases, the child goes from a broken home to a home in which he is a stepchild. What this involves has been referred to in an earlier chapter. In the case of a home broken by divorce, however, there are particular difficulties. The child must adjust to a stepparent while the real parent of that sex is alive. He may resemble the parent that is being replaced—a constant reminder of an earlier, unpleasant experience. Other children, born to the new union, compete and naturally have a better hold upon the parents. The child may resent the parent with which circumstances force him to live. He may resent the inferior position assigned to the parent with whom he does not live.

3. The child who is shifted back and forth between two parents must adjust to two different domestic milieus, and possibly to two stepchild situations. The two homes will differ, and in various ways. They may operate on different economic levels. The religious background may be different. Social differentiation may be present, perhaps in marked degree. Thus the child must learn to live at two domestic levels. A wide range of personal habits may have to be altered in going from one family to the other.

4. The foregoing suggests the problem of the restraints that are placed upon the child, on his conversational habits and other social relationships. Care must be taken not to speak of the other parent; reference to the past may be taboo. How should the new parent be addressed? How should he be described to friends? Is it advisable to bring friends home? How much should be told about the past? What comments are in order as one goes from one parent to the other? These are questions which merit the insight and restraint of an adult; for a child they must be both difficult and confusing.

5. The child with a broken-home background cannot but make comparisons with the home life of other children. When contacts with other children show that they have parents who live happily together, feelings of inferiority, self-pity, disappointment, or resentment may prevail. The average child is not a philosopher, nor is it of any comfort to know the statistical probabilities for a child to live in a complete and happy home.

6. The child, like the parent, carries the burden of a continuing awareness of his problems. He comes, at an early age, to sense the attitudes of kinsfolk, friends, and the community. The child from a broken home quickly becomes aware of furtive glances, incompleted sentences, crude innuendos, and tactless remarks from persons preoccupied, thoughtless, or vicious, as the case may be. The moral condemnation of divorce attaches to him and makes his position more difficult than it would be otherwise.

7. One must not overlook the fact that the child develops attitudes toward the parents which become an integral part of the situation. Not understanding the purposes of the parents' interference or their attempts to use him to maintain a guerrilla warfare with the other parent, the child may become confused; understanding them, there may develop disappointment and bitterness. Or he may develop a panicky terror over the prospects of a new parental alliance. Not a few children from broken homes come sooner or later to reject one or both of their parents with the callous air of "a plague on both your houses." This may subsequently take the form of a critical attitude toward the institution of marriage, or at least a critical awareness of it.

It requires no complete psychoanalytic equipment to understand that in some cases the child will identify himself with one of the estranged parents. It is in this connection that the feelings of guilt, failure, apprehension, defeatism, bitterness, and the like, which many divorced or separated mates develop, become so insidiously important in the development of their children. There is the added complication that the attitudes of child to parent and of parent to child change from time to time. The mother who is divorced by her husband when he has found a new attraction, clings to her child by way of comfort. She stimulates him to become a foe of his other parent. Later, when she finds a new romantic interest, she discovers that her child is a handicap. Or he may be critical of the new spouse-to-be. Thus the child may find himself at odds with, or rejected by, both parents. Or the father, established in his new happiness, may become reconciled with the child, who now leaves his mother. These shifting loyalties complicate the child's attitudes, as well as increase his general insecurity.

8. Finally, what cannot be emphasized too much is that the disruption of a child's home life breaks the continuity of his emotional and intellectual development. After all, what is involved is a crisis situation in the most intimate and sensitive aspect of his life, and the reverberations that follow extend into every phase of his life. He frequently must attend a new school in a different neighborhood, leave his old friends and find new ones. His economic

circumstances are disturbed, as a rule, demanding curtailments of some kind.

The Other Side of Family Disruption

Not all family disruptions are attended with bitterness or followed by aggravated personal problems for those involved. There are couples who are divorced with a minimum of ill feeling. Both parents may act like mature adults, frankly facing a mutual mistake and cooperating in the adjustment of their respective problems. There are divorces in which there is a substantial carry-over of good will, respect, and even affection. Also, whatever one's theories about separation or divorce may be, the fact remains that some marriages are a tribulation for all concerned. The child is apt to be the special scapegoat in these cases. The termination of such families, and possibly the new deal of another family setting, may mean only the stimulus of better conditions and new opportunities for the child and possibly the parents too. Divorce not infrequently is a solution which closes a whole chapter of family turmoil.

Family Conflict and the Child in Contemporary Culture

It seems not amiss to restate, by way of concluding this chapter, certain features of family culture in contemporary American society which make family conflict situations of such great importance in child development.

Four features stand out with impressing clarity. First is the prevailing emphasis upon, and the relative independence of, the immediate family as the unit of family relationships; second, and complementary to the first, is the secondary importance and lessened responsibility of the kinship group; third is the resultant high emotional concentration within the immediate family; and fourth is the equalitarian principle in regard to the child. Taken together—and in many ways they are but so many aspects of the same process—they carry great meaning for children in homes with conflict situations. Three results are noted as of primary importance. The first is that the development of the child's personality, the satisfaction of his deepest personal and emotional needs, as well as responsibility for his economic and social maintenance, rest upon the small immediate family of modern times. Second, when this unit falters or fails, there is no larger kinship group to take charge, to which parent and child can turn to assume responsibility. Third, there is no accepted principle on the basis of which responsibility for the child is guaranteed by parents, except the uncertain personal opinions of legally trained jurists. As pointed out before, the contemporary child in the American small-family system views the world from a very narrow ledge. When that ledge is wobbly, insecurity is as pronounced as it is inevitable.

SUMMARY

1. Many families are characterized by a lack of harmony among their members in personal relations or cultural patterns, or both. These situations, which have been considered chiefly in their bearing upon husband-wife relationships, are also significant for child development.

2. Quarreling is one form of conflict. It prevails to some extent in virtually every family. In a more exaggerated degree, it takes many forms of expression, each of which has its own meaning for child development. Parents who quarrel excessively create many problems for their children.

3. A second group of conflict situations grows out of cultural differences between the parents. These may focus upon some one cultural element, such as religion, or they may comprehend the range of a class or the entire ethos. They may express themselves in a continuing tug of war.

4. Second-generation children in homes of immigrants constitute an important part of the child population and are congregated particularly in large cities. The cultural world in which they grow up differs materially from that of their Old World parents, giving rise to the resultant problems of culture conflict, parental inadequacy, undue social pressure, and family disorganization. Common response patterns include the child's rejection of his parents, the appearance of the marginal man, frustration coupled with aggressive behavior, and the crystallization of mental conflicts.

5. Rapid cultural change tends to affect all families by lengthening the cultural distance between successive generations, thus creating problems of cultural differentials for additional groups of children, as well as intensifying those of the groups already mentioned.

6. Another group of conflict situations are those in which the unity of the family has disappeared, as in desertion, divorce, and the like. An enormous number of children are thus affected. Among the problems which such children face are basic internal conflicts; life in stepparent situations; frequent shifts from one family milieu

to another; usually restraints upon behavior and conversation; feelings of inferiority, self-pity, resentment, or disappointment; continuing preoccupation with personal problems; the development of critical attitudes toward parents; and breaks in the continuity of emotional and intellectual development.

7. There is sometimes another side to the termination of a family. It may mean a solution of unhappy situations and the opportunity of a new chance. This may be particularly fortunate and promising in the case of younger children.

8. The problems for children in conflict family situations are particularly important in our contemporary culture because of (a) the prevailing emphasis upon the immediate family, (b) the lessened responsibility of the kinship group, (c) a high emotional concentration within the immediate family, and (d) the equalitarian principle in regard to child care.

SUGGESTED READINGS

Adams, Romanzo, *Interracial Marriage in Hawaii,* The Macmillan Company, New York, 1937. Hawaii is said to have no problems of race relations although it is composed of many races. This book helps to explain why.

Barnett, James H., *Divorce and the American Divorce Novel, 1858–1937.* Doctoral Dissertation, University of Pennsylvania, Philadelphia, 1939. The author reveals changing attitudes toward divorce through an analysis of literature.

Barron, Milton L., *People Who Intermarry,* Syracuse University Press, Syracuse, 1946. A study of interethnic and interracial marriage in a New England industrial community.

Cannon, Poppy, *A Gentle Knight,* Holt, Rinehart & Winston, New York, 1956. This is an autobiography of a Negro-and-white marriage. Miss Cannon advocates it on principle and for love, but reveals many problems emanating from it, even in extraordinarily propitious circumstances.

Egleson, Jim and Janet Frank Egleson, *Parents Without Partners,* E. P. Dutton & Company, New York, 1961. A guide for the parent who must rear a child alone.

Gordon, Albert I., *Intermarriage,* Beacon Press, Boston, 1964. The newest and most comprehensive book on intermarriage. The author summarizes the literature on interfaith, interracial, and interethnic marriages and adds his own conclusions and proposals.

Healy, William, *Mental Conflict and Misconduct,* Little, Brown and Company, Boston, 1917. A psychologist tells of the relationship between mental conflict and behavior. A close parallel can be seen here with the sociologist's concept of culture conflict and its effects upon behavior.

Herberg, Will, *Protestant, Catholic, Jew,* Doubleday & Company, Garden City, N. Y., 1955. A sociological analysis of the religious aspects of structural changes in the American society.

Mayer, John E., *Jewish-Gentile Courtship,* The Free Press of Glencoe, New York, 1961. Through many excerpts from case records, this book attempts to reveal the feelings of persons involved in Jewish-Gentile courtship and marriage, as well as those of their parents and children.

Pike, James A., *If You Marry Outside Your Faith,* Harper & Row, New York, rev. ed., 1962. A book of counseling on interfaith marriage.

Plank, Emma N., "Must Children Bicker and Quarrel?" *PTA Magazine,* March, 1962, pp. 8–10. An article with a study-discussion program.

Stonequist, Everett V., *The Marginal Man,* Charles Scribner's Sons, New York, 1937. A classic, describing the effects of culture conflict on personality and behavior.

EXTRA FAMILY GROUPS AND CHILD DEVELOPMENT

Photograph by A. Devaney, Inc., N.Y.

PART VII

GROWING OUT OF THE FAMILY 15

Personality is a product of slow and gradual growth. Students of child behavior who analyze the emergence and early growth of behavior patterns place great emphasis upon the concept of development. This concept has been elaborated in particular by students of the physical and mental aspects of child life, and its philosophy has been made the lodestone of their constructive efforts. "Child guidance is growth guidance," write Gesell and his collaborators. "The refinements of the psychological care of normal and deviate child alike depend upon a developmental philosophy. A genetic approach is more important than rule of thumb and clever modes of discipline. A developmental outlook permits us to see the total tide of development in perspective. This gives a constructive forward reference to our methods and a more tolerant understanding of the difficulties of immaturity."[1]

Similar emphases appear today in the studies of the social behavior of the child. From the moment that life begins, the child is a social being. Even before birth, he has a profound effect upon those about him. At first, his role in social relationships is rather passive;

[1] Arnold Gesell, Frances L. Ilg, and others, *Infant and Child in the Culture of Today*, Harper & Row, New York, 1943, p. 5.

but with continued growth, his responses become more active and aggressive. From one point of view, these changes in behavior involve his individualization, that is, his emergence as an independent and relatively self-sufficient person; from the other, this is merely the story of his socialization, of his integration into group life and his acquisiton of values which have a social orientation.

This chapter is concerned with certain situational changes which underlie the process of the child's socialization, involving principally his growth beyond the world of his family into that of the larger society. The main emphases, following reference to selected aspects of these situational changes, will be upon the problems which they tend to create for the child and his family.

THE SOCIAL DEVELOPMENT OF THE CHILD

Obviously, the child's first social world is that of his family. In it the biological tasks of birth, protection, and feeding take place; within it develop those first and intimate associations with persons of different ages and sexes which form the basis of his personality development; from it are learned the manifold items which constitute its culture. It is a world in itself, in which the child learns to live, to move, and to have his being; and for a number of years his immaturity keeps him within the limits of its confines.

Early in life, however, the child begins to make forays into the other world outside. Gesell fixes the age for this at 18 months. "When a child reaches the age of 18 months, his behavior extends beyond the confines of his home. He goes abroad. He may attend a nursery school. His behavior has an enlarged cultural significance."[2] Certainly by the age of 2, instances of cooperative give-and-take, even if only of short duration, begin to appear. From this time on, response to the demands of other children and interest in the social world outside the family progress at a continuous even if irregular rate. Psychologists, observing manifestations of child behavior from year to year, tend to identify a sequence of relatively well-defined stages in this process of social development.[3] Five such stages will be identified briefly.

Five Stages of Childhood

1. First is the period of infancy, extending from birth to about the end of the second year. This is the period of the beginnings of

[2] *Ibid.*, p. 3.

[3] For a description of this sequence, see Elizabeth B. Hurlock, *Child Development*, McGraw-Hill Book Company, New York, 1964.

social behavior: the child learns to distinguish between persons and objects; shows selective attention to the human face, recognizing familiar persons; attempts speech; shows reactions to persons of the same age; imitates those about him; and manifests some degree of rivalry in play with other children.

2. Second are the years from 2 to 6, usually referred to as the preschool years, and sometimes as the pregang stage. During these years children progress from being relatively nonsocial to being distinctly socialized. Among observable changes are an increase in the size of the cooperating group, in the length of duration of cooperative activity, in capacity to identify oneself with a club or team, in ability to follow the complex rules of a game, in perception of social relationships, in awareness of status compared with that of others, in capacity for self-criticism with reference to the standards set by others, and in capacity to formulate in words the traits and characteristics of others which they like and dislike.

3. Third is the gang stage, which begins at about the age of 6, when most children enter school; it extends to about the twelfth year. During these years the child shifts his interests more and more from the social world of his family to the group life of his peers. Social consciousness develops rapidly, the chief interest is in group activities, group loyalty becomes highly important, sportsmanship is emphasized, there is growing susceptibility to social approval and disapproval, social discrimination begins to make its appearance, and there is a growing revolt against adult domination. Significant differences in these respects between boys and girls appear now, as a result chiefly of cultural determinants.

4. Just before the onset of puberty, from 11 to 13 in girls and from 13 to 15 in boys, the child passes through a stage in which various manifestations of antisocial behavior appear, with a definite backward trend in social adjustments. There is a critical attitude toward home, parents, society, and so on, coupled with a desire to withdraw from former friends and associates. Fortunately this phase is of short duration.

5. With puberty comes the beginning of adolescence. This stage customarily extends from the twelfth to the twentieth year. It is the transition stage from childhood to maturity, during which new patterns of behavior have to develop to meet the demands both of the larger and more diversified life of his peers, and of the adult society which he begins to enter. More will be said later about this stage.

The Social Crisis of Childhood

Obviously, there is a considerable variation from one child to another, not only as to the age when these successive stages occur, but also in the exact nature of their manifestations. Throughout this entire process of development, two changes continue to take place. First, the child spends less and less time with his family; and second, there is a corresponding increase in his association with children of his own age. At first, the separations from his family are relatively brief and incidental, but as time goes on, these separations increase not only in frequency and length of time, but also in their psychosocial implications. What comes basically to be involved is a shift in the center of the child's social orientation from his family to his peer group. Gradually and imperceptibly his loyalties to and his interests in his peer group grow until they equal, and finally tend to surpass, those he has for his family. To speak in situational terms, this transfer is a major social process in child development, precipitating what is for many persons life's first major social crisis. What actually happens during these years is that the child continues to live in the social world of his family, to whose requirements he must submit himself, while he is busy transferring his activities and allegiances to the social world of his peers, whose approvals and disapprovals come to have paramount importance for him. It is to the phases, factors, and problems associated with this process that we turn next.

TOWARD THE PEERAGE OF ONE'S AGE

The transfer from the social world of one's family to that of one's peers in childhood has been identified as a social process extending over a period of years. Although it begins very early in life in the form of casual excursions from the family fold, it is when the child starts attending school regularly that the process gets fully under way.

Going to school involves for the child a revolution in his situational setting. First, familiar objects and places are left behind. The child enters a new physical environment, different from his home. This difference may be quite pronounced, in the direction of either increased comfort and attractiveness or the reverse. Second, the population of this new world is much larger than that of his home. Perhaps the number is very large. Accordingly, freedom has to be curtailed. Contacts are multiplied, there are more rivals, more adjustments to other persons are necessary. This competition with other children takes one form in the schoolroom, another on the school playground, and often still another on the way to and from school. There are children who have to fight their way to school and back home again. Third, a new authority emerges in the child's life—that of the teacher, who now takes the place of the parent and in certain respects seems to supersede the parent. Furthermore, new responses to this person of authority are necessary. Instead of the shared intimacy with the parental authority, there is the more impersonal, ofttimes entirely impersonal, authority of the teacher. Truly, for the child this is a new world, with new criteria, new rules, new requirements. Viewed from his standpoint, the change must be revolutionary, and one cannot but speculate about its crucial meaning for the child and about two further questions involving social policy. First, how early in life may children be submitted safely to such a revolutionary transfer of social worlds; and second, what other obligations are more important than the mother's presence in the home in helping the child assimilate this experience?

Some Problem Aspects of the Transfer

Entrance into the school-peer-group world creates two sets of problems for the child: first, he has to learn to live in this new world; and second, he must learn to live in two worlds, for he continues also to live in his family world. In this continuing transfer from one world to another, many difficulties arise, some of which are selected for brief analysis. Throughout this entire discussion of the transfer process, its problems, and the child's responses to them, the children discussed are primarily below the age of 12.

1. First is the passage from protected to unprotected competition. This constitutes in large measure the early socialization of the child. Children gathered together in school or other groups in the earliest years come mostly from homes in which they have enjoyed protected competition, i.e., in which situations have been devised and manipulated to show them off, to let them win, and so on. When such children gather in groups, their first reaction is to play by themselves, without much reference to the presence of others, and to deal with each other only when conflicts arise. Subsequently, playing with each other begins, on the basis of unprotected or free competition. This is a most significant situational change that opens up an entirely new world, in which the child must gain status without benefit of adult manipulations. Parents and other adults

are prone to encourage child competition during this period, and in a form more stark and unrestricted than they employ in their adult relations. Viewed through the eyes of the child, this is a hard world, in which the contestants often are extremely cruel to each other.

2. A second set of problems involves the child's experience with patterns of response to his peers and to other persons as well. In the family world, he sees and learns to use certain ways of approaching people and responding to them. These may be patterns of friendliness, resentment, rebellion, submission, excessive volubility, or sullen silence. As was mentioned in Chapter 3, such patterns tend to become habitual and often unconscious.

Much of the child's early socialization is a trying out of these techniques or modes of approach. However they work at home, the peer world renders its own verdict. Some elicit favorable, others unfavorable, reactions. In one case a 7-year-old boy was under observation in a clinic because of a report from his school that he was an incurable bully. A therapist discovered that the child's father bullied the mother, the mother bullied the boy, and the boy bullied anyone younger and weaker than he. Though his peer group disliked his behavior, and him, to the boy this was merely the way one behaves. On the basis of experience with the peer group, there goes on in the child a continuous selection and valuation of responses, with a continuance of some and a modification or elimination of others.

Children differ markedly in the opportunities which they have to gain social experience of this kind. Some children have contacts during these early years with many other children, both at home and in peer groups outside the home. The ages of the children in these peer groups may be the appropriate ones to stimulate the socializing process. On the other hand, there are children who are the only children in the family group and who have very limited contacts, over a period of years, with other children of their own age. Parents often fail to consider situations of this kind in selecting the home and neighborhood in which they live, yet they are of basic importance in the child's social development.

In the course of this learning process, many a child comes to discover that there is a fundamental difference between the response patterns emphasized to him in the family world and those prescribed for him in the peer world. In the former, he is told by parents and teachers, and is shown by the examples of other children, to be obedient and submissive. He is to accept leadership and direction. Mother knows best, and it is not for him to question. But in the peer world the prescribed responses are apt to be those of self-assertion.

There the chief virtue is domination; the most important qualities are those of leadership. In fact, there is much evidence to show that the more dominating the parent is in his relations with his child and the more submissive he expects the child to be toward him, the more self-assertive he wants the child to be in his relations with other children.

3. A third group of problems for children arises from the differences between the culture of the family and that of the peer world. Such differences are very prevalent, and at times quite marked, in a country like ours, with its rich variety of cultural groups, its sectional traditions, its regional differences, and its class distinctions. Furthermore, the high rate of residential mobility of our population, with its changing contacts, increases the incidence of contacts between cultural groups. Thus the North Carolina small-town Protestant family comes to live among the Irish Catholic in Boston; the Polish Catholic family migrates to a Protestant German area; the Vermont couple, with their 7-year-old son, are transferred to a job in Georgia; the intellectually overstimulated son of a university professor lives on the edge of a changing urban neighborhood that is rapidly being taken over by Negroes; the child of wealthy parents, keenly alive to the social amenities, finds his peer contacts with a host of upper lower and lower middle-class children whose interests are for the most part considerably different from his own.

If we remember that the term *culture* includes ways of thinking and believing as well as material artifacts, the significance of cultural differences between family and peer worlds will be evident. From the family standpoint, the culturally different peer world stands for habits, ideas, and values which the family seeks to avoid in rearing its child; to the peers, the child's family appears as peculiar, old-fashioned, or unreasonable. From the standpoint of the child, the situation is both difficult and confusing. In his home world he is being trained, to the point of coercion perhaps, to certain cultural values, and his peers in the child world emphasize another set; he must live in both worlds, and at a time when he lacks insight into the peculiarities of life, his parents, and his peers. Sometimes these cultural differences are minor, and cause only a passing wonder in his mind; in other cases, they are broad or deep, or both, resulting in the direct conflicts between the two worlds in which he must live.

4. A fourth group of problems has to do with the reactions of the parents to this early socializing process of the child. Of the more commonly found parental attitudes, four, which tend to hamper the

child's social development, will be identified briefly. There are the parents, for example, who brook no competition. They tend to ignore or to reject the claims of the child or his peer world. They fail to realize its meaning to him or its role in his development. Second, there are the parents who seek to lure their child away from contacts with other children and try to restrict him to contacts within the family. "We and our children do everything together," say many parents with pride in their own exclusive parenthood. Again, some parents place themselves as a shield between the child and his social experiences with other children. Early in his life, they arbitrarily take him out of situations before he can learn to accommodate to them. This keeps the natural socializing process from functioning. It narrows the child's opportunity to develop the techniques of getting along with his peers. One of the major problems of parenthood is to learn one's proper place in this social learning process involving the child and his relations to other children. In a fourth type of situation the child is overpraised for even his more minor achievements, the obvious effect of which is to prevent him from learning the satisfactions of real achievement. In other words, the parent becomes a soft pillow between the child and the realities of life, and there is a resultant development of attitudes in the child which often continue into adult life. One can readily detect the persons in the adult world who expect praise and even outright flattery for doing only the more ordinary tasks.

In summary, how the child transfers from the world of family life to that of childhood, and later to adulthood, depends to a large extent on the parents, how they have functioned and what they have sought to achieve. Have they contrived to make the child independent and capable of dealing with his problems, have they sheltered him, has their major objective been to instill obedience, or have they kept him in ignorance of the realities of life? These parental attitudes toward the child's social experiences in his own world, and the child's responses to them, constitute an integral chapter in human development.

CHILD RESPONSES TO TRANSFER PROBLEMS

Child responses to these transfer problems are considered usually in terms of the rate and consequent age at which the transfer is made, and children are grouped as developing socially at (1) a normal, (2) an accelerated, or (3) a retarded rate of growth. This approach is important, particularly when related to measurements of other aspects of child development. Emphasis here, however, will be upon the type of response, in terms of social interaction, which children make to these transfer problems. To understand these responses, it seems pertinent again to recall the dual nature of the child's life. He is expected to learn to live with other children; he is compelled to live with his family. His problems are therefore basically twofold, centering in (1) his relations with his parents or his family world and (2) his relations with his peers in the child world; his responses are accordingly grouped under these two headings.

Responses in Relation to Parents

The ways of doing and thinking followed by the child or his peer world often do not meet the approval of the parent and the adult world. Most often this disapproval is mild, the peer world being regarded with amused tolerance as among the vagaries of childhood; at times, however, the disapproval may be so marked that his conduct is spoken of as "delinquent behavior." In making their judgments, parents tend to overlook the criterion by which the child is judging, in his desire for social recognition. The essential fact which parents are so prone to forget is that the child whom other children like and seek as a companion is succeeding in building up desirable habits of social behavior. From the adults' point of view his habits and attitudes may not appear satisfactory, but his own group has placed its approval on his manner of working and playing with them and from that standpoint his behavior may be called adequate and efficient. Hence a significant criterion in appraising the social behavior of growing children is the amount of recognition received from the group with whom the children are in daily contact under a variety of circumstances.

It is in the difference between these two criteria that many of the conflicts between child and parent begin; confronted with these conflicts, the following types of response are characteristic of many children:

1. Responses of hostility and resentment against parents are both frequent and inevitable, leading to open and direct opposition, to efforts at circumvention, or to compliance but with a sullen smoldering resentment. If deeply enough established, such attitudes naturally will be retained and carried over to the adult world.

2. Withdrawal from the child world, coupled with devotion to the teacher rather than the parent, occurs at times. These are the children who seek to become exemplary students in school; their behavior conforms to the teacher's demands; they develop the customary "bag of tricks" to draw attention to their own behavior

as well as to the nonconforming behavior of other children. They are the adroit "apple polishers" of the school world.

3. In some cases, however, the withdrawing child centers his allegiance upon the parent. Such children reject the peer world and remain loyal to the family world. Coupled with this, there is often a clever play upon parental generosity or sympathy. There may be hints to the parents about the discrimination of "other children"; and when the "other children" are of different cultural groups, the possibilities for the development of trouble are many and varied. Suggestions may be made to the parents to buy things so that the children may impress other children. Apparently, the opportunities in these situations for parents and children to exploit each other are numerous and tempting.

4. There are many cases in which the differing claims of the family and the peer worlds create conflicts which become crucial, and at times insoluble. Such children are early torn between loyalty to their families and the very human desire for social recognition in the world of other children. It is conflicts of this type which seem to relate themselves to the anxieties which Horney emphasizes as that "insidiously increasing all-pervading feeling of being lonely and helpless in a hostile world."[4]

5. There is, of course, always the possibility of dissociation as a response. This consists in keeping the peer world and the family world apart. Just as the adult learns to organize his Sundays about his duties as a pillar of the church and his Mondays about the realities of the business world, so children adjust early to conflicting situations by compartmentalizing their lives. It is amazing to discover how many children learn to lead double lives; the one, with their peers, and the other, in their families, straddling in one leap the differences between them and contriving steadily to keep one out of sight of the other.

Responses in Relation to Peers

Because responses in relation to peers will be dealt with in subsequent chapters, reference to them here will be brief. It will suffice only to point out that the normal child tends to give priority to the peer world over the family world in his deep desire to gain social recognition, and that when he does so, many a modern parent becomes alarmed. We cannot help recalling here the story of the distraught mother of such a child who rushed to a noted psychia-

[4] Karen Horney, *The Neurotic Personality of Our Time*, W. W. Norton & Company, New York, 1937, p. 89.

trist and asked where she could find a good psychiatric clinic. The psychiatrist gravely told her and added this terse bit of advice: "And while you are there, be sure you get a good examination."

Less than ordinary success for the child in his peer world often leads to other types of response, and these will be considered briefly.

1. The child may seek another child world in which special privileges will be given to him. He will search for playmates who will grant protected competition. It may be the neighboring child who has no one else to play with, or a smaller child, or a child of another color, or a child of lower status. Such responses, made by the child or suggested by the parent, are symptomatic and should receive early attention.

2. Some children seek to buy special favors, immunities, or recognition in the peer world. Out of such situations arise those inordinate demands for money which are often encountered in children. In some cases, these demands are met by the parents; in others, the child early seeks ways of earning the money; in still others, he makes theft the solution. Petty thieving among school children is very common and is, for the most part, overlooked or dealt with in a casual manner; it is usually only when large amounts of money or material are involved that a "hue and cry" is raised. There is little doubt but that much of the stealing by children who are old enough to distinguish between mine and thine results from their search for the means of achieving social success.

3. Children withdraw from the child world without transferring their allegiance to teacher or parent. They withdraw now in order to recapture it later. Here one finds the child who practices something in which there is for the time being no competition. This is the child who takes private lessons, usually in activities in which there is a possibility of individual achievement and subsequent success. Often such children are actuated by a strong driving force which seems to say, "I'll show them, I will." We find these children with particular frequence in certain ethnic groups who have peculiar problems in regard to social recognition. It is out of situations of this kind that the artist arises early, with his paradoxical combination of withdrawing from his fellows to achieve levels of performance which will enable him to gain their subsequent acclaim. The spiritual home of the artist has ever been on the terraced slopes of a social no man's land.

4. At times, the child who fails with his peers withdraws only from competition with his own sex, transferring his activities to the opposite sex. This group includes the girl who "hates" other

girls. She likes to play only with boys, among whom she finds protected competition. A little later, to enable her to retain her position with the boys, she may permit them special privileges. Some of these may be sexual in nature. One thus comes naturally to understand why sex delinquency and illegitimacy come to be spoken of as forms of compensatory behavior. There is the boy who wants to play only with girls. The other boys are too rough, he says, or uncouth, or uninteresting. To retain his position with the girls, he soon realizes his need for money, and theft may, in time, be his definition of the situation.

5. A great many children who fail or meet with inadequate success in the social life of their peer world seek early to compensate with success in their school work. School success serves many purposes for a child. Through it, he is proving to himself that he is no failure, he is showing other children that there is something in which he can surpass them, he is impressing his parents and other adults who regard such success as a virtue. Solutions of this kind are particularly feasible among middle-class persons, but in all classes there are children whose high levels of scholastic performance are a product of the withdrawing technique.

THE PROCESS OF SOCIAL WEANING

As the child grows older, the relative importance which he attaches to his peer and his family worlds gradually changes. At first, as has been noted, the family world is of primary importance to him, and the peer world is incidental. But by the time that the ordinary boy and girl reach their twelfth year, the peer world definitely surpasses the family world in its importance to them. From the twelfth to the twentieth year, the young person reorganizes his personality on an increasingly independent basis. Obviously, this entails the establishment of a new relationship between child and family, involving a modification of family attitudes and ties to meet the child's demands for self-affirmation. The child is growing away from the family, it is commonly said. There is an emotional detachment from the family, and a reorganization of habit patterns away from obedience and dependence to a relative independence permitting the young person to face the world "without turning back." For this growing-away process, the term *social weaning* seems appropriate.

To avoid possible misunderstanding, it should be pointed out that social weaning does not mean necessarily leaving the parental roof, although this is often involved; or defiance of the parents' legitimate authority, although this may have to be reinterpreted; or the manifestation of insolent or disorderly behavior, although this appears at times as a by-product. Social weaning means a reorganization of the child-parent relationship in recognition of the child's growing maturity. It is this aspect which is fundamental and needs to be emphasized.

Although this process is most obvious between the twelfth and twentieth years, its beginnings often are to be found earlier in life, as a by-product of childhood visiting. The way in which time and distance from family is gained has already been described in Chapter 6.

Social weaning is neither easy nor simple, being characterized often by a series of relative crises in parent-child relationships. Certain aspects of contemporary life are prone to complicate it. The role of the small-family system, early marriage and childbirth, and the increased health and longevity of parents have already been referred to as tending to create the possessive parent, i.e., the parent who will not let go. Another factor, generally overlooked, is the modern prolongation of childhood resulting from advanced standards of public education and child labor. Not only do these present-day standards postpone the child's entrance into the workaday world and, economically speaking, into the world of self-maintenance, but they also correspondingly prolong the period as well as the completeness of his dependence upon his parents. This situation is seen in its more exaggerated form among students at the collegiate and professional school level. A large proportion of young people have been going to college in recent years. To a large extent, this development has been assessed in terms of the intellectual sharpening of the younger generation. Two additional aspects may, however, be considered. One is the whole personality development of collegiate youth. Is their development balanced, or does the intellectual run beyond the emotional and the social? Does growth in the world of ideas too far exceed acquaintance with the world of reality? Questions of this kind, however important they are per se, are somewhat incidental to our main query here: what does this prolongation of dependence upon their parents do to young people? Does it tend to create a dependent, exacting, taking but not giving type of person—the abused citizen in a world of historically unparalleled luxury? How does a youth of 20 to 22, for example, define to himself his dependence upon his parents? Is it true that he develops often unconsciously a deep and intense emotional resentment against his parents? Is it inevitable that because he owes them so much which it would be so difficult to repay, he tends to rationalize the situation so as to excuse himself from his obligations: (1) his parents are unreasonable in their demands, (2) they do not understand him and are crippling the development of his personality, or (3) they are really much more blessed with this world's goods than they seem and can well afford the expenditures which they have made?

Some Symptoms of an Unweaned Condition

Social weaning, however, is unlike physical weaning in one marked respect—the fact that frequently it does not happen, wholly or at least in part. In everyday life, one constantly meets the people who have failed at being socially weaned, who have never learned or been allowed to let go of their dependence upon their parents, and who because of the characteristic symptoms that ensue are incapacitated for the activities of adult life. Two illustrations will suffice.

1. In the workaday world, the unweaned person is likely to be constantly expecting or asking for special consideration from his employer. The employer, being the person in authority, is expected to act as the parent did. When this is refused, the employee may indulge in temper tantrums, talk to himself, develop a persecution complex, act like a long-suffering hero, or resign in a huff. Many such persons become intolerable nuisances in the world of business and the professions. Undoubtedly, many a life spent in occupational drifting or failure results from the characteristics of social unweaning.

2. Many a matrimonial failure, too, goes back to a lack of social weaning. The unweaned individual expects his mate to act the way the parent did, to display the attitudes and to assume the roles of the parent in his earlier home life. "Better not marry a man who is tied to his mother's apron strings" is a very old adage which the very new insights are still revealing. One particular matrimonial manifestation of an unweaned condition is the choice of a much older person as a marriage partner. A young man still dominated by his mother is especially likely to marry a woman much older than himself. Statistics on the age of marriage reveal that in 10 to 15 percent of all marriages the bride is older than the groom.

A SOCIOLOGICAL THEORY OF ADOLESCENCE

Adolescence is one of the most discussed periods of the life span. Whatever conceptions and interpretations of it are presented, there is general agreement that it is a period of stress and strain for the maturing individual. Obviously, adolescence involves many things —complex changes in body structure and functions, accompanying changes in mental expansion and emotional maturing, developing self-consciousness, crystallization of life's values and plans, continuing experiments in social adjustment, and many other things. It is the purpose of the present discussion, not to develop or appraise any of these, but to advance a conception of adolescence in terms of its basic social situations.

The essential fact about this part of the life span is that a rapidly growing and not yet mature person is living, not in one, or two, but in three social worlds. One of these continues to be his family world. True, it is said that the child has been growing out of this world for some time, but there is still the stubborn fact that he remains in it. Whatever the individual variations of the situation may be, the basic facts are that the adolescent lives at home, is dependent upon his parents economically and otherwise, and continues to be subject to at least some of the rules and requirements of the family world. Moreover, the intangible bonds of family loyalty continue to hold him. To this family world the adolescent must adjust, at least in one large segment of his life.

The second world in which the adolescent lives is his peer world, i.e., the world of other adolescents. These are the years when the desire for social approval is stronger than perhaps at any other time of life, and there is the added fact of a shift to the adolescent world of the opposite sex. With this shift a whole new world opens, in which one must achieve status and recognition and to which one must adjust. It is as if the peer world had added another dimension.

Third, there is the adult nonfamily world, which has been creeping slowly over the horizon and has gradually been making itself known to the adolescent. Early contacts with this world are sporadic and incidental—through kinsfolk, in books, as a phase of neighborhood relationships, through the radio and daily press, perhaps in the realities of parttime employment, and finally in the prospects of and plans for future employment. Somewhere, sometime, in this adolescent period comes the realization, at times quite suddenly, of the stark reality of this adult world, its inevitability, its serious and exacting nature, its distinctive code and requirements.

Sometimes, however, the shift from the peer to the adult nonfamily world is very abrupt. This is particularly true in the case of many college and university folk. Four years of a happy and relatively carefree life in the peer world and the transfer into the adult world may occur within the twinkling of a week. The late William Percy has written about this with understanding. "Probably there is no nostalgia so long-lived and hopeless," he says, "as that of the college graduate returning to his native town. He is a stranger though he is at home. He is sick for a communal life that was and can never be again, a life merry with youth, and unshadowed by responsibilities. He is hungry for the easy intimacies which competitive anxious living does not provide. He is unproved when proof is demanded on every side. In this alien environment, the only one he may now call his own, he is unknown, even to himself."[5]

This, then, is the perennial sociological problem of the adolescent, that he must live in three worlds, each distinct in many respects from the others, each changing with the passage of time, and each changing in its meaning and importance to him. However intriguing, however romantically expectant, this is not an easy stage in the life span.

The modern age brings its own complexities. In olden times, in primitive societies, in sacred cultures, these three worlds are not too dissimilar. The ways of doing and saying tend to be much alike, and there is considerable overlapping of personnel. The peer world consists of siblings and kinsfolk, and the adult world is but an enlarged family. Today, the cultural patterns and pressures of these three worlds are often wholly or largely unlike each other, with little or no duplication of personnel. It is in the caldron of the modern American community that these conflicting values and colliding behavior patterns are thrown together and, heated by the fires of adolescence, attain at times an explosive force. This is the contemporary sociological problem of adolescence.

RITES OF PASSAGE

The social development of the individual, in all societies, involves a series of well-defined stages, each of which is characterized by its own pattern of obligations, privileges, and types of relationships with his fellows. We are concerned here with these stages in the earlier part of the life cycle. In terms of the frame of reference employed in this chapter, these changes mean the transfer from one world of childhood to another.

When these changes are so marked and comprehensive as to involve the individual's whole habitual interaction system, the term

[5] William Alexander Percy, *Lanterns on the Levee*, Alfred A. Knopf, New York, 1941, p. 125.

crises is applied to them. For example, when a person comes to puberty, gets married, or is initiated into some important new association, his relations to large numbers of other individuals are changed. To restore equilibrium after such crises, many peoples develop ceremonial rites which may be thought of as social techniques to restore equilibrium among the affected person on a new basis. When these rites are associated with the crises in the social development of the individual, they are spoken of as *rites of passage,* a term first introduced by van Gennep.[6] Several types of such rites will be described briefly.

1. Rites marking the transfer from infant to child or from the family to the child world are not found very frequently. When they do occur, they tend to be simple in character and limited in scope of observation to the family circle. "However, in societies in which children are used as an excuse for ostentation in connection with competitions for prestige they may become elaborate public affairs. Also, in societies having strong patterns of primogeniture, the early category transfers of an eldest child may be accompanied by elaborate rituals while those of younger children receive little or no attention."[7] In contemporary American society there is little of this character except the child's formal enrollment in school, or the children's social gatherings to signalize the beginning of the school career.

2. Much more frequent are the ceremonial rites marking the transfer from childhood to the adolescent stage. Many societies commemorate this in a rather spectacular way, by means of the well-known puberty rites which serve as symbols of membership and the new relationships being entered. Among many peoples, too, the puberty rite serves as a period of instruction, the accompanying physiological activities functioning to impress the novitiate with the importance of the lessons he is learning.

In our contemporary culture, there are certain observances which have a somewhat similar significance in this transitional process. Among these may be enrollment in a dancing class, the privilege of entertaining the opposite sex, entrance to high school, confirmation, or a little later, for girls in the upper classes, a formal coming-out party.

3. Marriage is the most universally observed and the most strongly emphasized of all the crises rites. It also serves the most functions. Among these are: (a) the founding of a new conjugal

[6] A. van Gennep, *Les Rites de Passage,* Nourry, Paris, 1909.

[7] Ralph Linton, "Age and Sex Categories," *American Sociological Review,* October, 1942, pp. 598–599.

family unit, (b) the establishment of new relationships between the two kinship groups, and (c) the transfer of the participants to the adult stage. This third function operates much more frequently for the male than for the female. "Except in the case of child marriage," Linton writes, "a first wedding always promotes a man to full adult status, but there are a number of societies in which women are promoted only with the birth of a first child."[8] The importance of this function is proved by the frequency with which remarriages receive slight or even no ceremonial accompaniment.

This reference to function serves to call attention to the basic purpose in all these rites. Van Gennep, who first recognized the significance of this type of ceremony, pointed out that in all such rites there were three consecutive parts, always occurring in the same order. These he termed *separation, marge,* and *aggregation,* which may be restated as *separation, transition,* and *incorporation.* These steps suggest what the crises rites really do. They call attention, in a formal and solemn manner, to the fact that the person is leaving one stage, group, age category, or social world, and entering another. This transfer is impressed upon the group that is left (separation), and the group that is entered (incorporation). Besides serving the ends of beauty and the nonrational needs of human beings, the ceremony indicates in a definitely precise manner what is happening, emphasizes the exceptional importance of the occasion, and makes it more impressive, just as the prestige of the law is enhanced by the ceremony of court procedure, or the majesty of the king by his coronation in church.

The Contemporary Status of Rites of Passage

Recent centuries have witnessed a definite trend away from public ceremonialism in our Western culture. Many factors have combined to bring this about. One goes back to the rise of Protestantism. An inevitable phase of this religious revolt was a rebellion against the elaborate ritual of the Roman Catholic Church, and its subsequent development of the barren and austere meeting house in New England and the general meagerness of the Protestant ritual. Second has been the increase of other forms of aesthetic satisfaction, for ceremony undoubtedly is often set up as an end in itself to satisfy the aesthetic needs of people. Similarly, education and individual judgment have come to be emphasized as ways of meeting crises, in preference to the prescribed routine of the ceremonial

[8] Linton, *Ibid.*, p. 598.

rite. Finally, the spread of the democratic cult, with its matter-of-fact tonal quality, has broken the hold of the conventional and traditional way of doing a thing. Obviously, it is in the United States that these factors have developed historically in very strong form, so that, coupled with the newness of the country and the sparsity of its cultural past, the lack of the ceremonial has come, in many ways, to be raised to the proportions of a national virtue.

Puberty ceremonials are few in the United States and those that exist are not related to actual changes in relationship of the adolescent to his social world. True, he impressively graduates from high school (after he has also graduated from kindergarten, elementary school and junior high!), but he may just go on to college for some years more with little change in his dependent state in the family and larger society. He may acquire a driver's license at about 16 years of age but he is still so immature socially and economically that his parents can make the decision as to whether he is capable of the responsibility of car ownership. The Jewish Bar Mitzvah means that the boy becomes man, but only in relation to his religion.

This lack, and indefiniteness, of rites of passage in the lives of modern American youth would seem to have great significance. To neither nonrelated adult, parent, nor child is there brought in a formal and impressive way a clear consciousness of the changes which the young person is really undergoing. Because the school career continues, because the financial dependence upon the parents remains unchanged, adult society continues to regard these young people as children, insists that they retain the submissive role of childhood, and, what is most significant, demands that they follow the behavior patterns of childhood.

SUMMARY

1. The child's social development involves his gradual growth from complete dependence upon his family to his emergence as a relatively self-sufficient person.

2. Five well-defined stages are customarily identified in this process. They are: (a) the period of infancy, (b) the pregang stage, (c) the gang stage, (d) the antisocial phase, and (e) adolescence.

3. Transfer from the family world to the school and gang or peer world involves revolutionary changes and major problems for the child, such as: (a) the passage from protected to unprotected competition, (b) the changed responses expected, (c) differences

between the culture of the family and that of the peer world, and (d) conflicts with parental attitudes.

4. In answer to these transfer problems, children develop a variety of responses toward their parents and the peer world, ranging from intense conflict to marked compensatory loyalty.

5. The concept of social weaning is applied to the process whereby the child grows away from his family and learns to reorganize his personality on an increasingly independent basis. Modern culture often makes this an exceedingly difficult process.

6. Some children are never weaned socially from their parents. The resultant symptoms often incapacitate them for the activities of adult life, especially in the occupational and matrimonial spheres of life.

7. Adolescence, conceived in situational terms, is a peculiarly difficult period, involving the combined problems of living in three social worlds: the family world, that of one's peers, and the adult nonfamily world. Often the demands and pressures of the three worlds are in disagreement.

8. Among many peoples, these crises changes are commemorated by ceremonial rites which serve to call the attention of all interested persons to the stages which are left behind and those which are being entered.

9. There is a definite trend away from ceremonialism in contemporary American culture. Current emphasis are upon education and individual judgment as methods of meeting life's crises.

SUGGESTED READINGS

Bandura, Albert, *Adolescent Aggression,* The Ronald Press, New York, 1959. A study of the influence of child-training practices and family relationship involved.

Blaine, Graham Burt, *Patience and Fortitude,* Little, Brown, and Company, Boston, 1962. A guide to parents on how to deal with teenagers.

Friedenberg, Edgar Z., *The Vanishing Adolescent,* Beacon Press, Boston, 1959. The author develops the point of view that rebellion is a necessary prelude to independent adulthood.

Gottlieb, David, and Charles Ramsey, *The American Adolescent,* The Dorsey Press, Homewood, Illinois, 1964. An examination of the adolescent within a sociological context.

Hall, G. Stanley, *Adolescence,* D. Appleton and Company, New York, 1905. Vols. I and II. One of the earliest, most extensive and now classic psychological studies of adolescence.

Havighurst, Robert J., and Hilda Taba, *Adolescent Character and Personality,* John Wiley & Sons, New York, 1949. The title of this book is, in itself, significant. Character, meaning "moral character" has not been a popular object of study recently.

Hurlock, Elizabeth, *Adolescent Development,* McGraw-Hill Book Company, New York, 1955. A psychologist explores a wide range of aspects of the adolescent period, from body changes to family relationships.

Mohr, George J., and Marian A. Despres, *The Stormy Decade: Adolescence,* Random House, New York, 1958. This book includes earlier developmental phases that lead up to and influence the nature of the adolescent.

Muuss, Rolf E., *Theories of Adolescence,* Random House, New York, 1962. A summary of eight different theories of the meaning of the adolescent group.

16

PEER GROUPS: PRESCHOOL AND LATER AGE

Reference has been made in preceding chapters to the fact that, in a given time in his development, the interests of the child begin to shift from his family to the group life of children of approximately his own age. On the negative side, this expresses itself in a growing revolt against parental control and often in a critical attitude toward home and parents; on the positive side, in the increase of interests in group activities and group loyalties. In Chapter 15 this process was analyzed in terms of a growth away from home. The purpose of the present chapter is to discuss: (1) the meaning and range of these contemporary age groupings among children, and (2) the nature and role of their development among children.

PEER GROUPS: THEIR MEANING AND RANGE

A peer in the common social sense of the word is a person whom one meets on terms of approximate equality, a companion or fellow. For a child, a peer, negatively considered, is a nonadult, a nonparent, a nonteacher; on the positive side, it means another child, relatively of the same age, in certain instances of the same sex, with whom he can associate on terms of equal status, at least so far as his elders are concerned. It is important that this dual nature of the peer concept be recognized, for the peer group is often more than an association of equals whose concern is with each other; it is, in a certain specific sense, also a grouping in which the adult is excluded. The peer group is the child's own social world, with its own language, its own mode of interaction, its own values and acceptable forms of behavior, many of which grownups cannot understand. It is a world in which the child has equal and even at times superior status with others, and not the subordinate status that he has invariably with parents and other adults.[1]

Chronologically, peer groups take form early in the child's life. The exact time varies, both with the nature of the family situation and the availability of age-mates. However, the process of moving away from the small world of the family to the engrossing world of one's fellows is usually under way before the fourth year. In the earlier years, these peer groups are relatively informal and transitory, adapted quickly to changing circumstances in the child's situation. Examples are the play group, the clique, and many gangs. Later come the more formally organized groups, such as clubs, fraternities, fighting gangs, and the like. Perhaps we should include here such character-building agencies as the Boy Scouts, Camp Fire Girls, and so forth. However, since the latter are not constituted and operated entirely as peer groups, they are omitted from consideration, although this is not to be interpreted as a lack of recognition of their very great importance.

THE PLAY GROUP

The play group is the most informal of the peer groupings and also the earliest in the child's life to develop. Conceived as a group, it is essentially an association of equals to share in a common play experience, with emphasis upon common rules and an understanding of the limitations which group activity places upon the individual. As most frequently used, the term is applied to groups of children in the lower age brackets. Gesell and Ilg,[2] as well as Hurlock[3] and others, have shown that from somewhere between the third and fourth year children prefer to play in groups, that

[1] Robert J. Havighurst and Bernice L. Neugarten, *Society and Education*, Allyn and Bacon, Boston, 1957, pp. 107–108.

[2] Arnold Gesell and Frances Ilg, *The Child from Five to Ten*, Harper & Row, New York, 1946, pp. 359–373.

[3] Elizabeth B. Hurlock, *Child Development*, McGraw-Hill Book Company, New York, 1942, p. 226.

the size of the group depends on the age of the children, and that the size increases with their age. Periods of preference for solitary play intervene from time to time, but gradually these begin to disappear, interest in organized play activities arises, and boys and girls begin to play separately. These play groupings tend to be temporary in character and limited in scope to some particular kind of play or the use of some common play space or equipment. In many cases, their origin is voluntary and spontaneous; in other instances, particularly at the lower age levels, they are engineered in large part by adult intervention as an adjunct to some other activity, such as that of a school, settlement house, or hospital. Play groups operate chiefly in schools and at neighborhood centers, and from the fourth to the twelfth year. They may be thought of as cliques and gangs in embryo.

THE PRESCHOOL PLAY GROUP

Play groups of children that form before school days have at least two characteristics which set them apart from later play groups. In the first place, the choice of playmates is relatively restricted, in kind and in number. Once in school, a child may select from many, and have ever-increasing power of locomotion to play away from his own neighborhood. This is not true of the preschool child, who must accept or reject whoever happens to be available in his immediate area. Secondly, the preschool play group is his *first* introduction to a group which assesses him as a child from a child's point of view, and teaches him the rules of behavior from the same point of view. That these are different from adult assessments and rules is generally acknowledged. The neat, obedient, and rather prissy youngster may be a joy to his parents, but usually has a few new lessons to learn before he can fit in with his peers. In similar vein, the "spoiled brat" may have to discover that peers can be more strong-minded than parents. Jean Piaget has described not only how children's rules are different from adults' rules but that they are considered differently by children. The latter are arbitrarily imposed, and to be broken as pleases. The former have the strength of federal law. An adult teaching youngsters to play a game can expect them to evade and argue about his rules. Left alone, the children will make up their own, and woe betide the peer who defies them.

These two characteristics of the preschool play group signify that the child is entering a new, different, and very powerful world when he joins the group, and that the composition of the immediate neighborhood has importance in his development. The matter of who is available and what he is like was considered by many parents long before sociologists became interested in the subject. One mother says: "Since Betty is destined to be an only child, I am glad we live where there are other nice boys and girls of her own age." Another complains: "We are looking for a new home in another community because we do not want to have to forbid our children to play with the little roughnecks in this one." Thus parents have manipulated, for their own purposes, their children's play-group environments, recognizing what may be said here in more "scientific" terms.

The play group is a social situation and has, as does any other group, its own specific structure, interactive process, and cultural content. The plasticity of the young child, so much stressed in the study of early family influences, still exists during the years of preschool play. It seems rather obvious, then, that the play group must have some importance in directing his development and behavior.

A child, however, is not merely a product of the play group but also of the rest of his environment which, before school days, is, for the most part, his family. Therefore, it is the interplay between these two groups which has real meaning for the child. In order to explore what this involves, 50 detailed case records were obtained by the William T. Carter Foundation. The following discussion is based upon analysis of them.

Family and Play-Group Structure

1. The relationship between size of the play group and number of siblings appeared to have a bearing upon the socialization process and ability to understand the behavior of peers. A few cases serve to illustrate this.

Jack, an only child, lived in a neighborhood composed mostly of foundry workers of foreign extraction, though his own family was not of this group. He was not permitted to associate with the children of the workers, and when he ran off to do so on several occasions he was brought home and spanked. There was just one approved playmate within his distance of free locomotion—a girl a year older than he. He admitted that he did not much care to play with her and felt she did not care to play with him, but she was the only available person. His one other playmate was the son of friends of his parents, three years older than he, who lived on the other side of town. Every time they played together they had to be taken and brought home by parents. This was unsatisfactory, as was the difference in their ages.

Another only child, Bill, lived in a neighborhood which consisted almost wholly of young family people and of college-educated parents. Most of the fathers were professional men, the major portion being college and high school teachers. There was a great deal of socializing among the parents who had many common interests. Quite naturally, their children grew up together. This boy had no difficulty in finding a continuous play group, easily accessible, from among nine children of both sexes and within one year of his own age.

Horace, a little Negro boy, whose father died when the child was 4 years old, moved at that time from his home where there had been no playmates available, to live with his mother who was 23; an aunt, 33; and two boarders (a married couple), 24 and 27. Formerly, he had been pampered as an only child and was *the* center of his parents' attention. With the move, he became the lone child "against" four adults, three of whom "took authority" because his mother taught school during the day. He wrote: "Limitations and frustrations began to pile up." He was aware that this could have been a very unhappy situation for him. However, the new neighborhood, by its constitution, enabled this lad to have a supremely happy preschool existence. The community was white middle class, with just five Negro families of college-educated backgrounds and good economic status. There was no race conflict whatsoever, but a mutual agreement not to mix socially. The five Negro families had a total of 10 children, within 3 years in age of the boy. Their social segregation made them stick together almost clannishly. The boy's need to get out from under adult domination made this group of children exceedingly important to him. He spent most of his day out "with the other kids, learning how to get along with other people." One cannot help but add here how much difference it could have made to the boy had there been no other children of his own race, age, and class status available to take a hand in his preschool development of behavior patterns and conceptions of himself as a person.

It was not just the only children who attributed their ease, or lack, of early socialization to the presence or absence of neighborhood playmates. The same sort of comment was made frequently in larger families in cases where the siblings were widely separated in age and/or of different sexes. Here, too, they directly related their own withdrawnness to an isolation from age peers, or spoke with gratitude of the playmates who reversed this tendency in them.

A study of social isolation and mental illness, made by Dr. Herman R. Lantz,[4] reveals an even more critical relation between numbers of friends and mental hygiene. Though cause and effect

[4] Herman R. Lantz, "Number of Childhood Friends as Reported in the Life Histories of a Psychiatrically Diagnosed Group of 1,000," *Marriage and Family Living*, May, 1956, pp. 107–108.

are not clear, the fact is that cases having no mental disease ranked high in reporting many childhood friends, and low in reporting few or none. The ranking of the psychotics was exactly reversed.

2. Some of the disadvantages of growing up without a sibling of the opposite sex have already been discussed in Chapter 2. In a truly situational approach, however, the absence of such a sibling cannot be considered as a unit factor, determining a certain kind of behavior. Rather, it must be thought of in relation to other aspects of life—in this case the sex makeup of the preschool play group. There may be considerable difference between a girl who has no brothers and knows no other boys, and one who has at least played with boys from her earliest years. A number of the case recorders commented upon the meaning of the sex makeup of the play group.

Ours was a very feminine household, and Mother was dedicated to making little ladies out of us. My older sister and I were even sent to private girls' academies until high school age. My sister had never played with anyone but girls up to that time and when, at the age of 14½, she started at a coeducational school, she got into various sorts of troubles. She was fascinated by suddenly being surrounded by boys who were quite ready to date her. But she didn't know anything about boys, really, nor their rules of the game, nor how to behave with them. The results were that first she got a badly turned head, then she got into trouble with the principal and finally she got her heart broken. She was "off men" for several years. It was so different with me. I went to the same schools at the same ages, but I grew up with a gang of boys and girls from the tender age of 3. We were together constantly and a little bit of Mother's "femininity training" was rubbed off me even before I went to the academy. Since my friendships with these same playmates continued for many years, I hadn't the slightest trouble in changing to the high school. Boys were "old hat" to me. I had had *their* ideas about proper girls' behavior pounded into me thoroughly and I had also learned a good deal about *them*.

I was the third daughter born to a man who desperately wanted a son. As chance would have it, the only children on my street were a number of young boys. Thus, while other little girls, I suppose, were busy playing with dolls or cutouts, I was out in the street tossing a softball or climbing lampposts. The boys accepted me as one of them and I was happy. The "rub" came when I entered grammar school and found myself face to face with the problem of learning, under social pressure, How to Act Like a Young Lady. This was indeed quite a problem. It seemed I had to learn, often by painful experience, the behavior patterns which were second nature to other girls. I had to learn what seemed at the time a whole new vocabulary, a whole new manner of dress, a whole new set of interests. It was not easy. I had to learn these things not only to fit in with the other girls, but I discovered, to my pain, that boys prefer tomboy girls only up to a certain age.

A boy whose only brother was three and a half years younger than he, and who had only one, and a very close and continuing, male playmate, wrote of being "terrified" by being in a classroom with girls, that he never made friends of them, and even at present is much more comfortable with men than with women. One sentence from his case record is of special interest. After describing the lifelong association with his friend, he wrote: "We were more like brother and *sister*."

3. Most preschool play groups are composed of children who are fairly close to each other in age, although wider gaps do emerge in some situations. Even in the former case, it should be remembered that slight age differences between very young children seem much greater than they do between adults. It is a common experience that age gaps increasingly diminish in significance as one grows older. In the case of very young children, the facts of maturation and muscular development and control add further highlights to age differences. Even 4 or 6 months, when one is 3, can make a great difference in actual ability, let alone in interests and in what Mother permits one to do. And a year or two makes a whole world of difference. For these reasons, the age composition of the play group in itself has been noted as important in our records.

A young lady who is remarkably competent at everything she undertakes, and for the simple reason that she studies each new problem carefully and keeps practicing until she is satisfied with the results, had the following experience. She was the youngest of seven playmates, the next closest in age being six months older. Apparently the greater motor abilities of the others challenged her. When she was just old enough to dress herself, she was found sneaking out into the yard one morning at 6 o'clock. When observed and questioned, her explanation was that she was going to "pwactice yumpin'." "Practicing jumping" has been characteristic of her behavior ever since. An extremely successful businessman, who has made his way by starting a number of times on jobs quite below his ability and economic value and then working himself upward, attributed his willingness to do this to attitudes formed in his earliest training. He had a sister five years his senior. The only other children in the neighborhood were girls of her age, and the little boy who tagged along was an abomination to them. He was very lonely and discovered that the only way he could "get in" was to offer to do the "dirty work" and "play the most menial roles."

When he did this, he was not only accepted, but achieved success in his goal for companionship.

A lad with a sister three and a half years older than he, and a group of eight playmates from seven to nine years older than he, wrote the following:

> Being younger, and with sister more or less of a boss, I became a follower and a cry-baby when I couldn't keep up with the older kids and when they made fun of me. I even developed stuttering, but, thanks to my mother who didn't sympathize with me, I got over it. She convinced me there was nothing organically wrong with me, that I could stop it if I wanted to. I did try hard, and it worked (although under extremely tense situations I feel it coming back, but I always suppress it). When my sister was in high school, my parents and she always insisted I go wherever my sister and her friends went (swimming, movies, to other girls' houses). I always felt out of place and not really wanted although everyone said I was very foolish to think such a thing.

A girl with a brother eight years older and a sister four and a half years younger tells this story:

> The only children in the block were about six boys all exactly my brother's age. As a result, there was no one for me to play with. But my brother's friends played with me, not regularly, but I was treated to bicycle rides, swings, etc., when they were in the mood. As a result . . . I never had a "till death us do part" bosom pal. I have a hard time talking to other people about things that are important. I enjoy being with myself. Reading is a favorite sport. And I sometimes wonder if the fact that I have always gotten along (on a dating basis) with fellows quite a bit older than I isn't caused by the earlier associations with my brother's friends.

Further light on the relation between age and sex of siblings and play groups has been shed in a study by Koch.[5] Children actually expressed a preference for playmates of their own sex, but a preference for those of the opposite sex was higher among children who had a sibling of the opposite sex. This decreased as the age between the siblings widened. It would seem, then, that those children who were not exposed to peers of the opposite sex in their families, and who might profit by playing with them outside the home, were the ones who would not seek them out by preference.

Finally, a 20-year-old girl with a brother two years her senior commented upon her good fortune in the healthy age and sex make-up of her family and play group as it had affected her up to

[5] Helen L. Koch, "The Relation in Young Children Between Characteristics of Their Playmates and Certain Attributes of Their Siblings," *Child Development*, June, 1957, pp. 175–202.

the present day, and of how different could have been the results had her and her brother's birth orders been reversed. As it was, the girl knew, played with, and became accustomed to boys a little older than she, grew up with them, and at dating age was "all set." Her brother had a similar experience, having learned to get along with girls of an age relationship from which he would normally choose a wife. Had the birth orders in this family been different, the girl felt that both she and her brother would have had to find new friends during adolescence and would have gone their separate ways. Instead of that, a continuing and comradely relationship had endured between them and with all their friends, promising, she hoped, close family ties and a sharing of social life in the future.

Interactive Processes of Family and Play Group

In situational analysis, the separation of a group into structure, process, and content is a necessary technique but a highly superficial one. It is necessary because it is impossible by word of mouth or in writing to analyze a situation in its total configuration. It is superficial because structure, process, and content are so completely interrelated that in a real life situation no one of them stands alone as a determining influence. Already, in the analysis of structure, there has been much reference to both interaction and cultural content. This is inescapable. However, as structure has been the chief emphasis in the preceding section, and content will be in the following one, so interaction is stressed here. Three aspects of it will be illustrated.

1. The general patterns of play-group interaction in our case records provided interesting contrasts. There were the very congenial ones in which even the parents sometimes helpfully participated when they were required, in which statuses and roles were clearly defined and agreeable to all the children, so that little or no friction resulted in the groups even during competitive play. "We all got along swell" is the tone of comments about such groups. At the other extreme were the play groups that battled incessantly, sticking together, but with a continuous jockeying for statuses and roles. In the records of such groups, the usual comment is something like, "I learned how to stand up for myself. I had to." Between these two polar extremes there were many-shaded mixtures of such interaction. Furthermore, there was one other distinct type: the close-knit group that achieved its closeness from an effort to protect itself against, or take it out upon, a second close-knit neighborhood play group. Interestingly enough, the respondents, both male

and female, who recorded this type of interaction, spoke of their groups as "gangs." The process described within them was very similar to that described in Thrasher's classic study of gangs,[6] here pushed back in time to preschool play.

2. Many studies in child development which are psychologically or psychoanalytically oriented stress that early psychic experience in family interaction may result in patterning a child's behavior and attitudes toward all other people and throughout life. For example, the family-rejected child may feel rejected by everyone else and even when he becomes an adult. Such cases do occur, and frequently come to light in clinics. Thus it is almost natural to attribute the results to family rejection. There are also, though, many obviously family-rejected children who do not react throughout life in this way. They do not usually show up in clinics (at least, not for rejection symptoms) and it is therefore very difficult to discover why their reactions have been so different.

A sociological, or situational, analysis of the total interactive group experience, rather than of just early family interaction, may shed light on possible answers to this question, and for the following reasons. For some people, the *realities* of their experiences throughout life correspond to, and reinforce, the influences of their intrafamily experiences. For others, this is not so; and at times quite abrupt reversals of behavior and attitudes result from new experiences. Our case records give indications that this does happen.

One very persistent story running through the records has to do with the ability, or lack of ability, to form close, intimate relationships with other people, to talk oneself out freely, to give confidences. In every case where a child had felt no such closeness with a family member, because of a variety of circumstances, and the play group offered no person of similar age and/or interests, the individual remarked upon a continuation of his "apartness" during school days and a lingering bit of difficulty in this respect up to the present. On the other hand, when the family situation was similar, but close pals had been found in the preschool period, the writer spoke of this as the beginning of learning to share himself with another.

The story, however, is broader than it appears on the basis of these comments. The authors have used the concept of "the empathic complex" to describe one of the ways in which personalities take form. The term *empathic complex* means "the particular emotional linkage between a child and the significant persons in his

6 Frederic M. Thrasher, *The Gang*, University of Chicago Press, Chicago, 1936; (rev. and abr. ed.), 1963.

environment."[7] A child does not respond to all the people in his environment with equal emotionality. Some, he loves because they fulfill his emotional and/or physical needs; others, he dislikes because they do not; still others seem neutral persons to him. Regardless of the actual social value of the behavior of these people, a child tends to react in two ways. First, he tends to adopt the behavior patterns of those he loves, and to avoid those of the ones he dislikes; second, he tends to develop a certain type of behavior pattern of his own which is appropriate to the relationship between him and the specific person. He is selective about this in his own family, and our cases indicate that he is equally selective among his own playmates. For example:

George had a circle of little friends whom he saw most frequently at birthday parties and Sunday school. Most of them were "neutrals" to him, and he rarely sought out their company. Jean, a girl one and a half years older than he, definitely appealed to him, however, and he spent most of his time with her. She was "likable," came from a "nice middle-class family of the same religious background," and "generally set a good example as to her character." Not only was she a "character example" to George, but he felt his association with her carried over into his later life. He prefers the kind of girl Jean was, now that he is at the dating age, and he thinks of girls as friends, and not just as "mere objects of sexual attraction." George had a strong emotional feeling about one other playmate, Harry. Harry was six months older but a "coward and not too intelligent." His character was "a little shoddy," he always told his parents lies and seldom got away with it. Through Harry, George discovered that "crime does not pay," and he felt that Harry influenced him negatively almost as much as Jean did positively—not because of the actual moral values represented, but just because George happened to like the one very much and despise the other.

In Grace's play group, Mary Louise was her favorite friend. Mary Louise was a year younger, and Grace always felt that she was "taking care" of the younger girl. The relationship was so pleasant and happy for both that when Mary Louise had a baby sister Grace extended her protective attitude to include the baby. Grace says that she loves young children, likes to work with them, and wants four of her own.

A similar case record involves a girl whose closest friend was a cripple. They spent a very happy childhood together; the recorder never lost her interest in people with physical incapacities and became a nurse, specializing in orthopedics. This case was in striking contrast to the statement of still a third girl whose next-door neighbor was a victim of paralysis of the right arm. She wrote that she

[7] James H. S. Bossard and Eleanor S. Boll, "Child Behavior and the Empathic Complex," *Child Development,* March, 1957, p. 37.

was forced to play with this boy and that his nasty disposition and vicious temper developed through frustration had made her steer very clear of anyone who had any kind of deformity.

3. Finally, the combination of interactive processes within the home and those encountered outside have their own specific effects.

Gloria writes that she was born when her parents were 39 and 41. Their first baby died at the age of 3. They had long since given up any hopes of parenthood before Gloria arrived. When she did, she was the apple of her parents' and kinsfolk's eyes, and very severely overprotected. She describes herself as "sensitive, isolated, and hesitant." The children in her neighborhood ran around in a "pack," and were boisterous and active. She wished so much for some one or few quiet children like herself to play with; but she could not become a member of the "pack" and she had no other resources than "imaginary playmates." She wrote: "Now that I have grown up, I realize the advantages of group play. Play is a great builder, not just of bodies and minds, but also of social awareness, for in play a child must take other children into consideration. He learns many valuable lessons in adjusting himself to the demands and ideals of his group as he will later have to adjust himself to the demands and ideals of his community."

Robert, an only child who lived on a large farm, contributed the following record:

I was quite lonely as a child, in fact, very lonely. My mother was not a talkative woman, and my father was a busy man. There were two groups of children available for me to play with and I was eager to play with them. One was a large family of about eight children. My parents did not think much of the family. The father was irregularly employed. One girl had had an illegitimate child. One boy had been in some kind of trouble. My mother thought they were trash, but she also had insight into the loneliness of a little boy. In addition to the social barrier between us . . . I early had to face certain problems. They cheated at play. They depreciated my superior toys but used them often and broke them. When I got a tricycle, they wanted to ride it all the time but yet it was not a good tricycle. They knew people who had better ones. Also, I envied them. They were a large family. They had a good time, it seemed. There was always somebody to do something with. These children did some petty thieving . . . I remember much talk about it in our home. My father wanted to go to the mat with them, but my mother said she didn't want trouble with them since they were, after all, our nearest neighbors and were the only children usually available for me to play with. About this time, the boy two years older than me began picking on me. My father told me the next time it happened to punch him. I did. I struck him and piled him up on the mud. This made a tremendous and lasting impression on me. He was older, he was a head bigger, yet I learned that fight can overcome what seemed like insurmountable obstacles. I don't think I was ever afraid after that of anyone, at least not for many years. The other thing I remember. These older children gave me my first introduction to sex. The girls as well as the boys joined in. I worried about this for years. The other children that I played with—and always separately from the first family—were my two cousins, a girl and a boy. The girl was a few months younger than I and the boy about a year and a half. The girl and I have always hit it off well together and we ganged up just a bit on the boy. We made him sort of fetch and carry for us. She and I always sort of understood each other and respected each other. Our parents liked each other and there were many happy days when her mother and she came to stay at our house. Then, she and I, and sometimes the boy cousin, ranged all over the place and the fields and played nicely and happily together. The psychoanalysts might well find in my happy play hours with her the development of a deep-seated need which it took many years to fill again. I think that my dual conception of women came from this far back. At 6, I was fully aware that there were two kinds, with two different statuses.

Culture of Family and Play Group

Two different aspects of the cultural content of family and play group seemed to affect significantly the writers of our case records. One was the similarity or dissimilarity of family culture and play group culture, so far as nativity, religion, race, and socioeconomic status were concerned. The other was the actual content of play activities within the play groups themselves. This section will be devoted to a brief consideration of each.

Three patterns emerged in the reports on group cultures.

One was that of a child living in a very homogeneous neighborhood in which the values, attitudes, interests, and general way of life of all the families coincided. The children attended the same school and, with their parents, the same church. Family, school, and church all reinforced each other in the acculturation of the children, and in the same manner. It almost goes without saying that the content of the play group was a close reflection of unicultural upbringing. There was, of course, some conflict between family and play group, based on "misbehavior" as interpreted by parents. There was little resentment against parents because of this, however, since the children all *knew* what was the approved way to behave and play. They broke the rules sometimes, and they expected to be punished for it. As adults, they commented on "the comfort of cultural consistency." "We always knew where we stood, what we shouldn't do, and what would happen if we did. There was no confusion in our minds." "It was not as if we were children *against* parents or children *against* each other. We all pulled together, amicably, and once in a while us kids would have a spat or decide to kick over the traces." The case of Bill, cited earlier, is an excellent illustration of such a pattern. The whole neighborhood was young, family-minded, social, college-oriented, of similar socioeconomic status. Bill, as a college student, still has as his closest friends some of his preschool playmates. Two are classmates at the same university. One is to be best man at his wedding after graduation. Bill is a conscientious, relaxed, self-assured young man, who says, in his own words, that he believes something about the continuities in his group experiences has resulted in making him comfortable and happy.

A second pattern was that in which the neighborhood was culturally divided into at least two distinct groups. Here the children were "told" with whom they could and could not play. Sometimes they were told by their own parents; at other times, they were rejected by the parents of the children with whom they wanted to play; and again, by those children themselves. The meaning of these divisions to children seemed to depend upon the specific group to which they belonged (high or low status, and majority or minority group) and the availability of playmates whom they liked within their own group. Striking contrasts appeared. Horace, for instance (the little Negro boy who was mentioned formerly), was of minority-group status in a sharply divided neighborhood; but he had his own social resources and cultural homogeneity within his own group. Now that he attends a university that is of heterogeneous makeup and liberal attitude, Horace preserves his social separatism of his own accord, with no resentment, and with self-confidence. A Catholic girl, however, who was the only child of her faith and age in a neighborhood divided between Catholics and strong anti-Catholics, did not have such a relatively easy adjustment. Under pressure of their parents, the other children rejected her from their play group. She was alone and lonely until her parents finally sent her to a parochial school. There she found that, though her religion was accepted, her person was not. She did not know how to get along with children—only with adults. She favored the Sisters and the Sisters favored her. This strengthened the notion of the other students that she was a "square." She relates that it took her years to find friends of her own age and to get over her hatred of Protestants. Then there was also the girl, in a divided neighborhood, who was a member of the minority group. This group, however, was superior in socioeconomic and educational status to the majority group. Her parents would not let her play with the children in the latter group; but the children in her own seemed "stuffy and cold" to her. She was intrigued by the adventuresome play of the others, and was determined to avail herself of it whenever possible. This resulted in constant intrafamily conflict and, during adolescence especially, a very rebellious girl. She is attracted only by peers of whom her parents do not approve, and is happy to be living away from home so that she can "get out from under."

The third pattern existed in "neighborhoods" which should not accurately be called by that name. They were found chiefly in urban areas of dense population whose makeup was so heterogeneous that there were few, sometimes no, cultural ties between the individual families. It was as if each family lived on its own cultural island. The play groups consisted of some rather exotic cultural combinations. Parents exerted little or no pressure. The children sorted themselves out. It was under such circumstances that the aforementioned "gangs" emerged even in preschool years. They ranged from the gangs that played tricks on each other, through the ones that vied for play localities and equipment, to several gangs that were surprisingly rough and vicious for children so young. It was in these situations that writers commented variously: "I learned that you had to be rough to make your own way," "It didn't pay to be alone, you needed some pal with you," "I think my fear of tough people stems from those gangs. I always avoid anyone who looks tough," and "My feeling has always been that if you aren't sharp you'll be outsmarted."

Activities within the play group proved to be varied. All of life is a learning process in which each new experience adds to the individual's cultural acquisitions. This is a selective process, however, and each individual learns only certain specific elements, or levels, of the wealth of cultural accumulations in his society. The specific selection is limited by the actual life experience of each person. In the family, the child learns his own family's version of the culture. In the play group, he is immersed in the content of children's activities.

Children's play is a direct reflection of the behavior and knowledge of the adult society. In a simple society, such as a fishing or agricultural tribe, one can fairly easily predict the forms that play will take—there are so few roles, behavior patterns, and forms of activity. In a complex society, this is not so; and the learning process, through play, is much more varied.

This proved to be so with our cases. In group activities, the children learned very different modes of behavior during their preschool years. The variations were so many that only a few are selected to illustrate some points on the gamut.

Andy, the 5-year-old son of an urban minister, was set upon by the local "gang"—first- and second-grade boys. They had thought the "minister's kid" would be an easy mark. Andy, however, was wiry and strong, fought back, and took his beating bravely. Instead of becoming a scapegoat, he achieved high status among this band of youngsters whose sole activity was composed of devising ways to throw stones at automobiles and through windows without getting caught. Aided by an older gang, some members of which had already become acquainted with the Juvenile Court, the play group taught the minister's son a great deal about the law and its evasion, and the excitement of "getting away with it." Andy says that he is the "black sheep" of his family. In school, he perpetually got into trouble for cheating. He said, "I knew it was wrong, but it's like a game and I get away with it more often than not. Even in college, I was up before the executive committee; but they don't do much to a minister's son."

In contrast:

Bill, who lived in an education-minded community, reported that most of his preschool play was "intellectual in nature." All the parents stimulated all the children, educationally. In their play, they taught each other the ABC's; how to count; the fundamentals of reading and spelling. When this group started to school together, they were well advanced over the rest of the students. They were soon set apart as the leading student group academically speaking. They remained so through elementary and secondary school. Bill recognized, as time went on, that he was not exactly a brilliant student. The work became increasingly hard for him. He applied himself very conscientiously, however, because he could not lose his status nor let his clique down. At present, with two members of his preschool group still in his own class, he is devoting all his energies to making "at least a B average," and is quite confident that he can do it.

One girl writes:

I spent all my days, before I went to school, playing house with my friends. We had dolls, and paper dolls, and kittens and puppies for the babies. We had all kinds of tiny housekeeping equipment—even a real electric stove on which we cooked real food, and a little hand sewing machine with which we made clothes for our dolls. We bathed our babies, took them for walks in their coaches, fed them (I had a hollow doll that had to be broken open once to remove the decayed food!), and I nursed them when they were sick.

And finally, another girl describes her preschool play in this way:

We did *everything*. We went "bird watching" in the woods and on nature hunts, and we drew what we had seen and collected specimens in albums. We gave our own little block parties, and sold lemonade in hot weather. We grew plants in eggshells, and in the winter we sledded, built snowmen, and knitted little wool squares for blankets for the Red Cross. We even tried to sell War Bonds, but we weren't very successful at that.

Added Observations

Up to this point, this study has attempted to describe some of the general aspects of child development as influenced by the structure, process, and content of the preschool play-group situation. It seems pertinent to comment further on two observations made during analysis of the materials.

1. Without having been asked to report on school adjustment, 36 out of the 50 cases did so. To them, their school adjustment clearly related to absence or presence of a play group and to the makeup and content of it. Since this has already been suggested in excerpts from case records, a very brief summary of what they reported will suffice here.

When the respondent was older than his playmates and the leader of them, and had only younger siblings, he had to cope with the problem of his "bossiness" in social relations at school.

When he was the baby of his play group, and was babied at home, his problems were those of establishing relations of equality among his age peers at school and of not being overly dependent upon classmates and teachers.

The child who had played, in family and neighborhood group, only with children of his own sex found some difficulties in adjusting to schoolmates of the opposite sex.

In the case of a child without siblings or playmates, entering a classroom with a number of other children was usually "terrifying."

The child who was used to playing with others of his own age and of both sexes found the transition to the classroom to be quite easy, as a rule.

Finally, the activity content of the play group, as it prepared the child, or did not prepare him, for participation in school learning, affected his interest, his status, and his adjustment in the school situation.

2. Twelve of our cases changed their play-group situations with a change of residence during their preschool days. These cases gave added conviction of the meaning of such groups to young children, for all of them mentioned the change as a real life crisis.

In seven of the cases, the move was a great relief. There had been no playmates available, or only wholly unsuitable ones. Here the move was spoken of as the beginning of better times or better adjustment. In four cases, the writers thought that their parents had made the move with this specific purpose in mind.

The other five cases were not so fortunate. They were "torn up by the roots" from their best friends and constant companions, to find loneliness, bad influences, or, at best, very poor substitutes for what they once had. All five of these mentioned that they could not find satisfactory associations until some time after they started school and got into some kind of amiable group once more.

LATER AGE PEER GROUPS

By the time the child reaches the age of approximately 8 to 12, peer groups become more definite, more stable, and, for the child, more important. Two distinctive forms of peer groups emerge.

First, when social distinctions begin to manifest themselves in the child's life, references appear with increasing frequency to "our crowd," "our set," and so on. The term *clique* has been used in sociological literature to designate this type of peer group.

A clique may be defined as a small, intimate social participation group consisting of persons of the same social status and in agreement concerning the exclusion of other individuals from the group. It has a definite membership which may vary in number from 2 to as many as 30. It may or may not be age-graded, and it may be unisexual or bisexual. Its organization is informal. It has no explicit rules of entrance or exit. The bond which holds it together is intimacy of interaction among the members, a strong sense of solidarity, and a common behavior pattern. Its significance for its members on the emotional side is very great. This expresses itself principally in two ways. First, as between members, it involves strong feelings of friendship and of responsibility to render mutual assistance in case of need; second, in regard to other groups and outside demands, the clique is given preference, even over the families of its members.

Cliques are essentially a prestige device to achieve, maintain or confirm status. They operate constantly in school, athletic, and social activities, and they are favored by children who seek to use them to gain identification with a higher status group. The life of the clique, however, is generally not of long duration.[8]

[8] For detailed description of the clique and its operation see, Ernest A. Smith, *American Youth Culture*, The Free Press of Glencoe, New York, 1962, chap. 4.

A second type of later age peer group is the gang. Thrasher, foremost among students of the gang, defined it as "an interstitial group originally formed spontaneously, and then integrated through conflict" (p. 57). "When it becomes a conflict group it becomes a gang" (p. 30). "To become a true gang the group as a whole must move through space (linear action) and eventually . . . must meet some hostile element which precipitates conflict" (p. 54).[9]

Current analyses identify the gang as a more integrated and, in a sense, a more formal group than the clique. It tends to have a longer life, and as a result of its greater experience it develops more in the way of tradition and morale. The bond of solidarity is often strong, but membership is less exclusive and more capable of being earned than in the clique. Its objectives tend more in the direction of activity, even if socially not acceptable, than is the case with the clique. Its greater concreteness tends to express itself through formal symbols, such as names, slogans, passwords, grips, uniforms, and so on.

For many years, the word "gang" has had a connotation of crime and delinquency only. Recently, however, the larger and more normal aspects of these peer groups have come to be recognized by students of social behavior. It is now realized that there are other peer groups than antisocial gangs, and their function in the lives of growing boys and girls is both natural and important. In other words, these peer groups take form for the most part naturally, even if at times riotously like weeds, in the area between the family group and such later adult institutions as the state, industry, or the church.

SELECTED CHARACTERISTICS OF PEER GROUPS

Peer groups, like the boys and girls who compose them, are singularly individual in many respects. Each is a separate sociological phenomenon; each is, in some way or other, unique. From the study of individual cases, however, certain generalizations concerning the development of these groups may be made and these are noted briefly.

Peer groups arise to satisfy definite needs. It involves a negative impulse to escape adult supervision, and a positive effort to function with like-minded persons. In both aspects there inheres the satisfaction and thrill of operating on one's own and of participating in forms of activity which one's peers, rather than one's elders, select. Peer groups, in this respect, serve a legitimate function in the de-

[9] Thrasher, *op. cit.*

velopment and socialization of the child. They represent his efforts to create his own world, an experimental and practice world, to fill in the transition from family domination to adult independence. James S. Coleman points out that this emergence of an adolescent culture is particularly important in a society which keeps prolonging the training period for adulthood.[10]

The development of peer groups follows the character of the need. This is shown partly in the adaptation of such groups to the age hierarchy, but much more in their adjustment to the prevailing cultural situations in which they arise and flourish. In an age span and in a cultural setting where social stratification is emphasized, the clique appears as the most important peer group. When children are younger and play is uppermost among their needs, the play group is the prevailing one. But it is in the studies of the gang that this relation is most evident. Most of the studies of the gang have emphasized it as a conflict group, emerging as a symptom of certain forms of community life. Ecologically, they have been shown to "congregate in interstitial areas, that is, in areas which represent fissures and breaks in the social organization,"[11] and which create conflict situations. Territorial clashes between nationality groups that have become segregated into relatively homogeneous groups often flare forth and at times develop into traditional feuds which are continued on a territorial basis after the originally antagonistic elements have lost their distinctive identity. Race riots among adolescent groups are a part of the same phenomenon.

Peer groups have natural histories. The conditions which call them forth, the experiences they undergo, the leadership which evolves, the treatment given them by outside agencies, the opposition they encounter, all combine to determine the specific course which their histories will take.

Peer groups arise spontaneously in most cases. That is to say, they are not consciously planned, but take form as children happen to gather at certain places and, because of certain common interests and needs, begin to function collectively. In many instances, their life is short; often the group bond is very loose; there is a continuous ebb and flow in the membership; conflicting personalities and contrasting diversions arise and break up whatever unity may previously have developed. For many children, and in various areas, the very conditions which create a strong need for peer groups make their strong and relatively long-lived development impossible. Here we

[10] James S. Coleman, *The Adolescent Society*, The Free Press of Glencoe, New York, 1961, pp. 2–3.

[11] Frederic M. Thrasher, "The Gang as a Symptom of Community Disorganization," *Journal of Applied Sociology*, January, 1926, pp. 3–21.

must note the importance of such factors as the high degree of mobility of many children and their families, the fact that children are subject to various interfering pressures and restraints from their families and other adult groups, and the fact that childhood interests are short-lived and often change with considerable rapidity.

On the other hand, the reverse of all this may happen. Under favorable conditions for the development of peer groups they may persist over many years. A strong we-feeling may appear, leadership may emerge, satisfactory common interests may be found, a strongly integrated organization may take form, and a heritage of memories and tradition may accumulate.

Thrasher has shown these contrasting courses of development in the natural history of the gang. In many instances, only a diffuse type of gang appears, with little solidarity and group loyalty, and a short life in point of time; in a lesser number of cases, a solidified type appears, with a longer history, a stronger morale, and a higher degree of integration. Either type, but more especially the latter, may in turn take a variety of forms; it may either veer in the direction of the more conventional club whose activities are socially approved and whose life is incorporated into the structure of the community, or it may become an integrated fighting machine, specializing in some one or several forms of delinquent behavior.

This concept of a natural history of peer groups has significant implications, particularly with reference to their treatment by family and community forces. The customary method of approach has been the direct frontal attack, which sees the peer group as a problem per se, and its breakup or elimination as the major end to be achieved. Obviously, the proper approach must be the indirect or flank approach, which recognizes it as arising to meet definite needs and developing on the basis of conditioning factors. Such an approach offers the possibilities of conscious and constructive direction of the peer group, to the end that its socially legitimate purposes may be served.

Peer Groups and Child Development

In order to emphasize some of these socially legitimate purposes, a few of the more outstanding ways in which peer groups operate in the field of child development should be pointed out.

1. Perhaps the first and most difficult step in the socialization of the child is the recognition of the rights of others. This involves a process of social education, more particularly in the lower-age brackets and principally through the medium of experience. This

process begins, of course, with the child's life with his family, as a number of the earlier chapters have shown. But the family, from one standpoint, is often an unnatural or inadequate socializing group. Frequently it is too small, especially the contemporary family; its personnel is too largely adult; and all its members tend to be emotionally disposed toward a type of relationship which differs from that prevailing in society as a whole. The peer group differs in these important respects from the family group: it consists of equals, that is, persons of the same approximate age and stage of development, and there is no emotional bond of the kind that is found in the family. The peer group involves association on a normal basis with equals who are equally bent on their own interests and self-expression. It is from experience in such groups, more particularly the earlier play groups, that the child gains an understanding of the limitations which group life places upon the individual. This is the first lesson learned in living with others, and it can best, and perhaps only, be learned through experience.

Early in this experience, common rules based on common experience begin to develop. These rules are requisite conditions for the existence of the group; the mere fact of group existence and action calls them forth. In part they are inventions of the group members, devised to meet a specific situation or problem; in part they are borrowed from other groups of children, usually older ones; in part they are obtained from or imposed by adults.

The acceptance of these rules, as in play groups, is characteristically slow and sporadic. For some years, usually between the third and the seventh year, the child partly accepts them and partly does not. Thus one sees children of this age playing, now in groups and in observance of the rules; now, off by themselves. Sometime after the seventh year, Piaget identifies a stage of *incipient cooperation,* in which "all begin to concern themselves with the question of mutual control and of unification of the rules."[12] Although some degree of agreement is reached, the rules remain rather vague and it is not until the eleventh or twelfth year that the codification of rules is made. Then, too, comes their acceptance by mutual consent. A child must respect the rules of the peer group if he wishes to belong. "This is the way we play the game." Cooperative teamwork develops, and the requirements for participation are now socialized.

Utilizing the terminology of morals, Piaget develops an interesting contrast between the morality of constraint and that of cooperation. Morality of constraint consists of a series of objective duties

[12] Jean Piaget, *The Moral Judgment of the Child,* Kegan Paul, London, 1932, p. 17. (Current edition: The Free Press of Glencoe, New York.)

based on respect for persons in authority. It is imposed upon the child from above, and is accepted because of the prestige and power of its source. Acceptance is much like that of language, as one of the realities imposed by the adult world. Morality is a duty. The right thing to do is to obey the will of the parent; the wrong thing is to have a will of one's own. Morality of cooperation rests upon mutual understanding between equals. It involves autonomy of conformity. Free from adult supervision, the child inspires his own rules. "As soon as the individual escapes from the domination of age, he tends toward cooperation as the normal form of social equilibrium."[13] These rules are accepted because the child realizes that they are necessary for the continuance of group life. As a result, he imposes these rules upon himself. Consciousness of a sense of justice now appears, and this sense of justice "requires nothing more for its development than the mutual respect and solidarity which holds among children themselves."[14]

2. Complementary to what has just been said is the fact that the peer group has great importance as an agency in controlling the behavior of its members. To be accepted, members must conform to the standards of the group. The peer group is a primary group among equals, its relationships are intimate in character, there is relative familiarity, and the members are closely identified with each other. As a result, they become very sensitive to each other's approval and disapproval, which means that group pressure upon the individual is great. Ogburn and Nimkoff point out two principles regarding the primary group in this connection: first, that the group frequently exerts a more effective control over the conduct of its members than can an outside individual charged with special authority; and second, that the most efficient regulator of all is a group of persons of the same age and interests.[15] These are commonplace facts in the sociology of primary group life; what happens is that most parents, and sometimes students of child development, fail to appreciate that primary groups among children operate in the same way as they do among adults. Several aspects of their operation will be noted briefly.

The peer group imposes its own rules or codes, that is, those which center around its activities and purposes. Piaget has shown this process in the play group, as has Murphy in her excellent study of a nursery-school group.[16] In fact, a large part of the purpose

13 *Ibid.*, p. 99.
14 *Ibid.*, pp. 195–196.
15 W. F. Ogburn and Meyer Nimkoff, *Sociology*, Houghton Mifflin Company, Boston, 1940, p. 266.
16 Lois Barclay Murphy, *Social Behavior and Child Personality*, Columbia University Press, New York, 1937.

and success of the present-day nursery school lies in its power to control effectively the behavior of its young members. Davis and the Gardners[17] have emphasized this in particular about the clique. Each clique has a common behavior pattern (p. 168). The behavior of its members is controlled, in their relations both with each other and with other persons (p. 169). Being an instrument of the class structure, the clique determines with what members of other cliques the member may have occasional informal and formal participation. The more stable the clique, the more marked is its control over the activities and associations of its members (pp. 169–170). Similarly, Thrasher has emphasized group control in the gang.[18] The gang, he says, is a unit which enforces its code upon its members in a variety of ways. Some of these are consciously and definitely directed, and others operate at the unconscious and unreflective level; but in virtually all cases there are emphases upon the common primary group virtues and the particular attitudes which focus about the group. Finally, we might include as examples of group control the various developments of the honor system, as in student examinations or in boys' reformatories.

Special mention should be made of the peer group's control over the attitude and behavior of its members toward persons outside the group. This has been most clearly emphasized in the case of the clique, but it is prevalent in all peer groups. Particularly evident is the control of attitudes toward adults with whom members of the peer groups come most often or most closely in contact, such as teachers, parents, and policemen. Since one purpose of many such groups is to ascribe the status of alien to adults with whom they are concerned, the next step often is to identify these adults as enemies, until at times a comprehensive pattern of behavior toward some adult may become the heart of the group's *esprit de corps*. Most persons can find ready illustrations of this in their own school experiences, usually in the junior or senior high school period. Proprietors of small shops in the neighborhood of a school—their importance in the social development of young boys and girls has never been adequately appreciated or studied—often play a significant role in the development of the attitudinal patterns of peer groups. This is well illustrated in the following case:

The "Union Avenue Crowd" had as their hangout a candy and tobacco store at Third and Union Avenue, which was two blocks away from the senior high school. Because of its nearness to the school, it was a con-

[17] Allison Davis, B. B. Gardner, and Mary B. Gardner, *Deep South*, University of Chicago Press, Chicago, 1941, chaps. 7 and 9.

[18] Thrasher, *The Gang*, *op. cit.*, chap. 15.

venient place to gather until the last minute before school time, as well as after sessions. Early in October, 19—, talk among the "crowd" that gathered there began to focus upon a new physics teacher. Apparently without experience as a teacher or facility as a disciplinarian, trouble developed between him and several members of the crowd. The proprietor of the shop was a former circus performer and small bit actor, with some special ability in mimicry. Having seen the new physics teacher, he was quick to seize upon several of his mannerisms as affording a special outlet for his powers of mimicry. This greatly delighted the crowd, and suggested a pattern of mimicry of the new teacher which was carried subtly and surreptitiously into the classroom by the more adept performers among the boys. The teacher's further disciplinary attempts only aggravated matters. The proprietor, because of his role as original imitator, was drawn increasingly, and as an active agent, into the tension between the teacher and the crowd. The matter subsequently passed from the control of the physics teacher to the school's administrative heads who, ignorant of the role of the shopkeeper and the existence of a definitely unified peer group, meted out disciplinary measures upon a few of the boys in the class.

Again, the peer group serves to correct extremes or deviations of behavior among its members, thus illustrating the well-known sociological principle that the primary group exerts a conservative influence on behavior. Among peer groups, these deviations are generally the ones that are out of line with the age, sex, or class range of its members. We might speak of them as the usual run of adolescent vagaries. For the boy who is a noisy braggart, nothing more subduing can be devised than close association with other boys, equally braggart if possible. The girl whose endless poses before the mirror are "a trial and affliction" to her parents can be cured, if at all, by several healthy young male extroverts. The lad who always insists on having his own way needs to run with the pack. Even more complex problems can be handled most effectively by the peer group, as Bill's case illustrates.

Bill was a late adolescent who began to run around with a girl who not only lived on the other side of the railroad tracks, but who had most of the traits associated with that oft-used phrase. Bill's family was upper class, Bill was personally most attractive, and his mother knew the power of a peer group. Calling Bill to her, she explained with disarming friendliness that she had heard of his new girl and wanted to meet her. Wouldn't he bring her to the house, and to make it less formal, she would invite a few of his favorite friends. Upon securing Bill's wondering and semireluctant consent, the mother proceeded to promote, secretly, a gala event, to which she invited all of Bill's extended clique. Bill's relations with the new girl just barely survived until the end of the party.

One final fact about the peer group as an agency of control over its members requires emphasis, and this is the priority it has in the mind of the child. Careful students of child development have emphasized repeatedly that it exercises a greater degree of control than the family.

Parents often fail to understand the logic of this, and berate the child as disobedient, incorrigible, or ungrateful. The problem becomes particularly keen when the family's culture differs from that of the peer group, as happens so continually and inevitably as a by-product of cultural change and residential mobility. Viewed objectively, the child's prior rating of his peer group is entirely normal and natural. Like calls unto like, the world over. A study of 280 girls in grades 9 through 11 showed clearly that in certain areas of their lives the girls considered their peers to be more adequate judges of behavior than were their parents.[19]

3. The peer group is a security device, and its hold upon its members is further strengthened in many cases by the very distinctive role which it plays in the modern urban area. By this we refer to the sense of safety and security which it gives the child. To understand the meaning and import of this, certain facts concerning the modern urban community and family need to be brought together here for brief recapitulation. The modern urban center tends to be large. School buildings and school populations are growing larger. The old-fashioned primary-group community has largely disappeared. Urban life tends to be impersonal. The families of children who go to school together often do not know one another. Populations are mobile, which means that families and their children are coming and going constantly. Among other things, this involves constant dislocations and readjustments of personal relationships among school children. In certain areas and among selected groups, the percentage of population turnover is particularly high. This is true usually of families whose children have, as a whole, more than their share of other problems and difficulties. Combined with all these is the further fact, previously referred to, that the present-day child comes from a small family, which means few if any siblings upon whom to rely.

One result of all this is that the peer group, in one form or other, becomes very important to the child because it gives security to its members. An obvious illustration is the necessity in many areas for white, Negro, Gentile, and Jewish children each to form groups, both for physical safety and for psychological assurance.

[19] Clay V. Brittain, "Adolescent Choices and Parent-Peer Cross Pressures," *American Sociological Review*, June, 1963, pp. 385–391.

But there are selective forces other than those which are racial or religious, and the child who stands out because of other characteristics has his problems, too. Moreover, the racketeering practices rife among adults in the past generation have seeped down into the lower age brackets. There are organized gangs in schools which levy taxes for "protection," systematically "invite" other children to "share" their lunches or lunch money, "borrow" written work, and engage in various other similar practices. Against threats and violations of this kind the isolated child is helpless; the peer group offers something, even for those with no immediate problems, that is both important and comforting. Considerations of this kind are often in the background when the child, forced into the cruel dilemma of choice, stands by his peer group against the dictates of his school or home, or both.

The Peer Group as a Cultural Entity

Each peer group tends to have a culture which is distinctly its own. More specifically, this means that every such group has its own range of activities, its own interests, its own values and choices, which unite to form the social pattern of the group. The development of this cultural identity begins early in the child's life with the formation of the play group. As has been pointed out the composition of the play group and the content of the play group indicate the first steps in this direction; the clique, the gang, and other groups merely carry on at a subsequent level.

The culture of the peer group is in large measure a reflection of the culture of its members and the community from which they come. In cliques, for instance, the values of the strata which they represent will ordinarily prevail, though innovations will be made so that the culture is uniquely the adolescents' own—innovations which are sometimes highly disturbing to the adults of the same strata.

Certain types of children are particularly important in fixing the cultural pattern of their peer groups. In studying the spread of a specific culture trait in a group, Murphy concludes that personalities "unusually intelligent and sensitive to the patterns of adults and aggressive in their social responses, were pivotal points in what might be seen as a process of cultural diffusion."[20] Similarly, the role of the child in the group is highly significant.

Recognition of the role of the peer group's cultural background in determining its pattern of social behavior enables one to under-

[20] Murphy, *op. cit.*, p. 132.

stand the role of the gang in criminal behavior. Gangs, it has been pointed out, are characteristic of interstitial areas, of intramural frontiers. They arise from the more or less spontaneous effort of boys to create a society for themselves in age spans and social areas where no others adequate to their needs exist. In developing their gangs, boys cannot go beyond their experiences and the observations and activities of their families and other elders, "and hence their codes and chosen activities must be studied with reference to the moral codes and activities they meet in the communities where they live."[21] In other words, just as the gang as a conflict peer group is a symptom of community disorganization, so it is a reflection of the culture of these disorganized areas.

The adult patterns of behavior in the areas in which most delinquent gangs arise and operate are dominated by or literally sprinkled with crime and vice. Many adults are connected with or interested in various forms of racketeering or "easy-money" pursuits of one form or another. Gambling is prevalent, as are stealing, the receipt of stolen goods, begging, panhandling, and the like. These areas will be considered more fully in the next chapter. Reference here is confined to the fact that in so many of these gang-breeding sections not only the overt activities but the argot, the current terminology, the subjects discussed, and all the forms and forces of community conditioning are likely to center around matters which the larger society labels as antisocial or nonsocial.

Furthermore, these areas are isolated from the culture of other areas. The gang member does not have access to the cultural heritages of the dominant social order. The reasons for this are obvious but are often disregarded. First, they are ethnic, racial, and social class segregation. Second, the reasons are developmental in part, for these gangs consist of individuals who are merely in the lower stages of a process of urbanization and social achievement through which other elements in the population have passed successfully. But for the time being, the social isolation and the socially deviant behavior of these sections and their inhabitants combine to call forth philosophies which seek to justify their present social patterns, and these, too, come to be absorbed by the younger boy and girl. Delinquent gangs, then, are a natural product of the social education process in areas where the prevailing patterns are antisocial.

A suggestive illustration of the foregoing is the concept of the socialized delinquency behavior syndrome pattern advanced by Hewitt and Jenkins. Three ideas are basic to this concept. One is

[21] Thrasher, *The Gang, op. cit.*, p. 255.

the fact that the individual children in many delinquent gangs are well socialized in the sense that they get along well with other children of their own type. Second, the group patterns of behavior to which they are loyal are directed, not against specific persons per se, but against formal property rights and conduct codes established by the larger society. Third, this group pattern is the product of the environment of the gang. In this environment many social deviation pressures are exerted. The homes of these children are located in deteriorated neighborhoods where traditions of delinquency and disrespect for the law are most likely to flourish. Their families offer little in the way of training in conforming to the rules of the larger society.[22] This antisocial group pattern explains the difficulty of dealing with gangs of this kind.

Cohen has spelled out the foregoing summary in clear detail in the area of delinquent behavior. Juvenile delinquents, he points out, are the products of a persistent subculture that is traditional in certain neighborhoods, usually of lower-class status. This subculture has its definite characteristics—malice, negativism, short-run hedonism, intolerance of restraint, and the like. This subculture envelops and conditions the development of its young, just as do other class and community subcultures.[23]

One final comment is necessary by way of warning against oversimplification in this connection. The social pattern of each peer group represents its own distinctive combinations of the culture of its members and their communities.

For many years there have been those students who have been impressed by a "novelty of behavior arising from the specific interaction or organization of a number of elements, whether inorganic, organic or mental, which thereby constitute a whole, as distinguished from their mere sum, or 'resultant.'" The simplest illustration of this idea is that of water—a combination of hydrogen and oxygen, in certain definite proportions, and under well-defined conditions, to form a liquid emergent, which exhibits very different properties, i.e., behavior, than either of its gaseous components. The existence and importance of this factor of special relatedness has been recognized by a number of thinkers of the nineteenth century, such as John Stuart Mill, Lester F. Ward, Spaulding, Wundt, and others, and various terms such as "heteropathic causation," "creative synthesis," "evolutionary naturalism," "holism," "organicism," have been used to designate it. Mr. C. L. Morgan's "emergent evo-

[22] Lester E. Hewitt and Richard L. Jenkins, *Fundamental Patterns of Maladjustment: The Dynamics of Their Origin*, printed by authority of the State of Illinois, 1946, pp. 28, 29, 43, 44.

[23] Albert K. Cohen, *Delinquent Boys*, The Free Press of Glencoe, New York, 1955.

lution" has apparently found most favor among the contemporary philosophers, biologists, sociologists, and the like, who utilize the concept.[24]

For the understanding and successful control of any peer group, this distinctive nonadditive character of its cultural pattern must be recognized. For the adult who is called upon to deal with a peer group, access to this distinctive pattern is not an easy matter, for its development is in part an effort to create a life to which the adult is an alien. One of the perennial traditions in most peer groups is the unassimilable alien character of the adult. Yet what the members of the peer group tell each other about subjects which are important to them, such as sex, their teachers, their studies, and so on, often constitutes the core of the problem they present to adult society.

The Individual's Role in the Peer Group

Thus far the peer group has been considered as a group; it is necessary next to analyze the interactive process within the group, with special reference to the emergence of the individualized roles of its members. In any group containing more than two persons, distinctions and divisions arise, since the members are not equal in nature or ability, nor do they have the same relationships to all the others. Just as the child's behavior cannot be understood without knowing his particular position in the family group, so also is it necessary to know his place in the informal social grouping which he forms with other children.

Three aspects of the process by which the individual role emerges within the peer group can be noted. First, common enterprise entails division of labor. Each peer group exists for certain purposes, and the more important and enduring the group, the more specific and clearly defined these ends will be. In order to bring about their achievement, organization and leadership are necessary, as is specialization of function. Second, the members of the peer group each have their own particular traits, interests, aptitudes, and skills, on the basis of which competition among them for these specialized functions develops. The peer group is a small society, and life within it, as in all societies, is competitive. Third, in the collective experience of the group, individual assignments of roles and functions come to be assessed. A consensus or generalized conception of individual members crystallizes, on the basis of which

[24] James H. S. Bossard, "Robert Ellis Thompson—Pioneer Professor in Social Science," *American Journal of Sociology*, September, 1929, pp. 246–247.

individual roles are definitely assumed and assigned, to be conformed to or revised on the basis of still further experience. The more complex and varied its activities, the more highly organized and integrated the peer group becomes, and the more distinct and individualized these roles become, until in many such groups every member has his place, his job, and his niche in the group's life.

The status or role gained by the individual member of a peer group may be ascribed by the group on the basis of age, sex, physical appearance, physical prowess, or physical disability. In many peer groups, however, there are a democracy of operation and a play of competition which make for a number of achieved statuses or roles. Thrasher has identified some of the better known of these specialized roles in the gang, and to a considerable extent these are typical of most peer groups.[25] Every group has its leader or leaders. If it is a play group under adult supervision, the leader may be the child who is unusually intelligent and sensitive to adult direction. If it is a social clique, the leader may be the suave and clever member who is well versed in class distinctions and traditions. If it is a fighting gang, leadership is achieved on the basis of size, strength, courage, foresight—good fighting. Most peer groups, especially at the older age levels, develop one reliable member who can be trusted to look after the details of peer activity. Here is the embryo secretary-treasurer of later organizations. Peer groups have their jealous custodians of group membership. This is particularly noticeable in cliques. Often the custodians are members who have themselves just "shaved in," and who rather quickly become zealous keepers of the keys. Most peer groups have their "funny boys" whose behavior and, at times, irresponsibility are tolerated because of the humor they contribute or may be expected to in the future. Few such groups are without their gossips, whose special role it is to gather, dress up in interesting fashion, and distribute the latest information about persons in whom the gang is interested. The gossip columnists of today are merely an adult commercialization of this role, originally developed in peer-group experience, usually to compensate for failure in performance. Often there is a "sissy" member of the peer group, who may be assigned this status for a variety of reasons. How undesirable it is can be gathered from the rather extreme lengths to which many boys and girls will go to avoid this role. "The other kids would think me a sissy" is the key to much behavior, of both commission and omission, at certain age levels. Virtually every peer group has its loud-

[25] Thrasher, *The Gang*, *op. cit.*, chap. 17.

mouthed member, the show-off, the braggart, whose account of anything comes to be discounted by the group. Akin to this member is the aggressive member. This one is an ambitious imperialist, always reaching out for more territory, always willing to engage in a fight, but with the others doing the fighting. "Let's fight them, fellows. I'll hold your coats." Every gang, according to Thrasher—and probably most other peer groups—have their "goats." These are the boys of lower intelligence, slow of wit, and not infrequently combining some special peculiarity of manner, speech, or appearance with their subnormalities. These are the members who invariably get caught, who are often sacrificed or used as a decoy or cat's-paw by the group.

That some of these specialized roles do not seem to adults to have any particular prestige does not mean that they are so regarded by either the peer group or the individual possessors of these roles. All studies of peer groups emphasize two facts that it is important to note. First, individual status within such a group is for most members a very real and highly important matter, bringing often keen and vivid satisfaction. Not only are these statuses achieved, but they have been gained in the child's own world. They involve recognition by his peers; and many a young boy or girl finds greater satisfaction in being the doorkeeper or errand boy for the gang than to receive the approval of adults. This role in the peer group becomes a powerful determinant in the formation of the child's conception of himself. It is for reasons of this kind, again, that an understanding of these roles is so important for parents, teachers, school attendance officers, probation officers, policemen, and others who deal habitually with children. The second fact is that peer-group status has special significance for children whose opportunities otherwise are relatively limited. The boy and girl who have not succeeded in gaining a satisfactory status within their family; whose family is nonexistent, inadequate, or in perennial conflict; whose relations with their parents and other older people at home involve a constant struggle against domination or neglect; whose school achievements are nil or unsatisfactory; whose opportunities to engage in other community activities are scant at best—all these and many other types of frustrated and underprivileged children can find in peer groups, especially conflict gangs, the opportunity for individual achievement otherwise denied. As a general rule, the less rewarding and the more drab the child's life outside of the peer group is, the more does a role within the group mean to him. Peer roles are often compensatory achievements affording great satisfaction to boys and girls.

Differentials in the Child's Experience with Peer Groups

In assessing the nature and role of peer-group situations in the process of child development, it is necessary to recognize the differences which prevail in the child's use of and experience with these groups. Two types of factors are particularly important in determining these differences.

First, there are wide variations in the number of years during which the child gives allegiance to peer groups. Keeping in mind the fact that they are transitional groups in the growing-up process, dominating the period between his social emancipation from his family and his integration into adult society, we see clearly that two variables are active in determining this time span. One is the age of emancipation from the family; the other, that of arrival at adulthood. All kinds of combinations exist, and we can readily identify from common observation types like the following. There is, for example, the child whose emancipation from the family occurs late but whose integration into the adult world takes place at the normal time. Here the period of peer-group life is relatively short. By way of contrast is the child for whom the former comes early and the latter is late. Emmy Lou, whose story is recorded in the files of the Carter Foundation, was withdrawn from family life at the age of 3, because of the death of her father. She was placed in an institution and remained there in several capacities until her twenty-sixth year, after which she made a slow and rather painful adjustment to adult life. On the whole, in analyzing the available cases, it appears that class differentials also prevail here. The lower the class status, the earlier the social emancipation from the family, and the earlier the entrance into adult life.

Second, the relative social need for peer-group activities varies to a considerable extent, and this naturally affects the child's utilization of these groups. Many details and circumstances are involved here, and these, too, seem to vary a good deal on a class basis. There are, for example, such factors as the pressure upon the child to acquire individual skills, involving music lessons, dancing lessons, art instruction, and so on, and the resultant time spent in practice; the scope and variety of family activities; and the extent to which community resources are available to the individual child. It will be recalled here that students of peer groups persistently emphasize their development as the result of children's efforts to meet needs not otherwise met. In short, the principle which operates here may be stated something like this: the number, appeal, and utilization of peer groups varies with the appeal and diversity of such competing groups as the family and the community.

If we think of the child's development in terms of process, it is evident that life in the peer group during the growing-up period is, for most children, one of life's major experiences, and that these peer-group experiences constitute one of the basic factors in the determination of the adult personality. A selected few phases of this process will be identified briefly.

To begin with, there are the children who have had no, or very little, peer-group experience. Perhaps the parents did not permit it, perhaps the circumstances of life did not, perhaps the child's traits led him to avoid it. Such children are often referred to as having had no childhood. What they have not had is experience in living and competing with and being disciplined by equals; growing up, they become adults who associate themselves first with persons much older than themselves, and subsequently, with those much younger. Having been inadequately socialized, they often are rather "difficult" individuals.

Some children make unsuccessful or painful adjustments to their peer groups so that memories of their experiences rankle and smart; but, because they do, there is often a spur to a much greater and more effective effort in the adult world. These are the persons who not infrequently turn out well, to the wonder of their adolescent friends. "I never expected him to turn out the way he did." "I didn't think he had it in him."

At times a lack of success in peer-group adjustments is found among children who mature relatively early in life, or who prematurely gain unusual insight into life situations and come to sense the serious imminence of the adult world. The adult world shines through the papier-mâché of the peer-group world. These are the young people who are impatient with adolescence. They will not take it in their stride. For this reason they become men before they learn to be boys. To become a man too soon may mean that one becomes a small man.

There are cases, of course, in which life presses hard upon youth. These are the young people who must go to work early in life, who are sobered prematurely by adult responsibilities. Perhaps they rationalize the appeal of the peer group, perhaps they actually are out of sympathy with it, perhaps they cast longing glances at it but are washed past it. When such persons attain financial success as adults, they often leave endowments or make contributions to youth activities in the community.

There are the children whose relations with peer groups are complicated unduly by their parents. The parents may be hard and unsympathetic to these groups; they may seek to keep the child away, tethering him with a silver cord; they may embarrass him whenever other children are about; they may disgrace the family name, or the home may be such that the child will not bring his associates there. Such children tend to marry early, often unwisely, or to affiliate themselves with peer groups which operate surreptitiously.

Finally, there are the children who adjust so well to peer-group life, who find so much personal satisfaction therein, that membership in them is continued unduly. Because they find in the peer group what life otherwise denies or makes too difficult for them to obtain, they cling to it. In the gang category and at the antisocial level, such persons perpetuate their gangs, shifting into various "easy-money" activities. Thus emerges the postadolescent and adult gangster. On the more conventional side, there are the people who grow up to be the joiners, the clubsters, the active organization men. Among college alumni, these are the old grads who never grow up and who insist at times on living at the "house" years after their classmates have vanished into maturity. The world is amazingly full of individuals who have not grown beyond the gang or peer-group stage.

SUMMARY

1. The term *peer* is used in this chapter to mean another child, that is, a nonadult. The peer group is an association of children or youth that operates in the child-youth world, and the chief concern of its members is with each other.

2. The preschool play group is the first peer group of a child. It is informal, relatively free from adult supervision, and is unique in that it is made up for the most part of whatever number and kind of children are available in the immediate neighborhood.

3. The play group, like any social situation, is composed of a specific structure, interactive process, and cultural content. The meaning of these to the development of any particular child is related to his experiences in his own home, that is, to his family situation.

4. The following factors seem to be significant for the development of personality and behavior patterns: (a) size of family and size of play group; (b) sex of siblings and of play-group members; (c) age of siblings and available playmates; (d) the relationship of patterns of interaction, and of cultural content, between family and play group; and (e) the specific activities content within the play group.

5. There are indications that a child's school adjustment may be related to the combined natures of his family and his preschool peer group.

6. Later-age peer groups have been studied largely in terms of one form, the gang, and in relation to antisocial behavior. This has created the idea that peer groups are vehicles of crime and delinquency. Recently their larger and more normal aspects have been recognized.

7. The later-age peer groups discussed here are the clique, a small, intimate social-participation group, operating as an instrument of class status, and the gang, developing chiefly as a conflict group and the product of an interstitial setting.

8. Peer groups are singularly individual. Each is a separate sociological phenomenon. To generalize their development, it is evident that (a) they are social products, (b) they take form on the basis of age gradations, (c) they arise to meet definite needs, (d) their development follows the character of these needs, (e) they have natural histories, and (f) they often reflect racial, national, and religious distinctions of the larger society.

9. Peer groups play an important role in child development (a) through their emphasis upon the rights of others, (b) as agencies controlling their members, (c) as a security device, (d) as a cultural entity, and (e) as a determinant of personality roles.

10. The child's use of and experience with peer groups varies considerably on the basis of (a) the number of years he belongs and (b) his relative need for peer-group activities.

11. The child's life in his peer groups is one of life's major experiences, and such experience constitutes one of the basic factors in determining the adult personality.

SUGGESTED READINGS

Bloch, Herbert A., and Arthur Niederhoffer, *The Gang,* Philosophical Library, New York, 1958. An interesting book to compare with that of Thrasher, it represents new thinking on the concept of gang.

Cohen, Albert K., *Delinquent Boys,* The Free Press of Glencoe, New York, 1955. Comparisons of delinquent and nondelinquent cultures in this book are especially thought-provoking.

Coleman, James S., *The Adolescent Society,* The Free Press of Glencoe, New York, 1961. An analysis of the adolescent subcultures in ten schools of varying student composition.

Kramer, Dale, and Madeline Karr, *Teen-Age Gangs,* Henry Holt and Company, New York, 1953. A story of three boys in New York and of the gangs they led.

Mays, John Barron, *Crime and the Social Structure,* Faber and Faber, Ltd., London, 1963. An attempt to underline the social components of crime and delinquency that are currently most overlooked.

Murphy, Lois Barclay, *Social Behavior and Child Personality,* Columbia University Press, New York, 1937. An exploratory study of some of the roots of sympathy in young children.

Piaget, Jean, *The Moral Judgment of the Child,* Kegan Paul, London, 1932. A description of the differing influences of the young peer group and of adults upon the development of rules and conscience in the child.

Powers, Edwin, and Helen Witmer, *An Experiment in the Prevention of Delinquency,* Columbia University Press, New York, 1951. A report on the Cambridge-Somerville Youth Study which attempted the prevention of delinquency by the use of friendly counselors.

Smith, Ernest A., *American Youth Culture,* The Free Press of Glencoe, New York, 1962. A description of the effects of current attitudes and institutions upon the youth group.

Thrasher, Frederic M., *The Gang* (rev. and abr. ed.), University of Chicago Press, Chicago, 1963. This book is the first thorough investigation of the gang, its processes and culture.

Tunley, Roul, *Kids, Crime and Chaos,* Harper & Row, New York, 1962. A reporter, journalist, and layman views juvenile delinquency throughout the world and attacks many current conceptions about its causes and treatment.

SCHOOL SITUATIONS AND CHILD DEVELOPMENT 17

It was once customary to think of the school primarily as an agency in the formal education of the child, with emphasis chiefly upon problems of curriculum, equipment, and pedagogy. In some parts of Europe, where there is careful selection of which children may continue their education past a certain age, this is still the case. In the United States, however, a revolution has occurred during this century that has made it necessary to consider the school in an added way; namely, as a complex of social situations in which children live, compete, perform, develop attitudes, form response patterns, fail, and succeed in the process of getting along in the world. The revolution is universal compulsory education on an ever-increasing scale, and to an extent realized in few other places in the world.

This chapter is devoted to a discussion of (1) the student population, its structure, process, and content, (2) teacher personnel in school situations, (3) cultural differences between home and school, and (4) current focuses in school situation problems.

THE STUDENT POPULATION

Once a child reaches the age of compulsory school attendance, he is introduced into a new life situation that is not of his making and not necessarily of his choosing. He may have little understanding of the aims of formal education, but he is very much aware that school is a social world quite different from the family world to which he has been accustomed. This awareness comes in the earliest years of school, but the school world becomes increasingly complex as the child grows older. Writing of Middletown, for example, the Lynds said: "The high school, with its athletics, clubs, sororities, fraternities, dances, parties and other 'extracurricular activities' is a fairly complete social cosmos in itself, and about this city within a city the social life of the intermediate generation centers. Here the social-sifting devices of their elders—money, clothes, personal attractiveness, male physical prowess, exclusive clubs, elections to positions of leadership—are all for the first time set going."[1] A student's adjustment, or lack of adjustment, to the school situation is one of the most significant facts in his life. First, he must remain in it for a considerable part of most of his waking days for ten or twelve years. Second, in a society like ours, his life chances correlate to a high degree with how long he continues his school career. There are notable examples, such as Winston Churchill, who were misfits in school and yet rose to eminence, but such people constitute a small minority. At present, the "union cards" of high school diploma and university degree are becoming more and more important in attaining the "good life" to which most Americans aspire. Some of the situations to which students must try to adjust will be described briefly.

The Size of the Student Population

The total enrollment of day pupils in public elementary and secondary schools rose from 75,995 in 1900, to 179,323 in 1960.[2] During the past ten years, pupil enrollment has grown faster than both the general population and the school-age population. These tremendous increases have resulted from the high birth rates during and following World War II, and also from the increased public interest in keeping children in school. In the near future, a further

1 Robert and Helen Lynd, *Middletown*, Harcourt, Brace and Company, New York, 1929, p. 211.

2 U.S. Bureau of the Census, *Statistical Abstract of the United States: 1963.* (Eighty-fourth ed.) Washington, D.C., 1963, p. 124.

increase is expected because of our attempts to get more younger children into schools and to prevent them from leaving before they finish the twelfth grade.[3] Between the school years of 1953–1954 and 1963–1964, the average pupil-teacher ratio declined by 9.4 percent; while at the secondary level it increased by 8.5 percent. Although improvement in numbers of teachers to pupils has occurred in some schools, many states still have critically high pupil-teacher ratios. This is especially true in urban areas.[4] In addition, the problem of classroom shortage is acute in many communities. The U.S. Office of Education has reported that 25.4 percent of current classrooms are obsolete, built of combustible material, nonpermanent, or located in off-site facilities.[5]

All of this means schools that are too large and classes that contain too many students. One difficulty that results is that teachers and administrators often become increasingly concerned with problems of discipline instead of teaching. Large numbers multiply contacts and thus problems of relationships, as well as create vague fears that situations may get out of hand. Many teachers in large schools seem haunted by an almost neurotic fear of student disturbances. The effect of large groups upon the social development of an individual member is a problem which has not been adequately studied or, may it be added, recognized as a problem. Common observation reveals many difficulties among individual students who are lost in the maze of the mass. It is far from easy for a 12-year-old to develop poise, self-assurance, and self-esteem when he finds himself identified as the eighth boy in the ninth row in Section 29 in a junior high school with a total of thirteen hundred students. The establishment of intimate personal relationships with students or teacher presents special difficulties. Moreover, the size of the school world takes on added significance when compared with the size of the child's family world. Whereas formerly a child came from a large family group, along with a number of other siblings, and entered a small school, the contemporary child tends to come from a small family, often alone, and to enter a very large school world. This change in the background of millions of children may prove, in retrospect, to be of revolutionary significance. At a time when the value of individual attention for the child is recognized as important and necessary, it appears that it is becoming less easy to attain. Although the city schools are largest and most crowded, the burgeoning suburbs

[3] *Financial Status of the Public Schools: 1964,* National Education Association, Washington, D.C., 1964, pp. 5–6.

[4] *Ibid.,* p. 11.

[5] *Ibid.,* p. 18.

in the great metropolitan areas are being confronted with a similar problem. In one study of 42 suburban school districts it was found that the percentage of students who received special counseling during one school year varied from 100 percent to 4.27 percent.[6] It is highly likely that in schools where such rates are low, it is the most flagrantly misbehaving student who gets the individual attention. A now classic, and widely publicized study was made of teachers' conceptions of behavior problems, in contrast to that of mental hygienists. Teachers in several large elementary public-school systems were asked: (1) to list the behavior problems they had encountered in their experience, (2) to check the frequency of the problems listed, (3) to rate the total behavior adjustment of each child, and (4) to rate the relative seriousness of the various problems. According to this study: (1) Teachers tended to stress behavior disturbances that threatened their standard of morality, obedience, orderliness, and application to schoolwork. On the whole, they seemed to be mostly concerned with the stubborn, disorderly, irresponsible, untruthful, and disobedient child. (2) The problems reported most frequently were those involving violations of specific classroom rules and the children's failure to meet prescribed standards of schoolwork. (3) The problem child, as identified by them, was antagonistic to authority, did not conform to classroom order and routine, did not make the expected application to prescribed school tasks, and violated standards of integrity. On the other hand, the purely personal problems of children which did not frustrate the immediate purposes of teaching were not regarded as symptomatic of significant maladjustment. (4) The ratings of the relative seriousness of behavior problems, by the teachers and the mental hygientists, were strikingly different. Teachers ranked as most serious the problems relating to sex, dishonesty, and disobedience, and as least serious such traits as shyness, sensitiveness, unsocialness, fearfulness, and dreaminess. This latter group, together with unhappiness, depression, resentfulness, cowardliness, and overcriticalness, was at the top of the mental hygienists' list. The items describing defiance to authority appear to teachers to be very serious; they are near the bottom of the psychiatric rating. Problems designating the failure of pupils to uphold classroom discipline were emphasized by teachers but greatly discounted by the psychiatrists, who rated them as the least serious of all. In short, teachers react mostly to the attacking, frustrating forms of behavior problems, counterattacking in turn; their response to the

[6] Eleanor S. Boll and Sara M. Brown, *Pupil Personnel in Eastern Pennsylvania Schools: 1962–63*, Educational Service Bureau, University of Pennsylvania, 1964, pp. 26–30.

withdrawing forms of behavior is sympathy and protective feelings aroused by the dependence and inadequacy of the pupils.[7] Although there may be some question as to whether the teachers are all wrong and the mental hygienists all right, the problems that the latter stress are important and require special attention. Yet, in overcrowded conditions when discipline and order must be stressed, it would not be surprising if teachers' attitudes, as described in this study, should become strengthened.

The Age Structure of the Student Population

The school system in the United States is very age-grade conscious. In most cases, depending upon the date of birth of a child, he may enter first grade this coming fall or will have to wait until the following one. The aim is to keep children of about the same age in the same class. During the early years of school there is some flexibility in retarding and accelerating students according to their ability. This flexibility becomes less, however, as the children grow older. Even if a child can learn little beyond fifth grade, he must remain in school, and it is unthinkable to retain a 15- or 16-year-old in a class with 10- and 11-year-olds. There are both pros and cons to this situation. The child who is unable to keep up with the classwork and is automatically promoted is a good candidate for failure, dropping out, and delinquency. Yet, maturation processes and the self-esteem of the child are of great importance. Also, the whole society tends to be age-grade conscious. We prefer to have people maintain their closest relationships, in dating and marriage, with those who are of fairly similar age. The young married set is supposed to socialize with others of that group, and the middle-aged couple who prefers the younger ones is commented upon. "He is a perennial Boy Scout." "She should act her age." It is wise, then, for children to learn to live with their own peers.

Too rigidly enforced age classification, however, does not allow for the fact that maturation does not occur for each child at the "average" age. Neither are intellectual, physical, emotional, and social age equal in every child. There result certain times of stress during school days. A generally recognized time of stress is when the girls start to ripen, and become interested in boys—but definitely not in those callow lads who are their classmates. Some teachers of experience feel that seventh and eighth grade boys and girls should never be permitted in the same classroom. Differences

[7] E. K. Wickman, *Children's Behavior and Teachers' Attitudes*, 6th printing, Commonwealth Fund, New York, 1937.

in individual children are striking also. There is the familiar case of the little boy, whose pals have grown beyond him, who copies their cavalier or Don Juan airs to the point of being obnoxious. There is also the immature girl who tries to keep up with her friends and finds herself a wallflower, before she should have been exposed to this type of social situation. There is some evidence that, in general, children in the United States are maturing earlier physically than they once did. For this, and other reasons, studies are being made of possible reorganization in the grades at which junior high school should start. The group in transition from childhood to adolescence should be separated, it is felt. Yet no one exact age requirement will fulfill this aim. Children develop individually. Another recent experiment has been continuous-progress programs, or educational streaming, in order to permit the intellectually able to progress at their own speed. Certainly, no American child should be prevented from stretching his mental potential to its highest limits; but in the life of the child, the mind is not the only consideration. One has to wonder a bit about the compartmentalization of the life of an 11-year-old boy who attains freshman status in a large university. Whatever the educational experiments adults visit upon children, there will be problems of maladjustment for some because of their specific mental, physiological, emotional, and social age. For these, the children need the individual help that is so difficult to give in overcrowded schools.

Pupil Relationships in the School World

School administrators and other adults may consider formal education to be the most basic function of the school, but there is some question as to the relative importance of that function to the students themselves. Dr. James S. Coleman has pointed out that separating adolescents, as a group, into the schools with their many extracurricular activities, and over a long period of time, has forced adolescents to rely for much of their social life on their peers and has made them of prime importance to each other.[8] His view was corroborated by interviews held with 300 students aged 6 to 18 which attempted to find out what the most important aspect of school life was to them.[9] For those students from 10 to 18 years of age, the answer was overwhelmingly, "the other children." Teachers ranked a not-too-close second, and success in schoolwork was not a popular reply. The general attitude seemed to be

[8] James S. Coleman, *The Adolescent Society*, The Free Press of Glencoe, New York, 1961, p. 3.

[9] Interviews given by the staff of the William T. Carter Foundation.

"teachers and failure in work can make life difficult part of the time, but not-getting-along-with-the-other-kids can make it miserable every minute." A result is that preadolescents and adolescents find it essential to meet the requirements of their own peer group, both for companionship and status. If these requirements conflict with those of the teachers, it is felt to be unwise to cater to the teachers' wishes. Many of the interviewees mentioned the need for subtlety in handling relationships with the school staff. They half-wanted and half-feared to be singled out by teachers. Only in cases of complete ostracism by their peers would they devote themselves to becoming teacher's pet. The following comments are those of a girl who was conscious of this situation and of her losing battle while fighting against it.

> My first experience meeting a large group was entering first grade. All I remember is sitting in a huge classroom of 35 children and feeling like a straw in a haystack. . . . The next thing I knew, my teachers began to take an interest in me. They used to call me in from the playground and sit me down at a classroom piano to play for them. They thought it was wonderful. I didn't mind—in fact I enjoyed the attention and fuss but also missed playing with the kids. When they came in from the playground I tried to slink away from the piano as soon as possible. I didn't like the idea of their seeing and hearing all this. I wanted to be one of them—another kid in the group. Later, I got in with four other girls. Then they placed us in sections according to how we made out in an exam. I was placed two sections below them. They didn't like this, and I was left out of their circle from then on. Two terms later I was in their section, but it was too late. I still wasn't accepted. I studied my music harder than ever. I received recognition on this basis, and it became my sole means for being accepted by people. I would have been lost without it. I still cling to my music for emotional satisfaction. It has become more of an escape from reality. I receive all sorts of honor for it. But that isn't the acceptance I wanted.

This girl, a talented pianist, was under psychiatric care during her junior and senior year in high school. It is not suggested that the school situation was the sole cause of her problems. It was, however, very clearly an aggravation of them.

In terms of child behavior and development the significant fact about the intensity of relationships between children and their peers lies not just in the interaction but in the content of the behavior and values that they expect from each other. Some of the more important aspects of this will be discussed.

The Culture of the School

Each school is a subculture, drawing from the larger American culture, but putting its own specific emphasis upon certain values, statuses, and ways of behaving. In a small school with a homogeneous student population there may be unity of opinion about these things. In our large schools, with their heterogeneous student bodies, however, it would be more accurate to say that within the schools there exist a *number* of subcultures. In a group that grows very large, it is impossible to maintain primary, face-to-face relationships without subdividing into smaller units.

In any large high school, "crowds" or cliques are clearly discernible. Although they differ from one school to another they have been labeled in many studies of schools. One of these classifies them as the Wheels (the top crowd), the Brains, the Outsiders (not school-oriented), the Mice, and the Outcasts (the ones you don't want to be with).[10] To the normal, healthy child, it is of greatest importance to be in with some crowd; but not all crowds are open to all children. A potential Wheel or Brain can become an Outsider or an Outcast, if the individual has personality or social background factors which close the preferred circle to him. For example, a boy writes of his fears of just this situation.

When I was in about the fourth grade I seemed to be the class leader. I was a very good student, and the teacher and children liked me. I loved school and would not have endangered my high position there for the world. Most of the kids in school I thought were much better off economically than I was. I knew we weren't well off. My father was just starting out in his own business and I didn't think my home was as nice as the homes of some of my friends. I never would bring any of them home, although they brought me to theirs. I lived in constant fear that if they ever saw my home I would lose status in school. It seems silly now but while in the fourth grade it was my greatest problem. Luckily the next year things took a turn for the better. We moved to a better apartment and from that point on, my home became a social center for the kids in my class.

Generally, from the child's point of view it is better to join any group than to be a loner. Thence stems some of the deep and hot loyalty of children for their school crowd no matter how unsuitable it may seem to adults. It is a fact, though, that identification with a clique lable tends to reinforce in its members the trait for which it receives recognition. The distinctive clique trait becomes a mem-

[10] Carson McGuire and Rodney A. Clark, "Age-Mate Acceptance and Indices of Peer Status," *Child Development,* June, 1952, p. 148.

bership card for each child. Outsiders, for their own protection, outwardly scorn the academic and extracurricular activities of the Wheels and Brains. Outcasts decry the conformity of the others. The Brains consider everyone else stupid. The Mice call the others loud, brash, and bold. The Wheels stress the lack of school spirit in the rest. Thus, while deriding the characteristics of the others, they give high value to their own. It is, to a great extent, the recognition of this fact that causes concern in parents when they see their child in a clique which they feel is not the proper one for him. Their concern grows deeper when their remonstrances cause only a deepening loyalty for the clique and hostility toward the parents. Enforced separation from the clique, however, may indeed result in the child's becoming a loner, with all the psychological problems that implies.

Dr. Coleman has attempted to discover exactly what it is that makes a high school student popular—in other words, what are the status-achieving values of modern American adolescents. In a detailed study of nine schools in different-sized communities and with student bodies of varying social backgrounds, he found some general patterns. In answer to the question of what it takes for boys to be popular with other boys the factors stressed in order of importance were: "to be an athlete," "to be in a leading crowd," "to be a leader in activities," "to have high grades," "to have a nice car," and "to come from the right family." In considering what it takes to be popular with girls, the order was the same except that "having a nice car" ranked higher than grades. For girls, the rating for popularity with other girls was "being in the leading crowd," "being a leader in activities," "coming from the right family," "having nice clothes," "having high grades," and "being a cheerleader." To be popular with boys, the ranking was different. "Having nice clothes" rose to third in importance, "being a cheerleader," to fourth; and high grades were of least importance.[11] It is rather clear, from these answers, that school culture is primarily social and secondarily academic to the students. Dr. Coleman suggests that we have set up an artificial situation for teen-agers in which they are cut off from the adult world for a long period of time and thrown upon each other to make their own world. They stress, and compete in, the things which most visibly lead them to activity and to some semblance of what they think is "growing up." Success in academic grades is not very visible, is individual, and is something that adults arbitrarily expect from them.

In spite of the above generalizations about peer culture, every

[11] Coleman, *op. cit.*, pp. 44–48.

school has its own specific values and statuses. There are schools in which the "top crowd" stresses scholastic achievement, or athletics, or dating, or delinquent behavior. Most children want to take on the behavior patterns of this crowd, for it is essential to membership in the highest-status group. It is when they cannot achieve this that they identify with another crowd, almost for self-preservation. Thus, in one school, a child may work hard, behave well and be in the top-ranking group. In another school, he may do the same thing and be at the bottom of the status ladder—a not too happy position. A recognition of this situation has led some parents to send their children to carefully selected private schools because of the cultural values of the students represented there. Other parents who cannot afford the expense have been able to solve the problem only by moving into another district where the schools are more to their liking. A part of the mobility of families with young children is for this very purpose.

Another approach to the school culture is in terms of the elements that compose it. First, there are the many cultural backgrounds from which the children come. The heterogeneity of the American population is reflected in the cultural diversity of its schoolrooms. This has been emphasized by a number of students,[12] and we quote briefly from Thrasher.

> A complicating factor for all educational programs is the number and variety of different social backgrounds which give conflicting definitions of social values. Among preliterate peoples and in simple European peasant communities cultural diffusion is largely absent. There is a consistent series of social definitions which govern all human activities. In the American city, on the contrary, we find a kaleidoscopic variety of natural areas representing many diverse cultural and nationality backgrounds which do not mutually support each other in the social definitions which they are accustomed to impart to their children. A further confusion is brought about by the concurrence of many different social worlds, not ecologically defined necessarily, but existing more or less independently in the same community. These social worlds, although of many types, often take on the character of racial or nationality groupings. Of importance also are the occupational groupings, such as those of the artist, the working classes represented by various labor organizations, the teachers, lawyers, the underworld, the Bohemians, and so on. . . . Even within a single nationality group-

[12] Robert J. Havighurst, Paul Hoover Bowman, Gordon P. Liddle, Charles V. Matthews and James V. Pierce, *Growing Up in River City,* John Wiley and Sons, New York, 1962; Hilda Taba, *School Culture,* American Council on Education, Washington, D.C., 1955; and Willard W. Waller, *The Sociology of Teaching,* John Wiley & Sons, New York, 1932.

ing one finds wide differences in language, tradition, customs and philosophies of life."[13]

It is the specific combination of these groups and their interrelations, which constitutes a separate and unique entity, and which gives any particular place or school its distinctive character or flavor. It is in these specific situations that the current problems of intergroup conflict are found. These are problems which seem destined to plague our educational system for many years.

TEACHER PERSONNEL IN SCHOOL SITUATIONS

Teachers constitute a small but important part of the school population. They represent the institutional type of leadership functioning in the school situation. They have a directive and supervisory responsibility. In the performance aspects of the school world, they set the tasks and direct their execution. In addition, they play various roles in the social life of the school. Often a personalized relationship develops between an individual teacher and child. In short, the teacher not only is concerned with the intellectual life of the child, but often carries a major responsibility in his socialization, playing the role of disciplinarian, counselor, confidant, and friend. To say that the teacher is often identified as a foe by the child is to comment upon the tone but not the roles of the teacher-child relationship. It is apparent, therefore, that a number of facts about teachers in addition to their scholastic equipment and pedagogical effectiveness become significant in the school world, especially from the standpoint of the child.

1. The sex of the teacher is important in terms of students' attitudes, discipline, teaching methods, pupil-teacher relationships and many other aspects of the school situation.

Possibly the most important problem involving the teacher's sex is the effect of the relative dominance of the educational process by women during the child's early and presumably the significantly formative years. There is widespread belief that this country has been experiencing a feminization of its culture in recent years, and that a very specific phase of this has been the feminization of child training.[14] Three factors may be identified in this connection. First is the fact that the modern father is away from home a large

[13] Frederic M. Thrasher, "Social Background and Informal Education," *Journal of Educational Sociology*, April, 1944, pp. 471–479.

[14] Roy Helton, "The Inner Threat: Our Own Softness," *Harper's Magazine*, September, 1940, pp. 337–343.

part of the child's waking day, thus leaving the responsibility for rearing him to his mother, or a woman substitute. Second is women's monopolization of the teaching process, especially below the high school level. Third is the fact that many of the functions performed earlier by the family, in which the father presumably had some share, are now delegated to social agencies of various kinds, staffed chiefly by women. In combination, these factors are interpreted to mean that women's dominance of the child-conditioning process is constant and pervasive—in the home, in the school, in many child and youth activities—and that, as a result, women determine not only the child's ways but also his attitudes, ideals, values, and, by indirection, his conception of what it is to be masculine. In spite of the general recognition of this problem, the teaching profession does not seem to be enticing to men at the elementary school level. A report on American public schoolteachers reveals that 87.9 percent of the teachers in elementary schools are women. At the secondary level men are slightly in the majority (56.8 percent).[15] This is rather late in the development of the child, however, to counteract the feminizing role. In fact, a sudden change from women to men teachers at this particular time can cause, and has caused, problems. Some girls develop crushes on male teachers, others are panicked by having to recite in front of them, still others "work them" for good grades. Even boys, who have been reared primarily by Mother and female teachers, have a real adjustment to make in confronting the male teacher.

The sex of the teacher is important also as concerns the ethnic and social class background of the student population. Women teachers, for example, often have severe disciplinary problems with male students who come from homes where the tradition of male dominance is very strong. Among such groups there is usually the complementary tradition that the mother is to be loved but not necessarily obeyed. It is the father who is to be feared and obeyed. The projection of early family-conditioned attitudes onto the teacher has been noted by many students of behavior, and the point emphasized here is merely a further elaboration of that fact. Perhaps the basic principle which should be stressed is that every distinct cultural group has its traditional conception of the respective roles of the father and the mother as disciplinarians, and that when these are transferred to the school world they become significant when related to the sex of the teacher.

2. There is also the age of the teacher to be considered, the signifi-

[15] "American Public School Teachers, 1960–61," *National Education Association Journal*, April, 1963, p. 48.

cance of which is difficult to assess, both because of the variables which must be considered and of the intangible nature of the evidence that is available. Obviously, the teacher's age is more than a chronological measurement; it involves more particularly poise, social experience, the maturing of understanding and judgment, the attitude toward children, and the manner in which one has adjusted to his age. The behavior of young teachers who grow beards and act stilted, and of those past 50 who insist on gamboling on the green, constitutes part of the age complex. In the report cited above, it appears that men, who are primarily in the secondary schools, are more apt to take on the first sort of behavior, for there are many more of them between the ages of 25 and 35 than there are women. The median age for all men teachers is 33.6 years, while for women it is 45.5 years.[16]

Perhaps the age of the teacher has meaning primarily when compared with that of his pupils, the age differential being an index of the personality-cultural distance between the two. This distance seems a highly significant factor, both in pupil-teacher relationships, and in determining the particular role played by the teacher in the school situation. When he is relatively near his students in age, he has the advantage of understanding better their cultural world and its problems, but he runs the danger of becoming too vitally interested in their activities and longing too intensely to participate in them. This frequently creates two types of problems. First, in becoming too friendly and perhaps familiar with his students, he is confronted with the problem of reconciling friendship with authority, and he often ends up by losing both. Second, if frustrated in his longing to participate actively in student life, the compensatory developments may take the form of "hard marking," a "tough attitude," or other unsympathetic manifestations.

Older teachers, by way of contrast, often have more difficulty in putting themselves in the place of students, and in sympathizing with the vagaries of behavior characteristic of the earlier years. On the other hand, older teachers seem more able to sublimate their own interests and ambitions in the development of their pupils, and to secure more easily their subordination because their students accept the teacher as a parent-substitute. The combination of these two sets of results creates the paradoxical problem peculiar to the teacher whose age separates him too far from his students: he has authority but little or no influence. The student's reaction to this situation is that he accepts the former fact while concealing

16 *Ibid.*

the latter. The most effective age differential, according to Waller, exists when the teacher is a young adult, sufficiently past adolescence to have solved its problems, yet still near enough to be understanding and tolerant of its challenge for others; old enough not to see the student as a rival but young enough to speak his language; old enough to be identified as an adult but not so old as to cease to have, for the student, the status of being a person.[17]

3. The marital status of the teacher has significance for the present discussion in a variety of ways. To begin with, it determines his status in the school world, particularly among students who have reached the adolescent stage. The teacher who is married, particularly if a woman, is one who has "made it"; the unmarried one has failed. To girl students, the latter personifies what is to be avoided; for school boys, the unmarried woman teacher retains some elements of intrigue only up to a certain age. From the teacher's status it is only a short step to the attitude toward what he teaches.

Reinforcing his status in the school world is the teacher's status in the adult (parent, community, etc.) world. Here, too, marital status is important. "Old-maid schoolteacher" has long been used by parents as a special weapon with which to disparage a teacher and thus dispose of what the child is expected to do in school or bring to it. Teachers have unusually difficult problems in many communities in acquiring a normal status, and the marital status may easily tip the scale in either direction.[18]

Fortunately, there is increasing diversity in the marital status of teachers. As a part of the influx of married women into gainful occupations outside of the home, the opposition to married women as teachers is rapidly disappearing, and more married women are teaching. Particularly noteworthy is the return of mothers who are going back to teaching after an interval of some years, during which they have reared their own children to school age. At the present time the majority of teachers in the public schools are married people—80.5 percent of the men teachers and 68.0 percent of the women. Of the latter, 32.1 percent have children all of whom are under 17 years of age. Some of these women have special problems. These arise chiefly from the extra responsibilities which marriage involves. Many a married woman teacher, in addition to being a full-time teacher, is trying to manage a home, be a wife, and possibly rear children of her own. To say that she may fail in one

[17] Willard W. Waller, *The Sociology of Teaching,* John Wiley & Sons, New York, 1932, p. 216.

[18] James H. S. Bossard, "Marriage as a Status-Achieving Device," *Sociology and Social Research,* September–October, 1944, pp. 3–10.

or more of these tasks, or may age prematurely, is merely to allude to the inevitable. Furthermore, if she fails with her own children or her husband or her household management, she may lose prestige in the school world or in the community, or in both.

The teacher's marital status is related, too, to the sex problems of the school world. The married teacher may be less actively involved in the cross-sex attractions of the classroom; he may show a less vicarious interest in the romantic activities of the students, a greater tolerance toward the "puppy love" stage, and a better understanding of the students' sex problems. Although not all married women are equipped to deal with the prime preoccupations of some secondary schoolboys, one does shudder to think of the young, unmarried girl fresh from her college degree having to teach them as "whole children."

4. The mental hygiene of the teacher has received considerable stress in the mental hygiene literature of recent years, with reference primarily to the importance of the teacher's mental adjustment as a factor in determining the mental health of the pupil.[19] Two phases of these discussions will be summarized briefly.

First, frequent reference is made to the large number of teachers who are not in good mental health and who give ample evidence of the fact in their relations with their students. To account for this, some of the motives are mentioned which lead people to enter the teaching profession, such as an escape (for women) from unpleasant home conditions, a refuge from the rigors of other occupations, the desire to dominate situations (made possible by working with younger persons), or a form of sublimation of a desire for children; but due recognition is given to the repressive pressures which society tends to exert upon the teacher. He is expected all too often to be a repressed person, a paragon of virtues, by a community that is seeking freedom from its own unconscious guilt. Nothing is said about the role of nervous fatigue in a profession in which the emphasis is upon the output of nervous energy but where the length of the working day is still measured in terms of ordinary manual labor.

Second, there is the role of the teacher in creating the mental attitudes of the students. Teachers dominate the child's work requirements, and thus may become a major factor in determining whether the child develops ennui over set tasks, boredom with meaningless content, intellectual satiety, and a distaste for thinking, or vitalizing drives exactly opposite in character. It is sig-

[19] Fritz Redl and William Wattenberg, *Mental Hygiene in Teaching*, Harcourt, Brace and Company, New York, 1951.

nificant to note how frequently students with fine records of achievement, both in school and afterward, attribute their records to the motivation given by an outstanding teacher.

Perhaps more pervasive and important are the subtle and intangible mental hygiene characteristics of the teacher which affect the atmosphere of the school. These include his morale, feelings of anxiety, worries, demeanor, voice, poise, tension, feelings of security, and relations with other teachers. Mental hygiene may be as airborne as are certain communicable diseases. Certainly the atmosphere of the home has been much emphasized in psychiatric literature; it seems equally important as an attribute of the school.

Mental hygiene is related to morale, and morale is related to adequacy of compensation for one's job and security in one's future. Teachers' salaries have been a popular subject of comment recently and much effort has been put into raising them. In spite of this, over a quarter of all teachers find it necessary to take extra jobs during the summer, and over 20 percent of them take extra jobs during the school year.[20] Teaching children is a nervous-energy-draining job, if the work is done with dedication. To add much other work to teaching and the preparation and "homework" can be physically and mentally exhausting. Efforts to improve the financial security of teachers might play a part in improving the mental-hygiene atmosphere of schools and the quality of teaching.

5. The status of the family from which teachers came has some bearing on teacher-pupil relationships and the education of the young. City schools, especially, have large populations of youngsters whose parents are unskilled laborers. Yet only 6.5 percent of the teachers in American public schools came from homes in which the father was an unskilled worker.[21] Enough has already been said about social class and occupational cultures to make clear that, in many respects, they represent different worlds of thought and behavior. In the United States, it is an educational goal to provide every child with the means to raise his own status. This cannot be done, however, by merely trying to force middle-class attitudes on lower-class children, or by degrading their own culture. It must be based, first, on true understanding of the content of that culture and on a subsequent building upon that foundation. That this has been too little understood is evidenced by the fact that until quite recently reading books in the lowest grades were written by middle-class people in the language of middle-class children. "A little white house with a picket fence," "Daddy sitting by the fireplace," and

20 "American Public School Teachers, 1960–61," *op. cit.*, p. 51.
21 *Ibid.*, p. 49.

"a cow in a field of daisies," are all images that connote absolutely nothing to many children. Some, indeed, when presented with a cake of soap do not know what it is and have to be shown how to use it. There are middle-class teachers who are baffled, or disgusted, by this sort of thing. Along with the growing heterogeneity of our schools and the attempt to raise levels of living, perhaps more stress should be put upon the education of teachers and prospective teachers in the realities and meanings of cultural differences.

CULTURAL DIFFERENCES BETWEEN HOME AND SCHOOL

Closely related to the above comments is the fact that cultural differences, particularly of an ideological nature, inevitably develop between the school and the family world. Many of these are minor in character or degree of difference, but some become so serious as to create major difficulties in either parent-child or school-child relationships, or both. Selected aspects of these differences will be considered briefly.

1. The school, as the formal and official instrumentality of middle-class American culture, runs counter to the culture of various other social groups. The differences that exist may cover the range of language, mores, family life, political traditions, conceptions of the universe, philosophy of man's role, and many other social values. In school, through formal instruction and informal contacts, the children learn to live in a world which is alien to their parents. Teachers in the school at times reflect the attitude that whatever is foreign is inferior. Frequently they put pressure upon the children to turn away from everything resembling the culture of the parents. Influenced by this attitude, the children begin to despise the customs and culture of their forebears. The school thus stimulates the child to reject his parents and their culture.

How fundamental and far-reaching these ideological differences may be is suggested in a contrast pointed out by Mangione.[22] The Sicilians, he says, lay everything on the doorstep of destiny. *E U Destino*—this single phrase explains everything. For centuries this has been the comforting philosophy of the Sicilians. Priests talked about it. Teachers emphasized it. But in America, children come home from school with the philosophy that every man is the archi-

[22] Jerre Mangione, *Mount Allegro*, Houghton Mifflin Company, Boston, 1942, p. 83.

tect of his own fortune, that anyone who works hard and has plenty of ambition can achieve anything he wants. When children talk about this at home, their parents only complain that the teachers teach them fairy tales.

2. The school as a nonpartisan, nonsectarian culture-transmitting agency naturally runs counter to the ideological patterns of many families. Some of these conflicts are open and avowed, but others arise by way of implication. In groups where religious affiliation is taken so seriously as to dominate the life and thought of the members, the resultant conflicts may be irreconcilable. Obvious illustrations include religious cults that forbid children to participate in patriotic exercises at school, such as flag-raising ceremonies; the observance of holidays other than those on the public-school calendar; and interpretations of and conclusions about life problems, imposed by a religious body and at variance with those developed in the school's regular courses of instruction. Most often, however, the differences which arise between the school's nonpartisan and nonsectarian approach and the insistences of specific groups do not take the form of overt conflict, but resolve themselves into a subtle game of cultural pressures and diplomatic avoidances and resistances, as in the case of the Roman Catholic opposition to the public-school program for sex instruction. The development of church schools, like parochial and other denominational schools, is an obvious device of the groups which seek to perpetuate their own culture in contrast to that of the public school.

3. There are social-class pressures which differ from those of the public school. As pointed out, the public school tends everywhere to be a middle-class institution, directed by middle-class officials and administrators, taught by middle-class teachers, and maintaining middle-class norms of behavior. Lower-class children tend not to fit in, and another of the reasons why they present behavior problems at times is the antagonisms to the school culture which are aroused in them by their parents. Many lower-class homes are in conflict with the schools, and the conflict is usually resolved by having the children withdraw from school as early as possible. Similarly, the cultural pressures of upper-class homes differ from those of the public school, but the conflict here is resolved in many cases by transferring the child to an upper-class private school. Such schools serve several purposes: they add geographic to social distance, they make possible the segregation of relatively homogeneous cultural groups, and they facilitate the transmission of the class culture. Upper-class children who continue in public school, on the other hand, often become the victims of the cultural conflict to which reference has been made.

4. One of the chief points of culture conflict between many homes and schools involves the patterns of child training. Obviously, this is basic to the parents' as well as the teachers' relations with the child. In many parts of the world, there are now and have been no problems in this connection, since both home and school agree on aims and methodology. But in contemporary America, the situation in home and school is in flux. In terms of the home, widely differing emphases prevail. In some homes, the fundamental purpose of child rearing is to train the child to conform; in others, it is to rear him so as to stimulate his development. Perhaps another way of bringing out the contrast is to ask if the child is parent-dominated, one on whom the parent imposes patterns of behavior; or whether the family is a democratic one in which the children have some leeway in developing their own patterns in response to their specific needs. The difference is basic, coloring many of the minutiae of family life.

There are similar differences in regard to the role of the school. Should the school impose upon the child a set of behavior patterns and a curriculum, so as to implement readily his induction into the prevailing culture, or should the child be encouraged to utilize the school to work out his own answers to the problems confronting him? This, in rather general terms, may be thought of as the contrast between conventional and progressive methods in education.

The development of many children is complicated by the fact that the systems of childrearing utilized at home and in school differ materially. Children from democratic homes go to conventional schools; the products of autocratic homes are sent to progressive schools. All kinds of combinations are possible, and the following case illustrates one of them:

Blankville is an upper-class residential community. Homes average in cost in normal times from $25,000 to $50,000. Parents are considerably above the average in intellectual interests and in their demand for the best for their children. In most homes, the emphasis is upon the strict training of children to accept the behavior patterns of their upper-class status, i.e., to conform to the prevailing code. On the other hand, the intellectual interest of the community expressed itself in a demand for a public school system "second to none." In pursuance of this interest, noted progressive educators were invited to Blankville to set up "an up-to-date" school system, and this was done for the first eight grades. The high school span was not included, and retained its traditional emphases. The result of all this, from the standpoint of the children of Blankville, has been somewhat as follows. From a home in which the training is directed toward conformity the child moves to a school system in which the emphasis for eight years is upon a progressive stimulation of the child's self-development, necessitating that he shuttle back and forth each day from one world to another. Then, having been trained in school by progressive methods for eight years, the child now proceeds to the high school in which the old conventional emphases are reasserted.

5. A final cultural conflict between school and home arises from their contrasting interpretations of life and the universe. The significant fact here is that much of our thinking and many of our modes of interpretation have been revolutionized within the span of a generation or two. Utilizing the Comtean terminology, the shift has been from a theological to a scientific interpretation of life. The result of this sudden and relatively complete shift has been that large numbers of parents and elder kinsfolk still think in theological terms, whereas the children have acquired a scientific approach and mode of interpretation. Here is a significant cultural conflict coinciding with the difference between generations. Its seriousness varies from one part of the country to another, but seems to be more marked in the South and parts of the West. In some cases, when families send their children to the universities, often at considerable financial sacrifice, only to find them returning with this "new nonsense," the problem becomes particularly keen. At times, parents or children or both personalize the issue, and then the deeper loyalties of family life become involved.

6. Whatever one's personal loyalties to the cause of education, the fact remains that, in our contemporary society, the school is often the creator of cultural conflicts for the child. At a very tender age, a child is taken away from his home to enter this specialized institution, which develops its own dual culture: that of the classroom and that of a more purely social world. Development of conflict between the schematized teaching of the school and the pervasive influences of the home is but the more obvious aspect of a much larger conflict situation. Some of this larger culture conflict is due to the cultural diversity of our population, some of it to the rapidity with which our culture undergoes change and the relative place of successive generations in that change. It is much aggravated when the school undertakes, as some educators insist that it shall do, to educate for cultural discontinuities rather than for cultural continuity.

The problems involved are not simple. Parents are voters and taxpayers, they have sired the children and are maintaining them. They have at least the prestige of maturity and the passing rights of trusteeship. Educators are trained to perform a specialized function in society, they are supposed to have superior knowledge and insight, and they are expected to prepare children for living in what today is a rapidly changing world, confident of its ability to remake itself in the interests of a better and more abundant life. Educators, in other words, have their responsibilities. Children are young. They owe allegiance to their parents, but they need preparation for life. They too have their needs and their rights. The problem of adjusting these conflicting interests becomes particularly keen and may reach pathological forms when totalitarian nations, backed by the resources of the state, take their children in hand to mold them into specific types of personalities, to the end that they may become an interchangeable cog or part in a vast human machine which is subject to the party in power. Such processes—and dangers, it should be added—are not confined to fascist cultures alone.

CURRENT FOCUSES IN SCHOOL SITUATION PROBLEMS

In any literature, popular or scientific, which concerns the schools, two special problems are apt to receive attention at the present time. They are high school marriage and school dropouts. Just at the time when we are considering it essential that children have all the education of which they are capable, and when financial success in life is related to years of schooling, students who marry and those who drop out before graduation are increasing in numbers. Some of the reasons and results should be given some consideration here.

High School Marriage

Until after World War II, married undergraduate students on a college campus were a rarity. Today married students and sometimes their children, are much in evidence. For a time, they became the subject of extensive research, but the reseach scene has now shifted to their juniors. The increased incidence of high school marriage has been causing concern to students of the family—and in exploring this situation some important facts have been uncovered.

1. The most popular age of first marriage for females in the United States is now 18 years, and the U.S. Bureau of Vital Statistics reports that almost one third of those who marry in their teens are between 14 and 17 years of age. The Population Reference Bureau revealed that in 1961 almost 40 percent of the brides in our country were teen-agers. During the same year the per-

centages of high school students married and with spouses present were as follows: 0.8 percent of those 14 and 15 years of age; 0.7 percent of those 16 and 17; and 5.2 percent of those 18 and 19. These percentages do not include married students who have already separated, deserted, or divorced. Although there are statistics pointing out that the rate of teenage marriage has not risen a great deal in the past few years, the rate of such marriage is misleading in terms of the measurement of the problem. According to Dr. Lee Burchinal, even if the rate of 1960 does not rise at all, there will be 50 percent more of these marriages in 1965, simply because of the increasing number of young people in our population.[23]

2. The reasons given for the popularity of high school marriage are numerous, and they come from observation of the society, of the students, from statements of high school administrators, and from the young married people themselves. There are several areas of agreement, and these seem deserving of some comment.[24]

A great deal of emphasis is placed on the romantic atmosphere of our country, where love is considered as the end to all problems and the beginning of perpetual individual happiness. Free and open discussions of the value of sex expression and gratification are also a growing part of our culture. These discussions are heard by small children at home. Mass media constantly reinforce the idea of making oneself attractive to the opposite sex and the triumph of catching a member of it for one's own. Since this is a prevailing ideology, parents are blamed for being lax in care, discipline, and supervision of their young children. In fact, some of them are accused of being so smitten themselves with the status that dating, engagement, and marriage bring that they are pushing younger and younger children into dating. The excitement with which certain mothers buy padded bras for their 11-year-old daughters has been commented upon by more than one observer of this situation. Also, teenage girls have reported on how disappointing it is to their parents if they do not have dates when their friends do. Another reason given is adolescents' desire for adult status and privileges. This is very closely related to their understanding of what adult privileges are. For reasons given above,

[23] Lee G. Burchinal, *The Early Marriage Problem in Public Schools*, Conference on Dropouts and Early Marriages in Public Schools, sponsored by West Texas School Study Council, Tech Station, Lubbok, Texas, and Phi Delta Kappa International, Bloomington, Indiana, May 1, 1963.

[24] See Lee G. Burchinal, *Ibid.;* Lee G. Burchinal, "Can Teen-agers Make a Go of Marriage?" *National Parent-Teacher*, February, 1961, pp. 4–7; Judson F. Landis, "Attitudes and Policies Concerning Marriages Among High School Students," *Marriage and Family Living*, May, 1956, pp. 128–136.

adolescents have come to see adult privileges as romance, sex, and freedom to do as one pleases.

This leads directly to another reason given for very youthful marriage—a completely unrealistic idea of what marriage involves. It seems impossible that children can live in a family and not know of all the responsibilities that it entails. Yet, as has been explained before, there are many youngsters who have little family life, who are sheltered from the unromantic facts of it, and who are confined largely to peer-group relationships for many years of their lives. Also, there are children who state that they fled into matrimony from a miserable home life. The faith that theirs will turn out happily is undaunted by past experience in the face of what romance is said to do for people. Still another reason given for the encouragement of early marriage is the continued affluence of our society and the attitudes it has bred in the young people who have been fortunate enough to live under its spell. "Money grows on trees," "The government will take care of us," "No, I don't have a job, but our parents have enough to get us started." All of these are attitudes seen clearly in the words of actual teen-agers contemplating matrimony. In many cases, parents have subsidized the marriage, sometimes ensuring its success, and at other times prolonging the immaturity of the couple and causing severe in-law tensions. In other cases, though, it comes as a sudden, shattering shock that the affluent society offers the greatest rewards to those who are prepared by their education to take an important part in its work. Finally, "personality problems" is given as a reason for early marriage. These cover a wide range of traits: lack of security and self-esteem, undermaturity, overmaturity, and the like.

3. The results of high school marriage have also been probed. Although there are those that grow into stable marriages, many do not—and the picture of these is dreary.

The Bureau of the Census reports that marriages for girls under 18 are 3 times as likely to end in divorce as for girls in their 20s. The actual rates are 12.6 and 4.8 respectively. One spot study showed the rate to be twice as high for those under 20 as for those 20 to 25 and 3 times that of couples married at 30 or over.[25] Divorce rates, however, do not reveal the whole story of tensions and unhappiness in marriage. Inselberg compared two groups of young people. In one (the experimental group), at least one of the spouses had married while in high school and before the age of 19. The other (the control group) was composed of those who married between the ages of 21 and 26 years of age. When they

[25] Lee G. Burchinal, "Can Teenagers Make a Go of Marriage?" *op. cit.*, p. 5.

were asked if they would still marry at the age they did, 40 percent of the experimental-group wives replied in the negative, compared to 6 percent of the control group wives. For the husbands, the percentages were 38 and 12, respectively.[26]

Beneath this statistical canopy of unhappiness lie specific reasons for the lack of success. A common problem is financial insufficiency related to low-educational achievement and occupational limitations. Inselberg found 10 percent unemployment among the experimental group husbands and 2 percent among the control group ones. The average annual incomes were $3776 and $6298. Because of financial hardship most of the teen-agers had to seek help from parents, usually in the form of living with them. Sixty-five percent of them did so. Aside from this one-fifth of the couples received other financial aid from parents. Half of the teenage group also had problems with the in-laws. In the words of the teen-agers, they complained, interfered, and discriminated against the spouse of their own child. Seven percent of the young wives in this situation said that they did not get enough emotional support from their husbands, who sided with their parents. Many of the girls admitted feeling jealous because their husbands had not settled down and ran around too much.[27] The United States Children's Bureau reports that over 250,000 teenage wives, with and without children, have had to find some kind of gainful employment in order to help support the marriage.

The coming of children increases financial and other problems—and children come soon to most of these couples. The rate of premarital pregnancy is high among couples both of whom are high school students. Estimates vary and run as high as 80 percent. Premarital pregnancy is not the cause of young marriage, but it is a precipitating factor, and a complicating factor after marriage. Christensen has shown a positive relationship between age of marriage and first birth, as well as between divorce and early arrival of children.[28]

A very frequent result of high school marriage is dropping out of school. An Iowa State survey shows that 80 percent of the girls drop out and only 8 percent re-enter. For the boys the figures are 43 and 9 percent.[29]

From the foregoing, one gets a picture of immature teen-agers, looking for a mirage that is a societal fancy—sometimes being

[26] Rachel M. Inselberg, "Marital Problems and Satisfactions in High School Marriages," *Marriage and Family Living,* February, 1962, p. 77.

[27] *Ibid.*, pp. 75–76.

[28] Harold T. Christensen, "Child Spacing Analysis Via Record Linkage," *Marriage and Family Living*, August, 1963, pp. 274–276.

[29] Lee G. Burchinall, "Can Teenagers Make a Go of Marriage?" *op. cit.*

pushed into it by adults, for their own reasons—but with the teen-agers rather quickly discovering that what they have seen has no reality. Stable family life involves maturity, employment, money, children who are well cared for, an adequate physical setup, and many other humdrum responsibilities. Disillusion sets in quickly.

Students of the family seem to be in agreement that high school students who marry are, in the majority, the very ones who should not marry. They are less mature than the other students, have more personality maladjustment, less adequate homes, a poorer educational background, are less employable and less adequate as husbands, wives, and parents. This is of concern not only because of the problems encountered by the teen-age parents, but also because of the needs of the children born to such marriages.

4. Although the extent of high school marriage has been largely blamed upon the society and parents, the school also has a role to play in this situation. Obviously, it is within the atmosphere of the school that such marriages are born.

If one of the reasons for early marriage is an unrealistic attitude toward its meaning, this is surely one area of education that the schools could tackle. The fact that some parents have opposed sex education as a part of the school curriculum has not prevented the spread of such courses. Some parents will oppose family-life education also, but sex education without family-life education may, in some cases, be as harmful as helpful. The survivability of that rugged institution, the family, has lain in the responsibilities it has assumed for its society and not in the liberty it offers for individuals. Surely, the functions of the family could be taught to high school students on the scale that such courses are taught in colleges and universities. Mrs. Elizabeth Force, formerly of Toms River, New Jersey, instituted one of the first such courses in high school with results that were widely acclaimed. One of the assignments for the students was to make a scrapbook of pictures of family life from magazines. There were then discussions of how much these romanticized pictures actually represented what went on within their own homes. Such excellent and direct teaching might persuade many immature young people that they should wait a while before tackling problems that only the mature can solve or live with happily.

An interesting study would be to correlate high school marriage with size of family. Although it would probably be found that some young people marry to escape from a houseful of siblings, the authors discovered that the age of marriage was higher for children of 100 large families than it was for the general population. Those who had grown up in large families had known what it was to be mother substitutes, unpaid housekeepers, diaper-changers and nose-blowers. They knew about family budgets and straitened circumstances. They were willing to wait for marriage until they felt they could manage a family. It is not entirely unthinkable that more schools might offer realistic courses on the family to parents themselves. It has been the author's experience that, because such students are parents, many of them quickly see the value of certain points of view—which they simply had not thought of—and are prompt to try to apply these ideas in their homes.

The school has yet another role to play. If high school marriages continue to grow in numbers, the issue of the education of these youngsters must be faced. If we permit them to marry, should they not, when possible, be permitted to continue to prepare themselves for the future? Laws preventing the expulsion of married students would not be enough, for many of them are only too eager to leave school. Encouragement and special help to remain in school are needed, but so far, the attitude in many schools is not to encourage. Rather, there is a sense of relief at losing the problem. Even when such young persons remain in school they are often penalized by not being permitted extracurricular activities and other social involvement. Though parents may complain that they do not want their single young people mingling with married young people, more than one school administrator has pointed out that single students who grow accustomed to seeing the real problems of the married students may have sober second thoughts about early matrimony.

School Dropouts

When the economy of the United States was largely agricultural the vast majority of its people had few years of formal education, yet managed to support themselves and their families. In 1800, the average person had only 82 days of schooling throughout life. In an industrial economy that is becoming more and more automated, however, eight or nine years of schooling is seldom sufficient to secure employment which affords what we consider a comfortable living. It is because of this situation and its effect upon individuals, their families, and the society that interest and concern has been centered recently on the matter of school dropouts.

1. Since a problem seldom comes to public notice until it is a large one, the extent of the dropout problem is significant. It is comforting to note that the dropout rate is decreasing. Whereas it was 50 percent a decade or so ago, it dropped to 40 percent in 1959

and is expected to drop to 30 percent in 1970. Again, however, rates are misleading, while numbers give a more accurate picture. In 1959, more than 900,000 students left high school before graduation. One-third of these dropped out before they reached high school. The number is expected to rise to 1,300,000 in 1965. Between 1960 and 1970, it is estimated that there will be 7,500,000 dropouts, 2,500,000 of whom will never reach high school.[30] In view of the general results of quitting school before graduation—results which will be discussed later—this is an alarmingly high number. In 1960, dropout rates were highest for American Indians—48 percent. For Negro Americans it was 44 percent; for native whites, 25 percent; and for those of Japanese and Chinese heritage, 10 percent.[31]

2. To the question of what causes students to drop out, many answers have been given. A summary of research on the subject lists the following reasons: low scores on intelligence test, reading problems, inadequate school curricula, nonparticipation in extracurricular activities, transfer from school to school, personality factors, and home-related factors. The last include a need for money, poor health of student or family member, marriage, and parental attitude toward school.[32]

Although children may be found who have dropped out for any of these reasons, current researchers believe that there is a dropout profile that can be drawn to portray the bulk of them. They come, largely, from neighborhoods and families that have no great interest in education, do not have good work habits, and do not inspire good work habits in their children. Generally, the parents have had little schooling and may have been dropouts themselves. They are hard-pressed financially and want their children to go to work as soon as possible. Because of lack of education and of sporadic employment away from home many such parents are unable to teach their children the most fundamental things—even speech—a skill that the average child takes in at home, as if by osmosis before he goes to school. Thus, the potential dropout has problems in learning to read which, if not corrected early, have a decidedly negative result on his academic work. He is conspicuous for being retarded beyond his age group, and for many failures in subjects. As he grows older, frustration, fear of more failure, lack

30 Eli E. Cohen, *How School People Can Help the Dropout,* National Committee on Employment of Youth of the National Child Labor Committee, New York, 1960, p. 1.

31 *Family Life,* February, 1965, p. 5.

32 James W. Tunnell, *What Research Says About the School Dropout Problem,* West Texas School Study Council, Lubbok, Texas, February, 1963, pp. 4–9.

of interest and just plain boredom with things which he does not understand make him slip back further. His attendance record is one of lateness, absences, and moves from one school to another. A teacher in a large school in New York described such a student as being in the classroom in body only, completely apathetic in mind. If the teacher could manage to stir up an argument in which that student showed some interest, the teacher considered himself successful.

The dropout is seldom involved in the extracurricular activities that are so meaningful to school children. One reason is that such activities usually require some outlay of money by parents. The parents are unable or uninterested. Also, most activities require some skills, many of which the potential dropout does not have. Then, too, the child who is a failure and is either apathetic or hostile is not the child who is welcomed into most school crowds and activities. The picture is one of family failure, and failure of the child scholastically, personally, and socially. He feels he cannot cope with school, and in many cases thinks it is of no use anyway, since he will be discriminated against in employment even if he does graduate.[33] In such a situation, the desire is to get out of school as soon as possible and to do something that seems to be more meaningful. For some dropouts, prime interests are making some money and having a car—symbols of status that permit freedom of action. Dr. Havighurst, when controlling a group of students and dropouts for socioeconomic level, found that 11 percent of the students and 26 percent of the dropouts owned cars.[34]

3. When young people leave school they have subsequent problems that are more grave than for the average graduate. Their rate of employment is lower. In 1961, the percentage of graduates of that year who were unemployed was 18. For the dropouts who would have graduated that year, it was 27. Types of employment were also different. Over 80 percent of the boy dropouts were operators and kindred workers, service workers, laborers, and farm laborers and foremen. Their hours of work are longer, and their chances of employment are best in the kinds of occupations that are expanding least rapidly.[35] Throughout life, the income of the dropout is apt to be less than for the high school graduate. In 1961, mean income for those aged 25 to 64 who had less than eight years of school was $3483; for those with eight years, $4750; and

[33] For the dropout profile see Eli E. Cohen, *op. cit.*, pp. 2–4, and Robert J. Havighurst, et al., *op. cit.*, pp. 59–64.

[34] *Ibid.*, p. 61.

[35] *Project: School Dropouts*, National Education Association, Washington, D.C., April, 1963, p. 5.

for those who graduated, it was $6102.[36] In addition, their social, cultural, and psychological experience is as limited as their financial status and prevents them from achieving the satisfactions enjoyed by others in our society.

At least two results of the dropout situation are threats to the society as well as to the individuals concerned. One is delinquent and criminal behavior. A member of a Board of Education of a large city reported that truants and dropouts accounted for 90 percent of the juvenile crime in that area. Such delinquent acts as are being committed on the streets are, in part, attempts to get money, to forget reality, to get status, and to get revenge. A second concern of the society lies in the vicious circle of the same kinds of families being reproduced in the subsequent generations. With the numbers of dropouts growing now, there could be a snowballing of such family and community situations in the future.

It should be stressed here that the above profile and consequences do not apply to all students who drop out of school. They come from all economic strata and drop out for many reasons, some of which are practical or unescapable. Many dropouts pick up their education at a later date, and some succeed in life without further schooling. The description given here is that of the hard-core problem which exists and which is a threat for the future.

4. There are, presently, many kinds of attempts to combat the dropout problem. President Lyndon B. Johnson's Poverty Program is obviously one such attempt, although its aims are much broader than for dropouts alone. Some schools are instituting cooperative work plans within the schools so that those who need money and want to work may combine jobs with schooling. School curricula are being carefully examined. It is felt by some that a fairly uniform educational system that is book-centered and college-oriented leaves no place for the potential dropout and that there should be much more concentration on special programs for him.[37] Carefully planned guides for teachers to follow have been prepared in an attempt to detect symptoms of dropout as early as possible. There has also been a stepping-up of counseling in some schools. For the child who is already well along in failure, the prognosis is not very optimistic. It is of vital importance to prevent children from getting into problems at school that would almost inevitably lead to dropping out. One experiment is to set up schools for culturally disadvantaged children—the younger the better. The idea behind this attempt is

[36] U.S. Bureau of the Census, *Statistical Abstract of the United States: 1963*, *op. cit.*, p. 122.

[37] Roul Tunley, *Kids, Crime and Chaos*, Harper & Row, New York, 1962, p. 121.

that by the time a child comes to first grade and has never seen, heard, or experienced what is taken for granted by the average first grader, it is already too late for him to catch up with others. Finally, there have been suggestions that something like vocational guidance should start as early as the first year of school and continue until the end of high school. In the beginning, such a program would involve opening the eyes of children to realistic possibilities, catching their interest, and detecting where the individual's specific interests and abilities lie. Later, it would more narrowly concern the means to attain a desired end.

SUMMARY

1. A school is a complex of social situations in which children live. In part, it is a workaday world in which they perform; in part, it is a social world in which the life of the intermediate generation centers.

2. The factors which affect this social world and affect the development of the child within it are the structure of the school, the interrelationships within it, and its culture.

3. Teachers constitute a small but important part of the school population. Many facts about teachers, in addition to their professional preparation, are important in this connection, such as their age, sex, marital status, and mental hygiene.

4. Cultural differences between the school and the home are inevitable and often serious. The culture of the school may run counter to that of specific cultural groups; its nonpartisan and nonsectarian role may differ from the ideological patterns of political, religious, and other groups; class cultural pressures may differ from those of the public school; systems of childrearing may show marked contrasts; contrasting interpretations of life and the universe may be accepted by home and school, respectively.

5. The problems of this cultural rift between school and home are difficult, and, in a sense, insoluble. Parents, educators, and children each have their own respective needs and rights and, because of rapidly changing ideologies, they tend to remain apart. The resultant conflicts and differences are imposed upon the child, another link in the chain of social causation which makes doubt and uncertainty such characteristic aspects of the philosophy of contemporary man.

6. Some special problems that have recently become of great public importance are the increasing numbers of high school marriages and of students dropping out of school before graduation.

SUGGESTED READINGS

Burchinal, Lee, *Dropouts and Early Marriage in Public Schools,* West Texas School Study Council, Box 4560, Tech Station, Lubbock, Texas, May 1, 1963. A publication of two speeches by the foremost authority on these subjects.

Bush, Robert N., *The Teacher-Pupil Relationship,* Prentice-Hall, Englewood Cliffs, New Jersey, 1954. A study of the relationship between learning, teacher, and pupil.

Conant, James B., *The American High School Today,* McGraw-Hill Book Company, New York, 1959. An analysis of, and recommendations concerning, the large and comprehensive high school in the United States today.

Conant, James B., *Slums and Suburbs,* McGraw-Hill Book Company, New York, 1961. A comparison of education in two parts of the metropolitan area.

Dahlke, H. Otto, *Values in Culture and Classroom,* Harper & Row, New York, 1958. The first word in the title recommends the book. Though "values" tend to be avoided in science, they are discussed here in a sociological approach to the study of the school.

Farnsworth, Dana L., *Mental Health in College and University,* Harvard University Press, Cambridge, 1957. A psychiatric approach to causes of emotional stress in college students, and to the ways for handling them.

Jacob, Philip E., *Changing Values in College,* Harper & Row, New York, 1958. A political scientist also has the courage to study values, and reports upon the impact of social science education upon the values of college students.

Mead, Margaret, *The School in American Culture.* Harvard University Press, Cambridge, 1951. This book represents a lecture given by Dr. Mead and is concerned with certain cultural differences between teachers and their students.

Odell, William P., and staff, *Philadelphia Public Schools,* The Board of Public Education, Philadelphia, February 1, 1965. A very controversial report of an 18-month study of one large city school system.

Spindler, George D., *Education and Culture,* Holt, Rinehart & Winston, New York, 1963. An anthropologist discusses education in America and cross-culturally.

Thayer, V. T., *Formative Ideas in American Education,* Dodd, Mead & Company, New York, 1965. A history of the ideas behind American education and the changes that created them, from the Colonial period to the present.

Waller, Willard W., *The Sociology of Teaching,* John Wiley & Sons, New York, 1932. Dr. Waller was among the first writers to recognize the educational institution as something more than a place for formalized learning. He describes it as a social situation.

MASS MEDIA AND CHILDREN'S HEROES 18

Only a hundred years ago most children grew up in their families and with their neighbors in relative isolation from the rest of the world. News travelled slowly and a stranger was an exciting rarity. The visit of the book salesman who came through the village once a year has been mentioned in more than one autobiography as an event to be remembered, and to which children looked forward with eagerness. It brought them face to face with a person from another world and the possibility of exploring far-off places through the literature he sold. The yearly carnival, with its strange people and intriguing animals, was something for which children saved hard-earned pennies. It made their small world more expansive and colorful.

It is hardly necessary to describe the change that has come about in the lives of children with the tremendous growth in mass communication of many kinds. Through reading, listening, and looking, modern children can know more about people and things in the farthest places of the world than the colonial child in New England knew about events taking place in another colony in America. Today's children not only *can* know, but they can hardly escape the impact of the information that bombards the public through books, newspapers, movies, radio, and television.

Mass communication has had far more effect than the mere expansion of children's knowledge. It has influenced the direction of their development, their behavior, their relationship with peers and adults, and the interaction with their families. In widening the range of their acquaintance with different personality types and kinds of occupation, it has also had an effect on the kinds of persons they admire, the heroes they worship, and the image of what they would like to be when they grow up.

Interest of students of child development in the mass media is relatively recent. It is growing, however, because of the inescapable fact that the lives of our children are immersed in the effects of mass media. Observations on the results are conflicting; there are few definitive studies; it is too early for long-range results to be seen conclusively. Yet there are some persistent threads of evidence that should not be overlooked. In the 1930 to 1940 decade, moving pictures and their effects on children was a topic of concern. In the 1940's comic books and radio came into their own as a point of focus. The popularity of television, less than 20 years old, has turned attention almost exclusively to this mode of communication. Actually its advent has appeared to decrease, to some extent, both movie-going and comic-reading for children. From 1943 to 1945, more than 1 billion comic books were published. This compared with 428 million others, including textbooks.[1] In 1960, a survey made by the Stanford University Institute for Communication Research showed that comic-book reading had been cut by more than one half.[2] In reviewing the literature, it is interesting to note that the observed effects to children of movies, radio, and comics are now being repeated as concerns television. More has been added, though. Television has dimensions in family life and child behavior that do not apply to the other mass media. This chapter, therefore, will be devoted to (1) influences of television on family and child, with comparative references to other mass media; and (2) children's heroes.

THE RANGE AND NATURE OF TELEVISION

Between 1946 and 1962, the number of families owning television sets grew from approximately 100,000 to 49,000,000, or nine out of every ten families in 1962. This represents more homes than are equipped with telephones, automobiles, bathtubs, or re-

1 Paul Witty, "Reading the Comics—Opportunity or Threat?" *National Parent-Teacher*, January, 1950, p. 14.

2 Charles Sopkin, "What is TV Doing to Our Children?" *This Week Magazine*, April 9, 1961, p. 9.

frigerators. It is estimated that in 1 out of 7 homes there are 2 or more television sets.[3] (There are about 17 million more sets in the United States than there are in all the rest of the world.) In contrast is the situation with moving pictures. Right after World War II, American producers made over 450 moving pictures a year; movie houses in the United States numbered about 22,000; and about 90 million people attended them. By 1960, attendance had been cut by more than half; there were 18,000 movie theaters, including the new drive-ins; and Hollywood produced 150 pictures in that year.[4] The growing popularity of drive-ins illustrates that selection of entertainment serves specific purposes. Whereas TV has drawn young children and adults away from the movies, this has not been so, to the same extent, for teen-agers—for whom the movies serve a social purpose that TV does not. It has been reported that 99 percent of all children, as compared with 87 percent of all adults, watch television daily.[5] A survey for the 1960 White House Conference, by Paul Witty, pointed out that school children in Chicago spent an average of 18½ hours per week watching TV; while the CBS Research Department, in a report covering 27 million children, shows that, between the ages of 4 and 11, children watch TV an average of 31½ hours per week. It is concluded that they spend more time this way than they do in activities with the entire family.[6] That this is not true of some children, does not mean it is not true of any.

It is inherent in the nature of television that it appeals to small children as no other medium can. Children must be taken to the movies and pay for attending; even comic books cost pennies and must be acquired from outside the home. Furthermore, books must be read to the preschool child in order for him to enjoy them. But what a wonderful experience in independence is the TV set. It is right there in the house, it costs nothing to the child, and a toddler learns early to manipulate the dial that sets the whole thing going! To do the same to a radio produces only music and talk; but television turns on a live world of picture and sound, and sometimes color. The preschool child often establishes cues as to when certain of his favorite programs are on the air even before he has learned how to tell time by the clock.[7] This is, indeed, a revolution

[3] Clara T. Appell, "Television Viewing and the Preschool Child; *Marriage and Family Living*, August, 1963, p. 311.

[4] Eric Johnston, "Getting the Most from the Mass Media: How and By Whom?" *Child Study*, Summer, 1960, p. 24.

[5] Paul Tripp, "The Programs That Aren't," *Child Study*, Summer, 1960, p. 31.

[6] Irving Gitlin, "Television and Children—A Look at the Research," *Child Study*, Summer, 1960, p. 33.

[7] Clara T. Appell, *op. cit.*, p. 312.

for children in determining what to do with "leisure time"—and they take advantage of it. It would be interesting to know to what extent television has decreased the incidence of that classic question, "Mother, what shall I do *now*?" One report indicates that most children start watching TV when they are 2 years old, and are "glued to the tube" by the time they start to school.[8]

It is also in the nature of television that it is a large and lucrative business. Those who profit from it are well aware of the interest of children and will do nothing to disenchant this captive audience. Pressures to produce what adults think children should see, rather than what children think they want to see have not proved too successful. Early mornings and late afternoons, when the average mother is busiest, are the hours primarily dedicated to small children by TV producers and advertisers. Whereas most of the advertising in magazines is directed to the adults who read them, much of the advertising televised during the children's hours is directed to children's interests. So effective is some child-centered TV advertising that family crises have developed over the specific choice of a breakfast cereal. Some parents have commented that their youngsters have learned to recite television commercials verbatim before they were old enough to understand the content of the programs. It would be strange, indeed, if these preoccupations and pressures did not have some impact on family life and child behavior.

TELEVISION CONTENT AND CHILD BEHAVIOR

Commercial television is an entertainment medium. Thus most of its content is not intended to be directly educational in nature. This does not mean, however, that no learning is involved in watching the content of television. The same distinction may be made here that was commented upon in an earlier chapter. When a parent stops indoctrinating a child in what he should know, the child does not stop learning. That process goes on unceasingly, as if by osmosis, during every minute of family living. The same may be said of television. It is this, perhaps, that most concerns those who wonder what TV is doing to children, their personalities, and their behavior. If children watch a program on mathematics, they may be quizzed afterward to determine what they have learned about the subject. When they view an entertainment program, it is difficult to discover what has been taken into their minds. There

[8] Charles Sopkin, *op. cit.*, p. 9.

have been studies, observations, and "educated guesses" about this, and a summary of the literature is offered here.

1. The type of TV content that has aroused the most interest is that of a violent nature—probably because of the amount shown. In a Stanford University study 100 hours of TV programs, shown during the times that children watch most frequently, were analyzed. They included murders, attempted murders, suicides, attempted suicides, gun fights, persons shot and stabbed, sluggings, stranglings, people pushed or falling off cliffs, cars running over cliffs, attempts to run over pedestrians, mob scenes, raving psychopaths, robberies, hired killers, a tidal wave, an earthquake, and so on.[9] In addition to this, the growing popularity of old movies on television brings into the home all the types of violence characteristic of the cinema formerly felt to be bad for children.

An important question is whether TV violence is related to juvenile delinquency and crime. Opinions vary. Judge Curtis Bok has stated that it is one of the five major causes. Dr. Spock urges parents to keep their children away from violent shows. What they see gives them the impression that it is widespread and taken for granted in the outside world. Even some people who have considerable vested interest in television have decried violent content as harmful to children. Ed Sullivan, for instance, fears that children imitate what they see and should not be permitted to watch man's inhumanity to man. Arch Johnson of "The Asphalt Jungle," would not permit his two children to see violent shows, including his own; and Bob Keesham (Captain Kangaroo) complains about the "mental garbage" with which children's heads are filled through TV viewing.[10] Children have been known to hurt each other seriously while enacting, in play, something they had seen on TV. A recent newspaper article reported on the suicide of a 66-year-old woman. She had shot herself, but no gun was found. Her two grandsons, age 4 and 5, had seen their grandmother dead on the floor, had taken the gun, wrapped it in a cloth, and hidden it in a cardboard box. Another small boy, when he heard that a relative's husband had died, immediately responded, "Who shot him?" Responses of this kind concern James Bennett, Director of the United States Bureau of Prisons, who notes that an increasing number of youthful crimes are committed by means similar to those the youths have seen on television.

There are others who feel that the horrors in television are not

[9] Sopkin, *op. cit.*, pp. 9–10.

[10] Bob Keesham, with Ed Linn, "We *Can* Have Better TV for Our Children," *Good Housekeeping*, January, 1963, pp. 51, 142–144.

worse than in other mass media, and that fairy tales and classic literature that sin in this direction have been in good repute for many generations. Children must learn of such things, they say; and until they are old enough to absorb the meaning it is not taken in at all. They add that children's imaginations can produce wild fantasies, passing those of any adult. Replies to this train of thought have to do with the difference between "pretend" and reality, and with the nature of television. Television *creates* reality as does no other medium of communication. Much of what is read to children passes over their heads. The radio has no frightening pictures. Cartoons are cartoons, and they do not move.[11] As an example, there is the little girl who sat quietly looking at the pictures in the book while her mother read "The Wizard of Oz," but ran crying from the room when she saw it on television.

Careful students of the effects of TV violence upon children are wary about concluding that all react in similar ways. Violence on TV upsets some children so much that they will not watch. Others, who are not *made* hostile or delinquent by the medium, nevertheless find very florid ways in which to act out the hostility that is already within them. A Senate committee on juvenile delinquents revealed that juvenile delinquents were great consumers of this type of program.[12] Still other children appear to take violence in stride. It makes no impression upon them. There are those who believe that this last reaction also is decidedly unhealthy. If the programs make no impression, they are simply a terrible waste of time, say some. Others go farther. Human beings *should* be moved by seeing violent passions directed against other human beings. Such comments raise the question as to whether there is any relation between television violence and the reports of people who see such things happen in real life, but who look, pass on, give no aid, and do not even call the police.

There are at least enough voices raised against violence on TV that some organized efforts are being made to exert some kind of control over it. Some years ago, public disenchantment over comic books led that industry to a self-imposed code, compliance with which carries a seal of approval on the books.[13] The private nature of television, plus the fact that it has never gone to the extremes indulged in by comic books, makes the problem more subtle and difficult.

[11] Eve Merriam, "We're Teaching Our Children That Violence Is Fun," *Reader's Digest*, February, 1965, pp. 39–45.

[12] Martin L. Hoffman and Lois W. Hoffman, *Child Development Research*, Russell Sage Foundation, New York, 1964, p. 324.

[13] *Ibid.*

2. Much of the content of television having to do with grownups, world events, the future, is said to create anxieties in children who are too young to cope with these subjects on an adult level. The consensus of several studies is that children's reactions vary from mild anxiety to nightmares. Symptoms emerge, such as bed-wetting or wanting to sleep in the parents' room.[14] Again, it is not necessarily the viewing that causes a child to be anxious but the fact that he can see so many programs that excite him. Some of the very parents who are most vocal about the idea that children should not be told things which they are not yet ready to understand are the same ones who give complete control of the TV to their children. Unexplained misconceptions then arise in the children's minds and produce worries that cannot be talked away.

3. In their summary of the effects of the mass media on children, the Hoffmans included references to studies as far back as the 1930's that indicate influences upon attitudes, values and beliefs. Specifically, these influences operated in areas such as war, gambling, capital punishment, minority groups, ethnic groups, and certain occupations. Conclusions are that some of these influences are positive and some negative. The important thing is that children's attitudes, values. and beliefs can be formed or changed, through television and other mass media. Stereotypes of people and groups can be set up in their minds which may have little to do with reality.[15]

4. It is generally agreed that children who grow up with television have about a one-year advantage in vocabulary when they enter school. The advantage, however, does not appear to be maintained.[16] Youngsters pick up words from TV that they would not ordinarily hear around the house, and learn the meanings by their usage—in much the same way children learn a lot of their basic vocabulary. This may give them a head start. TV language, however, is not the language of literature. It lacks the richness and the extensiveness of vocabulary. Thus, by sixth grade, the head start is lost. Furthermore, some children who become TV addicts early, remain addicts for many years. This tends to reduce their reading of good books and, in the long run, reduces rather than increases their vocabulary.

5. A positive side of television content is acknowledged by most people who have had any experience in watching its effects upon children. Never before in the history of man have children had an

14 Eve Merriam, *op. cit.*, p. 43.
15 Hoffman and Hoffman, *op. cit.*, pp. 340–343.
16 Ibid., p. 331.

opportunity to learn so much about so many things right in their own homes. The President is to them a very real living person, and they hear his ideas in his own words. They see important events as they are happening, such as the astronauts in orbit. They meet prominent people from all over the world, and are introduced to first-rate drama, science, travel, sports, music, dancing, arts and crafts, hobbies, nature study and the like.[17] Television makes it possible to introduce a great variety of constructive educational experiences to children at a very early age, when their attention span is too short to make this introduction practical in any other way.[18] Learning by television is also more effortless than many other modes of learning and is well adapted to the young child who may receive many short exposures to it.

6. Finally, the many kinds of television content are not viewed equally by all children. They have a certain selectivity. The smallest child is apt to be selective from among the programs devised especially for him, but rather indiscriminate otherwise—although, in general, the more exciting programs are preferred. As he grows older, the selection changes, and frequently viewing is reduced. By the time of adolescence, social activities with the crowd cut far into television time for the average teen-ager. Children with high intelligence levels are particularly apt to get bored with television, to select programs carefully and to get "entertainment" out of reading and schoolwork. Those with lower intelligence are more apt to continue being "glued" and to neglect the reading and homework. It has already been stated that delinquency-prone, or delinquent children, pursue the violent program avidly. A very significant study, that has yet to be made, would be the television selections of the culturally disadvantaged child—the one who has little else to do except to watch TV, who has little stimulation of any kind from parents, and as little control and supervision from them.

TV AND CHILD HEALTH

Among some children who are extremists about viewing television, consequences to health have been detected. In a study begun at Fairchild Air Force Base, two doctors identified what they called "the tired-child syndrome." Youngsters from 3 to 12 suffered nervousness, fatigue, headaches, loss of sleep, stomachaches and sometimes vomiting. They were watching TV from 3 to 6 hours

[17] Josette Frank, *Children and TV*, Public Affairs Pamphlet, no. 323, p. 10.
[18] Clara T. Appell, *op. cit.*, p. 316.

weekdays and from 6 to 10 hours over weekends. When they were denied TV privileges, the symptoms vanished in a few weeks. In cases where the rules were relaxed, the symptoms reappeared.[19] Eye experts warn that special care should be taken with TV-viewing, as with reading. Proper conditions are important. Improper conditions can cause eye problems. One study points out that although most children do not go to bed much later than during the pre-TV era, there are some who do, with serious loss of sleep.[20] The most common complaint against television, in respect to children's health, is that it attracts children away from outdoor exercise and other types of recreation that every growing child needs.

TELEVISION AND FAMILY INTERACTION

An Englishwoman once remarked that American family life much resembled the lives of a group of monks residing in their separate cells and joining together at times for certain purposes. Since each room in a house is heated equally (which is not the case in many homes in England), each person can repair to his room, with his own radio, television, or book. He can do as he pleases, without being interrupted and having to do what others wish. There is some food for thought in this remark, and one might look back to the days of the colonial family when all members *had* to remain together until bedtime, in the room where the fire was burning. While there, they had no mechanical diversions that kept conversation at a minimum. They talked together, made plans, played games, did chores, read aloud, and gave lessons to the children.

In contrast, here is a part of the history of one modern American family. Because all members were busy at different pursuits during the day, most of their interaction took place at the dining room table. For approximately an hour and a half every day, they were in intensive face-to-face conversation. When the dishes were done, they scattered.

The mother liked to sew while listening to the radio. The father preferred to read, in quiet. Thus, he went to bed where he could read in comfort. The two young teen-age girls went to their room, where they had their own radio. They liked to turn it on while doing their homework, but did not enjoy the same programs their mother did. Thus were their evenings spent until the advent of television. A large TV set was put into the living room and a change was made

19 "Tired-Child Syndrome," *Reader's Digest*, March, 1965, pp. 31–32.
20 Josette Frank, *op. cit.*, pp. 4–5.

in the family habits. While the set was still a novelty, dinner had to be planned at a certain time, and hurried, so that everyone could get back to the favorite programs. Little conversation was tolerated, and that little chiefly concerned what they were seeing on TV. Mother did not do as much sewing; Father stopped his reading; and the children's homework suffered. After a time, arguments began to occur over which of several programs the family should watch. The children usually won out in the selection. This bored the father, who found that he really did miss his reading. So, he resumed his former practice of retiring to his bedroom after dinner Even later in the history, the mother decided that there was no reason to continue the wrangling over program selection. She bought a small television set and put it in the girls' room. She learned to get on with her sewing while viewing, and the girls learned to do homework in the same way. The family interaction was thus back to "normal."

Television, it is sometimes said, brings the family together. The "togetherness," however, is usually of a peculiar nature. It is a spectator type of interaction rather than participating. Furthermore there is evidence, from Robert Blood, that family quarreling arises around television use and regulations.[21] He also found, in his sample, that two-set owners used them exclusively in bedrooms.[22] Clara Appell reports that some parents and children do play games together while the set is on. But in other cases, it replaces a bedtime story or prebed play period. Some parents admit that television conflicts with requests and interruptions from children, and also that it is used as a special reward or punishment.[23]

Family conversation is a two-way street. On one side, someone talks, on the other someone has to listen. This was well understood under the conditions described as they existed in colonial families. People took turns talking and listening and often came to family agreements during this process. Though parents were said to be autocratic, there was the possibility that both they and the children could become familiar with each other's points of view. It is a short step from being reared in this way to becoming a democratic adult who can listen to several sides of one issue without irritation. The town-meeting type of government in those days is an illustration of that. People with opposing viewpoints discussed them, and finally came to terms on programs that seemed best for all. There is some-

[21] Robert O. Blood, Jr., "Social Class and Family Control of Television Viewing," *Merrill-Palmer Quarterly of Behavior and Development*, vol. VII, no. 3, 1961, pp. 205–222.

[22] *Ibid.*, p. 212.

[23] Clara Appell, *op. cit.*, p. 315.

thing in the nature of radio and television that tends to reduce tolerance for hearing what one does not want to hear. One has only to turn a knob. How many times does one hear a Republican say about a Democratic candidate (or vice versa), "I just can't stand to listen to that line," and off goes the sound. This sort of habit can spread into other areas of life. Within the writer's lifetime, the increased noisiness of audiences at movies, plays, and concerts seems apparent. When they get bored or annoyed with what they are hearing, they will not listen. This can spread into family life, too—the tuning out of reception when the words do not please.

Television is also used sometimes as a mother substitute, or as an unpaid baby-sitter. There are accounts of infants in cribs who are lulled to sleep by the set which is put close to them and turned on softly. Much more frequent are reports of mothers who are happy to have the toddlers watch TV all day just as long as they keep quiet and out of her way. In one family with five preschool children, the TV set was the most important piece of furniture in the house. Most other furniture was partly broken and not repaired, but if a TV tube blew, it was promptly repaired.

Television, it seems, has introduced new anxieties, guilts, and responsibilities into the lives of some parents. "The prerogative of a parent to exclude unwelcome educational influences is not easily exercised in the home today," writes Selma Fraiberg.[24] What to watch, when to watch, how long to watch are all questions of concern. Some parents who feel that their children should not see television at all are torn about denying it to themselves. Some who find it such a convenient device for disciplining feel guilty, nevertheless, about using it in this capacity. Still others make firm rules, to the best of their ability, and are uncertain as to the wisdom of them. Though there are parents who say that good management alone is needed to put television into its proper perspective in family life, there are also the parents who refer to TV as "the Monster Box."

Many of the criticisms formerly directed toward the movies are now being applied to television. One of them has to do with the portrayal of adult interaction that children see repeatedly early in life. They are familiar with domestic quarrels, with infidelity, with the father who is a stooge and a joke to his wife and children, and all manner of other such situations. There has been little attempt to assess the influence of this upon children in their attitudes and their family relationship. Another theme has been given more atten-

[24] Selma Fraiberg, "The Mass Media: New Schoolhouse for Children," *Child Study*, Summer, 1960, p. 5.

tion, that of romantic love which conquers all obstacles and leads to eternal happiness between man and woman. Dysinger found that girls especially were emotionally aroused by such scenes.[25] It is generally agreed that the pervasiveness of such stimuli throughout our entire culture is not beneficial in terms of dating, courtship, marital choice, marital interaction, or family relationships. The accessibility of this kind of stimulus is much greater, and to younger girls, through television than through other mass media.

SOCIAL CLASS AND TELEVISION

Some differences in parental control over the use of television, on a social-class basis, have been found by Robert Blood, who studied 102 families with children from 2 to 18 years of age.[26] The sample was composed of families of lower-lower, upper-lower, lower-middle and upper-middle class. Children in lower-class families spent more time with TV, both during the week and over weekends. Most of the families did exert some control over viewing, but there were in the lower-class families some parents with a "laissez-faire" attitude toward numbers and kinds of programs, toward quarrels that arose, and toward interfering with bedtime. It is the lower-class parent who thinks of TV as a great positive in their family, feels that it has few disadvantages, and does not cut down on other activities. On the other hand, when lower-class parents do interfere with their children's viewing, they are more autocratic and less flexible about it than are the upper-middle class parents. The latter are more apt to forego rules in the case of some especially good program. They also solve the problem of too much time spent with TV by moving the set out of the living room to some place where it is less accessible. Their preference is to reason with their children about programs they should not see, and they prefer not to use the withdrawal of TV privileges as a punishment for unrelated kinds of misbehavior.

CHILDREN'S HEROES

Hero worship is not a new emotion in children or adults. "Hero worship," wrote Thomas Carlyle, "exists forever and everywhere . . .

[25] W. S. Dysinger and C. A. Ruckmik, *The Emotional Responses of Children to the Motion Picture Situation,* The Macmillan Company, New York, 1933.
[26] Blood, *op. cit.*

no nobler feeling than this of admiration for one higher than himself dwells in the breast of man. . . . Is not all loyalty akin to religious faith?" Knowing the weaknesses of human character, he recognized that not all those who have been set up as heroes are worthy of the worship, and he commented, "We can do with some forged false notes; with a good many even; but not with all, or most of them false!"[27]

"The Greeks had a word for it" says Fishwick, " 'heros,' the super man who was deified after death. In him people saw their values and dreams realized." Any hero, he continues, must reflect the social thinking of the times, people's innermost hopes and beliefs. Through hero worship we transcend our own stuffy backyards; and the specific qualities of the heroes at any given time are "barometers to national meaning."[28]

It seems that there is a gap in the literature on child development. Almost no one has set about trying to find out in scientific manner what the relationship is between the society, the family, child needs, and the idols they set up and adore. Yet popular writers have declared hero worship to be a universal emotion, and the nature of the heroes, a direct reflection of the times. Writers and parents have had considerable to say about the bad choices of today's children and the frenzied behavior resulting, without even trying to consider any of the reasons behind these things. A brief discussion of the subject seems to be pertinent, then.

First of all, not all children's heroes are ones that should bring complaints from adults, and many have exemplary influences on the worshipers' behavior. In a questionnaire given to several thousand boys and girls (age 11 to 18) by workers with the Boys' Athletic League in 1950, the top heroes were General MacArthur, Babe Ruth, and Franklin Roosevelt.[29] In a unpublished interview-study of children of prominent parents, heroes were chosen from among the many noted people whom the children met in their own homes or at public functions with their parents. The range was wide and attractive—statesmen, noted authors, famous actors and actresses from the legitimate stage, philanthropists, scientists, and the like. There are many great people on the current American scene who catch the admiration of children.

Dorothy Barclay suggests that if you ask children formal questions about who their heroes are you are apt to get a dignified

27 Thomas Carlyle, *Heroes and Hero Worship.*

28 M. W. Fishwick, "Making of a Hero," *Saturday Review,* August, 1964, pp. 12–15.

29 Dorothy Barclay, "Youth's Heroes and Hero Worship," *The New York Times Magazine,* November 4, 1951, p. 42.

answer. Ask them, however, whom they would like to be when they grow up, and the range is wider and often less attractive. At the turn of the century, this sort of question produced the following results: 78 percent of the heroes were historical figures; 12 percent, literary; and the remaining 10 percent, relatives or acquaintances. Fifty years later the answers were different: 33 percent were historical figures; 10 percent, relatives and acquaintances; and none were literary. The remaining 57 percent was made up by types never thought of in the earlier period. They were figures from sports (1/4); radio, movies, comics (more than 1/7). Some children answered on the basis of an occupation alone, such as columnist, writer, reporter, airplane pilot, hostess, etc. (nearly 1/5). Lawrence Frank's opinion is that children need someone to worship whose actions, gestures, words are a part of the child's everyday world, not merely a portrait of a great man.[30] Through the mass media a great variety of people are brought into the everyday world of a child.

Currently, adolescent and pre-adolescent hero worship is assuming proportions that disturb many people. The newest idol is the young popular music star, and the "worship" takes forms that make the erstwhile followers of Rudy Vallee and Frank Sinatra seem almost passive. Writes David Dempsey, "As our singers get progressively more frantic, their followers become increasingly frenzied, and an audience that once swooned in the presence of its favorite singer, or at best squealed, has given way to a mob that flips." Sometimes the singer is mobbed; teen-agers go into a trance, "a state of teenage Nirvana;" they jump up and down, scream, and protest their undying love for the hero.[31]

Explanations for such behavior have come from several sources. The anthropological interpretation is that everyone is instinctively primitive and that the jungle rhythm of much current popular music brings out the primitive and ritualistic in those youngsters who have no other kind of social focus for their energy and hero worship. The collective ritual operates as a group catharsis.[32] A psychological interpretation is that young people develop an hysterical reaction to a craze, are working off tensions, and that the singer's role is actually healing. Two types of fans are identified; the emotional type that merely gets a crush, is passive, and causes little trouble; and the "rhythmically obedient" type who must get into the beat and act with it. The wilder the music, the more they enjoy it,

30 *Ibid.*

31 David Dempsey, "Why the Girls Scream, Weep, Flip," *The New York Times Magazine*, February 23, 1964, p. 15.

32 *Ibid.*

and the more frenzied they become. This latter type has grown in increasing numbers, and they are products of a conformist and somewhat authoritarian society. Finally, there is the socioeconomic interpretation. Our affluent society, for the first time, has permitted the rise of a class of professional teen-agers who prosper financially and are known intimately through all of the mass media. These professionals have created a culture which is big business and is composed of heroes, worshipers, agents, fan clubs, and marketable symbols such as records, pins, rings, clothes of a certain type.[33] In a society such as ours, big business does not retire easily from making money just because the value of its service is questioned.

A point that seems significant is the faithlessness of the faithful. The hero of yesterday's teen-agers is not the hero of today's. He must not be far removed from his followers in age for he is an image to them of what can happen to people like themselves. Identity is important, and teen-agers, who feel most severely the schism between youth society and adult society, will not identify with their elders. Some of the frenzy, indeed, is a rebellion against the adults who constrain, or ignore youth, and who preach but do not practice their own preaching. When a teen-ager throws himself into the successful act of another young person it is as if he were telling the world of adults, and himself, that his own age group is effective, talented, and worthwhile. For young girls, of course, there is an added dimension—the romance of worshiping a peer who is glamorous and sought after.

The separateness of teenage culture, referred to in an earlier chapter, helps to promote the spread of any fad that takes hold upon some of them. It becomes a sort of contagion that draws more and more young people to a common altar. The sickness, however, does not afflict all to the same degree, and their symptoms are not identical. Many teen-agers "adore" the Beatles at a distance and do not indulge in wild behavior over them. To ignore the Beatles entirely would be to ostracize themselves from the popular temple of youth. Young people, however, who find satisfaction in their day-to-day relationships with family and friends can find more realistic heroes. For many, according to several polls of teen-agers' opinions, the hero is "Mom" or "Dad." James Coleman, in his study of ten schools, found considerable consensus surrounding which student the children most wanted to be like. The choice tended to be concentrated upon certain upperclassmen who were leaders in the schools.[34] A

[33] *Ibid.*, p. 70.

[34] James S. Coleman, *The Adolescent Society*, The Free Press of Glencoe, New York, 1961, pp. 98–103.

person, usually slightly older, who achieves modest success in acceptable areas seems to them a good enough model to try to imitate. Others find that kind of hero insufficient. The difference seems to lie in a lack of certain satisfactions in life. Fabian has commented that many of his followers are physically unattractive girls. The screamers and jumpers are made up of a majority of young people who are socially inept, lonely, and alienated from others of their own age. They are much in need of hero worship but can hardly set up as heroes the very people who reject them. Also, since they have not related well to people individually, they can spend their emotions most comfortably in a large group and on an idol that has no opportunity to reject them.[35]

Teenage hero worship of this sort is a phase that many adolescents go through; but for most of them it is a brief phase which passes with greater maturity. In this respect, it resembles juvenile delinquency, which is a phenomenon of an age group. Most juvenile delinquents do not become adult criminals. Both kinds of behavior —the worship and the delinquency—are results of stresses which are visited upon many youths in a specific culture. When the stresses are reduced, other forms of behavior develop.

SUMMARY

1. The growth of the mass media and its invasion into the intimacy of home life has created interest in its effect upon child development. Few conclusions are definitive, and opinions are often conflicting, although there are some persisting threads of evidence.

2. Most of the conclusions formed concerning earlier media are now said to be true of the effects of television. However, TV has dimensions in family life and child development that do not apply to the other media.

3. In the past 20 years there has been a great increase in the number of TV sets, the numbers of children watching TV, and the number of hours they spend watching.

4. Television has more appeal than other mass media to preschool children because of its sounds, pictures, color, and because they are able to manipulate it without cost and without adult help. Commercial television caters to their particular interests at important times of the day.

5. Much of the content of children's programs is of a violent nature. Though opinions vary as to the effects upon children, it has

[35] Dempsey, *op. cit.*

been noted that: (1) an increasing number of juvenile crimes are committed by means similar to those the juveniles have seen on TV, (2) the realistic nature of television makes it more difficult for a child to understand what is "pretend" and what is actual life, (3) some children are emotionally upset by the violent programs, while others become callous to man's inhumanity to man.

6. Much of the content of television which has to do with adults, world events, and the future can create anxieties in children with reactions varying from mild uneasiness to nightmares.

7. Children's attitudes, values, and beliefs can be formed and changed by the impact of TV, especially in such areas as war, gambling, capital punishment, minority groups, ethnic groups, and certain occupations.

8. Television may increase a preschool child's vocabulary, but the advantage does not appear to be maintained after sixth grade.

9. No mass medium has an opportunity like that of TV to educate the child about a wide range of subjects, current and past.

10. Program-viewing is selective with children. Those who have the highest intelligence and more of other resources in activity and entertainment are the ones likely to view less and with better choice.

11. Television, used unwisely, can have ill effects on children's health, energy, and eyesight. It reduces physical activity out-of-doors.

12. Television, and radio, can affect family interaction (1) by causing a spectator rather than a participating relationship, (2) by producing family quarrels over what to view, (3) by being used as a substitute mother or baby-sitter, (4) by producing new problems and anxieties for parents and, (5) by emphasizing the romantic complex already so pervasive in our society.

13. Parental control over children's viewing differs on a social class basis. Parents on a higher socioeconomic level have more control over time spent, are more flexible about regulations, and use reason rather than arbitrariness in exerting the control.

14. Hero worship is a universal emotion, and the type of hero set up is a reflection of the society. A growing trend for teen-agers is the frenzied worship of popular music stars. Those teen-agers who indulge most violently are identified as children who do not find normal satisfactions with adults and peers in their own day-to-day lives.

15. The separation of adult culture and teen-age culture is responsible for this passing phase of hero worship in which young people wish to identify with successful persons of their own approximate age group.

SUGGESTED READINGS

Blumer, Herbert, and Philip M. Hauser, *Movies, Delinquency, and Crime,* The Macmillan Company, New York, 1933. A good illustration of the fact that the bad effects on children now attributed to TV were once attributed to the movies.

Charters, W. W., *Motion Pictures and Youth,* The Macmillan Company, New York, 1933. A continuation of the studies in Blumer and Hauser.

Glick, Ira O. and Sidney J. Levy, *Living with Television,* Aldine Publishing Company, Chicago, 1962. The authors reveal that the group critical of TV is smaller than the groups who embrace it or who accommodate to it. They also describe what sorts of people belong to each group.

Himmelweit, H. T., A. N. Oppenheim, and P. Vince, *Television and the Child,* Nuffield Foundation, New York, 1958. An excellent, definitive study of the effects of British TV on children.

Mehling, Harold, *The Greatest Time Killer,* The World Publishing Company, New York, 1962. A tirade against the evils of TV.

Roe, Yale, *The Television Dilemma,* Hastings House, New York, 1963. One man's idea for improving television programming.

Schramm, Wilbur, J. Lyle, and E. B. Parker, *Television in the Lives of Our Children,* Stanford University Press, Stanford, 1961. An American study comparable to the Himmelweit British study.

Schramm, Wilbur (editor), *The Impact of Educational Television,* University of Illinois Press, Urbana, 1963. A series of reports on a specialized aspect of TV which is noncommercial and directed at its use in formally educating children.

THE LARGER SOCIAL SETTING FOR CHILD DEVELOPMENT

Photograph from Public Information Office, Los Angeles City Schools

PART VIII

CHILDREN AS A POPULATION ELEMENT

19

Preceding chapters of this book have been devoted to an analysis of the role of group interaction and the cultural milieu in child development. The emphasis has been upon the individual child and the situational factors in his rearing. There is, however, another phase of the whole process of child development which needs to be considered. This is the relationship of children as an age group to other age groups in the population. Basically this may be defined as the problem of the status of children as a population element, and it is to this phase of the sociology of child development that the remaining chapters of this volume are devoted. Included in the discussions of this phase are historical changes in the status of children, with particular reference to their present social position; social movements directed to further changes in directions which are considered desirable; and some basic problems of culture correlations which are involved. First, however, it is necessary to consider the age structure of the population, the factors which determine its form in any society, some indication of the forms it takes in various parts of this country, the nature of functional age groupings, the social significance of the age structure, and child status conceived in terms of social process. These constitute the substance of this chapter.

THE AGE STRUCTURE OF THE POPULATION

One of the basic facts about any given society is its age structure. This means the relative size and arrangement of the successive age layers that are represented in the population. At the bottom of the structure are the lower age groups. Arranged by years, the first layer consists of people under 1, next are those between 1 and 2, and so on through the length of life. For convenience in statistical tables and graphic representation, these ages are usually combined into five-year groups.

In a normally growing society, with no in- or out-migration and with conditions of life relatively stable and persistent, these age groups or layers take the form of an elongated isosceles triangle, and, because of annual depletions through death, each succeeding layer grows narrower. As the ages advance, there are fewer and fewer individuals in the respective groups, so the figure tapers off to a thin line after 65. The graphic representation of this is called a population pyramid.

In actual practice this population pyramid takes diverse forms in different populations, depending upon the relative operation of the factors which determine it. There are three such fundamental factors. The first is the birth rate. When the birth rate increases, the lower age groups broaden in relation to the rest of the pyramid; when it declines over a period of years, their relative width decreases. Obviously, either modification changes the shape of the pyramid as a whole. Second is the death rate, differentiated on an age basis. If a relatively large number of persons in the lower age groups die, the base of the pyramid contracts correspondingly; similarly, a low death rate in the upper age groups causes that part of the pyramid to bulge. The third factor is migration, with special reference to the age characteristics of those migrating. The migration of any particular age group from one area into another obviously creates a corresponding contraction and expansion, respectively, of the population pyramid at the age level involved.

Each society or social area, then, has its own distinctive population figure, a product of the operation of these three factors at the particular time and place involved. In the contemporary United States, the population pyramid of the South has a relatively broad base and a relatively narrow spread in the working age groups. In the Northeast, these facts are reversed. Rural areas show an excess of persons under 20; urban areas, of people between 20 and 45. In villages, many more persons are in the upper age groups, whereas suburban areas often contain an unusually large number of young couples and children. Pioneer communities have a preponderance of younger middle-class males. The foreign-born in the United States have an unusually small ratio of children.[1]

Just as each social area has its own distinctive age structure, so variations occur from one era to another in the same society. Changing birth, death, and migration rates over a period of several decades can bring about striking changes. Such a change has occurred in the United States in recent years and is generally referred to as the aging of our population. The operating factors which produced this change may be summarized as follows: First, during the generation after the Civil War, the birth rate tended to remain high. Second, from 1880 to 1914, there was a large-scale immigration of younger age groups into this country. These two factors in combination meant a relatively large population in the advanced age groups in recent years. Third, the death rate declined, particularly after 1900. Included here was the fact that many people in the older age brackets lived longer. Finally, since 1910, and most noticeably since 1920, the birth rate declined. In combination, these factors made for a marked contraction of the population pyramid in the lower age

Table 9 Five-Year Age Groups, by Percentage, U.S. Population 1880–1960

Age Group	1960	1950	1940	1930	1920	1910	1900	1890	1880
Under 5	11.3	10.7	8.0	9.3	10.9	11.6	12.1	12.2	13.8
5–9	10.4	8.8	8.1	10.3	10.8	10.6	11.7	12.1	12.9
10–14	9.4	7.4	8.9	9.8	10.1	9.9	10.6	11.2	11.4
15–19	7.4	7.1	9.4	9.4	8.9	9.9	9.9	10.5	10.0
20–24	6.0	7.6	8.8	8.9	8.8	9.8	9.7	9.9	10.1
25–29	6.1	8.1	8.4	8.0	8.6	8.9	8.6	8.3	8.1
30–34	6.7	7.6	7.8	7.4	7.6	7.6	7.3	7.3	6.7
35–39	7.0	7.5	7.2	7.5	7.4	7.0	6.5	6.2	6.0
40–44	6.5	6.8	6.7	6.5	6.0	5.7	5.6	5.1	4.9
45–49	6.1	6.0	6.3	5.7	5.5	4.9	4.5	4.4	4.2
50–54	5.4	5.5	5.5	4.9	4.5	4.2	3.9	3.7	3.7
55–59	4.7	4.8	4.4	3.8	3.4	3.0	2.9	2.7	2.5
60–64	4.0	4.0	3.6	3.1	2.8	2.5	2.4	2.3	2.2
65–69	3.5	3.3	2.9	2.3	2.0	1.8	1.7	1.6	1.4
70–74	2.6	2.3	1.9	1.6	1.3	1.2	1.2	1.1	1.0
75–	3.1	2.6	2.0	1.6	1.4	1.2	1.2	1.1	1.0

Source: Adapted from U.S. Bureau of the Census, *Statistical Abstract of the United States: 1963.*

[1] For an extended discussion of these variations, the reader is referred to Edward P. Hutchinson, *Immigrants and Their Children, 1850–1950*, John Wiley & Sons, New York, 1956.

groups and its relative expansion at the upper age levels. These changes are sometimes simplified and expressed in terms of the changing median age of the population, which shows an increase from 16 years in 1800, to 21.4 in 1890, and to 30.1 in 1950. More specifically, these changes are revealed in the data in Table 9.

FUNCTIONAL AND STATUS GROUPINGS WITHIN THE AGE STRUCTURE

Statistical summaries and graphic representations of the age structure are presented usually in terms of one- or five-year classifications. In the organization of the life of society, however, chronological ages are grouped on the basis of function and status. Reference has already been made to the universal practice of age grading, and Linton asserts that age and sex categories are more important for an understanding of the operation of most societies than are family systems.[2]

All societies recognize at least three age groups: child, adult, and elder. This corresponds roughly to a threefold functional classification on the basis of economic production and consumption. The child group is economically dependent, not yet part of the productive system. As a group, it is in process of preparation for subsequent usefulness. In financial terms, it is a liability at the moment but is considered as an investment in future values. The adult is the producing group; it carries the burden of maintaining the society, which includes the maintenance of the two dependent groups. The elders are the second dependent group, having reverted to this status after a span of usefulness, and being maintained now as an obligation for past contributions.

Each of these main classes may be divided in any given society into various subgroupings. Linton points out how in certain African tribes the entire male population is divided into units composed of those born in the same year or within two- or three-year intervals.[3] The Inca of Peru distinguished ten age groupings for males alone.[4] Our interest is centered upon the divisions recognized in the lower age groups in our contemporary culture. There are today four such divisions: infant, preschool child, child, and youth. The term *infant*

[2] Ralph Linton, "A Neglected Aspect of Social Organization," *American Journal of Sociology*, May, 1940, p. 872.

[3] Ralph Linton, *The Study of Man*, D. Appleton-Century Company, New York, 1936, p. 118.

[4] Ralph Linton, "Age and Sex Categories," *American Sociological Review*, October, 1942, p. 593.

is used customarily to mean a child under the age of 1. The preschool years cover the ages of 2 to 5, inclusive. The word *child* tends to be used in the literature in two ways, one general and the other specific. As a general term, the word means a young person ranging in age from birth to an upper level not exactly determined, but approximately the fifteen to the sixteenth year. Specifically, the term *child* is used for children from 6 to 14 years, inclusive. In recent years, the word *youth* has been used with the somewhat expansive interpretative range of 15 to 24, inclusive.

Modern Legislators Define Childhood

The drawing of precise lines identifying certain age groups and assigning them a legal status or function has become increasingly frequent in modern culture, chiefly because of various types of social legislation based on age distinctions. A large part of this legislation is aimed at the protection of childhood against certain social hazards; other laws are permissive in character, such as those having to do with the operation of motor vehicles, voting, enlistment for military service, and the like. Legislation of such kinds requires the designation of some age limit above or below which a particular law, function, or responsibility does not apply.

The more common attempts of legislators to define childhood have centered in recent years about such matters as age of adoption, rape, marriage, compulsory school attendance, employment, juvenile court jurisdiction, and dependency. Most of these laws in the United States have been enacted on a state basis and passed over a period of years, so that naturally considerable variation exists. Only certain general summaries will be made here. (1) Most laws requiring consent for adoption specify 12 to 14 years. (2) Legislation specifying rape mentions chiefly 16 or 18 years. (3) For marriage, the parents' consent is required for girls in most states up to 18 years, and for boys up to 21 years. (4) Compulsory school attendance is required in most states to age 16, with some recent advances to 17 and 18 years. (5) Age limitations on employment tend naturally to coincide with those on compulsory school attendance. (6) Federal legislation fixing the maximum age for aid to dependent children followed the school and employment ages commonly designated by the states, that is, 16 to 18 years. (7) The most frequently established age for juvenile court jurisdiction is now 18 years, having been advanced from 16 years in the more recent acts. In short, child protective legislation covers, with few exceptions, the first 15 years of life; the more recent legislation has advanced the ages by one or more years to protect children from being treated as adults too soon.

THE SOCIAL SIGNIFICANCE OF THE AGE STRUCTURE

Once the fact is grasped that age groups have differing functional roles in society, the fundamental importance of the age structure becomes apparent. Obviously, the structure sets the pattern of the human resources and social responsibilities of a society at any given time. Changes in this pattern over a period of time in the same society involve basic readjustments. Differentials between social areas in the same country, or between one country and another, may change not only the status of any particular age group, but also affect the relative position of the country as a whole. Some of the specific ways in which the age structure is of social importance will be considered briefly.

1. The age structure is one of the determinants of the productive capacity of a population. This is true for the very obvious reason that the economic maintenance of any society rests upon a designated middle age span, from which it follows that changes in the relative proportion of this age span result in corresponding changes in the labor potential. It is not possible to state categorically the productive years, for this age span varies with individuals and occupational groups. However, 65 has become the most popular age for enforced retirement; one cannot produce much until the age at which compulsory education ends; and one usually does not produce at top capacity for some years after that. The basic fact is that the age makeup has great importance for national efficiency and productivity.

2. Similarly, the age structure affects the consumption pattern of a society. Each age group has its own distinctive needs for commodities and services, and as these needs are expressed in the democracy of the market, the entire economic structure is affected thereby. Particularly is this evident when the larger age groups are compared, such as children with the aged. Children need baby carriages, baby clothes, milk, toys, scooters, sleds, express wagons, footballs, and ballet slippers. There is scant market for these goods among people past 50, just as children do not consume canes, whiskey, false teeth, wheelchairs, pipes, and bifocal eyeglasses.

3. The age structure, together with the sex ratio, is a determinant of the reproductive capacity of a society. First there is the con-

ventional age of marriage; hence the mathematics of the population for these periods are important. Normally, in this country, over 90 percent of reproduction takes place within the marriage bond. Second, reproduction is a physical function confined to a certain age span in the life of women, a period equivalent in our culture to about one-third of the life span. Specifically, therefore, the crude birth rate depends in large measure upon the proportion of married women in the population between 18 and 45 years of age. Other factors which determine the birth rate are significant only as they affect married couples in this age group. Another possibility, suggested by Landis,[5] is that a large grandparent quota (the group above 50) in proportion to the parent quota may have an effect on the birth rate, since many families with an increasing number of aged people to care for will reduce the number of their offspring.

4. The age structure is related to various social problems. The health needs and problems of a population of elders differ from those when there is a preponderance of children and younger married couples. Changes in the age structure are particularly important in their implications for problems of institutional care. The population in old folks' homes and institutions for the aged sick is expected to increase in the coming years.

Similarly, recreational needs differ. Each age group has its own recreational preferences, and these differentials express themselves in terms of equipment, space, activities, and nature of commercial facilities and programs offered. It has been suggested, for example, that the aging of the population in the United States will result in an increased sale of radios and television sets, and will affect the type of program put on the air. It is not unlikely that the problems of juvenile delinquency which have perplexed many areas in recent years have risen chiefly from sudden, large-scale changes in the age structure, involving the influx of many teen-agers into communities whose recreational life was adapted to, and dominated by, much older age groups.

5. The age structure determines the ratio of aged persons to the potential productive population. In contemporary analyses, persons 65 years of age and over are identified as the aged; those from 20 to 64, inclusive, are thought of as the economically supporting base of the population. While not all persons 65 and over are dependent and not all of those 20 to 64 are economically productive, the ratio between the two is an approximate index of the "old age" problem which society is called upon to carry.

[5] Paul Landis, *Population Problems*, American Book Company, New York, 1943, pp. 290–291.

A significant fact about this index is its changing nature. The percentage of the population 65 and over has been increasing rapidly. A glance at Table 9 shows that in 1880, 3.4 percent fell into that group, whereas in 1960 it was 9.2 percent. Meanwhile, the percentage in the 20-to-64 age span has increased from 48.4 to 52.5. While this, too, is a marked increase, it is less than proportionate to the relative increase in the proportion of elders.

The aged population poses many social and economic problems. Their increasing seriousness can be seen in the field of political development in recent decades. Two aspects will be noted briefly. One is the emergence of an old-age element as a pressure group. Constituting a substantial and increasing part of the electorate in this country, with leisure to devote to politics, they have the political voice to demand programs that are in their own best interests. The second aspect is the threat of such demands upon the public treasury in relation to other kinds of welfare activities, particularly those concerned with education and other child-welfare projects. This presents the unique situation of an age group with voting status competing with an age group that must rely upon other appeals.

6. Finally, the age structure determines the extent of the child-rearing responsibilities which a society must assume, according to the standards which it accepts. This, together with complementary facts, has much to do with the status of childhood.

Four sets of related data need to be considered in this connection.

a. First are the overall changes that have occurred in recent decades in the percentages of the population in the lower age brackets. Here again Table 9 tells the story. In 1880, of the total population, 38.1 percent was under 15 years of age, and 48.1 percent was under 20. By 1960, these percentages were 31.1 and 38.5, respectively. In proportion to the rest of the population this means a decline in familial, infant, preschool, and school responsibilities from 1880 to 1960.

The changes, however, must be related to those of the productive population, 20 to 64 years, and the aged, that is, those 65 and over. Table 9 indicates these changes, showing that between 1880 and 1960, while the percentage of the population under 20 declined from 48.1 to 38.5, the percentage in the 20 to 64 age brackets increased, as has been noted previously, from 48.4 to 52.5. In other words, the declining percentage of persons under 20, and the increasing proportion of the adult (20 to 64) population, have combined to make possible a higher status for children, in spite of the increase of elders, previously noted.

b. A second group of related facts concern the variations in the age structure from one part of the country to another. Some areas have a relatively high proportion of children, with a corresponding low proportion of persons in the economically productive years; in others, the reverse is true. The 1950 census reported that in the Northeast 30.7 percent of the population was under 20 years of age, and 60.4 percent was 20 to 64. Figures for the North Central were 33.2 and 57.7 respectively; for the South, 38.7 and 54.5; and for the West, 58.7 and 33.2.

Table 10 reveals these variations for 1960. Comparison with the 1950 figures shows three significant facts. First, the variations between regions are more pronounced in 1960. Second, in all regions the proportion of so-called "producers" to those under 20 has dropped. Third, in all regions the proportion of the aged to producers has increased.

Table 10 Age Structure, Percentage Distribution, 1960

Age Grouping	Urban	Rural non-Farm	Rural Farm	North-east	North Central	South	West
0–19 years	37.1	41.7	42.0	35.3	38.6	40.8	38.9
20–64 years	53.8	49.4	48.7	54.6	51.6	50.9	52.5
65 years, and over	9.1	8.9	9.3	10.1	9.8	8.3	8.6

Source: U.S. Bureau of the Census, *U.S. Census of Population: 1960,* vol. I, Characteristics of the Population, Part I, United States Summary, U.S. Government Printing Office, Washington, D.C., 1964.

c. The relative proportions of the child element of the population that must be reared by the adult productive population must also be related to the general economic status of the particular area under consideration. In this connection, the data on family incomes obtained in the 1960 census enumeration are particularly valuable. Tabulation of this information by regions is presented in Table 11.

Table 11 Family Incomes, by Income Class, by Regions, 1960

Income Class	United States	Northeast	North Central	South	West
Under $2000	13.0	7.9	11.2	21.4	8.9
$2000–4999	28.8	26.3	27.1	34.6	24.9
$5000 and over	58.2	65.8	61.7	44.0	66.2

Source: U.S. Bureau of the Census, *U.S. Census of Population: 1960,* vol. I, Characteristics of the Population, Part I, United States Summary, U.S. Government Printing Office, Washington, D.C., 1964.

Similar variations in age structure and family income distribution are shown in the census data for 1950 for standard metropolitan areas. This information is arranged for selected areas in Table 12.

Table 12 Age Groupings and Family Income Distribution, by Standard Metropolitan Area, 1960

SMA	Age Groupings			Income by Families in 1959			
	Under 15	15–64	65 and Over	Less than $2000	$2000–4999	Over $5000	Median Income
Akron, Ohio	32.4%	59.4%	8.2%	6.4%	19.3%	74.3%	$6735
Boston, Mass.	28.1	61.0	10.9	6.0	22.2	71.8	6687
Chicago, Ill.	29.7	61.7	8.6	6.3	17.5	76.2	7342
Los Angeles, Calif.	29.7	61.4	8.9	7.1	20.0	72.9	7066
Memphis, Tenn.	33.6	59.1	7.3	16.4	34.7	48.9	4903
New York, N.Y.	26.1	64.2	9.7	7.4	24.1	68.5	6548
Phila., Pa. and N.J.	29.1	61.7	9.2	7.4	24.1	68.5	6433
San Antonio, Texas	34.7	58.5	6.8	15.3	37.7	47.0	4766
St. Louis, Mo.	31.2	59.5	9.3	9.2	23.6	67.2	6275
Tampa–St. Petersburg, Fla.	26.0	56.9	17.1	16.5	40.0	43.5	4490
Wilkes Barre–Hazleton, Pa.	25.4	63.5	11.1	13.7	40.5	45.8	4722

Source: U.S. Bureau of the Census, *U.S. Census of Population: 1960*, vol. I, Characteristics of the Population, Part I, United States Summary, U.S. Government Printing Office, Washington, D.C., 1964.

d. A final group of facts which affects the situation in a comparison of one area with another is that of the nature and extent of their migration experience. Internal migration is thought of ordinarily as a means of maintaining something of a balance between people and resources. People tend to move from areas in which the pressure of population on resources is great to areas of less intense pressure. We are concerned here with the implications of such movements as reflected in their age makeup. Persons who migrate from one area to another are usually the youth or early maturity age brackets, or the more advanced years of complete or partial economic retirement. This means that certain areas which serve as reservoirs of population are bearing the economic responsibility of rearing the younger migrants, only to lose them when, or soon after, they reach the productive period of life. The South, for example, has, for several decades, been losing through migration while the West has been gaining. Similarly, areas to which the aged move carry unusual burdens. When such migratory movements occur on a large scale and over a period of years, the economic drain involved is great.

In summary, the more one ponders the national scene, studying the variations in the age structure of its population from one area to another, the economic differentials which obtain between them, and the internal movements of their peoples, the more it is apparent that variations in the status of childhood, as reflected in school, work, and child-care standards of all kinds, represent in large measure the relative size of the nonproductive and the productive groups, and the capacities of the latter to service the former.

CHILD STATUS IN TERMS OF SOCIAL PROCESS

Underlying the entire discussion in this chapter is the concept of a social process. This process is one of conflict, involving shifting balances between functional age groupings. Many social scientists have come to emphasize this as a fundamental social process. More than a quarter of a century ago, Lowie wrote: "The conception of society as a structure segmented into age-layers . . . reveals genuine insight into sociological dynamics. . . . Its importance must be acknowledged as overwhelming." It is "too deeply rooted in human nature not to loom largely amidst all the flux of cultural variation, though the class of greatest prominence will vary, as will the ideals of the age classes."[6] More recent is the implied emphasis upon the age conflict process in the study of the ascription of status by Linton and others. Similarly, Ross identified it as one of the basic conflict processes.[7] This process may go on between any particular age groups and it may take a variety of forms; we are concerned here with the relationship between the three groupings of dependent children, productive adults, and dependent elders as defined in this chapter. For purposes of clarity in discussion, they may be thought of in terms of a seesaw, the two dependent groups occupying the opposite ends of the board, the board resting upon the middle trestle, which is the adult producing group. This trestle is the supporting base of the social process; and its characteristics, such as size, virility, and strength, determine both the size of the

[6] Robert H. Lowie, *Primitive Society*, Boni & Liveright, New York, 1920, pp. 314–315.

[7] E. A. Ross, *Principles of Sociology*, D. Appleton-Century Company, New York, 1929, chap. 18.

dependent groups that can be supported and the stability of the process as a whole. Similarly, changes in any one of the three groups affect correspondingly the status of the other two.

It is this larger conception of the process as a whole that needs to be grasped by the reader. The status of childhood is not an independent development, capable of modification at will and without regard to the size and status of all the elements in the population. The status of children in any society and at any particular time is a phase or a product of the larger process of the interaction between the age groupings of the entire society. This is basic to an understanding of the remaining chapters in this volume. Not that child status is entirely a matter of the arithmetic of population; the role of other factors, ideological, traditional, sociopsychological, and cultural must be recognized. An appreciation of all these factors, as well as a sense of the larger social process involved, will, it is hoped, appear in the succeeding chapters.

SUMMARY

1. Each society has its characteristic age structure that reveals the relative size of the varying age groups in its population.
2. The age structure is the product of three factors: the birth rate, the death rate, and migration. Changes in any or all of these factors produce different age structures at different times and places.
3. Age classes are grouped on the basis of function and status. These vary from one society to another, but all societies recognize at least three: child, adult, and elder. This division is based largely on economic considerations, the adult being the producing and the other two the dependent consuming groups.
4. The drawing of precise lines at certain ages and the assigning of legal status on the basis of these lines have become increasingly frequent in modern culture. Attempts by legislators to define childhood have centered in recent years around such matters as adoption, rape, marriage, school attendance, employment, and juvenile court jurisdiction.
5. The age structure is socially significant because it helps to determine (a) the productive capacity; (b) the consumption pattern; (c) the reproductive capacity; (d) the nature of many social problems, such as health and recreation; (e) the ratio of aged dependents to supporting adults; (f) the extent of the childrearing problem.

6. Child status is the result of the social process of the conflict between age groups in the population.

SUGGESTED READINGS

Demographic Yearbook: 1963, United Nations, New York, 1964. For the person interested in population data a great deal about the status of children in the world can be inferred from this book.

Fairchild, Henry Pratt, *The Prodigal Century,* Philosophical Library, New York, 1950. Reflections on some of the problems that come along with population growth and economic growth.

Taeuber, Conrad, and Irene Taeuber, *The Changing Population of the United States,* John Wiley & Sons, New York, 1958. Two outstanding population experts have brought together in a not-too-large book the most important changes in the United States during 160 years.

THE STATUS OF CHILDHOOD IN SOCIETY 20

Childhood is humanity in its first and formative stages. Its history, therefore, coincides with that of the human race; its challenge is its inevitable continuity. If, then, there is any subject which ought to be approached historically, it is childhood.

Although there are wide gaps in our knowledge about the life of children in past ages, there is information on certain specific points that is helpful in our efforts to gain a historical perspective for our modern studies. One such specific topic is the status of childhood, by which is meant the position of children in relation to their parents and the larger social group of which they are a part. Possibly it is because the question of their status, rather than the children themselves, touched the interests of their elders that relatively more information is available on this subject. Fortunately, it is a topic of outstanding importance to the material in this volume, and to it this chapter is devoted.

THE CHILD IN PRIMITIVE SOCIETIES

There is every reason to believe that children were desired by primitive folk. The position of women in many groups turned on their ability to have children. The barren woman was despised. The childless husband appeared ridiculous. So fervent was the wish for offspring that it at times eclipsed the fact of legitimacy. To meet the problem of childlessness, the social fiction of adoption was developed as a restorative of the lapsed prestige of parenthood. With the domestication of animals, and as their other duties waned, women became much more important as bearers of valued property. Brides began to be bought. The barren wife was returned to the seller. Marriage became a durable bond for the protection of the young, and adultery was considered as a species of theft.

Children are a practical asset to primitive peoples; their value lies in the contribution they can make to the all-consuming struggle for existence. Supernatural advantages reinforce those of a more material kind, for children often become the caretakers of the parental spirits. Children spell not only comfort in this world but security in the next, and the relative value of boys and girls takes form early as they function in these respective ways to the advantage of their parents.

From the standpoint of the larger social group, the child assumes importance as the main instrument in the perpetuation of culture. Where there is no written language, it is only through the child that continuity of culture is assured. Then again, primitive society is based on kinship. The blood bond runs like an obsession through these simple forms of social life. It is, one might say, the organizing thread in primitive society. This bond is most obvious in the case of mother and child. It is a relationship easy to grasp, and obviously much was made of it in very early times.

In keeping with the foregoing picture is the fact that primitive elders seem only seldom to resort to corporal punishment of children. On the basis of a good deal of evidence, there seems to be a rather direct ratio between the crudeness of culture and gentleness with children, thus suggesting that as culture accumulates and comes to be taken more seriously, the pressure exerted on the child by the parent, to compel conformity, becomes correspondingly greater.

The picture of primitive childhood, however, is not entirely one of sweetness and light. There were times when the pressure of a high birth rate threatened the resources of the population. At such times, abortion and infanticide, including exposure and abandonment, were practiced. Many primitive tribes looked upon these methods without disapproval since it meant the better good of the living group. Infanticide was practiced not only as a population policy but as a eugenic program. The question was whether a particular baby should be allowed to live. Curious indeed are some of the earliest bases of selection. In addition to the obvious rejection of the physically defective, or babies who seem destined to be weak, there are cases where twins, one of twins, or the quieter of twins were not allowed to live. It might be pointed out that, though these practices seem very cruel, the unwanted baby was not permitted to be born or was not allowed to live after birth. Once he passed the test of survival, he was an accepted and valued member of the tribe because of the role he would perform in it at a later age. This is not always the case in a civilized society in which children are born, reared, and rejected as persons.

Another of the basic facts in the lives of primitive children is the short period of infancy. Just as the comparative study of animal life shows the shortest period of infancy among the simplest forms, so apparently, at the human level, the earlier the stage of social development, the shorter the period of infancy. During these years, the life of the child is much like that of young animals. The practices of many groups indicate a concept of young children as a sort of undifferentiated mass of humanity. The aim of the parents during this period is not to train the child, but to cleanse him and purify him of the ghostly influences of his prenatal life. It is significant that the child is not given a name until his seventh or eighth year, for it is then, only, that he is believed to assume a separate and distinct individuality.

The complement to brevity of immaturity is the early labor of children. The child in primitive societies must learn early to do his share of the work. Getting food is a communal effort of the kinship group, and the child is hardly weaned before he takes on his proportionate burdens. These tasks include stirring soup, kneading dough, hulling rice, washing roots, watching cattle, milking the goat, cleaning the cooking utensils, carrying water, and toting the inevitable younger child around. The primitive child, in other words, discovers reality before he has learned to play. The carefree, joyous child seems to be confined to the imagination of poets and the realities of these later days.

The early education of the primitive child contains few ideas of an ordered, purposeful instruction; rather it is a haphazard, uncontrolled, vague sort of training which can be bared in outline no more than can the growth of a puppy. What there is of more formalized instruction seems directed toward the dual purpose of emphasizing the uniqueness of his people and accepting the psychological domination of his elders. It is considered especially important that he develop the proper attitudes and disposition, parallel in point of time with his physical and economic maturing. The force of religion supplements the influence of such education. "The whole terrifying threat of the malignancy of the spirit world is let loose upon those who tend to dispute the power and threaten the interests of the predominant sex, class, or group. Those who stray from the beaten path of custom become tainted with moral iniquity."[1]

From what has been said, it appears that the child in primitive societies had little status as an individual with rights. During his short childhood, his status turned wholly upon the welfare of the group rather than on any right of the child himself.

THE CHILD IN EARLY CIVILIZATIONS

With social development comes differentiation of social structure, function, and value, all of which have to do with the way in which children are regarded and treated. The minutiae of child life would be quite different, for example, in caste-colored India than among the monotheistic Israelites or the sunbathing Greeks. We must guard, therefore, against the danger of generalizing too much with facts which of necessity vary a great deal; on the other hand, there are certain similarities in the fundamental outlines of the picture, and it is these which we shall consider briefly here.

Children in the early civilizations of Greece, Rome, India, China, Persia, and so on, were customarily welcomed at birth. Generally speaking, they were desired, even if there were limitations to the number that were genuinely welcomed. Thus feeling varied, as to both place and time, on the basis of socioeconomic circumstances; it was greater usually in the case of the birth of a male child. Available glimpses of parent-child relationships in those days, the games children played, the nature of the disciplinary controls customarily employed, indicate that child life had its happy and compensating features. On the other hand, there were darker practices involving children which, both in their direct effects and in their implications, are significant in their bearing upon our central theme, the status of children.

Infanticide was practiced in early civilizations, as it was in primitive tribes and for the same reasons. Sometimes it was under the direction of the state, as in ancient Sparta, or among the Romans, whose Twelve Tables forbade the rearing of deformed children; or at the discretion of the parents, as among the Athenians. In either event, the practice flourished with legal approval in actual

[1] Nathan Miller, *The Child in Primitive Society*, Brentano's, New York, 1928, pp. 33–34.

enactments, like those of Lycurgus and Solon or in the ideal legislative proposals of Plato and Aristotle.

The usual method of infanticide was by suffocation or drowning, but these more direct and unequivocal forms gave way early, in many cases, to abandonment and exposure. This was a definite step forward, since it allowed the possibility, and encouraged the hope, that the infant would not actually die but would be picked up and reared by strangers. This is clearly implied in the fact that infants were exposed so often where they could be seen—and saved: at the entrance to the temples, in the sacred grottoes, the hippodromes, the open highways, in vegetable gardens, on the banks of rivers or the seashores where bathers were wont to congregate. This practice of placing a child in a basket or earthen vessel and leaving it in a temple or some other public and accessible place was known among the Greeks as "potting the child." In Rome, costly ornaments were often put on the exposed infant in order to induce people to take him.

Significant in a number of ways are the measures taken against infanticide and its substitutes. Consider the situation in Rome. The first attempt to check the practice came apparently from Romulus, who, bent on the development of a powerful fighting machine, pledged his people to bring up all males except those who were lame or monstrous from birth, and at least the firstborn female child. More constructive, even if indirect, was the order of Augustus, emperor at the time of Christ, to set aside a reward of 2000 sesterces (about $40.00) for the person who would rear an orphan. About a century later, 97 A.D., came Nerva's order that assistance be given parents who found themselves without the means of bringing up their children. (By 100 A.D., there were 5000 such cases.) The fourth century witnessed a series of notable advances, possibly under the growing influence of the Christian religion. In 315 A.D., Constantine the Great issued an edict directing magistrates to give immediate and adequate aid to all parents who produced children which they were too poor to rear. An edict of 331 A.D. gave title to those who rescued an exposed child, against any subsequent claims of his parents. In 374, Emperor Valentinian definitely forbade, under stringent punishment, the exposure of infants.

Paralleling these secular measures and reinforcing their effect were the actions taken by the General Councils of the Church. Beginning in the fourth century, and for several centuries thereafter, these Council actions both denounced and ordered ecclesiastical punishments of varying severity for parents who killed or exposed their offspring. At the same time, the Church became active in the establishment of institutions for foundlings, which amounted in a sense to an attack upon the practice through the indirect approach of offering a substitute. The Xanodocheion, or village asylums, ordered by the Council of Nicaea in 325 were the first systematic step in this direction, and the development of a substitute approach to the problem had the sanction of the Church for more than a thousand years. This offer of an asylum for abandoned children was a wise policy on the part of the Church, both because it provided an effective answer to the problem and because it tended to identify the Church with mother love in the minds of many people.

Church and state united in the movement for the protection of children in the laws of Justinian, who, raised to the throne in 527 A.D., published a code of laws which have immortalized his name. Justinian proclaimed absolute liberty for foundling children, declaring that they were the property neither of the parents who exposed them nor of those who rescued them. The enactment of this legislation in the sixth century serves to indicate not only the obvious continuance of the practice, despite earlier decrees against it, but also the unending insistence upon its elimination.

Child selling was another common and widespread custom in the early civilizations. In a sense, it was a substitute for infanticide and exposure. Naturally it came later in the course of history, for obviously its spread was impossible before economic conditions were such as to make children's labor valuable to the purchaser.

The sale of children early attained extensive proportions in the Orient. Both Chinese and Japanese reports bear witness to its prevalence and to efforts to suppress it. In Japan, for example, from 1624 to 1734, no less than eight enactments appeared declaring it a crime punishable by death; yet as late as the famine year of 1905 there are reports of its widespread practice.

In the days of the later Roman Empire, the spectacle of children being sold became a sight so common that various regulatory measures against it were passed. Valentinian ordered that a child sold by its father become a free man after a certain period of servitude. In 451, it was decreed that a person who sold a freeborn son for the purpose of having that son sold to the barbarians would be fined six ounces of gold. In 500, Theodoric ordered that when a father, because of poverty, was obliged to sell his child, the child was not to lose his liberty. The Justinian Code of 534 contained a provision by which a father whose poverty was extreme was allowed to sell his son or daughter at the moment of birth and to repurchase the child at a later date.

The nature of this legislation and its continuance through the centuries clearly indicate that it had at best only partial success. The sale of children occurred in many lands over a period of centuries, and persisted to comparatively recent times. In modified form, the sale of children to satisfy the debts of their parents occurred in this country during the nineteenth century in the system of redemptioners. This was an arrangement whereby the children of immigrants who were brought here without money to pay for their passage were sold into service, as well as the immigrants themselves, for a number of years to persons who remunerated the carriers who had transported them across the seas.[2]

The paradox of happy child life on the one hand, and of infanticide or exposure or child sale on the other, which have just been outlined, can be resolved into proper perspective if we think in terms of the basic status of childhood. In these earlier and older civilizations, children had little if any status as a separate age group in the population. Of affection between children and parents, of happy compensations in their daily lives, there was no doubt a great deal; but in the sense of having rights and privileges which were their distinctive own, there was no such thing. The child had few or no rights, per se. Not only under the Roman law, but in the old Persian, Egyptian, Greek, and Gallic legal codes, a father was given absolute power over his children. "While, generally speaking, fathers loved their children and did not desire to kill them or sell them or rule them in an arbitrary or selfish way, they had the right to do so, and the state enforced this right instead of interceding in behalf of the child."[3]

Particularly striking were the rights of the Roman father. His relation with his child was known as the *patria potestas*; and nowhere else, in a highly developed society, does one find anything just like it. It gave the father the right to reject his children: he could sell them, he could disinherit them, he could select their wives and husbands, he could mutilate them and put them to death. This absolute right did not end when the child reached his majority; it ceased only at death or if the father lost his right of Roman citizenship. "In the forum, the senate or the camp, the adult son of a Roman citizen enjoyed the public and private rights of a person; in his father's house, he was a mere thing, confounded by the laws with the movables, the cattle, and the slaves, whom the capricious master might alienate or destroy without being respon-

[2] A. B. Faust, *The German Element in the United States*, The Steuben Society of America, New York, 1927.

[3] Grace Abbott, *The Child and the State*, University of Chicago Press, Chicago, 1938, vol. I, p. 3.

sible to any earthly tribunal. . . . Neither age, nor rank, nor the consular office, nor the honors of a triumph, could exempt the most illustrious citizen from the bonds of filial subjection."[4]

THE CHILD IN MEDIEVAL EUROPE

The Middle Ages constitute an intriguing period in human history. On the ruins of the greatest nation and the highest civilization that the world had known, there was imposed the crude culture of the invading barbarian. For a thousand years civilization seemed to be stagnant. First deterioration, then its continuity, and ultimately its standardization in feudal society, stand out. Yet always there were hidden influences working imperceptibly to happier ends, resulting ultimately in the rebirth of civilization that is commonly called the Renaissance.

There is an extensive and imposing literature on the history of this period, with full accounts not only of political and national affairs, but also of the daily life of the people and the institutional forces that operated within the social structure. But one turns the pages of this literature endlessly and all but fruitlessly to find any information bearing upon the status of children. The omission is eloquent in its meaning.

The medieval pattern of childhood was the product of three sets of ideas and practices. First was the one that had existed in the Roman world, just referred to as the highest civilization in the world up to that time. In the pages immediately preceding, the child's status among the Romans was indicated. Second were the practices of the lusty Germanic invaders. Of them, Tacitus writes as follows: "In every house you see the little boys, the sons of lords and peasants, equally sordid and ill-clothed, lying and playing promiscuously together on the ground and among the cattle, without any visible distinction. In this manner they grow up to that prodigious strength which we behold with admiration."[5] A healthy and disdainful disregard of children seems characteristic of these lusty ancestors of ours. The inhabitants of the northern part of Britain, prior to the introduction of Christianity, did not give their sons names until after they had performed some brave deed or given some indication of their disposition and character; this is reminiscent of similar practices among primitive folk. The youth of Germany, Gaul, and

[4] Edward Gibbon, *The History of the Decline and Fall of the Roman Empire*, The Macmillan Company, New York, 1898, vol. IV, pp. 473–474.

[5] Quoted from Oscar Chrisman, *The Historical Child*, Richard G. Badger, Boston. 1920, p. 288.

Britain, according to Caesar, received scant attention until they approached the manly age, for when a son was younger it was held shameful for his father to be seen in his company.[6]

The third source of the medieval pattern of childhood undoubtedly is to be found in the influence of Christianity. These influences were strangely mixed. The early Church fathers valued the ascetic life so strongly as to create almost an antagonism to married life. This, together with the lowered status accorded to women (despite the veneration of the Virgin) could not but have a marked influence upon family life and the status of the child. Children are seldom mentioned in the Christian writings of the second and third centuries, and almost nothing is said about their training. On the other hand, Christianity, from the first, condemned the practice of infanticide and denounced it as murder, thus becoming a powerful force for the protection of child life, of female children in particular. Out of this emphasis, and the general insecurity and poverty of the time, emerged the historic child policy of "easy come and easy go"—that is to say, a policy which insists upon natural and unlimited reproduction, accompanied by an excessively high child mortality.

Childhood in the Middle Ages was short. Betrothal and marriage took place at an early age, for boys customarily at 14 and for girls at 12. These ages, however, were often disregarded, children being married when even younger. Such matters were arranged by elders, and usually at their, not the children's, convenience. Another reason for the shortness of childhood was the early age at which people were put to work. An early marriage and an early age for work go hand in hand. Such early labor usually took the form of apprenticeship. The people of the Middle Ages accepted the fact that every child should be trained to do something. Boys of the upper classes were sent into the homes of nobles to serve a number of years in order to acquire the use of arms and become learned in the art of chivalry. Boys of the common classes were placed out under a master to spend several years in learning a trade or to carry on agriculture. Children of the very poor were put to work at a particularly early age, and their plight was often very pitiful. Orphans had the hardest lot of all; for if parents treated their own children as has been indicated above, it is obvious that they treated other people's even worse. The basic principle in the work and training of young people in the Middle Ages was embodied in the apprentice system. This principle took legal form as time went on; and by the sixteenth century, in England for example, the law required every child to receive such training as would fit him for business, a trade,

[6] *Ibid.*, p. 288.

or agriculture. Only the parents who could prove that they were able to maintain their children if they did not work were exempt from this requirement.

One hesitates to generalize upon so intangible a matter, but there is much reason to believe that there was less affection between parent and child during the Middle Ages than we today take for granted as a normal condition. Part of the evidence leading to this conclusion is gained from bits of information about parent-child relationships; much of it is based on inferences from certain existing practices which show that children left home at such early ages that relatively little affection had an opportunity to develop. Children who were sent to boarding school spent the entire year there, save for a few holidays. There was the custom of boarding children out or sending them out to be servants or persons-in-waiting. There were the away-from-home implications of the apprenticeship system, already referred to. Finally, we cannot but speculate upon the extent of remarriage among the people of the Middle Ages, because of the high mortality rate among adults as well as other age groups.

Children were brought up with relative strictness during the Middle Ages. It was the theory of the time that every child needed corrective discipline which was both frequent and severe. Offenses of a rather minor character were often punished with marked severity. When knighthood was in flower, the youthful aspirant to chivalry was soundly thrashed for evidences of disobedience. Young noblemen, princes, and even kings were beaten, brutally at times, by their tutors. Henry IV of France expressly ordered his son's governess to whip the prince, since "there was nothing in the world more profitable for him." He who was crowned king of France in 1610, at the age of 9 years, had the following experiences, as evidenced in diaries relating to him:

> October 9, 1603. Woke up about 8 o'clock. He was stubborn and was flogged for the first time. [He was born September 27th, 1601.]
>
> March 4th, 1604. At eleven o'clock, he wishes to dine. When the dinner was brought in, he had it taken out again, then brought back. Troublesome, severely whipped.
>
> May 14th, 1610. He was proclaimed king, went to Parliament, and received a delegation. For sundry offenses after his coronation, he was whipped. He reflects: "I would rather do without so much obeisance and honor, if they wouldn't have me whipped."[7]

[7] Robert H. Lowie, *Are We Civilized?* Harcourt, Brace and Company, New York, 1929, pp. 138–139.

THE ENGLISH CHILD IN THE EIGHTEENTH CENTURY

As every student of history knows, the eighteenth century was a period of tremendous upheaval and change which was particularly conspicuous in France and Great Britain. In France, these changes were most noteworthy in the realms of philosophy and politics, culminating in the French Revolution; in Great Britain, in the life and labor of the people, incidental to the development of the Industrial Revolution. It seems pertinent, therefore, to continue with a brief survey of child life in England in the eighteenth century, both because the changes in the life of the people were most pronounced in England, and also because of the more specific relationship of the English situation to that in the United States. In England in the latter half of the eighteenth century, the Industrial Revolution and the system of enclosures which was a forerunner to it brought poverty and misery to a great many people, and much wealth to a relative few. Any characterization of child life during this period must differentiate, then, between these two aspects of the picture.

For those elements who were on the upgrade, socially and economically, the century witnessed the appearance of new ideas in regard to social questions in general, and the problems of education and child status in particular. People began, says Mrs. Bayne-Powell, to take some interest in educational theories, to treat their offspring with less barbarity. A new spirit of humanity was creeping in. Parents were almost beginning to consider their children as of the same flesh and blood as themselves. Calvinism, with its theory of infant damnation and inherent juvenile depravity, was losing its hold. Complaints of indulgent parents multiplied. The old forms of address—"sir" and "madam"—yielded to "papa" and "mamma." Portraits of children were painted, some at considerable cost. The lack of discipline within the home was bemoaned. Toward the end of the century a more serious spirit was manifest. Fathers and mothers, although still talking at length about the duty of children to their parents, had some idea also of the duty of parents to their children.[8]

These new ideas are brought into bold relief by the grimness of much of the old which still prevailed, even among the wealthier classes. Cruelty still existed, notably in the schools and among the rough and ignorant. Many parents were stern and harsh. There are

[8] Rosamond Bayne-Powell, *The English Child in the Eighteenth Century*, E. P. Dutton & Co., New York, 1939, chap. 1.

many stories of children being flogged and wearing iron collars round their neck, with backboards strapped over their shoulders. Families were large, unusually so; and the very abundance of children kept parents from regarding them individually or even looking upon their death with aught but equanimity. Boys and girls entered adult life very early. The introduction of girls to society, the termination of school training for boys, and marriage all occurred at an early age. On the whole, childhood was regarded as a tiresome stage which it was hoped would pass quickly and painlessly.

If childhood was short among the upper classes, it was doubly so among those less fortunately situated. Children went to work at a tender age. Defoe was delighted to find in the Taunton neighborhood that "there was not a child in the town or villages round it of above five years old, but, if it was not neglected by its parents, and untaught, could earn its bread."[9] Long before the industrial revolution young children were working in mill and mine, and its advent gave new impetus and opportunities to the extension of the practice. Industry was almost entirely unregulated during the century under consideration, and there developed those abuses—whereby, for example, very young persons worked for 14 and 16 hours a day—which are well known to all students of the history of the modern industrial system and which led to the nineteenth-century movement for regulation of hours and conditions of labor.

The apprentice system continued to operate on a large scale. Children could be apprenticed at the age of 8. In some instances, this system fulfilled its theory of a training process for the young; in others it was only a subterfuge for exploitation. Many persons took apprentices, but for the purpose of securing cheap and stable labor. There were many complaints about "these weary years of service." Virtually the only safeguard under the system was the fact that an apprentice could apply to the justices if he were starved or ill used, and, if convinced, the justice could order that his indenture be canceled. As a practical matter, such an application, while feasible in the rural areas, was scarcely effective in the towns, where justices were not only "harder-faced" as a rule, but also not so accessible or so likely to be known to an aggrieved apprentice.

The legal status of children constitutes a tangible measure for the purposes of our study. The law of the eighteenth century dealt severely with children. They were imprisoned and hanged, for example, for offenses with which probation officers now deal. Thus children from 6 to 14 years of age were hung for theft and for other less serious offenses. To have their helpless children convicted of a

9 *Ibid.*, p. 32.

capital crime was for some parents a convenient way of ridding themselves of unwanted children. There are the all too numerous cases in which thieves and prostitutes "adopted" children to aid them in their business or hired them out to beggars. References are not infrequent, in the eighteenth as in preceding centuries, to the mutilation of the children used for begging, so as to increase their pity-inciting appeal. The penalty for such mutilation, in an age which hung offenders for theft, is highly relevant. In 1761, the Court of Hick's Hall committed Anne Martin, alias Chapbury, to Newgate. Convicted of putting out the eyes of children with whom she went begging about the country, she was sentenced to two years imprisonment! Other children languished in jail because their parents were confined there for nonpayment of debts. Large numbers were sent to America, as students of our early history well know.

There were, to be sure, bright spots in the child life of the eighteenth century. In a predominantly rural country, children had the liberty of ranging gardens and fields. Such a setting, with the inevitable large families, made possible the enjoyment of simple pleasures, and for many poor children these sufficed. In addition, however, there were a surprising number of other recreational facilities. The drama became exceedingly popular during the century, and the more careless parents might permit their children to accompany them to the theater. Puppet shows became prevalent during these years. A dictionary published in 1719 mentions the magic lantern. Fireworks, which have always delighted childish minds, were popular during the century. The country fair was an outstanding event for both young and old. Many of the children's games known to us were played by eighteenth-century children: blindman's buff, hide-and-seek (called hoop and hide), seesaw (known as teetertotter), prisoner's base, cricket, hockey, and football. The rocking horse was brought to England from France during the century, and the music boxes and dolls which delighted children in those years are of interest to us yet.

Despite these lighter aspects, the status of child life in England in the eighteenth century was but little higher than it had been for centuries. "If an age is to be judged by its treatment of the weak and helpless, the eighteenth century merits our condemnation. It must be remembered, however, that those horrible cruelties were nothing new. They had unhappily been going on all through the centuries; the new thing was that people were beginning to take notice of them and to ask each other whether they could not and should not be prevented. The nascent humanitarianism of the eighteenth century produced the great reforms of the nineteenth."[10]

[10] *Ibid.*, p. 44.

THE CHILD IN COLONIAL NEW ENGLAND

More than 300 years ago, the United States began its history with scattered settlements of adventurous or disgruntled Europeans, chiefly English. The culture they established here did not arise *de novo;* it was the culture that prevailed in the Europe from which they came. And yet it was not, and could not be, exactly the same. The early settlers were mostly dissenters, which meant that they would make changes when opportunity afforded. In addition, they transplanted their culture to a new world, which meant that although the broad outlines and the general features of the European culture would be established here, there would be variations in the picture in adjusting to the new scene. What has just been said was true regarding the treatment of children, as it was about other aspects of life. Beginning with the same basic concepts of child status which obtained in the England and Europe from which the settlers of America came, the detailed expression of these basic concepts took form in terms of the minutiae of colonial American life.

The picture of colonial childhood is most clearly revealed in New England, first because the forefathers there left comments and records to a greater extent than elsewhere, and second, because the greater homogeneity of the population (English) made for a more distinct cultural pattern.

The child of colonial days was emphatically " 'to be seen, not to be heard,'—nor was he even to be much in evidence to the eye. He was of as little importance in domestic, social, or ethical relations as his childish successor is of great importance today; it was deemed neither courteous, decorous, nor wise to make him appear of value or note in his own eyes, or in the eyes of his seniors. Hence there was none of that exhaustive study of the motives, thoughts, and acts of a child which is now so rife."[11]

In pioneer days, when many forms of social organization have not yet reached a high state of development, the home and family are naturally of great importance. In colonial New England, the patriarchal family prevailed, and the patriarch had tremendous power over his wife and his children. The family and the church were the two chief agencies of social control, and the family, in addition to being such an agency in its own right, was also important as the nursery of the church. It had, above all things, to be protected. "Ruin families and you ruin all."

Filled with biblical traditions, there was in these families a culti-

[11] Alice Morse Earle, *Child Life in Colonial Days,* The Macmillan Company, New York, 1899, p. vii.

vated desire for abundant posterity. Large ones were the rule. Families of 10 or 12 were quite common; 20 or 25 children in one family were not rare enough to occasion comment. Sir William Phips was one of 26 children, all with the same mother. Green, a Boston printer, had 30 children; Benjamin Franklin, another printer, came from a Boston family of 17. The Reverend Samuel Willard, the first minister of Groton, Massachusetts, had 20 children and was himself one of 17; the Reverend John Sherman, of Watertown, Massachusetts, had 26 children by two wives; the Reverend Moses Fiske had 16; and the Reverend Abigah Weld, of Attleboro, Massachusetts, with an annual salary of $220, had 15 children.

As one would expect, maternal mortality in colonial America was high. Many women died exhausted by maternity and labor, to be succeeded by another and younger wife who carried on the torch of fecundity. Most of the large families of earlier times were the offspring of at least two wives, and marriages three and four deep were no rarity. We might be tempted to think of these marrying colonial husbands as a species of chronological Mormons. Like maternal mortality, infant mortality was excessively high. Here, for example, is a portion of an early American family history that tells a story in itself:

In memory of
Mary the Daughter of John
and Effie Lewis who died 9th Nov. 1771
aged 4 years also
Seven children of Jno and Elizth Lewis

John Richard died	2d July 1787	aged 2 mo
Elizabeth	16th April 1789	11—
Richard	25th Feb 1791	7—
John	17th April 1795	1 yr
Eliza	24th July 1797	8 mo
Eliza	28th July 1800	3—
Jessy	3rd April 1805	4 yrs

Cases like these were not unusual. Of Cotton Mather's 15 children, only 2 survived him; of Judge Sewall's 14, only 3 survived.

Large families and child labor go hand in hand, and colonial America was no exception. In fact, parents increased the size of their families with an eye to their children's future usefulness. As early as 1629, Higgeson wrote in his *New England's Plantation* that "little children here by setting of corne may earne much more than their own maintenance," and less than a decade later the people of Rowley were praised because they "built a fulling mill and caused their little ones to be very diligent in spinning cotton wool."

Fortunately, as happens at times, self-interest and religious precept dovetailed neatly with each other. Following their favorite model, the Hebrews, the Puritans conceived of idleness as a sin. The value of the tasks performed by children in colonial days is obvious. Although there were some small industries which employed children, most of the work was on the farm. Here there were the customary chores to do—bringing in fuel, cutting feed, watering horses, picking berries, gathering vegetables, sawing and chopping wood; then too they could sow seeds, weed flax fields, hetchel flax, comb wool, split shoe pegs, make brooms, and the like. The custom of making Saturday a school holiday grew out of the necessity of catching up with the week's work in preparation for the Sabbath.

While these tasks were varied and often interesting, and constituted a phase of education not yet replaced in our modern system, the fact is that children, little children, worked hard. But adults worked hard, too. Hard work was a colonial necessity for both. The struggle for existence in the New World was a stern reality.[12]

The well-being of the family was conceived to depend on rigid family discipline. The behavior of children toward their parents and elders was formal and meek. Parents were addressed as "esteemed parent" or "honored sir and madam"; a pert child was thought to be delirious and bewitched. Reading both between the lines and the lines themselves of the following letter, written by an 11-year-old Long Island miss to her grandfather, tells us a great deal:

> Ever Honored Grandfather:
> Sir: My long absence from you and my dear Grandmother has been not a little tedious to me. But what renders me a Vast Deal of pleasure is Being intensely happy with a Dear and Tender mother-in-law and frequent opportunities of hearing of your Health and Welfare which I pray God may long Continue. What I have more to add is to acquaint you that I have already made a Considerable Progress in Learning. I have already gone through some Rules of Arithmetic, and in a little Time shall be able of giving you a Better acct of my Learning, and in mean time I am Duty Bound to subscribe myself
>
> Your most obedient and
> Duty full Granddaughter
> Pegga Treadwell[13]

The rod was universally accepted as the instrument of subjugation. John Robinson, the Pilgrim preacher, stated the prevailing philosophy in these words: "Surely there is in all children (tho not

[12] Arthur W. Calhoun, *A Social History of the American Family*, Arthur H. Clark Company, Cleveland, 1919, vol. I, pp. 124–127, 286–288.
[13] Earle, *op. cit.*, pp. 16–17.

alike) a stubbernes and stoutnes of minde arising from naturall pride which must in the first place be broken and beaten down so that the foundation of their education being layd in humilitie and tractableness other virtues may in their time be built thereon. It is commendable in a horse that he be stout and stomackfull being never left to his own government, but always to have his rider on his back and his bit in his mouth, but who would have his child like his horse in his brutishnes?"[14]

In this breaking and beating-down process, the school amply aided and abetted the home. Schools, like homes, resounded with strokes of the rod. Ferules, flat ladle-shaped pieces of wood to strike the palms of the pupils' hands, were a standard furnishing in colonial schoolhouses; birch rods, sold at goodly prices on the streets of London, were supplied in copious quantities on the New England hills; the flapper, a heavy piece of leather six inches in diameter, with a hole in the middle, and fastened to a pliable handle, was devised by a pitiless pedagogue of the times; and the cat-o'-nine-tails was widely known and used. Individual teachers, and no doubt particular parents, devised their own unique contributions to the corporal methodology of their day.

Colonial law was clear and positive in its support of paternal authority. For incorrigible disobedience to parents the death penalty was prescribed. The following law of New York, dating to the time that the colony passed from Dutch to English control, expresses the general attitude of the era: "If any Child or Children, above sixteen years of age, and of Sufficient understanding, shall smite their Natural Father or Mother, unless provoked and forct for their selfe preservation from Death or Mayming, at the Complaint of said Father or Mother, and not otherwise, they being Sufficient witness thereof, that Child, or those Children so offending shall be put to Death."[15] Punishment for lesser offenses of the kind were dealt with by the civil authorities. To deal with "divers children and servants" who "behave themselves disobediently and disorderly, towards their parents, masters and governors, to the disturbance of families," an early Massachusetts law gave authority to magistrates to "summon offenders and have them punished by whipping and otherwise."

A separate aspect of child life in colonial days, yet closely related to the matter of family discipline, was the marked emphasis upon

[14] Calhoun, *op. cit.*, vol. I., p. 112.
[15] Alice Morse Earle, *Colonial Days in Old New York*, Charles Scribner's Sons, New York, 1896, p. 16.

manners and courtesy. This was a carry-over from the earlier days in old England when children were sent to school or placed in great men's houses to learn the courtesies and formalities of life, and when these things were considered more important elements in education than philosophy and the classics. In her delightful and penetrating chapter on manners and courtesy in her *Child Life in Colonial Days*, Mrs. Earle shows how, at a time when neighborhood life comprised the whole outside world, these refinements of human relations were what made life endurable, and that, viewed from this angle, the legislation and lawsuits involving lying, name calling, scandalmongering, and so on, were really essential to the keeping of the peace.

Authors and readers of modern books on etiquette need to be reminded that similar books existed in days far removed from the present. Various such printed books go back to the fifteenth and sixteenth centuries, and these, together with those of later date written by colonial authors, were widely used. There was The Babees Book; the Lytill Children's Lytill Boke; the Boke of Curtasye; and the Schole of Vertue; and extracts of these will convey, as perhaps nothing else can, the emphases in child deportment in colonial days. The following is an often-used list of instructions for table etiquette.

> Never sit down at the table till asked, and after the blessing. Ask for nothing; tarry till it be offered thee. Speak not. Bite not thy bread but break it. Take salt only with a clean knife. Dip not the meat in the same. Hold not thy knife upright but sloping, and lay it down at right hand of plate with blade on plate. Look not earnestly at any other that is eating. When moderately satisfied leave the table. Sing not, hum not, wiggle not. Spit nowhere in the room but in the corner, and wipe it with thy foot.

Perhaps the best general picture of the deportment expected of colonial youth is given by the kinsman biographer of David and John Brainerd, who were born in Connecticut in 1718 and 1720, respectively:

> A boy was early taught a profound respect for his parents, teachers, and guardians, and implicit prompt obedience. If he undertook to rebel his will was broken by persistent and adequate punishment. He was taught that it was a sin to find fault with his meals, his apparel, his tasks or his lot in life. Courtesy was enjoined as a duty. He must be silent among his superiors. If addressed by older persons he must respond with a bow. He was to bow as he entered and left the school, and to every man and woman, old or young, rich or poor, black or

white, whom he met on the road. Special punishment was visited upon him if he failed to show respect for the aged, the poor, the colored, or to any persons whatever whom God had visited with infirmities.[16]

From all that has been said concerning parental authority, it is easy to understand the desire of parents to control closely the courtship of their children, particularly their daughters, and that the right to do so was granted to them by law. The Puritan lawmaker, especially, who meddled with so many detailed aspects of life, could not leave untouched so vital a part of family and individual relationships, and the early age at which courtship and marriage customarily occurred gave to such legislation the sanction of common sense. Although there were many cases in which legal barriers to courtship were more honored in the breach than in the keeping, nevertheless the court records of the time are dotted with indictments, convictions, fines, imprisonments, and whipping-post treatments for those who took matters into their own hands.

It is not to be assumed that parental control over courtship was supreme and unchallenged. Willful maids then, as now, overrode the parental mandate, and legal support for their independence was, at times, forthcoming. For above the parental authority was that of the general society or community. In a new country that needed population, discouragement of its legitimate increase by the personal motives of individual parents had to contend with the public interest; hence when parental prerogatives were exercised past a certain point to the undue delayment of marriage, the young people could appeal to the magistrates to bring their unruly parents to terms.

Looming large in the childhood of our forebears was the emphasis upon the religious aspects of life. The curing of souls began very early in life. For this there were two reasons. The first was the general tendency to regard the child as a miniature adult, which meant that the child's needs and experiences, and the procedure used with him, were the same as for the adult, an inference that was applied to spheres of life other than the religious. The second reason was the common acceptance of the idea of child depravity. Whitfield, the great preacher, likened children to rattlesnakes and alligators, which he said were likewise beautiful when small. Jonathan Edwards called them "young vipers." He said: "As innocent as children seem to be to us, yet, if they are out of Christ, they are not so in God's sight, but are young vipers, and are infinitely more hateful than vipers."[17]

The logical sequence of these two beliefs was a firm conviction

16 Earle, *Child Life in Colonial Days*, p. 224.
17 Works of Jonathan Edwards, New York, 1881, vol. III, p. 340.

regarding the necessity and propriety of infantile conversion. At the very outset of their lives, children were confronted with the terrors of hell, from which escape was possible only by accepting the procedures prescribed by their pious elders. What this implied in outstanding homes of the times may be gathered from the following recorded instances. For example, Cotton Mather wrote:

> I took my daughter Katy [aged four] into my study and there told my child that I am to dy shortly and she must, when I am dead, remember everything I now said to her. I sett before her the sinfull condition of her nature, and charged her to pray in secret places every day. That God for the sake of Jesus Christ would give her a new heart. . . . I gave her to understand that when I am taken from her she must look to meet with more humbling afflictions than she does now she has a tender father to provide for her.[18]

It is a relief to know that the Reverend Mather was spared to Katy for thirty years after this recorded conversation—indeed, he survived her.

It would be wrong to suppose that life for colonial children was wholly drab. That there were lighter and joyous moments is clear, even if we had only the complaints of the Puritan theologians to go by. The mere size of many families was enough to insure some recreational developments. But there is much evidence that, in spite of parental authority and the repressive spirit of the time, colonial children, in their search for fun and their love for sport, were much like children today. Even the colonial meeting house, sacred as it was and central to the life of the community as were its services, was not safe from the surgings of youth. Boys and girls were pests to many a parson, and had to be put under town surveillance. King Philip's War was considered a judgment from God on the Massachusetts colony for the "disorder and rudeness of youth in many congregations in time of worship of God, whereby sin and profaneness is greatly increased."

In 1772 the following action was taken in Farmington: "Where as indecencies are practised by the young people in time of Publick Worship by frequently passing and repassing by one another in the galleries; intermingling of the sexes to the great disturbance of many serious and well minded persons—Resolved that each of us that are heads of families will use our utmost endeavors to suppress the evils."

Then there were the various games which colonial children played—tag, stone tag, and wood tag; honey pots; kite flying; marbles; hop, skip, and jump; cricket; leapfrog hopscotch squares; wicket;

[18] Calhoun, *op. cit.*, vol. I, p. 108.

and many others. Coasting downhill became a most popular sport, although colonial youth had to win the right to enjoy it. A Massachusetts law of 1633 classified "common coasters, unprofitable fowlers and tabacco-takers" together as similarly detrimental. Even among the Dutch in Albany, the constables at one time were ordered to take the "small or great slees" in which "boys and girls ryde down the hills" and break them into pieces.

It is interesting to recall that football was played early in our history. In 1657, Boston passed a law which read: "Forasmuch as sundry complaints are made that several persons have received hurt by boys and young men playing at football in the streets, these therefore are to enjoin that none be found at that game in any of the streets, lanes or enclosures of this town under the penalty of 20s. for every such offence.

As was pointed out earlier in the chapter, this picture of colonial childhood has been drawn primarily with reference to New England. It was there that the lines of the picture are clearest and most distinct. In other parts of colonial America, the picture varied, even though, for the most part, the general features remained. These variations grew out of the cultural differences in the groups which settled the respective colonies. The Dutch who settled New York, for example, were a milder species of the genus to which the Puritans belonged. True, the tradition of paternal authority was as strong among the Dutch as in New England, and Dutch children were respectful and subdued in their manners; yet, on the whole, they were on more familiar terms with their parents and had more ample amusements. It is significant that schoolmasters, in complaining of youthful subordination, referred to maternal complicity in the children's mischief.

In the other middle colonies, paternal authority was likewise strictly upheld, although the minutiae of child life were much softer than in New England. The emphasis here was less upon worship and the restriction of play, and more upon work. Perhaps the outstanding fact in the history of the middle colonies was the unsettling influence of the heterogeneity of the population. Liberalizing influences operated from the beginning, but emphasis on work was an acceptable common denominator. Sons of wealthy Quakers in Pennsylvania and New Jersey were often indentured. Every man had to have a trade or occupation to follow. Daughters of wealthy Pennsylvania farmers worked as servants in other homes to complete their training in the domestic arts. This was their substitute for what in other places and times has been spoken of as a finishing school. The chief complaints against children and women in the middle colonies did not involve their religious activities and attitudes, as in New England, but "their going after fashions and ease to the neglect of butter-making, weaving, spinning and cooking."

Turning to the southern colonies, we find that the picture of early marriage, large families, excessive mortality, and youthful labor was much like that in New England. Concerning the spiritual and educational welfare of their children, colonial Southerners were solicitous to be sure, but the intensity was less and the vicissitudes were greater than among the Puritans. Family government in the southern colonies was patriarchal, but less harsh and forbidding than in other sections.

The Status of the Colonial Child

Enough has been said, it is hoped, to enable the reader to picture the colonial scene as the children were related to it. The basic concept concerning the child which the early settlers brought with them was that which prevailed in the Europe from which they came. This concept may be stated in its simplest form in these words: the status of the child was distinctly subordinate. A study of parent-child relationships of the time shows much that is interesting and unique, but seldom do we find the idea of children treated with any thought of their individual needs, capacities, or potentialities. Only as they fitted into the pattern of adult life in the community, only as their abilities and interests contributed to the welfare and interests of their elders were they considered to be of any importance. In the postfeudal period, as under feudalism and slavery, the personal and affectional relations of children to their own parents and to other older people were a distinctly secondary consideration. The dead hand of historical tradition, the pioneer conditions of colonial America, the emptiness of the country, the constant shortage of hands for labor all combined to reestablish the system of childhood exploitation in the early days of our history.

And yet, as we study this picture of colonial child life, we cannot but be impressed with the fact that, from the start, differences from the rigorousness of child life in Europe developed here in the New World, and that, as time went on, many of the harsh lines began to soften.

FACTORS IN THE HISTORY OF CHILD STATUS

In the preceding pages of this chapter an effort was made to present a series of slides, as it were, from the history of childhood. These pictures vary considerably in their detail, but they agree in their basic implication that the child, through the long centuries of man's upward climb, was per se of little importance. At this point there should be an effort made to generalize the factors which through the centuries have determined the status of childhood. These factors appear to be four in number.

The Arithmetic of Reproduction

The term *arithmetic of reproduction* is used here to include the birth rate, the death rate, and the change in population resulting from the relation of these two rates to each other. The population data available through the centuries of human history show that for the most part, in most countries and for the great mass of people, the combination has been a high birth rate, a high death rate, and a slow rate of population growth, if there was any growth at all. These are commonplace facts to population students, but little attention has been given to their bearing on the welfare of children. The proposition advanced here is that they constitute a fundamental factor in determining the status of childhood.

The mathematics of population has meaning for the individual, and in many ways. Pearl Buck has written recently of one aspect of it. "In all those countries," she says, "where population is too abundant, the cause of the individual is lost. Democracy is impossible in an overpopulated country. One needs only to read history with this in mind to discover how inevitably as population increases the form of government changes from any semblance of democracy into some form of despotism."[19]

This is much the same thought as is implied here in regard to the significance of high birth rate and a high infant and general mortality rate. They constitute the "easy come-easy go" method of reproduction. Life—infant life, child life—is cheap. Many children are born, many do not survive. Families are large, and the turnover within them is tremendous. It is the natural characteristic way of growth and reproduction in all forms of animal life.

The essential point to be recognized is this, that while the process of reproduction may be natural, its arithmetic is wasteful and its effect is a low value rating for the individual infant life. This individual fact, multiplied many times, dictates the relative status of infant and child life. Where the value of the individual unit is low, no group mores and programs based on a high status of child life are possible. As a social element in the population, children have little status because the individual child has little value.

[19] Pearl Buck, "Pearl Buck Writes on Birth Control," *Birth Control Review*, November, 1939, pp. 3–4.

Moreover, these effects are reinforced by the arithmetic of parenthood. Life for adults was considerably less certain in earlier centuries than it is today. The turnover among them was tremendous. The adult death rate was high. In particular, the birth of many children per family exacted a heavy toll from the mothers. Stepparents in earlier centuries were far more common than they now are. This affected parent-child relationships, for it meant that they could not be as individual or as stable as they are among us today. In other words, large families, a high turnover among parents and children, and short periods of infancy, all characteristic of earlier centuries, combined to these ends—shorter, less stable, less meaningful relationships between successive generations. Stated another way, the present high status of childhood was not possible until a more economical rate of reproduction and the small-family system came generally to prevail.

The Economic Factor

A second and obvious factor in determining the status of childhood is the economic one, that is, what people can afford. Tersely put, the argument advanced is that the status of the child depends historically upon the aid he gives in the struggle for existence.

The contemporary American, with his high plane of living, finds it difficult to remain aware of the fact that for endless long centuries man was preoccupied wholly or largely with the stark struggle for existence. In this struggle, the society that was able to exist was the one that sacrificed the individual for the group. This fact is revealed clearly by the work of all students of societal history. In the early stages of human society, people were forced to function in rather compact groups. Kinship, real or fictitious, was the bond which held individuals together. The relation of the individual to his group was all or nothing. Individual capacity was used to the advantage of all the members of the group; but if it was considered a serious handicap to the group, it was eliminated, often with blunt ruthlessness. Only by group solidarity and mutual aid could survival be made possible in the conflict with unconquered nature and hostile groups.

In this struggle, the child naturally was low in the scale of value; and when a choice had to be made, he and not the able-bodied adult was selected for elimination or exploitation. In the simpler stages of societal development, the problems of existence were immediate and the answers invariably were direct. A child was born, there was no room or food for him, so the parents snuffed out his life. At first, here and there, this was a personal, individual reaction. Repeated and continued, it became a social observance, and the practice of infanticide was established. The extent of its use, the degree of its social acceptance, the forms which it took, and the substitutes which arose vary in place and with time, but all the students of it emphasize poverty as its basic, precipitating factor.

What has been said about the relation of economic pressure to infanticide is equally true in regard to other practices which signify the status of childhood, or the lack of it. The heavy hand of economic want or scarcity lay heavy upon the heads of children through the ages. Parents loved their children, they indulged them when and as they could; but the institutionalized arrangements which determined the scope and scale of childhood were fixed by economic limits that were basic and distinct. It was and is not until the culture has reached the stage where economic surplus, or capital, is created that, first, individual parents in considerable numbers and, then, the social pattern are freed from the necessity of realizing present personal material gain from the child; only then can the parent and society afford to allow the child to devote himself to the development of his own individuality apart from parental demands.

The Ideological Factor

Against the dictates of necessity growing out of the economic factor is that deep and mystic bond which binds parent and child. Whatever form of neural hypothesis one supports concerning what is psychically inborn—whether parental affection is an instinct or an acquired emotional habit—the fact remains that it is real, deep-seated, and widespread. How then, we may ask, was it possible for many of the historic forms of child treatment to develop? Why did sheer mother love not suffice to safeguard the child during the centuries, even in the face of economic pressure?

The answer to these questions is to be found in the history of the social process of innumerable social groups, and it is this: The leaders in society invented plausible excuses to justify such practices because they considered it necessary to maintain them for other reasons. This is one of the functions of leadership: to take action which is necessary for some effective but not appealing reason, and to justify it in terms that are effective and in forms that are socially acceptable.

Consider infanticide. Direct want dictates its use in individual cases. As time goes on, it becomes customary. But mother love in many cases struggles against the custom. Social leadership, which accepts its necessity, must find—invent if you will—acceptable justification. There is recourse to many subterfuges. What more effective answer to mother love than fear of the gods? "Mother, the gods have need of your child. You must sacrifice him. If you do not, they will be angry, and they will visit their wrath upon all of us." Such an argument served a triple purpose: It offered the strongest kind of counteracting influence, it gave supernatural sanction, and it socialized the practice by making the entire group interested in its acceptance.

To the student of cultural history it is obvious that the various social and parental practices involving children, considered in the preceding sections, arose as scattered individual reactions to urgent and immediate needs, and that as these "answers" proved acceptable and effective they became general and customary. Thus arose the folkways of child care. As time goes on, these folkways are examined, challenged, criticized, and defended. Social leadership, convinced of their value, is intent upon their maintenance. Searching for support, the leaders develop justifying ideologies. A powerful ideology is the religious one. Throughout history, supernatural sanction has been constantly brought to bear in order to bolster up the folkways that have grown up. The whole terrifying threat of the malignancy of the spirit world is let loose upon those who tend to dispute the power and to threaten the interests of the predominant sex, class, or group. Those who stray from the beaten path of custom become tainted with moral iniquity.[20]

Although religious ideology has been used for purposes of concrete presentation, the idea advanced is this: What people have been taught to believe about children is the third basic factor in determining child status. Whether this factor is primary in character and original in time, or whether it is secondary, reinforcing, and rationalizing, is after all of minor importance, once it has developed and found social acceptance.

The Familial Factor

The familial factor is the final one which may be said to have basic significance in determining the status of childhood, and the two aspects of the family that are of outstanding importance in this connection are the structure or form of its organization, and the relative importance accorded to it as a social institution. The family is, of course, not an independent social institution capable of being fashioned as one wills. It is part and parcel of the organic life of society. From this it follows that the family's role as a determinant of child status is not separate and distinct from other factors; it

[20] Miller, *op. cit.*, pp. 33–34.

may be difficult to say which is the result of the influence of the family and which the result, let us say, of the economic factor. On the other hand, the family is the social vehicle through which the child customarily finds and makes his earlier way in the world; hence it seems obvious that what the family is and is not at any time and place in the history of a social group will have great meaning for the life and status of its children.

With reference to the form of the family, what all its historians have emphasized is the superiority of the monogamous type. The monogamous family has come to be the prevailing form because of its superiority over other historic competing forms. One of the bases of its superiority through the centuries of human experience is its high survival value. It is the best form of family life for children and the survival of child life. Polygyny, a competing form, is weak in its effect upon children. The care of the child tends, under this form, to rest more upon the mother. There is less biparental rearing of children.

In addition to the form, there is the relative importance of the family as a social institution. Among some peoples, the home and the family are of great significance, almost dwarfing at times other social institutions such as the state or the church. The family is the center of life and the outstanding vehicle for the transmission of the culture and values of the societal group. Because of this, the relationship between successive generations is closer and continues over a longer period of time than would otherwise obtain. On the other hand, there are and have been cultures in which the family seems of relatively minor importance. In ancient Sparta, for example, the state and not the family was considered paramount. In the Persia of classic times, the child remained with his mother until his fifth year; the father never saw him until then. At the end of this period, the boy left his mother and went under the care of the state to begin his physical training. But in China, through the centuries, the family has been of great importance and parental authority is strong, as a result of ancestor worship and the constant stress upon filial duty and piety. It is variations like these, in the relative position as well as the structure of family life, that have great basic meaning for the student of child problems.

THE STATUS OF CHILDHOOD IN CONTEMPORARY AMERICA

Against the picture set forth in the preceding pages stands the child in our contemporary society. Today, as can be readily perceived, the child and his interests and welfare are of prior and paramount importance. Not only is this the dictum of recent legislation and judicial decisions, it is the tacit assumption in the organization of the lives of millions of families and hundreds of communities. In the children's division of that new Magna Charta of human rights which a century and more of social struggle has evolved in our Western civilization, there are no emphases upon the rights of parents and relatively few upon the rights of society. Rather, they are upon the rights of children. Moreover, these rights are not simply new versions of the child's old prerogatives in the matter of food, shelter, and reasonable care; they are new rights, unknown and albeit inconceivable to parents and citizens of earlier centuries. The Children's Charter formulated by the third White House Conference on Child Health and Protection would have been as sacrilegious or unfathomable to the parents of a thousand years ago as the Declaration of Independence would have been to Louis XIV of France.

That the whole life of the modern child—all that is done and hoped and planned for him, either by individual parents or by organized social agencies—represents the opposite pole of the concept held 2000 or 200 years ago, is obvious; through the welter of changing circumstances and criteria we seek for the substance of the change. What is the essential change in the nature of the status of childhood?

The answer proposed is this: The essence of the change is the child's shift from a subordinate and incidental position in a family group dominated by an autocratic parent to one of acceptance as an equal with his own personality, needs, and problems of development. More tersely stated, it is a change from a position of subordination to one of equality, both in the family and in the larger social group. Use words to hide the truth as we will, the fact of the matter is that for centuries the child was dominated by his elders to be exploited in their interests. He had no rights, except as they fitted into the interests of his elders or his kinship group. That the bases of established authority upon which this exploitation rested came at various times and places to be clothed in ethical terms may confuse but does not alter the essential fact.

Today the child is recognized as a human personality in a peculiarly vital stage of development. He is a coequal personality in the emerging democracy of the family. The guarding of this personality is the child's precious right, and the dangers which threaten it are recognized social problems; the development of this personality is his most precious opportunity, and the furtherance and guidance of that development are the concern of his elders.

The great changes in human history occur, not in the mechanical gadgets which men use or in the institutionalized arrangements by which they live, but in their attitudes and in the values they accept. The revolutions of the past which have had great meaning for mankind are those which have taken place in the minds of men.

The outstanding change in the recent history of children has taken place in the minds of their elders. It has been essentially a change in the way in which older people, particularly parents, have come to regard children. This change has constituted a revolution in the life and status of children as a social element in the population.

Because this revolution has been achieved through gradual and voluntary concessions, rather than wrested by means of the more spectacular devices of bloodshed and riots, social historians have been slow to identify it or to appreciate its importance. Yet so profound and so far reaching in its consequences is this change in status proving to be that, viewed in the retrospect with a lengthened perspective, we may yet recognize it as one of the great revolutions of history.

Having in mind the nature and the epoch-making scope of this change, we propose in the remainder of this chapter to analyze the factors in American life which have been responsible for this transformation.

The Changing Arithmetic of Reproduction

It has been stated that the arithmetic of reproduction has operated through the ages as a basic factor in determining the status of childhood. Specifically, what was described there was the "easy-come and easy-go" method of reproduction—natural, wasteful, and involving a rather low value of the individual unit. This process, prevalent for centuries, was destined to change under the conditions attending the exploitation of the American continent and the emergence of the American culture. Although large families and high infant mortality rates continued in the New World for a time, the generally healthful conditions of life and the relative value of the individual resulting from the constant shortage of labor made for early emphasis on the conservation of child life. The result was the combination, for decades in our early history, of a high birth rate, a relatively low infant mortality rate, a rapid rate of population growth, and a high valuation of the individual unit.

The Economic Development of the United States

More than three centuries ago, small settlements of Europeans were being established along the east coast of this country. They were the beginning of that epic instance of nation building which is the history of the United States. In the course of three centuries, these small, scattered settlements grew into a nation of more than 190 million, and the continent which they opened and developed proved to be of unparalleled richness in the resources which Western civilization needed. During this same period, the economic system was transformed from medieval landlordism with its prevailingly simple and rural pattern, to modern capitalism with its huge complex and interrelated processes and its gigantic cities. Considering this development objectively, it must be obvious that these factors, and their combination in point of time, are so unusual as to raise the question whether anything like it, in both nature and scale, can ever again happen in world history; conceived in its comprehensive enormity, it must be equally clear that such a development would loom large and with intimate constancy in relation to the other elements of our emerging culture. In other words, we cannot understand American life without understanding and keeping this economic background constantly in mind, because for three centuries it colored every phase of our national development.

Although every aspect of this changing economic pattern is important for our purposes, one in particular needs to be emphasized. This is the continued existence of the frontier. The direction and speed of our settlement of this continent, and the tremendous transcontinental distance involved, accounted for one of the distinguishing features of American life, namely, the constant rebirth of our civilization for the 300 years of its history. This process of rebirth we have sensed on the westward-moving frontier, and its significance has been made clear by Turner, Paxon, and other historians.[21] The fact is that for several decades the arrival of large numbers of immigrants and the rapid development of industrial urban centers created, especially in our larger cities, a series of urban-industrial frontiers with many of the basic features of the earlier western frontiers, which operated after the early frontier on the slopes of the Pacific had ceased to exist. This process of rebirth, usually associated with the western frontier, has actually continued in the urban East down to the present time.

The relationship between the changing economic background

[21] F. J. Turner, *The Frontier in American History,* Henry Holt & Company, New York, 1920.

and the changing status of childhood is merely a phase of the larger story of the role of the economic factor in the development of our entire culture. It is well to keep this in mind here, for it means that while certain effects on the status of childhood were obvious and direct, many were indirect and touched child status only as it reacted to general changes in the culture as a whole. The discussion that follows, then, is meant to be selective and suggestive.

1. Migration is a highly selective process. This was particularly true in the case of colonial migration to the New World, for it involved a lengthy and uncertain voyage over an inadequately charted ocean to an unknown land beset with many dangers and difficulties. The bases of selection were bound to be definite and rigorous, and one of them clearly was a marked interest in the future. This interest would have to be more than a personal, self-centered one; it would be an interest in the family's future, in children, in the migrant's children, and in the future of society, which means other people's children. Selectivity on this basis meant that from the beginning the American colonist was relatively a lover of children. The whole process of colonial migration involved the continuing selection of persons sufficiently interested in the coming generations to make them exchange the certainties of the present for the prospect of the future. Building for the future is a child welfare process.

2. From the first days of our colonial history, children were wanted. All the social historians emphasize this fact. And the more the vastness of the unfolding continent and its needs impressed themselves upon the minds of the people, the more was the valuation of the child increased. It seems safe to make the generalization that in any situation in which the population is small and there are vast and valuable resources to be developed, children will tend to occupy an important position. Large families, under such circumstances, are an asset. The labor of grown sons and daughters is valuable. Children also give security against various foes and dangers—of man and beast and the forces of nature.

The continuing need for a rapidly growing population was a constant factor encouraging early marriage, large families, and a high status for childhood. As has already been intimated, it led public authorities to be rather impatient with parents whose strictness with their adolescent children interfered with these ends. Parents had the right to supervise and control the courtship of their children, it was true, but only within reason, and not so as to interfere with the interests of society. Here, as so often happens, the interests of the community take precedence over private rights.

3. In an old, settled society, what has been is accorded respect. The conventions of life have crystallized and are emphasized, traditions are revered, the old are consulted and obeyed. In a new world, men think primarily in terms of the future. In the face of new situations, the opinions of the young count for as much as those of their elders. In fact, the young are less likely to be encumbered by vestigial thinking. The hold of ancestral and paternal prestige is diminished; the trend is toward the transference of power to the more youthful members of the group. If the new country is rich, there is engendered a social optimism which tends to measure people by their future prospects rather than by the tokens of the past.

Expressed in terms of the family, all this means thinking in terms of descendants rather than of ancestors. "For the children" became the motto of many a pioneer family who broke new ground and endured loneliness and privation and danger, always with an eye to the consoling fact that their children would have a better chance, would grow up with the country and enter into their inheritance.

4. There were other reasons why the thoughts of many families in the New World should be directed so largely to the future. Unpleasant as it may be to recall, many people who migrated to America had no family tree which they could regard with much pride or satisfaction. American historians are not inclined to take literally Dr. Samuel Johnson's reference to the colonists as "a race of convicts," yet it is well known that from time to time the English authorities emptied their prisons upon the shores of America. Although it is true that many of these persons were guilty of what are regarded today as rather petty offenses, the fact remains that the families they established here in the New World would emphasize almost exclusively their future prospects rather than their past status.

The same thought applies to many other early settlers as well as the later immigrants. They may not have had criminal records, but they were individuals who had not succeeded signally in the Old World. Their coming to America was a new deal, it gave them a fresh start, it meant turning over a new leaf, it involved essentially turning their back upon the old life and hopefully facing the new. Expressed in terms of family life, this meant that the children embodied their dream of the future—the children were the future.

5. The ease with which young people could make their own way, independent of aid from their families, was another powerful factor in the emancipation of American childhood and youth. Land was the basis of the prevailing economy, it was cheap, and for many years there was an abundance of unoccupied land. The equipment needed to cultivate it was scant. As soon as a young man had

gathered a few dollars he could look forward confidently to establishing a family of his own. The customary wedding gift to a son was a horse, some farm implements, and some seed; a girl received a bed, a cow, some kitchen utensils, a table, and some chairs. The relatives might help in erecting a cabin and a crude stable. Life was simple, the prime necessities were abundant, subsistence was certain.

Such a situation made for self-sufficiency and independence at an early age. After their earliest years, children were not essentially dependent upon their parents. The tendency was toward the early loosening of the family bond. Undue prolongation of parental prerogatives was likely to result in estrangement. It was not that younger people always made their own way early in life, but that they so easily could, which was the emancipating factor.

As the nineteenth century wore on and land became less cheap and accessible, particularly in the older parts of the country, the factory system made its appearance, and many boys and girls went to work in these new industrial establishments at an early age. This development is usually referred to as part of the history of child labor, with rather definite condemnation of it. Whatever we may say about the employment of these children, measured by present-day standards, from the standpoint of our discussion here it had an emancipating influence in the relation of children and their elders. Give a child his own pay envelope, and the parent-child relationship is changed; have him share his wages with his parent, and he has gone a good part of the way in purchasing immunity to parental control.

6. The continuing process of vertical mobility in American society has been a far greater factor in parent-child relationships than is usually appreciated. Throughout their history, the people of the United States have been "on the up," economically speaking. Each generation has wanted to live better than preceding ones, and has succeeded so generally that such success has been accepted as natural and almost inevitable. This process has been viewed for the most part as an index of the economic progress of the country; what has only seldom been considered is its meaning in the relationship between these generations and their attitudes toward each other.

To speak more specifically, for 300 years the American child has been taught constantly to aim higher than his parents, to "begin where they left off." In this he has been aided and abetted, as a rule, by his parents, who have sacrificed, subordinated, driven themselves even, all to the end that he would have better advantages than they had. Even the unlettered immigrant, preoccupied with his own problems of adjustment to the New World, has felt impelled to give his children better advantages—often much better—than he and his forebears had.

7. Occupational mobility throughout the history of this country has played an important role in changing the status of childhood. Unlike the practice in older, more fixed civilizations, where a child customarily follows the occupation of his father, the very nature and needs of our rapidly expanding economic development made this largely impossible. The overwhelming proportion of the workers in this country have gone into jobs different from those of their parents.

The significance of this for parent-child relationships is easy to grasp. American youth has been freed from parental supervision while at work, and since this form of supervision cannot always be separated from more comprehensive supervision, it has often meant freedom from parental supervision in general. Then, too, differences in the economic careers of parent and child have involved and facilitated divergence of interests, and this is part of the larger process of growing apart.

8. The American population has been relatively very mobile. The exploitation of the continent would not have been possible by a race of "stay-at-homes." Earlier these movements were largely westward; but more recently, large-scale migrations in other directions have been taking place.

The population movements which have been a feature of American history have had their counterparts in family histories. The expansion of the United States has been in large measure a series of westward jumps of successive generations. The Middle West was the New England and Middle Atlantic States of a later date; Colorado and Utah, the more intrepid of the next generation; the Pacific coast is the contemporary edition of all of them.

This entire process has, from one angle, been disruptive, tending to weaken family ties. Particularly was this true in the case of successive generations. Mobility of residence put space between them, just as differences of occupation made for divergence of interests. These two factors were peculiarly complementary in their effects; taken together, they were of continued and fundamental importance in changing the status of American youth.

9. Thus far, the discussion has been in terms of children, with no reference to any differences on a sex basis. From the very beginning, however, certain factors operated particularly to affect the status of girls. In a rough, wild, new country, it is evident that conventions and restraints concerning women which are natural and necessary in more staid cultures become untenable. Everyone, re-

gardless of sex and, to some extent, age, must take a hand. The seclusion of women, for example, is not feasible. The frontier spirit is democratic, for young women as well as for the rest of the population; special treatment does not fit into the folkways.

Then, too, there was the effect of the arithmetic of the situation. For the greater part of our history, and particularly in the newer parts of the country, there has been a deficit of woman. Between the older settled East and the more frontierlike West there went on, for decades, almost a commercial traffic in unmarried women. This shortage of wives, actual and potential, tended early toward the breakdown of the parental control of courtship and marriage, and where the control continued, young girls exercised considerable independence in their love affairs.

Other factors particularly affecting the status of girls might be mentioned, but enough has been said to indicate that from the beginning of our history the relative freedom of the American girl was the natural product of conditions of life in this country.

10. The final aspect of the role of the economic factor in the changing status of American childhood to be emphasized here is the transition from a state of deficit to one of surplus, economically speaking. The reference here is to the enlarging capacity of our nation to finance the changing position and treatment of children, with special emphasis on the historical operation of this factor. Whether the surplus condition has passed permanently for the time being, whether it ceased with our large-scale discounting of the future in the huge borrowings during and since World War I—particularly since 1930—is an important question but has no bearing upon our historical analysis.

The rapid increase in the wealth of the United States, particularly between the Civil War and our entrance into World War I, is well known, and there can be no doubt of its fundamental importance in the tranformation of our life. Of the general social implications of this transition no one has written with more insight perhaps than the late Simon N. Patten. His concept of a pain and a pleasure economy and of the process of the change from one to the other, although described over a half century ago and not so well known to modern students, remains the most penetrating analysis of the fundamental changes involved. In an age of deficit, there exists what he called a pain economy. The primary purpose of this economy is the avoidance of pain, protection from enemies, the prevention of want, safety against destruction. The basis of the social institutions of such an economy is the fear of enemies and of pain. The purpose of its state is protection from enemies; of its morality, avoidance of destruction; of its religion, help from supernatural powers against foes; of its families, the satisfaction of primary physical needs. In a pleasure or surplus economy, the objectives of society are concerned with the promotion of welfare, with the enrichment and enlargement of the good life. Social values and ideals are recast and social institutions are remade to function toward these newer ends. The transition from a pain to a pleasure economy, Patten declared, was a difficult one, full of stresses and dangers.[22]

The child is a part of this economy and culture that is reconstructed as a result of this transition. In a pain economy, he is a pawn in the war against the constantly recurring threat of direct want, a pawn to be utilized, to be exploited. His function is to aid in the struggle for survival. Of affection between parents and child there may be a great deal, but life is hard and rigorous and imposes sharp and cruel limitations. In an age of surplus, the child becomes a luxury, the subject of social solicitude, the object of social planning. There is conscious promotion of his welfare. The question of how he can help in the struggle for survival is displaced by the question as to what can be done to develop him to the limit of his possibilities. The period of preparation for life is lengthened. Laws against child labor take form, and their age limitations are revised upward again and again. Schools multiply and the age of compulsory attendance is raised. Supplementary services and resources aimed at the more intensive cultivation of child capacities are developed. Children are reckoned in terms of their future possibilities, and the expenditure of the social surplus on them is conceived as a promising investment.

The Ideological Factor

American ideology is a colorful combination compounded of many elements. Some of these elements have changed from time to time throughout our history, others have remained rather constant. Our conception of and emphases on our ideology change too, for each generation recasts its ideas on the bases of its changing interests and needs. With this appreciation of the changing complexity of American ideology, the thesis is advanced here that this ideology has been compounded largely out of three basic and rather constant ingredients: humanitarianism, science, and democracy. The relationship of each of these to the changing status of childhood will be discussed briefly.

[22] Simon N. Patten, "The Theory of Social Forces," *Publications of the American Academy of Political and Social Science*, 1896, chap. 4.

1. HUMANITARIANISM AND THE CHILD. There is an abundance of evidence that humanitarianism has increased greatly in its range in recent years. We need not go back more than a century and a half in the most advanced countries of Western culture to find a good deal of abuse of animals and human beings—the extensive existence of slavery, marked cruelties in the treatment of criminals, the brutal beating of small children, little interest in the poor except on the basis of personal almsgiving, incredible horrors in the treatment of the feebleminded and insane. In the years since then, the condition of one after another of these groups has been transformed: the treatment of the sick, the insane, and various physically and mentally defective and sick persons has been humanized; there has been widespread amelioration in the condition of criminals; a large amount of social legislation has been passed to improve working conditions; slavery has been abolished; women have been placed more nearly on an equality with men; societies for the prevention of cruelty to animals have flourished; and extensive philanthropic movements have been directed toward the relief of distress and the reduction of poverty.[23]

Modern humanitarianism could not but affect the status of children. To begin with, children were bound to benefit from the ordinary implications of a general movement which affected the status and treatment of virtually all subject, exploited, and neglected groups. As one of these groups, children would naturally share in any general upward revision of the standards applied to such groups. But more than that, by their very nature they would be the particular beneficiaries of such a movement. After all, they were nearest and dearest to the persons who were influenced by these new humanitarian considerations, and no society could concern itself indefinitely with the freeing of slaves and better treatment for criminals without also taking thought of its children.

2. SCIENCE AND THE CHILD. Science is the architect of our civilization. Its achievements dominate modern culture, and its spirit shapes the character of our intellectual and spiritual life. To the Western mind, all other expressions of the creative spirit seem somewhat futile. The final appeal in all problems and disputed points is to the scientist, and his judgments we consider to be altogether true and righteous.

The history of science is the story of its progressive application to an ever wider range of phenomena. First applied to the material

[23] Maurice Parmelee, *Poverty and Social Progress*, The Macmillan Company, New York, 1916, chap. 17.

objects of the nonliving world, with the consequent development of the physical sciences, the scientific method came in time to be applied successively to the field of organic life, with the resultant renaissance of the biological studies, and then to the realm of psychic phenomena, with the emergence of the modern psychological sciences. Finally, the most complex phase of human life, namely, human association, has come to be studied scientifically, with the gradual emergence of the social studies as scientific disciplines.

One phase of this most recent extension of the scientific method has been its application to the social welfare movement. Conceived originally with good intention and born at the dawn of human history out of an emotional concern for the unfortunate, this movement has been going to school, figuratively speaking, in the temple of science. The lessons learned in that temple, the methods utilized, the attitudes emphasized, are revolutionizing social welfare just as science has revolutionized other fields of human effort. We are concerned, at this point, in appraising in somewhat broad terms how the application of the scientific method to social phenomena in general and to the social welfare movement in particular has affected our attitude toward the child and his importance.

One definite way in which this application of the scientific method has affected the status of work with children has been through its emphasis upon the genetic point of view. The point of view of modern science is genetic. Since the time of Charles Darwin, and as a result of his work, all science, broadly speaking, has become biological. Every science sees its problems against an evolutionary background, which means that everything is viewed in the light of its historical development. In other words, when we say that the point of view of modern science is genetic, we mean that every science sees its problems in a historical perspective, and that if we want to understand anything we must understand its origin and development.

Such a point of view applied to problems of human life has revolutionary significance for childhood, for it makes this period of life of paramount importance. Childhood is the period of origins, the stage of beginnings. It is the period in which so many problems arise and are manifest in their incipient stages. This can be illustrated with particular aptness in the history of the science of psychology. G. Stanley Hall, the Nestor of American psychology, was also its outstanding specialist in genetic psychology.

A second way in which the application of the scientific method to social phenomena and problems affects child study and work with children is through its emphasis on the principle of causation.

The point of view of modern science is causal; its object is the establishment of causal relationships. This is saying horizontally much the same thing we say vertically when we point out that the point of view of modern science is genetic; either approach has the same significance for childhood.

This is, perhaps, the essential difference in the way our ancestors and ourselves regard the child. Our ancestors saw these earliest years as a negative period of life, a sort of necessary evil full of idle deviltry and cantankerous mischief; the child survived it and his parents endured it as best they could, until late adolescence when life hesitatingly began. We, of a later vintage, regard childhood as a foundation period of great importance, a period of twig bending during which the shape of the future tree is determined.

To be sure, students of human problems have emphasized causal antecedents for many years. Only recently, however, has come the knowledge that these causal relations are neither so few in number nor so simple in their operation as had previously been supposed. In the study of these relationships, there has been a transfer of interest and emphasis from the broadly obvious to the subtly effective. It is this that is essentially new in the contemporary approach to the study of behavior problems. Modern psychiatry and the psychoanalytic procedure have multiplied many times the significance of the earliest years. Theories regarding the causation of crime, mental disease, distorted character, economic failure, and domestic maladjustment have had to be reconstructed on the basis of the contributions of the modern sciences and resolved into elements of juvenile conditioning.

Under the suggestive influence of the genetic and causal points of view of modern science, the social welfare movement is coming to a new and better understanding of its task. The cumulative effect of recent discoveries in the life sciences has been to make the social welfare movement more "child-minded." The modern mind, wrestling with the problems of human welfare, finds them where Plato dreamed his ideal state—in the directed development of the next generation. Science now dictates what our tender sympathies long have counseled. Society's "acres of diamonds" lies revealed in the cradle inside the door, and social statesmanship finds its task in the heart of a child.

3. Modern Democracy and the Child. It is interesting to speculate on what the status of the child would be today in this country were it not for the rise and dominance of democracy. What effect would the other factors working to emancipate the child have had without the favoring support of this comprehensive, conditioning

background? The emancipation of the American child must be considered, then, against the background, and as an integral part, of the general democratization of society. As such, it takes its place with other familial aspects of this democratizing process—the decay of patriarchy, the waning of paternal authority, and the greater freedom of and opportunities for women.

The most familiar instances of the operation of democracy are found in the political field. Political democracy has had direct and immediate significance for the status of children, for its basic tenet is to make the individual the ultimate unit of social development. The emancipation of the child, the decay of patriarchalism, the waning of the father's authority, and the changed status of the mother are all natural consequences of political democracy, which recognizes not clans or families, but individuals. "In a democracy the idea of superior fades before the idea of equal sovereignty. All men are sovereigns. Personality is exalted, and the political status overflows and democratizes family institutions."[24]

But democracy is more than a political creed or system. It is, in the ultimate analysis, an idea, an attitude, a value, a spirit, which permeates every phase of life. It expresses itself in and through our religious, economic, scientific, and social developments, as was pointed out in Chapter 4, and it is as a common core in these developments that it stimulated the changing status of childhood.

Perhaps all that has been said concerning the ideological factors —the rise of humanitarianism and the development of modern science and of the democratic way of life—comes to this: The current American ideology involves a new conception of the worth of the individual, and an appreciation of the child as the promise and hope of that individual.

The Familial Factor

The child is so inextricably a part of the family that no discussion of a change in his status is complete without reference to changes in the family. Changes in the status as well as in the structure and functions of the family must be considered, then, as factors in the changing status of childhood. For a more complete study of the changing family, the reader is referred to the excellent books on the family which are now available. Here only selected aspects of these changes will be dealt with briefly.

1. Historic Status of the American Family. "Families are the nurseries of the church and the commonwealth; ruin families

[24] Calhoun, *op. cit.*, vol. II, p. 53.

and you ruin all." This maxim of the early colonial fathers is indicative of the high status which the family as a social institution enjoyed in those days. This status was the natural result of the conditions of colonial settlement, and certain factors inherent in our national development have tended to maintain and increase this relative status until comparatively recent years. These factors will be outlined briefly at this point.

The American colonist of English stock was a home builder from the beginning. It was his interest in his family, his home, and his children, and his belief that their future was circumscribed in the Old World which led to his migration to the New.

Some of the other nationality groups which figured prominently in the settlement of the United States were noted for their domesticity. This was particularly true of the German colonists. From the beginning, they manifested a distinctive fondness for home life. They gave America a distinct type of woman, interested primarily in the household arts. German husbands and fathers in colonial America were noted for their interest in home life and their participation in the simple pleasures of their family groups. Similarly, the Dutch in New York were mentioned repeatedly because of their conspicuous success with the marriage relationship. Both they and the Huguenots farther to the south were a liberalizing influence as far as family relationships were concerned. The Huguenots were particularly noted for their pleasant home life.

Migration is always a selective process, and from the standpoint of the present discussion it is significant that the English migration to colonial America, as well as that of the Germans, Huguenots, Dutch, and Swedes who settled among them, occurred in the form of family units. Moreover, this family character persisted in the immigration stream until far down into the nineteenth century, and among such groups as the Russian Jews, until into the twentieth century. It is this movement in terms of family units that makes these migrations differ from those of the French and Spanish to colonial America, and this distinction does much to explain the differences in the success of these respective groups as colonizers.

The relative lack of development of other institutions in the early centuries of our national existence favored the family. The whole historical background of these population movements, the experience of the colonists in their home countries, was not such as to favor any immmediate development of a strong state, particularly because of the close connection of colonial governmental organizations with those of Europe. The school too, while not neglected, was relatively weak in those days. The church in New England, but apparently not so much so elsewhere, was the only social institution approaching the family in importance. The family was the one substantial social institution in a nation which had discarded hierarchical religion and reduced the power of government to a minimum. The entire colonizing process placed a premium upon the pioneers who moved in groups of families and tended to settle in areas contiguous enough to facilitate cooperation for defense, worship, and other prime social necessities, but for all other purposes utilized the family as the cradling and shaping agent of the new life.

What made possible this relative reliance upon the family was the self-sufficiency of the home as an economic unit. The almost complete self-sufficiency of the family in the economy of the time is pointed out by all economic and family historians. More will be said about this in the discussion of the functions of the family; the fact to be noted here is the importance of this self-sufficiency in support of the family's dominant role as a social institution.

Another factor of considerable importance was the relative isolation of the homes. This prevailed rather generally in the early history of this country, and in many cases persisted down to comparatively recent times. The general density of population for the greater part of our history and among our people has been very low. Rural settlements for the most part took the form of isolated homesteads rather than agricultural villages as in Europe. This isolation tended to throw the family upon itself, upon its own resources. It reduced tremendously the possibility or likelihood of much social control of the family, especially as far as detailed or continuing control was concerned.

Especially did the isolation of the frontier tend to turn the family within itself. The absence of social contacts, the silence and monotony, the lack of competing distractions, all characteristic of the frontier, made for strong family interests. This pioneer isolation tended not only to increase the importance of the family but also to soften and deepen its relationships. Husband and wife, parent and child, were partners in a common enterprise in work, and playmates in their recreational pursuits.

2. EFFECT UPON THE STATUS OF CHILDREN. The relatively high status of the family as a social institution did not per se have a softening effect upon the treatment of children or tend to raise their status. Conceivably the importance of the family, coupled with the relative lack of importance of the state in the earlier centuries of our history, might have formed the basis of a highly repressive policy toward children. Conceivably the autocracy of the Roman

parent might have been restored on the frontier. Who would there have been to say naught? Fortunately the other factors identified in this and the preceding chapter prevented that from happening. Neither the economic nor the ideological factors and incentives would have fitted in with such a turn of events. Rather they gave this strong family interest a liberalizing and democratic turn to aid still further in the emancipating process. The historic status of the American family operated, then, in the direction of a high level of parental interest in children, the mathematical, economic, and ideological factors and incentives combining to dictate the direction of that heightened interest toward more democratic objectives.

We must not be misunderstood when we say that the family today has a lower status in the institutional framework of society than it did in the earlier period of our history. In part, this has been due to the rise to pre-eminence of other institutions, notably the state and the school. The status of both of these has been revolutionized within the past century; hence the relative position of the family would be altered, even if no changes had occurred in it. But there have been changes, principally in its structure and functions, and it is to these that we turn next.

3. Changing Structure and Functions. All students of the modern family agree that the family has been transformed in recent decades. In so far as its structure is concerned, the older, larger, semipatriarchal form has given way to the contemporary, smaller, democratic, companionship type. Many of the aspects and factors involved in this change have been alluded to in the preceding pages. They include: (1) the passing of the family function of economic production; (2) the gainful employment of women, particularly married women, outside the home; (3) the mechanization, and the consequent lightening of the burdens of housekeeping; and (4) the small-family system and the resultant shrinkage in the physical basis of the home.[25]

With these changes in structure have come significant changes in the functions of the family. The decline of the home in the field of economic production has been accompanied by its increasing importance as a consumption unit, emphasizing rational consumption as a factor in the positive well-being of its members. In the area of protective functions, the rise of the civil authority and its agencies has led the family to shift its attention from dangers to life and limb to the protection of the interests of its members. The recreational needs of children tend to be satisfied less and less within

[25] W. F. Ogburn and M. F. Nimkoff, *Technology and the Changing Family*, Houghton Mifflin Company, Boston, 1955.

the home, with the result that parents are concerned more with the selection, evaluation, supervision, guidance, and coordination of the family's recreational life. The responsibility for the education of children is now turned over to the school, the parents devoting themselves to the supervision and supplementation of the educational process. The small-family system makes possible the development of a more intensive parenthood.

From the standpoint of the child, the changing functions of the family have involved, first, the decline of its control over, and responsibility for, various phases of child development; second, the development of various specialized agencies to whom is transferred the responsibility for selected segments of the childrearing process. The first has many consequences, but considered in relation to the status of childhood it tends to enable the family to give the child services that supplement those of the specialized children's agencies, and to stimulate in an increasing proportion of families the development of an improved technique of parenthood. The second has led inevitably to the development of new vested interests concerned directly with the raising and maintenance of the status of childhood.

When this latter development is examined objectively and in terms of social process, the following steps emerge rather clearly: The creation of specialized child development agencies and services means, from the occupational standpoint, specialized jobs. This leads in turn to the development of specialized training facilities—schools, courses, institutes, and teaching personnel. Not only do these function to satisfy the demands for specialized training, but, naturally perhaps, they magnify the importance of the jobs for which they offer training. Time passes, and a specialized group of jobholders develops in a particular field; gradually, these jobholders become conscious of themselves and their common interests; ultimately they begin to organize, both to protect their interests and further to exploit their field. Thus arises a vested interest. The claim having been staked off, the developing resources having been organized, the next step is intensive cultivation. Against the background of a constantly increasing emphasis on its fundamental importance, refinements of specialized service are developed. They are labeled *the technique*. A literature specialized in scope and ambitious in tone is fostered; public interest and appreciation are cultivated. The leaders in the specialty now tend to be of the promoter type, rather than concerned with ideals of service or research. There is a growing intolerance of any critical analysis of task or technique. Jobs are at stake, budgets are imperiled, funds are threatened.

This brief account of the natural history of the development of a specialized service is sufficient to indicate that the parceling-out of the care of children to specialized service groups results, as time goes on, in the creation of various vested interests vitally concerned in promoting the importance of children, their needs, their welfare, and their status. For decades this factor has been operating silently and subtly in the development of ideas, programs, legislation, and so on, for children, thus involving an obvious rise in the status of childhood.

The history of many of these specialized service activities and groups shows that they begin in an experimental way, supported by private philanthropic means. But as time goes on and the service is established and is sold more and more to the public, public interest and discussion increase. Legislative aspects gradually emerge, and still further public discussion follows. Ultimately a public program takes form, the services are taken over as an obligation of the public treasury, and public agencies plan comprehensive programs to cover the particular field. All this means that the child, his needs, and his importance, enter more and more into the public consciousness; standards of child care, which yesterday were the dreams of a few idealistic folk, tomorrow are the irreducible minimum below which no child must be allowed to live.

Finally, what has been described is a continuing process. These specialized types of child services are subject constantly to the forces of revision. New needs arise and stimulate new types of specialized services or modified forms of older ones. Sometimes these new types or modifications are added to those already established, resulting in marked growth and expansion of the range of the specialized services and agencies involved. This may proceed until the proportions attained are out of harmony with the group culture as a whole, raising problems of culture correlation such as are discussed in the closing pages of this volume. Or—and this is a second possibility—the new types of services may challenge the older, vested interests, with all the attendant evidences of conflict.

SUMMARY

1. Children constituted a relatively large population element in primitive society. Although they were desired, abortion, infanticide, child spacing, short infancy, and early labor were common in the primitive cultures of the past.

2. Certain changes in the status of children can be noted in the civilizations of classic antiquity. Infanticide often softened into aban-

donment and exposure, child selling developed as a substitute for both, and emphasis on the duty of children to support their parents became common. However, there remained the sweeping and arbitrary rights of parents to use their child in whatever way was to their advantage.

3. The status of the medieval child was the product of a blending of Roman, German, and Christian influences. Childhood was short, rigorous work came early in life, and childrearing was coldly severe and harsh, even at the level of royalty.

4. Newer attitudes toward children appeared in England during the eighteenth century. Despite the retention of historic practices, parents began to show some conception of their duties to their children. Such changes, however, were limited in extent and scope.

5. Colonial America reproduced, with certain modifications, the European pattern of child status. This pattern appeared most clearly in New England, and can best be studied there.

6. The colonial family had high status, was patriarchal in form and large in size. Maternal and infant mortality were high. Child labor was common, and from an early age. Family discipline was rigid, as was that of the school. Colonial law clearly supported both parent and teacher in their disciplinary measures. Manners and courtesy were markedly emphasized. Courtship was controlled closely by the parents. Religious experience was emphasized early in the lives of children. Large families seem, however, to have permitted some recreational developments, and references to children's games are numerous, even if sometimes in the form of complaints.

7. Contemporary America is seeing a revolutionary change in the status of children; they are viewed in terms of equality with other members of the family and recognized as coequal personalities in the emerging democracy of the family.

8. Reviewing the general history of childhood, we see four factors as the basic determinants in its status: (a) the arithmetic of reproduction; (b) the prevailing economic situation; (c) the ideological factor; and (d) the familial factor.

SUGGESTED READINGS

Ariès, Philippe, *Centuries of Childhod,* Alfred A. Knopf, New York, 1962. An interestingly written and comprehensive history of many aspects of child life, including dress, games, discipline, schools, and family.

Bayne-Powell, Rosamond, *The English Child in the Eighteenth Century,* E. P. Dutton & Company, New York, 1939. An interesting book on many phases of child life during this period, it includes letters written by children.

Calhoun, Arthur W., *A Social History of the American Family,* vols. I, II, III, Arthur H. Cook Company, Cleveland, 1919. Volume I covers the Colonial Period; Volume II, from the Revolutionary War to the Civil War; Volume III, from the Civil War to the time of writing.

Earle, Alice Morse, *Child Life in Colonial Days,* The Macmillan Company, New York, 1896. A very readable, intimate picture of the day-to-day life of the colonial child.

Gruenberg, Sidonie Matsner (Ed.), *The Family in a World at War,* Harper & Brothers, New York, 1942. A series of discussions by scholars and people prominent in public life. It illustrates that even in child-centered societies, national crisis takes first place over the welfare of children.

Hole, Christina, *The English Housewife in the Seventeenth Century,* Chatto and Windus, London, 1953. Customs surrounding critical steps in the life of the baby and young child are described in Chapter 8.

Ogburn, W. F., and M. F. Nimkoff, *Technology and the Changing Family,* Houghton Mifflin Company, Boston, 1955. The recent history of technological change in the United States which has so profoundly affected child status.

Payne, George Henry, *The Child in Human Progress,* G. P. Putnam's Sons, New York, 1916. A history of child status in his social, political, and humanitarian existence through many centuries.

Zimmerman, Carle C., *The Family and Civilization,* Harper & Brothers, New York and London, 1947. The author traces historically the status of the family in its society, and illustrates how child status changes with that of the family.

CHILDREARING IN THE UNITED STATES 21

The preceding chapters have sought to summarize the changing status of children considered as a separate population element. Emphasis has been directed to the broad historic changes that have occurred and to the basic factors that have been responsible. But broad social changes have a way of expressing themselves in specific movements and attitudes, and the changing status of childhood has been no exception. During this century a variety of ideas have crystallized concerning how children should be treated by the larger society, and how they should be reared by their parents. Most of these ideas are reflections of definite changes in our society and have resulted in new experiments in rearing children. This chapter seeks to examine some of the trends, in this respect, in the United States during the 1900's.

THE CONCEPT OF RIGHTS

The best-known statement of human rights is the American Declaration of Independence. "We hold these truths to be self-evident, that all men are created equal, that they are endowed by their Creator with certain unalienable rights, that among these are life, liberty and the pursuit of happiness. That to secure these rights, governments are instituted among men, deriving their just powers from the consent of the governed." This statement, together with the French Declaration of the Rights of Man and of the Citizen (1789), marked the inauguration of the modern age and inspired the triumph of modern democracy.

Recent years have witnessed a resurgence of interest in the subject of human rights, and some notable attempts have been made to revise the historic formulations. These have been directed chiefly toward the inclusion of economic and social rights, on the basis of the claim that we are living in a new world in which the central problems arise from new pressures of power, production, and population which our forefathers did not face. The proposed new rights center about the development of personality, the basic implication being that there are certain social and economic rights which are as essential as the civil and political rights already established.

The concept of the rights of childhood is a product of the larger program of human rights. When first applied to children, the alleged rights were little more than claims which children were said to have upon the consideration of society, especially if that society was blessed with social feelings and intelligence. These rights might be spoken of as a series of ethical insistences. Gradually, however, these claims found expression in organized efforts, first private and then public; in the "amiable purposes" of the philanthropic; in goals formulated by professional workers; in standards set by official and quasi-official bodies, as the White House Conferences; and lastly, in legislative enactments.

It is often contended that these rights are not "true rights" and that they have no validity in scientific treatises or in government documents, at least not until they become the specific statement of some legislative act. To this Merriam replies as follows: "That rights have not yet been fully recognized or realized does not remove them from the field of the political, for politics deals with ideals as well as with realities. Ideals indeed are themselves realities. The rights of man provide the domain of faith and hope in government, the court of appeal which is never closed, the law beyond the law and the jurists, the lawmakers, the managers, and the adjudicators. The rights of man go deeper and higher than institutional devices for interpreting or applying them."[1]

To clarify the point of view in this volume, it will suffice to say that

[1] Charles E. Merriam, "Essential Human Rights," *Annals of the American Academy of Political and Social Science*, January, 1946, p. 12.

the rights of childhood are conceived of as social values in process of translation into the realities of daily living. This process begins with the crystallization of the ideas on which these values rest; it passes through many forms of social expression; and each manifestation in its history is but another index of the changing status of childhood. Some of these rights or social values will be considered briefly.

The Right to Life

The basic right is the right to life. It involves the biological insistence for life expression, a social recognition of the eternal worth of the individual. Concretely, emphasis upon the child's right to life has been translated into the movement against infant mortality, one of the historic tragedies of childhood. Being a child has always been a dangerous occupation, and the earlier the stage in the life span, the greater has been the hazard. In all cultures and throughout the centuries, the first year was the most crucial one. A century ago, in this country, one out of every four babies born alive died before the end of the first year. As late as 60 years ago, a baby born in the United States had less chance to live a week than a person 90 years old, and less chance to live a year than an individual 80 years of age.

Following the series of fundamental discoveries in the second half of the nineteenth century which laid the foundation for the modern science of bacteriology, individual leaders like Pierre Budin in France, Benjamin Broadbent in England, and L. Emmet Holt in the United States began to develop and advocate new techniques which revolutionized pediatric practice. These in turn led to organized movements, first developed through private initiative and financial support, like the Strauss milk depots in New York City, and then through publicly authorized and financed efforts, like the establishment of the federal Children's Bureau, the passage (1921) of the Sheppard-Towner Act, and the Social Security Acts, beginning in 1935. As a result of these efforts and changes in attitude which they indicated, infant mortality rates today are roughly one-sixth of what they were at the turn of the century. Social effort has gone far in guaranteeing the child's right to life.

The Right to Be Wanted

The desire to control fertility apparently is age-old and universal, and it has taken a variety of forms. Once infanticide was widely practiced, with full consent of society and its leaders. The milder form of abandonment once was a recognized device. Abortion seems universal and frequent, by means of either bodily violence or internal concoctions. In primitive society, infanticide and abortion are the chief substitutes for control of conception. Most of the modern methods used are preventive, in that they seek control through the prevention of conception.

The past century has witnessed marked changes in the ability of parents to limit the size of their families. First, there have been great improvements in the techniques of contraception, and in their effectiveness. Today more than 200 mechanical devices are used in Western culture, in addition to chemical and other agents. Second has been the widespread diffusion and democratization of contraceptive knowledge, resulting both in its wider diffusion at upper-class levels and in its widespread penetration into the lower classes.

The third development has been the rise of cultural pressures favoring the limitation of family size. Particularly outstanding has been the stress upon its social and economic desirability. Four of these pressures might be mentioned briefly. (1) The maintenance of a large family in an industrial culture is much more precarious than in the older handicraft or agricultural system. (2) The economic value of a child to his parents has changed enormously. Formerly, the child, measured in economic terms, was an asset. His early and certain introduction to employment, often in his own family, resulted in his maintaining himself and being a source of income to his parents over a long period. Our contemporary industrial-urban pattern has changed all that. City life offers few opportunities for early and gradual employment. Industry eliminates the opportunities for homework. Child labor laws establish age limits for entering gainful occupations, and compulsory school requirements supplement these nonemployment factors. As a result, the child is today an economic liability to his parents, and definitely so, rather than an asset as formerly. (3) A relatively open class system is an important even if intangible factor. In any country where a considerable number of persons believe that they can raise their status by their own efforts, prudence combines with ambition to lead many families to seek to limit their size. (4) The status of women and their conception of their role in life has changed greatly during the past century. In former times, the chief or one of their chief functions was to serve as a breeding machine. In recent decades many factors have revolutionized the status of women—education, employment opportunities, changing functions of the family, etc. This changed status has expressed itself nowhere more than in sex attitudes and behavior. The modern woman refuses to have her sex exploited. She has definite and often precise ideas concerning the number of children she will have, and the space that shall separate their births.

The Child's Right to an Education

The right to an education which prepares the child for life is perhaps the most completely established and accepted of all the rights accorded American children. Its development has been an integral part of our national history. While it had its beginning in the transplanting of English practices and systems, its subsequent unfolding came in answer to ideas and needs peculiar to the New World. Following the Revolutionary War, the idea grew that the continuity and welfare of the new republic depended upon the enlightenment of its people, and that the nation must educate its youth as a duty to itself. By 1900, the period of pioneering in public education was over, for it was required in nearly all states outside of the South. From that time on, enrollments in schools and colleges have steadily increased, and the current quest is for equal quality in education for all children.

The Child's Right to Health

The child's right to health may be said to be on the road to public acceptance. Compared with developments in public education, those in the field of child health make an unsatisfactory showing in large areas of this country; but when contrasted with the child health work of two or more generations ago, the advances made in recent years are striking. Two developments in the latter half of the nineteenth century in particular focused attention upon this aspect of child development. One was the evolution of public health work to the stage where the economy of the preventive approach was recognized. Once this approach was made, it was quickly seen that all the diseases which, from the point of view of medicine or public health, were known to be preventable, occurred in the early part of life; that to prevent disease, the beginnings must be made in the age span when it can be prevented; that if the individual's resistance was to be utilized to fight disease, this resistance must be built up in the years of childhood; and that if health education was to be made an effective instrument in public health work, the foundations for it had to be laid in the years when persons were most educable. These ideas, now seemingly so simple and obvious, were hailed in this earlier period with all the enthusiasm given a new discovery.

The Children's Charter

Other rights have been advanced by various persons interested in child development. The standard statement of all of the rights of children is contained in the Children's Charter, drawn up in 1930 by the third White House Conference on Child Health and Protection. Its provisions follow:

I. For every child, spiritual and moral training to help him to stand firm under the pressure of life.

II. For every child, understanding and the guarding of his personality as his most precious right.

III. For every child, a home and that love and security which a home provides; and for that child who must receive foster care, the nearest substitute for his own home.

IV. For every child, full preparation for his birth, his mother receiving prenatal, natal, and postnatal care; and the establishment of such protective measures as will make childbearing safer.

V. For every child, health protection from birth through adolescence, including: periodical health examinations and, where needed, care of specialists and hospital treatment; regular dental examination and care of the teeth; protective and preventive measures against communicable diseases; the issuing of pure food, pure milk, and pure water.

VI. For every child, from birth through adolescence, promotion of health, including health instruction and a health program, wholesome physical and mental recreation, with teachers and leaders adequately trained.

VII. For every child, a dwelling place, safe, sanitary, and wholesome, with reasonable provisions for privacy, free from conditions which tend to thwart his development; and a home environment harmonious and enriching.

VIII. For every child, a school which is safe from hazards, sanitary, properly equipped, lighted, and ventilated. For younger children, nursery schools and kindergartens to supplement home care.

IX. For every child, a community which recognizes and plans for his needs; protects him against physical dangers, moral hazards, and disease; provides him with safe and wholesome places for play and recreation; and makes provision for his cultural and social needs.

X. For every child, an education which, through the discovery and development of his individual abilities, prepares him for life; and through training and vocational guidance prepares him for a living which will yield him the maximum of satisfaction.

XI. For every child, such teaching and training as will prepare him for successful parenthood, homemaking, and the rights of citizenship; and, for parents, supplementary training to fit them to deal wisely with the problem of parenthood.

XII. For every child, education for safety and protection against accidents to which modern conditions subject him—those to which he is directly exposed, and those which, through loss or maiming of his parents, affect him indirectly.

XIII. For every child who is blind, deaf, crippled, or otherwise physically handicapped, and for the child who is mentally handicapped, such measures as will early discover and diagnose his handicap, provide care and treatment, and so train him that he may become an asset to society rather than a liability. Expenses of these services should be borne publicly where they cannot be privately met.

XIV. For every child who is in conflict with society, the right to be dealt with intelligently as society's charge, not society's outcast; with the home, the school, the church, the court, and the institution when needed, shaped to return him whenever possible to the normal stream of life.

XV. For every child, the right to grow up in a family with an adequate standard of living and the security of a stable income as the surest safeguard against social handicaps.

XVI. For every child, protection against labor that stunts growth, either physical or mental, that limits education, that deprives children of the right of comradeship, of play, and of joy.

XVII. For every rural child, as satisfactory schooling and health services as for the city child, and an extension to rural families of social, recreational, and cultural facilities.

XVIII. To supplement the home and the school in the training of youth, and to return to them those interests of which modern life tends to cheat children, every stimulation and encouragement should be given to the extension and development of the voluntary youth organizations.

XIX. To make everywhere available these minimum protections of the health and welfare of children, there should be a district, county, or community organization for health, education, and welfare, with full-time officials, coordinating with a state-wide program which will be responsible to a nation-wide service of general information, statistics and scientific research. This should include: (a) Trained full-time public health officials, with public health nurses, sanitary inspection, and laboratory workers. (b) Available hospital beds. (c) Full-time public welfare service for the relief, aid, and guidance of children in special need due to poverty, misfortune, or behavior difficulties, and for the protection of children from abuse, neglect, exploitation, or moral hazard.

For every child these rights, regardless of race, or
color, or situation, wherever he may live
under the protection of the
American Flag.

Impediments and Questions

A basic problem involved in contemporary social programs for child development arises from the stubborn realities of financial limitations. The economic capacity of a society is a constant and fundamental factor in the determination of child status. Two outstanding aspects of this relationship in modern society will be noted briefly. First, it determines the nature and scope of the public financing of child development programs which is possible. The public treasury is not an inexhaustible reservoir. Over an appreciable period of time it presents a specific and inevitable problem in the balancing of income and expenditures. Moreover, all kinds of demands are made upon it: to maintain order within, to give protection against attacks from without, to conduct the ordinary business of government, to meet emergencies, and to promote the social welfare of the society. This last named category includes many programs other than those involving children—those for the aged, the sick, the mentally diseased, and many others. Time was, in the history of this country, when all these financial obligations of the public treasury were paid out of small-change levies on a generous citizenry; today they have become an integral problem in public finance, pressing heavily upon a taxpaying public increasingly resistant to existing demands. Because of the contemporary emphasis upon public responsibility for all kinds of social welfare programs, these facts about the basic conditions of public finance are of direct importance in child development.

In the second place, the existing tax structure, as well as its foreseeable form for some years to come, is also related to what individual families are able to do for their children. Federal income tax payments alone now exact, and will continue to do so for a number of years, a proportion of the family income which, until recently, financed many of the opportunities afforded to American children beyond those available to children in other lands. Our present standards of child care and education pose a relatively heavy financial obligation upon parents, and their maintenance constitutes a financial problem which many careful thinkers are considering with gravity. The lack of funds to provide every child with all of the rights of childhood has resulted in unequal distribution of them. Much of the discussion in foregoing chapters makes it clear that there has been considerable success in winning such rights for some of our child population, but not very adequately for others.

There have been questions raised as to how much we *should* do for our children. Two contrasting philosophies can readily be identified in the literature and discussions of recent years. One emphasizes the overwhelming responsibility of parents and society. Children are what we make them. They cannot be more, they dare not be less. Wise and adequate parenthood requires that parents assume the responsibility for child development, creating the necessary opportunities for their children to grow into healthy and happy adults. Wise statesmanship, through the public provision of the requisite conditions, seeks to supplement parental efforts in the controlled development of the next generation. The major responsibility for child development lies with parents and the larger society.

The opposite point of view is rather critical of this emphasis; it contends that too much concern has been shown for children in our contemporary society, that modern parents tend to pamper rather than discipline them, that society gives them too much and expects too little, and that proper child development calls for more emphasis upon child self-help. Adult life, it insists, is grim and hard, and adequate preparation for it dares not partake too much of the soft, the easy, and the effeminate. To show the broad front of this "harder" approach to the problems of child development, three comments regarding it will be presented. They were made by a psychiatrist, a former educator and journalist, and a sociologist, respectively.

The psychiatrist is Dr. E. A. Strecker, who served as special consultant to the Secretary of War and to Surgeons General of the Army and Navy in World War II. Emphasizing the fact that 1,825,000 men were rejected for military service in that war, that another 600,000 were discharged from the Army alone for neuropsychiatric reasons or their equivalent, and that another half million attempted to evade the draft, Dr. Strecker attributes the basic inability of these three groups out of 15 million persons to their immaturity, that is, to the fact that they had not grown up. This condition, he points out, is in turn the result in large measure of parental domination, of oversolicitous "moms," of lack of child weaning—in short, of the failure of parents to allow or compel their children to grow up. This one-fifth of the manhood of America failed to measure up to their country's crisis because their parents, particularly their mothers, did too much for them, and too long.[2]

The former teacher, later a research worker and writer, is Roy Helton. He also has expressed himself in unmistakable terms:

> It is not that we do too much for our children, for we all agree that their health and education are vital responsibilities not yet fully discharged, but rather that we do permit them to do too much to us. We

[2] Edward A. Strecker, *Their Mothers' Sons,* J. B. Lippincott Company, Philadelphia, 1946.

allow them to direct our taste in amusement, to control our time, and to determine our outlays. They compel us to insist on easy courses for them in their schools, and to badger educational authorities, not for the parental aim of better and more intensive education, but for the adolescent aim of better football teams. In short, they have so far taken over that a growing characteristic of modern life for the past twenty years has been not its youthfulness but its juvenility. . . .

An era of plain clothes for the young, an era of the divorcement of youth and gasoline, an era in which active and self-generated recreation is necessary as a prime condition, is the very beginning of a program for justice and intelligent help of our youth, in meeting the grave problems life is certain to present to them. Today we rob them of their future because we are too tender to deny them anything they now demand. We pity them, as we pick their pockets. We do too little for our children because we give them too much.[3]

Kingsley Davis, sociologist, has put it this way:

An individual's most important functions for society are performed when he is fully adult, not when he is immature. Hence, society's treatment of the child is chiefly preparatory and the evaluation of him mainly anticipatory (like a savings account). Any doctrine which views the child's needs as paramount and those of organized society as secondary is a sociological anomaly, although a personal evaluation of particular children above other ends (mainly by parents) is a normal phenomenon which fits the cultural system for socializing the young.[4]

The fundamental problem at issue in these conflicting points of view is that of relative responsibilities in the field of child development. How much parents and society should do for children, what they should do, when they should project themselves into the processes involved and when they should studiously withdraw from them, what status of childhood makes for its best development—these are moot questions. The answers to them cannot and should not be made arbitrarily. Some of them may be determined by scientific measuring sticks; others will come as by-products of the art of human living together. In the last analysis, child development means life, growth, development, socialization, adjustment—and these are the universals of each generation.

There is a final group of questions that is being asked. These concern the complementary part of child development. For example, we have just discussed the rights of children. What now are their responsibilities? In return for the years of their rearing and preparation to play their role as adults, what do children owe in return? In

[3] Roy Helton, "Are We Doing Too Much for Our Children?" *Annals of the American Academy of Political and Social Science*, November, 1940, pp. 233–234.

[4] Kingsley Davis, "The Child and the Social Structure," *Journal of Educational Sociology*, December, 1940, p. 217.

contrast to the current emphasis upon the rights of children, the necessity for maintaining high standards for their development, and the need for ever prolonging the period of their preparation, one finds very little reference to reciprocal responsibilities. Is this a proper balance? Is life all take, and little or no give? What do children owe their parents? Their schools? Their college? Their community? The larger society? Are these questions not equal in importance to the standards of their development? Is not the price of early development that of subsequent responsibility? Does not the balance scale of life demand this? Does anything less spell inevitably the anomaly of social bankruptcy?

We talk constantly about developing the individual child. Into what sort of child are we developing him?

Are there abiding verities in life which could serve as the basic goals of child development? Is self-discipline one of these? In a society in which the role of the intimate primary groups has given way largely to the impersonal specialized controls of secondary groups, must not much more reliance for the behavior of the individual rest upon the inner springs of conduct? Is consideration for one's family one of these verities? The family is not only a vehicle for the development of the personalities of its individual members, but it is also the connecting link between successive generations, a group device for the perpetuation both of life and of civilization. Can a society survive without the general acceptance of familism as a supreme value?

Is consideration of one's fellows one of the eternal verities? Is the revival and detailed expression of this the basic remedy to the "institutional chaos" and "moral anarchy" which modern scholars decry? Does the right to one's own development inevitably involve recognition of the rights of others to their growth and development? Is one possible, in the last analysis, without the other? After all, the developing individual is surrounded by other individuals who also seek their respective developments.

This problem of values is one which social scientists in general, and sociologists in particular, tend to evade. While the role of the learned man in the past was generally that of emphasizing and conserving traditional values, the modern scientist claims that values "may not be derived by science, and therefore science should have nothing to do with them. . . . It prefers to say that for science the word 'ought' ought never to be used, except in saying that it ought never to be used."[5]

Actually, this is a good deal of a pose, without foundation of fact.

[5] Robert S. Lynd, *Knowledge for What?*, Princeton University Press, Princeton, 1939, p. 181.

Values inhere in everything the scientist does—the problems which he selects, those which he avoids, his evaluation of data, his methods of research, and his treatment of conclusions. "Research without an actively selective point of view becomes the ditty bag of an idiot, filled with bits of pebbles, straws, feathers, and other random hoardings."[6]

Yielding to no one in the insistence that the sociologist be pure in his lack of bias and detached in his gathering and appraising of data, it still seems relevant to us to point out that the values of society are what give direction, scope, and significance to scientific analysis, whatever its particular value may be. The concepts, the methods, and the content of the sociology of child development all take meaning from their relation to the needs and values of children *and of the society* in which they live. The determination of these needs and values may well constitute the next stage in the development of the sociology of childhood.

TRENDS IN CHILDREARING THEORY

Since 1900, with the tremendous growth in mass communications of all kinds, including books and magazines, the American public has been bombarded with advice and theories on childrearing, as no public has been at any time or in any place before.

Theories do not arise out of a vacuum, but are related to social movements and ideologies of the times. Often they are ephemeral and seem more like fads than theories when they have passed away for a newer one. This is especially true in a fast-changing culture. Rapid change means also that a theory of childrearing may not be tested out long enough to assess accurately its results. Certain unfavorable aspects of it may appear and a frequent reaction to it sets in—if this way of rearing children does not seem effective, the opposite way must be the correct way. Thus, the possible good is thrown out with the suspected bad and another extreme is launched upon for a time, even though the results of that cannot be predicted either.

That much of this cyclical change of childrearing theory has existed in the United States has been spelled out by Celia Stendler in a survey of materials in popular women's magazines from 1890 to 1950.[7] During the early period of this century the articles stressed the physical development of the child, specific behavior problems, and the instilling of good moral character through such traits as

6 *Ibid.*, p. 183.

7 Celia B. Stendler, "Sixty Years of Child Training Practices," *The Journal of Pediatrics*, January, 1950, pp. 122–134.

"courtesy, honesty, orderliness, industriousness, and generosity; character, not personality development, was the focal point."[8] A "Christian" atmosphere in the home was stressed as an essential, and the mother was thought of as the keystone of the home. Although they were given advice, "Mothers occupied a position of importance which they have never since recovered. This was the day when Mother knew best; there was no book, no scientific authority to shake her maternal self-confidence, and she could tend her flock with the calm assurance that her 'instincts' were right."[9] The modes of operation suggested were setting a good example for the children to imitate; invoking God's help; and disciplining through love.

By 1910 a change was taking place. Apparently love, spiritual influences, and imitation were not effective enough. Now the advice turned to strict upbringing through punishment for misbehavior, and this was to be started early by rigid schedules, letting the baby cry it out instead of being picked up, and by being restrained in demonstrations of affection. The medical profession, during this period, were concerned over the high rate of infant mortality and urged careful regimens in order to combat it. Their advice on physical regimen, in itself not tested out, was taken over by the literary "experts" and extended to the general area of childrearing.

In the 1920s period, J. B. Watson began to influence theories about raising children. Their behavior, he said, was conditioned by very specific stimuli. If parents catered to them in moments of bad behavior they would be conditioned to continue it. Thus, strict regulation of the child continued to be the advice although it was not merely for their physical benefit but also for the sake of rearing properly conditioned human beings.

Under the growing influence of Sigmund Freud, G. Stanley Hall, and others, the advice of the 1930s softened greatly toward children. Fixations can occur at any point in life and the budding personality of the baby must not be repressed. That would inevitably mark the kind of adult he is to become. At the same time nutritionists were coming into their own and mothers became vitamin and diet conscious. "Interestingly enough, along with increased interest in scientific feeding in the twenties and thirties went more attention to feeding problems. There were more articles devoted to finicky eaters and slow eaters during these two decades than at any other time."[10] (Quite recently, pediatricians have been pointing out that too much

[8] *Ibid.*, p. 125.
[9] *Ibid.*, pp. 126–127.
[10] *Ibid.*, p. 130.

anxiety in the mother concerning feeding can definitely cause eating problems.) Also, at this time, the moral behavior of children took second place to their personality development, a concept almost unheard of in the earlier literature.

By the 1940s, the change from toughness to permissiveness in rearing was almost complete. Permissiveness would produce two important things, a sense of security and a healthy personality. It was during this period that developmental theory also became popular. Arnold Gesell and Frances Ilg's writings became bibles for many parents who watched with interest, and sometimes with dismay, the process of maturation in their children as compared with the children in the studies.

Orville Brim has interpreted these variations against the background of cultural change rather than explicit scientific knowledge about children and their rearing.[11] The first part of this century, he says, witnessed the beginning of women coming into their own after a nineteenth-century male aggressive attitude toward children. The 1910–1930 period represented "the age of mother"—women coming, perhaps, too much into their own, and resulting in a subjugation of baby to her own needs. The rigid scheduling may have worked out better for mother than for baby. Dr. Brim calls the after 1935 period "the baby's decade" when the child came into his own.

As of 1965, there are voices being raised suggesting that the child has now come too much into his own, and that some balance should be struck between developing their personalities and giving them discipline and good character—a word that was almost lost in the literature for a long period. No less a figure in advice to parents than Dr. Spock has recently been spelling out a modified program of childrearing aimed at these very things. There are, also, many voices, not always professional ones, advocating a return to the "get-tough-with-them" school of thought. Enough are heard in order to indicate that what was considered the proper way in one era may be thought of as entirely foolish in another. A superintendent of police has recently blamed the increasing delinquency in suburban areas to parental lack of discipline. A poll of more than a thousand young people, from coast to coast, revealed that those who had the most lenient discipline were the very ones most in favor of the get-tougher theory. A similar poll of college students showed that when they themselves become parents they expect to give their children more responsibility, more discipline, and more spankings. More than one teen-ager has construed the lack of limitations put on him as mean-

[11] Orville G. Brim, Jr., "Changes and Trends in Child-Rearing Advice," *Child Study*, Fall, 1959, pp. 23–27.

ing that his parents do not care enough about him to concern themselves. A teen-age girl asked her mother to *tell* her what she could and could not do. "Then I can tell them I'm not allowed to and can blame it on you, instead of having to decide against the other kids on my own!"

Another recent trend is a theory that there is no specific right or wrong way to rear a child. Neither permissiveness nor strict discipline are the things that affect the child. Rather, it is the manner in which the parents administer their discipline and the way in which they and the child relate to each other. The "atmosphere of the home" is the all-important thing. Unfortunately, no one has so far spelled out very concretely just what "manner" and what "atmosphere" are conducive for proper childrearing, nor, indeed, what is our desired end in the childrearing process. An attempt to define these things and explain them may be the next step toward new advice for parents.

THE AMERICAN PARENT

The American parent in the midst of many conflicting opinions about childrearing, has been characterized by a cultural anthropologist as being unsure of *what* to do.[12]

> In all societies except the United States, and, to a lesser degree, the countries facing her across the Atlantic, at all periods except during the last hundred years, the answer could be given without hesitation; the proper way to bring up children is the way we were brought up . . . When a woman bore her first child, she had the accumulated wisdom of her whole society to help her; the grandmothers, the midwives, the neighbors all spoke with one voice; every baby she had seen since she could first notice anything was being brought up in the same way; her path was clear.[13]

In our "new world," most things that come from the past are suspect. In terms of raising children this often means that the way in which we were reared must be wrong and another way would be better. But the question is, what way? There are so many different kinds of advice. The United States Government itself, through the Children's Bureau, tries to help parents by publishing the latest word of advice for parents on all aspects of childrearing. Dr. Gorer points out, "these pamphlets are completely revised every few years;

[12] Geoffrey Gorer, *The American People,* W. W. Norton & Company, New York, 1948, chap. 3.

[13] *Ibid.,* pp. 71–72.

a comparison of the different editions gives an interesting synopsis of the vagaries of the most accepted theories of child rearing."[14]

A result, for many mothers, is that a particular method of handling a particular child at a particular time comes from the "expert" she happens to consult at that time. Since she is aware of other ways, she is not only unsure but anxious. One form that her anxiety takes is to compare her child's development with that of "the average child" or the child next door. If the progress of her own is slower, it must be her own fault, she feels guilty, her anxiety increases, and also her pressures on the child to measure up. The fact that most parents in the United States have small families tends to make them continue this "sidewise" comparison with other children, as well as the reliance upon the advice of others. The mother of two does not gain much experience in watching the great differences in the developing process of different children.[15]

That the unsureness Dr. Gorer suggests does exist in the United States can be evidenced by the increasing numbers of agencies which offer help and advice, and the popularity of them among parents. Some psychiatrists have themselves said that many children are rushed to their offices when the only thing wrong with them is their mothers' anxiety. Yet there is another side to the picture.

SUCCESSFUL AMERICAN FAMILIES

The majority of families in the United States are not problem families and do not rear problem children. A great many of them, at all social levels and from all subcultural groups, never seem to feel the need of expert advice in the childrearing process and do exceptionally well alone. They, too, are subject to the social change that makes some of the old ways of dealing with youngsters inappropriate. They nevertheless are adaptable. They decide what they believe are the eternal verities involved in family life, as well as how to adjust to new times. An important question is, what *do* they decide and how *do* they rear their children? Such families, themselves, it would seem, are a very rich source for finding this answer. Yet the most popular approach to the study of the family has been to select problems and try to figure out how to solve them. Perhaps this too may change, and a greater interest be brought to bear on a truly preventive approach to child problems. One such effort was made by Carle C. Zimmerman and Lucius Cervantes, who studied many thousands of "successful" families. They write:

[14] *Ibid.*, p. 73.
[15] *Ibid.*, pp. 86–87.

We have taken the families which have demonstrated their success by getting their children into the senior class of high schools under the most difficult circumstances and we have delved deeply into a key, if not *the* key process in the development and enrichment of coming American culture. Our study is of an "ideal type," or of a group most conspicuous in achieving a fundamental goal against great odds.[16]

A great deal more of concentration upon how the successful families are actually doing the job might provide better answers from the experts for those parents who do feel the need for help and advice. It might also serve to furnish better information to families just forming and, hopefully, decrease the need for correction of childrearing practices at a later date. More refined methods of study and increasingly greater funds for research have not been too effective in reducing the incidence of problem behavior. Yet, the answers to the question of how to do so is usually more research and more money. Perhaps, in this particular field, there should also be a re-evaluation of the research itself and the sources of its data. Along with this might come greater efforts in constructive education for parents based on what successful parents do, as well as a continuation of help with problems. Orville Brim has said:

It has been argued that using "rules" as content in parent education has resulted in an increase in parents' dependency on professional students of human behavior . . . usually accompanied by rigidity or inflexibility in child care, by a decrease in creativity and in spontaneity on the part of the parent . . . the trend toward giving child rearing advice in terms of suggestions and hypotheses should mitigate some of these efforts . . . cultivate in the parent himself an attitude of scientific inquiry.[17]

CONCLUDING COMMENTS

This book has not been concerned with telling parents how to rear their children. Its aim has been, rather, to explore as widely as is possible in limited space, the many factors that make up the total life situation of a child and influence his behavior and development. Many of these facets of life have been brought to our attention by people who have felt their importance—and we have explored their possibilities. Our approach has been not to study problems primarily, but to suggest many influences in a situation that are representative of most children's lives and to assess some of the positives and negatives of these. Our point of view has been that it is not merely the

16 Carle C. Zimmerman, and Lucius F. Cervantes, *Successful American Families*, Pageant Press, New York, 1960.

17 Brim, *op. cit.*, p. 27.

critical and spectacular parts of a child's life that mold his behavior. Rather, his development is a result of an interrelated network of large events and of the minutiae of daily living—the latter of which probably carries the greater weight. A system of childrearing is but one small part of the experience of a child and has meaning only in terms of his total life situation.

SUMMARY

1. The twentieth century in the United States has brought a general acceptance of certain rights that should be extended to all children. These are expressed in the Children's Charter.

2. Efforts to insure these rights are limited by the economic capacities of the country, and at present the rights are distributed unevenly.

3. The identification and maintenance of the proper balance between those who want to do too much for children and those who want to do too little is one of the fundamental and abiding problems of child development.

4. Another concern is a proper balance between the responsibilities of society and parents toward children, and the responsibilities of children toward them.

5. Theories as to how to rear children have, in some respects, been cyclical during this century. Along with this, the proliferation of sources for advice about childrearing has created a confusion, anxiety, and dependency upon the expert characteristic of many American parents.

6. The majority of families in the United States, however, are successful in raising their children in spite of the many exigencies of modern life and social change. Such families might prove to be good sources for research, for advice and for general parent education of a preventive nature.

SUGGESTED READINGS

Bruch, Hilde, *Don't Be Afraid of Your Child,* Farrar, Straus and Young, New York, 1952. The author attempts to help parents find confidence in their own judgment despite the maze of contradictory advice about childrearing.

Brim, Orville G., Jr., *Education for Child Rearing,* Russell Sage Foundation, New York, 1959. This volume describes the contributions of the social sciences to parent education theory and practice and points to areas of research that have been neglected.

Davis, Allison, and Robert Havighurst, *Father of the Man,* Houghton Mifflin Company, 1947. This is a case record approach to the study of child personality with suggestions for parents added.

Hoffman, Martin L., and Lois W. Hoffman, *Child Development Research,* Russell Sage Foundation, New York, 1964. A thorough review and evaluation of recent research on children.

La Pierre, Richard, *The Freudian Ethic,* Duell, Sloan, & Pearce, New York, 1959. The author takes umbrage at permissive-rearing and progressive schools.

Lear, Martha W., *The Child Worshipers,* Crown Publishers, New York, 1961. The author develops her theory that the child in America is used as a status symbol by parents.

Miller, Daniel R., and Guy E. Swanson, *The Changing American Parent,* John Wiley & Sons, 1958. This description of the actual childrearing practices of 600 families in the Detroit area illustrates the selectivity of parents in adopting past and current theories.

Sears, Robert R., Eleanor E. Maccoby, and Harry Levin, *Patterns of Child Rearing,* Harper & Row, New York, 1957. Interviews with 379 American mothers are analysed to show how they brought up their children from birth to kindergarten age.

Zimmerman, Carle C., and Lucius Cervantes, *Successful American Families,* Pageant Press, New York, 1960. A study of over 54,000 "successful" families, their social systems and friendship groups. Of special interest is the weight given to the influence of friends on family stability.

INDEX